ADULT
PSYCHOPATHOLOGY

A Social Work Perspective

SECOND EDITION

Edited by

Francis J. Turner

THE FREE PRESS

THE FREE PRESS
A Division of Simon & Schuster Inc.
1230 Avenue of the Americas
New York, NY 10020

Designed by MM Design 2000 Inc.

Manufactured in the United States of America

10 9 8 7 6 5 4 3 2

Library of Congress Cataloging-in-Publication Data

Adult psychopathology : a social work perspective / edited by Francis
     J. Turner.—2nd ed.
          p.   cm.
     Includes bibliographical references and index.
     1. Psychology, Pathological.   2. Psychiatric social work.
     I. Turner, Francis J. (Francis Joseph)
     RC454.4.A38   1999
     616.89—dc21   99-25899
                                                                     CIP

ISBN 978-1-4516-2429-8

To my mother,

"Her ways are ways of pleasantness,
and all her paths are peace."

Proverbs III:17

CONTENTS

PREFACE TO THE SECOND EDITION

The driving forces that led to the decision to re-edit this book are fourfold: The first, the very strong reception given to the first edition. In my travels it has been most satisfying to receive positive, supportive comments from students, teachers, and practitioners as to its utility. As well, of course I have received criticisms and suggestions for change in recent years, as it became evident that much has changed since the first edition.

Secondly, similar to the motivation for the first edition, we are living in an era with a rapidly growing awareness that as our knowledge expands, at a pace at times overwhelming, so too does our appreciation of the complexity and multifaceted aspects of the human condition. This is true whether as individuals or intimate groups, we are functioning at our optimum level or when we are handicapped by the myriad of potential biopsychosocial blocks to our seeking fulfillment. But thankfully, knowledge as to the understanding of and responses to various forms of mental illness is also expanding—perhaps not as fast as we would hope, but we are moving forward. Social work of course has contributed to this knowledge growth in our transdisciplinary world of practice, and this in a much more confident and assertive stance than years ago.

A third motive for preparing a second edition relates to the ongoing development of knowledge just mentioned. Thus, with increased awareness of the intricacies of normal and abnormal growth and development, our professional terminology has changed. New clusters of disorders have emerged and new vocabulary has been formulated as situations we once thought to be pathological have become reformulated and better understood as normal. Further, important distinctions between concepts such as *variations* and *deviations* are much more a part of our thinking and understanding. This has been assisted by, as well as contributing to, our own growing understanding of the vast dimensions of cultural differences that exist in our society and how things perceived as psychopathological in one situation are viewed as normal in another.

I remember well a young female adolescent of First Nations origins with whom I worked several years ago. Her mother had just been killed in an auto accident. Following the accident she told, I believe it was a teacher, that her mother visited her each night and talked to her. This was assessed as hallucinatory activity; combined with her extreme diffidence toward persons in authority and some limitations with English it resulted in a diagnosis of schizophrenia, leading to institutionalization where I first met her. As I came to know this young woman I learned that the mother's nocturnal visits were what would ordinarily be called her dreams, phenomena that in her culture were viewed as very important and real, even though a different type of reality. Further, I learned that her marked diffidence in relationships with perceived authority figures was a sign of respect. Whether I helped her or not I don't know. I do know, however, that she taught me a great deal.

A fourth motive for this re-edition is to ensure that the content is up to date, the vocabulary correct and precise, and the concepts discussed contemporary.

Overriding these motives is the awareness of two things: the fact that social work plays a major role in the provision of services and treatment to the mentally ill and the fact that busy practitioners and students need to have a ready-to-hand desk resource that will give them immediate information about particular forms of mental illness, from the perspective of social work colleagues and in a vocabulary understood by us. Thus all of the articles but one in this volume are written with social workers as the primary authors. One other is cowritten with a psychiatrist. The one written by a colleague in another discipline is the chapter by a psychiatrist-gerontologist, David Millard. I invited Dr. Millard to write the chapter on the multidisciplinary aspects of mental illness so as to include someone who knows the field well, who has worked closely with social workers, and who could look beyond our own social work purview and talk about the complex yet essential reality of transdisciplinary practice in today's world.

Overall I am pleased with the final outcome of this endeavor. As with other edited books, as it developed it took on a life of its own, one which reflects a common base of social work knowledge, but as well the range of individual perceptions of a group of highly competent colleagues, who in their individuality contribute to the advancement of knowledge. From this perspective I am keenly aware and appreciative of how much my knowledge and understanding of this critical aspect of our contemporary practice has grown.

Wilfrid Laurier University
Waterloo, Ontario, Canada
March 1998

ACKNOWLEDGMENTS

Now that my editing of this book is completed, I am most conscious of the many people and processes that were involved. As with the previous edition, I am strongly aware of the highly positive contributions of the group of colleagues who provided chapters for the book. I have known and worked with some of these people for many years. Others are new colleagues whose work I have come to respect. They each bring to their chapter their own views of the world of practice and suggest how social work can respond to a particular problem. I have learned much from each of them, and I am appreciative.

I am also grateful to the staff of The Free Press, who saw the need for a second edition of this book much sooner than I did. Together we have struggled to meet deadlines, respond to editors' queries, and ensure a commonalty of format. These academic/corporate communications have been cordial, with a mutual understanding of various perceptions of time and urgency by all concerned.

As always, my family has been supportive. Since we moved to Toronto my work has taken place in "Dad's new library." Although some family members are now geographically distant from the process, they knew that it went on. Anne-Marie and Sarah, even though many miles away, especially assisted with the index. Their superior understanding of the potential of technology and utility of the courier network speeded this process. Francis observed the work from a closer vantage point. Joanne—who understands well the rules of scholarly publishing—has been supportive and understanding.

Finally, I am grateful to the many colleagues who have found this work useful. I hope that it will continue to assist their practice in a manner that will in some small way enhance the lives of clients and their families.

ABOUT THE CONTRIBUTORS

DANIEL C. ANDREAE is president of the Ontario Association of Social Workers, first elected in 1993. Dan has served as the executive director of organizations including the Alzheimer Society, where he served as the first executive director for Metropolitan Toronto. He is pursuing his doctorate at the Ontario Institute for Studies in Education, University of Toronto, and has authored several publications on social and health-related issues. He has been awarded the Governor General's Commemorative Medal from the 125th anniversary of Confederation for his contribution to social services. He has also been the recent recipient of the Continuing Education Teaching Excellence Award for Outstanding Academic Contribution, Humber College, Toronto.

PETER BOHM is currently a clinical manager for the Child and Family Centre in Parry Sound, Ontario. From 1991 to 1996 he was an assistant professor (adjunct) with the Department of Psychiatry, Queens University, and an instructor in the St. Lawrence College Addictions Services Diploma Program, while serving as clinical director at Beechgrove Children's Centre in Kingston, Ontario. Prior to that he served in senior clinical positions with the Addiction Research Foundation of Ontario and taught on the part-time faculties of social work at both the University of Toronto and York University. His master's degree is from Indiana University and his doctorate from the University of Toronto. He has extensive (public and private) clinical experience in both addictions and mental health, with publications in both of these areas. He is particularly interested in working with families and dispute resolution.

CATHRYN BRADSHAW is in private clinical practice. Her master's degree is from the University of Calgary. She practices in the areas of counseling and mediation. She has a particular interest in clients who have experienced trauma related to child maltreatment and domestic violence. She is actively involved in research, development, and dissemination as part of her clinical practice. She has published in the areas of sexual abuse trauma and social work practice.

MARCIA BRUBECK provides therapy for children and families in Hartford, Connecticut, and is the author of *Law as Symbol: A Jungian Analysis.*

ROSLYN H. CHERNESKY is professor and chair of the Administration Concentration at the Fordham University Graduate School of Social Service in New York. She received her doctorate from CUNY (Hunter College School of Social Work). She publishes and teaches on administration and organizational theory, program development, and service delivery. She has written extensively on women and management. She has just completed a project on AIDS/HIV case management in the New York City metropolitan tri-county region, and previously was project director of the Comprehensive Medicaid Case Management Training Project for the New York State Department of Social Services.

KATHLEEN JOYCE FARKAS is an associate professor at the Mandel School of Applied Social Sciences at Case Western Reserve University in Cleveland, Ohio. Her career has included both clinical practice and research in the areas of gerontology and substance abuse. She is currently involved in local and national research projects in perinatal substance abuse and reentry services for incarcerated and ex-offender women. At the Mandel School, she teaches in both the doctoral and master's programs. She has completed a faculty fellowship in perinatal substance abuse sponsored by the National Institute on Alcoholism and Alcohol Abuse and is a trustee of the Ohio Credentialing Board for Chemical Dependency Professionals in Ohio.

GRAHAM D. GLANCY achieved his M.B., Ch.B., from Victoria University in England and completed his postgraduate studies in psychiatry at the University of Manchester and University of Toronto. He is presently an assistant professor of psychiatry at the University of Toronto and at McMaster University in Hamilton. He is a founding member of the PSILEX Group, which provides consultation to the legal/medical community, correctional facilities, and others. Previously he was chief of the Forensic Service of the Clarke Institute of Psychiatry, where he helped to institute the Sex Offender Treatment Program. In his capacity as president of the Canadian Academy of Psychiatry and the Law, he has served as a special consultant to federal and provincial government agencies, particularly the Federal Ministry of Justice, regarding matters pertaining to forensic psychiatry.

HARVEY L. GOCHROS is a professor of social work at the University of Hawaii in Honolulu. He is a pioneer in developing social work education in human sexuality and is the author of several books and numerous journal articles on sexual problems in social work practice. He has contributed articles on sex-related issues to the last three editions of the *Encyclopedia of Social Work*. His most recent works have focused on the sexual concerns of long-term survivors of HIV disease.

IRENE A. GUTHEIL is an associate professor and director of the Ravazzin Center for Social Work Research in Aging at the Fordham University Graduate School of Social Service in New York. Her master's degree and doctorate are from the Columbia University School of Social Work. She teaches social work practice, clinical practice, and case management with diverse populations, and has published in the fields of aging and direct social work practice. She was director of training of the Comprehensive Medicaid Case Management Training Project for the New York State Department of Social Services.

MARILYN A. HERIE received her bachelor of arts (sociology) from Queen's University and her master's degree in social work from the University of Toronto. She has been a project manager, trainer, and therapist at the Addiction Research Foundation division of the Centre for Addiction and Mental Health since 1993. Her experience in addictions includes group and individual treatment of adults and youth, as well as research and clinical training in the use of brief, outpatient treatment for alcohol- and drug-dependent individuals. She has coauthored books and journal articles on relapse prevention and dissemination research.

She is currently a Ph.D. candidate at the University of Toronto, Faculty of Social Work, where she is conducting research on computer-based education of social work practitioners.

DANIEL E. JACOME is a board-certified clinical neurologist in private practice in western Massachusetts. He is an adjunct clinical assistant professor of neurology at Dartmouth Hitchcock Medical Center in Lebanon, New Hampshire. Dr. Jacome previously held clinical teaching appointments with the University of Minnesota at Minneapolis and the University of Miami, Florida. He specializes in epilepsy and clinical neurophysiology and has published in many neurologic subjects, both in the United States and overseas. In addition to book chapters, he has authored an atlas in electroencephalography and a book that represents a large collection of exotic cases studied by him during his many years of clinical practice. Dr. Jacome is originally from Colombia, South America, and received his training in neurology at Georgetown University. His subspecialty training was completed at the University of Minnesota and at the National Institute for Medical Research (INSERM) in Paris, France.

HARRIETTE C. JOHNSON is a professor at the University of Connecticut School of Social Work, West Hartford, Connecticut. She combines many years of clinical experience with a record of publication in the areas of mental health, human behavior in the social environment, parent/professional collaboration, and issues in clinical practice. Her most recent book, *Psyche, Synapse, and Substance: The Role of Neurobiology in Emotions, Behavior, Thinking and Addiction for Non-Scientists*, introduces students of human behavior, mental health, and addiction to the contemporary scientific knowledge base for the biopsychosocial paradigm.

BERT L. KAPLAN is Professor Emeritus of the School of Social Work, Adelphi University, Garden City, New York, where he was professor of social work and served as director of the Behavioral Sciences Division, director of the Post-Master's Certificate Program in Clinical Practice, and chair of the Clinical Track of the Doctoral Program. He also served on the New York State Board for Social Work for ten years, during which time he spent two years as chair and vice chair of the Board. Additional professional activity includes more than twenty years in private practice and seven years as director of the Psychotherapy Study Center. Dr. Kaplan also held adjunct faculty status at the Smith College School of Social Work and the School of Social Work at New York University.

Dr. Kaplan has authored numerous books, and articles that have appeared in *Clinical Social Work* and *The International Review of Psychoanalysis,* including "The Art of Intervention in Dynamic Psychotherapy." Dr. Kaplan received his M.S.W. at the Columbia University School of Social Work, his Ed.D. at New York University, and his Certificate at the Institute for the Study of Psychotherapy.

CAROL P. KAPLAN is associate professor of social work at the Fordham University Graduate School of Social Service. She received her M.S.W. from Hunter College School of Social Work and her Ph.D. from New York University. She has many years of experience as a clinical social worker in the field of community mental health. She has published in a number of areas including child and adolescent mental health and resilience, and is actively engaged in mental health research. In addition to teaching at Fordham, she has taught social workers in South Africa and Vietnam.

M. DENNIS KIMBERLEY is a professor of social work at Memorial University of Newfoundland, where he is chair of the Diploma for Clinical Counselling in Addictions. He is a former director of the Alcoholism and Drug Addiction Research Foundation of Ontario. He has appeared as an expert witness on the link between addictions and sexual abuse and between addictions and sex offending. Among his current research interests are parenting assessments of the addicted parent, sex addiction, and internet addiction, especially as it relates to pornography. He maintains an active clinical practice with Advanced Therapy & Consulting Services. He has taught in the addictions field for over thirty years.

KAREN KLINE is a licensed clinical social worker in Illinois. She is currently working in schools, private practice, and as an adjunct faculty member in the George Williams School of Social Work at Aurora University. She received her M.S.W. from Jane Addams School of Social Work, Chicago Circle.

JAN LACKSTROM is a social worker in the Eating Disorders Program at the Toronto Hospital, Toronto, Ontario. She also works as a sessional instructor at the York University School of Social Work and is an associate professor in the Department of Psychiatry at the University of Toronto.

JIM LANTZ is director of the Midwest Existential Psychotherapy Institute, Codirector of Lantz and Lantz Counseling Associates, and a professor at Ohio State University College of Social Work. He received his M.S.W. in 1970 and a Ph.D. in Counselor Education in 1981 from Ohio State. Dr. Lantz is a graduate of the Viktor Frankl Institute of Logotherapy and the Cincinnati Family Therapy Institute. He has studied with a number of pioneers in both existential psychotherapy and family therapy, including Ernest Andrews, Andy Curry, Viktor Frankl, Virginia Satir, and Carl Whitaker. He is a member of the Academy of Certified Social Workers, the International Family Therapy Association, and the American Academy of Psychotherapists, and serves as president of the Society for the Study of Philosophy and Psychotherapy. He is the author of four books and over 125 articles on family treatment, group psychotherapy, existential psychotherapy, and mental health intervention.

JACINTA MARSCHKE is an assistant professor at Fordham University Graduate School of Social Service, where she teaches clinical practice and psychopathology. She holds an M.S.W. from Fordham, a Ph.D. from Smith College, and a Certificate in Psychotherapy from Washington Square Institute in New York City. She maintains a private practice in New Paltz, New York, and is an active member of both NASW and the NYS Society for Clinical Social Work. She has special interests in dialectical behavioral therapy, borderline personality disorders, and the provision of support to family members of the mentally ill.

DONALD E. MEEKS is Professor Emeritus, Faculty of Social Work, University of Toronto, and a retired senior executive of the Addiction Research Foundation of Ontario. He earned his clinical doctorate in social work from the Smith College School of Social Work in Northampton, Massachusetts. At the Addiction Research Foundation, he served as associate director of the foundation's hospital, was founding director of the School for Addiction Studies, and served as coordinator of International Programmes. For over 25 years, he functioned as a consultant for WHO and the UN to universities and governments in Africa, Europe, Southeast Asia, and the Caribbean region. He is presently director of the United Nations–sponsored Caribbean Regional Certificate Program in Addiction Studies, delivered by the

University of the West Indies. He is also codirector of the Caribbean Institute on Alcoholism and Other Drug Problems, which conducts an annual summer school in Tobago.

DAVID W. MILLARD has recently retired after working for 38 years as a psychiatrist in the UK National Health Service. For part of this time he also taught in the Department of Applied Social Studies and Social Research at the University of Oxford, where he is a Fellow of Green College. He has broad interests in the social and psychological aspects of psychiatry.

JUDITH MISHNE is a full professor at New York University School of Social Work. In addition to her doctorate from Hunter College, she has further training in psychoanalytic child therapy. She has taught in several schools of social work, including a recent Visiting Scholarship to Bar Ilan University in Israel. She has published extensively including authorship, coauthorship, and editing of several books relating principally to practice with children. She is the recipient of various scholarly awards, including The Distinguished Practitioner in Social Work award.

MARY KAY O'NEIL is a training and supervising analyst of the Canadian Institute of Psychoanalysis, an assistant professor in the Department of Psychiatry, University of Toronto, and visiting scholar, Department of Psychology, Concordia University. She is in private practice in Montreal and Toronto. Her principal area of research has been emotional problems in young adult development. Her master's degree is from the University of Ottawa and her doctorate from the University of Toronto.

CHERYL REGEHR obtained her M.S.W. and Ph.D. from the University of Toronto. She is presently an assistant professor of social work at Wilfrid Laurier University. Her practice background includes direct service in mental health, sexual assault recovery programs, and sex offender treatment programs; and administration of community and emergency mental health programs and sexual assault care centres. At present she is clinical director of the Critical Incident Stress Team at Pearson International Airport. In addition she remains involved in the practice of forensic social work, specializing in civil litigation and criminal court assessments of trauma victims and violent offenders. Dr. Regehr's program of research involves examining aspects of recovery from trauma in such diverse populations as victims of rape and firefighters witnessing traumatic events.

MICHAEL ROTHERY holds an M.S.W. from the University of British Columbia and a Ph.D. from the University of Toronto. He is currently with the Faculty of Social Work at the University of Calgary. His practice has been in the fields of child welfare and mental health, and his current research interests are in family violence.

GARY B. SELTZER received his M.S.S.W. from the University of Wisconsin-Madison and his Ph.D. in clinical psychology from Harvard University. He has been on the faculty of Brown University School of Medicine and Boston University School of Social Work. He is currently professor, School of Social Work, at the University of Wisconsin-Madison, where he directs the Program on Aging and Developmental Disabilities at the Waisman Center. Presently his research interests are in the study of aging in persons with Down's syndrome and persons with cerebral palsy. Dr. Seltzer has published widely in the areas of aging, intellectual disability, and health. In addition to his research activities, Dr. Seltzer has developed clinical demonstration projects such as a tertiary care, interdisciplinary assessment program for older persons with developmental disabilities and their families.

MARY SHERIDAN is an associate professor of social work at Hawaii Pacific University, Honolulu. She received her M.S.W. from the Jane Addams School of Social Work, Chicago Circle, and her Ph.D. in American Studies from the University of Hawaii. She has many years of experience and many publications in medical social work, and special interests in infant apnea and Munchausen syndrome by proxy.

BARBARA THOMLISON obtained her Ph.D. from the University of Toronto and her M.S.W. from the University of British Columbia. She has considerable practice experience in family and child therapy, as well as teaching and publishing extensively in these areas. As visiting professor at Miami's Florida International University, she is acting director of the Institute for Children and Families at Risk, which promotes research, training, and technical assistance to address the needs of children, youth, families, and the social networks and systems that support them.

RAY THOMLISON is professor and director of the School of Social Work at Miami's Florida International University. He obtained his doctorate from the University of Toronto, and was dean of social work at the University of Calgary for 14 years. His interests span the areas of applied behavioral analysis, family therapy, child welfare, and international social work and social work education. As well as academic social work activities, he has considerable experience as a board member of social work agencies and organizations. He has publications in all of these areas.

FRANCIS J. TURNER is Professor Emeritus and former dean of the School of Social Work, Wilfrid Laurier University, Waterloo, Ontario. Currently he is editor of the journal *International Social Work*. He is the author and editor of several books on practice, including *Differential Diagnosis and Treatment in Social Work*. His master's degree is from the University of Ottawa and his doctorate from Columbia University in New York.

HOWARD M. TURNEY is director of the School of Social Work at the University of Arkansas at Little Rock. His doctorate is from Florida State University (in marriage and family therapy). In addition to his academic appointment, he has had extensive experience with children and families in his private practice in Little Rock.

JOSEPH WALSH is an associate professor of social work at Virginia Commonwealth University in Richmond. He earned his M.S.W. and doctoral degrees from the Ohio State University. He has an extensive practice background in psychiatric hospitals and community mental health center settings. He still engages in clinical practice while teaching courses in social work practice and research. His scholarship is focused in the areas of serious mental illness, psychotropic medication, and clinical social work practice.

MARY E. WOODS recently retired as adjunct associate professor, Hunter College School of Social Work, New York City. She has also recently retired from clinical practice with individuals, couples, and families and from an extensive practice of supervision and consultation. She coauthored, with Florence Hollis, the third and fourth editions of *Casework: A Psychosocial Therapy.* As *Adult Psychopathology II* goes to press, she is completing the fifth edition of *Casework.* She has recently moved from New Rochelle, New York, to Clinton, Connecticut.

1

INTRODUCTION

Francis J. Turner

The term *psychiatric social work,* a term once highly status laden, is now rarely seen or heard in the profession's lexicon. In its heyday the concept was seen as denoting some form of higher-level position and practice than "just" social work. This attitude prevailed partially because social workers with this designation appeared to have a close connection to other human-service colleagues in the mental health field, a connection that was thought to give some degree of status. The designation also implied possession of a specialized body of knowledge relating to the then identified types and forms of mental illness. These two factors in combination were seen as putting the title and those possessing it above colleagues without it. This term was prevalent at a time when in most countries there was in fact a very clear division between general social work practice and that encompassed by the term *mental health services.* This segregation of services, only one of many that existed, further added to the perception of a differential role in the profession.

In practice this identification of social work in the mental health field as a separate specialty was never as definitive as the terminology indicated and in recent years has blurred. Experienced social work practitioners in all direct service roles understood all too well that over a period of time, regardless of practice setting, one met the entire gamut of human psychopathology. Hence knowledge about it and skills in responding to it were necessary for all practitioners. As well, even if one did not meet such clients on a face-to-face basis, it has always been necessary that social workers understand these patterns of problematic mental functioning to ensure that policies and services meet the specific needs of clients.

Thankfully the blurring of this artificial division of the profession has continued at a rapid pace, facilitated by changed community attitudes,

1

great advances in pharmacology, and of course the broad impact of deinstitutionalization. These factors have both increased the nature of social
workers' involvement with the mentally ill and, as well, expanded the
extent of this involvement. Today all social workers are in reality in the
mental health field and all must have an enriched knowledge of psychopathology. Hence the need for volumes such as this.

As with the first edition, this volume starts from the premise that accurate diagnosis is the essence of contemporary, skilled, and responsible
social work practice. This statement immediately opens up another question of terminology. If one uses as a reference point most of the current
social work practice texts in North America, the current "politically correct" position appears to be that *diagnosis* is itself a somewhat pejorative
term and thus one to be avoided. This for a long list of supposed negative
connotations of the concept. Instead the term *assessment* is to be substituted. Here is not the place to continue this debate, apart from stating my
own position. It is my strong conviction that we underserve our clients,
weaken our relationship with our coprofessionals, and avoid the discipline
inherent in the term *diagnosis* if we fail to include it in our conceptual
purview and professional vocabulary.

As I have studied this issue I remain increasingly convinced that for a
variety of sociological, political, historical and turf issues we have "misdiagnosed" what is meant by *diagnosis,* made it a scapegoat onto which we
have loaded all the failings of the misuse of labels and categories, and
attempted to drive it out of our practice lexicon. But for me, and clearly for
my fellow contributors to this volume, and to an ever increasing number of
senior colleagues, it is still a critical term that needs to stand, as it once was,
at the heart of our clinical responsibility.

This discussion, as with many that need to take place around the misuse of designated categories of behavior, relates of course to the question of
"labeling." Thankfully, *the antilabeling movement,* itself a label, seems to
have greatly diminished in intensity in professional circles since the first
edition. To a welcomed increasing extent, we have come to understand that
our concern about labels is correctly one about their misuse; we can, if not
most careful, make them all-inclusive, overgeneralized, depersonalized, and
disempowering.

But we need a precise vocabulary. We cannot practice without an
accepted terminology to convey large bodies of essential information to
each other about individuals and groups by means of a single word, phrase
or sentence. However, all of us who have practiced have seen how destructive and limiting can be the misuse of such labels and hence the awesome

responsibility to use them carefully. We need to ensure they work for us and not we for them.

Clearly the basic structure of this volume is built on a commitment to the skilled and effective use of a common nomenclature within and between human-service professions. This presumes that over the centuries we have learned much about the myriad ways in which the human person can develop patterns of behavior that reflect some internal dysfunction of the mental apparatus, or some responses to complex interpersonal or societal realities that also cause dysfunctions or intensify the internal condition. As well, we have learned much about the complex ways in which the biopsychosocial spheres are interconnected. (It is hoped that we soon can add to this multifaceted understanding the spiritual dimensions of human existence as well.)

We have learned that these responses are not random; they can be understood and classified and in so doing, to an increasing extent, they can be managed and modified in a manner that brings comfort and enhanced autonomy and empowerment to persons.

But to make use of this accumulated wisdom we need to understand the degree of precision or lack thereof that we possess in each category and the extent to which we, as a profession on our own or in conjoint activity with other professions, have or lack strategies of intervention that can assist in particular ways. We, especially social workers, also need to understand the extent to which many of our perceptions of, and responses to, various patterns of behavior can often reflect more of society's views and attitudes to them than signs of internal suffering or dysfunction. In a related way we need to be aware that differential perceptions of and reactions to similar behaviors exist in different cultures. This latter becomes of increasing importance in the highly culturally diverse practice context of many parts of the world.

Certainly as our knowledge expands so too does our awareness of the need to alter vocabulary through deletions, additions, regrouping, or modifications of categories. The fact that our vocabulary changes, at times rapidly, is a humbling declaration to each other, and to the world, that our knowledge is far from perfect, that our categories do not—and must not—stand as unchangeable, that today's apparent convictions must be ready to yield to new insights and understandings. We also know that a term that today is viewed as useful and neutral can later become loaded with socially generated negative connotations and thus be more harm producing than helpful. But the process of knowledge development only takes place through the proper use of categorizations based upon a commitment to precision in the development of concepts–which in turn are subject to empirical reification.

Hence this process of knowledge building must be carried on in a manner that keeps constantly before us the risks and potential harm of the misuse of the vocabulary by which we communicate with each other. An especially relevant facet of this discussion relates to the title of this book, *Adult Psychopathology*. To date no one has challenged me on the use of the label "Adult," but it had been suggested that the label "Psychopathology" is no longer acceptable. Indeed one of the participants suggested that combining the subtitle *Social Work* with the title *Psychopathology* was an "oxymoron." *Psychopathology* for him is a medical term only. Obviously we disagree, but these different perceptions about appropriate vocabulary remind us that we need be very sensitive to terminology and how it is differentially used and perceived both within our profession and by other professions.

It is my position that no profession owns any words or labels. It is how we understand, interpret, and make use of such words in our practice that creates differences between disciplines. Hence for some the word *psychopathology* is to be eschewed. It is viewed by such persons as being out of date, overmedicalized, and reflecting a too narrow view of mental disorders. Whether in a future edition we may change the title remains to be seen. I think not!

However as with the term *diagnosis,* I view the word *psychopathology* as a most useful term that stands clearly as one of the anchoring points on the health–nonhealth continuum. If we accept that "healthy" is a legitimate concept, a much-to-be-sought-after state of existence for all of us, then we need to have a term that conveys states of nonhealth, or less health, which is exactly what the term *psychopathology* does.

The essential point for all of us is to avoid dichotomizations of those aspects of our clients' realities in which we become involved. Rather we must view various facets of clients' situations as continua. Having a clear perception of both ends of a continuum in regard to particular presenting situations helps us to assess severity and to decide whether we can help or not as well as the intensity of the help required. It also helps us to recognize when change is taking place in either direction. Mary Woods's chapter on Personality Disorders (chapter 16) is particularly helpful in understanding this concept of continuum. As social workers, in addition to a focused interest in our clients' mental functioning we bring a commitment to view this from a very broad base of interacting systems, few if any of which can be correctly seen as yes/no situations. Hence the utility of an understanding of continua.

Our responsibility as social workers is to be aware that many persons we meet have a myriad of problems originating from a plethora of inter-influencing causes that interfere with their mental health, which in turn influences their ability to function in many life roles. We need to understand all persons as individuals of course, but also as individuals manifesting similar situations, as do other groups of persons—which similarities help me to understand them and in turn to help them. In seeking to understand it is equally important that we learn to assess the myriad of strengths and resources a person possesses in his or her biopsychosocial realities, not only the nature and intensity of problems. Our diagnostic question is always, how is this person in his or her profile of strengths and limitation like no other person I have met, and as well how is he or she like some others I have met? Following from this is the further challenge that says, "Based on this understanding of who they are, what do I bring of knowledge, skills and resources that can be of help to them or what do others bring that are not within my competence?"

Our present situation, in North America at least, is that, unlike in earlier days, fewer people are institutionalized for any forms of mental illness or psychopathological behaviors, apart for very brief periods. Hence, to an increasing extent, community-based social workers in all practice settings will come into regular and frequent contact either directly or indirectly with the entire gamut of types and severities of psychopathologies. Thus, to respond responsibly and effectively, with understanding, wisdom, and competence we must be knowledgeable about this range of human problems.

This responsibility implies the ability to accurately diagnose, as mentioned earlier. Here of course we are talking of diagnosis from a social work perspective. We do not, nor must not, assume the responsibility of formulating our diagnoses from the perspective of other professions. That is for them to do. Social workers do not make medical diagnoses; we make social work diagnoses. Social workers do not make psychological diagnoses; that is for psychologists to do. Similarly, physicians nor nurses nor psychologists do not make social work diagnoses; they make medical or nursing or psychological diagnoses. Understandably and appropriately and to an increasing extent, there will be elements of commonalities across professions. Hence the richness of transdisciplinary practices discussed by David Millard in the next chapter. Certainly in an era of close interprofessional team practice it will and should happen that at times many aspects of our diagnostic formulations will be similar to those formulated by colleagues in other disciplines. So be it! It is a social work diagnosis that we must make based on the spectra of judgments we make, and for which we must be prepared to be held responsible. This in turn requires that we have the requisite knowledge to do so, to ensure that our responses to clients are as appropriate, ethical, and helpful as possible.

In our days a new reality has emerged as a part of social work practice: the question of practitioner safety. This is a topic rarely, if ever, mentioned in the standard textbooks on social work practice until very recently and then only on occasion. As well, it is a topic rarely considered in practice except in those specialized areas where there is a known high probability of violence.

Unfortunately it is now a factor that needs to be considered by all practitioners. We know all too well that there are people whose mental state is such that they are frequently a high risk danger to us, to themselves, or to others. Fortunately we know something of the patterns of mental upset or illness of those persons who are high risk. I consider it totally unethical for practitioners or teachers of practice to tell our beginning colleagues that diagnosis and use of labels are of no value and instead one must learn only to trust one's "gut reaction." An accurate and skillful understanding of the process of diagnosis and the sensitive use of diagnostic categories as a part of this process can alert us to high risk situations and lead us to take appropriate steps for our own and others' security. Failure to do so can result in death. Let us not forget this!

We cannot help everyone we meet in our practice. Hence an essential and conscious determination we need to make in all situations is: Is this is a situation for which I am prepared to take professional responsibility, or is it one that should best be handled by some other profession, or is it one that requires a multidiscipline approach, or is it one I or others do not understand sufficiently well and thus we must seek further input? We, or any profession, just do not have enough knowledge to help everyone. I do emphasize, however, that turning our backs on the knowledge that is available out of a distorted misunderstanding of the accurate meaning of *diagnosis* is unethical, irresponsible, and in relation to this point dangerous. I am not suggesting that mastering the content of this volume or the material of *DSM* will ensure that there be no risk to our practice. But it certainly will help us to be more responsive.

We have just mentioned *DSM*, a volume now in its fifth revision. This is a project that reflects an ongoing search for more precision and common usage of concepts across professions. Certainly all of us in social work are aware of the major contribution this work has made to broaden our view of psychopathology and to help other professions to broaden theirs. *DSM* has helped to ensure that psychopathology needs to be multiaxially understood, to foster an ongoing search for increased precision, to open the doors of richer interprofessional cooperation, mutual understanding, and multidiscipline practice and to foster the need to understand categories of pathology from a multifaceted perspective. It was because of the importance and influence of this work on social work practice, especially in North America, that we invited Dr. Marcia Brubeck to write a chapter for this volume on *DSM*, a topic not specifically addressed in the first edition. This she has done in a highly useful and objective way.

Although strongly influenced by *DSM* this volume does not want to, nor pretend to, nor attempt to cover all that it contains. Rather what we have done is to identify those situations most frequently met in front-line social work practice that require a more detailed knowledge of particular forms of presenting situations of pathology in various forms of intensity

In addition to new topics, in this edition there are several new themes that emerge across the spectrum of chapters. First there is a growing emphasis on the concept of multicausality and interinfluencing factors in psychopathology, which in turn require a multifaceted knowledge base. Implied in this is the renewed emphasis on the need for social workers to be much better informed about the neurological and physiological aspects of many presenting situations—not of course that we attempt to be neurologists, but that we have sufficient knowledge and appreciation of the importance of being appropriately sensitive and responsive to this critical area of understanding.

In a similar way there is the need for social workers to be much more understanding of, and thus responsive to, the role of pharmacology in assisting various types and intensities of pathology in the varying levels on which we meet it. Again not that we attempt to be pharmacists; but to a much greater extent than we have heretofore, we must also be more sensitive and responsive to our need to see our colleagues in pharmacy as resources of considerable import in our practice. Failure to do so can result in our misunderstanding of many aspects of clients' functioning, or a failure to be aware of pharmaceutical resources for clients that can be of considerable assistance to them and in turn to their significant others. Both of these latter topics receive much more attention by the various authors in this edition than in the first.

As well, there can be noted two very mature additional trends. The first is the comfort that there are limitations in our knowledge, and thus the extent of our ability to help in many situations. That is, we do not have to pretend to ourselves or to society that we have a level of effectiveness that does not exist. But we must never cease our efforts to expand our levels of competence. Thus the second trend reflects a corresponding readiness to identify areas where social work-based research is needed to advance our ability to improve our effectiveness with particular types of situations from a multimethod and multitheory perspective. As we become more comfortable in our awareness of limitations in knowledge we also grow more confident in what we do know. We have much to contribute to the multidiscipline team. Our current literature strongly reflects this, as seen in the greatly increased amount and quality of strong research writing. There is as well as an expanded confidence in using this knowledge. One of the challenges faced by each author was that of condensing into single chapters material which could easily fill a book. As knowledge grows about each topic, the task of presenting it in a manner that makes it succinct enough for front-line workers is formidable.

However, as befits good social work practice two further themes emerged loudly and clearly from this group of colleagues. The first was the need to individualize each situation with which we are confronted. As mentioned earlier, categories and subtypes and classificatory labels are very useful tools to help us to understand both strengths and limitations and areas of vulnerability and to assess risk—but, as we have said, they must only be tools to be used skillfully, compassionately, carefully, rarely, and partially. But they cannot be ignored.

A second theme critical in the content of these chapters is to remind ourselves of that dictum we were all taught in Casework I for some of us many years ago: "We must start where the client is." Often a client only wants and needs something to eat and nothing more. Recognizing that such a person is manifesting some psychopathological symptoms does not mean necessarily that these will be the focus of our interventions. Such recognition may and should help us to develop a sensitive base from which to respond to where individual clients are and what they want. That is, understanding that a client is manifesting a high degree or range of symptoms of behavior that attend a specific form of pathology can help us to help him or her and help others to find a needed resource not necessarily related to his or her pathology in a manner that is sensitive, helpful, nonthreatening, and sustaining. To not recognize and identify and respond appropriately to these aspects of our clients' profiles can result in hurt, rejection, misunderstanding, and failure to help.

We have come far in social work in learning to respond helpfully to clients and families and communities who are involved with or in touch with or touched by some aspect of human psychopathology. We have come far in our comfort with both a multitheoretical and multimethod perspective. We have yet far to go. But this need not daunt us. What must drive us is the need to be as knowledgeable, responsive, and accountable as possible to all whom we dare to serve.

2

A TRANSDISCIPLINARY VIEW OF MENTAL DISORDER

D. W. Millard

W hat sort of phenomenon is mental disorder? Although most people who are in contact with mental disorder may not often ask this question consciously, their every action implies that they have in mind some kind of answer to it. The nurse feeding a patient in a depressive stupor is saying that mental disorder is something to do with problems of self care; the physician prescribing an antidepressant is saying that it is something to do with biological mechanisms; the social worker's contribution is saying it is something to do with a mismatch between psychosocial resources and needs. The patients' and their carers' behavior is also implying an answer to the same question.

This chapter attempts to build a bridge between concepts and practice. Multidisciplinary teamwork is of course commonplace in contemporary mental health practice. While it would be too extreme to claim an exact parallel between the varying ideas concerning mental disorder held by the different professions in the clinical team and the precise contribution each member might bring, there is perhaps a fairly close relationship between the two. Thus, we shall attempt to identify certain essential components in these concepts and to consider what may fairly be called a transdisciplinary view of mental disorder within the team approach to practice in this field.

SETTING SOME LIMITS

Mental disorder is not free of cultural relativities; how it appears is influenced by the viewpoint one takes. This chapter takes first a pluralist view, then a professional view, and lastly a British view.

A Pluralist View

The term *pluralist view* indicates that we shall take seriously a number of different standpoints, both philosophically and professionally. The basic assumption is that we cannot speak of mental disorder without having in mind some concept of mental order (or orderliness). Thus, the question, *"What kind of phenomenon is mental disorder?"* is part of what we wish to say about human nature in general. Mental disorder is not outside the common stock of accounts of general human experience and behavior.

Modern philosophers are interested in examining the ways in which people sometimes describe things by reference to various possible "worlds." Perhaps the simplest of these is a model of two worlds: a physical world of matter and energy in which occurrences have extension in space and time, and a symbolic world. The characteristic of the first world is that events within it (like gravity) occur independently of human volition; we may certainly choose how to describe them but they occur whether or not anyone notices or labels them. The symbolic world is the world of ideas or information dependent, ultimately, on the human mind and on human volition. In sociology, the study of the first is often associated with *positivist* and the second with *hermeneutic* approaches (Giddens, 1976). The relationship between the two worlds comes to a crux in that most persistent philosophical dilemma—the mind/body problem.

Both worlds are, of course, inescapably "real"; and each includes the capability of influencing the other; the relationship between them is one of interaction. We are here asserting an essential place for both physical (chiefly, but not exclusively, brain) events and psychological events in the characterization of mental disorder—and our introductory question must be understood in this sense. Both the phenomena and also the determinants of mental disorder exist within these two worlds.

There are aspects of every mental disorder that belong to the physical world; after all, we know of no examples of mental events, including mental disorders, which are not related in some way to the existence of one or more particular human bodies which exist in space and time. It is the anatomical or biochemical abnormalities that chiefly account for such facts as the fairly consistent prevalence rates found in cross-cultural studies of schizophrenia, and modern psychiatric research is heavily involved in neurophysiology. But equally there are no mental disorders of which certain aspects do not belong to the second, or symbolic world; these aspects are there because of choices of the human mind—not necessarily the choices of the individual sufferer, or of those in his own family or other social group, but freely choosing human minds nevertheless.

In a different sense, pluralism involves attending seriously to the contributions of a variety of different approaches. This method is not new: for example, M. Siegler and M. Osmond, a sociologist and a psychiatrist, described in 1974 eight "models of madness" (medical, moral, chronic impairment, psychoanalytic, social, psychedelic, conspiratorial, and family interaction); for each, they include a range of definitions of mental disorder, statements about causes and effects, and prescriptions for the professional behavior of the caregivers and of the rights and duties of all involved. But while Siegler and Osmund conclude that the medical model is superior, we shall argue here for team practice and for a transdisciplinary view of mental disorder.

In modern practice, the transdisiplinary view seems to have developed through a number of phases. Starting from a largely unchallenged medical hegemony, the first phase was perhaps one of a rather overdone blunderbuss attack. The second has been a much more reasoned phase, which, drawing on a developed sociology of work and the professions and a sophisticated study of social policy, leads to a detailed conceptual analysis of teamwork. And the most recent phase—which, indeed, we are only just entering—is that of the empirical study of such matters as the effectiveness of members of different professional groups in the accomplishment of defined clinical tasks, and of the distribution of power and responsibility among various roles within the caregiving team.

A Professional View

We shall deal in this chapter only with what we may describe as the "established" professions.

The range of those who have some claim to offer a contribution to the conceptual task of characterizing mental disorder is very wide. There are, of course, the obvious health services professionals—*physicians*, especially *psychiatrists; nurses; social workers; psychologists,* especially *clinical psychologists; psychotherapists* and *behavior therapists;* the *clergy; physiotherapists;* and *occupational therapists.* Persons ordinarily included when describing psychiatric hospital settings would, in Britain, increasingly also be found in the wider community: *speech therapists* and *remedial teachers* contribute in child psychiatric settings; within special schooling for children with a variety of mental and physical handicaps specialist *teachers* and *residential social workers* find their place; the *police* and *lawyers* have their own roles; the staff and the members of a very wide range of *voluntary associations and societies* make a substantial contribution to mental health care; a vast network of *informal caregivers,* and—undoubtedly the largest group of caregivers to the mentally disordered—their *relatives.*

Among this extensive array, whose views count? This question becomes very pointed as soon as a further matter is raised: Where are the mentally disordered? A recent overview by Goldberg and Huxley (1980) produces some instructive figures. These authors summarize from a number of investigations in the United States and in Britain the one-year prevalence rates (the number of people who suffer from a disorder during a calendar year on at least one occasion) per 1,000 population at risk. Taking five levels of analysis, they suggest that the rate of morbidity from psychological disorder in *random community samples* is about 250 per 1,000 at risk per year; about 230 will present themselves to a *primary medical care* facility (in Britain, a general practitioner) of whom 140 will be *recognized* by the primary care physician as having conspicuous psychiatric morbidity. Of these, about 17 will be *referred to a specialist psychiatric service* and will therefore come to the notice of a psychiatrist, whereas only 6 of the original 1,000 at risk per year will be *admitted* to psychiatric inpatient care.

There are three broad categories of those who might decide whether or not a particular state of affairs should count as a case of mental disorder: the patients, their relatives, or the observing and caregiving professionals. Moreover, there may be a considerable disagreement in specific cases between these judgments: the patient's "Am I going mad?" the close relative's "Surely this is madness?" and the psychiatric "Is this person diagnosably sick?" frequently yield very different answers.

The point here plainly has to do with the identity of the classes of individuals listed above, and their role in the social situations represented by the five levels of analysis in Goldberg and Huxley's 1980 study. It is appropriate to recognize that, in limiting ourselves to a professional viewpoint, alternatives with powerful claims to be heard are being set to one side.

Nevertheless, we shall consider only the concepts of mental disorder embedded in the identity of some of the professionals involved. Occupational or professional identity is of course a matter of the range of expertise deployed by members of each profession and, therefore, of the form and content of each worker's education and training. But it is also connected with such matters as the relative status and power of different professional groups and the varied forms of professional organization with which they work. It is not intended to imply an exclusive "ownership" of a particular view, but it is the case that the training and practice of physicians will be linked with a predominantly medical view, that of social workers a view which more strongly emphasizes social interaction, that of nurses or psychologists or of occupation or industrial therapists, or of ministers and clergymen, other views, and so forth.

Yet, despite the fact that psychiatrists and other psychiatric hospital-based personnel come regularly into contact with only a limited and unbalanced sample of those identified in the community as mentally disordered, in practice it is the medical viewpoint—or what people take to be the established medical viewpoint—against which all others are set to be considered. Whatever reservations may be advanced, it is in relation to "the physician"—the psychiatrist—that the viewpoints, powers, roles, and statuses of patients, their relatives, volunteers, and other professionals are currently debated.

The present writer would not wish to join in the wholesale condemnation that has sometimes arisen from radical commentators of the psychiatrists' attitudes towards the management of mental disorder: they have frequently been very much more insightful and sensitive than they have been given credit for. But we are constrained by history to start our analysis from this point, and we shall in fact confine ourselves to views which may broadly be associated with the identities of physicians, nurses, social workers, clinical psychologists, and the clergy.

A British View

Finally, the author's professional experience has been almost wholly within the United Kingdom, and this chapter is therefore written within the context of British experience. This is not too dissimilar from that throughout Western society; but no claims are made for the application of what follows in the culture of the developing countries.

We now proceed by taking individually the five professions mentioned above, and to consider aspects of mental disorder that are loosely linked with the professional identity of these key members of the multidisciplinary team.

BIOLOGICAL MEDIATION: THE PSYCHIATRIST'S VIEWPOINT

We ask first how it has come about that the medical view of mental disorder commands today the central position it clearly holds. Historically, the earliest recognition is of the social aspects of the individual's disorder. For example, in fourteenth-century Britain the *Statute of Prerogatives* of

Edward II made the distinction between the "born fool" (*fatuus naturalis*) and the person of unsound mind who might have lucid intervals (*non compos mentis*). This enactment related to property: in the case of the mentally ill person its control reverted to the Crown during the period of his lunacy, and in the mentally handicapped it reverted permanently except for an obligation to provide for his person and estate.

During the following centuries, where any interest in mental disorder existed the focus continued to be upon its social consequences—vagrancy, pauperism, and sometimes crime; and also on such interpretations of individual behavior as could be assimilated to notions of witchcraft or demonic possession (K. Jones, 1972). The impetus for any change in the unhappy situation of such people came from social reformers, public-spirited persons who were no doubt influenced by growing national affluence and the general spread of enlightened ideas in the seventeenth and eighteenth centuries. There was growing concern about the plight of a poorly understood group, disadvantaged to the point of helplessness, residing in the lunatic hospitals and madhouses, in prisons and workhouses, and in attics and closets in private residences. Writing of this movement in the eighteenth century, K. Jones (1972) notes:

> [But] William Tuke had proved at The Retreat* that "lunatics" could respond to kindness and trust, and Godfrey Higgins defied an Archbishop of York in making the story public. In London, a group of members of parliament investigated Bethlem, the oldest lunatic hospital in England, and others forced their way into the filth and the squalor of the private madhouses. In Gloucester, Sir David Onesiphorous Paul set in train a series of events which led to the passing of the County Asylums Act of 1808, and the first local authority institutions designed for "criminal and pauper lunatics."

Medical practitioners played only a peripheral part in these developments; the early asylums usually had a layman as Master, and relations between such a person and the visiting apothecary or physician varied but were often very strained. Jones notes that it was essentially not until the middle of the nineteenth century that there appeared "a new spirit of humanity and treatment, a rising class of competent asylum doctors and the beginnings of training for nurses" (K. Jones, 1972).

The development of a psychiatric view of mental disorder is closely

---

*A Quaker hospital for the mentally disordered, opened in York, England in 1796.

interwoven with developments occurring, also in the nineteenth century, in general medicine's concepts of disease. At least from the time of Hippocrates, there had been available the notion of a combination of signs and symptoms occurring together so frequently and characteristically as to constitute a recognizable clinical picture. He distinguished as three separate entities "the patient," "the environment," and "the disease." By the seventeenth century an English physician, Thomas Sydenham, had suggested that these disorders might be classified "with the same exactness as we see it done by botanic writers in their treatises on plants" and he too thought of such disorders as having a kind of autonomous existence with natural histories of their own—invading the body from without.

The fundamental change—indeed it constitutes little short of a revolution—was the introduction of the cellular theory of disease by the German pathologist Rudolf Virchow (1821–1902). This relocated the source of disease within the tissues of the body; instead of the concept of disease as extraneous pathology attacking normal life from outside, there grew the concept of pathological life itself (Clare, 1976).

By the nineteenth century there were several humane and enlightened medical men working in the mental health field: Dr. John Connolly, for instance, went as Superintendent to Hanwell Asylum in West London in 1839 and there introduced the "moral treatment" of the insane. But it is in the thought of a layman, the great Victorian philanthropist Lord Ashley, later the seventeenth Earl of Shaftesbury, that the two streams of social reform and medical development begin to be brought together. As a Commissioner in Lunacy writing in his annual report for 1844 (in which further revision of the existing legislation concerning the mentally ill was advocated) he first used:

> an analogy which, though common today, must have been novel to his readers. He enquired of them what would be the reaction of the general public if patients suffering from acute physical ailments, such as inflammation of the lungs, were commonly sent to workhouses, and allowed to remain there until the disease was incurable before being sent to hospital; and stressed that the insane person was a sick person urgently in need of specialised treatment. . . .
>
> The similarity between mental and physical illness was repeatedly stressed by reference to "patients," "hospitals," and "nurses," avoiding the derogatory and emotionally coloured terms then still in common use. (K. Jones, 1972, pp. 143–144)

The medicalization of care for the mentally disordered—and, with it, a medicalized view of the nature of mental disorder—developed over the next century or so from the sowing of that seed.

The determinative power of the analogy between physical disease and mental disorder can scarcely be overstressed. It inspired the great observers of psychopathology—Freud and his followers, Karl Jaspers and others—to more and more detailed descriptions of mental phenomena in parallel with the work of histopathologists, bacteriologists, and the like. It inspired the work of the great classifiers from Emile Kraepelin and Eugene Bleuler down to the devisers of the World Health Organization's *International Classification of Mental and Behavioural Disorders* (ICD, 1993) or the American Psychiatric Association's *Diagnostic and Statistical Manual of Mental Disorders* (*DSM IV*, 1994). It inspired research into the causes and mechanisms of mental disorder in such areas as focal infection, degeneration, or genetics and the details of subtle but disruptive biochemical changes. It inspired the search for better treatment than the old practices of physical restraint and unpleasant experiences like the cold shower and the rotatory swing, along lines such as the removal of septic foci and malarial or insulin treatment down to the prescription of effective drugs, convulsive therapy, and the like. And it seems certainly to have brought to psychiatrists an aura of authority that they derived, at least in part, by association with the more obvious successes of their surgical and general medical colleagues.

The establishment of the preeminence of a medical view of the nature of mental disorder, symbolized by the adoption of the phrase *mental illness,* thus seems to have resulted from the combination of political pressures that it should so be seen, the corresponding willingness of psychiatrists to accept and use the power and prestige thus ascribed to them, and developments in the natural sciences, which fed the growing clinical and technological expertise of medicine at large. The familiar *medical model* (though in fact, there exist several medical models, e.g., Clare [1976], Siegler & Osmond [1974] acquired and retains its predominance.

We must, however, note several refinements. First, psychiatric disorder does not reside entirely within the individual but exists also in terms of that person's relationships with his immediate social environment. Nevertheless, the manifestations within the individual are sufficiently distinct to be classified in a system (see MD–10, *DSM-IV*) about which, especially if standardized interviewing techniques and relatively precise definitions of the technical terms are used, respectably high degrees of agreement between practitioners can be obtained. In modern psychiatry both research and practice rest upon this foundation.

Second, the cause of any mental disorder is always multiple. Three broad classes of causal factor are involved. Two are

- *genetic:* fixed at the moment of conception, and establishing a program whose working out involves biological mechanisms and adequate environmental conditions; and
- factors acquired as a consequence of *subsequent life experience* from conception onwards and somehow "stored up"; (Psychodynamic, behavioral, cognitive and other learning or socialization theories exist to explain how such "storing-up" occurs, and how past events are influential in contemporary life. Biological mechanisms are also involved, and the massive research enterprise into brain function, using techniques such as brain scanning and Magnetic Resonance Imaging [MRI] is rapidly expanding our knowledge of these matters).

Factors drawn from these two classes are held to interact with one another to produce an individual with certain personal characteristics ("premorbid personality" factors) which themselves interact in turn with influences drawn from:

- the *current situation*—(the sense organs and central nervous system being, of course, a unique apparatus for converting environmental events into internal events).

This complex sequence of interactions manifests itself in the subjective experience and overt behavior of the person concerned.

Third, management, like causation, is almost always multidimensional. It frequently calls on some combination of social and environmental adjustment, psychodynamic or behavioral, individual or group, methods of psychological management, and physical treatments. The relationships existing between causes, the phenomena of disorder, and management plans are more influenced by the individual characteristics of a particular case than by the class characteristics of the diagnostic category to which any particular individual belongs.

Finally, the prediction of the course and outcome of mental disorders is less certain than that of physical disease because such disorders are not abnormalities of a mechanistic system; indeed there may be absolute limits which may occur as a matter of principle to the predictability of human behavior, whether in health or in disorder.

It is clearly because of the importance of biological mechanisms in mediating the interaction between genetic, earlier life experiences and the current situation in producing mental disorder that the claim of the psychiatrist to a place in the transdisciplinary team is so strong. And this fact colors his attitudes and that of others towards him. All concerned have a tendency to ascribe to biological mediation a kind of primacy over the social or psychological dimensions of mental disorder (about which the expertise of the psychiatrist is shared with other members of the team)—doubtless a part of the Western culture's tendency to ascribe a primacy to the physical world over the symbolic world. So the practice of the team sometimes implies an assault on the authority of the psychiatrist.

PERSONAL COMPETENCE: THE NURSES' AND PSYCHOLOGISTS' VIEWPOINTS

From the time of Hippocrates, the literature has made clear that never in practice has the physician unaided been responsible for the care of the sick. In this section we consider the views of mental disorder contributed by two professions, nursing and clinical psychology, which emphasize deficiencies in personal competence—albeit of rather different kinds.

Nursing

It is said that a Madame Le Gros attempted in 1645 to provide special training for those looking after the mentally ill in the Petites Maisons in France, and some legal recognition for such training was obtained in that country in 1801. Once the tradition that the mentally disordered were cared for adequately in the various Religious Houses had faded, the history of the development of nursing from its origins in low-status domestic service calling for little or no education or occupational organization is closely related, so far as mental disorder is concerned, to the development of the institutionalized care of the insane outlined in the previous section. In the nineteenth century the attendants, both male and female, working in mental institutions were seldom sufficient in numbers; nor in general were they the right kind of people for that type of work. As in the case of psychiatry, so with psychiatric nursing—the parallels with general medical developments are important.

Developments in general nursing originated in the Crimean War (1854). There were no army nurses; most of the orderlies were feeble old pensioners, many of whom were unfit even to carry a stretcher. Thus Florence Nightingale introduced women nurses into the hospital at Scutari and, in response, public funds were raised to endow the first British School for Nursing at St Thomas's Hospital, London; it opened in 1860.

The Earl of Shaftesbury's reference to psychiatric hospital "nurses" has already been noted; training and an examination for them in Britain was begun by the Royal Medico-Psychological Association (the predecessor of the Royal College of Psychiatrists) in 1891, but is now superseded. The General Nursing Council in Britain, established in 1919, instituted its mental nursing certificate two years later, so that by the early 1920s there were two separate forms of qualification for mental nurses, but many people employed in this role had ". . . neither the will nor the ability to take either" (K. Jones, 1972).

In the early stages of its development, nursing training was very dependent on medical doctors—who therefore taught nurses a simplified version of what they themselves knew, i.e., basic anatomy, physiology, an elementary account of pathology and treatment of disease, and so forth—material which was only of partial relevance to the essential nature of the nursing task. This emphasis tended to identify both general and psychiatric nurses with the doctor's interest in biological mediation and to impel them into the role of simply carrying out "doctor's orders" in their management of the mentally disordered.

But the developed concept of the professional role of the nurse has as its central purpose to carry out aspects of self care which the patient, temporarily through illness or permanently through disability, is incapable of carrying out for himself. Although this is a matter related to medical treatment it is, in fact, a response to the patient's illness (and, indeed, its treatment) different from the physician's response. The emphasis here is on a greater independence of nursing from medicine, seen not only in the care of the individual but also of his personal and material environment—so that the management of a ward regime and working with relatives becomes part of the job.

This rise in the status, educational expectations, and achievement of nurses, and in their power and responsibility has implications for psychiatric nursing both in hospital and in the wider community. The end point of this development is the identification of a nursing view of mental disorder significant enough to modify the psychiatric viewpoint.

A theologian, David Jenkins, has offered a distinction between:

. . . *interdisciplinary* co-operation (where everyone contributes his or her bit of a clearly defined sort from a clearly defined discipline) and *transdisciplinary* work where everyone finds his or her bits (and therefore his or her discipline) changed by the effects of the common work in hand. (Jenkins, 1960)

This distinction is reflected in the title of the present chapter.

In considering the persuasiveness of the nurses' contribution to the transdisciplinary view of mental disorder, three areas are important: the nurse in relation to the hospital; the nurse in relation to the patient; and the nurse in relation to the community.

The participation of nurses in the evolution of hospital style residential care from its poor-law precursors was for both good and ill; they were part of the shift from the perception of the mentally disordered as people who created uncomfortable problems for society to their perception as individuals with certain kinds of personal incompetence, or "need," or, indeed, "illness." And such a shift was, in its time, a necessary and humane development. But they were also part of the social mechanisms which produced the pathologies we now call *institutionalization,* familiar from the technical contributions of Barton (1959) and Goffman (1961) and cruelly portrayed in novel and film, as in *One Flew Over the Cuckoo's Nest).* On the other hand, their influence in maintaining high morale and open institutions (Revans, 1976) is paramount, as is their role in such specialized regimes as the therapeutic community (M. Jones, 1952).

Secondly, at the individual level nurses, being in contact with the mentally disordered day and night, saw mental disorder in a rather different light, and exerted powerful influences in understanding it that differed from those of the physicians. Their view was of mental disorder as a much more detailed matter—as a range of interferences with the competence of the individual to manage his or her own life. At its most fundamental, the problems of such patients might include eating or drinking enough to sustain life, attending to bowel and bladder function or to the details of personal hygiene, and so forth. At a higher level, they might include matters to do with table manners, dressing, and generally presenting oneself in a socially acceptable fashion; at a higher level still, they would include problems of occupying one's time in a way both satisfying to the self and contributing something to the common good. Plainly such problems include questions of relationship, not only between patient and staff but between members of the patient community and between individuals and their families, employers, and society at large.

The contribution of nursing to the multidisciplinary team derives from this analysis. It ranges from very fundamental physical caregiving (e.g., for the profoundly mentally handicapped, psychotic patients in grossly autistic phases, the brain damaged, or older persons with advanced degrees of dementia) through therapeutic activities such as detailed planning of the hospital patient's day (both in its group aspects and for individuals) to highly specific interventions in which the psychiatric nurse is the key worker in behavioral therapy, counseling, family therapy and the like.

The third factor is that, as part of the growing emphasis on community care and (in Britain) a relative failure on the part of the personal social services to take over adequately from National Health Services, psychiatric nurses have increasingly followed their patients out into the community or gone out to meet them there. The range of functions is similar to that noted above: aspects of physical care, the supervision of medical treatment such as long-term maintenance drug regimens, coping with psychiatric emergencies, the observation and reporting back of the patient's clinical condition, the management of interpersonal and family relationships, and so forth.

> In the context of the comprehensive service, it is likely that a generic role will be assigned to the nurse, and that she will acquire legitimate therapeutic and preventative function in dealing with the relationship problems and social difficulties of the patients . . . . Nurses should profit from the experience of other related disciplines (especially health visiting and social work) in the development of interactional skills; and, until a frame of reference specific to psychiatric nursing is developed, they must draw relevant concepts from related fields. (Sladden, 1979)

We see here, then, progress towards the full development of the psychiatric nurse in his or her therapeutic role in the multidisciplinary team, both in the institution and in the community—where, as Goldberg and Huxley (1980) have made clear, most of the patients are. However, the starting point is not the biological mediating mechanisms central to the physician's expertise, but rather strengths and weaknesses of personal performance that are not relevantly categorized by the medical systems of classification.

Clinical Psychology

Clinical psychology is a younger, numerically smaller profession whose influence is founded more on an independent knowledge base than on its members' availability to undertake a central role in the team. As an experimental discipline, psychology began with the establishment by Wilhelm Wundt of the first laboratory in Leipzig in 1879.

For the purposes of this chapter, the emphasis is upon the contribution of scientific psychology to defining with some accuracy the aspects of behavior that represent defects in personal competence. Following the contributions of people like Alfred Binet, who was chiefly interested in education and who is remembered for his work on intelligence in school children and in establishing the techniques of psychometrics, psychologists in clinical posts with the mentally disordered made increasing use of psychological tests in the characterization of a wide range of the abilities of mentally disordered individuals. Throughout the first half (broadly speaking) of the twentieth century the contribution of psychologists on the side of therapy was largely confined to the work of those who became psychoanalysts or who drew on dynamic theory as psychotherapists.

Both contributions were particularly notable within child psychiatry. But in recent decades psychologists have increasingly abandoned formal psychometric testing for much more detailed behavioral analyses of patients' problems, and with this has come greater involvement in the planning and management of programs of behavioral therapy. Patients with certain forms of mental disorder have benefited particularly. It is not too much to say that this contribution has, in Britain, revolutionized the prospects for the mentally handicapped. And the other notable area of application of these principles is in the field of the neuroses, particularly in phobic anxiety and obsessional states.

The result of these changes has been to promote clinical psychology to a much more prominent place in the clinical team—and the associated viewpoint to greater influence on the transdisciplinary view of mental disorder. Of course, the psychiatrists had always contemplated psychological symptoms in their descriptions of mental disorder. But their main interest has been in looking behind these phenomena, as their medical and surgical colleagues looked behind the patients' symptoms and signs, to understand a more fundamental reality—the "disease" lying beyond them.

A classical protagonist of the view that the behavior disorder ought not to be the province of the psychiatrist was Hans Eysenck, who wrote (1975, p. 5) that

[T]he behavioural part of psychiatry deals with disorders of behaviour acquired in large part through the ordinary processes of learning, unlearning, or failure to learn. Neurotic disorders, personality disorders, and many types of criminal conduct probably come under this heading; these are not to be constructed as disease in the usual medical sense of the word, and their treatment is subject to many ethical and social considerations which would be largely irrelevant to the medical disorder discussed above . . . . And let us note that the subject which is fundamental to an understanding and the treatment of behavioural disorders is psychology, not medicine.

Eysenck proceeded to propose a "divorce" in which the organically based part of psychiatry is left in the hands of conventionally trained psychiatrists (assisted where necessary by clinical psychologists operating, for example, token economy regimens to counteract the effects of institutionalization) but the behavioral-psychiatry side would be taken over either by behaviorally trained psychiatrists—whom he envisages as omitting much of the general medical content in their current training—or by psychologists.

This development has not occurred in practice, but its underlying significance is that the mental disorder is to be viewed as a problem in personal competence—the individual case to be investigated and treated in terms of its own characteristics (rather than as a member of a diagnostic class in the medical system)—and that the relationships between one aspect of the characteristics of the case and others are sufficiently described in purely psychological terms. Thus the links between previous experience and the behavior and experience that currently constitute the "mental disorder" are psychological; the biological apparatus can be assumed to be invariant in this relationship, and so ignored. The major theoretical systems of psychology—Freudian, Kleinian, those derived from learning or socialization theory and so forth—are alternative accounts relating past to present. Similarly, the links between the current behavior and experience and the treatment process and outcome are conceived in psychological terms—in the construction of counseling or behavioral modification programs, their implementation, evaluation, and the like. Although the methods of psychologists approximate as closely as possible to positivism, these phenomena belong to our second, symbolic, world.

SOCIAL SIGNIFICANCE — THE VIEWPOINT OF SOCIAL WORKERS AND THE CLERGY

Most multidisciplinary teams working in the field of mental disorder in Britain today would include a social worker as a member, often in a fairly prominent role. It would be rather less common to find a clergyman in this situation. But every hospital will have a chaplaincy service, and in some the chaplain may be the "key worker" for the individual client or family—a reflection of the part now played by instruction about the behavioral sciences in general, and mental disorder in particular, in the training of many ordinands. There is some justification for discussing social workers and clergy together—the similarities are such that it is not surprising that the social worker is often popularly thought of as the twentieth-century successor to the priest. In fact, this popular notion is highly misleading; nevertheless, it is characteristic of both these professions to understand and to account for the phenomena of mental disorder by reference to the wider context in which it is placed.

Social Work

We shall consider both the general development of social work and its application in the field of mental disorder. Social work in Britain emerged in the nineteenth century from the application of the provisions of the Poor Laws. It attempted to make distinctions between individual cases—at least in terms of the two famous classes, the "deserving poor" and the "undeserving poor"—and it set itself to alleviate the position of some in the former. The account of these earliest beginnings in Woodruffe's *From Charity to Social Work* (1968) makes it clear that, although the focus of work was the individual case, the conceptual framework for understanding and responding to the client's predicament was entirely one of socioeconomic forces. It was not until social work had spread from Britain to North America in the closing decades of the nineteenth and the early years of the twentieth centuries, and American social work had become influenced—indeed, swamped—by what Woodruffe calls the "psychiatric deluge" that the profession started to develop a vocabulary and a system of ideas that enabled it to consider social work problems on the basis of personal psychopathology. Early in the century this personal emphasis was not particularly Freudian but it rapidly became so; the espousal by social work of psychoanalytic theory dates from this time. This tendency was never as wholehearted in Britain as in America, and in recent decades the pendulum has returned to a more central position. Thus, it is perhaps fair to characterize social work today as being concerned with problems of *psychosocial adjustment*—problems that are located neither exclusively within the individual nor within the environment, but precisely in the interaction between the two.

The involvement of social work in the mental health field began in America during the phase of the "psychiatric deluge" in the setting of the law courts and in child guidance. Recrossing the Atlantic in the 1920s, practice in this area understandably emphasized psychology and individualism. But the growing professional education of social workers (in such institutes as the London School of Economics, and later in many other centers) held the balance for successive generations of practitioners between the psychological and the sociological, the individual and the environmental aspects of mental health problems both in childhood and adulthood.

This balance is manifest in the social work contribution to a transdisciplinary view of mental disorder. At the macrosociological level it stresses that a person's disorder cannot be wholly accounted for without considering such matters as that person's place in a class structure or ethnic group or that person's occupational, economic, or housing status; moreover, at a microsociological level, family interaction, peer group, or school influences are regularly found to be significant. Both predisposing and precipitating factors ("life events") are relevant—e.g., Brown and Harris's work on *The Social Origins of Depression* (1978). Yet not every person exposed to such influences in fact develops mental disorder, so individual and psychological components also play their part in accounting for the particular case.

The reemphasis on the social aspects of mental disorder might seem in the psychiatrists' historical perspective to be a turning back of the clock toward an early nineteenth century understanding from which medicalization rescued the sufferers; it might seem as if a century of progress were being thrown away. But this is clearly not so; an emphasis on social causation does not involve judgments of social culpability.

Some of the factors that are represented particularly clearly by the social worker's membership of the transdisciplinary team belong to the world of physical reality, others to the symbolic world. Thus their contribution in practice will include both the provision of material resources: money, places of residence or day care, and so forth, and also efforts through counseling or psychotherapy to modify how the mentally disordered person and relevant others construe or symbolize and their relationships. The emphasis, ultimately, is upon the individual's place in society—objectively or subjectively conceived. And the large involvement of social workers in many centers, not only in the conjoint assessment of patients but in treatment independently or as cotherapist, exemplifies the fruitfulness of the social approach.

The Clergy

It is largely a reflection of the limitations of the author that this section is written from the Christian perspective. In general, the political and cultural assumptions of Western societies were Christian in origin. But beginning somewhat before the first edition of this book and, I judge, accelerating markedly since, such societies have been increasingly making space for non-Christian religions old and new. This multifaith emphasis is reflected in the literature—see, for example, *Psychiatry and Religion: Context, Consensus and Controversies* edited by Dinesh Bhrugha (1996)—but it has become exceedingly difficult for any individual to represent the whole breadth of these considerations. In any case, it remains true that in the English-speaking world the best explored interface between mental health and religion is that involving Christianity.

We should not fall into the trap of equating the view of "the Church" with that of the clergy—still less with that of any individual clergyman or minister. But just as we have attached a particular viewpoint concerning mental disorder to other members of the clinical team, so it will be convenient to regard the clergy as embodying a religious view. Like social workers, their concern is with the individual's place in a larger context: in this case, a cosmic context. Going back in history no further than the Renaissance, two points of impact of the Church on the mentally disordered may be noted: the Church as the only effective form of public care, often through the monastic hospices, for this as for other needy groups; and the Church as the source of theories of mental disorder. The modern successors of both are relevant to our theme.

Although the Church's role in providing institutional care for the mentally disordered has been taken over in Western societies by the secular authorities, certain influences remain. Some of these are vestigial: hospital organization still has overtones of obedience, disciplines like plain food and early rising, and nurses' salary scales which hint that work satisfaction might offset a vow of poverty; but others are not. For instance, in Britain, the National Health Service made from the outset formal provision for hospital chaplaincy services, and the significance of the chaplain as personifying the churches' presence in the institution is clear.

The chaplain's presence symbolizes, first, the importance of the individual patient or staff member: insofar as persons are thought of as the objects of Divine regard, there is no source more absolute of the value systems that surround them. Of course, proponents of atheistic philosophies would reject the fundamental assumption, but where it is granted the ultimate significance of the individual is further affirmed. The premise of a personal God further asserts that the significance of humankind is diminished unless due care is taken of each individual as a biological and psychological being having status in a social and historical—and in some sense, an ultimate—context. In addition, while it is not possible to read off from this point any particular ethical decision concerning a particular patient, the general necessity to take seriously questions of values and ethics is established by it.

It may be objected that formal chaplaincy arrangements are not made in the same way in the community at large where, as shown by Goldberg and Huxley (1980), the overwhelming majority of mentally disordered actually are found. But the hospital is not only a place of care and treatment, it is also for staff and patients alike a source of ideology (Wilson, 1971). Experience in a hospital tends to establish norms in the minds both of patients and their relatives—and, even more powerfully, of students in the various caregiving professions who are trained there—concerning life and death, health and disease, technology, human relationships and so on. And such norms pervade the wider society and there influence the attitudes and behavior of us all. The hospital is *A Place of Truth* (Wilson, 1971) and the chaplain will expect to contribute as teacher and learner to the development of this understanding.

Some clergy will interpret their duty of pastoral care towards individuals to explicitly include working as a psychotherapist; others will maintain a greater degree of separation between psychological and spiritual forms of care. Some will take it as a duty to involve themselves in the management of the health-delivery organization; others will confine their institutional activities to the conduct of public worship. Many will take the view that the distance between religion and mental health provision has become too wide in Western societies.

It is perhaps worth rehearsing the basis for this view. The following is a condensed quotation from Fulford (1966) that refers to empirical research bearing on this theme:

> It is said that religions attract the mentally unstable—but the mental health of the followers even of new religious sects is if anything above rather than below average . . . . It is said that religions may have their origins in madness . . . but madness can also be a source of creativity in art and science . . . . It is said that religious experience is phenomenologically similar to psychopathology (visions are like hallucinations, for example)—but this is to confuse form and con-

tent: normal and pathological varieties of religious experience stand to be differentiated by essentially the same criteria as normal and pathological varieties of non-religious experience . . . . It is said that paranormal experiences are a product of definable patterns of brain functioning—but . . . paranormal experiences are no less invalidated by their grounding in physiology than are normal experiences. It is said that religions are harmful, that they induce guilt, for example . . . but religion, no more than psychiatry is not harmful as such. It is also said, conversely, that religious belief is ineffective—but there is empirical evidence that it is not, improved "coping" for instance being correlated with religious faith in a variety of adverse situations . . . . (Fulford, 1966, pp. 5–6)

Thus, the interpretation of healing both as the gift of God and as part of the mission of the Church does not make it in some way "special" or even opposed to secular clinical social work, but rather leaves it consistent with that endeavor.

THE MULTIDISCIPLINARY TEAM AND THE TRANSDISCIPLINARY VIEW

We have assembled a collection of stereotypes of mental disorder that have developed within five professional groups commonly represented in multidisciplinary clinical teams working with adults. By the sixteenth century, the Old English word *team* (originally, a group of animals harnessed together to draw an agricultural implement) was being applied to a number of persons jointly involved in a common action (as in tug-of-war) and, later, to examples (such as a football or cricket team) where there is considerable differentiation of function. The principles from these two sporting illustrations also exist in the organization of any caregiving team; once *role definition* is achieved with respect to each member it is possible to emphasize *role blurring* or *role differentiation*.

Role blurring is held to be valuable in, for example, therapeutic community ideology, which stresses the importance of the common therapeutic potential of all staff and, indeed, also of the patients. In mental health practice more generally, however, most members of each profession would probably claim that their expertise extends significantly into adjacent fields.

Role differentiation—having defined what each person must do, then let each stick to his or her own task—is frequently advocated in the interests of efficiency. In the management of that complex system comprising the individual suffering from mental disorder together with his or her relevant personal and social environment a better quality of care is achieved; care offered by an individual being seen as in some way inferior, harmful, or actually impossible. A second argument concerns cost-effectiveness: a less expensive but equally adequate service may be offered by one team member rather than another. However, in practice, both some degree of differentiation and also some degree of overlap of function are likely to be usual, and the discrete stereotypes we have described appear to be influential.

In this final section, we consider team relationships in the light of our analysis of the transdisciplinary view of mental disorder through the phases outlined earlier: the attack on medical hegemony, the phase of conceptual analysis, and the empirical study of teamwork in various settings.

Regarding medical hegemony, there exists a large literature reporting investigations of the mutual perceptions of members of different occupational groups. In an early example, Miles (1977) studied in three British psychiatric hospitals the roles of psychiatrists (n = 6), nurses (n = 16), social workers (n = 17), and occupational therapists (n = 12). All respondents ranked the psychiatrist highest in order of importance, but there were disagreements concerning other groups, physicians and nurses ranking second in importance only the nurses, and members of the other groups ranking themselves equally as second. None of the psychiatrists were willing to concede to any other specialty a so-called "area of exclusive competence," while senior practitioners in the other disciplines working in the same hospital wards did claim areas of such competence.

Too much weight must not be placed upon a single small study, but the conflicting attitudes revealed here probably remain very widespread. They represent an implicit claim on the part of the other professionals that the nature of mental disorder is such that the viewpoint of the psychiatrists, derived from their medical background, is only partial.

The phase of conceptual analysis applied to such matters may be represented by the work of the Health Service Organisation Research Unit of Brunel University (Brunel Institute, 1976). As a profession develops an increasing specific body of knowledge and practice that nonmembers can recognize, several things follow. First, members will tend to form a variety of professional associations; second, they will begin to take an interest in training and setting qualifications for practice and influencing conditions of employment for members, and, third, they develop:

> . . . certain very specific standards and norms of behaviour. Certain
> things are invariably (and therefore "properly") done this way;

other things should be avoided. Of particular interest from the organisational point of view are any standards which are regarded as absolute and binding . . . . (Brunel Institute, 1976)

Standards, as represented, for example, by a voluntary code of conduct or by the authority of a statutory registering body may require an accountability to professional norms which overrides any accountability to colleagues within the team. But it is the duty toward other team members that more directly concerns our theme.

The Brunel workers' terminology will help us here. Thinking chiefly of the issue of "the physicians versus the rest," they define four models of relationship: *managerial, prescribing, monitoring* and *coordinative*. The first and last need not concern us here. In a managerial relationship, the manager has responsibility for the direct and constant appraisal of the subordinate's performance: even if practicable, such a relationship could not have an ethically defensible place in the life of a multidisciplinary team. At the other end of the spectrum is a coordinative relationship, in which someone is

expected to take the lead in suggesting specific action or programmes and in reviewing progress, but does not have managerial rights and cannot issue binding rulings or instructions in situations of sustained disagreement . . . . (Brunel, 1976)

This seems only common sense if teamwork is, in fact, to work at all. A physician might sometimes take this role but clearly need not do so. There is an obvious professional duty upon members to be coordinated, and a right to expect that the team relationships will be limited in this way.

The real debate has surrounded the extent to which physicians may have prescribing or monitoring relationships in respect of other team members. Of monitoring which, the Brunel terminology suggests, is a relationship

. . . in which the monitor is expected to keep himself aware of certain specifically defined areas or aspects of activity, to discuss deviation from acceptable standards in these areas and to report serious or continual deviation to higher authority . . . . (Brunel, 1976)

Some would be doubtful although others might accept this. A structure of rights and duties would follow fairly obviously from this kind of arrangement if it was in force.

The chief discussion surrounds the question of whether the physician has, or should have, prescribing authority in relation to other team members. A prescribing relationship, according to the Brunel workers:

> . . . arises where a member of the occupational group has by virtue of his membership of that group the right to determine the objectives to be pursued and the contexts to be observed in specific cases by members of certain other occupational groups *whose knowledge base is encompassed by that of his own* [italics added]. (Brunel, 1976)

It is that matter of the *encompassing profession* that is at the heart of the problem.

The analysis offered in this chapter suggests both why it is that psychiatrists should claim the role of an encompassing profession and also why the nature of mental disorder is such as to make such a claim inappropriate.

This view is beginning to percolate through the empirical literature. Two examples must suffice. First, in relation to the assessment and management of patients with acute self-poisoning, studies in London (Newson-Smith & Hirsh, 1979) have compared the effectiveness of psychiatrists and social workers and in Oxford (Catalan, Marsack, Hawton, Whitwell, Fagg, & Bancroft, 1980) psychiatrists and nurses had found the nonmedical professionals to be equally effective. And, second, in relation to the rehabilitation of long-stay psychiatric patients, a study from a British mental hospital of a quite successful program (Barker, Woods, & Anderson, 1977) notes without differentiation that the primary therapists were "nurses, social workers or chaplains." In practice, this kind of approach has become increasingly widely accepted in the mental health field.

The Transdisciplinary Team

How, then, may role differentiation and role blurring be reconciled? We may think of this in terms of the image of a cartwheel. Each spoke represents one of the contributing professions, and the patient is at the hub. At the rim, each profession is at its furthest from its neighbors; this represents the extreme of professional identity and specialization. Individual practitioners may be thought of as moving in and out along their own spoke. As the spokes converge on the hub of a wheel, the closer team members get to being able to undertake one another's tasks, the closer are they likely to be to territory which is also shared with the patient—who is, of course, less preoccupied with the technicalities of the pathology but more concerned with his or her suffering and its alleviation. Conversely, the further they are from one another, the further each is from the patient and the more they are in their separate worlds of high specialization in traditions, institutions, training, and the like.

Consider a situation where the particular task performed for and with the patient appears the same whether the worker be physician, nurse, psychiatrist, social worker, chaplain, or member of any other professional group. This may occur particularly, perhaps, in respect of psychotherapeutic or counseling tasks (but other examples exist). Borrowing a concept from Gestalt psychology, we may suggest that individual practitioners will see this work figured against the background of their own discipline. The psychiatrist engaged in psychotherapy is not prescribing a drug; the social worker is not providing a material resource; the nurse is not substituting for self care; the psychologist is not engaged in mental measurement; the clergyman is not conducting a public rite. The psychotherapeutic task may be the same; but the varied backgrounds against which this ostensibly identical task is performed are also relevant. Transmitted by all manner of nuances of attitude and language, they influence the task performance and enrich the range of possibilities available to the patient. Thus it is legitimate within a team that a particular function may be allocated more upon the basis of, say, the personal qualities of those involved than on their professional identities.

Returning to our image of the cartwheel, the rim thus represents professional separation, with its preoccupations with part-function, pathology, and, often, high technology. The hub represents the less constrained territory sufficient to enable the professionals to enter into a therapeutic alliance with the patient and collaboration with one another. It is the territory of the holistic approach, in which the transdisciplinary view of mental disorder is matched by the multidisciplinary practice of the clinical team.

REFERENCES

American Psychiatric Association. (1994). *Diagnostic and statistical manual of mental disorders, fourth edition.* Washington, DC: Author.

Barker, G. H. B., Woods, T. S., & Anderson J. A. (1977). Rehabilitation of the institutionalised patient. *British Journal of Psychiatry, 130,* 484–488.

Barton, R. (1959). *Institutional neurosis.* Bristol: John Wright.

Bhugra, D. (Ed.). (1996). *Psychiatry and religion: Context, consensus and controversies.* London and New York: Routledge and Kegan Paul.

Brown, G. W., & Harris, T. (1978). *The social origins of depression*. London: Tavistock Institute.

Brunel Institute of Organisation and Social Studies. (1976). *Professionals in health and social service organisations: A working paper*. Uxbridge, England: Author.

Catalan, P., Marsack, P., Hawton, K. E., Whitwell, D., Fagg, J., & Bancroft, J. H. J. (1980). Comparison of doctors and nurses in the assessment of deliberate self-poisoning patients. *Psychological Medicine, 10*, 483–492.

Clare, A. (1976). *Psychiatry in dissent*. London: Tavistock Institute.

Eysenck, H. J. (1975). *The future of psychiatry*. London: Methuen.

Fulford, K. W. M. (1966). Religion and psychiatry: Extending the limits of tolerance. In Bhugra, D., op. cit. (pp. 5–56).

Giddens, A. (1976). *New rules of sociological method*. London: Hutchinson.

Goffman, E. (1961). *Asylums*. New York: Doubleday.

Goldberg, D., & Huxley, P. (1980). *Mental disorder in the community*. London: Tavistock Institute.

Jenkins, D. (1960). Resources for being human. *Contact, 36*, 2–19.

Jones, K. (1972). *A history of the mental health services*. London: Routledge and Kegan Paul.

Jones, M. (1952). *Social psychiatry: A study of therapeutic communities*. London: Tavistock Institute.

Miles, A. (1977). Staff relations in a psychiatric hospital. *Britain Journal of Psychiatry, 130*, 84–88.

Newson-Smith, J. G. B., & Hirsch, S. (1979). A comparison of social workers and psychiatrists in evaluating parasuicide. *British Journal of Psychiatry, 134*, 335–342.

Revans, R. W. (1976). *Action learning in hospitals*. London: McGraw Hill.

Siegler, M., & Osmond M. (1974). *Models of madness, models of medicine*. New York: Macmillan.

Sladden, S. (1979). *Psychiatric nursing in the community*. Edinburgh, Scotland: Churchill Livingstone.

Wilson, M. (1971). *The hospital—A place of truth*. Birmingham, England: University of Birmingham, Institute for the Study of Worship and Religious Architecture.

World Health Organization (WHO). (1993). *International Classification of Mental and Behavioural Disorders* (10th Revision). London: Her Majesty's Stationery Office.

Woodruffe, K. (1968). *From charity to social work*. London: Routledge and Kegan Paul.

3

CASE MANAGEMENT AS A STRATEGY OF SOCIAL WORK INTERVENTION WITH THE MENTALLY ILL

Irene A. Gutheil and Roslyn H. Chernesky

C ase management is an approach to service delivery that works to ensure that clients with complex, multiple problems and disabilities receive all the services they need in a timely, effective, and appropriate fashion (Rubin, 1992). Its primary goal is to organize, coordinate, and sustain a network of formal and informal supports and services that individuals may require for optimal functioning and well-being (Moxley, 1989). Case management has always had a dual focus: It is both client-oriented and system-oriented. Therefore, a second goal is to redress shortcomings in service delivery in order for services to be both available and accessible to individuals who may need them. To be effective, case managers must understand individual clients, their needs and supports, as well as be knowledgeable about agencies, communities, and service delivery systems.

This chapter examines case management in mental health, reviews recent thinking about this method of practice, and considers some issues faced in implementing case management. After more than twenty years of case management programs and practice, a considerable body of knowledge has emerged that illustrates the breadth and diversity of what has become a critical intervention strategy for services to vulnerable individuals who

The authors wish to acknowledge the contribution of case material by Basia Kinglake, MSW, Program Coordinator of Family Matters. Family Matters is a collaboration between Westchester Jewish Community Services and The Center for Preventive Psychiatry with the support of the Westchester County Department of Community Mental Health.

show a high level of internal impairment, who have a low level of access to external resources, and who are faced with overwhelming stressors (Gitterman, 1991). The chapter's focus on the strengths model of case management reflects the increased attention to strengths in social work practice.

APPLICATION OF CASE MANAGEMENT TO MENTAL ILLNESS

Case management is especially appropriate for clients with serious and persistent mental illness (SPMI). The term *SPMI* includes individuals with diagnoses such as schizophrenia and major depressive disorder that reflect enduring symptoms, neurocognitive impairments, disabilities, and deficits in everyday functioning. When symptoms are controllable through a continuing course of medication, periods of remission may nonetheless be interrupted by episodes of crisis and decompensation.

Despite limitations in skills or information, many persons with SPMI retain basic strengths and are able to function at a level sufficient to maintain a reasonable quality of life in the community when provided with adequate supports. Persons with SPMI have great difficulty arranging for the kind of support that is necessary. Their networks and support environment are frequently inadequate, highly complex, and difficult to access (Tracy & Biegel, 1994).

Sullivan (1997) notes that persons with SPMI are particularly at risk of being caught in limiting environments, referred to as "entrapping niches."

> Entrapping niches are highly stigmatized, and people who occupy them are defined by their social category, or in this case, their illness. Because of stigma and the lack of opportunities, people must turn to others in like situations, and ultimately their social world becomes highly constricted. In the most dire situations, the individual is segregated to such a degree that there is little reality and feedback, and this limits the opportunity to learn from real-life experiences. Over time there is little expectation, on the part of self or others, that growth and change will occur. (Sullivan, 1997, p. 192)

Too often, the mental health system itself contributes to the entrapping niche of individuals with SPMI. Psychiatric institutions, sheltered workshops, and specialized community residences keep people segregated from the mainstream. Eventually it is accepted that specialized care and environments are essential because those with mental illness could not manage otherwise (Sullivan, 1997).

Case management moves clients toward competency in community living. It builds on client and community resources to assist clients to cope with basic life tasks, to develop daily living skills, and to grapple with environmental stressors and with the multiple demands associated with their illness. For individuals being discharged from a psychiatric facility and reentering community living, case management addresses a range of issues including housing, income, maintaining a medication regimen, making friends, and acquiring and applying daily living skills.

History of Case Management and Mental Health

The need for case management with the mentally ill grew in response to two major forces: the unprecedented growth in human service programs through federal and state monies to communities beginning in the 1960s and continuing through the next decade, and the deinstitutionalization of the mentally ill after the advent of psychotropic medications (Intagliata, 1992; Blodgett, 1993). Services developed through highly categorical funding, resulting in a complex, duplicative, and uncoordinated service system spread among many different types of agencies and all levels of government. Each component of the system had its own requirements for determining which clients were eligible for which services, contributing to a service environment that was difficult to decipher and negotiate. With the advent of deinstitutionalization mentally ill persons, who previously had had all of their needs met in large institutions, were discharged to communities ill prepared to manage their needs in the context of a fragmented, bewildering service network (Intagliata, 1992).

The availability of community services was further complicated by the fact that some agencies were unresponsive or even rejecting. Social service agencies and community mental health centers, which had been established primarily to facilitate reintegration of the seriously and persistently mentally ill into the community, often preferred not to serve the deinstitutionalized population, whom they considered unsuitable for their treatment approaches. Instead of finding a network of support, deinstitutionalized persons found that the services they needed were inaccessible, and they were likely to fall through the cracks or get lost in the system.

Although case management had been identified as a core aftercare service in the 1963 Federal Community Mental Health Center Act, community mental health centers (CMHC) operated from a medical model of psychiatric aftercare (McGurrin & Worley, 1993). Because the medical model primarily addresses symptom reduction, medication management, and provision of therapeutic services, other needs of persons with SPMI such as employment, housing, recreation, and necessities of daily life were not adequately attended to. At best, these services were provided by agencies other than the CMHC where clients received psychiatric care (McGurrin & Worley, 1993). There was generally little contact between these agencies and the CMHCs, leading to another source of fragmentation.

Communities began to raise their voices in response to the realization that large numbers of mentally ill persons were unable to successfully integrate into the community. At the same time, pressures toward accountability, cost effectiveness, and cost containment increased. In a effort to deal with the increasingly disappointing situation, the National Institute of Mental Health (NIMH) responded with the development in 1978 of the Community Support Program (CSP). This was a milestone in the history of case management in mental health. Demonstration projects were funded in 19 states and the District of Columbia (Intagliata, 1992). Local agencies designated as core CSP agencies used case managers to assess the needs of persons with SPMI in their area, negotiate interagency linkages and arrangements for providing needed services, and develop new services to fill gaps in the existing service networks. In this initiative, the case manager played a key role, coordinating various system components and making them more responsive to client needs (Rose, 1992).

The 1986 Omnibus Reconciliation Act required case management services for all individuals with SPMI who receive substantial amounts of public funds or services (Raiff & Shore, 1993). Case managers once again emerged as pivotal players in the system, with the primary responsibility for clients—linking them with essential services, coordinating and monitoring these services, and following the clients to ensure their ability to remain in the community.

Today, case management continues to be an integral component of services for individuals with SPMI. Federal funding currently supports "intensive case management" (ICM), which is intended to meet the unique needs of the most difficult SPMI individuals. Through State Offices of Mental Health, ICM programs target services to heavy users of inpatient or hospital emergency services, persons with a history of irregular or unreliable aftercare service, and individuals who are unable or unwilling to maintain a medication regimen. ICM clients are among the most unserved and undeserved, and include the homeless mentally ill, and those who might not otherwise be discharged from psychiatric hospitals because they would be unable to adjust to community living. State guidelines establish program eligibility, caseload size, staff qualifications and training, and basic program requirements such as 24-hour access to services by clients, a commitment to long-term support to clients, and work with clients in their communities rather than by office appointments (Degan, Tamayo, & Dzerovych, 1990; Landsberg & Rock, 1994; McGurrin & Worley, 1993).

SOCIAL WORK AND CASE MANAGEMENT

Although the term was not then used, case management activities can be attributed to Mary Richmond, an early-1900s social work pioneer. Called *social casework,* these activities were carried out to involve the community at large in assisting persons who were experiencing problems in daily living. Thus, case management's roots are in social work (Johnson & Rubin, 1983).

Case management is also grounded in the social work tradition of problem-solving, its values and principles regarding respect for the individual, client self-determination, and equal access to resources. The social work perspective focusing on the person-in-environment and the significance of the practitioner–client relationship further place case management in the social work arena.

The values and assumptions that undergird case management are the cornerstones of good social work practice: the uniqueness of the individual and the need to design service in response to each individual's needs; the importance of understanding that clients' needs change over time, and that the services provided must be responsive to these changes; the importance of working to maintain maximum client self-determination and independence.

Although social work's professional mandate, values, knowledge base, and skills suggest that social workers ought to be fulfilling case manager roles, the profession's place in case management is ambiguous. Today, case manager roles are filled by other professionals, including nurses, and nonprofessionals. Social work may have abdicated its place in defining and implementing case management for the mentally ill. One reason for this may be the misconception that case management is limited to coordination of concrete services and does not draw on clinical skills (Soares & Rose, 1994). The argument for social work assuming leadership in case management of the chronically mentally ill goes back some time (Johnson & Rubin, 1983). Perhaps, recent social work initiatives to reconceptualize case management from a strengths perspective will revitalize social work commitment to case management practice.

CASE MANAGEMENT FUNCTIONS

Case management practice is comprised of core functions or activities. These are seen as a phased series of sequential, discrete yet overlapping and interactive activities. Although as few as four and as many as fifteen have been identified since 1992 (Rothman & Sager, 1998; Rubin, 1992), five primary functions are widely accepted.

- Assessing needs
- Planning for services
- Linking clients to resources appropriate to their needs
- Monitoring and evaluating services to ensure that they are both appropriate and effective
- Advocating with other people or providers on behalf of clients

There is no consensus on the operational definitions of these functions. In general, the literature describes what case managers do but not necessarily how they do it (Fiorentine & Grusky, 1990).

Without specific protocols, case management has adapted to different situations, agencies, client populations, problem fields. Duration varies (brief to ongoing), as does intensity and staff-to-client ratio, frequency of staff-client contact, case manager availability (up to 24 hours), and site of service. Moreover, the case management process is hard to standardize because it is influenced by numerous factors: program structure and staffing; case manager education and training; case manager authority (from control of resources to persuasion only); funding; and agency auspices (Ridgely, 1996).

MODELS OF CASE MANAGEMENT

It has been suggested that a number of case management models coexist (Korr & Cloninger, 1991; Raiff & Shore, 1993; Rothman, 1992) based on the extent of the case manager's clinical involvement with clients, and the range of functions or activities than the models provide. Although there are no clearly defined, universal models of case management, four are referred to most often in mental health case management: expanded broker, strengths-based, rehabilitation, and full support (Solomon, 1992).

The expanded broker model is both client and system focused. Case managers link clients to needed resources and services, monitor clients' progress and the delivery of services, and, when necessary, advocate for services clients may need. The strengths-based model stresses the importance of the case manager's relationship with the client in identifying individuals' strengths and securing critical resources to help clients achieve a better quality of life. The rehabilitation model emphasizes individual needs assessment and goal formulation and the teaching of personal, social, and daily living skills necessary for clients to meet their goals. The full support model combines traditional service planning with clinical case management, treatment and rehabilitation services.

A major distinction among case management programs in mental health is between "clinical" and "nonclinical" case management. Clinical case management (Raiff & Shore, 1993) involves the delivery of mental health and support services by the case manager in a program characterized by intensity of service and small caseloads. It draws upon the clinical expertise of case managers and is usually targeted to people with severe mental illness who use emergency or inpatient services but have difficulty following through with aftercare plans and community reintegration.

Other case management programs focus on the coordination of services of a range of health and social service providers without clinical care provided by the case manager. Clients in these programs are referred to treatment programs for actual clinical services such as counseling or psychotherapy. Even when the focus is coordination of service, to be effective, the case manager does more than simply coordinate treatment. Effective case management relies on skillful assessment, and results in strengthening clients' inner resources and cognitive and emotional capacities in order for them to make better use of the services and supports to which they have been linked. The result is enhanced functioning and the greater likelihood of their integration into the community. Harris and Bergman (1992) contend that close relationships with case managers offer clients the opportunity for identification and, ultimately, internalization of the case management process.

STRENGTHS-BASED CASE MANAGEMENT

The past decade has witnessed the growth of a new paradigm in social work practice: the strengths perspective. The strengths-based approach, centered on discovering, mobilizing, and nurturing clients' strengths, has had a growing impact on case management practice (Saleebey, 1997). A growing body of literature describes this approach as a powerful intervention for assisting persons with serious and persistent mental illness. It is predicated on the belief that clients will be most successful when the focus is on their strengths and they are meaningfully involved in directing their own treatment. It was first used with persons being discharged from long-term hospitalization for mental illness (Rapp & Chamberlain, 1985), and struggling to become integrated into communities. It has become an aid in the recovery process of people with SPMI (Sullivan, 1997).

The six principles that drive strengths-based case management are the following.

1. The focus is on individual strengths rather than pathology.
2. The case manager–client relationship is primary and essential.
3. Interventions are based on client self-determination.
4. The community is viewed as an oasis of resources, not as an obstacle.
5. Aggressive outreach is the preferred mode of intervention.
6. People suffering from severe mental illness can continue to learn, grow, and change. (Rapp, 1992, p. 46)

The case manager begins by exploring the wants, desires, dreams, and goals of the individual, gathering information from the client's (generally referred to as the consumer in this model) view. The focus is on assets, both in the individual and in his or her environment, in contrast to the traditional deficit-oriented approach (Rapp, 1998). The case manager must earn the client's respect and confidence by nurturing a collaborative relationship rather than playing the role of helper (Kisthardt, 1997). Relationship is key to successful case management. As Perlman wrote almost twenty years ago: "If services to human beings are to fulfill their alleged purposes, they must attend not only to the problems people have but to the people who suffer and struggle to cope with these problems" (Perlman, 1979, p.11).

Because creating an accepting climate is critical to developing a collaborative relationship, initial engagement efforts aim to establish trust through accepting and validating the client. The case manager may draw on a range of interactions to connect with clients, including talking about common interests or engaging in activities together (Kisthardt, 1997). Providing a concrete service communicates to the client that the case manager is reliable and can be trusted to help. Because many clients have had previous involvement with insensitive or damaging service systems, they may be fearful of losing control of their lives yet again. There are times when not trusting is a strength, demonstrating that a client has learned from damaging past circumstances (Rapp, 1998). Overcoming fear, anger, or mistrust and demonstrating that case management can return to clients control of their lives is a crucial step in engagement (Rothman & Sager, 1998). This takes time, and must be recognized as a process that evolves naturally and cannot be hurried by the case manager (Rapp, 1998).

The case manager may be the one person in clients' lives that believes in their capacity to grow and to improve their lives (Rapp, 1992). In addition, the relationship with the case manager may be the one relationship clients can rely on for continuity as they move across institutional, agency, and community boundaries. For individuals devalued by society, this relationship offers reassurance, stability, and hope, and may strengthen clients' motivation and capacity to use available supports (Rubin, 1992).

Clearly, the quality of the personal commitment that case managers develop toward their clients is a critical aspect of the case management process, perhaps the most critical. The case manager, concerned with and responsible to and for the whole client, can be the one who humanizes the service delivery system and personalizes it to clients' needs (Intagliata, 1992). As Intagliata (1992) notes: "The human relationships that develop between case managers and clients should be considered a fundamental strength of the case management model, and case management programs should be structured to facilitate and capitalize on this process" (p. 33).

A recent study of the key elements of the recovery process of 46 current and former consumers of mental health services found that the relationship and the caring atmosphere and protection the case managers and programs offered was one of the two highest factors identified as critical to their success. The friendship, companionship, encouragement, and sense of being looked after offered by the case managers were highly valued. In addition, case managers helped with basic problems in living and the daily life stresses (reported in Sullivan, 1997).

In strengths-based case management, the strengths of the environment are primary in planning. Instead of focusing on the limitations of community resources, the case manager looks for areas of strength in the community where it is possible to nurture collaborative relationships that can be mined for the benefit of clients. Rapp (1998) underscores the importance of recognizing and utilizing "naturally occurring resources" such as neighbors, volunteer opportunities, and junior colleges. Instead of bemoaning the deficiency of the traditional mental health system to adequately provide for the needs of persons with SPMI, strengths-based case management looks to new, creative avenues for tapping the potential of communities to care for and about their members.

Working from the strengths perspective, case managers cannot operate primarily from an office. The process requires aggressive outreach in the community (Rapp, 1998). It is essential to see clients in their communities to have an accurate understanding of their skills and behaviors. In addition, clients are best able to integrate into their communities when they learn and practice skills "in vivo" (Kisthardt, 1997). Also, case managers need to see the resources they are linking clients up with to be certain that they are accessible and welcoming, or, when there are difficulties, to help clients find ways to cope with these difficulties. Nurturing collaborative relationships with the resources that can be of help to clients, be they family members, neighbors, or potential employers, cannot be accomplished without getting out into the community.

When Mrs. T, a 37-year-old single mother of six, first came to the attention of the case management program, none of her children, aged 7–17, was attending school regularly. Although undiagnosed at the time, Mrs. T was suffering from Major Depressive Disorder and had taken to her bed. The household consisted of Mrs. T, her six children, and her 17-year-old daughter's son. The family history includes placement of the children in foster care and subsequent return home, homelessness, violence against Mrs. T by former partners, use of alcohol by Mrs. T to self medicate, and current involvement by protective services for the children (CPS). The family lives on public assistance.

Despite hardships and multiple stressors, the family is currently intact.

Based on a referral from CPS, a team of two case managers initiated contact with this family, one to work with and for the children, and the other for Mrs. T. At the time of the referral, the family became homeless and was moved into a shelter. The case manager visited regularly, bringing food for the family and

By providing a concrete service, the case manager (CM) demonstrates that she is trustworthy and reliable.

The CM honors Mrs. T's agenda.

Relationships with the service network enable quick response to client needs.

focusing on finding permanent housing, Mrs. T's priority. The case manager was able to arrange for the family to move into subsidized housing for formerly homeless mentally ill adults, a resource previously used by the program.

Although it took a long time to develop a relationship, Mrs. T was appreciative of the assistance with the food and housing. She indicated that she would accept help around her children's needs. Therefore she was linked with a community-based parent support program which offered support groups and parenting classes. However, she attended intermittently and with great difficulty.

The CM helps the mother regain control of her life by identifying the areas she can accept help.

The case manager working with the children was able to proceed more quickly. Over a period of time, each of the children was connected with the appropriate school and school-based support services to deal with developmental disabilities and hyperactivity. Two of the children were referred to a psychiatrist and were placed on medication.

To carry out this plan arrangements for transportation were made using several resources.

Arrangements were made for a parent aide to arrive at the home every weekday at 7:00 A.M. to help Mrs. T manage the children and get them off to school. Day trips with a Big Brother/Big Sister and weekend visits with a respite family were arranged to give Mrs. T a break from some of the children. Resources within the schools, such as teachers' aides and other parents, were identified and used to support the family with respite, transportation, mentoring, and trips to special events. After-school programs were used whenever available. The oldest daughter was included in the program's newly created recreation program for adolescent girls. Arrangements

Through outreach into the community, the CM uses naturally occurring resources to support and sustain the family.

When needed services do not exist, the CM helps establish them.

were also made for several of the children to attend summer sleep-away camp for the first time.

The relationship with Mrs. T deepened, and, with the support of the case manager, after nine months, Mrs. T began to see a psychiatrist. She was prescribed Paxil. Her continuing use of the medication as prescribed was one of the areas case management focused on. The case manager also provided supportive therapy in Mrs. T's home two to three times a week. Their work focused on helping Mrs. T deal with her past traumas, understand her current relationships and disappointments, and begin to take care of herself, including seeing a physician. Mrs. T expressed her hope to some day go back to school. Mrs. T's lack of an informal support network was a poignant reflection of her isolation. While ongoing efforts focused on building supports in the community and helping develop positive relationships with the various schools and services working with her children, Mrs. T identified a long-term goal of reconnecting with an aunt who lives nearby.

The CM validates Mrs. T by listening to her aspirations and taking them seriously.

The case manager convenes monthly meetings in her office of Mrs. T and all the agencies and services working with this family, including the psychiatrist. These meetings are referred to as "support circle" meetings and help foster the goal of developing a healthier community around the T family. The meeting also provides a forum for Mrs. T to develop basic skills. For example, the case manager gave Mrs. T a calendar to bring to the meetings and helped her develop a system for keeping track of the children's various appointments and activities.

By participating in the meetings, Mrs. T begins to have greater control of her life.

The CM teaches Mrs. T new skills and provides opportunities for her to practice them.

In working to coordinate a number of community agencies, the case manager found it particularly helpful to be open about the differing agendas of the various systems involved with this family. The mental health system is concerned with healing trauma; the child welfare system, protecting the children; the school system, educating the children; and the housing system, maintaining the living facility in satisfactory condition. The support circle meetings provide an opportunity to find a common ground among the systems as well as to avoid duplication.

> The CM nurtures collaborative relationships.
>
> The meetings are a potential arena for advocacy when necessary and monitoring that services are being provided as planned.

Other than the monthly meetings, case management services to this family are provided in the field. The case manager working with Mrs. T sees her in her home and may accompany her into the community. For example, when Mrs. T first visited a school for a parent-teacher conference, the case manager went along with her. The case manager working with the children works primarily with their various schools, developing and nurturing individualized supports for the children.

> The CM supports Mrs. T as she takes on a new challenge.

Work with Mrs. T and her family over the course of almost three years, despite setbacks, has resulted in significant gains. Mrs. T gets up every day, gets dressed, and, with the help of an aide, gets her children off to school. She straightens up the apartment, does the laundry, and cares for her grandson while the oldest daughter is at work. Mrs. T is now ready to work on her goal of developing a relationship with her aunt, and hopes to begin work toward her other goal: completing her own high school education and getting a job.

> The CM has been available 24 hours a day should crisis arise.
>
> The CM will continue to work with Mrs. T, tailoring the case management to her changing needs.

EVALUATION OF MENTAL HEALTH CASE MANAGEMENT

There have been many efforts during the 1980s and through the 1990s to describe and examine the process of case management and the factors that affect it (Baker & Weiss, 1984; Franklin, Solovitz, Mason, Clemons, & Miller, 1987; Goering, Wasylenki, Farkas, Lancee, & Ballantyne, 1988; Harrod, 1986; Intagliata & Baker, 1983; Kurtz, Bagarozzi, & Pollane, 1984; Modrcin, Rapp, & Poertner, 1988; Perlman, Melnick, & Kentera, 1985). These studies provide a picture of case managers, the design of their jobs, the array of case manager roles, client characteristics, and identify some of the difficulties associated with case management practice. Other research on case management has aimed to determine whether case management actually benefits clients and their quality of life (Curtis, Millman, Struening, & D'Ercole, 1992; Hornstra, et al., 1993; Macias, et al., 1994; McGurrin & Worley, 1993; Quinlivan, et al., 1995; Solomon, 1992).

Experimental studies examining the impact of case management services resulted in contradictory findings. Solomon (1992) reviewed 20 empirical studies of four models of case management for severely mentally disabled adults, conducted from 1980 to 1991, to determine their outcomes and conclusions. She concluded that:

> [T]he evidence seemed to indicate that case management is most effective in reducing the number of rehospitalizations and, in the event of hospitalization, reducing the length of stay. Furthermore, with a reduction of hospitalization, if a number of highly costly services are not substituted, case management appears to be cost effective. Case management also seems to improve the quality of life of severely mentally disabled clients. (p. 176)

Later studies have not confirmed the effectiveness of case management in reducing the number of rehospitalizations (Curtis, 1992; Hornstra, et al., 1993). In contrast, Quinlivan and his colleagues (1995) found that frequent users of inpatient care assigned to intensive case management rather than traditional case management or no particular services had fewer inpatient days. In addition, case management resulted in reduced overall costs for mental health services.

Findings regarding use of outcomes other than rehospitalization have similar functioning and symptomatology. McGurrin and Worley (1993) did not find that client behavior or daily functioning in the community improved dramatically after three years of intensive case management, although client level of functioning was maintained and was a little better than when inpatient. Macias and her colleagues (1994), however, found that individuals who received case management along with psychosocial rehabilitation functioned at a higher level of competency and experienced significantly lower psychiatric symptomatology than those who received only psychosocial rehabilitation.

The discrepancies in findings among the empirical studies evaluating the value of case management are most likely the result of wide variation in case management models, agency context, program emphasis, and objectives (e.g., to reduce rehospitalization), case manager and client characteristics, and the service and resource environment. Research design, choice of outcome measures, data sources, and the timing of the evaluation also impact on findings, as do differences between programs received by those in the experimental (case management) and the control groups (Bond, 1994).

The mental health field has gone beyond relying upon evidence of effectiveness from anecdotes, case studies, and clinical observations but, despite the number of empirical outcome studies, the field lacks reliable evidence of case management's effectiveness. The need for rigorous evaluation of case management to determine its effectiveness remains. Nevertheless, in the absence of such data, case management continues to be viewed as a critical and valuable component of community care for mentally ill individuals.

PRACTICE ISSUES

A number of issues that impact on work with clients and the overall effectiveness of social work case managers have been identified (Fiorentine & Grusky, 1990; Moore, 1992; Roberts-DeGennaro, 1993). It is critical that case managers be aware of these issues and the ways in which they may be affecting their practice.

- *Client participation:* Since maximizing clients' capacities to manage their own lives is the goal of case management, client participation is of particular concern. Case managers are expected to empower clients who feel helpless and defeated. At the same time, they must link clients with necessary services. To accomplish this in times of crisis often means that the case manager must act for the client. The case manager is challenged to balance the need to intervene with helping clients remain in control of their lives.

- *Client self-determination:* Closely linked to client participation, a commitment to client self-determination raises the need for case managers to balance the benefits of supporting clients' autonomous decision making with the risks of not intervening in potentially dangerous situations. Case managers must resist the pull toward paternalism, although at times it may be necessary for them to influence clients' decision making.
- *Confidentiality:* In a complex service system, case managers may deal with many professional and nonprofessional resources on behalf of their clients. The questions of what information service providers need to have, how to ensure that this information is used appropriately, and how to best involve clients in decision making are ongoing concerns.
- *Gatekeeping:* In some instances, case managers are expected to be mindful of the most cost-effective service options and to direct their clients to these services. When case managers are expected to contain program costs and, at the same time, provide clients access to services, they face a potential conflict of interest.
- *Community resources and services:* Characteristics of the resource and service network impact the delivery of case management services. Case managers need to be careful not to let the existing resources inappropriately dictate what services clients receive. When there are relatively few resources or when needed services are unavailable or even ineffective, case managers must spend more time on developing naturally occurring supports as well as advocating for more community-based services.
- *Burnout:* Situations that are overwhelming to clients may be overwhelming to case managers as well. Case managers may become frustrated when they are unable to meet clients' needs because essential services are not available. Case managers need to look for ways to reduce or prevent the potential for overload and burnout. Case management teams or partnering, peer/agency support groups, and continuing education are all tools for coping with a stressful and demanding job.
- *Boundaries:* Because case managers may interact with clients in ways that are more associated with friendship than with a professional relationship, such as engaging in activities together or talking about common interests, the case manager and the client may experience some difficulty being clear about the boundaries of the relationship.

The case manager's twenty-four-hour availability further complicates the situation.

CONCLUSION

Case management is a critical component of the mental health system serving persons with serious and persistent mental illness. Regardless of whether clients need continuous involvement with a case manager or someone to turn to at times of crisis, their case manager may provide the one reliable and stable relationship in clients' lives. The case manager humanizes an overwhelming or unresponsive service system and helps individuals with SPMI remain in the community.

Although there is a perception by some that case management is not clinically challenging, working with clients struggling with severe mental illness to help them grow and maintain themselves in the community requires refined clinical skills. In addition, skills in negotiating complex systems, crucial to effective case management, are of increasing importance to all clinical social workers as they deal with today's managed-care environment.

As social work continues to focus on ways to build on clients' strengths, case management will continue to evolve as an essential, creative, and humanizing component of services to persons with severe mental illness.

REFERENCES

Baker, F., & Weiss, R. S. (1984). The nature of case manager support. *Hospital and Community Psychiatry, 35,* 925–928.

Blodgett, B. P. (1993). Case management in mental health. *Journal of Case Management, 2,3,* 96–100.

Bond, G. R. (1994). Case management and psychosocial rehabilitation: Can they be synergistic? *Community Mental Health Journal, 30,4,* 341–345.

Curtis, J. L., Millman, E. J., Struening, E., & D'Ercole, A. (1992). Effect of case management on rehospitalization and utilization of ambulatory care services. *Hospital and Community Psychiatry, 43,9,* 895–899.

Degan, K., Cole, N., Tamayo, L., & Dzerovych, G. (1990). Intensive case management for the seriously mentally ill. *Administration and Policy in Mental Health, 17,* 265–269.

Fiorentine, R., & Grusky, O. (1990). When case managers manage the seriously mentally ill: A role-contingency approach. *Social Service Review,* 79–93.

Franklin, J. L., Solovitz, B., Mason, M., Clemons, J. R., & Miller, G. E. (1987). An evaluation of case management. *American Journal of Public Health, 77,6,* 674–678.

Gitterman, A. (1991). Social work practice with vulnerable populations. In A. Gitterman (Ed.). *Handbook of social work* (pp. 1–32). New York: Columbia University Press.

Goering, P. N., Wasylenki, D., Farkas, M., Lancee, W. J., & Ballantyne, R. (1988). What difference does case management make? *Hospital and Community Psychiatry, 39,3,* 272–276.

Harris, M., & Bergman, H. C. (1992). Case management with the chronically mentally ill: A clinical perspective. In S. M. Rose, (Ed.). *Case management and social work practice.* New York: Longman, pp. 91–100.

Harrod, J. B. (1986). Defining case management in community support systems. *Psychosocial Rehabilitation Journal, 9,* 56–61.

Hornstra, B. K., Bruce-Wolfe, V., Saduyu, K., & Riffle, D. W. (1993). The effective of intensive case management on hospitalization of patients with schizophrenia. *Hospital and Community Psychiatry, 44,9,* 844–847.

Intagliata, J. (1992). Improving the quality of community care for the chronically mentally disabled: The role of case management. In S. M. Rose, (Ed.). *Case management and social work practice* (pp. 25–55). New York: Longman.

Intagliata, J., & Baker, F. (1983). Factors affecting case management services for the chronically mentally ill. *Administration in Mental Health, 11,2,* 75–91.

Johnson, P., & Rubin, A. (1983). Case management in mental health: A social work domain? *Social Work, 1,* 49–55.

Kanter, J. S. (1992). Mental health case management: A professional domain. In S. M. Rose (Ed.). (1992). *Case management and social work practice* (pp. 126–130). New York: Longman.

Kisthardt, W. (1997). The strengths model of case management: Principles and helping functions. In D. Saleebey (Ed.). *The strengths perspective in social work practice* (pp. 97–113). New York: Longman.

Korr, W. S., & Cloninger, L. (1991). Assessing models of case management: An empirical approach. *Journal of Social Service Research, 14,1/2,* 129–146.

Kurtz, L. F., Bagarozzi, D. A., and Pollane, L. P. (1984). Case management in mental health. *Health and Social Work, 9,* 201–211.

Landsberg, G., & Rock, M. (1994). Mental health systems coordination: The Intensive Case Management Program in New York City. *Administration and Policy in Mental Health, 22,2,* 115–131.

Macias, C., Kenney, R., Farley, O. W., Jackson, R., & Vos, B. (1994). The role of case management with a community support system: Partnership with psychosocial rehabilitation. *Community Mental Health Journal, 30,4,* 323–339.

McGurrin, M. C., & Worley, N. (1993). Evaluation of case management for seriously and persistently mentally ill persons. *Journal of Case Management, 2,2,* 59–65.

Modrcin, M., Rapp, C. A., & Poertner, J. (1988). The evaluation of case management services with the chronically mentally ill. *Evaluation and Program Planning, 11,* 307–314.

Moore, S. (1992). Case management and the integration of services: How service delivery systems shape case management. *Social Work, 37,5,* 418–423.

Moxley, D. P. (1989). *The practice of case management.* Newbury Park, CA: Sage Publications.

Perlman, H. H. (1979). *Relationship: The heart of helping people.* Chicago: University of Chicago.

Perlman, B. B., Melnick, G., & Kentera, A. (1985). Assessing the effectiveness of a case management program. *Hospital and Community Psychiatry, 36,* 405–407.

Quinlivan, R., Hough, R., Crowell, A., Beach, C., Hofstetter, R., & Kenworthy, K. (1995). Service utilization and costs of care for severely mentally ill clients in an intensive case management program. *Psychiatric Services, 46,4,* 365–371.

Raiff, N. R., & Shore, B. K. (1993). *Advanced case management.* Newbury Park, CA: Sage Publications.

Rapp, C. A. (1992). The strengths perspective of case management with persons suffering from severe mental illness. In D. Saleebey (Ed.). *The strengths perspective in social work practice* (pp. 45–58). New York: Longman.

Rapp, C. A. (1998.) *The strengths model.* New York: Oxford University Press.

Rapp, C. A., & Chamberlain, R. (1985). Case management services for the chronically mentally ill. *Social Work, 30,5,* 417–422.

Ridgely, M. S. (1996). Practical issues in the application of case management to substance abuse treatment. In H. A. Siegal & R. C. Rapp (Eds.). *Case management and substance abuse treatment* (pp. 1–20). New York: Springer Publishing.

Roberts-DeGennaro, M. (1993). Generalist model of case management practice. *Journal of Case Management, 2,3,* 106–111.

Rose, S. M. (1992). Case management in mental health: Social work contributions, concepts, and questions. In S. M. Rose (Ed.). *Case management and social work practice* (pp. 73–76). New York: Longman.

Rothman, J. (1992). *Guidelines for case management: Putting research to professional use.* Itasca, IL: F. E. Peacock.

Rothman, J., & Sager, J. S. (1998). *Case management.* Boston: Allyn & Bacon.

Rubin, A. (1992). Is case management effective for people with serious mental illness? A research review. *Health and Social Work, 17,2,* 138–150.

Scheid, T. L., & Greenley, J. R. (1997). Evaluations of organizational effectiveness in mental health programs. *Journal of Health and Social Behavior, 38,* December, 403–426.

Saleebey, D. (1997). Introduction: Power in the people. In D. Saleebey (Ed.). *The strengths perspective in social work practice* (pp. 3–19). New York: Longman.

Soares, H. H., & Rose, M. K. (1994). Clinical aspects of case management with the elderly. *Journal of Gerontological Social Work, 22,3/4,* 143–156.

Solomon, P. (1992). The efficacy of case management services for severely mentally disabled clients. *Community Mental Health Journal, 28,3,* 163–180.

Sullivan, W. P. (1997). On strengths, niches, and recovery from serious mental illness. In D. Saleebey (Ed.). *The strengths perspective in social work practice,* (pp. 183–197). New York: Longman.

Tracy, E. M., & Biegel, D. (1994). Preparing social workers for social network interventions in mental health practice. *Journal of Teaching in Social Work, 10,1/2,* 19–41.

4

THE BIOLOGICAL BASES OF PSYCHOPATHOLOGY

Harriette C. Johnson

In social science, the nature/nurture controversy has shaped causal models of behavior. . . . Now, [we] will need to be trained in the new person-environment paradigm, which includes the integration of nature and nurture. . . . [We] need to be open to new concepts. *Do not fear integration of social and physical science, but welcome it. This is the future* [emphasis added].

—A. M. Johnson and S. Taylor-Brown (1997)
Genetics research and social work education
Social Work Education Reporter, 45(2):10

S ince the first edition of this book 15 years ago, knowledge about the neurobiological bases of psychopathology has advanced at a phenomenal rate. Research unequivocally supports a biopsychosocial model of psychological function, putting to rest the dichotomies of nature versus nurture and biology versus environment that have influenced our thinking for so many decades. The avalanche of new information in the past decade about the relationship of neurobiology to psychological functioning has been activated by major technological advances in brain imaging, biochemical analysis, electrophysiological measurement, and other procedures. The new discipline of *neuroscience* now provides a scientific foundation for understanding the psychological events of emotion, behavior, thinking, and addiction that was missing from all theoretical models until recently. It has generated new knowledge about child development. As we approach the twenty-first century, no theory of human behavior or human development that runs counter to this knowledge base merits serious consideration, beyond historical interest.

In this second edition, central concepts of today's knowledge will be emphasized. The first edition of *Adult Psychopathology* reviewed studies prior to 1984. It will be assumed that readers are familiar with much of this literature. For those who are not, the chapter on the biological bases of psychopathology in the first edition provides a foundation on which this chapter will build.

New information about biology–environment interactions falls within several intellectual frameworks. In each of the following conceptual approaches, neurobiological knowledge is an important component. *General systems theory (GST)* (Miller, 1978) represents the world as a complex entity comprised of hierarchically structured, interacting, and mutually influencing components (systems, suprasystems, and subsystems) that range from very small particles (atoms, molecules) to very large national and international forces (economic, political, cultural). *Ecological theory* considers the mutually influencing interaction between people (human organisms) and their environments (Germain, 1991). *Contemporary developmental psychology* incorporates mutually influencing biological, interpersonal, cultural, organizational, economic, and political variables into an understanding of human development (Kagan, 1994). *Epidemiology* (the knowledge base for the field of public health) views the human organism in its interaction with the environment to assess *risk factors* and *protective factors* for human conditions, problems, and disorders. The concepts of risk and protective factors pertain to biological and environmental variables, interacting through time, *to prevent or minimize* (protective factors) or *cause or exacerbate* (risk factors) health, mental health, and social problems.

The criticism leveled by Steven Hyman (1993), now director of the National Institute of Mental Health, against his fellow psychiatrists, also applies to social workers and other nonmedical human service professionals:

> It is common in psychiatry . . . to construct certain disorders (e.g., personality disorders) as environmental and developmental in origin, and as a result—so the Cartesian inference goes—to be treated with psychological therapies. In contrast, other disorders (e.g., manic-depressive illness) are generally construed as biological in origin and are therefore to be treated with somatic therapies. These formulations are nothing short of absurd. Both personality disorders and mood disorders represent the product of gene–environ-

ment interactions, and either psychological or somatic therapies could in principle be effective for both. (Hyman & Nestler, 1993, p. 203)

From social work's person-in-environment perspective, the rubric "psychological therapies" (as distinct from "somatic therapies") requires expansion to include a range of psychosocial interventions such as husbanding resources, advocacy, respite care, education, support groups for persons with mental illnesses and for family members, and coping-skills training for the individual and for families.

A stressor introduced at any point in the complex chain of events comprising psychic functioning can set off reverberations throughout the entire chain. Interpersonal and social stresses cause changes in brain chemistry (function, or process) and eventually can even alter brain structures that regulate emotion and thought. Biological variables also alter brain chemistry and/or structure, arising from genetics, excesses or deficiencies of certain substances in the system, ingestion of toxic substances such as lead, scar tissue from lesions in the brain, deficiencies of brain enzymes that govern transmission of nerve impulses, or myriad other physical causes (Johnson, 1984). These biological events can induce behavioral and emotional responses that in turn evoke reactions from the environment. Bizarre or deviant behavior provokes responses from relatives, neighbors, friends, colleagues, employers, caretaking persons, police, judges, and social workers. These environmental responses may further upset the individual with the disorder, escalating imbalances in the recursive cycle, or conversely may defuse and deescalate the disruption. Any number of different interventions—medication, diet, detoxification, or altering the environment—can operate to restore equilibrium. The following example is illustrative.

A six-year-old boy was referred to a child psychiatric facility because of constant trouble at school, at home, and in the neighborhood. He had changeable moods, was sometimes wild and violent, punched and poked other children, knocked them down, and took their toys. He often provoked his father, who would then fly into violent rages himself and beat the boy quite mercilessly. It would have been natural to ascribe all the child's difficulties to the chaotic and punitive environment at home.

EEG abnormalities were identified and the boy was treated with methsuximide (an anticonvulsant) and amphetamine and placed in a special class for brain dysfunctional children. His behavior improved markedly.

Within eight months his arithmetic and spelling performance had increased by three grade levels and his reading by four grade levels. The atmosphere at home improved considerably *as the father responded to the improvement in the child* [emphasis added]. When the amphetamine was discontinued for a few days, the boy reverted to hyperactive and hyperaggressive behavior. (Gross & Wilson, 1974)

Three models of biological and environmental influence on psychic function are relevant to the etiology of psychopathology. Influence on some psychic functions may be *predominantly biological, with contributions from the environment.* Examples include biologically based brain disorders such as schizophrenia, bipolar disorder, attention deficit hyperactivity disorder, obsessive-compulsive disorder, learning disability, Tourette syndrome, panic attack, and some major depressions. Influence may be *predominantly environmental, with contributions from biology,* as in posttraumatic stress disorder. Finally, there may be *strong influences by both.* Examples include addiction, substance abuse, some kinds of violence, borderline personality, antisocial personality, and other personality disorders. But in every instance of psychological function, there are ongoing interactions between the biological organism and its environment. These interactions are *recursive*—they go on continuously, back and forth. Biology affects environment, and environment affects biology.

Some early case examples from the 1970s and 1980s illustrate the interactive effects of biological, intrapsychic, social, and economic factors in psychological problems.

A married mother of three in her forties was subject to severe depression. She was treated unsuccessfully with psychotherapy and finally hospitalized at the nearby state hospital, where she remained for two years. Her husband spoke with the social worker about getting a divorce, although, he said, they had been happy together before her illness. When an in-depth physical examination revealed the presence of hypoglycemia, treatment with diet was instituted. Within a few months, she was home with her family, fully recovered. Her husband appeared surprised when the worker alluded to his earlier plans for divorce, stating that the family was very happy and that separation was totally out of the question. (Johnson, 1984, p. 9)

In this example, *family dynamics* improved in response to *biological* therapy of a family member. That is, the *environment* changed in response to *biological* therapies. Another example shows changes in *individual psychiatric status* in response to *macroenvironmental* forces.

> A group of 32 unemployed older persons (mean age 63) was interviewed. Symptoms of depression such as suicidal thoughts, sleeping and eating difficulties, self-deprecation, and nervousness were widespread. After placement of these people in CETA jobs, these symptoms vanished. (Briar, 1979)

Family dynamics, too, change in response to *macroenvironmental* forces. In a 20-year longitudinal study of 145 children reared during the Great Depression, family members attributed the fathers' joblessness to personal inadequacies, weakening the fathers' prestige, attractiveness, and perceived power (Elder, 1974).

BIOLOGICAL FACTORS IN PSYCHOPATHOLOGICAL CONDITIONS

Recent research on psychopathology has produced a deluge of information about neurobiological underpinnings of psychiatric disorders. We will illustrate with a few examples of research-based knowledge, but we emphasize that these illustrations comprise only a tiny fraction of the specific research-based information now available about virtually every *DSM-IV* diagnosable condition (Johnson, 1999).* These neurobiological differences may show themselves in structures, such as enlarged ventricles or unusual organization of neurons, or in functions or processes, such as abnormal levels of neurotransmitters or abnormal activity in certain regions of the brain.

> *Attention-deficit hyperactivity disorder* may arise from various influences. In many cases, genetics are decisive, involving possibly three or more genes. In ADHD boys, the anterior frontal region of the brain has been found to be 5% smaller on average than control groups of "normals." The right caudate and the globus pallidus (structures through which the cortex inhibits behavior), and the cerebellum, may be somewhat smaller than normal. These anatomical differences could be due to fetal or other early event. Differences may be related

---

*Much of the material that follows has been quoted by permission from Johnson (1999).

Figure 4–1
PET Scans of Adults With and Without Attention Deficit Hyperactivity Disorder (ADHD)

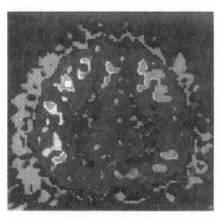 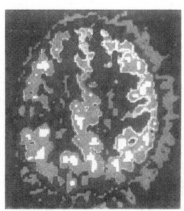

Source: Alan Zametkin, National Institute of Mental Health, Rockville, MD.

PET (positron emission tomography) scans of the brain of an adult with ADHD (left) and the brain of an adult without ADHD (right). In the original PET scan, the person with ADHD has more areas of greens and blues, indicating that less glucose is being burned up and therefore that there is underactivity in certain areas of the brain. The brain systems that inhibit behaviors are underactive. The person without ADHD has more areas of reds and oranges in the original PET scan, indicating more glucose is being burned up. The brain systems that inhibit behaviors are normally active in the person without ADHD. This *underactivity in the brain* in people with ADHD is believed to result in *impulsive behavior* arising from deficits in inhibition.

to maternal smoking during pregnancy, low-level lead toxicity, or allergies. People with ADHD may have elevated mental activity compared with controls, possibly leading to overarousal and difficulty mentally judging stimuli. In certain parts of the brain, decreased activity is characteristic (see Figure 4–1). When the frontal cortex and caudate nucleus underperform, poor attention span may result. The motor cortex is sometimes overactive, possibly explaining hyperactivity. ADHD symptoms are responsive to dopamine-increasing drugs (stimulants), a norepinephrine-decreasing drug (clonodine), and some antidepressants. Newer drugs are being tried (Levin, 1995; Leutwyler, 1996; Castellanos et al., 1996; Jensen, 1996; Zametkin, 1991).

Schizophrenia is often the result of strong genetic influence, involving several possible genes, or derailing of neural development due to

Figure 4–2
Monozygotic Twins Without and With Schizophrenia

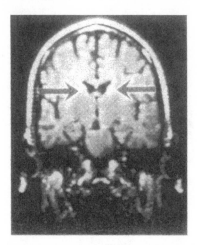 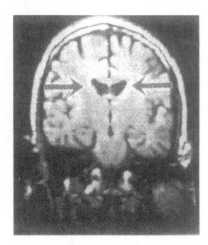

Source: Daniel Weinberger, MD, NIMH Clinical Brain Disorders Branch.

Loss of brain volume associated with schizophrenia is clearly shown by magnetic resonance imaging (MRI) scans comparing the size of ventricles (butterfly shaped, fluid-filled spaces in the midbrain) of identical twins, one of whom has schizophrenia (right). The ventricles of the twin with schizophrenia are larger. This suggests structural brain changes associated with the illness.

viral disease or obstetrical complications. Structural characteristics may include enlarged ventricles (spaces in the brain) (see Figure 4–2), or pathological orientation and organization of neurons in the hippocampus. Functional differences may involve the limbic system, frontal cortex, and basal ganglia, all of which are interconnected. High levels of dopamine are associated with symptoms of schizophrenia. When dopamine levels are reduced by medication, symptoms often remit. Other neurotransmitters likely to be involved include serotonin, norepinephrine, and amino acids (GABA and glutamate). Symptoms of schizophrenia are often responsive to drugs that block action of several dopamine receptors. Some newer drugs also act on other transmitter systems (for a list of sources, see Johnson, 1999).

Obsessive-compulsive disorder is associated with decreased size in the caudate, increased brain activity especially in the frontal cortex (see Figure 4–3), basal ganglia, and cingulum, and dysregulation of serotonin. OCD is frequently responsive to serotonin reuptake

Figure 4–3
Brains of Patients With and Without Obsessive-Compulsive Disorder

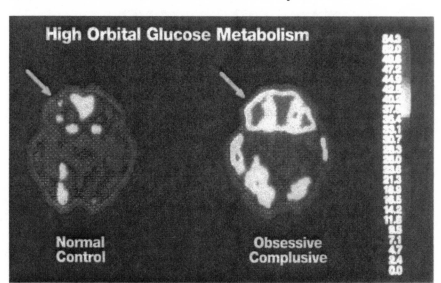

Source: Lewis Baxter, M.D., University of Alabama.

inhibitors. It is strongly genetically determined (Leonard, Rapoport, & Swedo, 1997).

Mood disorders involve pathology of the hypothalamus, other structures of the limbic system and the basal ganglia. Enlarged ventricles are present in some bipolar disorders. In some major depression, there are smaller caudate nuclei or smaller frontal lobes as compared with controls. In depression, reduced brain activity is typically found, especially in the frontal cortex (see Figure 4–4). Abnormalities occur in several neurotransmitter systems: serotonin, norepinephrine, and dopamine; also possibly GABA, vasopressin, and endogenous opioids. Neuroendocrine abnormalities involve the adrenal or thyroid axes. Dysregulation of circadian rhythms may occur. There may be abnormal hypothalamic regulation of the immune system. Interactive influences of environment and genetics may cause major depression, whereas the origins of bipolar disorders are almost entirely genetic, involving complex mechanisms of inheritance. Most bipolar disorders are responsive to lithium, with anticonvulsants or calcium channel blockers often effective when

Figure 4–4
PET Scans of the Brains of Persons Without and With Depression

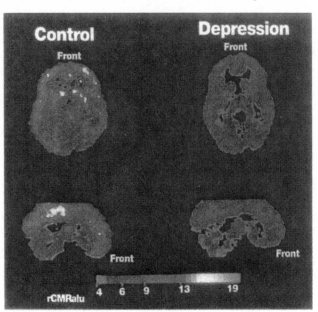

Source: Mark George, M.D., NIMH, Biological Psychiatry Branch.

PET scans of the brain of a person without depression (left) and the brain of a person with depression (right) reveal reduced brain activity (darker shading) during depression, especially in the prefrontal cortex.

lithium cannot be used. Drug actions are not fully understood and continue to be researched. Major depression is responsive to serotonin reuptake inhibitors, other new antidepressants, and older antidepressants such as tricyclics and monoamine oxidase inhibitors that affect other transmitters as well as serotonin (Grinspoon, 1997a; see also Johnson, 1999, for list of sources).

Panic disorder may involve pathology in the temporal lobes, the hippocampus, the brain stem (particularly noradrenergic neurons of the locus ceruleus and serotonergic neurons of the median raphe nucleus), the limbic system, and/or the prefrontal cortex. Cerebral blood flow is constricted during panic attack. The autonomic nervous system may show slow adaptation to repeated stimuli and excessive response to moderate stimuli. Panic attack may be associated with a surplus of natural anxiety-producing chemicals or a deficiency of natural anxiety blockers. It is responsive to high potency antianxiety drugs such as alprazolam (Xanax) and other drugs in the benzodiazepene family, and antidepressants (selective serotonin reuptake inhibitors and newer related antidepressants). Panic disorder and associated agoraphobia have a strong genetic component (see Johnson, 1999, for list of sources).

HOW THE BRAIN WORKS: SOME FUNDAMENTALS OF BRAIN STRUCTURE AND FUNCTION

Neurobiological differences that underlie psychological disorders can best be understood in relation to *brain systems* (such as the basal ganglia), *large structures* that form components of these systems (such as the striatum and the substantia nigra), *microstructures* that comprise these larger structures (such as neurons and receptors), and *brain functions or processes* (such as release, reuptake, and inactivation of neurotransmitters). These hierarchically arranged brain systems and subsystems interact continuously with suprasystems (larger systems) such as the entire human body, families, social groups, organizations, and social forces (cultural, economic, political).

Larger Structures in the Brain

The *frontal cortex* is the thinking part of the brain. The outer surface of the brain, called the cortex, is made up of folds and has multiple functions. The frontal cortex is a part of the entire cortex. In humans, the frontal cortex comprises 29% of the entire cortex. The frontal cortex continually receives messages from and sends messages to the limbic system and other brain regions. The frontal cortex is the part of the brain that distinguishes us from other animals. The higher the percentage of the cortex that's in the frontal area, the more complex the thought process. By comparison, on average the frontal cortex comprises 17% of the cortex in chimpanzees, 7% in dogs, and 3.5% in cats. (See Figure 4–5.)

The *limbic system* is the inner section of the brain, once known as the "old brain" because animal species that pre-dated *Homo sapiens* had limbic systems, and animals today whose brains are much less developed than ours, such as lizards, have them. The limbic structures regulate drives (hunger, thirst, sex), emotions and passions (love, rage, joy, fear, sadness), arousal, and levels of attentiveness; they also transmit messages of pleasure or pain

Figure 4–5
Larger Structures in the Brain

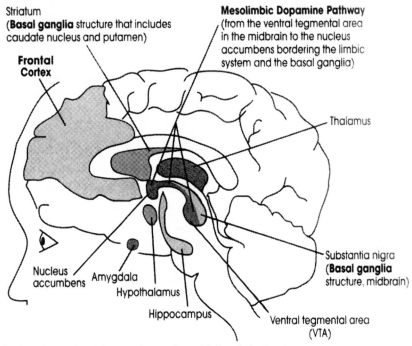

A view from the side, cut down the middle of the brain.

into memory. These memories are put into storage by a biochemical process that results in actual changes in microscopic brain structures.

Structures of the limbic system perform a range of functions. The *amygdala* mediates rage reactions. When a person flies into a rage, his or her amygdala is revved up. Fight/flight reactions occur in the amygdala. The amygdala also plays a role in learning and memory. Recent research indicates that the amygdala is also involved in the pleasures of doing drugs. The *hippocampus* plays a critical role in learning and memory. Damage to the hippocampus can result in loss of short-term memory in laboratory animals as well as humans. The *thalamus* is a relay station that transmits messages back and forth between different regions of the brain, the entire body, and the external environment. The *hypothalamus* (below the thalamus), working in conjunction with the *pituitary gland,* regulates sleep, appetite, and sexual activity. These two structures are the major endocrine regulators in the body—they regulate hormones. Stimulation of the hypothalamus can produce upsurges in sexual behavior. The hypothalamic–pituitary circuit also has significant influence over the immune system and the autonomic nervous system. The *nucleus accumbens* is the limbic structure that receives messages from dopamine neurons that pertain to pleasure. It is crucial in the process of becoming addicted.

The *mesolimbic dopamine pathway* is the reward circuit in our brain. The *ventral tegmental area* (VTA) in the midbrain (or mesencephalon, Greek for "middle brain") hooks up with the *nucleus accumbens* (NAc) in the limbic system to create this pleasure pathway. The mesolimbic dopamine pathway has a role in creating privileged memories of highly rewarding novel stimuli. A "privileged" memory is a memory that is so powerful that it keeps popping up, even when you wish it wouldn't. The limbic system plays a key role in determining what is salient enough to be remembered. Intensely positive memories can cause addicts to have cravings and risk of relapse even after years of abstinence.

Why do we have this reward circuit? It's for survival of the species. It motivates animals to eat, drink, and copulate. This pleasure pathway is in the region of limbic system. The limbic system also mediates fear—another survival emotion. Less developed species, such as reptiles, also have limbic systems (the "primitive" brain). The limbic system occurs in almost all levels of species and does not depend on consciousness.

The *basal ganglia* are a group of structures deep within the brain adjacent to the limbic system. These structures regulate normal and abnormal movement and are also implicated in many psychiatric disorders, for example paucity of movement in depression and abnormal grimaces in schizophrenia. The basal ganglia contain the highest concentration of dopamine D2 receptors in the brain, receptors that are the primary target of action for many antipsychotic medications. Basal ganglia structures include the *striatum* (region that includes the *caudate nucleus* and the *putamen*), the *globus pallidus,* the *substantia nigra,* and others. These structures interconnect with each other and with other brain regions.

Microscopic Structures in the Brain

Neurons are tiny cells in the brain, spinal cord, and throughout the body that carry out the brain's functions of receiving messages, making decisions, and sending out commands—see Figure 4–6. There are an estimated 100 billion neurons in the human organism. Neurons come in different sizes and shapes. There are some neurons with long axons (as much as a

Figure 4–6
The Neuron

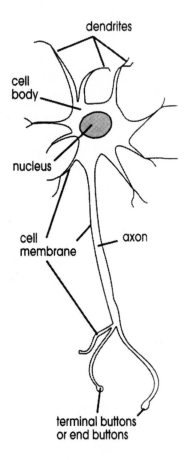

meter in length) and some with short axons. Each neuron connects with between 1,000 and 10,000 other neurons through tiny spaces called synapses. In the brain and spinal cord, neurons are tightly packed together in bundles. The basic structures and functions of human neurons are similar to those of less differentiated species, such as the squid, the snail, and the leech!

The neuron, like other cells in the body, is covered around its entire surface with a thin *cell membrane* and has a *cell body* containing a *nucleus*. It has many tiny filaments (threads) called *dendrites* (singular *dendron*) that receive chemical messages from adjacent neurons. Each neuron has many dendrites but only one *axon*. The *axon* is another threadlike structure that sends chemical and electrical messages to the receiving neurons. (Although messages can also go from the axon of one neuron to the axon of another neuron, or from an axon to the cell body of an adjacent neuron, we shall only discuss the usual transmission route from the axon of one neuron to dendrites of adjoining neurons.)

Although there is only one axon per neuron, at its end the axon divides into numerous projections with tiny bulbs at their ends, called *terminal buttons* or *end buttons*. At these end buttons, chemical messengers called *neurotransmitters* are manufactured and then dispatched to other neurons.

The *synapse* (Figure 4–7) is also called the *synaptic cleft*. Synapses are tiny spaces between the cell membranes of adjacent neurons. The dendrites of neurons are very near (but don't actually touch) the axons of adjacent neurons. They are separated by these tiny spaces. There are an estimated 100 trillion synapses in the human body. Synapses are where the action is! The activity of transmitting messages from neuron to neuron takes place at the synapse, not in the nucleus or the cell body.

Vesicles are round containers that store neurotransmitter molecules in the end buttons.

The *presynaptic membrane* is the section of the sending neuron's cell membrane (the thin membrane that covers the entire surface of the neuron) that is adjacent to the synapse.

The *postsynaptic membrane* is the section of the receiving neuron's cell membrane that is adjacent to the synapse.

Receptors are protein molecules embedded in the surface of postsynaptic and presynaptic membranes. Although the presynaptic membrane as well as the postsynaptic membrane has receptors, we will mostly be discussing receptors on the postsynaptic membrane.

Receptors have many different chemical structures. Each receptor molecule combines only with those neurotransmitter molecules that fit with its chemical structure, like a lock (the receptor molecule) and a key (the neurotransmitter molecule).

BRAIN FUNCTIONS OR PROCESSES

In order to understand brain processes or functions, it is necessary to be able to identify a few of the chemicals that are active in these processes.

Chemicals in the Brain

Precursor substances (substances that *come before* something else) are building blocks for neurotransmitters. They are protein molecules that

Figure 4–7
Terminal Button and Synapse

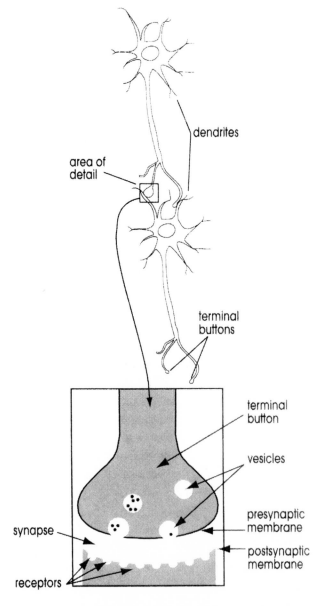

come from digestion of protein-containing foods. Many of these proteins have been broken down during digestion into amino acids. These amino acids are transported to the brain by blood vessels, enter the neuron, and are transformed into neurotransmitters inside the neuron.

Enzymes are compounds that trigger chemical reactions without themselves being chemically changed. We have many enzymes throughout our bodies that perform essential functions. Enzymes can be recognized because they end in the letters -**ase**. For example, monoamine oxid**ase** is the enzyme that causes monoamine compounds to be broken down chemically.

Glucose is the simple sugar that the brain uses as energy to do its work. Remember, the brain scans that measure how much activity is taking place in different regions of the brain do it by forming color-coded images of glucose in the brain.

Neurotransmitters are molecules that act as chemical messengers. They transmit messages directing all our psychic functions. There are at least 50 known neurotransmitters and as many as 250 transmitters called "putative" (chemicals that meet some but not all criteria to join the neurotransmitter club). Neurotransmitters are manufactured from precursor substances in the axon terminal buttons (most transmitters) or the cell body (peptide neurotransmitters), stored in synaptic vesicles, released from the vesicles into the synapse, cross the synapse, and combine with postsynaptic receptor molecules to start off a chain of events in the receiving neuron.

There are several families of neurotransmitters, such as the monoamines, amino acids, and neuropeptides (see Table 4–1). Neurotransmitters often play more than one role in the human body. For example, *epinephrine* is the same substance as *adrenaline,* the chemical that gives you butterflies in the stomach. Epinephrine and norepinephrine used to be called adrenaline and noradrenaline. When you come across the terms "adrenergic" and "noradrenergic," they are referring to systems involving norepinephrine and epinephrine. *Histamine* is related to the histamine that makes you sneeze, itch, or have watery eyes. *Estrogens* and *androgens* are sex-related hormones.

How the Brain Sends Messages — Neurotransmission

The brain sends messages through the firing action of neurons, a process that goes on continuously, day and night, waking and sleeping. The firing action of a neuron consists of sending electrical impulses through the entire neuron, then setting off chain reactions of similar firing action in adjoining neurons.

Neural (nerve) impulses are motions of electrically charged particles (called *ions*) that pass back and forth across the neuron's membrane. The impulse travels the entire length of the neuron (starting with the dendrites

Table 4–1   Families of Neurotransmitters, and Names of Some of the More Common Transmitters

Monoamines: dopamine, norepinephrine, epinephrine, serotonin, histamine
Amino acids: γ-aminobutyric acid (γ is the Greek letter gamma), called
     GABA for short; glutamate, glycine
Neuropeptides (made of short chains of amino acids):
     hypothalamic hormones: vasopressin, oxytocin, somatostatin,
          arginine-vasotocin, thyrotropin-releasing hormone (TRH),
          luteinizing-hormone-releasing hormone (LHRH)
     pituitary opiomelanocortins: corticotropin (ACTH),
          α-endorphin, ß-endorphin, γ-endorphin (endorphins are referred to
          as opioid transmitters), dynorphin, leu-enkephalin, met-enkephalin
     other peptides: substance P, delta sleep-inducing peptide (DSIP),
          glucagon, bradykinin
Acetylcholine
Other substances that generally act as "neuromodulators": growth hormone,
     prolactin, adenosine, prostaglandins, corticosteroids, estrogens,
     androgens

and ending at the axon's terminal buttons). It is propelled down the neuron like a row of dominoes, as each ion exchange across the cell membrane sets off another ion exchange in the next section of the neuron.

These electrical impulses are then set off in adjoining neurons by chemical messengers, the neurotransmitters that cross the synapse from neuron to neuron. This network of interconnecting neurons is so complex that by comparison, the world's most complicated computer looks like a child's toy.

To understand neurotransmission, it is sometimes helpful to think of the process in two phases, transmission of electrical current down the neuron, and biochemical events at the terminal buttons. It is important to remember, however, that the electrical activity itself is also biochemical. The ions are tiny particles of chemical substances that have lost or gained electrons, thereby becoming electrically charged.

Four Steps in Neurotransmission

1. Neurotransmitters cross the synapse and bind with receptors on the postsynaptic membrane of dendrites of receiving neurons—see Figure 4–8(a).
2. When the neurotransmitters bind with postsynaptic receptors, an

Figure 4–8
The Steps in Neurotransmission

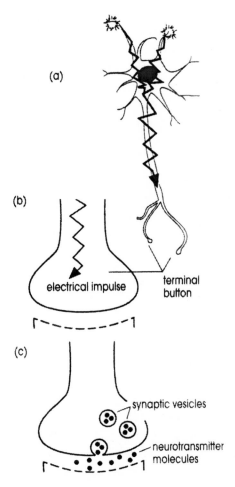

(a)

(b)

electrical impulse

terminal
button

(c)

synaptic vesicles

neurotransmitter
molecules

electrical impulse is set off in the receiving neuron and travels down the neuron, as electrical current, from the dendrites, through the cell body and the axon, to the end buttons—see Figure 4–8(a).

3. Electrical current arrives at the terminal buttons—see Figure 4–8(b).

4. When this electrical message arrives at the terminal buttons, it sets off biochemical events in the terminal buttons that cause neurotransmitters to be released into the synapse. These messages are carried by the neurotransmitters from the presynaptic membrane of the sending neuron, across the synapse, to the postsynaptic membrane on the dendrites of the receiving neuron—see Figure 4–8(c).

These messages can be either *excitatory* (telling the receiving neuron to fire at a faster rate) or *inhibitory* (telling the receiving neuron to fire at a slower rate). The rate of responding of the receiving neuron depends on whether there is a preponderance of excitatory or a preponderance of inhibitory messages coming into the receiving neuron. Remember, the neuron is receiving several hundred messages at the same time from other neurons adjacent to it. When the chemical messengers called neurotransmitters arrive at the postsynaptic membrane, they combine with postsynaptic receptor molecules. Each kind of postsynaptic receptor molecule only receives the specific neurotransmitter molecule whose chemical structure fits with it, like a key in a lock. That is, each different neurotransmitter has its own special receptor molecule.

However, sometimes receptor molecules can be fooled. Sometimes they accept imposters, such as therapeutic or street drugs that are *similar* but *not identical* in chemical structure to the natural neurotransmitter that fits with the particular receptor.

Pathways for Sending Messages

A pathway is a bundle of interconnecting neurons that performs specific tasks. Transmission pathways for different neurotransmitters extend throughout the brain. Examples are *dopamine pathways* and *serotonin pathways* (see Figure 4–9). Notice that in many areas the different transmitter systems run parallel to each other. That means they pass through, and act in, many of the same regions of the brain.

The *mesolimbic dopamine pathway* is the bundle of neurons that carries pleasure messages from the ventral tegmental area (VTA) in the midbrain to the nucleus accumbens (NAc) in the limbic system (see Figure 4–5).

Neurotransmitters from Birth to Decay

Synthesis of Neurotransmitters
Your hamburger or tofu meal is transformed into neurotransmitters in your body in a multistep process—see Figure 4–10.

1. You eat protein-containing foods.
2. Your digestive system breaks the foods down into many proteins, such as amino acids, that are the building blocks for neurotransmitters.
3. Your circulatory system carries these protein molecules to your brain. These precursors are called *precursor substances* because they are

Figure 4–9
Pathways for Sending Messages

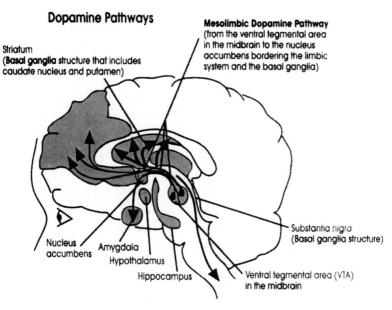

Dopamine Pathways

Striatum
(**Basal ganglia** structure that includes caudate nucleus and putamen)

Mesolimbic Dopamine Pathway
(from the ventral tegmental area in the midbrain to the nucleus accumbens bordering the limbic system and the basal ganglia)

Nucleus accumbens
Amygdala
Hypothalamus
Hippocampus

Substantia nigra
(Basal ganglia structure)

Ventral tegmental area (VTA) in the midbrain

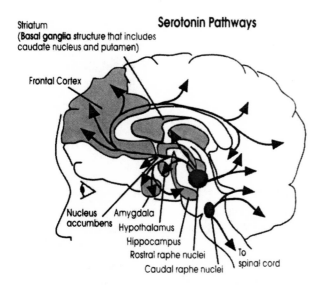

Serotonin Pathways

Striatum
(**Basal ganglia** structure that includes caudate nucleus and putamen)

Frontal Cortex

Nucleus accumbens
Amygdala
Hypothalamus
Hippocampus
Rostral raphe nuclei
Caudal raphe nuclei
To spinal cord

precursors—that is, they *come before*—neurotransmitters. Once in your brain, they cross through the walls of blood vessels and through the cell membrane of neurons. (The blood vessel walls and the nerve cell membranes, taken together, are called the *blood–brain barrier*—see Figure

4–10(a).) Neurotransmitter factories are inside the neurons. Once these precursors get into the neuron, the neurotransmitter factory swings into action with the help of enzymes.

4. Enzymes in the terminal buttons promote chemical reactions that convert the precursor molecules into new substances; see Figure 4–10(b). Let's call the first enzyme that acts on the precursor substance Enzyme 1— see Figure 4–10(b).

5. The transformation from precursor substance to neurotransmitter molecule can involve only one change (using one enzyme), or there can be a series of changes, a series of different new substances, using several different enzymes. Let's call the second enzyme in this chain of events Enzyme 2. Enzyme 2 promotes chemical reactions that convert the new substance into neurotransmitter molecules, or into another new substance. We are using the term *new substance* as a generic term for any chemical compound that is produced during this process of transformation from precursor substance to neurotransmitter—see Figure 4–10(c).

Once the final products have been manufactured (the final products are neurotransmitter molecules), the life cycle of the neurotransmitter is at Step 2.

Storage of Neurotransmitter Molecules
To prevent various enzymes from continuing to change neurotransmitters into other compounds, the newly created little transmitter molecules need protection. So they get into the round containers called vesicles. They are stored in the vesicles until the next phase of release—see Figure 4–11(a).

Release
The electrical impulse coming down the axon stimulates release of the neurotransmitters from their vesicles into the synapse. Electrically charged calcium particles (calcium ions) sit outside the neuron's cell membrane in the area of the axon terminal buttons (end buttons)—see Figure 4–11(b). The electrical impulse comes down the neuron—starting from the dendrites, through the cell body, and on down the end button via the axon.

When the electrical message hits an end button, it stimulates channels in the cell membrane to open and let the calcium ions into the neuron. There, the calcium ions in turn stimulate the vesicles to move down to the

Figure 4–10
Synthesis of Neurotransmitters

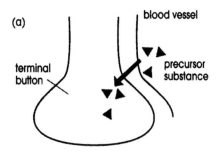

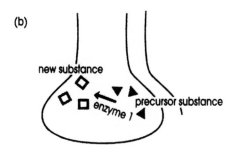

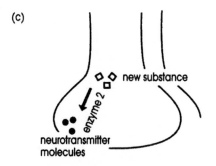

(a) Precursor substances cross the blood-brain barrier
(b) Enzyme 1 converts precursor substances to new substances
(c) Enzyme 2 converts those substances to neurotransmitters

presynaptic membrane, where they fuse with the presynaptic membrane, open up, and spill their contents (the neurotransmitter molecules) into the synapse—see Figure 4–11(c) and (d).

After dumping most of their contents into the synapse, the vesicles close

Figure 4–11
Storage of Neurotransmitter Molecules

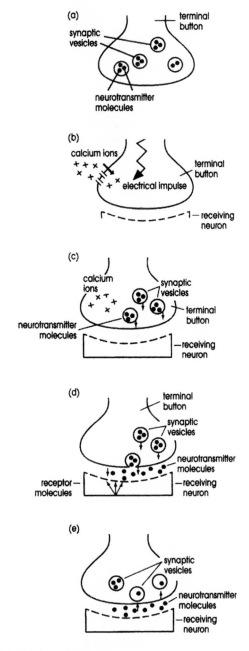

(a) Storage of neurotransmitters in vesicles
(b) Entry of calcium ions
(c) Action of calcium ions on vesicles
(d) Vesicles spill neurotransmitters into the synapse
(e) Vesicles close up and move back into terminal button

up and move back up into the end button, where they receive more neurotransmitters and go through the cycle again—see Figure 4–11(e).

What Happens Next?
There are several possible outcomes:

1. Neurotransmitter molecules can bind (combine) with postsynaptic receptor molecules to *excite* or *inhibit* the receiving neuron's firing action—see Figure 4–12(a).

2. Neurotransmitter molecules can be taken back up into the sending neuron, a process called *reuptake*—see Figure 4–12(b).

3. Some of the reuptaken neurotransmitters get back into vesicles and are recycled through the process again—see Figure 4–12(c).

4. Other reuptaken molecules don't make it into the vesicles, because they get broken down by the action of an enzyme—(let's call this Enzyme 3) into end products of chemical degradation, called metabolites—see Figure 4–12(d). Now they're out of circulation—they're not neurotransmitters any more.

5. Still other neurotransmitters don't make it out of the synapse at all. They get broken down by the action of an enzyme in the synapse (let's call this Enzyme 4), into metabolites—see Figure 4–12(e). Now they're out of circulation too. Putting neurotransmitters out of circulation by breaking them down into metabolites is called *inactivation*.

HOW DRUGS AND OTHER CHEMICAL COMPOUNDS ACT IN THE BRAIN

Psychoactive drugs (legal and illegal, therapeutic and recreational) and other chemical compounds can interfere with normal processes of neurotransmission at any stage in the life span of neurotransmitters in any of six ways.

1. They can *interfere with the synthesis of neurotransmitters. Example:* Low levels of lead, ingested over time, impede the action of enzymes that promote the synthesis of neurotransmitters from precursor substances—see Figure 4–13(a).

2. They can *facilitate or inhibit the release of transmitters. Example:* Calcium channel blockers, such as Verapamil, sometimes used to treat bipolar disorder, affect the action of the calcium ions that stimulate release of neurotransmitters, by blocking the channels on the cell membrane that allow calcium ions to pass through—see Figure 4–13(b).

Figure 4–12
Possible Outcomes for Neurotransmitters

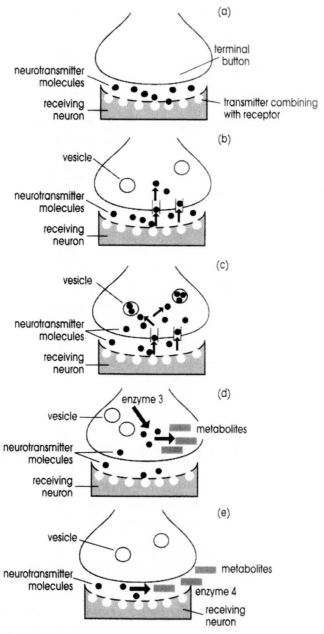

(a) Binding to receptor molecules
(b) Reuptake into terminal button
(c) Recycling back into vesicles
(d) Degradation into metabolites in terminal button
(e) Degradation into metabolites in synapse

Figure 4–13
How Drugs and Other Chemical Compounds Act in the Brain

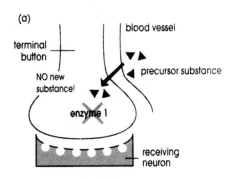

(a)

terminal button

NO new substance!

blood vessel

precursor substance

enzyme 1

receiving neuron

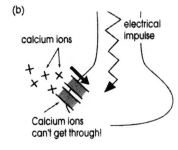

(b)

calcium ions

electrical impulse

Calcium ions can't get through!

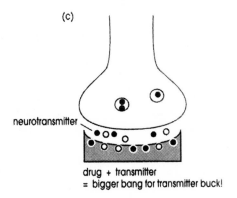

(c)

neurotransmitter

drug + transmitter
= bigger bang for transmitter buck!

(continues)

3. They can *potentiate (increase, strengthen) the action of neurotrans-mitters. Example:* Opiates such as heroin and morphine have molecular structures similar enough to the structures of natural neurotransmitters (endorphins) that they can fool natural opioid receptor molecules into think-

ing they are the natural transmitters. They act in similar fashion to the natural transmitters, thereby adding to the action of the transmitter. In this situation, you have natural transmitters doing their stuff *plus* opiate drugs doing the same stuff. Drugs that do this are called *agonists*—see Figure 4–13(c).

4. They can *block action of transmitters at postsynaptic receptor sites.* *Example:* Neuroleptics (antipsychotics) such as Thorazine, Haldol, Stelazine, Prolixin, Mellaril, and newer antipsychotics (Clozaril, Risperdal). These drugs also fool receptors, especially dopamine receptors. However, unlike the previous group, they do *not* act like the natural transmitters they resemble. They grab receptor slots away from the natural transmitters by binding more quickly and more tenaciously to the receptors, thereby preventing the natural transmitters from doing their work. This process is called "competitive binding at the receptor site." Drugs that behave this way are called *antagonists*—see Figure 4–13(d).

5. They can *block reuptake of transmitters into the presynaptic neuron.* *Example:* Selective serotonin reuptake inhibitors (SSRIs) block the reuptake of the neurotransmitter serotonin into the sending neuron, thereby increasing the amount of serotonin available in the synapse to combine with receptors on postsynaptic membranes. The SSRIs relieve symptoms of depression, obsessive-compulsive disorder, and other psychiatric conditions by remedying the inadequate supply of serotonin that is causing the symptoms—see Figure 4–13(e).

6. They can *prevent inactivation of transmitters by enzymes.* *Example:* Some enzymes promote the degradation, or breaking down, of neurotransmitters into the end products, called *metabolites.* When there isn't enough of a neurotransmitter, inhibiting the enzyme—that is, causing it to break down—increases the supply of that neurotransmitter available in the synapse to combine with postsynaptic receptor molecules.

For example, monoamine oxidase (note ending -*ase,* designating an enzyme) breaks down monoamine neurotransmitters. Monoamine oxidase inhibitors (MAOIs) inhibit the action of the enzyme monoamine oxidase in breaking down the monoamine transmitters, thus increasing the amount of monoamines available to do their work. Serotonin is one of the monoamine group. Some others are listed in Table 4–1. So the MAOIs also increase serotonin, as well as other monoamines, thereby relieving symptoms of depression related to inadequate supply of the transmitters—see Figure 4–13(f).

Figure 4–13 continued

(d)

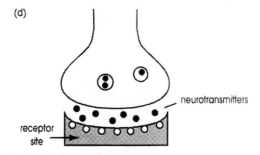

Drug won't let transmitters into their postsynaptic homes (receptor sites)

(e)

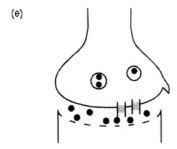

Transmitters can't get back up!

(f)

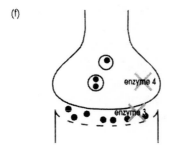

NO metabolites!

Table 4–2   Categories of Therapeutic Drugs

Category	Used to Treat
Neuroleptics (antipsychotics)	Schizophrenia, and as adjuncts in other conditions
Antidepressants	Depression, obsessive-compulsive, and eating disorders, aggressivity, attention-deficit hyperactivity disorder (if stimulants can't be used), some addiction cravings
Mood stabilizers (lithium, anticonvulsants)	Bipolar and schizoaffective disorders, episodic aggression
Anxiolytics (antianxiety)	Anxiety
Psychostimulants	Attention-deficit hyperactivity disorder

Dopamine and Serotonin

Two neurotransmitters that have a great deal to do with psychic activity are the monoamines *dopamine* and *serotonin*. These neurotransmitters are extremely versatile; they do lots of things.

For example, dopamine is active in the pleasures of eating, drinking, and sex. Its receptors come in several different forms, known as D1, D2, D3, D4, and so on. It is too abundant in schizophrenia. It is also overabundant when a person is high on any of numerous street drugs. Sometimes people who come into an emergency room having overdosed on amphetamines are misdiagnosed as undergoing an acute episode of schizophrenia. The symptoms can look a lot alike. Serotonin is deficient in depression, obsessive and compulsive thoughts and behaviors, eating disorders, some forms of pathological aggression, and other conditions. Increasing serotonin sometimes helps chronic fatigue syndrome, migraine headaches, and nausea and vomiting due to cancer therapy. The most widely used way to increase serotonin is to block its reuptake into the presynaptic (sending) neuron.

MEDICATION AND SOCIAL WORK INTERVENTIONS

The beliefs that practitioners hold about the etiology of mental illness have important consequences for the treatment they provide. A case example

(George P) may illustrate the relationship between theory of etiology and choice of practice approach.

George P is 30 years old, has been hospitalized twice, for several months each time, with a diagnosis of schizophrenia, chronic paranoid type, and currently lives with his parents, Mr. and Mrs. P. He has been on Risperdal for the past year. Mr. P works as a machinist and Mrs. P is a housewife. George is unemployed and spends his time either watching television or walking back and forth to the town center, not far from his home. George has never displayed any assaultive behavior but seems to be in his own world much of the time. He sometimes hallucinates, as evidenced by his holding conversations with nonexistent persons. The content of his hallucinations is strongly flavored with persecutory ideation. Mrs. P worries constantly about George, urging food on him, cautioning him about talking to strangers when he goes out, and insisting that he come home before dinner. Mr. P is extremely irritated by George and snaps at him when they are together. Mostly he tries to avoid his son and leaves his care to Mrs. P.

The situation of George and his family is typical of patients and families seen in outpatient psychiatric agencies. Workers in such facilities might approach this case in different ways, depending on their personal preferences for different aspects of the biopsychosocial model. I shall use this vignette to illustrate four approaches to practice, highlighting essential features while eliminating confusing or distracting detail. In real life, the "walls" between these approaches are by no means so clearly delineated as they are here.

Workers who believe that psychopathology is caused primarily by *interpersonal factors* (even when they acknowledge the existence of innate predispositions to psychopathology) stress interpersonal forms of therapy. They often regard drug therapy as a necessary evil needed to quiet patients or relieve their symptomatology in order to make them amenable to psychological treatment. Individual and/or family therapy is used to approach the "real" causes of the condition, which are viewed as stemming from interpersonal psychogenic pathology. Worker A, using this paradigm, might work with George and his family in the following manner.

> I see George once a week individually and meet with the family twice
> a month for family therapy. I am working with George on trying to
> help him express his feelings of rage toward his mother. I am trying
> to help Mrs. P be less controlling toward George and allow him to
> grow up. I am trying to engage Mr. P in a more supportive and pos-
> itive interaction with his son.

Practitioners who believe that *neurobiological factors* are the predominant cause of psychopathology (even when they acknowledge contributions of interpersonal events) interpret observable phenomena such as
delusions, hallucinations, or assaultive behavior as the outward manifestation of internal biochemical imbalance. Hence, alteration of underlying
neurobiological events through pharmacotherapy is the preferred intervention. Worker B, using this approach, might work with the family in
the following way.

> George is currently receiving Risperdal, which he sometimes forgets
> to take. I call Mrs. P to verify this when George appears agitated or
> more disoriented than usual. I am now asking George to call me
> every Friday to report on how he has been doing with his medica-
> tion. He has been given a calendar to check off each time he takes his
> medication.

Worker C sees *interpersonal stressors and larger system factors* as the
targets of intervention. Families are viewed as needing therapy, leading to
heavy emphasis on individual and family therapy. This is combined with
such services as day treatment, contacts by the worker with income support sources (e.g., to obtain supplemental security income for disabled and
elderly persons), and development of natural support systems. The worker
engages in activities to promote linkage with resources, together with interpersonal therapy intended to modify what are believed to be illness-
generating interpersonal phenomena. Worker C, practicing in this model,
might proceed as follows.

> I see George once a week individually and meet with the family
> twice a month for family therapy. I am working with George on try-

ing to help him express his feelings of rage toward his mother. I am trying to help Mrs. P be less controlling toward George and allow him to grow up. I am trying to engage Mr. P in a more supportive and positive interaction with his son. I am working with George toward getting him to attend a day treatment center and have also contacted the state employment service to see whether any part-time maintenance work might be available. George has done custodial work and lawn care in the past. I am also helping Mrs. P explore the possibility of joining a women's activity group, where she could socialize and find some companionship without having to travel too far. I have been in touch with the social security administration because George's supplemental security payments are often late.

In the the fourth approach, *neurobiological factors and larger systems* are the targets of intervention. Families are viewed as needing support and education, not therapy. Practitioners using this approach emphasize enhancement of the quality of life of the patient and the family by directing a wide range of practice behaviors toward amelioration of environmental conditions. There is less emphasis than in interpersonal approaches on trying to promote communication and express feelings, and more emphasis on husbanding resources, ensuring accountability by community service providers, and looking for as many kinds of social supports as possible. Worker D, using this approach, might work with George and his family as follows.

George is currently receiving Risperdal, which he sometimes forgets to take. I call Mrs. P to verify this when George appears agitated or more disoriented than usual. I am now asking George to call me every Friday to report on how he has been doing with his medication. He has been given a calendar to check off each time he takes his medication. I am working with George toward getting him to attend a day treatment center and have also contacted the state employment service to see whether part-time work might be available. George has done custodial work and lawn care in the past. Mrs. P feels enormous stress because of George's constant presence in the home. We are exploring the possibility of a group home for George, as well as resources for Mrs. P. where she could socialize and find some companionship without having to travel too far. Mr.

P has expressed resentment at never being able to go away with his wife on a vacation because of George. The last time they left him alone for a week to go on a trip, he had an acute psychotic episode that resulted in hospitalization. They have never left him alone since that time. We are currently exploring possibilities for overnight care for George so that his parents can get away together. There have been recurring problems with George's SSI payments. I have made several calls to the social security office about this and finally went there to talk with the supervisor.

THE NEUROBIOLOGICAL FOUNDATIONS OF ADDICTION

Addiction is a vulnerable individual's response to taking addictive drugs with adequate dose, frequency, and chronicity (Hyman, 1995). Vulnerability is not a permanent state; rather, an individual can have different levels of vulnerability in different environments and different life situations at different times in his or her life. Vulnerability is a function of the number of risk factors to which a person is subject at any given moment in time. *Individual risk factors* can include genetic loading, psychiatric disability, chronic pain, feeling stressed and user goals (such as experimentation or escape from psychic pain). *Environmental risk factors* include drug availability, peer-group pressure to use, lack of behavioral alternatives to drug use (no other opportunities for fun or satisfaction), settings in which drugs are used such as religious ceremonies, family holidays, and presence of conditioned cues (such as a place where the addicted person formerly used frequently, or running into drug-using friends).

Other risk factors are the *specific characteristics of a particular drug* such as the drug's addictiveness, purity, and route of administration.

Chronic use of drugs causes long-lived molecular changes in the signaling properties of neurons. Depending on the drug and the circuits involved, these adaptations have different effects on behavior and different time courses of initiation and decay. With chronic drug use, three types of long-term changes may take place in the brain centers that control (a) somatic functions (body functions), (b) rewards and pleasures, and (c) emotional memories (Hyman, 1995).

Physical effects of drugs that affect somatic functions are visible when the drug is withdrawn. We can't see the physical effects of drugs on reward/pleasure pathways in the brain or on emotional memories, but these effects are physical too: They are just as real, just as physical, as the somatic effects of withdrawal from *alcohol* (e.g., tremor, hypertension, grand mal seizures, tachycardia, irritability, delusions, hallucinations), *caffeine* (e.g., headache, fatigue), or *opiates* (e.g., severe muscle cramps, bone ache, diarrhea, tearing, insomnia, restlessness, nausea, gooseflesh).

Only a few drugs involve somatic dependence, but almost all drugs of abuse are believed to induce the other two kinds of long-term changes in brain structures and functions. First, changes take place in brain reward and pleasure pathways, involving *motivation* and *volition,* both in microanatomic structures and in chemical processes. Motivational aspects of withdrawal are *dysphoria* (feeling sad, blue, down in the dumps); *anhedonia* (inability to experience pleasure—things once enjoyed are no longer fun); and *cravings.* The person suffering from these feelings experiences a change in behavioral priorities: now, getting the drug of abuse becomes the most important goal in life.

Second, changes occur in memories. Many memories during a lifetime are eventually lost through decay of memory traces in the brain. However, memories of powerful experiences remain. Cues evoke these memories of intensely pleasurable experiences leading to cravings, as in addiction, or intensely painful experiences leading to to traumatic flooding, as in post-traumatic stress disorder (PTSD). These memories are referred to as "privileged" memories because they take precedence in affecting the individual's emotional state and in motivating behavior. These latter two types of long-term changes—changes in structures and functions affecting *motivation and volition,* and changes in *emotional memories*—are actual physical effects that we cannot see (Hyman, 1995).

The *mesolimbic dopamine pathway,* also called the reward circuit or the pleasure pathway, originates in the ventral tegmental area (VTA) of the midbrain (see Figure 4–14), where neurons manufacture dopamine. A bundle of nerve fibers projects from the VTA to the nucleus accumbens (NAc) in the limbic system bordering on the basal ganglia (see Figure 4–14). This mesolimbic dopamine pathway has a role in creating privileged memories of highly rewarding novel stimuli. These memories cause addicts to have cravings and risk of relapse even after years of abstinence. The limbic system plays a key role in determining what is salient enough to be remembered.

We used to distinguish between "physical" and "psychological" addiction by the presence or absence of somatic withdrawal such as tremors, nausea, hallucinations, muscle cramps, seizures, and other obviously phys-

Figure 4–14
Sites Where Addiction Takes Place

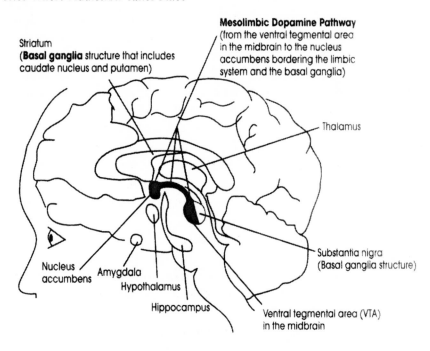

Striatum
(**Basal ganglia** structure that includes caudate nucleus and putamen)

Mesolimbic Dopamine Pathway
(from the ventral tegmental area in the midbrain to the nucleus accumbens bordering the limbic system and the basal ganglia)

Thalamus

Nucleus accumbens   Amygdala

Hypothalamus

Hippocampus

Substantia nigra
(Basal ganglia structure)

Ventral tegmental area (VTA) in the midbrain

ical symptoms. Now we know that all drugs of abuse produce actual physical changes in the brain. Even though many of the physical effects of drugs on the brain are not directly observable, we now know they are just as real as seizures and muscle cramps.

These changes last varying amounts of time. Somatic withdrawal may last days, weeks, sometimes even longer. Motivational aspects of withdrawal may last from several weeks to months, even years. Emotional memories may last a lifetime; we may never shake them off. That is, once addicted, you may never "withdraw" from the memories of intense pleasure associated with drug use. That is why AA members with years of sobriety call themselves "recovering," not "recovered," alcoholics (Hyman, 1995).

Each Drug Has Its Own Special Neurotransmitter

Drugs of abuse work in the brain through different neurotransmitter systems. Some drugs affect several transmitters through a chain of reactions. Here are some of the transmitters that are active with different drugs.

Table 4–3   Drugs Mediated by Neurotransmitters

Drug	Neurotransmitter
Opiates/Heroin	Endrophins/Enkephalins
Cocaine/Amphetamine	Dopamine
Nicotine	Acetylcholine
Alcohol	GABA, opioids, and others
Marijuana	THC receptor ligand, anandamide
Hallucinogens	Serotonin
Caffeine	Adenosine

However, it is now believed that most or all drugs of abuse either directly or indirectly act on dopamine systems. Moreover, it seems likely that other forms of addiction, such as gambling or binge eating, also create feelings of pleasure, excitement, or satisfaction through dopamine pathways.

How Certain Drugs Behave in the Process of Becoming Addicted

Cocaine

To understand the process of addiction, let's take cocaine as an example.

The pleasure pathway (mesolimbic dopamine pathway) is composed of neurons that transmit the neurotransmitter dopamine. The bundles of dopamine neurons that form the mesolimbic dopamine pathway extend from the ventral tegmental area in the midbrain to the nucleus accumbens in the limbic system. Everyday pleasures such as eating or listening to music touch off little spurts of dopamine. Figure 4–15 shows the normal dopamine neuron, without cocaine.

Cocaine blocks the reuptake of dopamine into the presynaptic neuron by jumping on board the shuttle that carries the dopamine back up into the sending neuron. Cocaine grabs the slots on the shuttle away from the dopamine neurons that are floating around in the synapse, so there is a lot more dopamine left in the synapse than before the person had a hit of cocaine.

Thus, cocaine makes a direct hit on the dopamine pathways. This means that a lot of dopamine is now available to combine with the postsynaptic receptor molecules that are located on the surface of the receiving neuron. The dopamine is what gives the rush. That is, cocaine users get high on their own dopamine.

Figure 4–15
A Normal Dopamine Neuron

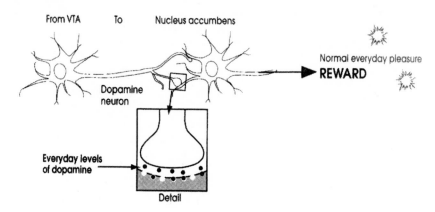

Figure 4–16 show what happens in response to a hit of cocaine. The cocaine blocks the normal reuptake of some of the dopamine molecules into the presynaptic neuron, flooding the synapse with dopamine.

However, continuing floods of dopamine triggered by cocaine *sledgehammer* the dopamine system. The brain tries to adapt to this sledgehammering. After a person has been using cocaine at a sufficient dose, often enough, over a long enough period of time, DNA (genetic material) is acti-

Figure 4–16
A Dopamine Neuron Reacts to Cocaine

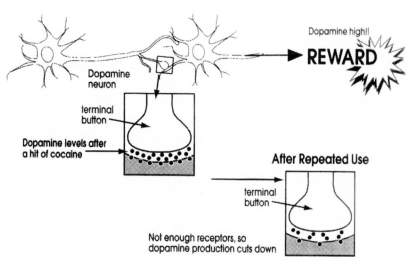

Figure 4–17
How Amphetamines Affect Dopamine Release

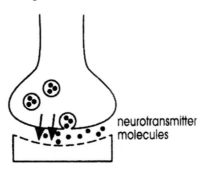

neurotransmitter
molecules

vated and is turned into RNA. This RNA makes a neurotransmitter *dynorphin,* which directs neurons to cut down on dopamine production. The brain's adaptation to too much dopamine is to reduce the number of dopamine receptors. So the brain adapts to the presence of cocaine, and when the cocaine is taken away, the person is in an adapted state. The user now has insufficient dopamine, which produces symptoms of depression and anhedonia (inability to experience pleasure). All this leads to cravings. The individual is in a worse condition than before taking drugs, because withdrawal when in an adapted (addicted) state causes *severe psychic pain.* This psychic pain is neurobiological in origin. It comes from molecular changes in the brain brought about by genetic activity in response to drug use.

Amphetamines
Amphetamines make a direct hit on dopamine systems as well, but they do it a little differently. They facilitate the release of extra dopamine into the synapse from the presynaptic neuron. Although the mechanisms differ, the effect is the same—see Figure 4–17.

Opiates
Remember that neurons come in different sizes and shapes, and that each neuron connects with between 1,000 and 10,000 other neurons. Short neurons make connections with longer neurons. These interconnecting short neurons are called *interneurons.* There are lots of interneurons in the brain that transmit an inhibitory neurotransmitter called GABA (γ-aminobutyric acid). These inhibitory interneurons inhibit the action of receiving neurons.

Figure 4–18
Inhibitory Interneuron (GABA) Keeps Dopamine Neuron in Check

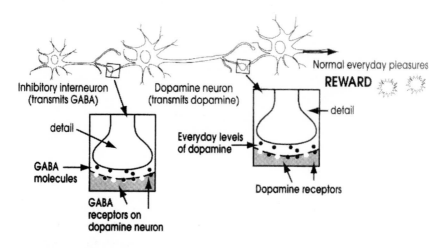

Figure 4–18 shows a dopamine neuron, in its everyday state, giving little ordinary pleasures. The short GABA interneuron is keeping the dopamine neuron in check by sending it some inhibitory messages. The GABA interneurons send inhibitory messages to receiving neurons and balance out the messages they're getting at the same time from excitatory neurotransmitters. When the right amount of GABA is coming through, you get modest amounts of dopamine—just the right amount of dopamine to enjoy simple everyday pleasures. But when the GABA neurons stop squirting GABA onto the dopamine neurons, inhibitory messages decrease. The balance between excitatory and inhibitory messages is disrupted. The dopamine neuron gets overexcited and fires faster and faster.

When opiate drugs get into the system (Figure 4–19), they have inhibitory effects too: They *inhibit* the *inhibitory* GABA neurons. When opiates inhibit GABA neurons, the GABA neurons *stop* inhibiting the dopamine neurons. In Figure 4–19, neurotransmitter molecules being sent from the GABA interneuron to the dopamine neuron in Figure 4–18 have now diminished, because the opiate drug has inhibited the GABA neuron. The result is a flood of dopamine, which gives the high. We've seen that cocaine and amphetamines affect dopamine action directly. The opiates affect it indirectly through GABA neurons.

Alcohol (Ethanol)
The molecular action of alcohol in the brain is very complex and is not yet well understood. Alcohol consumption changes concentrations of sev-

Figure 4–19
Opiate Inhibits Inhibitory Interneurons

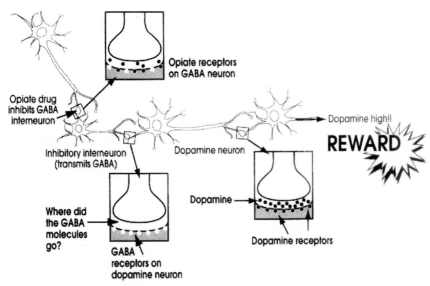

eral neurotransmitters (dopamine, GABA, endogenous opioid peptides, serotonin, glutamate, and noradrenaline). These changes are associated with activation of reward centers in the brain. Dopaminergic and noradrenergic mechanisms, together with the endogenous opioid peptides, are thought to play important roles in the reinforcing properties of ethanol (alcohol) through activation of positive reinforcement pathways.

Ethanol is thought to potentiate GABA (causing relaxation) and stimulate release of dopamine from mesolimbic neurons (causing euphoria). Ethanol also reduces the firing rate of pars reticulata (PR) neurons, which are believed to have an inhibitory effect on dopamine neurons (thus, ethanol *dis*inhibits the dopamine neurons). Low doses of ethanol produce significant enhancement of the release of dopamine in limbic structures in mice (DeWitte, 1996).

An exciting recent discovery was that opioid peptide neurotransmitters are involved in a range of effects of ethanol. Drugs that block the effects of opioid peptides decrease self-administration of ethanol by laboratory animals. Clinical trials have shown that opioid peptide *antagonists* (substances that block effects of opioid peptides) can decrease relapse rates in detoxified outpatient alcoholics; see Froelich et al., 1996, for a review of this research. Some recovering alcoholics report that opioid antagonists such as naltrexone take away their *cravings for alcohol,* even though these same opioid blockers *don't* take away cravings for opiate drugs (Holloway, 1991). In fact in the early 1900s morphine, an opiate drug, was used to treat alcoholism!

Nicotine

Nicotine acts at the receptor for the neurotransmitter acetylcholine, causing an increase in number and sensitivity of acetylcholine receptors. This process probably accounts for withdrawal symptoms when the drug is withheld. These acetylcholine receptors in turn stimulate the release of dopamine in the mesolimbic dopamine pathway. Another substance in cigarettes also increases dopamine levels by blocking the action of monoamine oxidase, the enzyme that breaks down dopamine and other monoamines into metabolites (Panagis et al., 1996; Rowell, 1995; Grinspoon, 1997b).

Caffeine

Caffeine is an antagonist to a transmitter that blocks dopamine D1 receptors, called *adenosine* (another double negative). Caffeine *blocks the dopamine blocker,* hence it enhances dopamine levels. Caffeine induces dopamine-dependent behavioral arousal and enhances motor activity in rodents. It also activates norepinephrine-producing neurons (Okada, Mizuno & Kaneko, 1996; Popoli, Giminez-Llort, et al., 1996; Wu, Mercuri, & Johnson, 1995).

Marijuana

The psychoactive component of marijuana, delta 9-tetrahydrocannabinol (delta 9-THC) enhances ventral tegmental dopamine levels, suggesting evidence for local neuronal action by delta 9-THC. In addition, a possible *ligand* (compound that has an affinity for a certain receptor), anandamide, is thought to represent the endogenous marijuana-like substance that binds with cannabinoid receptors. Anandamide may play a role in modulating neural activity, or it may be a neurotransmitter itself. Marijuana research has progressed rapidly during the past five years and is continuing to progress (Adams & Martin, 1996; Chen et al., 1993; Onaivi et al., 1996).

Addiction as a Self-Destructive Process

Practitioners and family members often wonder why the addicted person persists in using despite such obvious drastic consequences as job loss, abandonment by significant others, and trouble with the law. It is often hard for people not themselves addicted to comprehend why a person would give up virtually everything of value in his or her life in order to maintain the addiction. The answer lies in neurobiology. Addiction usurps brain mechanisms that are prime movers in motivated behavior. It commandeers the parts of the brain that control motivation and set behavioral priorities. The addict is intensely aware of dysphoria and craving. The "strange" behavior of an addicted person *is not strange* because *the person's brain has really changed.*

PSYCHOSOCIAL INTERVENTIONS IN THE CONTEXT OF A CHANGED BRAIN

Interventions for substance abuse include support groups such as Alcoholics Anonymous and Narcotics Anonymous, cognitive-behavioral strategies, therapeutic communities, other psychosocial interventions, and medication. Like a person who has had a stroke, an addicted person has lost certain nerve cells, but can recover some functions because other parts of the brain are sometimes able to take over what the damaged part of the brain used to do. Psychological, social, and contextual treatments act as prostheses for the person's broken brain. By asking addicted people to take responsibility for themselves, practitioners or family members are asking for other thinking parts of their brain and other emotional parts of their brain to do things the damaged part of their brain used to do.

The action of the intact parts of the brain doesn't make the changes brought about by addiction go away. The problems are still there, especially long-term emotional memories that predispose to relapse. But psychosocial treatments enlist other parts of the brain to act as bulwarks against these parts of the brain that want nothing more than to get another hit. Similar principles work in trauma as well. Traumatic emotional memories almost never go away, but other parts of the brain learn to manage and suppress these memories, to focus on other things, and to engage in positive behaviors and actions.

Treating Drug Abuse With Drugs — Doesn't That Just Substitute One Drug for Another?

Medications, usually in conjunction with psychosocial interventions, often help people in recovery stay clean. This is especially true for medications that diminish cravings. In each individual case, we need to ask these questions: What are the risks of our proposed intervention? What are the likely benefits of our proposed interventions? and—the question most often neglected—What are the possible risks of *not* doing the proposed intervention?

The last question is really on target with respect to treating drug abuse with drugs. If we had a drug that could take away cravings, that would help a person to stay clean or sober, and that person was at high risk for relapse, wouldn't there be a risk attached to *not* giving that medication?

There are at least three types of drugs for treating addictions: agonists, antagonists, and aversive agents.

Agonists
Agonists bind with receptor molecules in a fashion similar to the drug of abuse, prevent withdrawal symptoms, but do not give the high of the drug of abuse. For example, methadone binds to opiate receptors in place of heroin, prevents heroin withdrawal syndrome, and takes away the craving for heroin. Nevertheless, the street marketability of treatment drugs such as methadone suggests that they do give some kind of a high. Another problem with agonists is that they are also likely to be addictive, so that the user substitutes one addiction for another. The advantages are that the person may be able to function (e.g., hold a job) better than when using the original drug, and that the prevention of withdrawal symptoms and cravings diminishes the need for criminal behavior to get money for the drug of abuse.

Antagonists
Antagonists bind with receptors in a different way from the drug of abuse ("competitive binding at the receptor site"), so taking the drug of abuse gives no effect, but does not satisfy the addict's craving. For example, naltrexone binds to opiate receptors, blocks the effects of heroin, but does *not* remove the craving for heroin and other opiates. A problem with antagonist drugs is that the user still craves. Since the antagonist therapeutic drug now blocks the effect of the original drug, the user may just substitute a different drug of abuse for the original drug. Researchers are developing and testing new drugs that combine agonist and antagonist actions, in the hopes of remedying the limitations of each type of medication. An interesting discovery is that naltrexone, which acts as an antagonist at opioid receptor sites, does not take away the craving for opiate drugs but *does* diminish the craving for alcohol in some cases.

Aversive Agents
Aversive agents, such as disulfiram (Antabuse) for alcohol addiction, deter drug use by making the user violently nauseated if the drug is used while taking the medication.

SSRIs (selective serotonin reuptake inhibitors) have also been found to diminish cravings for alcohol or obsessive cravings for food in some people. How? We don't know for sure. Various psychotropic medications have been used to treat addiction. For more information about these, readers are urged to search Medline (a computerized index of articles in medical and addiction journals), to obtain the most up-to-date information. Medline can be found in medical libraries and on the Internet.

SUCCESSFUL TREATMENT

Successful treatment requires that the addicted person eventually take personal responsibility for himself or herself, overcome denial, commit to sobriety, and take active steps to achieve it. We can then provide ways of propping up the compromised brain. The same principles apply in most serious chronic diseases. The individual is asked to comply with treatment and to avoid behaviors that put him or her at high risk of relapse or of worsening the condition. For example, a person is at high risk for a heart attack because he or she is obese, has a family history of heart disease, smokes, and is a couch potato. Only he or she can actually change that situation by following the doctor's orders to lose weight, change eating habits, stop smoking, and exercise. The person with the disease must take responsibility for compliance. Just because a user was unlucky enough to have been more at risk than some other people doesn't change the fact that *only he or she* can choose to behave in ways that will either perpetuate or overcome the addiction.

SUMMARY

This chapter has reviewed some aspects of the neurobiological foundation of psychopathology. Advances in technology, notably brain imaging, have radically changed our knowledge base about human behavior, both typical and atypical. All psychiatric conditions as well as "normal" states are the product of highly complex biology–environment interactions through time, states that can vary greatly at different points in time according to the relative inputs of risk and protective factors at any given moment. Nature-versus-nurture dichotomies have been replaced by an integrated biopsychosocial understanding of conditions that we refer to as "psychopathology." This chapter has attempted to give readers some tools for understanding neuroscience research as it pertains to our daily work with consumers of social work services.

REFERENCES

Adams, I. B., & Martin, B. R. (1996). Cannabis: pharmacology and toxicology in animals and humans. *Addiction, 91*, 11, 1585–1614.

Briar, K. (1979, March). The human costs of unemployment for young, middle-aged, and aged workers. Paper presented at the Annual Program Meeting, Council on Social Work Education. Boston.

Castellanos, F. X., Giedd, J. N., Marsh, W. L., Hamburger, M. D., Vaituzis, A. C., Dickstein, D. P., Sarfatti, S. E., Vauss, Y. C., Snell, J. W., Rajapakse, J. C., & Rapoport, J. L. (1996). Quantitative brain magnetic resonance imaging in attention-deficit hyperactivity disorder. *Archives of General Psychiatry, 53*, 7, 607–616.

Chen, J., Marmur, R., Pulles, A., Paredes, W., & Gardner, E. L. (1993). Ventral tegmental microinjection of delta 9-tetrahydrocannabinol enhances ventral tegmental somatodendritic dopamine levels but not forebrain dopamine levels: evidence for local neural action by marijuana's psychoactive ingredient. *Brain Research, 621*, 1, 65–70.

DeWitte, P. (1996). The role of neurotransmitters in alcohol dependence: Animal research. *Alcohol and Alcoholism, 31*, Suppl. 1, 13–16.

Diana, M., Rossetti, Z. L., & Gessa, G. (1993). Rewarding and aversive effects of ethanol: interplay of GABA, glutamate, and dopamine. *Alcohol and Alcoholism, 28* Suppl. 2, 315–319.

Elder, G. (1974). *Children of the Great Depression.* Chicago: University of Chicago Press.

Froehlich, J. C., Charness, M., Wand, G., Di Chiari, G. & Koob, G. (1996). The neurobiology of ethanol-opioid interactions in ethanol reinforcement. *Alcohol Clinical and Experimental Research, 20*, 8 Suppl., 181A–186A.

Germain, C. (1991). *Human behavior in the social environment: An ecological view.* New York: Columbia University Press.

Grinspoon, L., Ed. (1997a). Mood disorders: An overview, Part 1. *Harvard Mental Health Letter, 14*, 6, 1–4.

Grinspoon, L., Ed. (1997b). Nicotine dependence. (Part 1.). *Harvard Mental Health Letter, 13*, 11, 1–4.

Gross, M., & Wilson, W. (1974). *Minimal brain dysfunction.* New York: Brunner/Mazel.

Hoffman, P. L., & Tabakoff, B. (1996). Alcohol dependence: A commentary on mechanisms. *Alcohol and Alcoholism, 31*, 4, 333–340.

Holloway, M. (1991). Treatment for addiction. *Scientific American, 264*, 3, 94–103.

Hyman, S. E. (1995). What is addiction? *Harvard Medical Alumni Review,* Winter.

Hyman, S. E., & Nestler, E. J. (1993). Toward a new psychiatric neuroscience. In *The molecular foundations of psychiatry* (pp. 193–211). Washington, DC: American Psychiatric Press.

Jensen, P. (1996). Treatments for child and adolescent mental disorders: Recent research progress. *Decade of the Brain, VII*(1), 2–4.

Johnson, H. C. (1999). *Psyche, synapse, and substance: The role of neurobiology in emotions, behavior, thinking, and addiction for non-scientists.* Greenfield, MA: Deerfield Vally Publishing.

Johnson, H. C. (1984). The biological bases of psychopathology. In F. Turner (Ed.), *Adult psychopathology* (pp. 6–72). New York: Free Press.

Kagan, J. (1994). *The nature of the child.* New York: Basic Books.

Kaplan, H. I., & Sadock, B. J. (1998). *Synopsis of psychiatry* (8th Ed.). Baltimore: Williams and Wilkins.

Leonard, H. L., Rapoport, J. L., and Swedo, S. E. (1997). Obsessive-compulsive disorder. In J. M. Weiner (Ed.), *Textbook of child and adolescent psychiatry* (2nd Ed., pp. 481–490). Washington, DC: American Psychiatric Press.

Leutwyler, K. (1996). Paying attention. *Scientific American, 8,* 12–14.

Milberger, S., Biederman, J., Faraone, S. V., Chen, L., & Jones, J. (1996). Is maternal smoking during pregnancy a risk factor for attention deficit hyperactivity disorder in children? *American Journal of Psychiatry, 153*(9), 1138–1142.

Miller, J. G. (1978). *Living systems.* New York: McGraw-Hill.

Levin, G. M. (1995). Attention deficit/hyperactivity disorder: the pharmacist's role. *American Pharmacy, 35*(11), 10–20.

Littleton, J., & Little, H. (1994). Current concepts of ethanol dependence. *Addiction, 89*(11), 1397–1412.

Nevo, I., & Hamon, M. (1995). Neurotransmitter and neuromodulatory mechanisms involved in alcohol abuse and alcoholism. *Neurochemistry International, 26*(4), 305–336.

Okada, M., Mizuno, K., & Kaneko, S. (1996). Adenosine A1 and A2 receptors modulate extracellular dopamine levels in rat striatum. *Neuroscience Letters, 212*(1), 53–56.

Onaivi, E. S., Chakrabarti, A., & Chaudhuri, G. (1996). Cannabinoid receptor genes. *Progress in Neurobiology, 48,* 4–5, 275–305.

Ortiz, J., Fitzgerald, L. W., Charlton, M., Lane, S., Trevisan, L., Guitart, X., Shoemaker, W., Duman, R. S., & Nestler, E. J. (1995). Biochemical actions of chronic ethanol exposure in the mesolimbic dopamine system. *Synapse, 21*(4), 289–298.

Panagis, G., Nisell, M., Nomikos, G. G., Chergui, K., and Svensson, T. H. (1996). Nicotine injections into the ventral tegmental area increase locomotion and Fos-like immunoreactivity in the nucleus accumbens of the rat. *Brain Research, 730*(1–2), 133–142.

Popoli, P., Giminez-Llort, L., Pezzola, A., Reggio, R., Martinez, E., Fuxe, K., & Ferre, S. (1996). Adenosine A1 receptor blockade selectively potentiates the motor effects induced by dopamine D1 receptor stimulation in rodents. *Neuroscience Letters, 218,* 3, 209–213.

Rowell, P. P. (1995). Nanomolar concentrations of nicotine increase the release of [3H] dopamine from rat striatal synaptosomes. *Neuroscience Letters, 189,* 3, 171–175.

Terenius, L. (1996). Alcohol addiction (alcoholism) and the opioid system. *Alcohol, 13,* 1, 31–34.

Wu, Y. N., Mercuri. N. B., & Johnson, S. W. (1995). Presynaptic inhibition of gamma-aminobutyric acidB-mediated synaptic current by adenosine recorded in vitro in midbrain dopamine neurons. *Journal of Pharmacology and Experimental Therapy, 273*(2), 576–581.

Yan, Q. S., Reith, M. E., Jobe, P. C., & Dailey, J. W. (1996). Focal ethanol elevates extracellular dopamine and serotonin concentrations in the rat ventral tegmental area. *European Journal of Pharmacology, 301,* 1–3, 49–57.

Zametkin, A. (1991). The neurobiology of attention-deficit hyperactivity disorder. *CHADDER,* Spring/Summer, 10–16.

5

PSYCHOPHARMACOLOGY AND CLINICAL SOCIAL WORK

Jacinta Marschke and Carol P. Kaplan

C linical social workers in the field of mental health today face new challenges, brought about not only by changes in mental health services but
by ongoing advances in psychopharmacology. Practicing in a variety of settings, social workers confront clients with diverse problems, who either
may be taking prescribed drugs that affect their psychosocial functioning
or may be candidates for such medications. In addition to the seriously and
persistently mentally ill, examples of such client groups include those with
other mental disorders or dual diagnoses, alcohol abusers, children diagnosed with attention deficit hyperactivity disorder (ADHD), and a diverse
group who are the patients of primary care physicians.

This chapter will identify and discuss the subject of pharmacology from
three perspectives. Basic information about psychotropic medications will
be provided in the form of tables. Since new drugs are constantly being
developed, additional references will be provided so that social workers
can continue to remain up to date. The various roles that social workers
adopt with their clients in relation to psychotropic medications will be
described and case examples provided. Also, certain ethical concerns that
arise for social workers when clients are either taking or considering psychotropic drugs will be discussed.

PSYCHOACTIVE DRUGS AND SOCIAL WORK ROLES

In public mental health settings today, social workers serve as primary care
providers to over 70% of all patients with acute and chronic mental illness (Peterson et al., 1992). In fact, a study of mental health providers conducted by the National Center for Social Policy and Practice (1988)

concluded that social workers were the only mental health treatment providers in 25% of the counties surveyed. This role as mental health treatment provider has been enhanced by the efforts of managed care to control costs. Severe time restrictions on psychotherapy prevail. Emphasis has been placed on symptom alleviation primarily through use of medication, and increased reliance on general physicians rather than psychiatrists in the prescribing of psychotropic drugs (Krizay & Oss, 1990). These changes in the provision of mental health services require flexibility on the part of social work. Not only must workers become reasonably knowledgeable about pharmacology in general, they must be prepared to adopt a variety of roles with clients in regard to psychoactive drugs.

Psychotropic Medications

The social worker in the field of mental health must have basic knowledge about psychoactive medications, as well as access to references that provide more comprehensive and updated information.* The tables included in this section offer basic information about the psychotropic drugs currently used to treat psychiatric disorders, but they do not pretend to be either exhaustive or definitive. Rather, the drugs currently in use have been grouped with those conditions for which they are given. We suggest that social workers whose clients may be candidates for medications think conceptually in terms of general classes of drugs, rather than attempting to memorize specific ones.

Because new medications are constantly being introduced, social workers have the obligation of remaining informed about developments that may impact their clients, even though the physician has ultimate responsibility for prescribing drugs. In addition to the references cited, many medical and nonmedical mental health professionals consult frequently appearing publications like the *Harvard Mental Health Letter,* a monthly newsletter published by Harvard Medical School. Ultimately, however, the social worker must consult the psychiatrist or other prescribing physician when in doubt about any client's medication.

The tables presented later in this chapter list medications in four categories: Table 5–1: Antipsychotics, Neuroleptics and Major Transquilizers; Table 5–2: Antianxiety Medications; Table 5–3: Antidepressant Medications; Table 5–4: Mood Stabilizers and Other Medications. Each table lists behavioral symptoms, drug class (i.e., chemical composition), generic (i.e.,

*The authors would like to thank Michael Kaplan, M.D., for his valuable assistance in preparing the section on psychotropic medications.

chemical compound) and trade (i.e., trademark) names, daily dosage in milligrams, side effects, and other special considerations. Common medication side effects associated with psychotropic drugs include sedation as well as extrapyramidal symptoms (EPS) and anticholinergic symptoms (ACH). EPS refers to Parkinson's dystonias, akathesia, and tardive dyskinesia. ACH refers to dry mouth, constipation, urinary retention, and blurry vision.

Certain general points should be kept in mind with regard to all psychoactive medications.

1. In choosing a psychoactive medication of any type, the physician will always consider the following factors: the targeted symptoms or behaviors, known side-effect profile including sedation level, motoric effects, prior client and physician experience with medication, lethality and abuse potential, and current or potential medical complications.

2. Although all drugs within a class share a common chemical structure, they differ in their clinical effectiveness with individual clients. These differences are not fully understood, but they account for physicians' decisions to switch to another drug in the same class when one does not work.

3. Because some behaviors or symptoms are manifest in a variety of conditions, some medications typically associated with one disorder may be prescribed for someone with a different disorder. For example, low doses of antipsychotic medications are sometimes prescribed to dissipate impulsive acting-out behavior associated with borderline personality disorder. Also, antidepressants are used at times to treat clients with anxiety disorders.

4. Even though the doses cited in the tables reflect general practice standards, higher or lower doses may be prescribed for particular clients.

5. Special considerations may apply when prescribing medication with older clients (Giannetti, 1983), children (Green, 1991), and patients with confounding medical conditions. In the case of older people the potential for drugs to produce cognitive impairment may be greater, while prepubertal children may respond differently or not at all to certain medications, such as tricyclic antidepressants.

In addition to these general considerations, certain points should be emphasized in regard to each of the four tables. Table 5–1 (Antipsychotic, Neuroleptic, and Major Tranquilizer Medications) conceptualizes neuroleptics into high and low potency, according to their side-effect profiles. In addition, this chart reflects the developmental history of these drugs: i.e., the phenothiazines are older, while the atypical neuroleptics are much newer. Table 5–2 (Antianxiety Medications) lists some drugs that carry a

Table 5-1 Antipsychotic, Neuroleptic, and Major Tranquilizer Medications

Behavioral Symptoms	Drug Class	Generic Name (Trade Name)	Dosage[a]	Side Effects: Sedation, EPS/ACH[b]	Special Considerations
Positive Symptoms Hallucinations, Delusions, Impaired thinking, Confused and impaired judgment, Severe anxiety, Agitation and emotional dyscontrol	Phenothiazines	Fluphenazine hydrochloride (Prolixin)	1–20	Low, High/Low	
		Trifluoperazine (Stelazine)	6–20	Low, High/Low	
		Perphenazine (Trilafon)	up to 24	Midlevel, High/Low	
		Thioridazine (Mellaril)	200–700	High, Low/High	
		Mesoridazine (Serentil)	75–300	High, Low/High	
		Chlorpromazine (Thorazine)	30–600	High, Low/High	
	Thioxanthenes	Thiothixene (Navane)	15–60	Low, High/Low	
	Butyrophenone	Haloperidol (Haldol)	2–40	Low, High/Low	
	Diphenybutylpiperidines	Pimozide (Orap)	2–30	Low, High/Low	
	Benzisoxazoles	Risperidone (Risperidol)	2–6	Low, Low/Low	
	Atypical neuroleptics	Sertindole (Serlect)	12–24	Low, 0/0	New drugs, see 1997 data sources
		Quetiapine (Seroquel)	150–300	Low, 0/0	
		Olanzapine (Zyprexa)	5–20	Low, Low/Low	
	Dibenzazepine	Clozapine (Clozaril)	200–600	High, 0/High	Risk of agranulocytosis[c] and seizures

Source: Data from Butler, Jeffries & Martin, 1994; Preston & Johnson, 1995; Arvanitis, 1997; Tollefson, 1997.
[a]Dosage refers to the average milligrams prescribed per day.
[b]Severity of sedation and EPS/ACH side effects range from 0 to high.
[c]Agranulocytosis is a deficiency of white blood cells.

risk for abuse and dependency. Table 5–3 (Antidepressant Medications) addresses medications that target all the specific symptoms listed and that are also used to treat other disorders in which similar symptoms are manifest. These include anxiety disorders, obsessive-compulsive disorder (OCD), bulimia, posttraumatic stress disorder (PTSD) and ADHD. Moreover, when one antipressant alone does not prove clinically effective, physicians may add adjunctive agents or other antidepressants. Table 5–4 (Mood Stabilizers and Other Medications) is actually a hybrid table, inasmuch as it includes drugs used for three distinct groups: bipolar disorders, ADHD, and borderline personality disorders. They have been grouped together solely for convenience. Finally, various medications included in the tables may be used for disorders not listed, such as Tourette's syndrome.

SOCIAL WORK ROLES

Social workers assume a variety of roles with clients who are candidates for, or current users of, psychoactive medications. These roles include clinical assessor/collaborator, client/family educator, client advocate, and case manager. In this section a clinical case illustration, followed by a discussion of the unique clinical issues that arise with each social work role, will be provided.

The Clinical Assessor/Collaborator Role

The Case of Joan

Joan, a 45-year-old nursery school teacher, seeks counseling for the first time in her life because she is unable to "shake her rage" after learning of her husband's five-year extramarital affair. He has broken off the relationship and states he is committed to making their 18-year marriage work, but she is ambivalent. Since the revelation three months ago, Joan reports, she has withdrawn at work because she feels "ashamed," easily breaks into tears, has had trouble sleeping, has lost ten pounds, and frequently flies into rages with her 16 year old son, her friends, and her husband. During these rages she blurts out "mean" and "cruel" things that are not appropriate or true. Until now she has always been an "upbeat" person with high energy and enthusiasm. Her friends have viewed her as a "fun-

continued on p. 108

Table 5–2 Antianxiety Medications

Behavioral Symptoms	Class	Generic Name (Trade Name)	Dosage[a]	Special Considerations
Generalized Anxiety Disorder	Azaspirodecanedione	Buspirone (Buspar)	20–60	Must be taken on an ongoing basis. Not found helpful in other anxiety disorders. No potential for addiction/dependence.
Situational or Stress-Related Anxiety, Insomnia, Panic Attack Symptoms, Acute Mania (with antidepressants or alone)	Benzodiazepines Long acting	Clonazepam (Klonopin) Clorazepate (Tranxene) Diazepam (Valium) Flurazepam (Dalmane) Prazepam (Centrax) Quazepam (Doral) Chlordiazepoxide (Librium)	.5–4 15–60 5–40 15–30 20–60 7.5–30 15–100	For all benzodiazepines, there is a high risk of dependency/addiction & withdrawal symptoms. Thus, most effective for short-term use. Klonopin also an effective anticonvulsant, an alternative mood-stabilizer (rapid cyclers) & antidote for behavioral/emotional dyscontrol. Used primarily for acute alcohol detoxification.
	Short acting	Midazolam (Versed) Triazolam (Halcion) Estazolam (ProSom)	7.5–45 .12–.50 1–2	Also for stress-induced insomnia
	Intermediate acting	Halazepam (Paxipam) Lorazepam (Ativan) Oxazepam (Serax)	60–160 2–6 30–120	Also for stress-induced insomnia
Panic Attacks/Disorder, Situational Anxiety		Temazepam (Restoril) Alprazolam (Xanax)	15–30 .50–4	Also for stress-induced insomnia. Antidepressants an alternative
Stress-Induced Insomnias	Sedatives and hypnotics Antihistamines	Hydroxyzine (Atarax) Diphenhydramine (Benadryl) Doxylamine (Unisom)	10–400 25–300 25–150	More sedating and less effective than benzodiazepines but no risk of addiction. ACH side effects common.
	Sedative	Zolpidem (Ambien)	5–10	No risk of dependence or increased tolerance.
	Heterocyclic Triazolopyridine	Trazadone (Desyrel)	50–100	Used with other antidepressants
Performance Anxiety	Beta blockers	Propranolol (Inderal) Atenolol (Tenormin) Metropolol (Lopressor)	60–160 50–100 150–300	Known to treat hypertension but also used for aggressive behavior and mania.
Social Phobia	MAOs and SSRIs	See Antidepressants		Dependency/tolerance risk low. Also used for social phobias with/without depression.

Source: Data from Gitlin, 1990; Butler et al., 1994; Preston et al., 1995; Bentley et al., 1996.
[a]Dosage expressed in average range of milligrams prescribed per day.

Table 5–3   Antidepressant Medications

Behavioral Symptoms	Drug Class	Generic Name (Trade Name)	Dosage[b]	Side Effects: Sedation Levels, EPS/ACH[c]	Special Considerations
Diurnal fluctuations in and depressed mood Significant anhedonia;[a] Appetite increase/decrease with weight gain or loss; Insomnia or hypersomnia; Restlessness, agitation; psychomotor retardation; Fatigue, loss of energy; Feelings of worthlessness or guilt; Impaired concentration, forgetfulness	Heterocyclics Tricyclics	Amitriptyline (Elavil) Clomipramine (Anafranil) Doxepin (Sinequan) Imipramine (Tofranil) Nortriptyline (Pamelor) Desipramine (Norpramin)	150–300 150–200 100–200 150–350 75–200 150–300	High/Moderate High/Severe High/Minimal Moderate/Moderate Moderate/Minimal Low/Severe	All antidepressants can cause impotence & lower sexual drive. May be used with mood-stabilizers &/or additional antidepressants. Also used for panic attacks.
	Dibenzoxazepine	Amoxapine (Asendin)	150–450	Low/Minimal	
	Monocyclic	Bupropion (Wellbutrin)	100–300	Low/Minimal	Also used for ADHD
	Triazolopyridine	Trazodone (Desyrel)	150–400	Moderate/Minimal	
	Selective Serotonin Reuptake inhibitors (SSRIS)	Fluoxetine (Prozac) Paroxetine (Paxil) Sertraline (Zoloft) Fluvoxamine (Luvox) Venlafaxine (Effexor)	20–80 20–50 50–200 50–300 75–375	Very low/0 Low/0 Low/0 Low/0 Low/0	SSRIs also used for OCD, Bulimia, and Panic Disorder.
	MAO inhibitors	Isocarboxazid (Marplan) Phenelzine (Nardil) Tranylcypromine (Parnate)	30–50 45–90 20–60	Low/0 Low/0 Low/0	Dietary restrictions for all MAOIs. Cannot be used with SSRIs.
	Alpha-2 receptor antagonist	Mirtazapine (Remeron)	15–45	High/Minimal	New drug. Risk of agranulocytosis. Not to be used with MAOIs.

Source: Data from Gitlin, 1990; Preston & Johnson, 1995; Bentley et al., 1996.

[a]Anhedonia refers to the loss of ability to experience pleasure.

[b]Dosage refers to the average number of milligrams prescribed per day.

[c]Sedation/ACH Levels: Sedation levels range from low to high; incidence of ACH effects range from 0 = to serve.

Table 5–4 Mood Stabilizers and Other Psychoactive Medications

Behavioral Symptoms	Class	Generic Name (Trade Name)	Dosage[a]	Special Considerations
Bipolar I: Elevated self-esteem, grandiosity, pressured speech, racing thoughts, distractibility, irritability, agitation, expansiveness	Lithium	Lithium carbonate/Lithium	900–2100	Risk of toxicity requires regular blood levels. Also used with antipsychotic or antidepressant meds when symptoms concurrent.
Rapid cycling of mood	Anticonvulsants	Carbamazepine (Tegretol) Valproate (Depakene, Depakote)	300–1600 750–3000	Anticonvulsants first choice for rapid cyclers. Also an alternative for nonresponders to lithium. There is an associated risk for liver toxicity and/or bone marrow suppression.
	Benzodiazepine	Clonazepam (Klonopin)	4–24	Also an anticonvulsant and antidote for emotional/behavioral dyscontrol.
Bipolar II: Intense depressive episodes with less severe manic phases	MAO inhibitors(An add on or an alternative to lithium)[b]			MAOIs involve complex medication management.
ADHD/Attention Deficit	Psychostimulants	Dextroamphetamine (Dexedrine)	5–40	These stimulants improve attention and concentration.
Hyperactivity Disorder[c]		Methylphenidate (Ritalin) Magnesium pemoline (Cylert)	5–50 37.5–112.5	
	Adrenergic antagonists	Clonidine hydrochloride (Catapres)	0.1–0.4	Antihypertensive medication
	Heterocyclic/Monocyclic	Bupropion (Wellbutrin)	100–300	Antidepressant
Borderline Personality Disorder: Impulsivity and emotional instability	Antidepressants: SSRIs	(Prozac, Zoloft, Paxil)		Used briefly for specific symptoms because of proclivity for abuse.
	Anticonvulsants	(Tegretal, Klonopin, Depakote)		Klonopin, a benzodiazepine, also used as an anticonvulsant and mood stabilizer (rapid cyclers).
Transient psychotic symptoms	Antipsychotic meds	None specified	Low doses	

Source: Gitlin, 1990; Butler et al., 1994; Bentley et al., 1996.
[a]Dosage: average number of milligrams prescribed per day.
[b]Preston & Johnson, 1995
[c]ADHD symptoms include impulsivity, impaired concentration, distractibility, restlessness, hyperactivity, and impaired organizational skills.

loving leader." Although she states that she is in good health, she has a history of ulcerative colitis, which required a permanent colostomy in her late 20s. Also, 8 months ago she consulted a neurologist for what she believed were migraine headaches. The physician prescribed Prozac, which she never took because she read that it could cause people to become violent.

This case raises two diagnostic issues relating to pharmacology: Social workers need to know what psychological symptoms suggest the need for medication; and presenting psychological symptoms may mask an underlying medical condition. In both cases a medical consultation would be indicated. Joan presented with many symptoms of depression including sleep disturbance, irritability, weight loss, tearfulness, social withdrawal and low self-esteem. At the same time, she described both a recent and a past history of physical concerns that might indicate an additional or underlying organic problem. Whereas antidepressant medication often helps clients with the symptoms associated with depression, it may be contraindicated for clients with other medical disorders. Furthermore, sometimes psychological difficulties are secondary to an underlying physical problem. Illnesses such as diabetes, high blood pressure, thyroid conditions, colitis, and migraine headaches may precipitate secondary psychological symptoms that will remit once the medical disorder is addressed. In the case of Joan, the social worker deferred to a physician to determine whether her recent headaches were organically based. Once an organic problem was ruled out, a referral to a psychiatrist for a medication evaluation could be considered.

When clients apply for services at outpatient mental health clinics, it is generally a social worker or other nonmedical provider who completes the initial assessment and develops the initial intervention plan (Johnson, Atkins, et al., 1990). Due to limited resources, psychiatric consultations are typically conducted only upon request, for diagnostic purposes, when planning treatment in complicated cases and when clients need evaluations to initiate or monitor psychotropic medications (National Center for Social Policy & Practice, 1988). As the Clinical Assessor/Collaborator the social worker must determine whether a medical and/or a psychiatric consultation is indicated, and must prepare both the client and the examining psychiatrist for the face-to-face consultation. To be effective in this role the social worker must have basic knowledge of psychoactive medications, as we have noted. In addition, the worker must provide the clinical data, in the form of a written or oral report, so that the physician can establish the differential diagnosis and consider various medications. The report should include:

- a specific rationale for, and objectives of, the consult, which are clear to both the physician and the client.
- a succinct summary of the client's current clinical status, prior experience with medications, prior psychiatric inpatient admissions and treatment, and risk of impulsive, suicidal, or homicidal behavior.
- an assessment of alcohol or drug use, abuse or dependency (including prescription and over-the-counter drugs). This perspective is frequently overlooked by social workers.
- a review of the client's current and historical medical problems, including any drugs currently being taken for a medical condition.

The social worker must also prepare the client for the psychiatric consultation. First, the client should be told how it will be conducted, how it differs from the typical worker–client interview, and how important his or her honest participation in the process will be. Second, the worker needs to explore any fears, misconceptions, or biases regarding psychiatry and medications the client may have. For example, Joan feared that Prozac might make her violent. Other clients may have different concerns: e.g., that the physician will read their minds, that they will be compelled to comply with any medication recommendation, or that the drugs will "control" them. Paranoid clients, in particular, may require lengthy and careful preparation for a psychiatric consultation. Clients with a history of substance abuse, especially those attending certain 12-step recovery programs, may fear that they will become physiologically or psychologically dependent on the medications.

In summary, the Clinical Assessor/Collaborator role requires that the social worker be able to identify those behaviors, symptoms and disorders that warrant a medical consultation, provide the physician with the clinical rationale and client data to conduct the assessment, and ensure that the client understands and is able to work collaboratively with the physician.

When psychoactive drugs are recommended by the consulting psychiatrist, the social worker may then need to assume additional roles in relation to client use of the medications. We have termed these roles Client/Family Educator, Client Advocate, and Case Manager, but in reality these roles may overlap both one another and that of Clinical Assessor/Collaborator. The social worker may need to play any one of these roles at different times with the same client or family.

The Client–Family Educator Role

The Case of Anna and Joseph

Anna, age 28, married and pregnant with her third child, came to the support group for family members of the mentally ill with concerns about her 32-year-old brother Joseph, who had been diagnosed with schizophrenia. Until six months ago Joseph resided with Anna, her husband, and two young children. At that time Anna had to insist that her brother leave, because he became argumentative with her husband and threatened suicide. Following a brief hospitalization Joseph was discharged with medication to a single-room-occupancy hotel. He was taking his pills as prescribed and seeing a psychiatrist at the local mental health clinic monthly, but staying in his room and refusing to go to the continuing treatment program because it was "boring and full of crazy people." Anna accepted that her brother had a serious and persistent mental illness that requires medication, but believed that the current dosage was turning him into a "zombie." This, she felt, compounded his feelings of hopelessness and incompetence. She was hesitant to approach Joseph's psychiatrist with these concerns because she feared the doctor would rebuff her for inappropriate interference.

The social worker educated Anna about the psychoactive medications used for schizophrenia, and explained the benefits and limitations of the particular drug that Joseph was taking. Once Anna understood these facts she became still more convinced that his current symptoms were a function of the medication rather than his mental illness. She and the worker concurred that a review of the medication was warranted. With the worker's support and her brother's approval, Anna contacted the psychiatrist and effectively negotiated for a medication consultation. Subsequently Joseph's dosage was reduced, and his energy, interest, and involvement with both the family and the continuing treatment program increased.

In the role of educator the social worker can serve both the identified client and his or her family members. When clients are given accurate information, their anxieties and distorted beliefs about the medications dissipate and they are more apt to take them as prescribed. As informed consumers they are also better able to communicate and participate in the management of the medications. With knowledge clients are able to keep the physician apprised of the clinical impact of the drugs, to recognize untoward side effects, and to proactively adopt strategies that address these side effects (Hayes & Gantt, 1992; Goldman & Quinn, 1988).

Because family members are the primary caretakers for over 50% of those released from mental hospitals (McFarlane, 1983), it is equally important that they too be fully informed about psychotropic medications. In the role of educator the social worker can help family members appreciate the benefits and limits of different drugs, identify potential side effects, and understand the purposes and symptoms addressed by the medications. This educational process, conducted in the context of the worker–family relationship, enables family members to support the client's compliance with medication treatment, to process their own feelings about the illness and about medications, and to develop skills that help them relate more effectively with the mentally ill client (Hatfield & Lefley, 1993; Walsh, 1988).

The need for psychoeducation—i.e., education about mental illnesses and associated issues, including psychotropic medications—with both clients and their family members has increased in recent years for a number of reasons. More and more clients are being treated with the plethora of psychoactive drugs that have been developed in the last 30 years. "Informed consent" laws mandate that clients be educated about the options and the risks associated with pharmacological treatments (Beck, 1987). Moreover, the mental health profession supports psychoeducation because of the early success that was achieved using psychoeducational models with family members of patients with schizophrenia (Anderson et al., 1986; McFarlane, 1983; Hatfield & Lefley, 1993). Finally, the reduction of mental health services has led to a demand for psychoeducational programs by patients and family members who lack other sources of support and knowledge (McFarlane, Lukens, et al., 1997). Bentley and Walsh (1996) reviewed the literature on psychoeducation and schizophrenia and found that clients and family members who attended psychoeducation groups knew more about the types of medications and their side effects, and that informed clients did become more involved in their own treatment and reported fewer symptoms and relapses than did those who received no education.

The Client Advocate Role

The Case of Katie

Katie, a 32-year-old mildly retarded woman, was referred to the psychiatric emergency service by the staff at the sheltered workshop of Aid to Retarded Citizens (ARC) after she became hysterical and verbally abusive on the job. Katie explained that she was "emotional" and "out of sorts" at work but she felt desperate and "didn't know which way to turn." One month ago her supervisor threatened to suspend her if she arrived late again. As a result, she stopped taking her "nerve" medication to ensure that she arose and got to work on time, but then she found that she because easily agitated at work. Now, because of this agitation, the ARC staff threatened to drop her from the program unless she agreed to resume taking medication to "calm her down." Katie feared that if she were let go from this job she would be unable to afford her apartment and would be forced into a supervised group home.

Consultation with ARC staff revealed that Katie's performance at work had deteriorated and her emotional volatility had increased after she had moved into her own apartment the previous year. Prior to this she had functioned consistently well at the workshop, and only became "obstreperous" when someone "invaded her space" or criticized her work. Now other program participants looked up to her because she had moved from the group home to her own apartment, and the ARC staff thought her tardiness and emotional outbursts suggested that she was incapable of living on her own. Also, Katie's volatility was negatively affecting the morale and productivity of the entire work group.

The examining psychiatrist appreciated both Katie's and ARC's perspectives. He observed Katie's emotional lability and was not surprised that the stimulation at work was at times agitating her. In addition, he noted that she suffered from a mild case of Parkinson's disease, which could explain her emotional lability and sensitivity to even low doses of psychotropic medications. He recommended that she return to living at the group home. He believed that the structure and support provided at the group home would help to stabilize her and offset the need for medication. Although another consulting neurologist concurred that the Parkinson's disease would eventually require both medication and supported housing, he felt that this might not become necessary for years. Physically, at least, she was capable of living on her own.

Ultimately, Katie agreed to weekly counseling with a social worker to learn new behavioral skills to deal with her feelings, so that psychotropic medications would not be necessary. She hoped to continue at ARC and to maintain her own apartment. The worker agreed to advocate with ARC on Katie's behalf. ARC staff were receptive to the plan of counseling for Katie, and relieved that someone would be monitoring her more closely. All involved hoped that her strong desire to remain independent, coupled with ongoing social work support and skill building, would make it possible for her to continue living in her apartment and avert the need for medication, at least for the present.

Social workers have historically acted as client advocates, to help clients effectively adapt to their environment and to support client empowerment and self-determination. Pharmacology does not change this mandate; rather, it requires social workers to include knowledge about medications in the service of these core values. In Katie's case the social worker advocated with ARC to support cessation of medication and maximize the client's independence and autonomy. In this situation, Katie's problem with medication seemed to be having a negative impact on her life, so that the social worker agreed to assist her by developing alternate means of coping. In the case of Anna and Joseph, on the other hand, the social worker empowered Anna to advocate with the psychiatrist on her brother's behalf, not to eliminate the medication but to reduce the dosage.

Sometimes clients ask the social worker to help them advocate with the prescribing physician because they have had negative prior experiences with psychoactive drugs. They may report that the psychiatrist has been unresponsive to their complaints about common side effects like dry mouth or blurry vision. While these side effects may not be alterable, the social worker can validate the client's complaints with a working knowledge of psychotropic medications and a readiness to share this knowledge with the client in the role of educator. Clients are more apt to advocate for themselves when they feel knowledgeable, their concerns have been validated, and they are confident that the worker will support them should the need arise. In fact, because the social worker is often the one who knows the client best, her advocacy—with the client in order to encourage medication compliance, and with the physician to hear and attend to client needs—may be crucial to successful treatment.

The Case Manager Role

The Case of Tim

Tim, aged 35, requested services at the Family Service Agency when the local Mental Health Clinic threatened to discontinue his treatment because he was verbally abusive and argumentative with the assigned psychiatrist, whom he saw monthly regarding his medication. Tim felt that the psychiatrist resented his raising questions about his medication and treatment. After his request for a transfer to a new "more respectful" physician was refused by the Mental Health Clinic director, Tim "blew up" verbally and stormed out of the clinic. He came to Family Services with a letter from the clinic director stating that Tim would have to follow all the physician's recommendations without question if he wished to return. Tim had so alienated the staff at the Mental Health Clinic that they were not receptive to his request for a new physician. They hoped Family Services would accept him because they felt "burned out" by his "demanding" and abusive manner.

Tim's history revealed that both of his parents and a sister had died from alcohol and drug-related causes by the time he was six years old. He was raised at a residential treatment center after multiple attempts at family foster care failed due to his conduct disturbance. When he aged out of the residential facility, he joined the Marines. Throughout the period of his military service in Grenada and the Persian Gulf Tim's drug habit escalated.

At the time when Tim returned home on leave from Operation Desert Storm, eager to meet his pen pal, Annie, he was using pot and alcohol daily. He dreamed of marrying Annie and eagerly joined her and a male friend to "party" at a local motel. After they all got high and drunk, Tim believed that Annie began to make fun of him. He "lost it" and beat her and her friend severely. As a result he was remanded to a locked psychiatric unit of the Veterans Administration hospital.

After a 16-month inpatient stay Tim left the hospital reluctantly because, as he said, "I felt more at home at the hospital than anywhere else in my whole life." He chose to settle close to the residential treatment center in which he had grown up. Now, one year later, he was employed at a sheltered workshop for the developmentally disabled, and was living with a new girlfriend. He enjoyed having money and a prestigious and challenging job at the workshop, and he felt proud to be living with a girlfriend, "even if she is not very smart."

At the time of his referral to the Family Service Agency, Tim was taking heavy doses of antipsychotic medication to control persecutory thinking, to allay his anxiety, and to regulate his impulsive behavior. Urine screens confirmed his reports that he was drug free. The V.A. hospital and Mental Health Clinic physicians, as well as the Family Service worker, agreed that without medication and close monitoring Tim was at risk of relapsing into drug and alcohol abuse and becoming more impulsive if he felt anxious or overwhelmed. The Family Service Agency consented to accept Tim if he agreed to take his medication, travel monthly to the VA hospital for medication reviews, remain in the sheltered workshop program, and engage in weekly sessions with the social worker. He agreed to the contract in order to avoid returning to the Mental Health Clinic.

It took several months before the side effects of Tim's medication became manageable. He was understandably impatient and needed support to take and track the effects of the medication, to learn about the purpose and properties of the drugs, and to effectively communicate his concerns to the prescribing psychiatrist. He characterized his client–social worker relationship by saying, "She looks out for me, keeps me on the straight and narrow, and stands up for me when I need it." His worker viewed her role similarly even though she used more sophisticated language to describe it. She believed that she served as case manager; advocate; coordinator of services between Tim, his psychiatrist, and his sheltered workshop counselor; and an ego-supportive clinician for a man with a serious emotional disorder. His adjustment in the community required services associated with all of these social work roles.

Over the course of the next three years Tim continued with the worker. Although he was admitted to the hospital five times on a voluntary basis for brief stays, both he and the worker arranged for these stays in order to afford him the respite to "get a grip." There were no relapses into substance abuse and no incidents of violence. Clearly the worker, by serving multiple roles, including case management, enabled Tim to continue to function in the community. Without the medication and her participation this outcome would have been unlikely.

ETHICAL CONCERNS ASSOCIATED WITH PSYCHOPHARMACOLOGY

Because a firm value base and an ethical commitment to the best interests of clients has historically characterized the social work profession, the actual or potential use of psychotropic medications by clients may raise ethical concerns for the social worker. In discussing the following concerns, the authors do not intend to suggest that the use of psychoactive drugs is contrary to the best interests of clients. Rather, ethically informed social workers need to bear in mind both benefits and risks as they assume various roles with respect to these medications.

Long-Term Risks of Medication

The long-term risks associated with any medicine, even one that has clear benefits, is not always known until the drug has been in widespread use for years. One example involves the discovery, many years after they were first introduced, that the phenothiazines—which enabled thousands of patients with schizophrenia to leave mental hospitals and function in the community—had a severe side effect in 20% of patients taking them long term (Marsden, Mindham & Mackay, 1986). This side effect, tardive dyskinesia, produces a persistent and irreversible neurological disorder manifested by continuous and abnormal involuntary movements of the face and extremities. Although psychiatrists are now aware of this potential risk, and are able to utilize various methods to counteract it and minimize its incidence, new psychoactive drugs are constantly being introduced. We may appreciate the obvious benefits they produce, but we cannot forget that their long-term effects are still unknown (Cohen, 1988; Cohen, 1989; Johnson, 1989).

The Impact of Medication on Children

Gadow's (1991) review of the literature cited multiple concerns related to the use of psychoactive medications with children. These included the possibility that children would attribute all their difficulties to an organic problem, taking no responsibility for learning to control their behavior. Similarly, caretakers might neglect teaching their children new coping skills, seeing the medication as a total solution. Finally, there was concern that the use of medication in childhood would lead to abuse of psychoactive substances later in life.

A related question is whether many children are being medicated inappropriately as a way of addressing societal or environmental problems. Diller (1996), in exploring the extensive use of methylphenidate (Ritalin) with children, questions whether the increased incidence of ADHD diagnosed in children may actually be a function of stressors produced by social phenomena such as more parents working, children attending school for longer periods of time each day, and—due to decreased revenues—overcrowded classes and a lower teacher–child ratio. He suggests that society may be overmedicating them in order to make them more compliant and less troublesome to overwhelmed parents and school personnel. Other writers, on the other hand, point to the benefits of Ritalin in helping children with ADHD to concentrate in school so that they can more effectively learn and sustain relationships with peers.

Cost-Driven Versus Client-Need-Driven Treatment

The emergence of managed care has seen an increasingly heavy reliance on treatment consisting exclusively of medication, despite the fact that this kind of treatment (i.e., medication alone) for psychological disorders has been shown to be both less effective and ultimately economically unsound. Research has demonstrated that the relapse rate and functional outcome of clients who received medication alone for anxiety disorders (Lindsay et al., 1987), depressive disorders (Hollon, Shelton, & Loosen, 1991), panic disorder (Michelson & Marchione, 1991) and Attention Deficit Hyperactivity Disorder (Barkley, 1990) is much worse than for clients who receive both medication and adjunctive treatments. Clients who receive partial or temporary relief from drugs without the additional skill-building, supports, and understanding derived from other interventions incur greater expenses due to hospitalizations, lost productivity and absences at work, and additional health problems.

Yet the increased number of prescriptions for psychotropic drugs, the increase in those written by general practitioners and primary-care physicians, and the heavy use of psychotropics in nursing homes and with children (Giannetti, 1983; Butler et al., 1994; Diller, 1996) all suggest a trend that may represent misuse or abuse of these medications. It raises the question of whether psychoactive drugs, rather than serving to facilitate or supplement other less intrusive treatments, are coming to replace them simply because they appear to be cheaper. The social worker must therefore remain aware of the ethical imperative to place client needs ahead of economics when planning interventions, and to advocate for those interventions that have been demonstrated to serve clients' needs in both the short and the long term.

"Conventional Wisdom" Versus Client Self-Determination

The visibility of psychotic individuals who either refuse to take or discontinue taking medication has increased since deinstitutionalization, and has created tensions between those who support the client's right to self-determination and those who support the right of the community to be shielded from the bizarre, erratic, or threatening behavior of floridly psychotic individuals. Those concerned with the rights of the community believe that these clients should be forced to take medication or involuntarily hospitalized. Legal statutes, on the other hand, support the right of the individual to refuse medication. New York State's landmark decision in the case of *Rivers v. Katz* (1986) established the right of individuals to refuse medication unless they are judged to be in imminent danger of harming themselves or others. Other states have cited this decision to assert the same rights (Clayton, 1987) and to establish state rules and procedures in dealing with patients who resist medication (*New York State Code 14,* Section 527.8).

Some have argued that the guiding principle in such cases should be the question of competence or incompetence. Bentley & Walsh (1996) suggest that for social workers client self-determination should be paramount, until incompetence and/or imminent danger can be definitively demonstrated. They are among many who assert that social workers who are faced with this kind of dilemma should place client self-determination at the forefront, in the absence of some other compelling factor (Reamer, 1986; Cohen, 1988).

CONCLUSION

In order to practice effectively in the mental health field today, social workers must include in their professional knowledge base facts about psychotropic medications, the roles that they as clinicians may be called upon to assume with clients, and ethical issues that may arise in the course of their practice. This chapter has addressed these three areas, with particular attention to the overlapping social work roles of clinical Assessor/Collaborator, Client/Family Educator, Client Advocate, and Case Manager. As new psychoactive drugs appear, so may new challenges for the social worker. But the core values and ethics of the social work profession will continue to guide the social worker in her interactions with clients, physicians, agencies, and the community.

REFERENCES

Anderson, C., Reiss, D., & Hogarty, G. (1986). *Schizophrenia and the family.* New York: Guilford Press.

Arvanitis, L. (1997). Quetiapine (Seroquel). *The Decade of the Brain: A Publication of the National Alliance for the Mentally Ill, VIII,* (3), 9–11.

Barkley, R. (1990). *Attention deficit hyperactivity disorder: A handbook for diagnosis and treatment.* New York: Guilford Press.

Beck, J. (1987). Right to refuse antipsychotic medications: Psychiatric assessment and legal decision-making. *Mental and Physical Disability Law Reporter, 11,* 368–372.

Bentley, K., & Walsh, J. (1996). *The social worker and psychotropic medication: Towards effective collaboration with mental health clients, families, and providers.* Pacific Grove, CA: Brooks-Cole Publishing.

Butler, K., Jeffries, J., Martin, B. (1994). *Clinical handbook of psychotropic drugs.* Seattle: Hogrefe & Huber Publishers.

Clayton, E. (1987). From Rogers to Rivers: The rights of the mentally ill to refuse medication. *American Journal of Law and Medicine, 13,* 1, 7–52.

Cohen, D. (1988). Social work and psychotropic treatments. *Social Service Review, 62,* 576–599.

Cohen, D. (1989). Good intentions are not enough. *Social Service Review, 63,* 4, 660–664.

Diller, L. (1996). The run on Ritalin: Attention deficit disorder and stimulant treatment in the 1990s. *Hastings Center Report, 26,* 2, 12–18.

Gadow, K. D. (1991). Clinical issues in child and adolescent psychopharmacology. *Journal of Counseling and Clinical Psychology, 59,* 6, 842–852.

Giannetti, V. (1983). Medication utilization problems among the elderly. *Health and Social Work, 8,* 262–270.

Gitlin, M. (1990). *The psychotherapist's guide to psychopharmacology.* New York: Free Press.

Goldman, C. & Quinn, F. (1988). Effect of a patient education program in the treatment of schizophrenia. *Hospital and Community Psychiatry, 39,* 282–286.

Green, W. (1991). *Child and adolescent clinical psychopharmacology.* Baltimore: Williams and Wilkins.

Hatfield, A., & Lefley, H. (1993). *Surviving mental illness: Stress, coping and adaptation.* New York: Guilford Press.

Hayes, R. & Gantt, A. (1992). Patient psychoeducation: The therapeutic use of knowledge for the mentally ill. *Social Work in Health Care, 17,* 1, 53–67.

Hollon, S., Shelton, R., & Loosen, D. (1991). Cognitive therapy and psychopharmacotherapy for depression. *Journal of Consulting & Clinical Psychology, 59,* 88–89.

Johnson, H. (1989). Resisting the evil empire: Comments on "Social work and psychotropic drug treatment." *Social Service Review, 63, 65,* 657–660.

Johnson, H., Atkins, S., Battle, S., Hernandez-Arata, L., Hesselbrock, M., Libassi, M., & Parish, M. (1990). Strengthening the "bio" in the biopsychosocial paradigm. *Journal of Social Work Education, 2,* Spring/Summer, 109–123.

Krizay, J., & Oss, M. (1990). Pro and con: Are psychiatrists an endangered species? *Open Minds.* November.

Lindsay, W., Gansu, C., Mc Laughlin, E. (1987). A controlled study of trial of treatments for generalized anxiety. *British Journal of Clinical Psychiatry, 26,* 3–15.

Marschke, J. (1997). An alternative support model for family members of the mentally ill: Modifying dialectical cognitive-behavioral skill-building. *Smith College Studies in Social Work, 68,* 32–55.

Marsden, C., Mindham, R. H. S., & Mackay, A. V. (1986). Extrapyramidal movement disorders produced by antipsychotic drugs. In Phillip Brady & Stephen Hirsch (Eds.). *The psychopharmacology and treatment of schizophrenia.* (pp. 340–402). Oxford: Oxford University Press.

McFarlane, W. (Ed.). (1983). *Family therapy in schizophrenia.* New York: Guilford Press.

McFarlane, W., Lukens, E., Link, B., Dushay, R., Deakins, S., Newmark, M., Dunne, E., Horen, B., & Toran, J., (1995). Multiple-family groups and psychoeducation in the treatment of schizophrenia. *Archives of General Psychiatry, 52,* 679–687.

Michelson, L., & Marchione, K. (1991). Behavioral, cognitive, pharmacological treatments of panic disorders with agoraphobia: Critique and synthesis. *Journal of Consulting and Clinical Psychology, 59,* 100–114.

National Center for Social Policy and Practice. (1988). Preliminary report of the geographic distribution of mental health providers. Silver Spring, MD: National Association of Social Workers.

New York State Code of Rules & Regulations (NYCRR); 14, section 527.8.

Nordmann, R., & Wargo, C. (1990). Negative Prozac publicity offers buying opportunity. *Paine Webber: Health Care Group Report,* July, 23.

Peterson, M. P., Christianson, J. B., & Wholey, D. (1992). *National survey of mental health, alcohol and drug abuse treatment in HMO's: 1989 chartbook.* Excelsior, MN: Interstudy Center for Managed Care Research.

Preston, J., & Johnson, J. (1995). *Clinical psychopharmacology made ridiculously easy.* Miami: Medmaster, Inc.

Reamer, F. (1986). The use of modern technology in social work: Ethical dilemmas. *Social Work,* November/December, 469–472.

Rivers v. Katz, *67 New York Supplement 2d (NY2D),* 45 (June 10, 1986).

Ruffolo, M., (1998, January). *Evaluating a multiple family group psychoeducational intervention for parents of children and adolescents with serious emotional disorders.* Paper presented at the International Conference on Research for Social Work Practice. Florida International University, Miami, Florida.

Silber, C. (1997). Sertinole (Serlect). *The Decade of the Brain: A Publication of the National Alliance for the Mentally Ill, VIII,* 3, 11–13.

Tollefson, G. (1997). Olanzapine (Zyprexa). *The Decade of the Brain: A Publication of the National Alliance for the Mentally Ill, VIII,* 3, 7–9.

Walsh, J. (1988). Social workers as family educators about schizophrenia. *Social Work.* March, 138–141.

6

SOCIAL WORK AND THE *DSM*

Marcia Brubeck

T he *Diagnostic and Statistical Manual of Mental Disorders (DSM)* of the American Psychiatric Association, now in its fourth edition, sets forth a diagnostic system with objective diagnostic criteria that uses five axes: axis I for clinical syndromes; axis II for personality disorders and mental retardation; axis III for physical disorders and conditions; axis IV for psychosocial stressors; and axis V for global assessment of functioning.

Clinical therapists often use the *DSM*'s diagnostic system (in particular axes I and II) to diagnose a mental disorder preliminary to treatment.[1] A *DSM* diagnosis may be a prerequisite for a provider's reimbursement by government agencies and private insurers alike. Treatment plans and medication may be selected on the basis of diagnosis. Once assigned, a *DSM* label may become as much a part of an individual's medical record as a history of rubella or chicken pox.

Although the *DSM* is the creation of an organization of psychiatrists, it is now employed extensively by social workers, a development that has been attributed to the requirements of state examinations for professional licensing, the increased employment of social workers in mental health settings, the proliferation of *DSM*-related resources for counselors, and the emergence of programs sponsored by the American Psychiatric Association (APA) for training counselors in psychiatric diagnosis using the *DSM* (Kutchins & Kirk, 1986; Velasquez et al., 1994).

The *DSM*'s increasing dominance of the mental health field has created a professional boundary problem for nonmedical practitioners. What does a manual that embodies the values, assumptions, and outlook of the medical profession offer social workers? Can social workers use it in ways that benefit their clients? If use of the *DSM* is mandatory, how can it be integrated into a practice that upholds the long-standing ideals of the social work profession? The present chapter considers these questions in the context of broad ethical issues and other concerns that have been voiced about the *DSM* in its various editions.

HISTORY OF THE *DSM*

As the tool of mental health practitioners, the *DSM* is of fairly recent vintage. The ancient Greeks described madness and its subtypes, but until the second half of the twentieth century, the medical profession contented itself with a few unofficial broad categories. Epidemiology spawned the modern preoccupation with classification, as it promoted the counting and sorting of people (Kirk & Kutchins, 1992). Imitating the approach of medicine, and accommodating the scant knowledge of etiology by focusing on overt symptoms rather than causes, psychiatry in the person of the German doctor Emil Kraepelin in the late nineteenth century produced the first taxonomy of mental disorders.

In the United States the federal census takers nurtured the classification of mental disorders. The 1840 census included the term "idiocy," understood to encompass insanity. By 1880 seven terms had emerged, but not until after 1904 did census officials pursue a psychiatric taxonomy in earnest. The American Medico-Psychological Association, the predecessor of the American Psychiatric Association (APA), at the government's request produced the first standard, the *Statistical Manual for the Use of Institutions for the Insane,* which enabled the diagnostician to choose from 22 categories. Despite criticism from some psychiatrists, notably Adolf Meyer, who cautioned his colleagues that the use of one-word diagnostic labels was fraught with hazards, the manual went through 10 editions between 1918 and 1942. The experience of psychiatrists working with combat veterans during World War II gave rise to the next nosology, which reflected greater concern with the role of the environment and with less severe forms of mental disturbance and placed greater stress on psychodynamic and psychoanalytic perspectives. The *DSM-I,* produced in a year by an appointed working group, was published in 1952.

The *DSM-II,* which was prepared by an APA committee in three years and was published in 1968, increased the number of recognized diseases and encouraged users to give the patient more than one diagnosis. It also eliminated use of the term "reaction," which in the *DSM-I* had reflected the psychobiological view of Adolf Meyer that mental disorders were responses to psychological, social, and biological factors. Like its predecessor, the *DSM-II* embodied the current practice of psychiatry. The successor editions, the *DSM-III* and the *DSM-III-R*, were published in 1980 and 1987, respectively.

The *DSM-III* brought a descriptive, atheoretical approach to classification with objective diagnostic criteria and introduced the five-axis diagnostic structure. The manual was touted as providing "the most up-to-date and valid criteria for diagnosing mental disorders," a new classification system that "should lead to improved treatment of [social work] clients" (Williams, 1981, p. 101). Nevertheless, critics expressed concern about the value-laden language and the objective stance taken by the manual.[2] Cutler (1991) offered the following interpretation:

> The *DSM-III* places the maximum amount of distance between clinician and client through their position as dualistic opposites. . . . The reason for distance in the first place [becomes apparent from their opposition]: the distance is based on clinicians' desire to see clients as other than themselves; the desire is based on clinicians' fears of being or becoming like clients—sick, confused, hurt. Distance allows the clinician to view the client as other without having to examine self in relation to mental disorders. (p. 157)

The *DSM-III-R* during its preparation received considerable publicity in connection with proposed diagnoses regarded as being unfair to women. Misgivings were also expressed about the way in which diagnostic categories were established and about control of the decision-making process (Kutchins & Kirk, 1989a; Kirk & Kutchins, 1992; Caplan, 1995). The timing of revision and publication meant that data needed to assess the empirical basis for a new edition were not available until after it had been published (Kirk & Kutchins, 1994). The *DSM-IV*, currently in use, was published in 1994.

With each successive edition, the number of diagnostic categories has mounted. In one survey, psychiatrists complained that the *DSM-III* focused on signs and symptoms so much that it detracted from understanding, promoted a "cookbook approach" to assessment, and misrepresented the current state of knowledge regarding mental disorders (Kutchins & Kirk, 1988, p. 215). While it has been suggested that the *DSM* is merely an effort to organize behavioral manifestations in a field that is "still far from scientific clarity" (Anello, 1989, p. 186), questions about proposed new disorders have spawned questions about the manual's basis in clinical trials and about its validity and reliability (Mattaini & Kirk, 1991; Kirk & Kutchins, 1992).

Proponents of the *DSM-III* declared that it solved the central scientific problem of unreliability by providing "explicit diagnostic criteria that made diagnosis more systematic and replicable" (Widiger et al., 1990, p. 190). Field trials of proposed *DSM-IV* criteria were said to have yielded a high rate of agreement across sites and between raters (Kline et al., 1993). Studies of reliability typically refer to *kappa,* a measure of the extent of agreement between raters (clinicians diagnosing the same patients); a kappa of 0 indicates chance levels of agreement, whereas a kappa of 1.0 indicates perfect agreement.

Comparison of kappa ranges for studies of different editions of the *DSM* suggests that reliability has remained approximately the same for three decades, from the publication of the *DSM-II* to the present day (Kutchins & Kirk, 1986; Kirk & Kutchins, 1994). Furthermore, the statistic has several inherent problems. First, a given level may be interpreted differently, depending on the study (if, as has been claimed, no major diagnostic category in the *DSM* achieved a kappa of .70, should this standard be regarded as poor, satisfactory, or quite good?). Second, kappa responds to hidden factors that may not be immediately apparent from discussions of results. These factors include variations in sensitivity (the tendency of the clinician to make a positive diagnosis when a disorder is present), specificity (the tendency of the clinician to make a negative diagnosis when a disorder is absent), and the base rate, or prevalence of the disorder in the population under study (Kutchins & Kirk, 1986; Kirk & Kutchins, 1994).

Indeed, patients may be diagnosed differently by clinicians for many reasons.

> It is well established that unintentional diagnostic mistakes in mental health are commonplace, whether due to the limits of professional knowledge, the inadequacy of clinical training, or the unreliability of diagnostic classification systems. But mistakes stem not only from the limits of knowledge and technique or from careless practice but also from perceptual distortions that occur in interaction. For example, we know that social context affects the psychiatric interpretation and labeling of behavior. Clinicians' assessments are also unwittingly influenced by suggestions or prior labeling by colleagues. And, of course, there are situations where two clinicians simply disagree about the diagnosis. This situation is frequently illustrated by contradictory psychiatric testimony provided at criminal trials. These events, and a host of diagnostic stud-

ies, suggest that psychiatric diagnosis is easily influenced and unreliable. (Kirk & Kutchins, 1988, p. 227)

The five-axis approach, designed to make possible a more balanced assessment of biological and environmental factors contributing to mental illness, has also inspired some misgivings. Although axis IV has been welcomed because it introduces environmental concerns into the diagnostic formulation, the identified stressors may—confusingly—be both cause and consequence of mental disorder (Kirk, Siporin, & Kutchins, 1989, p. 301). Some concern has also been expressed about the use of the *DSM* by nonmedical practitioners on the ground that axis III calls for an evaluation of organic conditions, which physicians alone can perform (Kutchins & Kirk, 1987).

Within the medical profession the fit between disorder and enumerated symptoms has been the subject of debate. The manual's critics have attacked the effort to categorize symptoms as environmental or biological in origin without acknowledging that all disorders reflect gene–environment interactions: "Genes affect the relevant environment for psychological development as much as the environment affects the expression of genes" (Hyman & Nestler, 1993, p. 202). Indeed, the biological/psychological dichotomy is increasingly being discredited: "Urgently needed advances in the diagnosis, treatment, and prevention of severe mental disorders depend on the identification of specific neuronal and intracellular factors involved in the pathophysiology of specific diseases" (Hyman & Nestler, 1993, p. 203). Moreover, the utility of the *DSM*'s diagnostic categories would be compromised if phenotypically indistinguishable psychiatric disorders were found to be genetically heterogeneous in etiology or due to environmental causes, as may well be the case (ibid., p. 207).

Apart from disputes about the *DSM*'s validity and reliability, there has been broad controversy about the relationship between classification and assessment.

SCIENTIFIC CLASSIFICATION

Diagnosis entails translating subjective experience into an objective list of symptoms that fit into a codified diagnosis (Cutler, 1991). Like other forms of categorization or classification, diagnosis summarizes information for administrative purposes, defines conceptual categories in a way that gives structure to research, promotes communication between professionals, and facilitates the control or prevention of undesirable events.

Systems that involve such classification, it has been noted, can distort phenomena. Diagnosis alters the information available to the clinician. Rather than illuminating the full range of a client's attributes, diagnosis highlights some parts, obscures others, and subtly suggests that a hitherto unnoticed but nonetheless independently existing entity—a disorder—has been discovered. This tendency is sometimes derogated as assigning blame (implying deficiency) and suppressing the wealth of contextual information that is often present in descriptions (Mattaini & Kirk, 1991). Social workers have traditionally been ambivalent about the value of classification, in part from professional distrust of standards that threaten to be judgmental (Kirk, Siporin, & Kutchins, 1989; Abramovitz & Williams, 1992).

In addition, the *DSM* presents a fixed-rule diagnostic system: the diagnostic criteria do not alter across settings. Fixed-rule systems of classification have been faulted for failing to take into account variations in treatment practices that relate to region, time, situation (whether research or practice), and clinician (Finn, 1982).

Diagnosis need not necessarily involve a categorical system of the sort represented by the *DSM*, however. Dimensional systems of diagnosis describe human activity as occurring on a continuum and thereby accommodate the reality that similar behaviors may serve different functions and may have different origins, depending on the individual. Because dimensional systems of diagnosis and the description of behavior in observable, reliable terms point the way to specific interventions without imposing value judgments and permit a more contextual, relational view of human problems, they find favor among social workers (Mattaini & Kirk, 1991).

SOCIAL WORK ASSESSMENT

A concern with diagnosis, or more accurately with assessment, has a long tradition in social work, dating back at least to publication in 1917 of Mary Richmond's *Social Diagnosis*. Richmond identified betterment at the level of the individual rather than the collective as the goal of the caseworker practicing with individuals. Social work assessment of the individual has traditionally focused on the person in interaction with the overarching environment and has reflected a tension between the systemic and the individual approaches.

Richmond declared, "Although the affixing of the correct label is an advance, no such label standing by itself has a practical bearing upon prognosis and treatment" (quoted in Kutchins & Kirk, 1988, p. 215). Richmond was concerned less with pigeonholing than with the gathering and sifting of information to develop a plan of intervention. In social work assessment, the aim is not to explain apparently aberrant behavior but "totally to apprehend human beings, their inner minds and their feelings, and the way these are expressed in their outward actions and achievements" (Rodwell, 1987, p. 232).

Purpose—whether the objective is understanding or the creation of a clinical formulation or an agenda—largely determines procedure. In any inquiry, the answers produced reflect assumptions (regarding the nature of the problem, for example) implicit in the questions asked. "The ways in which we select, collect, order, and interpret case data are shaped by the perspectives we bring to bear upon them, and the knowledge upon which we draw shapes the way we understand and intervene . . . assessment is both an objective and subjective process" (Meyer, 1992, p. 299).

Social workers have traditionally regarded the assessment process as complex and ongoing, continuing throughout the work, with new hypotheses being tested as new information emerges (McPhatter, 1991). In contrast, the diagnostic system set forth in the *DSM* is often used prior to treatment, with the aim of producing a diagnosis that will dictate interventions. Regardless of the approach selected, a valid instrument cannot be devised until research has determined what information practitioners need (Kirk, Siporin, & Kutchins, 1989; Mattaini & Kirk, 1993).

SOCIAL WORK RESPONSE TO THE *DSM*

The *DSM* has been credited with increasing the ability of master's-level counselors to conceptualize clients' problems, to plan counseling strategies and referrals, to communicate with other mental health professionals about clients, to access resources, and to establish professional status (Waldo et al., 1993). It has also been called a valuable tool for teaching about mental illness and psychopathology (see Raffoul & Holmes, 1986, and sources cited therein).

Still, social workers required to use the *DSM* on the job have not been uniformly enthusiastic about it. In one survey, clinical social workers

. . . in general . . . rejected the medicalization of mental disorders and thought that *DSM-III* placed medical labels on psychosocial problems. . . . many believed that *DSM-III* labels too many problems of childhood as pathological. Half of the respondents thought that *DSM-III* does not serve the purposes of clinical social work. . . . only a third found *DSM-III* helpful in treatment planning or in determining what medications may be needed. . . . A third believed that *DSM-III* sometimes leads to inappropriate treatment.

Furthermore, many . . . were concerned about the extent to which *DSM-III* inhibits understanding of individual clients. . . . More than 40 percent thought it obscures individual differences and detracts from understanding clients or their problems. More than 70 percent believed that *DSM-III* is of no real help in understanding marital and family problems, . . . a serious limitation because these constitute a significant portion of their caseload. (Kutchins & Kirk, 1988, p. 217)

Survey respondents also expressed concern that the manual gives the "impression that social work's understanding of mental disorder is greater than it is, and [a concern that the manual] allows the overuse of certain diagnoses because of the theoretical orientation of the practitioner" (Kutchins & Kirk, 1988, p. 218). Of survey respondents, 60% asserted that they would not use the *DSM-III* if they were not required to do so (ibid.).

One study of the *DSM-III* found that diagnoses did not correlate with the type of treatment received except that major psychiatric syndromes are associated with the subsequent use of medications (Longabaugh et al., 1986). The absence of a clear-cut, established link between diagnosis and treatment has reinforced a tendency among counselors to regard the latter as separable from the former and more deserving of attention (see Velasquez et al., 1994, p. 1336).

Critics have also charged that the *DSM*, because it views the individual in isolation, fails to address interactional problems and thereby obscures the role played by the family system (Kutchins & Kirk, 1988, p. 219). Although problems within this system may be described by *DSM* V-codes, disorders so labeled are not third-party reimbursable; therefore they are formally relegated to second place in treatment plans. Family therapists have found the scientific paradigm underlying the *DSM* fundamentally different from their own and incompatible with it (Denton, 1990).

Social workers' concerns have been echoed by other mental health professionals. Educators asked about their use of the *DSM-III-R* to train counselors expressed reservations and some ambivalence about integrating the manual fully into their programs. In the words of one survey respondent, "While our students should learn to use the *DSM-III-R* because it is the official system . . . , we (counselor-educators) should be very careful about giving the message to students that they accept the medical model as a framework for diagnosis and treatment" (Velasquez et al., 1994, p. 1336).

An earlier study (Smith & Kraft, 1983) surveyed APA member psychologists about their opinions of *DSM-III* and other diagnostic approaches and found that 47% of respondents regarded a focus on social-interpersonal forces as the preferred option, followed by nondiagnostic and behavioral analysis, with the *DSM-III* coming in third (p. 781). Fifteen years have passed since publication of this study, and the biological basis of mental disorders is now more fully understood. It remains true today, however, that the manual encompasses not only clusters of symptoms rooted in an individual's biology but also problems in living that are linked to the external environment. Whatever their biological aspects, these difficulties often require psychotherapeutic interventions for lasting results rather than pharmacotherapy alone. Examples include conflictual relationships, phobias, some forms of anxiety, and grief or bereavement issues involving anger, separation, loss, and abandonment.

Such considerations call into question the definition of a disorder as residing exclusively within the individual and suggest the efficacy of the relational approach, traditional in social work, which addresses the fit between the individual and the environment. The importance of this approach is particularly plain when the relevant matrix is understood to comprise not simply a person struggling to survive in the modern world but also a conglomeration of genetic strengths and vulnerabilities (the individual) pitted against a heterogeneous collection of stressors (the environment)—both internal (biological) and external (nonbiological).

Advocates of the *DSM* suggest that social workers should collaborate with other mental health professionals to improve future editions of the *DSM;* still, it may be asked how such a collaboration should proceed, given the fundamental conceptual differences between the medical view of the problem under study and the perspective of the social work profession.

SCIENCE AND SOCIAL WORK: THE NORMATIVE APPROACH AND THE NATURALISTIC

The rise of science in the nineteenth century brought with it greater emphasis on linear cause-and-effect reasoning and a disease model of social ills that was consonant with Social Darwinism (Rodwell, 1987;

Kirk, Siporin, & Kutchins, 1989). The scientific approach reflects various familiar assumptions: there is a single knowable reality; inquiry properly seeks to uncover a lawlike body of knowledge divorced from time and context; identification of such knowledge is desirable to promote prediction and control; knower and known are independent and separable; every event has a real cause that explains it.

As applied to the profession of social work, whose emergence paralleled the rise of science, this normative approach presupposed that the proper goals of treatment were knowable, and could be imposed, by sources outside the client. By locating disorders in the individual, the system precluded calls for change in the external environment. Furthermore, in this scheme of things a problem between people did not constitute a disorder, since disorders had been defined as occurring only within the individual (Denton, 1990). Once social workers had collectively adopted the scientific framework, the profession could claim scientific respectability, with a panoply of analytical tools, scientific principles, and objective descriptions. A diagnostic system was required to permit the development of a treatment typology and differential effective methods of helping.

The normative approach is not, however, the only option. Standing in sharp contrast, the naturalistic perspective involves five fundamental assumptions: there is not one reality but many; inquiry properly seeks not to generalize but to describe the individual case; inquiry is value bound; knower and known interact and are separated by no objectively knowable distance; causes are impossible to distinguish from effects (Rodwell, 1987). Such a perspective harmonizes with social work's traditional values.

Social work often views the problems of a client as functional responses to relational stressors and to the environment and perceives clients as wanting or needing to alter maladaptive behaviors so as to manage their lives more effectively (Carlton, 1989). The focus in psychiatry, however, is on pathology: patients have symptoms that must be eliminated to restore well-being (Raffoul & Holmes, 1986). The behavioral model of mental health treatment familiar to social workers dictates a plan of action that encompasses assessment, intervention, and desired outcome; in contrast, the medical model sets clinical practice in the framework of diagnosis, treatment, and cure.

In short, whereas scientific research characteristically seeks to move from the specific to the general (in pursuit of broadly applicable knowledge, or rules that permit the manipulation of reality), social work practice traditionally moves from the general to the specific (in pursuit of interpretive understanding). Both approaches are needed. Throughout its history, social work has struggled to see human beings in context while achieving scientific legitimacy.

ETHICAL CONCERNS

Viewed in broad historical context, the use of the *DSM* by social workers presents a variety of ethical concerns. Perhaps foremost among these is the intrusion of the marketplace into clinical practice. Decisions regarding the nature and quality of care that social workers provide to their clients, once driven by assessment and by clients' expressed needs, today increasingly reflect the dictates of insurance companies whose medicalization of the mental health field confers supreme authority upon physicians.

Although physicians have long enjoyed considerable prestige in our society, psychiatrists have not historically been on equal footing with their medical colleagues, in part because scientific knowledge about disorders of the brain has lagged well behind that amassed about illnesses principally associated with other parts of the body. A desire for parity with medical professionals generally has been a powerful force motivating psychiatrists, psychologists, and social workers in their efforts to determine how clients' problems are defined (Valenstein, 1986; Carlton, 1989; Oppenheim, 1991; Dawes, 1994). The *DSM*, then, is noteworthy not simply as a diagnostic method but also as a statement endorsed by the medical profession.

Today any group of mental health treatment providers that rejects the methodology and outlook of the *DSM* risks being excluded from power, here understood to be the coverage of services by third-party payers. Lack of access to such coverage places practitioners at a serious economic disadvantage (Denton, 1990, p. 120) and makes financial considerations a major determinant of the type—and quality—of care available.

The *DSM* may invite or encourage deliberate misdiagnosis in response to financial concerns in the case of particular individuals. A clinician may overdiagnose with the aim of helping the client secure insurance reimbursement; conversely, a clinician who worries about the label's long-term stigmatizing effects once it has been recorded in a client's file may deliberately underdiagnose (Kutchins & Kirk, 1987; Kirk & Kutchins, 1988).

Still other ethical problems may inhere in the requirement that social workers hew to a medical definition of their task. Is it appropriate for all mental health professionals to be required to use a manual that is the property of one professional organization (Kutchins & Kirk, 1989a)? Does use of the nosology set forth in the *DSM* require social workers to believe that the problem being treated is a disorder as defined by the manual—and are reimbursement and treatment properly denied if it is not? Are clients—to whom social workers owe their primary duty—well served when mental health professionals privilege the psychiatric viewpoint over others?

As two thoughtful social workers have asked:

> What are the long-term consequences of defining increasing numbers of human problems as "mental disorders," or of adopting a categorical classification that suggests that people either have a "disorder" or are normal, of minimizing the influence of social context on behavior, of allowing increasing numbers of behaviors to fall under the professional domain of medicine, or of participating in the design of a system of reimbursement that impels many mental health providers to act dishonestly in completing insurance forms? (Kutchins & Kirk, 1989b, p. 188)

Such questions are of course framed by larger considerations. How should we properly define problems that are eligible for reimbursement? Finally, how large a role should medical insurance play in the maintenance of an individual's health and well-being?

CONCLUSION

The *DSM* is likely for the foreseeable future to remain a tool that must be used by social workers employed in mental health settings. Social workers familiar with its terminology and methodology will be able to participate more fully in dialogue with medical practitioners than they otherwise could. In addition, *DSM* diagnostic categories afford the clinician ready access to the latest medical research in the databases. Finally, the *DSM* diagnostic criteria may assist social workers who are monitoring the side effects of medication.

Playing as it does a pivotal role in the reimbursement of social work services, the *DSM* invites mental health professionals to ask a threshold question about the nature of the problem being treated: whose definition should determine treatment, that of the psychiatrists or that of the practitioner's profession? Surely the client's best interests should determine the answer.

Diagnostic criteria afford a starting point for dialogue between the client and the clinician. Discussion of them can promote self-monitoring, the identification of treatment issues, and the worker's understanding of the client. By coming to terms with current medical thinking, the client can assume greater responsibility for himself or herself and can become a more informed consumer of mental health care. The *DSM*, in short, can be used to empower clients.

However imperfect the manual may currently be as a diagnostic guide, the pathophysiology of psychiatric disorders will eventually be understood. The criteria set forth in future editions of the *DSM* will presumably meet increasingly rigorous standards of validity and reliability. As scientific knowledge advances and as social workers become better educated regarding the neurobiological basis of their clients' problems, social work values and forms of assessment will continue to play a role in the treatment of the mentally ill. The fit between the person and the environment will remain an important focus of attention. The utility of a medical "cure" in any specific case will depend not just on its efficacy but also on the personal priorities of the client—the context of each individual's life.

Social workers have traditionally sought to avoid reductionism and the pure cause-and-effect analysis of complex human problems. For the present, the *DSM* must be regarded as one tool of many, offering only one point of view. Providers of mental health care can continue to avail themselves of this resource while promoting awareness of its limitations and also drawing on the perspectives of other disciplines. Indeed only by doing so can social workers serve their clients to the full and thereby discharge their primary professional responsibility.

NOTES

1. According to the *DSM-IV* definition, a mental disorder is "a clinically significant behavioral or psychological syndrome or pattern that occurs in an individual and that is associated with present distress (e.g., a painful symptom) or disability (i.e., impairment in one or more important areas of functioning) or with a significantly increased risk of suffering death, pain, disability, or an important loss of freedom. In addition, this syndrome or pattern must not be merely an expectable and culturally sanctioned response to a particular event, for example, the death of a loved one. Whatever its cause, it must currently be considered a manifestation of a behavioral, psychological, or biological dysfunction in the individual. Neither deviant behavior (e.g., political, religious, or sexual) nor conflicts that are primarily between the individual and society are mental disorders unless the deviance or conflict is a symptom of a dysfunction in the individual, as described above" (American Psychiatric Association, 1994, pp. xxi–xxii).
2. The diagnostic criteria employ language that presupposes that clinicians will agree not only about what they are seeing but about the degree to which it deviates from the norm; the criteria for 301.83, Borderline Personality Disorder, for example,

presume that the words "frantic," "real or imagined," "unstable," "intense," "chronic," and "inappropriate" will be applied in precisely the same ways by all clinicians performing an assessment. Interestingly, a member of the *DSM-IV* Task Force expressed this viewpoint in writing about stressors enumerated on axis IV: "To avoid ratings of individuals' idiosyncratic vulnerabilities, clinicians should rate the severity of the stressors according to how they judge an 'average' person would experience them. Thus, even though a particular individual reacted catastrophically to a change in a work schedule, the stressor itself would only be rated as 'mild,' because that is how an average person would experience it" (Williams, 1981, p. 104).

REFERENCES

Abramovitz, R., & Williams, J. B. W. (1992). Workshop 2: The pros and cons of the *Diagnostic and statistical manual* for social work practice and research. *Research on Social Work Practice, 2*(3), 338–349.

American Psychiatric Association. (1994). *Diagnostic and statistical manual of mental disorders, fourth edition.* Washington, DC: Author.

Anello, E. (1989). *DSM-III* is a useful tool: Response to Kutchins and Kirk. *Social Work, 34*(2), 186.

Caplan, P. J. (1995). *They say you're crazy: How the world's most powerful psychiatrists decide who's normal.* Reading, MA: Addison-Wesley.

Carlton, T. O. (1989). Classification and diagnosis in social work in health care. *Health and Social Work, 14*(2), 83–85.

Cutler, C. E. (1991). Deconstructing the *DSM-III. Social Work, 36*(2), 154–157.

Dawes, R. M. (1994). *House of cards: Psychology and psychotherapy built on myth.* New York: The Free Press.

Denton, W. (1990). A family systems analysis of *DSM-III-R. Journal of Marital and Family Therapy, 16*(2), 113–125.

Finn, S. E. (1982). Base rates, utilities, and *DSM-III*: Shortcomings of fixed-rule systems of psychodiagnosis. *Journal of Abnormal Psychology, 91*(4), 294–302.

Hyman, S. E., & Nestler, C. J. (1993). Toward a new psychiatric neuroscience. In S. E. Hyman & C. J. Nestler (Eds.). *The molecular foundations of psychiatry* (pp. 193–212). Washington, DC: APA Press.

Kirk, S. A., & Kutchins, H. (1988). Deliberate misdiagnosis in mental health practice. *Social Service Review, 62*(2), 225–236.

Kirk, S. A., & Kutchins, H. (1992). *The selling of DSM: The rhetoric of science in psychiatry.* New York: Aldine de Gruyter.

Kirk, S. A., & Kutchins, H. (1994). The myth of the reliability of DSM. *Journal of Mind and Behavior, 15*(1–2), 71–86.

Kirk, S. A., Siporin, M., & Kutchins, H. (1989). The prognosis for social work diagnosis. *Social Casework, 70*(5), 295–304.

Kline, M., Sydnor-Greenberg, N., Davis, W. W., Pincus, H. A., & Frances, A. J. (1993). Using field trials to evaluate proposed changes in DSM diagnostic criteria. *Hospital and Community Psychiatry, 44*(7), 621–623.

Kutchins, H., & Kirk, S. A. (1986). The reliability of *DSM-III*: A critical review. *Social Work Research and Abstracts, 22*(4), 3–12.

Kutchins, H., & Kirk, S. A. (1987). *DSM-III* and social work malpractice. *Social Work, 32*(3, May/June), 205–211.

Kutchins, H., & Kirk, S. A. (1988). The business of diagnosis: *DSM-III* and clinical social work. *Social Work, 33*(3, May/June), 215–220.

Kutchins, H., & Kirk, S. A. (1989a). *DSM-III-R:* The conflict over new psychiatric diagnoses. *Health and Social Work, 14*(2), 91–101.

Kutchins, H., & Kirk, S. A. (1989b). Human errors, attractive nuisances, and toxic wastes: A reply to Anello. *Social Work, 34*(2), 187–188.

Longabaugh, R., Stout, R., Kriebel, G. W., McCullough, L., & Bishop, D. (1986). *DSM-III* and clinically identified problems as a guide to treatment. *Archives of General Psychiatry, 43,* 1097–1103.

McPhatter, A. R. (1991). Assessment revisited: A comprehensive approach to understanding family dynamics. *Families in Society,* January, 11–22.

Mattaini, M. A., & Kirk, S. A. (1991). Assessing assessment in social work. *Social Work, 36*(3, May), 260–266.

Mattaini, M. A., & Kirk, S. A. (1993). Misdiagnosing assessment. *Social Work, 38*(2, March), 231–233.

Meyer, C. H. (1992). Social work assessment: Is there an empirical base? *Research on Social Work Practice, 2*(3, July), 297–305.

Oppenheim, J. (1991). *"Shattered nerves":* Doctors, patients, and depression in Victorian England. New York: Oxford University Press.

Raffoul, P. R., & Holmes, K. A. (1986). *DSM-III* content in social work curricula: Results of a national survey. *Journal of Social Work Education, 22* (1, Winter), 24–31.

Rodwell, M. K. (1987). Naturalistic inquiry: An alternative model for social work assessment. *Social Service Review, 61*(2, June), 231–246.

Smith, D., & Kraft, W. A. (1983). Do psychologists really want an alternative? *American Psychologist, 38,* 777–785.

Valenstein, E. S. (1986). *Great and desperate cures: The rise and decline of psychosurgery and other radical treatments for mental illness.* New York: Basic Books.

Velasquez, R. J., Callahan, W. J., Evans, D., & Ishikuma, T. (1994). *DSM-III-R* training in master's-level counseling programs. *Psychological Reports, 74,* 1331–1338.

Waldo, M., Brotherton, W. D., & Horswell, R. (1993). Integrating *DSM-III-R* training into school, marriage and family, and mental health counselor preparation. *Counselor Education and Supervision, 32,* 332–342.

Widiger, T. A., Frances, A. J., Pincus, H. A., & Davis, W. W. (1990). DSM-IV literature reviews: Rationale, process, and limitations. *Journal of Psychopathology and Behavioral Assessment, 12*(3), 189–202.

Williams, J. B. W. (1981). *DSM-III:* A comprehensive approach to diagnosis. *Social Work, 26* (2, March), 101–106.

7

NEUROLOGICAL DISORDERS

Harriette C. Johnson and Daniel E. Jacome

The distinction between psychological and biological disorders is now known to be a false dichotomy (see chapter 4). Neurobiological events influence psychological functions, and environmental forces trigger neurobiological responses. The rationale for including this chapter in a volume on psychopathology was that diseases considered neurological are still misdiagnosed as psychiatric. Moreover, psychiatric and neurological conditions frequently overlap; neurological conditions often manifest psychiatric symptoms. This chapter first summarizes current knowledge about the characteristics of major neurological disorders, their prevalence, etiology, course, and interventions. It then considers psychosocial issues faced by individuals with these disorders and their families, and social work responses to these issues.

THE MAJOR NEUROLOGICAL DISORDERS

Characteristics of neurological disorders include symptoms and signs. *Symptom* refers to a subjectively experienced event, such as a headache; a *sign* can be seen by others, such as paralysis.

Cerebrovascular Disease

Apart from migraine headache, cerebrovascular disease is the most common neurological disorder in adults. Symptoms and signs of cerebrovascular accident—stroke—vary greatly depending on the location and the extent of the area(s) involved. In most cases, signs and symptoms of a cerebral vascular episode have a sudden onset and reach maximum intensity within minutes or hours. Common symptoms and signs are paralysis, speech and language deficits, and sensory loss. Headache, vomiting, confusion, convulsions, and coma may also occur.

Each year 275,000 Americans die and 300,000 others are disabled by cerebrovascular disease. About 2 million Americans (approximately 1%) suffer from the disease at any one time, of which 30% are under 65 years of age. Roughly 15% of admissions to institutions for chronic care in the United States result from cerebral atherosclerosis and related neurological disability. Approximately 20% of cerebrovascular accidents—strokes—are due to hemorrhages. The remaining 80% are caused by blockage of the veins or arteries to the brain by clots of blood, tumor, fat, or air.

Stroke occurs at the end stage of cerebrovascular disease and results from either atherosclerosis (accumulation of substances on the walls of blood vessels, ultimately causing blockage) or hypertension. Noninvasive evaluation of intracranial circulation is now possible, employing transcranial Doppler and magnetic resonance techniques (magnetic resonance angiography, or MRA). Safe removal of arteriosclerotic plaques obstructing the carotid arteries can be accomplished quickly under local anesthesia, reducing perioperative complications. Intravenous administration of recombinant tissue plasminogen activator (rt-PA) in acute stroke is a promising new modality of treatment which may substantially reduce morbidity and long-term disability in the future (Rt-PA Study Group, 1995).

Stroke patients show great variability in return of functions. About half the patients who survive stroke remain permanently disabled. Typical sequelae include difficulty walking, using the hand, and speaking. Recurrence is frequent, and fear of recurrence is a major source of stress for stroke patients and their families.

Brain and Spinal Cord Injuries

Traumatic brain injury, most often resulting from automobile accidents, is a leading cause of acquired neurological disability at all ages and commonly gives rise to sequelae that significantly affect the individual's ability to function again at previous levels. Severe head injuries, with prolonged periods of coma, usually result in major deficits in both physical and mental functioning. However, even mild head injuries carry the risk of later development of convulsive seizures in predisposed individuals.

In addition to physical disabilities, significant personality alteration, memory loss, and impairment of mental abilities are often seen, resulting in a need to gradually acknowledge and accept the extent of the individual's altered functioning and its implications for the future. Less severe head injuries may leave the individual unaffected physically but nonetheless significantly handicapped with regard to intellectual and emotional functioning. Transient psychotic episodes, memory loss, and confusion are often seen during the early stages of recovery, with resolution of the more severe behavioral and emotional disturbances a usual outcome. Permanent aftereffects, however, can include personality disorder, memory loss, and deterioration of mental abilities.

Posttraumatic syndrome appears in about 30%–40% of patients who sustain minor head injuries, but there is no direct relationship between the severity of the injury and the development of symptoms. Adults experience headache, dizziness, insomnia, depression, irritability, poor concentration, and restlessness. Patients are bothered by noise—for example, by the presence of children or by television. They cannot enjoy themselves and have poor control of their temper and emotions. Children are likely to suffer behavioral and personality changes. Symptoms may be present for a few weeks or may persist for years. Typical sources of stress for adult patients with posttraumatic syndrome are financial worries and anxiety about legal proceedings, which are usually in progress with regard to insurance or other liability claims. Such external sources of stress can impede recovery and aggravate psychological symptoms. Although prognosis in posttraumatic syndrome is uncertain, usually progress is noted with the passage of time.

Convulsive seizures are the most common late complication of head injuries, occurring in 5% to 15% of hospitalized head injury victims. Risk of seizures is proportional to the severity of the injury. Geometric deformation of traumatized nerve cells and secondary electrophysiological alterations, nerve fiber tears, and gliosis or scar tissue formation, are the basic mechanisms underlying posttraumatic epilepsy. Treatment with antiepileptic agents may prevent subsequent seizures.

Cerebral Palsy

The term *cerebral palsy* refers to a variety of nonprogressive conditions involving motor and cognitive dysfunction caused by damage to the brain early in life. Many factors are thought to be causative, including genetic defects associated with chromosome abnormality or inborn errors of metabolism; head injury in infancy or early childhood (including that caused by child abuse); infectious disease such as meningitis; and difficulties arising during pregnancy or at birth, particularly lack of oxygen to brain cells.

There are three main types of cerebral palsy. In the *spastic type,* the arms and legs are stiff and movement is restricted due to the extreme tightness of the muscles. In the *athetoid type,* involuntary, sudden, and uncontrolled movements are seen. In the *ataxic type,* disturbance of balance is present, along with varying degrees of tremor. Common manifestations include difficulty in muscular control and coordination; awkwardness of gait; seizures; inability to see, hear, speak, or learn normally; and psychological and behavioral problems. Mental retardation is present in about half the cases. New antispasmodic pharmacologic agents provide relief from painful spasms in limbs and other symptoms.

Spina Bifida

Spina bifida, a condition in which the spinal column fails to close property due to a defect in early fetal development, is fairly common and varies in severity, occurring in about 100 per 100,000 live births in North America. It is frequently associated with other physical anomalies and neurological defects, especially hydrocephalus and mental retardation. Direct and indirect complications of spina bifida may require numerous hospitalizations over the years for infections and orthopedic and neurological operations. Spina bifida ravages many body systems. Patients who survive into adulthood usually require lifetime supportive services.

Seizure Disorders

The term *epilepsy* refers to recurrent seizures or episodes of altered states of consciousness, often but not always accompanied by convulsive body movements. Epilepsy is extremely common. Prevalence is estimated at 2% of the population, or about 4 million Americans.

Epilepsy is an acquired or hereditary (genetic) condition characterized by frequent recurrent seizures caused by a neuroanatomical, neurochemical, and electrophysiological disturbance of the brain. Clusters of cortical nerve cells discharging in unison constitute the epileptic focus. Secondary spread of spontaneous or induced focal discharges recruit distant nerve cells via anatomic pathways that become part of the epileptic process over time ("secondary epileptogenesis"). Seizures may be *focal,* with limited clinical expression (i.e., transient twitching of one hand, transient detachment from reality) or *generalized,* engaging the whole brain and resulting in convulsions. However, because even patients with genetic or primary generalized epilepsy may harbor microscopic lesions of the brain, this classic distinction between focal and generalized epilepsy is mostly theoretical. Either acquired or genetic epilepsy may manifest with focal seizures,

generalized seizures, or both. In clinical practice, it is customary to desig-
nate epilepsy according to the expected site of seizure origin, i.e., frontal,
temporal, occipital, etc. Finally, a distinction must be made between
"symptomatic" epileptic seizures, which are acute, limited, and secondary
to obvious causes such as meningitis or severe head trauma, and "true"
epileptic seizures—recurrent, stereotyped episodes arising from an established epileptic process. Currently, seizures are classified by performing
simultaneous video and electroencephalographic recordings of seizures at
epilepsy units in tertiary medical centers.

Symptomatic seizures are treated by eliminating the underlying cause,
such as infection, brain tumor, or endocrine abnormalities. Epileptic
seizures are successfully suppressed by antiepileptic agents in most cases. A
minority of patients with refractory epilepsy benefit from neurosurgical
procedures to remove abnormal tissue. Selection of surgical candidates is
a very complex endeavor that requires advanced imaging techniques such
as positron emission tomography (PET) superimposed on tridimensional
magnetic resonance images. These techniques diagnose with almost math-
ematical precision the epileptic focus and patterns of seizure spread.
Appropriate physical care, such as regular eating and sleeping, moderate
exercise, and avoidance of alcohol, is also important. Social interventions
are designed to encourage the patient to live as normal a life as possible,
and to avoid lapsing into a state of invalidism.

Grand Mal Seizures

Grand mal seizures are generalized convulsions sometimes preceded by a
warning sign or *aura,* variously described by the patient as dizziness, weakness, or poorly defined sensations. The aura is, in fact, the beginning of the
seizure, and can help identify the location of the seizure. Seizures of temporal lobe origin may begin with sudden fear or a sensation of "butterflies in the stomach," while the emission of a loud cry at onset is typical
of seizures arising from the supplementary motor area of the frontal lobe.
Loss of consciousness and violent jerking movements of the limbs follow
the aura or may appear from onset. The patient may bite his tongue, have
urinary or fecal incontinence, salivate at the mouth (saliva may be mixed
with blood if the tongue or cheek has been bitten), and on rare occasions
ejaculate. Then the patient lapses into a deep sleep, from which he awakes
minutes or hours later. After awakening, the patient may have headache,
stiffness in the muscles, nausea, and fatigue. The patient may be confused
or may behave in an automatized fashion for hours or days after a severe
attack. There may be residual paralysis or sensory disturbance. The attack

itself may vary in length from less than a minute to 30 minutes or more. Frequency varies from many attacks in a day to one in several years. Grand mal seizures can be controlled by medication in 50% of cases and significantly reduced in at least another 35%. Absence (*petit mal*) seizures are controlled by medication in 60% and improved in 33% of cases. Mortality is increased in patients with grand mal seizures by lethal cardiac arrhythmias or sudden development of pulmonary edema, mediated by neuronal excitation during seizures. Morbidity is increased due to trauma during falls and pneumonia caused by aspiration of gastric contents while the patient is unconscious (Leetsma, Walczak, Hughes, Kalelkar, & Teas, 1989).

Jacksonian Seizures
Jacksonian seizures, sometimes called partial seizures, usually occur in patients with an organic lesion in the cortex. The seizure starts with convulsive twitching in a particular part of the body and may spread to involve an entire extremity. If the seizure activity involves the language area of the brain, speech may be impaired during the seizure itself. If the abnormal electrical activity caused by the seizure spreads to involve both hemispheres of the brain, the seizure becomes generalized and consciousness is lost.

Psychomotor Seizures
Also called "temporal lobe seizures" and "complex partial seizures," psychomotor seizures show enormous variability in their manifestations, and may range from brief interruptions of consciousness without associated body movements to prolonged periods of confusional or dreamlike states lasting many hours. Often heralded by an aura of anxiety and visceral symptoms such as a sensation of welling up in the throat, the seizure itself may be characterized by an alteration in but not a loss of consciousness, accompanied by brief stereotyped movements such as lip smacking or manipulation of the patient's clothing. Some patients experience hallucinations (visual and auditory) and bodily delusions; others manifest affective disturbance such as expressions of anger, fear, or depression. In 28% of patients, the disorder can be controlled with medication; another 50% improve with medication.

Absence Seizures
Absence seizures, also called *petit mal,* are more common in childhood and consist of transient loss of contact with the environment. Absence seizures are typical of the generalized genetic epilepsies. They become infrequent or

disappear in adult life. Approximately 50% of patients with absence seizures also have grand mal seizures. In some patients, the attack may last only a second or two and may consist of a blank expression or fixed gaze, which may pass unnoticed. Longer attacks may last 15–90 seconds, during which time the patient is out of contact with the environment and may show a few jerks of the arms or the eye muscles, a drooping head, or a stagger. After the attack, the patient immediately becomes alert again and resumes activities. Patients with absence seizures may have very frequent attacks, from a few daily to as many as 30 in a single hour.

Intracranial and Spinal Tumors

Intracranial tumors presently afflict the largest portion of admissions services after cerebrovascular and infectious diseases. Symptoms and signs of these lesions vary according to whether the tumor is benign and slow growing or malignant and rapidly progressive. The location of the tumor determines whether the major symptoms and signs are those of increased intracranial pressure (headache, vomiting, blurred vision, lethargy) or dysfunction related to a particular area of one or the other cerebral hemisphere (emotional or behavioral disorder, weakness of one side of the body, convulsive seizures). The effectiveness of surgery varies according to the location of the tumor and its type, with outcomes ranging from complete cure to rapid deterioration and death. Even when a relatively good outcome is achieved with surgery and/or radiation therapy, the individual may be left with the mental and physical residual deficits that characterize other forms of neurological disability.

Spinal cord tumors are uncommon. Like brain tumors, however, they vary in their presenting signs and symptoms according to location and type of tumors. As with brain tumors, the outcome varies considerably. Many survivors of spinal cord tumors sustain residual paralysis, with the complications similar to those of spinal cord injury. Advances in imaging procedures have made it possible to identify tumors in their early stages, prior to becoming inoperable. Neurosurgical technology has been refined by the use of the intraoperative microscope and stereotaxic ablations that have significantly reduced the operative morbidity of cerebral and spinal tumors.

Neurofibromatosis

Neurofibromatosis, also called "von Recklinghausen's disease," is a genetic disorder with varied manifestations. Most commonly, patients develop multiple growths (benign tumors) on the skin and along nerves, including those of spinal or cranial origin. Associated complications may include seizures, learning difficulty, and mental retardation, as well as malignant tumors. The disease is quite common; prevalence has been estimated at about 50 per 100,000 in the United States. The majority of cases are mild, but severe disability occurs in some patients. Existence of the disease in an individual is usually indicated by excessive numbers of large, coffee-colored birthmarks. Two types of neurofibromatosis are recognized: multiple skin fibromas and other lesions are present in type 1 (a specific gene for which is localized on chromosome 17), whereas lack of skin changes and the presence of bilateral acoustic nerve tumors typify type 2 (gene on chromosome 22) (Mulvihill, 1990). The disease may remain stationary for many years, but periods of rapid growth of lesions occasionally are experienced.

Headache

Headache is a complaint expressed by more than half of patients seeking attention from a physician. Headache can be caused by intracranial or systemic disease, external stressors, sensitivity to foods or chemicals, or a combination of factors. The most important tool for evaluating the source of the headache is the patient's history. A severe headache with sudden onset may indicate a life-threatening condition, such as cerebral hemorrhage or an infectious illness, such as meningitis or encephalitis. Headaches that first appear late in life are seldom due to migraine, tension, or psychiatric disturbance and should be investigated thoroughly by a physician.

Migraine

Migraine (popularly called "sick headache") is an intensely painful headache often accompanied by nausea. Prevalence is estimated at 5–10% of the population, 70% female. Migraine is a systemic disorder with neurologic manifestations. Headache, although the most striking symptom, is only one of the manifestations of migraine. A hereditary predisposition is present and migraine episodes may occur without headaches ("acephalgic migraine"). Migraine has been related to estrogen level; sensitivity to chemical additives and to foods such as ripened cheese, chicken liver, red wine, citrus fruits, and caffeine; sensitivity to inhaled chemicals such as perfume or natural gas; stress; and weather changes or high altitude. In most instances, however, migraine attacks occur without obvious antecedents. Current advances in therapy have enabled the vast majority of migraine sufferers to experience significant relief from this condition. Medications can help prevent the occurrence of the attacks or significantly alleviate pain at the time of an episode.

Multiple Sclerosis

Multiple sclerosis (MS) is a chronic disease with very diverse symptoms and signs. These may include muscle weakness, visual disturbance, urinary problems, pain in the legs or abdomen, speech disturbance, clumsy gait (ataxia), loss of libido, impotence in males, and mental symptoms. Studies have revealed disturbances of affect in 54% of cases, mental deterioration in 26%, and psychotic episodes in 4% (Merritt, 1979, p. 787). Cognitive impairment may be present even when neurologic examination shows intact mentation. Other symptoms include bizarre or transient complaints such as loss of color vision, tinnitus (buzzing in the ear), and vertigo. Because of the transient and unusual nature of some of its manifestations, MS is sometimes misdiagnosed as hysteria.

The cause or causes of MS are unknown; current research centers on theories relating to altered immunity and viral infection. It has repeatedly been verified that the incidence of the disease is much higher in countries at higher latitudes than in countries closer to the equator.

MS may follow a steadily progressive course over one or several decades; rarely, the disease may progress rapidly to death. MS is generally not fatal. Death usually occurs from infections of the urinary tract, respiratory infections, and septicemia and, in older patients, from heart disease, stroke, and cancer.

About one-third of patients continue to be able to carry on their lives without significant disability; another third have enough impairment to require altering their lifestyle; and the remaining third become severely disabled. Currently there is no cure for multiple sclerosis. Steroids may shorten acute exacerbations. Some patients repond to plasmapheresis (a type of transfusion), which removes antibodies that attack the white matter of the brain. Others respond to immune modulation achieved by the infusion of immunoglobulin G (I.V. Ig). Beta interferon injections slow down the progress of the disease by approximately 30%. Identification of specific protein precipitates (oligoclonal bands) in the spinal fluid and employment of high resolution magnetic resonance imaging of the brain (MRI) allow early detection of MS (Rudick, Goodkin, & Jacobs, 1997; Filippi, Yousry, Campi, et al., 1996). Unfortunately, as with any chronic disabling condition without a known cure, patients and their families are often pressured by well-meaning family or friends to try unproven or faddish treatments.

Neuromuscular Disorders

Amyotrophic Lateral Sclerosis (ALS)
ALS is a disease of the motor nerve cells of the brain and the spinal cord. Progressive muscle wasting, with weakness and atrophy, is the major sign, accompanied by diffuse twitching of muscle fibers. As the disease progresses, paralysis ultimately occurs. Pain in the extremities may occur in about half the cases, and urinary frequency or incontinence occurs in about 15–20% of patients. Emotional lability related to neurologic dysfunction occurs in about one-third of patients at some stage of the disease: manifestations include uncontrollable laughing and/or crying. Intellectual abilities remain intact, with acute awareness of the decline in physical functioning, often resulting in depression. Prevalence is thought to be 5–7 cases per 100,000; as many as 30,000 persons are believed to have the disease at any one time in the United States. Recently a mutant form of an enzyme involved in antioxidation and nerve cell protection (superoxide dismutase) was identified in the familial form of ALS (Rosen, Siddique, Patterson, et al., 1993).

In about 50% of cases, the disease progresses rapidly to death within three years; another 20% survive five years; 10% survive ten years or more; and 20% reach a plateau as the disease ceases to progress. Riluzole (Rilutek) and insulin-like growth factor offer some hope of prolonging survival to individuals affected by this devastating illness.

Muscular Dystrophy
There are a number of progressive muscular dystrophies of different types. These are usually inherited conditions, but the underlying mechanisms for the diseases are unknown at the present time. The age of onset and the distribution of muscle weakness vary according to the particular condition. Most common is Duchenne's muscular dystrophy, an inherited disease affecting only males that is passed on through the mother.

The disease first manifests itself as progressive muscle weakness, with waddling gait and hypertrophy (overenlargement) of the calves of the legs in the early school years. Learning disorders and mental retardation are sometimes seen. A significant minority of muscular dystrophy cases are considered to be the result of genetic mutation not involving maternal transmission.

The course of the muscular dystrophies is variable. Duchenne's dystrophy is uniformly fatal by the late teens or early twenties. The other forms of progressive muscular dystrophy are compatible with long life, but the patient is significantly handicapped. Duchenne's muscular dystrophy is caused by mutations in the dystrophin gene, resulting in abnormal dystrophin, an essential structural protein of the cytoskeleton of striated muscles. Abnormal dystrophin-associated proteins have been identified in other variants of muscular dystrophy.

Myasthenia Gravis

Myasthenia gravis involves a defect in neuromuscular transmission. Prevalence estimates are 3–10 per 100,000 in the United States. It results from the blocking effect of antibodies directed against acetylcholine receptors located at the neuromuscular junctions. This defect prevents effective transmission of nerve impulses to the muscles, thereby limiting the ability of the muscle to contract. Manifestations include muscle weakness, which is worse at the end of the day. Weakness first affects the muscles of the eye in about 40% of cases and ultimately affects these muscles in about 85% of cases. Weakness of facial muscles and muscles of the mouth and throat is also common. Limb and neck weakness also occurs frequently. Respiratory muscles are affected only when the patient is in a crisis condition such as respiratory infection.

Myasthenia gravis is a disease of varying progression and severity. In a very small proportion of cases there is progression to death. The majority of cases are milder and may intermittently go into remission. The severity of the disease is usually established within weeks or months after the symptoms first appear. For example, if symptoms are restricted to ocular muscles at that time, the disease is likely to remain restricted; only rarely will it become generalized.

Myasthenia gravis responds to cholinergic drugs so uniformly that this response is now considered one diagnostic criterion in establishing the presence of the disease. Definite diagnosis is possible with electromyography (EMG) and nerve conduction studies. Complete remission may be achieved with the administration of steroids, plasma exchange that removes the offending antibodies, and intravenous immunoglobulin G (I.V. Ig) infusions. Young women, in particular, respond over time to the surgical excision of the thymus gland, normally overactive in myasthenia gravis.

Movement Disorders

Huntington's Chorea

Huntington's chorea is transmitted by a dominant gene that affects 50% of the children of sufferers. Chronic progressive chorea, named after George

Huntington, who first described this disorder in 1872, is characterized by choreiform (jerky, involuntary, and abrupt) movements and mental deterioration. These two types of signs may occur together at onset or one may appear first, to be followed years later by the other. Profound depression and/or severe emotional disturbance with hallucinations may occur years before physical symptoms appear, resulting in frequent misdiagnosis as schizophrenia. The disease is caused by a defective protein due to a gene mutation that interferes with glycolysis, the metabolic process by which cells convert the sugar glucose to energy.

Typically, the disease progresses over a 10–20 year period and ends in death, usually from infection, heart failure, or choking. Beginning signs and symptoms are fidgetiness, irritability, slovenliness, and neglect of responsibilities. Early manifestations also often include fits of violence, bouts of depression, or impulsive behavior. Mental deterioration is similar to that encountered in organic dementia: progressive loss of memory, loss of intellectual abilities, apathy, and failure to attend to personal hygiene. As the disease progresses, choreiform movements become more pronounced.

Huntington's disease is fairly common: recent evidence suggests that it may occur in 10 per 100,000 in the United States. Because of frequent misdiagnosis and because families sometimes conceal the disease, accurate prevalence estimates have been difficult to obtain. A particularly poignant aspect of this disease is the fact that its symptoms and signs do not become manifest until the early 30s, usually after the individual has decided whether or not to risk passing on the disorder by having children. Issues relating to genetic counseling, alleviation of guilt when the disease becomes manifest, and other facets of reproduction are prominent aspects of counseling of these patients and will be discussed at length later in this chapter.

Tourette Syndrome
Onset of Tourette syndrome occurs between the ages of 2 and 13. Signs and symptoms include facial twitching and grimacing; abrupt, jerky movements of the neck and shoulder and, later, the limbs; explosive and often foul language; obsessional thinking; and hyperactive behavior. The disease increases in severity during childhood but sometimes spontaneously remits by adulthood. However, the disease is generally lifelong and chronic. It has been estimated that there may be as many as 50,000 patients in the United States, a prevalence of about 25 per 100,000. It is a hereditary disorder affecting some individuals in every generation. It arises from reduced cell volume in the basal ganglia of the brain, and acquired

supersensitivity of the dopamine D2 receptor of the caudate nucleus. This probably results in enhanced connections between the hemispheres and hyperactivity of the orbitofrontal cortices of the frontal lobes and the limbic system. Hormonal-nerve cell interaction during development may play a role in the appearance of this syndrome and its amelioration after adolescence. Tourette syndrome is treated with dopamine blocking agents, e.g., pimozide, or with norepinephrine agonists, e.g., clonidine, with relative success (Wolf, Jones, et al., 1996).

Parkinson's Disease

Parkinson's disease, named for James Parkinson, who first described it in 1817, is a common disease. U.S. prevalence is believed to be 100–150/100,000. Manifestations include tremor (shaking), muscular rigidity, and loss of postural reflexes. Parkinsonism is a leading cause of neurologic disability in persons over the age of 60. Onset occurs most frequently between the ages of 50 and 65. Tremor is the initial symptom in 70% of cases. Patients with parkinsonism may have extreme difficulty in walking, in feeding themselves, and generally in performing ordinary activities (e.g., dressing and washing). Treatment with levodopa alone or in combination with dopamine agonists (drugs that increase levels of dopamine, e.g., bromocriptine or pergolide) is usually recommended. Dopamine agonists seem to slow the progression of this highly incapacitating condition. There is a renaissance of the surgical treatment of Parkinson's, which includes *stereotaxic ablation* of the globus pallidus (creation of small brain lesions with thin microprobes) and deep cerebral electric stimulation to ameliorate rigidity. Transplant of fetal nervous tissue or adrenal gland tissue offers no long-term relief, and is of greater risk to the patient. Recently the gene that causes familial Parkinson's was identified (Polymeropoulos, Lavedan, Leroy, et al., 1997).

There is a difference of opinion as to whether dementia is an intrinsic characteristic of the disease. Cognitive, memory, and perceptual deficits have frequently been found, but do not appear to be severe. All forms of parkinsonism are progressive, resulting in considerable motor disability. Some forms have a fatal outcome within 5 years, while other forms progress very slowly. Thus, patients sometimes continue to function for 30 years or more.

Motor disability resembling Parkinson's disease is sometimes seen as a complication of treatment with antipsychotic drugs and other medications. Many forms of this acquired parkinsonism can be successfully treated by reducing the dose or adding antiparkinson medication.

CHARACTERISTICS OF NEUROLOGICAL DISORDERS

The diseases and conditions described above share certain characteristics and differ in others. *Chronic progressive diseases* include those with progression toward death (80% of cases of amyotrophic lateral sclerosis, some brain tumors, Huntington's chorea, some types of muscular dystrophy, and a few cases of parkinsonism) and those with progression of disabling symptoms not resulting in death in most cases (multiple sclerosis, most cases of Parkinson's disease). *Chronic nonprogressive diseases* include cerebral palsy, brain and spinal cord injury, spina bifida (when victims survive childhood), epilepsy, neurofibromatosis (in most cases), and Tourette's syndrome (after initial progression in childhood).

Some diseases are characterized by remissions (multiple sclerosis, myasthenia gravis, migraine headache, some cases of Tourette syndrome). Variation in symptomatology, sometimes from day to day or even from hour to hour, may occur (myasthenia gravis, sequelae of brain injury, parkinsonism). Acute onset conditions include those that result in severe, chronic disability (some strokes, some brain injuries) and those in which no serious disability results (about one-half of strokes, migraine headache, some cases of brain injury). Some conditions are characterized by sudden onset of symptoms without warning (epilepsy, stroke). The psychological factors in patients and families associated with various conditions differ according to whether the disease is progressive or nonprogressive, the predictability of its effects on a day-to-day basis, the severity of disabilities, and the degree to which symptoms are socially embarrassing.

COMMON DIFFICULTIES FACED BY PATIENTS WITH NEUROLOGICAL DISORDERS AND THEIR FAMILIES

The majority of neurological disorders entail varying degrees of loss of both physical and mental functions. As frustrating and frightening as the loss of physical abilities is, observers tend to agree that the prospect of losing mental faculties—of becoming "crazy"—is more devastating. In progressive diseases, the pain of today's disability is made immeasurably worse by the prospect that as time passes, impairment will become more severe.

Loss of Physical Functions

Patients with parkinsonism, multiple sclerosis, Huntington's disease, muscular dystrophy, and amyotropic lateral sclerosis face progressive worsening of symptoms such as tremor, unsteady gait, difficulty in dressing and feeding themselves, difficulty with bladder and bowel control, drooling, and inability to swallow. Fear of choking may be common in advanced stages, as is fear of falling and bumping into things. Slowness in perceiving, responding, and moving are characteristic of some diseases. Ability to follow conversations may be seriously impaired. Loss of speech, even when the intellect remains completely intact, is an enormous source of frustration.

Persons suffering chronic nonprogressive conditions (cerebral palsy, traumatic brain injury) may experience any of the symptoms that patients with progressive disorders experience. The chief difference between the two groups is that in nonprogressive disorders, the patient does not have to fear continual worsening of an already bad situation. Adjustments that individuals have made to the condition, therefore, can be expected to continue to be appropriate. In progressive diseases, new adjustments are continuously required.

It is sometimes difficult for patients to cope with physical symptoms, both because they often have very low energy levels and because they lack control of their muscles. The well spouse must often assume a parental role with the patient in relation to physical care. Breakage and spillage often result from loss of manual dexterity. Simple activities like making a cup of coffee or smoking a cigarette pose hazards of spilling boiling water or setting a home on fire.

Psychological Distress in the Patient

Psychological reactions to the diagnosis of a progressive disease have been conceptualized in terms of stage theory, for which the Kubler-Ross (1969) model of stages toward the acceptance of impending death serves as a prototype. The Kubler-Ross progression (denial, anger, bargaining, depression, and acceptance) may be applicable to conditions expected to result in death in the near future, such as many cases of amyotrophic lateral sclerosis. Models applicable to chronic disability also have been proposed (e.g., Falek, 1979). The Falek model includes denial and shock, anxiety, anger or guilt, depression, and psychological homeostasis.

The most common initial reaction to a diagnosis of a serious progressive disorder, such as multiple sclerosis or Huntington's disease, is denial: "It can't be me. The doctor made a mistake." The patient and/or family members may seek other medical opinions in the hope of finding someone who will give a different diagnosis. Falek (1979) pointed out that counselors often consider patients "firmly entrenched in denial" to be good clients because they "accept [the diagnosis] so well" (p. 40). This appearance of maturity, however, is misleading. The individual has avoided acknowledging the real stress at an emotional level and is therefore not motivated to make the behavioral changes necessary to deal with the new reality. For example, in some Huntington's patients, decisions to have children are made despite the knowledge that every child of a Huntington's disease patient has a 50% probability of developing the disease. (Progress in human genome research may soon alter available choices.) During the denial phase, the individual's capacity to absorb new information about the situation may be very limited. Denial in patients with such diseases as multiple sclerosis, in which there is a fair chance that the patient may continue to live without significant disability, may not, however, be pathological. Rather, denial can be seen as an adaptive coping mechanism in the early stages of the illness when, in fact, the individual is not disabled.

Feelings of hopelessness may cement denial. Patients may be failing to perform at work, may have escalating interpersonal stresses within the family, may have withdrawn from hobbies formerly enjoyed, and may have withdrawn from social activities in which their disabilities cause embarrassment, humiliation, and avoidance by other people. Wexler (1973) reported two cases of Huntington's disease in which rigid denial, which had persisted for many years, gave way when the patients were given new hope. One patient was given a new medication, which proved effective in controlling his chorea. Another became aware of research and fund-raising activities that a national advocacy group, the Committee to Combat Huntington's Disease, were carrying out. For the first time, he admitted to having the disease and began to attend local committee meetings.

The second phase in Falek's (1979) model of the coping sequence is a period of anxiety, during which reality testing forces cognitive recognition of the illness. Bouts of anxiety may show themselves in irritability, nervousness, headaches, fatigue, insomnia, loss of appetite, and somatic complaints. The patient is still trying to retrieve the "good old days" but is finding it impossible to continue pretending that nothing has really changed.

The frustrations aroused in this phase lead to a period of anger. Patients may show resentment toward well relatives or acquaintances and hostility even toward the people who care most about them. Caretakers may become the focus of hostility because they act as constant reminders to patients of their dependence and lack of competence. Patients may belittle or heap complaints, accusations, and demands upon the caretaker or even threaten physical violence such as striking with a cane, tripping with a crutch, pushing, or slapping.

Depression occurs over the loss of one's former capacities, unfulfilled hopes and desires, increasing need to be physically dependent on other people, loss of control over one's life, and deprivation of formerly enjoyable activities, which have become painful or embarrassing. Depression is a salient feature of most disabling illnesses.

The final stage, psychological homeostasis, is conceptualized as the desirable but not always achievable resolution of earlier stages. Like the Kubler-Ross (1969) model, the Falek (1979) model of stages in chronic disability does not necessarily progress in chronological order. One Huntington's patient described experiences as a Huntington's victim:

> My ailment seems to have two parts, the uncontrollable movement you see on the outside plus small continuous movements inside that no one can see. I can feel it, but no one can see it; others might interpret this as my being just "nervous and highstrung." I remember the inner movements began at least 10 years before the outer movements. . . . It is important for others to realize that because the disease is progressive and so much of it is not observable to the naked eye, things are constantly going on internally that are upsetting.
>
> I am aware of the usual progression of Huntington's so I want to keep myself in as good physical condition as possible for as long as possible. I do this through extensive exercising. . . . walking was important because I would sleep better and not disturb others in the house. As beneficial as walking was, it was not without its concerns because when I walked, I staggered, and people thought I was drunk. I finally solved this by going out and telling the neighbors that I had Huntington's Disease and that I don't drink.
>
> With the progression of the disease I sometimes act hardheaded or angry because it is so difficult for me to ask for help, and even when I ask, it is difficult for me to get the kind of help I need. It is difficult for people to understand that I can paint an entire room but be unable to remove the light switches and door knobs to begin the job. (Nee, cited by Falek, 1979)

Embarrassment or Humiliation

Many neurological diseases subject sufferers to signs that range from mildly embarrassing to repulsive. These include tremors (parkinsonism), jerky movements, drooling, bladder and bowel incontinence, speech impairment, tics, facial and other bodily distortions (present in several disorders), bizarre noises such as grunts (Tourette syndrome, Huntington's disease), and even large multiple wartlike bumps (neurofibromatosis). Feelings of shame, embarrassment, and humiliation are common among patients who have outwardly visible manifestations of this nature. Individuals with epilepsy are frequently mortified by having grand mal seizures in public. Family members are also embarrassed by patients' symptoms.

Uncertainty
Difficulty in diagnosis creates ambiguity about the status of the patient's health. In diseases such as multiple sclerosis, early manifestations are often intermittent and ambiguous. The diagnostic process can be protracted and uncertain. This causes patients and families to be apprehensive and often to fear the worst. Physicians may be unable to make a diagnosis or, having made it, may be reluctant to tell the patient. Uncertainty is enormously anxiety provoking. Even after the diagnosis has been made, the great variability in both the rate of progression and the ultimate degree of disability makes uncertainty a prominent feature of the disease throughout most of its duration. With MS, drastic symptomatic changes occur, ranging from symptom-free periods to periods of severe disability. In myasthenia gravis, symptoms can occur and disappear within minutes.

Social work practitioners have found that discussion of the problems of adaptation to the stress of chronic uncertainty enables some patients to take positive steps in their lives that they had previously been unable to take. Hartings et al. (1976) gave an example of a 31-year-old MS patient, an accountant, who was unable to decide whether to apply for Social Security disability (thereby resolving the ambiguity of his health status by planning for a downhill course) or to try to retain his faltering position at the office in the hope that the disease would not get worse. Encouraged by discussions in an ongoing peer group, he came to the conclusion that "life gives no guarantees to anyone" and that "even people without MS have troubles." He decided to ask for a raise. The point of this anecdote is not to advise patients to resolve ambiguity by choosing a course of action based on a more hopeful assessment of the future course of the illness, but rather to illustrate the effect of ambiguity on making life decisions.

Fear of Fatal Attack
Patients as well as family members may live in fear of a fatal attack, both when the condition is clearly life threatening, as in stroke, and when ramifications of the disease—falling, choking, losing consciousness—may

result in severe physical harm or even death (Williams, 1994). Fears of the latter kind are common in epilepsy, Huntington's disease, and other disorders that disrupt motor function.

Marginality

The term *marginality* refers to situations in which disability is minimal and patients live on the borderline between health and sickness. Patients are often fatigued, weak, or uncomfortable but do not as yet have outward signs of illness. They may feel ambivalent about this situation, wishing both to maintain an appearance of normality and to surrender to the fatigue or to other distressing symptoms. Family expectations of the patient remain the same as they were before the onset of illness, as do expectations of people outside the family. These expectations can create added stress for the patient. Hartings et al. (1976) gave an example of a 34-year-old mother of three who prior to the onset of her illness had been energetically involved in her children's extracurricular activities. On a particularly bad day she was called and asked to bake a cake for the Brownie troop. Aware that she was going to have difficulty making it through the day as it was, she declined to bake the cake. She then felt discontented with herself and worried that the other mothers would think that she was avoiding responsibility.

Redefinition of Lifelong Social Norms

Adaptation to chronic disease with physical disability requires that patients redefine their daily experiences and unlearn internalized social norms (Hartings et al., 1976). An obvious example relates to loss of bladder control. Patients may have to wear diapers. The stark physical realities may occur long before the individual has made the cognitive and emotional shifts that alleviate the sense of humiliation and failure that accompanies the physical problem.

Asking for help in situations in which the request is entirely appropriate may represent weakness and defeat to the patient with a neurological disorder. An example was given of a middle-aged father of two children who had been in a wheelchair for more than a decade because of multiple sclerosis (Hartings et al., 1976):

> One Saturday afternoon while watching a TV football game he got thirsty for a beer. Knowing he would feel bad asking his teenage daughter, sitting nearby, to get a beer for him, he considered getting it for himself; but as the kitchen was some distance from the

den, he knew it would take him several minutes to maneuver his chair through the house by himself. So he deliberated on whether he would be better off to get it himself, putting his independence "to the test" as it were, or to "just this once," ask his daughter to help out. After much deliberation he meekly, as if defeated by an internal foe, enlisted his daughter's aid, thus conceding to himself weakness and defeat. She cheerfully obliged. Dinner was ready shortly afterwards and our patient wheeled himself briskly to the table, forgetting to bring his half-full beer can along. And again, more grist for the mill: "Should I get it myself or ask Karen?" Now it seems that a person who has been confined to a chair for 10 years ought not to go through that every time he is thirsty. Yet we continually find patients immobilized for years in the lonesome job of bringing their thoughts and feelings into harmony with actual physical capability. (p. 70)

This issue was dealt with in group counseling sessions with MS patients. Group members helped the patient change his viewpoint and recognize that fetching a beer is a small task unworthy of inner turmoil. Viewing oneself as an independent adult does not have to depend on such capabilities.

The response of family members to the needs of the patient for physical assistance requires sensitivity. On the one hand, it is important not to reinforce patients' feelings of inadequacy by doing for them things that they are quite capable of doing for themselves. Patients should be allowed to take as much time as they need to complete a task and should not be rushed by family members. It may be tempting to complete tasks for the patient because it saves time and may relieve the patient's (or the relative's) frustration momentarily. However, it may also decrease the patient's motivation to held himself and may compound feelings of helplessness. On the other hand, it is important that family members give help when needed or even, as in the preceding example, when not strictly needed, if a small service by a family member will add to the patient's comfort.

In some conditions such as Parkinson's disease, there is extreme variability even during a day in the severity of symptoms. For example, tremor, slowness of movement, or rigidity may be more pronounced during the morning than during the afternoon. The patient may be fully capable of dressing at one time and not at another. This unpredictability and variability is extremely confusing for family members and promotes misunderstanding and frustration on the part of everyone. The family needs to be aware that the patient is most probably not malingering and that variability in the disease itself causes the fluctuation in ability to perform daily living activities.

Aggression

Expression of aggression takes on new meaning in families with a disabled member. It is not considered acceptable to be angry at ill persons. Sick and disabled persons themselves may fear to express irritation or anger as they used to do before the onset of illness, because they acutely feel that they are burdens to spouse, children, or to other relatives; to give vent to anger might risk abandonment or loss of affection by the already taxed relative on whom the patient is so dependent.

Sexuality

In working with 150 MS patients in group counseling, Hartings and colleagues (1976) found that sexuality was the issue most difficult for patients to address. Difficulty in sexual function, or inability to perform, appeared to be a highly charged issue. Although the topic of sexual functioning was raised routinely by group leaders, only 2 out of 10 groups expressed interest in exploring this area. In these two groups, attendance dropped by 50% or more when the topic was scheduled to be discussed. The subject is sometimes approached indirectly through discussion of body image. Patients talk freely about their feelings pertaining to the first experience with a cane or a wheelchair. A common attitude is bravado: "There is nothing to be ashamed about. Dammit, it doesn't bother me at all!" Once the topic of body image is opened some patients can go on and discuss aspects of the disease affecting sexual functioning.

Competence

Competence is a highly charged topic that profoundly concerns the patient's dignity and self-esteem. When this issue relates to physical matters, such as the ability to drive a car, patients often resent attempts by relatives or outside agents, such as licensing departments, to deter them from an activity. The issue of driving is particularly salient in epilepsy since the patient is fully capable except when having a seizure. States either stringently monitor or entirely prohibit the driving of motor vehicles by persons with epilepsy. When the issue of mental functioning arises, the question of competence is even more charged and traumatic. Doubts about the patient's mental competence, whether based in reality or not, often lead family members, physicians, and other professionals to treat the patient as a nonperson by withholding information, offering "reassuring" lies, preventing patients from participating in the process of making decisions about their own lives, or talking about them in their presence as if they were not there. Such behavior is demeaning and often very frightening to patients. It reinforces their worst fears about the seriousness of their condition and the loss of their mental functions.

Psychological Distress in Family Members
Families with a physically disabled member experience certain common concerns and emotions. Spouses and others close to the patient may go through stages in reaction to learning the diagnosis similar to those the patient goes through. Initially, denial is common. Anger, often suppressed, may accompany realization of the meaning of the illness. Spouses may feel extremely burdened by the constant physical care necessitated by the patient's illness. Round-the-clock care can become extraordinarily wearing even for healthy, energetic, and devoted relatives. Patients may embarrass family members by loud or bizarre behavior, getting lost, or becoming upset in unfamiliar places. The trauma of going out with the patient may lead the family to stay home. Entertaining in the home may also become difficult or uncomfortable. Thus, relatives may find themselves deprived of sources of enjoyment and companionship that they enjoyed prior to the onset of the illness such as work, hobbies, or social visits. At the same time, spouses may have to assume new and unaccustomed responsibilities: breadwinning; childrearing; bathing, feeding, diapering, and/or lifting adult patients; management of financial affairs; and a plethora of household chores. Anger is an appropriate reaction to excessive burdens combined with decreased pleasure and enjoyment in life. Family members need to be helped to acknowledge and accept their angry feelings when previously learned prohibitions against being angry at sick people cause them to suppress or deny these feelings. Depression is also common among spouses and other family members. The spouse (or child) may lose companionship, affection, and nurturing as the ill member's disability causes him or her to become more and more self-engrossed.

Loss of Mental Functions

In neurological disease, deterioration of mental functions can take a variety of forms. Patients may become disoriented or forgetful. They may have difficulty following conversations. They may become depressed, withdrawn, secretive, suspicious, or hostile. There may be marked fluctuations

in mood, with inappropriate crying or laughing. Hypochondriacal preoccupations may occur. Occasionally, overt psychosis may appear, with hallucinations or delusions. Violent or aggressive outbursts are characteristic
of certain conditions, notably Huntington's chorea. In Tourette syndrome
and some dementias, sufferers may call out obscenities. Brain injured persons may display characterological changes ranging from mild to severe.

Reactions of others to illness vary according to its manifestations. Physical sickness, observable deformity, or mannerism may evoke disgust or
revulsion combined with pity. Mental disorders evoke avoidance reactions,
as well as a sense of embarrassment at inappropriate behaviors. Diseases
that cause a combination of bodily defect and mental disturbance tend to
evoke the most extreme avoidance, rejection, ridicule, or revulsion.

Falek (1979) described in stark terms the reactions of others to patients
with Huntington's disease:

> Similar to that which occurs with elderly people, particularly with
> those who show signs of deterioration, individuals diagnosed with
> Huntington's Disease are frequent treated as socially dead when
> they are still physically alive. Social death . . . results in a mecha-
> nistic approach to health care for the diagnosed patient. This is par-
> ticularly true for those with Huntington's Disease when patients
> show increased difficulties with speech, and exhibit grossly abnor-
> mal movement patterns. Grotesque movement patterns and long
> periods of muteness are considered by most medical personnel,
> many family members, and friends as evidence of mental deteriora-
> tion. Treatment for the patient is discussed with others (family and
> medical staff) but never with him or her. Difficulties in communi-
> cation and awkward body movements produce embarrassment,
> frustration and distaste which are dealt with by treating the patient
> as a non-person. This is often done without determining his com-
> petency to understand and make decisions about his own treatment.
> Similar to that found with elderly patients, the individual we are
> treating as socially dead may be sensitive to his or her environment
> and able to understand all or most of what is said and done in his
> presence. (p. 36)

Researchers have identified several types of characterological alterations in brain-injured persons that are likely to create problems for families. Brain-injured patients tend to have an impaired capacity for social
perceptiveness, manifested in self-centeredness, lack of empathy, and

diminished or absent capacity for self-reflective or self-critical attitudes. Impaired impulse control causes patients to be impulsive, restless, impatient, and irritable. Patients may be disorganized and unable to plan and execute activities. They may verbalize intentions that they do not carry out. They may exhibit dependence on others, overreactivity to stimuli, and a seemingly imperative need for immediate gratification. Emotional changes may include irritability, silliness, emotional overreactivity, apathy, or greatly increased or decreased interest in sex. Patients are frequently unable to learn from experience even though their intellectual ability to absorb information appears intact.

These characterological changes are often bewildering to family members, who remember the patients as they were prior to the disability. Family interactions may remain geared to the patient's previous personality for some time after the changes have occurred. Even small changes such as mild irritability or diminution in drive can create stress for families. Any changes may leave family members feeling cheated, angry, or guilty about harboring such feelings toward a disabled person.

When major changes have occurred in the patient's personality, so that he is demanding, irresponsible, excessively dependent, or possibly violent or dangerous because of impaired judgment, stress in the family escalates. As Lezak (1978) pointed out, the burden is felt most critically by the person or persons who have assumed major responsibility for the patient's care. Caretaking relatives usually feel trapped. Embarrassment arising from the patient's behavior may isolate family members at home since it may no longer be possible to invite friends into the home. Lezak (1978) gave the example of a teenage girl who stopped bringing female friends to her home because her brother, who was physically fit but brain injured, could not keep his hands to himself.

Even when family members maintain their social contacts, they may feel lonely because their friends, who have not experienced similar situations, lack empathy or understanding. The extended family, too, may withdraw from the immediate family both physically and emotionally as the patient's disabilities generate discomfort. Relatives who have not had to assume caretaking responsibility tend to be liberal with criticism of the caretaking relative (Lezak, 1978).

Without day-to-day experience of the patient's irresponsibility, impulsivity, or foolishness, or of the onerous duties, vigilance, and sacrifices undertaken by the caretaker, they can easily misperceive the caretaker as being too protective or restrictive, too neglectful or uncaring. Only relatives who have experienced the caretaker's burdens are likely to be genuinely grateful and emotionally supportive. (p. 593)

Some brain-injured patients become abusive toward family members, especially spouse and children (Lezak, 1978). Unrealistic expectations for the patient based on the person she was before onset of the disorder arise from misinterpreting deteriorating behavior. Family members may wonder what they are doing wrong and believe (sometimes with professional reinforcement) that their behavior toward the patient is causing the behavioral changes. When patients are recovering from a sudden-onset brain condition, such as stroke or head injury, family members are likely to be solicitous and supportive initially. Delight at survival, however, can turn into impatience and exasperation as some capabilities improve, but an irritable, demanding patient makes little effort to resume prior responsibilities. Considerable time is often needed for families to realize that their loved one is not the same person that he or she was prior to the disability.

Family members may provide more care than the patient actually needs due in part to the personality characteristics of the brain-injured patient (demandingness, dependence, childishness, negativism). Brain-injured patients may be overindulged, fostering the dependence and demandingness that are part of the problem to begin with. Family members may do more for a patient than is necessary in order to silence critical relatives, to give purpose to their own lives, or, they hope, to ameliorate the patient's condition. Accordingly, caretaking relatives are likely to be exhausted, resentful, and deprived of outlets of their own.

Spouses of brain-injured persons are subject to multiple stresses. The spouse may have lost a person who supplied companionship and affection and sexual gratification. Since many brain-injured patients no longer have the capacity for empathy and interpersonal sensitivity, their ability to satisfy their spouses' needs is strictly curtailed. There may be a disparity between their sexual competence and their demands for sexual attention; for example, many patients make incessant demands whether or not it is realistic to expect the spouse to keep satisfying them. The sexual act may be one-sided, without regard for the partner. When a husband is impotent, he may blame his wife and pursue her all the more vigorously. And while the spouse has lost a companion, she is not free to seek another. Divorcing a disabled spouse is often condemned by relatives and regarded as unethical by the healthy spouse. At the same time, the spouse cannot mourn the loss of a partner, although the loss is real.

When there are young children in a family with a brain-injured parent, the healthy parent may lack sufficient time and energy to devote to the children because of the burden of running the family single-handed while caring for a difficult or demanding spouse. Disabled parents may "bully and belittle their children in childish competition for their spouses' attention and affections, and to recover a few shreds of self-esteem as their children's developing competencies begin to surpass their own" (Lezak, 1978, p. 594). The well parent may be faced with a painful choice: to remain with the ill parent at the expense of the children or to abandon an ill and dependent mate.

Given the stresses of living with a brain-injured person, it should not be surprising that family members sometimes become seriously depressed and occasionally seek relief in drugs or alcohol. Some degree of depression should be expected in all family members. Those who can escape or avoid the situation, finding their satisfactions elsewhere, are likely to be less prone to serious depression than are those who are trapped with the patient.

Mental deterioration in Huntington's disease takes on a special and grotesque significance for family members. Since the illness tends to appear after the early childbearing years, families may not know whether their children will stand a 50% risk of contracting the disease until after the children are born. Children and other close relatives of Huntington's disease (HD) victims live in dread of contracting the disease. Wexler (1973) described the reactions of 35 at-risk men and women:

> For all these men and women at risk no matter how mature and well-adjusted they were to the presence of the illness in the family, the nature of HD symptomatology seemed to strike at the core of their physical and psychological self-esteem. The peculiarities caused by uncontrollable movements and mental deterioration became translated for many into a vision of a Frankensteinian monster, one who approaches others with affection but from whom others recoil in horror. Subjects spoke repeatedly of how "disgusting," "repulsive," "grotesque," "ugly and horrible" the HD patient becomes. There was a particular dread of losing bladder and bowel control. Some reported feeling nauseated at the sight of their ill parents.
>
> Most fantasize the period following diagnosis to be a prolonged wait on death row. . . . None of the at risk individuals mentioned feeling afraid of death per se. On the contrary, death is often cited as

a welcome relief from life with symptoms. . . . Approximately half the sample felt that they would seriously consider suicide as an option if and when they started to deteriorate. (pp. 201–204)

Spouses of persons who contracted Huntington's chorea after their children were born experienced resentment and rage that the existence of the disease in the patient's family, known to the patient and in-laws, had in most instances been concealed from the spouses prior to the marriage (Hans & Koeppen, 1980).

Environmental Sources of Stress

Economic and social factors burden patients and families. An almost universal problem is financial hardship. Income maintenance programs for the disabled provide no more than poverty-level subsistence for most. Loss of earning capacity by the patient and also possibly by the relative who must stay home to care for the patient, enormous medical bills, and the need for expensive supportive services, all contribute to making financial problems a major component of disability for both patient and family.

In order to qualify for Medicaid to finance whatever care is needed, families must often spend their life savings on medical services for the patient before they become eligible for assistance. This means, in effect, that many families lose everything they have worked for during a lifetime because of the misfortune of having an ill member.

Shortage of absence of necessary services such as home health care, transportation, socialization opportunities for the patient, and, above all, service to provide respite to the family immeasurably adds to the grief and anguish that patients and families experience. The inadequacy of treatment and care options is particularly striking in the area of part-time alternatives to home or institutional care. Full-time hospitalization or other institutionalization may deprive patients of family life, separate them from any community other than that of the institution, dehumanize them, and frequently amounts to de facto incarceration. Patients often feel that families have deserted them. Families, too, are burdened with guilt at having abandoned their family member. Partial hospitalization (day, night, weekday, or weekend), group homes, supervised apartments, and foster family placements are sometimes available and offer patients and families relief from the stresses of home care while avoiding the suffering inherent in full-time institutional living.

SOCIAL WORK INTERVENTION WITH NEUROLOGIC PATIENTS AND THEIR FAMILIES

Various approaches have been developed by social workers and other helping professionals to try to alleviate the inevitable hardships and pain of neurological illness and its attendant disabilities.

Open Communication with Patients and Family Members

When a diagnosis is catastrophic, as is the case in neurologic diseases such as Huntington's chorea, the affected individual is often deprived of the right to make decisions about the future course of her life by both family members and physicians. This is so even when the patient is still fully competent intellectually and has no impairment in ability to communicate (Falek, 1979). Families and professionals inadvertently heighten, rather than diminish, the patient's anxiety by attempting to explain away symptoms while becoming increasingly solicitous. The patient, who is well aware that the disability is not going away (it may even be obviously progressing), worries that information is being withheld—an unmistakable signal that something too terrible to talk about is occurring. The use of euphemistic language reinforces stigmatization experienced by the patient. Maintaining the deception over a period of time increases everyone's burden, as family members try to protect each other from the truth and carry their burdens alone.

Sensitive workers support denial when there is good reason to believe that the patient will be better off not knowing the whole truth, but this does not mean that workers should ever tell outright lies. Omission of devastating information is not a violation of honesty; stating falsehoods is. Although both patient and family experience an initial shock when a diagnosis is given and its meaning explained, most people can begin to work through the feelings such information generates. Knowledge about the realities of the situation is often necessary to make realistic plans, involving care for the patient, location of new sources of income if the patient has been a breadwinner, readjustment of lifestyle, and understanding some of the most emotionally charged facets of the disability such as loss of sexual function. These issues can be dealt with only when the condition is identified and its possible course considered.

Depriving patients of knowledge about what is happening and information about possible ways of responding to the situation may strip them of dignity. Early information giving can favorably influence the course both of treatment and of the disease if positive aspects, such as things the patient can continue to do or the possibility of trying a new medication, are presented.

Ordinarily, it is the physician who communicates, or fails to communicate, with the patient and family about the diagnosis. The social worker should elicit feedback from both patient and family to try to ascertain their understanding of the information they have received. Frequently, the shock of the initial diagnosis prevents people from absorbing all the information that has been presented. At a later time, the worker should again try to ascertain the patient's and family's level of comprehension and knowledge about the condition. The worker may reintroduce information at this time to help patient and family deal with their feelings, make realistic plans, and pursue efficacious treatment. It is often useful to provide written information about the condition, so that patients and relatives, who are likely to forget much of what has been told them initially, can read and reread about the disease at their leisure, in the privacy of their homes (Appolone, 1978). Advocacy and self-help organizations now exist for most disorders. One of the functions of these groups is to prepare written material about the condition for the public. Practitioners should routinely distribute literature from advocacy groups pertaining to their client population.

Drug regimens are often crucial for preventing symptoms or attacks, as in epilepsy. Misconceptions and fears may contribute to "forgetting" to take the medication. In such situations, the information exchange process may have a decisive influence on the course of the illness.

Chronic illness and the life circumstances of families dealing with chronic illness are subject to vicissitudes, therefore the communication process must extend over a long period. Patients and family members should be encouraged to call whenever the need arises. Long-term stress requires long-term supportive service. Continuity of providers is desirable but often not possible with current funding and institutional arrangements.

The role of the social worker as individual and family counselor can be critical throughout the duration of contact. Patients need to receive recognition of their fear, frustration, anger, and disappointment, combined with positive input pertaining to constructive actions that they can take to gain meaning in their lives. The literature on chronic neurological disease repeatedly emphasizes the importance of maintaining hope by identifying positive goals and steps to take toward these goals. The crucial message is that life can still be worth living despite the pain and inconvenience associated with disability.

Workers must be knowledgeable about the client's condition so they can relate to realistic problems (how to get to the bathroom), as well as to feelings and attitudes. A worker who brushes aside nitty-gritty physical concerns in order to delve into feelings will quickly be perceived by patients and families as lacking understanding of the very real problems encountered in getting through the day.

Peer Self-Help and Advocacy Groups as a Major Treatment Modality

Peer support groups have been widely used both at the stage of initial diagnosis and during the course of disabling conditions (Becu, Becu, Manzur, & Kochen, 1995; Collings, 1990; Pasquarello, 1990; Kasarkis, Bishop, & Spears, 1997; Feenberg, Licht, Kane, et al., 1996; Good, Bower, & Einsporn, 1995; Richardson, Warburton, Wolfe, & Rudd, 1996; Printz-Feddersen, 1990). Purposes of these groups are to educate patients and relatives about the condition, mobilize support of others experiencing a similar problem, break down social isolation, disseminate information about resources, expose patients to a range of coping strategies being used by their peers, enhance self-image, and help patients redefine their lives in relation to changed abilities and opportunities. Peers may be more effective in helping each other in these areas than professionals. However, professional skills are helpful in planning and convening groups, producing structure and direction when needed, facilitating communications, and resolving conflict or alleviating disruption when it occurs.

Geronemus (1980) presented a model of care based on the concept of crisis prevention and predicated on normality rather than pathology. In this model, chronic illness is viewed as a developmental life crisis. Different types of services are suggested for different degrees of disability. For newly diagnosed, nondisabled patients and their families, a major therapeutic strategy is the use of time-limited, educationally oriented groups whose composition can vary (couples, patient or family groups, or combinations thereof). These groups focus on increasing knowledge about the disease: ways to prevent complications, possible effects of medication, introduction of patients and families to available resources, enhancing patient and family ability to negotiate the medical system, and helping to increase the patient's ability to exert control over the illness and over daily activities. These groups provide a nonthreatening, goal-oriented support system.

Minimally to moderately disabled patients and their families receive individual, group, and family therapy; sexual counseling; and vocational rehabilitation counseling. Treatment is tailored to individual needs. Social workers with extensive knowledge about the disease itself may collaborate with nurses or rehabilitation counselors.

Group therapy for the moderately disabled population is long term and emphasizes therapeutic rather than educational goals, including relieving tension, enhancing self-esteem, helping the patient adjust to a changing self-image, developing methods for coping with stress, recognizing feelings and needs and learning ways to deal with them, understanding the effects of one's behavior, confronting one's own illness through shared experience with group members, and using group feedback and support to test newly acquired behaviors.

Groups for family members break down social isolation; relieve family members' concern that they are too impatient with the patient's difficult behavior and symptoms; reduce anger arising from the need to assume new roles and additional burdens; help families to understand changes in the patient; learn new ways of responding to the changed family member; recognize needs of other family members despite the illness; promote maintenance of ties with other relatives and with friends; learn to set limits on patient demands, promoting the patient's independence; and promote constructive patterns of using medical and social support services. Individual and family therapy are possible alternatives for patients and families who do not appear to be able to benefit from groups, but groups are the first line of intervention.

A model has been developed for working with groups of young adult epileptic patients in order to help them reject the "sick role," often based on a lifetime of reinforcement (Appolone & Gibson, 1980). These groups have been used to reeducate patients about opportunities to assume other roles. The group process is conceptualized as a series of stages of group development. The following case summary reflects the use of groups:

> In the first stage, a sense of identity is confirmed. Many members had never talked to other epileptics prior to the inception of the group. Some had an ever-present fear of disclosure ("closet epilepsy"). One young man had never discussed his condition with his wife, although she had witnessed several of his grand mal seizures. A school administrator whose seizures were well controlled kept his epilepsy a secret for fear of losing his job. Group members shared feelings of shame and mortification about having grand mal seizures in public.
>
> Development of trust is an important task of early meetings.

Leaders are supportive, nonconfrontational, and active in giving encouragement and praise. Information giving is another important component of early meetings. Epileptics were found to harbor many of the same misconceptions about their illness as does the public. Accurate information was provided to groups both by leaders and by pamphlets.

Exploration of goals is the focus of the second stage. Members were asked to state what they would like to be doing five years from now and then each member was required to form a plan of action. Leaders saw passivity as epidemic in this population. They fantasized about ambitions and aspirations but "waited for magic to carry them there." Confrontation may be used to get members to explore how they have been using their epilepsy as a crutch or a manipulative tool. "What can you do about it?" became a group litany once members had heard the leaders say this repeatedly.

Modification of behavior patterns characterizes the third stage. Direct confrontation is used intensively (e.g., "If you're sleepy all the time, see your doctor about changing the medication," or "If your job counselor isn't helping you, be assertive about what you want."). At this point in the process, a meeting was called for family members, including the extended family, to give them information about the condition, to give them the opportunity to share experiences and feelings, and to enlist their support for the changes that were occurring in the patients.

In the final stage, members evaluated their progress and the group was terminated, with two follow-up meetings scheduled for 6 months and 12 months after termination

Husbanding Resources: The Linkage Function

Throughout the course of a protracted illness or a chronic disability, the social work function of linking consumers with community resources that provide financial assistance and other services is essential. Referrals may be needed to income support resources, health care services, lawyers or financial counselors for such matters as guardianship, wills, and financial concerns, educational and vocational counseling, and day care, sheltered workshops, homemaker services, and respite care. In order to be effective, social workers must inform themselves about available services through online information and printed material.

Case Management

Case management is a crucial function of the social worker. All too often, fragmentation of services, staff turnover, poor communication between agencies, and other obstacles impede use of services. The social worker is the logical professional to assume the role of monitoring the combination of services received by the patient and the family, to stay in contact with service providers to assure maximum accountability, and to serve as a coordinator of information. Changes in patient or family status or in the nature of available resources may require the case manager to help patient, family, and service providers reassess needs and service plans and to supervise implementation of new plans.

Advocacy

The social worker must often become an advocate for the patient or the family to obtain financial entitlements, home care services, transportation, or other services. For severely disabled patients, even greater advocacy efforts are likely as the need for supportive services escalates and existing resources become inadequate. When institutional placement is decided upon, advocacy may be necessary to overcome obstacles to the patient's admission.

Family Counseling

Family counseling can be enhanced by attention to common problems families face. Lezak (1978) outlined issues that are frequently salient for families of patients with brain injury. Many of these issues also pertain to care of physically disabled persons. When families do not raise these issues, it is desirable for the counselor to do so.

The worker should emphasize that anger and frustration, as well as grief, are natural emotions for close relatives:

> It is bad enough feeling chronically annoyed or tied down by a once-beloved person; but these feelings become harder to endure when complicated by guilt. After months of caring for an unhappy, ungrateful, difficult patient, with no end in sight, close kin are apt to be frightened or upset by their irrepressible wishes for the patient's early demise. (Lezak, 1978, p. 595)

Family members need continual reassurance that these feelings are natural.

Caretakers must attend to their own needs in order to be effective in caring for the patient. This issue should be brought up early and often, since the notion of enlightened self-interest runs counter to moral axioms about the virtue of self-abnegation and duty. The caretaker needs to understand that the patient's well-being depends directly on his or her own well-being.

When patients have impaired judgment or when relatives offer well-intentioned but inappropriate advice, caretakers may have to rely on their own judgment in opposition to the patient's or relatives' wishes and opinions. This may be extremely difficult for the caretaker, since unilateral decision making may be contrary to the nature of the relationship that existed prior to the disability.

The counselor needs to help patient and family members clarify and identify the type of the role changes demanded by the disability. Adult patients often become irresponsible or dependent, but assuming a parental role toward the adult patient can be very upsetting. Role changes involve reversals of patterns established over many years of interaction, involving complex, subtle, and often automatic behaviors. The counselor should identify these behaviors and indicate how they are being changed by the illness or need to be changed to accommodate the changed circumstances of the family.

Family members are frequently confused by shifts in the patient's behavior. Reference to developmental stages can sometimes ease their puzzlement. For example, when a patient's impulsiveness or poor judgment is likened to that of a three-year-old, the family may be helped by being told that a new, unfamiliar, and uncomfortable role (authority figure) is now necessary. It is important to include all the family in counseling sessions to clarify these issues.

Family members can do little or nothing to change the patient's condition, hence they do not need to feel guilty or inadequate when their ministrations do not result in the patient's improvement. The practitioner should make sure that family members understand that trying harder cannot, in most instances, be expected to ameliorate a disability.

An agonizing issue for responsible relatives is that of conflict between the interests of the patient and the interests of other family members. When children are belittled or even physically abused by a brain-injured patient, the responsible parent may have to choose between the children's welfare and the needs of the patient. Management using behavioral principles of extinction and reinforcement of alternative behaviors is often helpful.

For many of these childish adults, the most effective tool for gaining the patient's cooperation that the spouse has is his/her own presence or absence, judiciously applied. Just as childhood temper tantrums can be reduced and often eliminated by benign neglect, so do tantrums of adult patients tend to dissipate when the spouse leaves the room—or the house if necessary—quietly and predictably, and in turn, desired behavior, such as setting the table or picking up dirty clothes, can be fostered by the spouse's undivided attention. . . . In many ways, managing an irascible, bullying, brain injured spouse is not much different than disciplining a refractory two- or three-year-old. (Lezak, 1978, p. 595)

Placing a patient in an institution, when home management becomes too difficult, is an enormously traumatic step for all concerned. However, in many situations it may be the only realistic alternative. The social worker's sensitivity to the needs and feelings of patient and family around the time such a decision is being considered may play a crucial role. Alleviation of family guilt is a major task at this stage.

Natural Helping Systems

In addition to peer groups, other natural helping systems are very important resources. An example of a natural helping resource is a neighbor housewife who may feel isolated or unimportant. Engaging such a person to help care for the patient on a short-term basis in order to allow the caretaker to go out might meet the needs of all concerned. An example of a quasi-natural helping system is a local organization (such as a church or fraternal organization or even schoolchildren willing to do community volunteer work). The practitioner should explore the availability of such supports to help ease the burden on the family and to provide companionship or stimulation for the patient.

Social Action

Lack of needed services, financial resources, and job opportunities for disabled persons is critical in many parts of the United States, Community organization efforts to develop and coordinate resources on the local level can do much to promote adequacy of services. Ultimately, however, organized social action on the national and state levels will be necessary to bring about significant improvement in care. Self-help groups often engage in legislative and public education activities. Social workers should ask these groups how they as professionals can support the groups' efforts to gain benefits and services and to educate service providers and the general public.

No amount of counseling and therapy can prevent some of the serious casualties of our economic and social welfare systems, which bankrupt ordinary, hard-working families unlucky enough to be stricken with a chronic disability. Existing laws demand that families become destitute before financial assistance is given, subject them to demeaning investigations before providing needed assistance, and define the individual family as the social unit with sole obligation to care for disabled members. In some other countries, such burdens are distributed throughout society by the provision of adequate and timely financial assistance, group care facilities, and respite resources for families. In the United States, the enormous responsibility of full-time care of chronically disabled persons is compounded by the gnawing and realistic fears that families have of being destroyed financially as a result of an unlucky roll of the dice. Governmental financial assistance for disabled individuals, in the absence of private wealth, condemns both patient and family to subsistence below the poverty line (Goldberg, 1991). Lack of needed services, financial resources, and job opportunities for disabled persons is severe in many parts of the United States. Community organization efforts to develop and coordinate resources on the local level can help promote more adequate services. Ultimately, however, organized social action on the national and state levels will be necessary to bring about significant improvement in care.

Social workers must, as part of their everyday practice, join with advocacy groups for welfare recipients, disabled persons, the elderly, and others to lobby for more humane government policies. However, many people who become active in promoting social change devote their energies exclusively to a particular group in which they have a special interest. In today's political climate, single issue activism, if effective, may benefit one group at the expense of another, equally needy group. Advocates for disabled citizens, therefore, should form coalitions with advocates for other groups in order to press for increasing the overall size of the pie, rather than simply redividing an undersized pie so that some get larger and some get smaller slices.

CONCLUSION

This chapter has reviewed some of the more common neurological disorders resulting from injury, infection, and genetic causes. Social work is challenged to keep up with advances in research on these conditions on an ongoing basis, as new knowledge continues to emerge. The various conditions have differing major characteristics which give rise to different constellations of problems that patients and families must face. The common issues that arise with neurological disorders have been discussed and illustrated with case material. Finally, approaches to social work intervention, geared to alleviating the multiple stresses and burdens created by neurological disorders, have been presented.

REFERENCES

Appolone, C. (1978). Preventive social work intervention with families of children with epilepsy. *Social Work in Health Care, 4,* 139–148.

Appolone, C., & Gibson, F. (1980). Group work with young adult epilepsy patients. *Social Work in Health Care, 6,* 23–32.

Becu, M., Becu, N., Manzur, G., & Kochen, S. (1993). Self-help epilepsy groups: an evaluation of effect on depression and schizophrenia. *Epilepsia, 34* (5), 841–845.

Collings, J. A. (1990). Correlates of wellbeing in a New Zealand epilepsy sample. *New Zealand Medical Journal, 103* (892), 301–303.

Falek, A. (1979). Observations on patient and family coping with Huntington's disease. *Omega, 10,* 3542.

Feenberg, A. L., Licht, J. M., Kane, K. P., Moran, K., & Smith, R. A. (1996). The online patient meeting. *Journal of Neurological Science, 139* Suppl., 129–131.

Filippi, M., Yousry, T., Campi, A., Kandziora, C., Colombo, B., Voltz, R., Martinelli, V., Spuler, S., Bressi, S., Scotti, G., and Comi, G. (1996). Comparison of triple dose versus standard dose gadolinium-DTPA for detection of MRI enhancing lesions in patients with MS. *Neurology, 46,* 379–384.

Geronemus, D. F. (1980). The role of the social worker in the comprehensive long-term care of multiple sclerosis patients. *Neurology, 30,* 48–54.

Goldberg, G. S. (1991). *Government money for everyday people: A guide to income support programs* (4th ed). Needham Heights, MA: Ginn Press.

Good, D. M., Bower, D. A., & Einsporn, R. L. (1995). Social support: gender differences in multiple sclerosis spousal caregivers. *Journal of Neuroscience Nursing, 27* (5), 305–311.

Hans, M. B., & Koeppen, A. H. (1980). Huntington's chorea: its impact on the spouse. *Journal of Nervous and Mental Diseases, 168,* 209–214.

Hartings, M. F., Pavlou, M. M., & Davis, F. A. (1976). Group counseling of MS patients. *Journal of Chronic Disease, 29,* 65–73.

Kasarkis, E. J., Elza, T. A., Bishop, N. G., & Spears, A. C. (1997). The amyotrophic lateral sclerosis (ALS) support network of Kentucky: an informational support group using interactive video. *Journal of Neurological Science, 152* Suppl. 1, S90–S92.

Kubler-Ross, E. (1969). *On death and dying.* New York: Macmillan.

Leetsma, J. E., Walczak, T., Hughes, J. R., Kalelkar, M. B., & Teas, S. S. (1989). A prospective study on sudden unexpected death in epilepsy. *Annals of Neurology, 26,* 195–203.

Lezak, M. D. (1978). Living with the characterologically altered brain injured patient. *Journal of Clinical Psychiatry, 39,* 592–598.

Mulvihill, J. J. (1990). Discussants Parry, D. M., Sherman, J. L., Pikus, A., Kaiser-Kupfer, M. I., & Eldridge, R. Neurofibromatosis 1 (Recklinghausen Disease) and

Neurofibromatosis 2 (Bilateral Acoustic Neurofibromatosis). *Annals of Interna. Medicine, 113,* 39–52.

Pasquarello, M. A. (1990). Developing, implementing, and evaluating a stroke recovery group. *Rehabilitation Nursing, 15* (1), 26–29.

Polymeropoulos, M. H., Lavedan, C., Leroy, E., Ide, S. E., Dehejia, A., Dutra, A., Pike, B., Root, H., Rubenstein, J., Boyer, R., Stenroos, E. S., Chandrasekharappa, S., Athanassiadou, A., Papapetropoulos, T., Johnson, W. G., Lazzarini, A. M., Duvoisin, R. C., DiIorio, G., Golbe, L. I., & Nussbaum, R. L., (1997). Mutation in the α-synuclein gene identified in families with Parkinson's disease. *Science, 276* (5321), 2045–2047.

Printz-Feddersen, V. (1990). Group process effect on caregiver burden. *Journal of Neuroscience Nursing, 22* (3), 164–168.

Richardson, E., Warburton, F., Wolfe, C. D., & Rudd, A. G. (1996). Family support services for stroke patients. *Professional Nursing, 12* (2), 92–96.

Rosen, D. R., Siddique, T., Patterson, D., Figlewicz, D. A., Sapp, P., Hentati, A., Donaldson, D., Goto, J., O'Regan, J. P., Deng, H.-X., Rahmani, Z., Krizus, A., McKenna-Yasek, D., Cayabyab, A., Gaston, S. M., Berger, R., Tanzi, R. E., Halperin, J. J., Herzfeldt, B., Van den Bergh, R., Hung, W.-Y., Bird, T., Deng, G., Mulder, D. W., Smyth, C., Laing, N. G., Soriano, E., Pericak-Vance, M. A., Haines, J., Rouleau, G. A., Gusella, J. S., Horvitz, H. R., & Brown, R. H., Jr. (1993). Mutations in Cu/Zn superoxide dismutase gene are associated with familial amyotrophic lateral sclerosis. *Nature, 362,* 59–62.

Rt-PA Study Group, National Institute of Neurological Disorders and Stroke. (1995). Tissue plasminogen activator for acute ischemic stroke. *New England Journal of Medicine, 333,* 1581–1587.

Rudick, R. A., Goodkin, D. E., Jacobs, L. D., & Multiple Sclerosis Collaborative Research Group (MSCRG). (1997). Impact of interferon beta-1a on neurologic disability in relapsing multiple sclerosis. *Neurology, 49,* 358–363.

Wexler, N. S., Ed. (1973). Living out the dying: HD, grief, and death. In *Huntington's disease handbook for health professionals.* New York: Committee to Combat Huntington's Disease.

Williams, A. (1994). What bothers caregivers of stroke victims? *Journal of Neuroscience Nursing, 26* (3), 155–161.

Wolf, S. S., Jones, D. W., Knable, M. B., Gorey, J. G., Lee, K. S., Hyde, T. M., Coppola, R., & Weinberger, D. R. (1996). Tourette syndrome: prediction of phenotypic variation in monozygotic twins by caudate nucleus D2 receptor binding. *Science, 273,* 1225–1227.

8

SENESCENCE

Kathleen Joyce Farkas

For many years, clinicians often viewed therapeutic work with older people as less than attractive. Among their reasons for veering away from therapeutic work with older people were the ideas that older people were not willing to change, that older people were not intellectually or emotionally able to engage in therapeutic process, and that the time they have left is so short that therapeutic efforts should be spent with people who could enjoy the benefits of change for a longer time. Robert Butler (1975, 1990) coined the term *ageism* to describe negative stereotypes toward aging and aged people. This type of ageist reasoning against work with older people has changed with the growth in the numbers of the old, the increases in the health and educational status among older people, and with the dissemination of results of practice interventions which have shown that older people can and do benefit from therapeutic interventions.

SENESCENCE

Senescence is the term used to characterize the biological changes related to the aging process (Rybash et al., 1995, p. 52). Senescence encompasses the normal aging process and the impact that process has upon the person's physical, psychological, and social well-being. Senescence or late life has been characterized by theorists in a variety of ways. Butler (1989) characterized life as a time for reflection and reminiscence. Erikson (1982) talked about late life as the period when an individual develops ego integrity—the ability to see one's life as meaningful and to accept both positive and negative aspects of the self. Burack-Weiss (1992) discusses Kaufman's idea of the ageless self (1986), the aspects of the self

174

that do not change with age, but become more evident with age. The study of senescence, or normal aging, focuses on the biological processes that are associated with growing older. It is a process that affects all human beings and one that is filled with variation. Rowe and Kahn (1987) have made the distinction between normal aging and successful aging. While normal aging is dictated by biology, successful aging encompasses the adaptive interplay between biological, social, psychological, and environmental processes and accounts for the heterogeneity of the aging experience. For some people, late life is a time of fulfillment and creativity; for others it is a time of continual loss and difficulty. Burack-Weiss (1992) writes that the goal of social work treatment is the restoration of past abilities and the maintenance of current functions. Social work practitioners who work with older people are witness to the many challenges of later life and to the variety of abilities and skills that older people use to adapt to these changes. Gerontological social work began in 1935 and therefore is a relatively new field. It is an area of practice that has continued to grow, both in numbers of practitioners and in the size of the research and practice literature. However, we are still just at the beginning of understanding the biopsychosocial complexities of aging, the delicate interactions and balances among biopsychosocial resources, and the ways to intervene to resolve problems in late life.

The term *senescence* is used in this chapter to refer both to a time period and to a process. As a time period, senescence is a person's later life, usually demarcated by age 60 or 65. As a process, senescence is the continuation of biological, social, and psychological changes that have occurred for an individual over his or her entire life as well as the additional changes that happen as a person moves through his or her later years. Senescence is seen as a dynamic and unique process for all human beings who reach later life and who continue to grow and change with each year of life.

DEFINITIONAL PERSPECTIVES OF AGE

At what point does a person become old? How can we best define the concept of old age? Age can be defined in terms of the number of years a person has lived, by the physical and mental abilities a person has, by the person's physical appearance, and by the culture's expectations of age-related behaviors (Atchely, 1997). Chronological age is the most commonly used indicator of age. Government programs and voluntary organizations have used 60 or 65 as the threshold for later life. The origins of the use of 60 or 65 as the cut-off point go back to European bureau-cracy and social welfare programs of the 1880s. Some researchers and practitioners divide the older population into two subgroups: the young-old and the old-old (Neugarten & Hagestad, 1976). The old-old are peo-ple aged 85 and older; this group accounts for 10% of the population over age 65 (U.S. Bureau of the Census, 1994). The old-old group is increasing rapidly and the Census Bureau projects this group to increase to 25% of the older populations within 30 years. Among the old-old, the group of people aged 100 or older, centenarians, is also increasing. The old-old group, because of the increased incidence of age-related physical and men-tal problems, use the most health and social services.

Chronological age, however, is rarely an accurate indicator of a per-son's physical, cognitive, or social abilities. One person may be mentally active and physically vital at age 65 whereas another may be easily fatigued and confused. Knowledge of the chronological age does not give accurate information about an individual's mental, physical, or social resources. *Biological age* takes into account a person's physical appearance and pro-vides a first impression of age status. Biological age typically includes hair color, posture, skin texture, strength, and sensory acuity. While a person may be 75, she may not "look a day over sixty." *Functional age* is a devi-ation from biological age and is the ability to perform specific tasks, such as the activities of daily living (ADL). While 80% of all older people have some level of functional impairment, the majority of older people are inde-pendent and able to care for themselves. A person who cannot perform basic ADLs can be described as functionally older than someone who can perform these tasks. *Psychological age* is determined by a person's atti-tude and point of view. The adage, "You are as young as you feel" describes psychological age. Someone who keeps up to date with current events and maintains an active interest in people, organizations, and/or topics can be said to have a younger psychological age.

All of these definitional issues are couched in the ideas of age norms in society. Age and aging are greatly influenced by the society in which a per-son lives. The roles that older people can and do play in a society are cen-tral to the individual's ability to enjoy a productive and meaningful later life. More people are living longer and the number of successful late-life role models is limited. For many people, advanced age is a foreign territory, and society does not often offer a clear guide for behavior or expectations. A useful definition of age will include not only the physical and psycho-logical characteristics of the individual, but also will consider cultural and societal needs and attitudes.

WHAT'S DIFFERENT ABOUT WORKING WITH OLDER PEOPLE?

Assessment Issues

Working with older people has several unique aspects. First, the sheer volume of information to be explored and understood with each client can be daunting. Interviewing skills in gerontological social work must include not only the ability to understand the presenting problems, but also knowledge of how similar problems were solved in the past. In the lives of older people, the past is often the gateway to understanding the future. However, not all pieces of information from the past are relevant to the clinical task and it is incumbent upon the interviewer to separate the relevant from the irrelevant pieces of information, which sometimes spans a distance of over 80 years.

Onset of problems can provide an important diagnostic insight into problems an older person experiences. Although information about onset is important in the diagnosis process with any age group, it can be of special help to practitioners working with the elderly. Practitioners will want to understand whether a problem has occurred earlier in the client's life or whether it has emerged for the first time in later life. A recurring problem has implications for treatment and recovery processes and leads to questions about how that problem was dealt with in earlier life. A recurring problem allows the practitioner to evaluate the existence of long-standing coping strategies. Late-life onset can be often interpreted as a reaction to losses and changes associated with older age.

Biopsychosocial Perspective

The biopsychosocial perspective is useful with all populations, but it becomes central in understanding the sometimes fragile balance among physical, mental, and social systems for older people. The interdependence and complexity of systems can create a difficult diagnostic picture for older clients, but this same interdependence and complexity can be used in developing creative options for problem solving. More than any other area of practice, gerontological social work requires a comprehensive and holistic approach to medical and psychological assessment and treatment. The extent to which older people are embedded in a social network and tied to social roles presents another layer of complexity. The social context of an older person's life is often the deciding factor in how well he or she can function in the community. For frail older people especially, the balance between the formal and the informal care system can be crucial to the ability to continue to live safely in the community. Given the overlay of social, emotional, and physical problems among older people, there is a need to collaborate with other professional disciplines. Interdisciplinary teams for assessment, diagnosis, and treatment are common in care settings that serve older people. Interdisciplinary teams usually are composed of physicians, social workers, and nurses, but other disciplines are part of teams too, depending upon the nature of the work and the orientation of the organization.

Not only is working with older people interdisciplinary, but also it is often intergenerational. Most older people have friends and/or family who are involved in their lives in some way. Work with older people usually means becoming involved with adult children and their spouses, grandchildren, or other family members on some level. The intergenerational nature of gerontological social work is frequently overlooked, but most work with the elderly involves people from at least two generations in assessment, planning, and treatment.

Motivation for Treatment

Engaging elderly people into treatment, especially into treatment for mental health problems, can be difficult (Butler et al., 1991). There are a variety of reasons why older people and their families are cautious about seeking any type of help, but especially about seeking help for mental health problems. One area of resistance involves older people's perceptions of problems and expectations about solutions to problems. Older people may not recognize physical and mental health changes as problems to be addressed and treated. Many older people and their families harbor the idea that symptoms of depression or arthritis, for example, are aspects of normal aging. Family members may not mention issues of fatigue, sleeplessness, loss of appetite, joint stiffness, or chronic pain to a health care provider because they believe that the cause of these problems is age and that age cannot be reversed. Stigma might present another barrier to older people and their families seeking help for mental health problems (Biegel et al., 1997). Older people may still feel that having a mental health problem is a sign of weakness, and may fear for the reputations of themselves and their families if they are labeled with a mental problem. Interview protocols and assessment techniques must be adjusted to account for these issues in working with older clients and their families.

Treatment Issues

Once engaged in a therapeutic relationship, older people can be successful in dealing with the problems of later life. The pace of therapeutic interaction, however, might need to be slowed with older clients. Sensory impairments must be addressed initially, to evaluate the extent to which hearing or sight problems impede a person's ability to participate in treatment. Large print for handouts and instructions are a good investment for anyone working with the older population. Hearing impairments typically require professional assessment and treatment, but clinicians who speak slowly and clearly are often better understood by all older people. The pace of treatment may need to be adjusted for work with older people. A thorough assessment may take longer because of the sheer volume of information and because of the communication issues. Treatment sessions may need to be spaced between appointments for medical problems or may be canceled if the client does not feel well. Practitioners treating older clients using a cognitive-behavioral framework may consider a longer time to complete homework assignments or breaking homework into smaller tasks. Practitioners using insight-oriented models may find that they want to provide more time for reflection or to spend more time in interview to understand the dimensions and resolutions of similar issues earlier in life. Practitioners should calculate treatment progress based upon the individual's abilities and upon the practitioner's experiences with other older people, not with the young.

Another aspect of work with older people is the amount of clinical work that takes place outside of the agency. Gerontological social workers have emphasized the importance of in-home assessment and treatment and have developed a variety of tools to facilitate in-home work (Emlet et al., 1996). The nature of work with the elderly often requires the practitioner to meet with the client in her home and to bring the information about health and well-being back to the interdisciplinary team. Although the quality of the information about the person's environment and the extent of the problems is often superior from a home visit, the practitioner must be able to operate independently and to record all of the relevant information during the visit. In addition, the home visit approach also requires the practitioner to be versed in personal-safety practices and to have immediate agency backup in the case of an emergency.

Attitudes Toward Aging

Work with older people also requires the practitioner to have a clear understanding of his or her own views about old age and the process of aging. Breaking down the myths and stereotypes of aging is one of the basic training issues in gerontology. Practitioners must learn how to clarify their own values and ideas and to recalibrate these values as they gain experience and as they themselves move through life. Older people who seek the help of social work professionals are often those who are in crisis; social work practitioners must be sure that they do not develop a distorted view of aging in general based upon the problems of their clients.

The age difference between practitioners and clients may mirror parent–child relationships, and older clients may trigger personal feelings regarding issues of authority and respect. The fact that all of us are subject to the aging process and that all of us will face issues of death and dying makes clinical work with aging people more accessible and more personal. Practitioners working with older people are likely to see their clients fall ill and die, and therefore must be secure in their own professional and personal resources in coping with loss. A focus on the diagnosis and treatment of grief is key to successful work with older people. Grief is the human response to loss and is a part of the healing process. Practitioners working with older people must be able to offer supportive help in the grief process and to detect and treat complicated grief reactions. Not everyone responds to grief in the same way, and there are cultural and ethnic norms that guide an individual's expression of grief.

Losses in Late Life

Regardless of the developmental perspective taken, many of the problems of later life are associated with losses. Older people experience loss associated with physical illness, with death of family and friends, and with changes in social roles. Chronic and acute illnesses increase in later life and often bring limitations in functional ability and independence. Pain associated with illness and treatment means a loss of enjoyment of life and isolation from social activities. Two primary causes of social losses are death and retirement. The older a person is, the more likely he or she is to have experienced the death of a close family member or friend. An elderly person's loss may be compounded by multiple deaths within a short time. Death of a spouse, for example, may suddenly cut a person's income and reduce the number of opportunities for social interaction. Not only does the widower or widow lose a close companion and helper; he or she may become socially isolated. Retirement is another challenge for some older people, bringing a change in social status, self-image, and financial well-being.

Assessment of loss in late life involves questions about changes in a person's life and the extent to which those changes have meaning. A typical assessment strategy is to ask a client about the changes that have occurred during the past several months and to rate the extent to which those events have produced changes in his or her daily life. It is important to understand the client's perspective on these changes; are the changes for better or worse? A death of a spouse, for example, would be expected to produce a great deal of negative change. Retirement might bring a lot of change, but the change might be seen as very beneficial and welcome. The presence or absence of a particular loss is not the issue, but the amount of change and the type of change are important.

A social network map is a useful tool to assess an older person's social network and the social supports available (Biegel, Shore, & Gordon, 1984). A social network map provides feedback on the number of people in the older client's network and the type of relationship held with that person. An inventory of social support provides information on the availability of aid, affirmation, and affection from the people in the network. Since the social environment often shifts for older people, an assessment of the social network and social supports should be repeated periodically.

Although many of the losses in later life cannot be predicted or avoided, these losses do not cast a pall over all of later life. The adaptive responses to loss are varied and depend upon a variety of personal and social resources available to the individual. Many older people adapt well to the losses they are dealt and overcome these losses by using the supports available to them. Typical responses to loss usually include depression and grief. In older populations, these responses can also give rise to symptoms that mimic dementia and that can worsen an underlying memory problem. It is important that practitioners be able to distinguish depression from dementia in these situations, so that a true dementia will not be missed and a depression will be detected and treated. Maladaptive responses to loss include severe depression, substance abuse, and complicated grief reactions. The tasks of screening and assessment are essential for successful differential diagnosis of complex problems so that effective treatments can begin.

The following sections discuss three mental health problems common during senescence: depression, suicide, and dementia. While these problems are not typically thought of as part of normal aging, they are common among older people, and clinicians working with older people must know the basics about screening and assessment issues. Readers are directed to chapters in this volume that provide a more thorough discussion of these problems.

COMMON MENTAL HEALTH PROBLEMS IN LATE LIFE

Screening and Assessment for Depression

Depression, of all the mental disorders prevalent in older populations, is among the most difficult to diagnose. The reasons for this diagnostic difficulty are varied (National Institutes of Health, 1991). The symptoms of depression are easily confused with ageist stereotypes. These symptoms include weight loss or gain, sleep problems, fatigue or loss of energy, feelings of worthlessness, diminished ability to concentrate (American Psychiatric Association, 1994, p. 327). Families, professionals, and older people themselves often mistake the symptoms of depression for inevitable and irreversible aspects of aging. Depressive symptoms are also associated with medical problems. Older people often report somatic symptoms rather than depressed mood, and these somatic complaints are often explored, and the medical problems are ruled out, before depressive disorders are evaluated. Since depression does coexist with various acute illnesses and chronic conditions, any investigation of medical complaints should include an assessment of depression. Medications, both prescription and over the counter, can give rise to symptoms of depression as well as the disease process itself (Condon, 1997). A change in medication followed by an increase in depressive symptoms indicates an evaluation of the effect of the drug upon the older person's mental state.

Depressive symptoms of confusion, memory impairment, and inability to concentrate can be mistaken for signs of dementia. Depression is often associated with true dementia, and may also worsen cognitive function in a person who suffers from dementia. Antidepressant medication may decrease cognitive impairment in people who suffer from both dementia and depression (National Institutes of Health, 1991). Differential diagnosis for depression and dementia is especially important, to sort out the symptoms that the two conditions share and to determine which of the symptoms can be reversed or ameliorated.

Low expectations and stigma play a role in the underdiagnosis of depression among older people, who may feel that depression and feelings of sadness are not problems that can be treated and that one should just "tough it out." Older people and their families may feel ashamed or afraid to be labeled with a diagnosis that might be seen as a mental illness or weakness. These barriers to diagnosis may be especially high for older minority members (Biegel, Farkas, & Song, 1997).

Fortunately, there are a variety of tools available for screening and assessment of depression among older people. The purpose of a screening tool is to identify those clients who are candidates for further assessment of depression. A clinically useful screening tool should be easily administered, suitable to the population group, and easily interpreted. A useful screening tool will assist the practitioner's assessment and treatment decisions. One of the most frequently used screening tools is the Geriatric Depression Scale (GDS) (Yesage et al., 1983; Corcoran & Fischer, 1987). This is a 30-item questionnaire which asks yes-or-no questions about how a person has felt during the past week. One point is scored for each depressive answer; a score of 11 to 20 is indicative of the need to continue the assessment process and consider treatment. The 20-item self-rating depression scale (SDS) is another option for screening (Zung, 1965; Corcoran & Fischer, 1987). Although not normed for elderly populations, the SDS has demonstrated validity in distinguishing between depressed and nondepressed samples. The Zung scale (Zung, 1965) asks questions about feelings at the time of testing.

Assessment for depression must include questions not only about current functioning, but also for past episodes of depression in an older person's life. The issue of onset of depression is important because people with a history of depression are at increased risk for recurring problems with depression during later life. A careful interviewer will ask questions about prior depressive episodes as well as information about the treatment the person received and the response to that treatment; information about prior treatment experience is useful in designing treatment approaches and expectations for older people.

Also warranted in a screening process are questions about alcohol and other drug use. The Geriatric version of the Michigan Alcoholism Screening Test is a useful clinical tool for determining which people need to receive further assessment efforts for substance abuse (American Medical Association, 1995). Alcohol is often used to cope with loss and to deal with depression. Alcohol is a central-nervous-system depressant and can lead to increased symptoms of depression in older populations, especially in older persons whose metabolic processes are slowed or those who take medications that may interact with alcohol. For older clients who are assessed to have a substance abuse problem, treatment can include primary rehabilitation at an inpatient or outpatient setting and/or twelve step treatment through Alcoholics Anonymous. Older people respond well to alcohol and other drug treatment programs tailored to their special needs (Farkas & Kola, 1997).

Treatment Options for Depression

Treatment options for depressed older people include psychosocial treatment, pharmacological approaches, electroconvulsive therapy, and a combination approach. The knowledge base on treatment effectiveness is growing as larger numbers of older people seek treatment for depression. The psychosocial treatment of depression includes psychodynamic, cognitive-behavioral and social support approaches. There have been relatively few controlled studies on the effectiveness of various psychosocial treatment methods. In general, old people who do not see themselves as depressed or who do not recognize the usefulness of treatment are likely to reject therapeutic attempts. Special adaptations such as large type, hearing devices, and slowed pace may be needed. Since many depressed old people have experienced devastating losses, psychosocial treatment approaches must incorporate ways to recognize these losses as well as to strengthen adaptation and coping mechanisms.

Antidepressant medications are a treatment option for the elderly. Three general classes of drugs are available: tricyclic antidepressants, selective serotonin reuptake inhibitors, monoamine oxidase inhibitors (MAOIs), and lithium. The general issues in drug treatment of depression in older people are the issues of compliance, medication interactions and dosage. Older people who have cognitive impairment from depression or from dementia must have additional support to comply with drug regimens. Antidepressant medications must be evaluated for their interaction with other prescription medications and over the counter medications. Since older people take 25% of all prescription medication dispensed, the possibility of adverse drug interactions must be carefully evaluated (Condon, 1996). As with all medication, the dosage level for antidepressants must be adjusted for the older patient's metabolic system and body composition.

Tricyclic antidepressants are frequent choices for older people because they present fewer side effects than some of the other types of antidepressants (National Institutes of Health, 1991). One caution is that tricyclic medication in doses 10 to 30 times the usual can be lethal, so seriously depressed and/or suicidal people must be monitored to ensure that they are not building up a lethal supply (National Institutes of Health, 1991). Selective serotonin reuptake inhibitors work by their ability to block the neurotransmitter's ability to uptake serotonin. There are few studies of this class of drug in older patients, but these drugs have shown few side effects, little weight gain, and relative safety in overdose in younger groups (Valente, 1994). Monoamine oxidase inhibitors have been used to treat atypical depression, but are less widely used in general. People taking MAOIs must not eat food containing tyramine to avoid a hypertensive crisis (National Institutes of Health, 1991). Lithium is the drug most often thought of in the treatment of bipolar depression, but it can be added to other antidepressants to boost their effects. Lithium treatment requires added monitoring of blood levels, thyroid function, and renal function, and is not the first drug offered in the treatment of depression.

Electroconvulsive therapy (ECT) is a treatment option for depression and has been used successfully with elderly people (National Institutes of Health, 1991; Gaylord & Zung, 1987). Although the exact therapeutic mechanism remains unknown, ECT has been shown to be an effective treatment for people suffering from severe depression and for people who cannot tolerate the side effects of antidepressants. The risks of ECT include initial disorientation several hours after the treatment and memory impairment for two weeks after the treatment. Cardiac arrest is a risk, but a minimal one. The course of ECT for older people is typically six treatments offered every other day. ECT is not the first line of treatment for depression, but should be considered as an option for severely depressed older persons.

Suicide Risk Assessment

Once an older client's needs have been identified through the screening process, more detailed questions about various aspects of depression are warranted. The risk of suicide is an important area for assessment with all people who show signs of depression, especially older people. The suicide rate for some groups of older people is approximately twice as high as the rate in the general population (Stillion et al., 1989). The rate of suicide in the general population is 12.4 suicides per 100,000 and the rate for people aged 80 to 84 is 26.5 per 100,000 (Tice & Perkins, 1996). Tice and Perkins (1996) have compiled a list of suicide risks specific to the elderly. These risks include bodily changes, retirement, decrease in mobility, institutionalization, deteriorating health conditions, and dependency increased by chronic conditions and loss of friends and extended family. Depressed people are at increased risk for suicide, and all clients who are screened into assessment for depression should be evaluated for suicide risk. Suicide questions are often omitted by practitioners, who tend to underestimate the risk of suicide among older clients. Suicide assessment should be done routinely and nonjudgmentally. Questions must be answered thoroughly and the practitioner must be sure that he or she can support an assessment of no risk as well as the assessment of risk. Questions about suicide often create anxious feelings for the practitioner, especially for those practitioners who are unsure about what to do if the older person is found to be suicidal.

The basic elements of suicide risk include specific questions about suicidal thoughts and about plans. Questions about suicidal thoughts need to include how often the client has thoughts about harming him- or herself and how intense these thoughts have been. For clients who acknowledge suicidal thoughts, the practitioner should ask about feelings and hopelessness and what problems the suicide will solve. Practitioners should also take into account the severity of the depression; the more severe the depression, the more likely a person is to commit suicide. The next set of questions should ask if the person has a plan to commit suicide and what that plan is. The practitioner should listen for the lethality of the plan and the availability of the means to carry out the plan. For example, if overdose is part of the plan, does the client have the ability to obtain a lethal dose of the chosen drug? Evaluation of a suicide plan should also include questions about accessibility to guns and other weapons. Risk assessment should include questions about plans the client has made to avoid discovery or any suicide attempt in the past. People who have articulated a plan to commit suicide are at higher risk than those who merely voice the idea of suicide. Presence of substance abuse, psychiatric illness, persistent pain, social isolation, and/or past history of suicidal behavior provide additional support for the need to take suicide precautions. Suicide precautions with the older client are similar to precautions with other age groups. Immediate steps are necessary in cases that present multiple risk indicators for suicide. Immediate steps include 24-hour observation, usually in an inpatient setting under the care of a psychiatrist. Intermediate steps may include increased interaction with family, friends, and professionals and a no-harm contract. A no-harm contract is a written document that specifies the agreement between the client and another person that the client will "do no harm"of any kind to him- or herself without first contacting the other person. A no-harm contract is most useful as a transition to facilitate the referral to additional mental health services for people who are assessed as suicide risks but not at risk of immediate harm. A person who refuses to sign a no-harm contract should be assessed as a immediate suicide risk and be placed on suicide precautions.

Screening and Assessment of Dementia

Dementia is defined as multiple cognitive deficits manifested by both memory impairment and one or more additional cognitive problems (*DSM-IV,* pp. 133–155). *DSM-IV* defines the additional cognitive impairments as including *aphasia,* which is a language disturbance; *apraxia,* impairment of the ability to perform motor activities despite intact motor functions; *agnosia,* the failure to recognize or identify objects despite intact sensory function; and any disturbance in executive functioning—the ability to plan, organize, sequence, or abstract information. The person must show a significant decline in memory and cognitive ability in order to be diagnosed with a dementia. A widely used brief screening tool for memory impairment is the Mini Mental Status Exam (Folstein et al., 1975). This 30-point form consists of two parts: a verbal part and a written part. The MMSE takes about 15 minutes to administer and assesses orientation to time and place; memory, registration, and recall of three objects; language skills; and calculation and constructional abilities. Caution must be used in interpreting the written portion, to avoid misdiagnosis of persons with visual impairments. Pfeiffer (1975) offers another useful tool to assess cognitive abilities in the Short Portable Mental Status Questionnaire, which is part of the Older Americans Resources and Services scale. This is a 10-question scale that assesses recall of information, orientation to times and place, and calculation abilities. Both tools are valuable to clinicians who are looking for screening tools to be used with the general populations of elderly people.

There are several types of dementias; the correct diagnosis of the dementia is important to developing treatment goals, treatment approach, and expectations for progress. These dementias include dementia due to multiple etiologies, vascular dementia, dementia due to a general medical condition, dementia of the Alzheimer's type, and dementia not otherwise specified. Classification of the dementia depends, in part, on the etiology of the problem. Vascular dementia, for example, is diagnosed when there is evidence that a cerebrovascular disease is related to memory and cognitive problems (*DSM,* p. 690).

The incidence of dementia increases with age. At 65, 1% of the populations is cognitively impaired; 5% of the population aged 65–84 show signs of cognitive impairment; and 20% of the population aged 85 are cognitively impaired. Dementia resulting from Alzheimer's disease accounts for two-thirds of all dementias and is the most prevalent cause of dementia. Alzheimer's disease is a progressive neurological illness that is characterized by loss of memory and changes in mood and behavior. Alzheimer's disease is a progressive, debilitating disease for which there are no known causes or cures. The average length of time from diagnosis to death is 10 years (Hanin, Yoshida & Fisher, 1995; Mace & Rabins, 1981). Alzheimer's disease cannot be diagnosed definitively until autopsy; the supportive evidence for diagnosis is the presence of neurofibrillary tangles and senile plaques in the brain.

Symptoms of dementia do not always indicate the presence of a dementia. Nutritional problems can mimic the symptoms of dementia. Fluid and electrolyte disturbances secondary to dehydration can result in memory problems in an older person. A folate deficiency or a vitamin B_{12} deficiency can result in impaired memory function. Health problems also can be responsible for declines in memory function. Chronic health problems such as cardiovascular disturbances, respiratory diseases, metabolic and endocrine disturbances, central nervous system disorders, and collagen and rheumatoid diseases can all play a role in the diagnostic picture. Acute illness such as septicemia and influenza could be a root cause of cognitive problems. Surgery, pain, and trauma can also produce cognitive impairments in an older population. Cognitive decline can accompany psychosocial changes in an older person's life. Changes associated with relocation, bereavement, and retirement may be causative agents. Alcohol and drug abuse, as well as prescriptions and medication interactions, must be evaluated to determine their role in cognitive problems. Depression can often accompany true dementia and exacerbate the cognitive problems, but depression can also present itself as dementia. Careful differential diagnosis for depression and dementia is especially warranted in work with older clients.

The central questions to ask in assessment of a dementia are: What are the causes of this memory impairment? and, Is this impairment reversible? The evaluation and diagnosis of memory impairment is an area where interdisciplinary work becomes most visible. The evaluation of a dementia must include a thorough physical examination to rule out medically based causes. A comprehensive psychosocial examination must include questions about recent and past losses, the emotional reaction to those losses, depression, alcohol and other drug use, and family supports. Working together, physicians, social workers, and nurses should sort out the possible causes of the dementia and treat those causes which might be contributing to the memory impairment and other cognitive problems. It is never acceptable to make a diagnosis of dementia without stating the cause of the memory impairment and without attempting to rule out medical, social, and psychological problems thought to contribute to memory problems.

Treatment of Dementia

Treatment of dementias will depend upon the type of dementia diagnosed. The first step is, of course, treatment of problems that will reverse memory problems. Dementia of the Alzheimer's type is a progressive disease and there are no known cures. Treatment of Alzheimer's involves work with both the patient and the family, since caregiving issues are salient in the treatment (Hamdy, 1998). Treatment of Alzheimer's disease revolves around efforts to enhance the areas of competence that remain and to provide support and assistance in areas where the person has lost function. Communication issues are important in dealing with people with dementia (Wykle & Ripich, 1996). Clear, direct communication is necessary to avoid unnecessary confusion and frustration. The needs of the family members include knowledge and understanding about the disease process, dealing with grief and loss, and service planning to meet increasing needs. Most families will struggle with efforts to maintain the individual's independence within a protected environment. The timing and sequence of the stages of Alzheimer's disease are not predictable, so work with each family must be tuned to their individual needs and efforts to adapt (Hamdy, 1998).

The Case of Dr. C. B.: A Challenge in Differential Diagnosis

Dr. C. B. is a 70-year-old physician who recently retired from his general practice of 40 years. He had planned to stay involved part-time in the practice, but the physician group who bought the practice joined a managed care organization that did not want to pay for malpractice insurance for part-time employees. Dr. C. B. decided to retire, since the malpractice premium for single practitioners was very high. He belongs to the local Academy of Medicine and subscribes to several medical journals in his field.

Dr. C. B. and his wife celebrated their 45th wedding anniversary and they have four children, none of whom live in the area. The children are all accomplished professionals and all have careers and families. They come to visit during the holidays and call their parents about once a month. Dr. C. B. says he has a good relationship with his wife and with his children, but he admits that he did not spend much time with them while they were growing up. He says he felt dedicated to his patients and this dedication often meant he was not at home.

After Dr. C. B. retired, he and his wife took a long trip across the county. When they returned home his wife noticed several changes in his behavior that alarmed her. He has been suffering from bouts of insomnia and will stay up most of the night several times a week. He sometimes takes naps during the day, but he doesn't sleep soundly. His appetite is diminished and he doesn't seem to enjoy any of the foods he used to love. He tells his wife to go out to dinner without him because he feels she "needs to learn to get along without him." He doesn't seem to be able to concentrate and does not spend much time reading or reviewing journals, something he always enjoyed and made time to do. He says he is in good health, and he has had no major illnesses or mental health problems during his life. His wife thinks he has lost weight in the past two months. Dr. C. B. has recently begun to have difficulty remembering small details such as phone numbers and where he has left objects around the house. He recently could not remember his address when he was writing out a return address. Dr. C. B.'s father died of Alzheimer's disease when he was in his late 70s. Dr. C. B. denies feeling sad or depressed. He became irritable with his wife when she suggested that he talk to one of his colleagues about his insomnia. Lately he has been taking long walks alone and will not allow his wife to come with him, nor will he tell her where he has been when he returns. Sometimes he is gone for over four hours and his wife worries about his safety.

Psychosocial Assessment and Treatment Suggestions

Dr. C. B. presents a variety of issues in need of exploration. His retirement from his longtime medical practice represents a significant loss in his life. This retirement was unplanned in that he intended to stay involved with the practice, but finds now that he is not able to do so. Not only is he cut off from his daily routine and his long-term patients, but also he has experienced a change in social status; he is no longer a practicing physician and his opinions and expertise are no longer in demand at his practice. Using only the perspective of social loss, Dr. C. B.'s insomnia and eating problems could be attributed to feelings of grief and depression at the loss of his role as physician. However, Dr. C. B. experiences additional symptoms which indicate that his problems may be more serious than adjustment to retirement. He evidences a lack of interest in activities and food that he previously enjoyed. This lack of interest coupled with insomnia indicate the need to rule out depression. The loss of role as physician as well as the reflection that his role as a physician had overshadowed his family commitments may add to his depressed feelings. His recent memory loss may be caused by the presence of a depression, by lowered nutritional status, by a dementia such as Alzheimer's disease, or by an interaction of all of these reasons. Each of these possible causative factors must be evaluated thoroughly in order to determine if the memory loss is a reversible one. The symptoms of depression and dementia may be in reaction to his retirement, or they may be part of a longer-standing problem that was not evident while he was working. The most serious problem evident in this case is that of suicide risk. While all depressed people should be screened for suicide risk, Dr. C. B. presents several warning signals. His demographic profile, highly educated male professional, puts him in a high-risk category for suicide. The fact that he takes long walks and does not want his wife to accompany him is a sign of social isolation. His cryptic remark that his wife needs to learn to get along without him must be addressed directly to understand his meaning. It is important to investigate whether Dr. C. B. has thoughts of suicide and if he has developed a plan to harm himself. Suicide risk assessment and, if necessary, suicide precautions are the first priority in this situation.

What are the causes of Dr. C. B.'s dementias and are these symptoms of dementia reversible? Is his depression tied to his retirement alone or are there other issues involved? To what extent is his retirement responsible for the emergence of these symptoms or did the retirement allow the symptoms to be revealed? The interplay between the social, biological and psychological issues is crucial to untangling the issues in this case and to determining the treatment strategies necessary.

CONCLUSION

While all humans experience the aging process, not all experience senescence in the same ways. There are as many variations within senescence as there are between senescence and other life stages. The idea of senescence as a life stage as well as a dynamic process can be a useful tool for clinicians who work with older people and their families. The successful clinician will use the concept of normal aging as a guide to determine the parameters of functional behaviors and attitudes among older clients and families and to diagnose problems and disease. The use of senescence as a life stage provides a context to interpret individual case materials and clinical issues. The use of senescence as a process provides a way to synthesize the interplay of the biological, psychological, and social forces at play in a person's life. This synthesis is at the core of understanding later life and is essential to developing effective strategies to enable older people to maintain their independence as long as possible.

REFERENCES

American Medical Association. (1995). *Alcoholism in the elderly: Diagnosis, treatment, and prevention: Guidelines for primary care physicians.* Chicago: American Medical Association.

American Psychiatric Association. (1994). *Diagnostic and statistical manual of mental disorders, fourth edition.* Washington, DC: Author.

Atchley, R. C. (1997). *Social forces in later life* (8th Ed.). Belmont, CA: Wadsworth Publishing.

Biegel, D. E., Shore, B., & Gordon, E. (1984). *Building support networks for the elderly.* Beverly Hills, CA.: Sage Publications.

Biegel D. E., Farkas, K. J., Song, L. (1997). Barriers to the use of mental health services by African-American and Hispanic elderly persons. *Journal of Gerontological Social Work, 29* (1), 23–44.

Burack-Weiss, Ann. (1992). The losses of late life: Elderly responses and practice models. In F. J. Turner (Ed.). *Mental health and the elderly: A social perspective.* New York: Free Press.

Butler, R. N. (1975). *Why survive: Being old in America.* New York: Harper & Row.

Butler, R. N. (1989). Productive aging. In V. L. Bengtson, & K. W. Schaie (Eds.). *The course of later life* (pp. 55–64). New York: Springer.

Butler, R. N. (1990). A disease called ageism. *Journal of the American Geriatric Association, 38,* 178–80.

Butler, R. N., Lewis, M., & Sunderland, R. (1991). *Aging and mental health: Positive psychosocial and biomedical approaches* (4th Ed.). New York: Merrill Publishing.

Condon, V. A. (1996). Medication management and the elderly. In C. Emlet, J. Crabtree, V. Condon, & L. Treml. *In-home assessment of older adults* (pp. 107–130). Gaithersburg, MD: Aspen Publishing.

Corcoran, K., & Fischer, J. (1987). *Measures for clinical practice: A sourcebook.* New York: Free Press.

Emlet, C., Crabtree, J., Condon, V., & Treml, L. (1996). *In-home assessment of older adults: An interdisciplinary approach.* Gaithersburg, MD: Aspen Publishing.

Erikson, E. H. (1982). *The life cycle completed: A review.* New York: Norton.

Farkas, K. J., & Kola, L. A. (1997). Recognizing and treating alcohol abuse and alcohol dependence in elderly men. In J. Kosberg and L. Kaye. *Elderly men: Special problems and professional challenges* (pp. 175–192). New York: Springer Publishing.

Folstein, M. F., Folstein, S. E., & McHugh, P. R. (1975). A practical method for grading the cognitive status of patients for the clinician. *Journal of Psychiatric Research, 12,* 189.

Gaylord, S. A., & Zung, W. W. K. (1987). Affective disorders among the aging. In L. L. Carstensen & B. A. Edelstein (Eds.), *Handbook of clinical gerontology* (pp. 76–95). New York: Pergamon Press.

Hamdy, R. C. (Ed.). (1998). *Alzheimer's disease: A handbook for caregivers,* 3rd Ed. St. Louis: Mosby.

Hanin, Y., Yoshida, M., & Fisher, A. (Eds.). (1995). *Alzheimer's and Parkinson's diseases: Recent developments.* New York: Plenum Press.

Kaufman, S. (1986). *The ageless self.* Madison: University of Wisconsin Press.

Mace, N., & Rabins, P. V. (1981). *The 36-hour day: A family guide to caring for persons with Alzheimer's disease, related dementing illnesses and memory loss in later life.* Baltimore: Johns Hopkins University Press.

National Institutes of Health. (1991). *Diagnosis and treatment of depression in late life.* Consensus Statement, Vol. 9, 3. Bethesda, MD: National Institutes of Health.

Neugarten, B., & Hagestad, G. (1976). Age and the life course. In R. H. Binstock & E. Shanas. *Handbook of aging and the social sciences* (pp. 35–55). New York: Van Nostrand Reinhold.

Pfeiffer, E. (1975). A short portable mental status questionnaire for the assessment of organic brain deficit in elderly patients. *Journal of the American Geriatrics Society, 23,* 433–441.

Rowe, J. W., & Kahn, R. L. (1987). Human aging: Usual and successful. *Science, 237,* 143–149.

Rybash, J. M., Roodin, P. A., & Hoyer, W. J. (1995). *Adult development and aging* (3rd Ed.). Madison: Brown & Benchmark Publishers.

Stillion, J. M., McDoeill, E. E., & May, J. H. (1989). *Suicide across the life span.* New York: Hemisphere Publishing Corporation.

Tice, C. J., & Perkins, K. (1996). *Mental health issues and aging: Building on the strengths of older persons.* Pacific Grove, CA: Brooks/Cole Publishing Company.

U.S. Bureau of the Census. (1994). *Statistical abstract of the United States: 1994.* Washington, DC: U.S. Government Printing Office.

Valente, S. M. (1994). Recognizing depression in elderly patients. *American Journal of Nursing, 94* (12), 19–24.

Wykle, M., & Ripich, D. (1996). *Alzheimer's disease communication guide. Caregiver's manual: the FOCUSED program for caregivers.* San Antonio: Psychological Corporation.

Yesage, J. A., Brink, R. L., Rose, T. L., & Leirer, V. O. (1983). Development and validation of a geriatric depression screening scale: A preliminary report. *Journal of Psychiatric Research, 17,* 37–49.

Zung, W. K. (1965). A self-rating depression scale. *Archives of General Psychiatry, 12,* 63–70.

9

ALZHEIMER'S DISEASE: PATIENT AND FAMILY VICTIMIZED

Daniel C. Andreae

The purpose of this chapter is to provide social workers, those new to the field as well as established practitioners, with an awareness, an understanding, and a practical knowledge about Alzheimer's disease. This includes an overview and discussion of such key issues as what Alzheimer's disease is and what it is not, symptoms and diagnosis, possible causes and treatments, stages of the disease, care and planning for the Alzheimer patient, and the role of the social worker in a multidisciplinary context, working with patients and families on psychosocial dimensions. In a relatively brief chapter such as this, space does not permit an in-depth discussion of all pertinent aspects of interest to social workers. Nevertheless, the goal is to equip the practitioner with a broad-based grounding of the disease that has been labeled "the silent epidemic" as well as "the disease of the century." Social workers, whether in clinical, community, policy or administrative positions, will increasingly come into contact with this insidious affliction and its impact as Canada's population continues to age. Undoubtedly, many readers will personally know of someone who has or is suffering from this disease, has treated patients, or has served in the capacity of caregiver to a victim—including relatives, friends, neighbors, and coworkers.

Alzheimer's disease is a neurodegenerative brain disease for which at present there is no known cause or cure. It affects primarily those who are over age 65 but can strike as young as 40 (Turner, 1992). Indeed, the earliest known case was diagnosed in a 27-year-old patient (Davidson, 1996). Considerably less than 1% of the population is cognitively impaired by age 65, but this proportion escalates to approximately 20% of those aged 80 or older (Aronson, 1988). There is disagreement among experts as to the actual and projected percentages of individuals who suffer or may suffer in the future from Alzheimer's disease, with one study indicating that 10% of people over age 65 will develop Alzheimer's rising to 47.2% for those over age 85 (Turner, 1992). The Harvard Letter on Alzheimer Disease states, "It affects predominantly older persons (less than 5% of patients with the disease are younger than 65) and the risk rises with increasing age. About 1% of the population aged 65-74, 7% of those aged 75-84 and 25% of those older having severe dementia" (Harvard Health Letter, 1996). It is estimated that roughly 250,000 people currently have Alzheimer's disease and related disorders, but by the year 2030, according to Dr. Serge Gauthier, professor and director of the McGill University Centre For Studies In Aging in Montreal, and Dr. Jules Poirer, Associate Director of the same Centre, this will increase to 750,000 people, about 70% suffering from either "sporadic" or the less common "familial" form of the disease (Bayley, 1996). These figures do not include the countless family members who have coped with the devastating effects of Alzheimer's. Approximately 10,000 Canadians die each year from this illness and it is estimated that Alzheimer's disease is a fourth leading cause of death after heart disease, cancer, and stroke (Lobray, 1995).

Virtually anyone is at risk for developing Alzheimer's disease. It is found in all societies and in all classes and types of people across the world, from the Western world to the South Sea islands, to China, India, and Japan. There are some variations in groupings: a lower incidence in Japan and a high incidence in the Marshall Islands; at present it is not known why this should be the case (Davidson, 1996). It occurs more frequently in men than women although this could arise because women in general outlive men, and it is not contagious.

Although Alzheimer's disease has steadily gained a higher profile and greater exposure in the last several years, in part due to public figures such as former U.S. President Ronald Reagan, who announced that he has Alzheimer's disease, it is not a new disease nor confined to this century. The earliest documented mention of a condition that now looks like Alzheimer's disease was in 500 B.C. when Solon, the famous Greek lawyer and philosopher, wrote that impaired judgment from old age could cause a will to be invalid (Davidson, 1996). Approximately 100 years later, in his *Republic,* Plato recognized the loss of capacity in some aged people when he wrote that certain crimes could be excused if committed in a state of madness, disease, or extreme old age (Turner, 1992). Esquinol outlined a similar condition to Alzheimer's disease in a French textbook on psychiatry in 1838, in which he referred to *démence senile* as an illness that is characterized by a weakening of the memory for recent experiences, drive, and will power. Esquinol stated that the condition appears gradually and may be accompanied by emotional disturbances (Reisberg, 1986, p. 4, cited in Cutler & Stramek, 1996).

In the past, Alzheimer's disease was commonly referred to as "senility" or "hardening of the arteries." Often when an aging person or relative began to act strangely, he or she was labeled senile, crazy, dotty, confused or demented. *Senility* is a term commonly used by lay persons to describe the general declines in memory, concentrating ability, and thought processes that are believed to accompany aging. Professionals in the field of aging generally dislike the term *senility* because it is so imprecise and because it can be used to describe conditions that could be successfully treated if correctly diagnosed. Senility, properly speaking, is not a medical diagnosis at all. Indeed, some professionals call the word an unestablished or meaningless term. The word *dementia* is much more precise; it is derived from two Latin words meaning "way" and "mind" and refers to a group of symptoms, not to the name of the disease that causes the symptoms (Turner, 1992). Although estimates vary, Alzheimer's disease accounts for approximately half of all dementias and is the most prevalent nonreversible type. About 20% of nonreversible dementias are attributed to vascular blockages; 20% to multiinfarctorial or uncertain origin, and 10% to secondary dementias. Only 3–8% of diagnosed secondary dementia cases are truly reversed partially or completely (Ganesan, et al., 1994). A very small percentage are due to rare nerve diseases such as kuru, Pick's disease and Kreutzfeldt-Jacob disease. However, there are over 60 potentially reversible and treatable conditions that exhibit symptoms similar to Alzheimer's disease and other related dementias. These include the following (Turner, 1992; Harvard Health Letter, 1996):

- Hyperthyroidism or hypothyroidism
- Dehydration
- Tumors
    - Direct CNS invasion (e.g., brain)
    - Remote effect: mostly lung, but occasionally ovary, prostate, rectum, or breast
- Drugs and alcohol: beta-blockers, methyldopa, clonidine, haloperidol (Haldol), chlorpromazine (Thorazine), phenytoin, bromides, phenobarbital, cimetidine, steroids, procainamide, disopyramide, atropine
- Addison's disease

- Head trauma with subdural hematoma
- Hyperglycemia
- Nutritional disorders
    - B_{12} deficiency (dementia may precede anemia)
    - Folate, pellagra, Wernicke-Korsakoff's syndrome
- Inflammatory disorders: systemic lupus erythematosus
- Congestive heart failure
- Anesthesia
- Kidney disease
- AIDS
- Low sodium or magnesium
- Infection: syphilis, abscess, encephalitis
- Hypopituitarism
- Psychiatric/neurological disorders
    - schizophrenia
    - seizures
    - normal-pressure hydrocephalus (dementia, ataxia, incontinence)
    - depression

Alzheimer's disease is named after Dr. Alois Alzheimer, a German physician and psychiatrist who made his discovery in the late 1890s and who in 1907 described his landmark case with a 51-year-old woman brought to him by her husband. Because the patient was younger than 65, he referred to her condition as "presenile dementia" but it is now known that Alzheimer's disease, whether presenile (under age 65) or senile, is the same condition and is commonly referred to as *senile dementia of the Alzheimer's type,* usually abbreviated to *SDAT* or *DAT.* As both a practicing physician and researcher, Dr. Alzheimer became known for his expertise in bringing together what information he had from his patients' lives and the results of brain autopsies to make important new discoveries in the studies of dementia. Using a newly developed high-resolution microscope, Dr. Alzheimer found brain deterioration in those patients diagnosed with dementia. He found a pattern of tissue change, including large numbers of senile plaques and neurofibrillary tangles in the brain cells; these were the visible signs of degeneration in the nerve endings and the reason why the person had become so impaired in functioning. Other associated histological features include cortical neuronal loss, loss of dendrites, neural atrophy, and granulovascular degeneration. Alois Alzheimer thought that this microscopic evidence proved the presence of the disease, but it was his superior and sponsor Dr. Ernst Kraepelin, who named this Alzheimer's disease in his own clinical textbook in 1910 (Davidson, 1996).

POSSIBLE CAUSES: RESEARCH

Why do some people develop Alzheimer's disease, while others with similar genetic makeups and social histories do not? An adult's chance of succumbing to Alzheimer's disease is approximately 1 or 2 in 100 after age 65, but the odds increase by a factor of 4 if a close relative has the disease. This familial factor, combined with evidence that the disease may be linked to other diseases such as Down syndrome or mongolism that are known to be caused by a defect in chromosome 21, and the fact that Down syndrome patients over age 40 invariably develop Alzheimer's disease, indicates that there is a genetic predisposition in at least some of the cases (Mace & Rabins, 1984; Kociol & Schiff, 1989). It has been estimated that familial Alzheimer's disease accounts for approximately 10% of all cases, which makes genetics an important but not exclusive factor. Other possible causes that are currently under investigation include biochemical imbalances in the brain, such as a shortage of the enzyme acetyltransferase, which is necessary to produce the vital neurotransmitter acetylcholine; the possibility of a slow virus that may lie dormant for many years only to express itself later in life, although no evidence has yet been found to validate this etiology; and the high concentration of certain proteins in, and the decreased blood and oxygen supply to, the brains of Alzheimer's patients.

Aluminum in acidic drinking water may also be a contributor to the development of Alzheimer's disease. Epidemiological studies conducted in Norway and Britain indicate that the risk of developing the disease in areas in which water contains high levels of aluminum is 1.8 times greater than it is in geographic regions with low levels of aluminum in the drinking water (Kociol & Schiff, 1989). Researchers continue to debate whether an elevated level of aluminum in the brains of Alzheimer's patients is a cause or an effect of the disease and whether aluminum pots and pans and products containing high levels of aluminum, such as deodorants and lipstick, should be discarded.

Interesting studies have determined other possible risk factors for the onset of Alzheimer's disease, including a previous head injury, which increases the risk factor by 3, and the possibility of thyroid gland dysfunction, which raises the risk by 1.5 times over those who do not manifest signs of thyroid gland disease. Thus an understanding of the effect of thyroid gland disease upon the brain function may prove extremely important in determining the causes of Alzheimer's disease (Kociol & Schiff, 1989). Ultimately, it is likely that a series of cofactors, rather than a single factor, will be shown to cause the disease. The challenge is to identify these various factors and to determine how they interrelate with and affect each other. Canada is among the world's leaders in research on Alzheimer's disease, and several excellent research centers have been established across the country, including the Centre for Research in Neurodegenerative Diseases at the University of Toronto (Turner, 1992).

TREATMENT

Although the progression of Alzheimer's disease is irreversible, there are limited treatments, including drugs, that can alleviate the symptoms in the absence of an effective cure. However, there are always risks and unpleasant side effects with drugs, some of which may result in further cognitive impairment.

Tranquilizers can help to control outbursts, but the prolonged use of major tranquilizers may cause serious and chronic effects. For example, tardive dyskinesia, a syndrome resulting from the prolonged use of antipsychotic drugs, results in involuntary rapid, uncontrolled jerky movements and lip smacking. Haloperidol (Haldol) is an antipsychotic medication that appears to have an effect in managing such symptoms as depression, agitation, anxiety, and sleep disturbances; however, the fact that it is a sedative and anticholinergic means that it can increase memory loss (Powell & Courtice, 1983). Indeed, several medications that are commonly prescribed for heart disease, hypertension, diabetes, or anxiety may also exacerbate cognitive impairment.

It has been estimated that persons aged 65 and older who are living in the community are taking an average of 5 medications per day and that those in nursing homes are consuming more than 10 drug mixtures. This mixture of drugs may be dangerous because many drugs interact with each other to cause a wide variety of physical problems in addition to agitation, sedation, drowsiness, or memory loss. The result of multimedication may be symptoms that mimic Alzheimer's disease, but once the patient is taken off the drugs or has the dosages decreased, the symptoms subside or disappear. This is not to indicate that drugs do not have a positive purpose and effect; however, it is important for the physician, caregiver, and patient, when appropriate, to weigh the potential benefits of particular drugs against their possible adverse side effects.

In addition to drugs, exercise may help to reduce a patient's restlessness and anxiety. The Alzheimer's patient may engage in such activities as walking, dancing, or basic calisthenics. Also, a well-balanced nutritious diet can increase the patient's resistance to disease and alleviate digestive problems, such as diarrhea and constipation, as well as dehydration, malnutrition, anemia, or vitamin and mineral deficiencies (Turner, 1992).

DIAGNOSIS

The diagnosis for Alzheimer's disease is complicated by the fact that the symptoms of different illness and dementias tend to look more or less the same from the outside, even though the causes may be quite different. Therefore, the first thing that a physician must do after having eliminated all other diseases and dementia look-alikes from the diagnostic picture is to establish the cause of a particular dementia; then he or she must determine whether it is reversible or irreversible, progressive or nonprogressive, temporary or permanent. Currently there are no definitive tests that can confirm whether a person has Alzheimer's disease. Therefore, the diagnosis is essentially based on the exclusion of other possible diseases and can only be confirmed at the time of autopsy through a biopsy of brain tissue, in which the neuropathologist looks for the telltale signs of neurofibrillary tangles and senile plaques. A postmortem diagnosis is not simple to make because these neurological changes also occur to some extent in the brains of normal patients, so the pathologist must be certain to locate affected tissue from the frontal and temporal lobes of the brain, which are the areas most ravaged by this affliction. In Europe a brain biopsy is occasionally performed on living patients, who are administered a local anesthetic while a small piece of brain is removed for the examination of pathological trademarks under the microscope. Since a brain biopsy involves some risk of infection or hemorrhage, as does any surgical procedure, it is performed only when a clinical diagnosis of Alzheimer's disease in indicated. This procedure is never performed in Canada exclusively to validate a diagnosis of Alzheimer's disease, but a biopsy may be done when another medical condition, such as a brain tumor or abscess, is indicated (Turner, 1992).

The diagnostic process involves two steps: (1) determining if the patient is suffering from real dementia or from a dementia look-alike, and (2) once it has been established that dementia is present, determining what kind of dementia the person is suffering from. The physician will want the patient to first undergo a complete physical examination, including blood chemistry and other laboratory tests. Later a series of mental examinations ranging from simple to more complex may be administered by a social worker, physician, or psychiatrist. These mental tests are designed to determine the extent of possible brain damage and to distinguish between Alzheimer's disease and other conditions such as depression. The interviewer will pose simple questions usually from a standard questionnaire, such as "How old are you?" "What day is it today?" "What place is this?" etc.

A key initial step is to obtain a history of the illness; this is usually obtained from a family member or a close relative, since the demented individual may no longer be capable of providing accurate information depending on what stage of the illness he or she is in. The physician will want to know when the symptoms began; rarely is it possible to provide the exact date. A detailed description will be obtained of the changes in mental abilities, personality, mood, and behavior, including when and how the changes began and how they have affected the person's ability to function. Letters, checkbooks, household lists or other materials that illustrate changes in cognition may also be helpful. The history will include a complete medical history, including injuries and recent illnesses, as well as a list of medications the patient is taking, including nonprescription drugs (Harvard Health Letter, 1996).

In addition to the history, both general and neurological exams should be performed. Their purpose is to find impairment of organ systems or evidence of localized brain disease. For example, physicians may find evidence of liver or kidney failure or evidence of localized disease of the brain, such as may be seen with a brain tumor or clot. Alternatively the physician may find evidence of multiple areas of the brain and brain stem that are injured, as is typical of multiinfarct dementia. The patient will undergo a complete physical examination, which will include blood tests for detecting metabolic disorders: X-ray and electrocardiogram (EKG) and other tests for problems that result in the symptoms of Alzheimer's disease, such as special studies of the spinal fluid system. An electroencephalogram (EEG) may be done to detect abnormal brainwave activity. Although the EEG is usually normal in patients with Alzheimer's disease and many other types of dementias, EEG abnormalities do occur in delirium and Kreutzfeldt-Jacob disease. If infection of the central nervous system or hydroencephalus is suspected, a lumbar puncture may be performed. In evaluating unexplained dementia, a physician typically orders brain scans with either computerized axial tomography (CAT) or magnetic resonance imagery (MRI) to rule out tumors, stroke, and hydrocephalus. Electroscopic changes associated with Alzheimer's disease cannot be seen with brain scans. Atrophy of the brain is the only abnormality visible in Alzheimer's disease and other degenerative dementias (Harvard Health Letter, 1996).

DSM-IV contains the most widely utilized criteria for dementia; it refers to Alzheimer's disease as "the development of multiple cognitive deficits that must be sufficiently severe to cause impairment in occupational or sound functioning and will represent a decline from a previously higher level of functioning" (see Table 9–1).

FUNCTIONAL ASSESSMENT

Cognitive problems affect a person's daily functioning in many different and sometimes surprising ways. An objective assessment can help determine what a patient can and cannot do. This information is invaluable for caregivers, especially when the patient has other health problems that complicate the situation, such as arthritis or poor vision. Moreover, a functional assessment can determine the appropriate stage of Alzheimer's disease that a patient has reached, which can then help family members decide what type of care and support services are needed.

Nurses and occupational or rehabilitation or physical therapists perform functional assessments. The therapists obtain some information by interviewing the patient and family members. Part of the assessment focuses on how the person manages in a controlled setting that simulates real-life situations. Therapists observe while the patient performs activities of daily living. These include the basic self-care tests of eating, bathing, dressing, ambulating, and using the toilet, as well as managing common daily tasks such as using the telephone, preparing a meal, and handling money. By noting what activities are completed successfully, done partially, or not managed at all, the therapist can suggest ways of preserving as much of the patient's independence as possible (Harvard Health Letter, 1996).

PSYCHOSOCIAL CRITERIA

Another key assessment area involves a psychosocial evaluation, which is normally conducted by a social worker and is designed to help the patient's family plan how to manage care. The social worker will discuss the emotional, physical, and financial impact of Alzheimer's disease and guide the family through an evaluation of their own circumstances. Social workers can help coordinate community services, or suggest alternatives to the patient's present living arrangements and provide a list of resources and locally available services such as day-care programs (Harvard Health Let-

Table 9–1 Diagnostic Criteria for Dementia and Alzheimer's Disease

Dementia	Alzheimer's disease

A. Multiple cognitive deficits manifested by both 1 and 2
   1. Impaired short- or long-term memory
   2. One or more of the following cognitive disturbances:
     a. Impaired language ability
     b. Impaired ability to carry out motor activities
     c. Impaired ability to recognize objects
     d. Impaired abstract thinking (e.g., planning, organizing)
 B. Deficits in A are sufficient to interfere with work or social activities and represent a significant decline in function
 C. Deficits do not occur exclusively during the course of delirium
	Dementia as determined by A through C, plus
	 D. Disease course is characteristic by gradual onset and continuing cognitive decline
	 E. Cognitive deficits are not caused by any of the following:
	   1. Another progressive central nervous system disorder (e.g., Parkinson's disease, Huntington's disease)
	   2. A systemic condition (e.g., hypothyroidism, niacin deficiency)
	   3. A substance-induced condition
	 F. Disturbance is not better accounted for by another disorder (e.g., major depressive disorder, schizophrenia)

Source: Adapted from American Psychiatric Association (1994), *Diagnostic and statistical manual of mental disorders*, 4th Ed., pp. 142, 143, 151, 152, Washington, DC, Author.

ter, 1996). Once the battery of tests and evaluations has been completed the physician will need some time to evaluate and determine the results.

No matter how certain the physician feels about the diagnosis, after all exams and tests have been done, technically the diagnosis will be "probable Alzheimer's disease" or if the symptoms are not typical but no other cause is found, "possible Alzheimer's disease" (Harvard Health Letter, 1996). The physician will undoubtedly request that the patient return in approximately six months and on a continuing basis to gauge whether, and how much, further cognitive deterioration has occurred. At that time, the physician will be in a better position to confirm the original diagnosis or to decide which additional tests are required to determine the cause of the symptoms. Evaluation by an experienced physician is about 90% accurate, as confirmed by autopsies. It is difficult enough for families to cope with the shock of learning the diagnosis; now the question arises as to whether, and what, to tell the Alzheimer's patient if the physician has not already informed him or her. There is no correct answer to this question, and the merits of both disclosing and withholding the diagnosis from a patient can be argued. There may be an advantage to informing the patient if he or she is in the earlier stages because the patient still has time to participate in planning the rest of his or her life. It also discourages the formation of a barrier to communication between the family and patient, and provides the patient with an explanation for his or her condition, and the fact that he or she is not "crazy." Some patients prefer to know and are reassured by the labeling of a specific medical diagnosis. The key is to take the lead from the Alzheimer's patient, and to base the decision to tell or not to tell on the patient's personality and behavior in previous circumstances, as well as on the types of questions that the patient has asked. Different approaches are appropriate for different patients (Turner, 1992).

STAGES

Each Alzheimer's patient progresses through a series of stages of deterioration; however, the duration and intensity of each of the three major stages is idiosyncratic to that patient. Some individuals decline rapidly in the initial phases, but then reach a plateau for a while, and even show occasional glimmers of improvement, before they lapse into further deterioration. Others may decline more slowly in the early stages, but then degenerate more quickly toward the end. Every individual does not suffer the same symptoms during the course of the disease or suffer them at the same time or to a similar degree. There is no way to predict the rate at which a patient will move through the stages that make Alzheimer's disease so frustrating, unpredictable, and frightening for patients, families, and lay and professional caregivers.

In addition to the generally utilized three-stage model, a seven-stage model, developed by Barry Reisberg, is used by professionals primarily for diagnostic and assessment purposes (see Table 9–2). Reisberg's research demonstrates that Alzheimer's patients lose abilities in the reverse order that they were initially learned. This knowledge may assist professionals in deciding whether an individual has Alzheimer's disease. For example, according to the Reisberg model, if a person is able to function in a difficult work environment, yet forgets appointments and major responsibilities, one would suspect that Alzheimer's disease is not the cause of the memory loss (Turner, 1992).

Table 9–2 The Seven Stages of Alzheimer's Disease

Stage 1	No cognitive decline	No functional problem
Stage 2	Very mild cognitive decline	Forgets names and location of objects
Stage 3	Mild cognitive decline	Has difficulty traveling to new locations
		Has difficulty in demanding employment settings
Stage 4	Moderate cognitive decline	Has difficulty with complex tasks (finances; marketing; planning for dinner guests)
Stage 5	Moderately severe cognitive decline	Needs help to choose clothing
		Needs coaxing to bathe properly
Stage 6	Severe cognitive decline	Needs help putting on clothing
		Requires assistance in bathing; may have fear of bathing
		Has decreased ability to handle toileting
		Is incontinent
Stage 7	Very severe cognitive decline	Has vocabulary of six words
		Has single-word vocabulary
		Loss of ambulatory ability
		Loss of ability to sit
		Loss of ability to smile
		Stupor and coma

Source: Kociol & Schiff, 1985.

The onset of Alzheimer's disease is gradual and at times imperceptible. The person may begin to suspect that something may be wrong, but often hides this suspicion from family members, other relatives, friends, and coworkers. Since there is little or no physical sign of deterioration until the late stages, it is difficult to determine in the early stages whether a person has Alzheimer's disease because he or she appears physically normal. Thus, in the early stages, people in the community may think that the person is simply intoxicated, upset, or emotionally unstable.

The first stage is characterized by slow, subtle changes in the person's ability to learn; problems in communication; memory loss for recent events; difficulty making decisions; impaired judgment; a shortened attention span; problems in coping with new situations; and a decreased desire to attempt new things and to meet people.

A typical characteristic of all examples of Alzheimer's disease is its effects on recent memory, which involves recollections of events that occurred a few minutes to several days in the past. Recent memory is distinct from immediate memory, which refers, for example, to the short time it takes to look at an address and write it down. Not all recent memory is affected during Alzheimer's disease; for instance, the person still remembers the sensation of pain. Recent memory is also different from remote memory—the remembrance of events and people from childhood or adolescence. Remote memory is usually permanent, but it may deteriorate. This variable memory loss is both random and unpredictable. Indeed, it is not unusual for a patient to forget where he or she has just left the keys to the house but be able to recall in detail some aspect of childhood 60, 70, or 80 years before. Some examples contributed by caregivers to illustrate the first stage include these:

Since my wife had always described herself as being absent-minded, it was easy for her to excuse and laugh off memory lapses such as forgetting names of grandchildren and missing appointments. It was only after she became anxious after getting lost on the way home that we were able to persuade her to see a physician. (Kociol & Schiff, 1985, p. 21)

My wife was cooperative and when it was suggested that she wash up for dinner, she would go to the appropriate place. However, she would consistently emerge from the bathroom without having washed. We realized that she had forgotten what "wash" meant, so she had not been able to carry out this task. (Ibid.)

My husband was a bus driver. He began coming earlier and earlier for work because he couldn't remember what time his shift started. (Ibid.)

Another wife related that the first thing she noticed in her 55-year-old husband was "poor memory, slow movements and occasional weak legs." (*About Alzheimer's Disease*, 1987, p. 7, quoted in Turner, 1992)

During the second or middle stage, memory continues to deteriorate. The ability to concentrate lessens, errors in judgment increase, and word-finding problems emerge. There are also marked difficulties in speech, language, and communication and a decreasing ability to conduct daily activities without supervision or guidance. There is a disconnection between time and place, and the patient may not be able to recognize himself or herself in the mirror. The Alzheimer's victim may still be able to read aloud and repeat words, but numerical functions and other cognitive abilities decline. It is difficult to know what is still intact and what the person can feel, understand, interpret, and experience because further intellectual and behavioral changes are occurring.

During the second stage, it is important to reduce the amount of stimulation and to establish as predictable a schedule as possible. The patient may respond to people or objects in an aggressive manner because he or she misperceives what is happening. For example, someone who approaches the patient suddenly to assist with dressing may be perceived as a threat, particularly if the approach is made from behind or from one side at the edge of the patient's peripheral vision.

In this stage there is often a struggle to maintain bodily functions, some of which are retained longer than are others. The loss of dexterity and the slowing down of bodily movements may impede such tasks as dressing and other self-care routines, but the patient physically resists help. Some Alzheimer's victims may begin to wander from home, often just in a housecoat and in the middle of the night, and may be unaware that they are wandering and that they are placing themselves in potential danger. Wandering can cause extreme anxiety and upset for family members and caregivers.

Typical problems associated with the middle stage are illustrated in the following examples:

Mrs. S stated that her 53-year-old husband showed an "inability to concentrate and work at figures." She added that he seems a different person but is not too hard to handle. Later, however, she said that he had visual and speech impairments, as well as the loss of bladder and bowel control. (*About Alzheimer's Disease,* 1987, p. 7)

Mr. W said: "When the phone rings I don't let my dad answer it anymore because it could be business. He can't take messages even. The person at the other end of the phone will ask 'Where's Jim' and I'll be standing next to him, and he'll say 'He's not here today.'" (Powell & Courtice, 1983, p. 170)

Mrs. L remarked that her brother now shows so much impairment that "comprehension is too poor to determine if there is still memory." She added that he is "fearful, suspicious, has episodes of depression and weeping—and sometimes of giggling. He needs to be guided for he has just fallen down and broken his hip." (*About Alzheimer's Disease,* 1987, p. 7)

In the third and final stage, 24-hour nursing care is usually required. The patient may need complete assistance with daily self-care routines, such as feeding, toileting, and dressing. In addition, the patient may require hospitalization to treat increasing physical infirmities and illness. The ability to speak or communicate disappears or may consist of only randomly spoken phrases with no apparent meaning, as well as immobility. Bowel and urine control decrease greatly, leading to incontinence, and twitching and jerking may develop. Seizures, delusions, and delirium may occur. There may be virtually no spontaneous movements or reactions to people or other stimuli as the patient assumes an almost vegetative state. Reflexes may develop, such as the one that causes the patient to suck anything put in his or her mouth. The person with Alzheimer's disease becomes increasing susceptible to bedsores, pneumonia, and heart failure, the last two of which eventually result in death. Although the immediate cause of death is in reality Alzheimer's disease, often a secondary cause of death is listed on the certificate; however, this practice is slowly changing as physicians become better educated about Alzheimer's disease.

This difficult final stage was described by two members of an Alzheimer Society:

Mr. G stated that his 69-year-old wife is now showing a "general slowing of movement and recently has become bedridden due to a complete loss of mobility."

Mrs. G reported that she has been nursing and caring for her 65-year-old husband at home for about two years, "but finally I could no longer stand the physical and emotional strain and was able to have him placed in a nursing home three months before he died." (*About Alzheimer's Disease*, 1987, p. 7, quoted in Turner, 1992)

IMPACT ON PATIENTS AND FAMILIES

Alzheimer's disease has a devastating psychological, emotional, social, and even financial and legal impact on the family system, including the victim, that often extends over a period of years. According to the Alzheimer's Disease and Related Disorders Association in the United States (ADRDA), caregivers feel alone and disconnected from friends; need assistance but are reluctant to ask; often are unable to do errands and complete household tasks; experience stress, sometimes severe; need a break from caregiving but may not have anyone to relieve them or refuse assistance when offered; and are looking for someone to listen. Those with Alzheimer's disease feel an uncertain future; must adjust to new schedules and changing roles and responsibilities; worry about overwhelming family caregivers; strive to maintain an active and independent lifestyle, and may look the same but act differently. Marion Roach, the daughter of an Alzheimer's patient, writes, "It goes on and on, and just when we can't stand another phase, we don't have to because it's succeeded by another one—a worse phase, a more outrageous phase, a quieter phase, a sloppier phase, a more confused phase, a phase of hushed panic—seen in the eyes of the victim, seen by us."

The patient, family members, and caregivers will experience a myriad of constantly changing emotions in response to the evolving and challenging conditions associated with this unpredictable disease. These feelings and reactions are perfectly normal and should be openly acknowledged, accepted, and resolved to ensure that they would not become barriers to caregiving in the future, according to Dr. Eva Philipp, a social worker, adult educator, and psychotherapist in private practice in Toronto, where I interviewed her in May 1998. Often these emotions seem overwhelming, conflicting and confusing but they are shared by many others who are witnessing the gradual disappearance of the traits that make up the unique personality of the sufferer. It is important to realize that family members are not alone in experiencing the roller coaster impact of their feelings (Turner, 1992).

A key difficulty experienced by family members, especially those who are caregivers, is that they are prevented from experiencing the normal grieving process by which people come to terms with their losses. Grief is an emotional response to loss, and in the case of death, can be overwhelming at first, becoming less intense over time. In a chronic illness, however, just when you think you have adjusted, the person may change and you go through the grieving process again.

The feelings of sadness, anger, fatigue, guilt, and despair that accompany grief are restimulated each time another element vanishes that made the patient a person.

The grieving process experienced by family members has also been documented by Elisabeth Kubler-Ross, who identifies the stages of denial and isolation, anger, bargaining, depression, and acceptance (Turner, 1992).

It is important for family members to realize that although these patients are increasingly unable to articulate what is occurring inside them, they require constant compassion, support, and understanding, however difficult it is to provide them. Even though they may not be able to express their feelings in words, they are still experiencing their feelings. In the beginning, Alzheimer's patients feel confused as they realize that something is happening to their memory or ability to work, but are unsure what is occurring and why. They feel frustrated because, regardless of how diligently they try, they are unable to perform the same tasks that they once could. Many patients feel angry at the loss of their abilities and question, "Why is it happening to me?" They experience fear as the loss of memory makes the world seem a frightening place and feel uncertain because the symptoms and progression of their illness are so unpredictable that they do not know what the future will hold. Alzheimer's victims also experience grief and depression as they mourn the loss of their abilities and feel hopeless about their future (Turner, 1992).

For families, denial is common in the first stage, when the symptoms begin to appear and are diagnosed. Families frequently express hope that the diagnosis is incorrect and that the patient will recover. Indeed, denial may be functional in protecting against the traumatic reality of the disease. However, if families continue to deny, they may suffer serious problems of coping and adjusting in the long run. As the disease progresses and the patient becomes increasingly dependent, role adjustments become necessary in the family (i.e., adjustments as to who will now assume legal and financial responsibilities). The spouse, children, or caregiver must assume the role of guardian. As the Alzheimer's patient becomes too debilitated to do previously simple tasks, such as cooking, cleaning, or money management, the family must take over these chores. Because Alzheimer's patients begin to display many behavioral symptoms such as wandering, forgetfulness, the continued repeating of questions, paranoia, and occasionally violence, family members are constantly uncertain as to when the patient will exhibit aggressive behavior or inappropriate outbursts arising from the patient's distorted view of reality. Often these behaviors are seen as rude and unacceptable, but they are caused by the patient's misperception of the situation. Caregivers may feel guilty because they are embarrassed by the person's bizarre behavior or the need for constant reminders in public. These unpredictable behaviors, in conjunction with disrupted family routines and the exorbitant amount of time, energy, and money that are involved in the care of the Alzheimer's patient, lead to frustration, anger, and resentment.

Families may also feel guilty because they believe that they are somehow responsible for the illness, although it is not the result of anything they may have done or could have prevented, or because they are angry at the patient's inability to perform even the most routine tasks. During the later stages of the disease when the patient becomes immobilized, families need to be given permission to begin the mourning process because the patient is still alive. They need to be able to grieve the loss of a personal relationship that no longer exists (Turner, 1992).

Because the daily routine of the family, sometimes involving school-age children, is severely disrupted, with attendant reactions, stresses do occur that need to be acknowledged and constantly dealt with. According to ADRDA, 80% of Alzheimer's caregivers report high levels of stress and stress related illness. Too often caregivers do not recognize their own needs, fail to do anything about them or simply do not know where to turn for help. For these reasons, the Alzheimer's caregiver is called the hidden, or second victim of the disease (ADRDA, 1997).

THE ROLE OF THE SOCIAL WORKER

The social worker plays an indispensable role in the ongoing care of the Alzheimer's patient and family members. Working in concert with a multidisciplinary team of allied professionals, such as general practitioners, neurologists, psychiatrists, psychologists, neuropsychologists, nurses, physiotherapists, occupational therapists, speech pathologists, rehabilitation counselors, recreational therapists, and the clergy, the social worker contributes a set of intervention skills that combine clinical and community foci. Social workers, especially those with some training in gerontology, can help family members to work through emotional difficulties arising from the illness and to cope with the changing disease process, offer practical suggestions and techniques to improve caregiving, provide case management, educate and provide information about the condition, and conduct support groups for patients and families in the community and in institutional settings. They can also engage in ongoing psychotherapy with family members, when required; assist families to resolve disagreements about caregiving; help families plan for the legal and financial consequences of the disease; assist in the diagnostic process by conducting a thorough family history to ascertain the family's strengths and deficits and to identify needs; refer the patient and family to appropriate community resources and allied professionals, when required; conduct research on psychosocial issues associated with Alzheimer's disease; and help the family to plan for and select an appropriate long-term-care facility.

Many social workers conduct or facilitate support groups for caregivers, as well as for patients, primarily in institutional settings. They and other health care professionals have successfully employed group work techniques with the elderly for years (Turner, 1992).

INSTITUTIONAL CARE

The choice of an institutional facility is one of the most traumatic and agonizing decisions a family has to make, and the social worker can provide much needed support and practical assistance in this regard. At some point, the overwhelming majority of Alzheimer's patients require institutional care. There are several circumstances in which residential care must be considered. For example, the patient may be residing alone and not be able to handle violent episodes of incontinence, or the patient's need for medical attention may require the family to place him or her in residential care. Family members should deal openly with the circumstances of, and options for, long-term care and should talk about them in advance because institutions often have long waiting lists and the number of facilities that accept patients may be restricted. Indeed, many institutions are reluctant to admit, or even refuse to admit Alzheimer's patients. Options for residential care may include homes for the aged; chronic-care hospitals; nursing homes, both private and nonprofit; and psychiatric institutions (for brief assessments).

As well as helping the family to deal with the emotional turbulence associated with this decision, the social worker can also help the family with admissions procedures; assist the patient to adjust to the institutional environment; and consult with the institution's staff concerning the psychological and social needs of the patient, including the selection of a roommate and a dining partner. If appropriate, the social worker can help the family look at alternatives to institutionalization.

Most families consult a social worker in a time of high stress—once the diagnosis has been made or when they feel they are no longer able to cope with the strain of caregiving. This situation presents the social worker with a unique opportunity to intervene. Often a physician refers the family to a social worker who works in the hospital (if the patient is hospitalized), in a home for the aged or nursing home, in a senior citizens' center, in a family service agency, in a public housing project, or in private practice.

When they visit a social worker, most families require both information and education about the disease and emotional reassurance and support. It is imperative that the social worker attend to both areas, for providing only one type of assistance will prove ineffective, since it neglects the holistic needs of the caregiver (Turner, 1992).

INDIVIDUAL COUNSELING

Most social work intervention involves individual counseling with the primary caregiver; in this type of counseling, it is important that the social worker keep focused on the caregiver's ability to cope with the daily rigors of caring for the Alzheimer's patient. Family counseling may also be effective in facilitating decision making, and thus may prevent conflicts from emerging over such issues as finances and placement and allow the family members to cathect and resolve feelings that could stand in the way of cooperative behavior.

However, the social worker's main objective is to ensure the well-being of the patient and caregivers and to avoid being sidetracked into dealing with other difficulties in family members' relationships. The social worker should focus on improving the patient's functioning and problem-solving abilities and should not become a sounding board for long-standing unrelated conflicts. The social worker should be internally secure enough to deal with the caregiver's intense feelings of anger and depression and to remain focused on these feelings.

It is important to remember that the social worker also has feelings, and that he or she will experience them during the counseling sessions. All feelings should be accepted nonjudgmentally, and if the social worker has difficulties accepting feelings, then he or she will have problems accepting the caregiver's feelings. The social worker should provide a comfortable and secure haven in which the caregiver can talk openly about the difficulties and can experience, express, and resolve his or her feelings, so that the caregiver's energy is liberated to focus on practical issues (Dr. Eva Philipp, interviewed in Toronto, May 1998).

In addition to providing the necessary clinical support, the social worker is equipped to engage in community intervention, such as referring the patient and caregiver to a local Alzheimer's Society, a support group, outside respite care, in-home respite care, and a day program, if appropriate. Adult day care for patients provides stimulation and socialization, as well as a link to services that maintain or enhance their health status.

Social workers should also utilize their advocacy skills throughout the counseling process on both the individual level and the macro level. Individual advocacy provides caregivers with the courage and the means to regain control and adjust to unpredictable circumstances. By giving support and information, the social worker is in a position to empower patients and families to engage in macro-level activities in relation to policy and care issues through letter-writing campaigns, telephone blitzes, petitions, and visits to government officials and representatives. The personal and political empowerment of caregivers is a key element in the counseling process, since it helps caregivers focus their anger outward toward social change (Turner, 1992).

The social worker also should be in the forefront of meeting the needs of multicultural communities. Currently, the vast majority of information on Alzheimer's disease is available only in English, even though both Canada and the United States are rich, diverse multicultural mosaics. Because Alzheimer's disease affects all cultures and ethnic groups, families, caregivers, and practitioners from every linguistic group must be able to receive information, support, medical assistance, and vital community services in the appropriate language. For many reasons, some ethnic groups often prefer to care for their elderly relatives and utilize the services available solely within their own communities. Also for valid reasons, many ethnic groups are wary of outside interventions from established institutions, community agencies, and other sources that they view as being unsympathetic or insensitive to their unique concerns. It is the role of the social worker to attempt to overcome these barriers, to facilitate the training of culturally appropriate practitioners to provide sensitive information and support, and to promote awareness of multicultural issues and foster attitudinal changes in the society at large. These are challenging tasks, but fortunately several ethnic groups have already begun to initiate steps to deal with Alzheimer's disease in their own environments (Turner, 1992).

POLICY DEVELOPMENT

Social workers also can contribute enormously to policy development, both in institutional settings and in the government. Silverstone & Weiss (1981, cited in Dobrof, 1986, p. 74) indicated that the challenge of the social worker is heightened by the changes that inevitably occur in long-term care, in which "goals are defined by the problem and the needs of the frail impaired client wherever encountered along the continuum."

The involvement and expertise of social workers in the planning, conceptualization, and development of these environments is crucial. Social workers must play key roles in the decision-making and organizational processes to achieve institutional change. They must expand their role from their traditional work with individual clients to include work with the systems and staffs of long-term care facilities in an effort to influence the establishment and maintenance of positive, pleasurable, and supportive environments.

Social workers should also encourage governmental policymakers at all levels to pay serious attention to the looming public-health crisis of Alzheimer's disease in Canada and the United States. As the older population grows, there will be a dramatic increase in the number of Alzheimer's victims, a situation that will have health, social, economic, demographic and political ramifications. Currently 10% of hospitals are occupied by senior citizens, but by the year 2030 this patient population will increase to over 20%. This encouragement can be accomplished through such measures as meeting with politicians at every level of government to educate them about the facts and to alert them to the burgeoning demographic realities of their constituencies. Informational meetings can be held in the community; articles can be written for major as well as community-based newspapers. Written briefs can be presented to parliamentary and legislative committees on the impact of the disease as well as outlining the services required, in addition to using all media through interviews and publicizing events focusing on Alzheimer's disease, such as Alzheimer's Awareness Month, which occurs in Canada each January. Social workers can make themselves available to various government ministries involved in policy development and offer to serve on committees and task forces. Social workers and their clients can become involved during election campaigns and can ask potential candidates running for elected office what resources they intend to make available for the research, treatment, and care of Alzheimer's disease. Governments in a pluralistic democracy have an obligation to arbitrate among many different societal interests, but it is difficult to capture the attention, interest, and financial commitment of politicians and policymakers. However, the costs of ignoring this silent epidemic will be exorbitant. Social workers, employing their array of advocacy skills, must mobilize patients, caregivers, and allied health professionals to insist that governments provide much greater funding for such areas as long-term care facilities, hospital beds, respite and in-home respite care, day care centers, transportation, and biomedical and psychosocial research. The future well-being of tens of thousands of Canadians and Americans will literally depend on it.

The stigma associated with Alzheimer's disease is still evident, although the situation is changing, thanks to the work of public education programs and the Alzheimer's Societies. The future with regard to Alzheimer's disease is grim yet hopeful. Despite the pain, loss, and tragedy that lie in its wake, there is hope because of recent medical discoveries throughout the world and because of the caring, compassion, strength, and concern shown by caregivers, citizens, families, and friends.

The profession of social work, armed with a theoretical base and practical understanding of the biopsychosocial dimensions of human behavior, combined with a wealth of knowledge of community-based resources and services, is poised to make this unbearable situation brighter and more tolerable. There are challenges that must be faced, but social workers, steeped in a commitment to human values, will be in the forefront of caregiving and in the vanguard of institutional and societal change (Turner, 1992).

REFERENCES

Alzheimer's Disease and Related Disorders Association (ADRDA). (1997a). *Is it Alzheimer's? Warning signs you should know.* Chicago: Author.

Alzheimer's Disease and Related Disorders Association (ADRDA). (1997b). *Memory and aging.* Chicago: Author.

Alzheimer's Disease and Related Disorders Association (ADRDA). (1997c). *Signs to watch for: Steps to take.* Chicago: Author.

Alzheimer's Disease and Related Disorders Association (ADRDA). (1997d). *Steps to enhancing communication.* Chicago: Author.

Alzheimer's Disease and Related Disorders Association (ADRDA). (1997e). *Steps to planning activities.* Chicago: Author.

Alzheimer's Disease and Related Disorders Association (ADRDA). (1997f). *You can make a difference: Ten ways to help an Alzheimer family.* Chicago: Author.

Alzheimer Society of Canada. (1991). *Just for you: For people diagnosed with Alzheimer disease.* Toronto: Author.

Alzheimer Society for Metropolitan Toronto. (1996). Home support services help keep people in their homes. *The Alzheimer Alert.* Toronto: Author.

Alzheimer's update: Caregivers suffer from behavioural problems, too. (1994). *The Medical Post* (Canada), April 12.

Aronson, M. K. (1988). *Understanding Alzheimer's disease: What it is, how to cope with it, future directions.* Gen. Ed.: Alzheimer's Disease and Related Diseases Association. New York: Macmillan Publishing Company.

Bayley, G. (1996). The commonsense approach to Alzheimer's. *Patient Care Canada 7,* 1, January.

Caroline, M. *Alzheimer disease: Unraveling the mystery.* Bethesda, MD: National Institute on Aging. Public Information Office.

Cutler, N. R., & Stramek, J. T. (1996). *Understanding Alzheimer's disease.* Jackson, MS: University Press of Mississippi.

Davidson, F. G. (1996). *The Alzheimer sourcebook for caregivers: A practical guide for getting through the day.* Los Angeles: Lowell House.

Diagnosis of Alzheimer's disease. (1997). *Postgraduate Medicine* (Canada), 1, 1, 6, June.

Dippel, R. L., & Hulton, T. (1991). *Caring for the Alzheimer patient.* Buffalo, NY: Prometheus Books.

Dobrof, R., ed. (1986). *Social work and Alzheimer's disease: Practice issues with victims and their families.* New York: Haworth.

Ganesan, R., Standish, T., Mollow, D. W., Darzins, P., & Orange, J. B. (1994). *Canadian Family Physician, 40,* June.

Harvard Health Letter. (1996). Alzheimer's disease. Boston: Harvard Medical School Publishing Group.

Kociol, L., & Schiff, M. (1985). *Alzheimer: A Canadian family resource guide.* Toronto: McGraw-Hill Ryerson.

Lobray, D. (1995). Alzheimer disease. *Community Health,* May–June.

Philipp, Dr. Eva. (1998). Interviewed by chapter author. Toronto, May.

Roberts, D. J. (1991). *Taking care of caregivers: For families and others who care for people with Alzheimer's disease and other forms of dementia.* Palo Alto, CA: Bell Publishing Group.

Turner, F. (1992). *Mental health and the elderly: A social work perspective.* New York: The Free Press.

10

PSYCHOPHYSIOLOGIC DISORDERS

Mary S. Sheridan and Karen Kline

P sychosomatic illnesses raise fundamental questions about why people become sick and what can be done about it. Clinicians are used to a linear medical model: dysfunction generates symptoms, symptoms lead to diagnosis, and diagnosis decides treatment. Attempts to understand psychosomatic illness often lead into a labyrinth. Scientific knowledge and ignorance, and ideas about self, others, religion, philosophy, ethics, and even reality itself must be explored. The simple becomes so complex that we speak about it authoritatively at our own peril. Nor are the issues limited to the body and mind of the sick person. Families, cultures, and social issues create, maintain, prevent, and treat illness. These considerations make psychosomatic illness an especially appropriate field for social work study and intervention.

Terminology

The term *psychophysiologic disorder* properly denotes any illness in which mind and body interact. The authors of this chapter believe that mind and body cannot be separated, and thus that all illness is psychophysiological; the psychological aspects of physical illness must be understood, just as the physical aspects of mental illness must be understood. Health care professionals acknowledge this view (Lask, 1996) but in practice usually give it no more than lip service.

Western culture perceives the physical as real, but is less sure about the nonphysical. To the average person, health care professional or not, *psychosomatic* still means an illness that is imaginary—"all in the head," a sign of personal pathology or weakness (Courts & Bartol, 1996). Even professional nurses were unable to agree on a definition of *psychosomatic* (Bartol & Eakes, 1995). In medicine, only verifiable symptoms from an organic cause are viewed as fully valid. A more useful approach is to recognize that psychosomatic illness involves both mind (*psyche*) and body (*soma*). Thus, psychosomatic illness is a range of possibilities. A "psychogenic continuum" includes illness entirely caused by internal conflict, illness that involves a physical predisposition plus stress, organic illness that has psychological effects, and all possible points between. Any illness can be located on this continuum from psychogenic to somatogenic (Sheridan & Kline, 1984). According to this approach, all illnesses are combinations of physical and nonphysical factors. More important, the resources of the body become available to the mind, and the resources of the mind become available to the body. This is consistent with social work's emphasis on strengths and empowerment. Lask (1996) asks:

> In what conceivable way can it be helpful to our patients to continue to differentiate organic from psychosomatic (or for that matter somatoform, somatization, psychogenic, or psychophysiological) disorders? What we should be doing is practicing "psychosomatic medicine," as defined by Lipowski so many years ago: "the scientific study of the relation among psychological, social and biological factors in determining health and disease" . . . rather than perpetuating false dichotomies. . . . It is sad that nearly 20 years later we need to be reminded that our task is to pay due attention to each of these processes at all times, whatever the presentation and course of the disorder. (p. 459)

This chapter will discuss: (a) the physical illnesses considered to result from disordered mental processes (*psychogenic* illness); (b) common psychological challenges to coping for persons with physical (*somatogenic*) illness and for their families; and (c) situations of unclear etiology. All these situations are subtypes of *psychophysiological illness*. Social work approaches will be suggested for each category.

Social work's "person in environment" problem-solving model allows consideration of both mental and physical aspects of disease. The social worker can serve as an advocate for a perspective that locates both problems and solutions in a variety of systems. The traditional health care approach to psychosomatic disease has been to apply physical treatments to physical disorders and psychological treatments to psychological disorders. However, this presumes that we can separate the two easily. This is not so! Many mistakes have been made over the years. For example, the effects of a disease have often been confused with its causes. It has also been assumed that the same cause (whether psychosocial or physical) always produces the same symptoms in the same way.

More modern approaches recognize that diseases also affect emotions in ways that may look causal, and that multifactorial causation is complex and chaotic. It is not always easy to categorize diseases as psychogenic or somatogenic; both physical and mental treatments may be appropriate for both physical and mental disorders. Two principles guide safe work in this area: first, when physical symptoms are present, there should be close collaboration between social workers and physicians, and second, one should always keep an open mind.

Psychogenic Disease: Physical Illness Resulting from Mental Processes

In psychogenic disease, there must be strong evidence that physical symptoms are linked to unconscious psychological factors or conflicts. (Failure to find a physical cause is not sufficient to make this diagnosis.) It is important to remember that these illnesses are not under the voluntary control of the patient—the conflicts or the mechanism generating the disease are unconscious. In this, they differ from malingering (voluntary symptom production or exaggeration) and factitious (self-induced) symptoms. These have conscious goals in the individual's environment—e.g., attention or the prospect of material gain. By contrast, patients with a psychogenic disease may have a false but sincere and persistent belief that they are sick. They may have unconsciously created symptoms to express conflicts. Or they may be preoccupied with the possibility of disease and thus overattend to normal physical phenomena. Often they are anxious or depressed. Occasionally they have a delusional system. Following adequate medical evaluation of symptoms, the physician and social worker can reassure the patient that no physical disease has been found. If this is ineffective, further counseling may be undertaken. Currently, desensitization (treating the hypochondriasis as a phobia) or cognitive/educational strategies have become more popular. Patients are taught that their symptoms may be distressing, but are not severe. Their job is to "tune out" the symptoms. If they succeed, they may then be able to work on underlying problems (Kellner, 1992). Saarmann (1992) suggests that if reassurance fails and the patient lacks insight, the patient can at least be told that serious disorders have been ruled out. The patient can be given a simple physiological explanation for symptoms (e.g., "tension" headache), and should be directed to a single practitioner who will coordinate all medical care.

Case Example: Psychogenic Illness

An 18-year-old single woman, Ms. V, came to a community mental health center and was seen by a social worker. She spoke of depression, extreme anxiety, and many physical conditions from which she had suffered for the past few years. She had severe headaches, heart palpitations, nausea, and sleep disturbance. Her family physician found no physical reason for the difficulties. The social worker asked Ms. V to see the clinic psychiatrist for further discussion of the physical complaints and for evaluation of the need for antidepressant medication.

In therapy with the social worker, Ms. V could talk about her depression. In time, she recognized that her headaches were worse during periods of tension in the family. She acknowledged her low self-esteem and constant need to receive reassurance from the people close to her. Ms. V. could transfer some of her needs to the social worker and could learn healthier ways to relate to her family. As she gained insight and management skills, Ms. V's symptoms diminished. When she understood them to be a learned reaction to stress, she was less frightened. She could put more energy into getting her needs met in better ways.

Psychogenic diseases may present dramatically or, as here, take the form of subacute maladies experienced by everyone. Ms. V's difficulty functioning in everyday roles and her degree of distress marked this case as appropriate for intervention. The worker first made sure that physical factors had been ruled out. Once the worker had received this assurance, she could engage Ms. V in a reflective consideration of her life situation. This included a look at her symptoms to see what they could tell her about herself. This reflective discussion—the exploration of life issues and their relation to medical symptoms—was not very different from what it would have been if Ms. V had a chronic illness or a nonphysical problem. The focus was on the whole situation, the here-and-now, not on symptoms and their etiology.

Today, because of popular books and talk shows, some patients will be willing to consider the idea that physical problems are caused or made worse by emotion. To accept that this is happening in themselves, however, and to change their behavior accordingly may be very different issues!

Because there is a good deal of uncertainty in this area, social workers can help by taking a middle position: "Let us work together on the emotional side of these issues, while you and your physician work on the physical. We can try many different things and see what benefits you."

Interactions between mind and body are complex and still debated. There is substantial evidence that the classical "psychosomatic" diseases (e.g., colitis, high blood pressure, ulcers, asthma, etc.) are not simply physical representations of specific psychological conflicts. In recent years researchers have found physical mechanisms for many of these diseases. (It is still possible that psychological factors are "behind" the physical/neural mechanisms, or that multiple or variable causes—including emotional factors—contribute to diseases [Moran, 1991].)

Because of the stigma attached to psychosomatic and mental illness, the physician or social worker may have difficulty convincing clients that counseling will be useful. Clients often believe that the symptom is physical. They may have an unconscious need for it. Consequently, many individuals with psychological components to their illness do not receive appropriate treatment.

In the initial interview with the patient manifesting psychosomatic illness, the social worker should not attempt to break down defenses. The focus should be on the frustrations of living with illness and what this means to the individual. The interviewer should be empathetic, not confronting (Pankrantz & Glaudin, 1980). Watzlawick, et al. (1974) write: "In helping the psychosomatic patient cooperate with assessment and treatment, the experienced clinician is ever mindful of the threatening nature of this material, the importance of minimizing defensiveness, and the value of using the patient's own language to promote agreement and subsequent change." Sometimes clients are open to the idea that "stress," "nerves," or other emotions are making them sick. In any case, "It is important to see clients as they see themselves and to deal with the person as a whole rather than as a conglomeration of 'real' and 'imaginary' symptoms" (Hossenlopp & Holland, 1977).

The initial interview lets the worker investigate underlying psychosocial problems. Questions about the frustration and loneliness of illness and its effect on family members may uncover depression, frustration, interpersonal difficulties, or secondary gain. This information is essential in assessing the individual's situation.

As treatment progresses and the defenses weaken, discussion can move to the interaction between the individual's psychosocial situation and the illness. The client can be helped to deal better with stress and to express the emotions relating to stressors in more productive ways. As the relationship of stress to the symptoms comes into the client's conscious awareness, physical symptoms tend to decrease in both frequency and intensity (Hossenlopp & Holland, 1977). However, it is not unusual for the individual with psychogenic symptoms to terminate treatment prematurely if the elicited material is too threatening. Thus, every contact with the individual should be a helping experience focused on what can be accomplished here and now.

Somatogenic Disease

Physical illness, especially when it is serious, threatens the integrity of the self. If the challenge of adult life is to preserve continuity through change, this goal is even more problematic in illness. Medical and surgical procedures assault and may even change the body image. Following an amputation, the diagnosis of terminal illness, or the discovery of diabetes, patients must confront themselves in new ways, which will differ with each individual. Their families must also adjust to changed relatives, and will have their own anxieties and concerns.

Adaptation never occurs in a vacuum. Whether a patient emerges from illness diminished, enhanced, or unchanged depends on personality structure, previous coping experiences, and present conditions. The supports available in the family, hospital, and community also affect adaptation. Depression, increased dependence, and impaired self-esteem are common problems, since our society values independence so highly. However, the experience of illness is not always negative. Attention, expressions of caring, and freedom from daily life stresses often accompany it. Illness frequently brings people into contact with others around them and with their own philosophical, emotional, and spiritual beliefs. It may, then, be a source of growth and affirmation, or contain both positive and negative elements.

Care of Patients with Physical Illness

Social work tasks with diagnosed physical illness commonly include the following:

1. *Assistance with feeling issues.* Allowing and encouraging patients and family members to express feelings about illness is the most traditional

form of medical social work. The social worker listens, encourages insight, and promotes both cognitive and emotional understanding. Patients who are socially isolated, introspective, for whom the illness has great personal meaning, or who have not shared feelings before may benefit greatly from this service. Family members' needs are often overlooked in the focus upon the sick person. They also appreciate having their feelings understood and legitimized. Health care can be so objective and focused on symptoms that the presence of someone genuinely concerned about the patient's *experience* is often welcome.

A social worker sat with Mr. Izumi, an elderly cancer patient, while he was receiving chemotherapy. The social worker's simple comment, "Having cancer must be difficult for you," unleashed a flood of feelings. Tears came to Mr. Izumi's eyes as he described his worries about his own future and how his wife might cope if the illness progressed. He told the social worker that he had never shared these feelings with anyone before, as his cultural heritage encouraged stoic behavior. Later he introduced the social worker to his daughters as "the lady who helped me so much."

Although many popular lecturers and authors stress the importance of a positive and optimistic attitude in recovery from serious illnesses such as cancer, this is controversial. Many assertions about cancer etiology and prognosis are not supported by high-quality empirical evidence (Levenson & Bemis, 1991). Patients who are optimistic and remain interested in the world or display a "fighting spirit" are more likely to have a good quality of life whatever the outcome. Social workers should teach and support affirmations, visualization, meditation, and other forms of self-help. However, they should be presented as adjunctive, not curative. Patients should not blame themselves if these do not provide relief or if the disease progresses or recurs (Rittenberg, 1995).

Not every patient or family member needs or appreciates the opportunity to share feelings. Some patients are highly defended against feelings, or simply have no pressing need for ventilation now. Others have friends and family who provide sufficient support. In today's environment of cost-conscious, "downsized" health care, the skilled service of simply listening to troubled patients is becoming a luxury. Social workers must look at their own institutions and consider the patient's wishes and best interests, balancing these against their other duties. The authors believe, however, that social workers ought to defend their historic role of helping patients to understand and cope with the feelings associated with illness.

2. *Support to patients and family members during illness-related crises.* By definition, this kind of crisis is a temporary upset in normal functioning, often associated with an unusual and upsetting occurrence. In times of crisis, clients or family members are overwhelmed by feelings. Often their coping resources are diminished to the point that they cannot deal with necessary practical tasks. Social workers can help patients and family members understand the emotions associated with the crisis and cope with decisions that must be made. Social workers can also watch for and help with feelings that are potentially problematic.

Mr. and Mrs. Williams were on their "second honeymoon" when Mr. Williams suffered a heart attack while swimming at Waikiki. He was taken to the hospital in an ambulance, with cardiopulmonary resuscitation in progress. The social worker met Mrs. Williams at the door of the emergency department. The worker kept her informed of efforts to save Mr. Williams's life, and gathered necessary information. She assisted Mrs. Williams with phone calls, and was present when the physician informed her that Mr. Williams had died. The worker hugged Mrs. Williams as she cried, went with her to view her husband's body, and remained through the routine police interview. Later the social worker helped Mrs. Williams to inform her children and to make arrangements to fly Mr. Williams's body home. Mrs. Williams was a competent woman with good coping skills. During this crisis, however, she needed emotional support and practical information.

---

3. *Information about feelings normally associated with the diagnosis or situation.* Education is often an important part of social work practice in health care. Providing anticipatory or concurrent information about feelings can improve patients' and families' coping abilities. As emotions associated with illness can be unexpected or counterintuitive, the guidance of a knowledgeable and experienced social worker may help resolve problems.

Mr. and Mrs. Gonzalez had experienced the loss through Sudden Infant Death Syndrome (SIDS) of their second baby. At the support group meeting, Mrs. Gonzalez complained that her husband was not grieving properly. She cried; he did not. She wanted nothing to do with sex, feeling it was disrespectful to the child that was lost. Mr. Gonzalez wanted to try for another baby as quickly as possible. The social worker explained that these kinds of differences are often seen, and that people grieve in different ways. The worker asked other couples at the meeting to discuss their different styles of grieving. Building on their contributions, the worker helped all the families to see that different ways of showing grief were equally valid. At the next group meeting, Mr. and Mrs. Gonzales reported that this explanation and discussion had decreased the tension at home.

4. *Assistance with the practical details of living with physical illness, especially when referral to community resources is involved.* With today's increased emphasis on decreasing the costs of health care, social workers have assumed significant responsibility for discharge planning—which has also become more complex. Patients are going home with more health care needs. The agencies that meet these needs, and their regulations, are constantly changing. Social workers have the knowledge and skill to help families navigate difficult systems. Social workers also help staff coordinate logistics and sort out ethics. A full discussion of discharge planning is beyond the scope of this chapter. It should be said, however, that workers should not allow discharge planning to become an automatic function that bypasses social work values and patient/family advocacy. An institution's focus on expedient discharge should not be allowed to crowd out other roles for social work.

Mr. Moore suffered a devastating stroke. After two weeks of hospitalization, a resident physician said that hospital policy "required" that Mr. Moore go home immediately, or his son would become financially liable for his bill. The son and his family reluctantly took Mr. Moore into their home, in spite of a long-standing poor relationship. A unit secretary arranged home care nursing and respite care, with little information exchanged. Mr. Moore proved to be a difficult patient at home. He would obey the directions of the nurse when she was there, but would not cooperate with his family. Although his gait was unstable, he insisted that his son could not tell him what to do, and that he "would rather fall" than walk with his walker. There were many battles that ended with the son's wife in tears, the son's children resentful, and the son confused about where his duty lay. Within a few days Mr. Moore did fall, requiring rehospitalization.

A senior social worker was asked to meet with this family, now labeled "difficult" and "uncooperative" by home care staff. The social worker discussed with the family the hospital's policy on aggressive discharge. He also clarified that, under state law, the son could *not* be held financially liable for his father's care. The social worker explored the family's resources and their understanding of Mr. Moore's condition. He discovered that they had unrealistic expectations for recovery and arranged a conference for them with the neurologist. This was the first time the family had spoken with the attending physician, and the social worker facilitated thorough and realistic information exchange. Based on this and Mr. Moore's continuing refusal to cooperate with his son, the family decided that nursing-home placement was the only alternative. This was a difficult decision for the son, who had hoped that his relationship with his father would improve. The social worker helped him see that the father's safety was at stake, and that their own family well-being was also important. With the social worker's assistance, the family located a good nursing home and applied for Medicaid benefits on Mr. Moore's behalf. The social worker also used this case as an opportunity to discuss with hospital staff the need to give accurate information to families and agencies.

5. Improving the environment in which physical illness is treated. Social workers should be alert for environmental or staff conditions that might be causing patient stress and thus hindering recovery. For example, if there is no natural lighting in an intensive care unit, patients may become disoriented as to time. A clock that also differentiates day from night may reduce this source of stress. On another level, if staff tensions spill over into patient care the social worker can intervene, or at least to bring this situation to the attention of management.

Psychophysiological Diseases, and Diseases of Unclear Etiology

In many conditions physical changes are far more marked than in psychogenic disease, yet there is an enduring suspicion that emotions are also involved. There has been much debate about whether certain illnesses are purely psychogenic, purely somatogenic, or a combination of the two. If a combination, how is the illness produced? The current belief is that both emotional factors and underlying physical predisposition contribute to some (not fully specified) disease states. Both the emotions and the physical conditions probably have a synergistic effect (Koo, 1995). This suggests new roles for social workers in prevention and intervention. Applying mental health insights to these conditions in challenging.

A growing body of literature suggests that stress and other emotional factors can influence susceptibility to illness, perhaps through the mechanism of neurotransmitters (Biondi & Zannino, 1997; Lechin, et al., 1996). For example, one study deliberately exposed volunteers to viruses associated with the common cold. Even with other factors held constant, those volunteers with few social ties were found more likely to become ill than the volunteers with many social ties (Cohen, Doyle, et al., 1997). The field of "psychoneuroimmunology" has developed to study these interactions (Cohen & Herbert, 1996).

There is a well-documented association between hostility and heart disease (Miller, et al., 1996). Acute or chronic stress is implicated in heart attacks and other forms of cardiovascular disease (Niaura & Goldstein, 1992). Lack of social support is also implicated in gastrointestinal ulcers (Fukunishi, Hosaka, et al., 1996; Fukunishi, Kajr, 1997). High blood pressure may be related to stress, particularly stress that is not acknowledged by the patient (Nyklicek, et al., 1996). Emotional suppression may be associated with the development of cancer, and pessimism may decrease survival in patients with cancer and AIDS (Scheier & Bridges, 1995). Animal studies suggest that stress raises blood sugar levels in Type II diabetes (Surwit & Williams, 1996). Programs to provide social support or stress management can help manage cardiovascular diseases (Williams & Littman, 1996), and perhaps other forms of medical illness (Saravay, 1996). However, diseases other than cardiovascular ones have not been studied as extensively, and practitioners must also be careful not to "blame the victim." Other physical factors, as yet undefined, may be implicated in these results.

Beyond their work with patients, families, groups, and staffs, social workers are often involved in community organizational and educational efforts to make systemic change. This change could reduce tensions in the environment as a whole, and thus have the effect of preventing tension-induced illness. For example, providing more support to working parents may reduce their own risk of stress-related illness and decrease the risk of abuse to their children. Overcoming oppression and discrimination would reduce frustration and hostility as well as stress (see Taylor, et al., 1997). Social workers should be alert for opportunities to support legislation or policy changes, to write, to conduct research (including documentation of the efficacy of psychosocial treatment), to support professional organizations and serve on their boards, to supervise field students, and to teach about health care issues and methods in schools of social work. If they are unable to engage in these activities personally, they may have opportunities to support organizations or individuals engaged in change efforts.

Behaviors such as smoking, use of alcohol or drugs, or malnutrition (including eating disorders and overnutrition) predispose to many diseases (Stoudemire & Hale, 1991). Such behaviors, and the feelings that underlie them, can be a useful target for social work intervention. Other illnesses are complicated by a lack of health care or poor compliance with health care; diabetes, hypertension, and asthma are just examples of illnesses in this category. Many psychosocial factors contribute to poor health care and poor compliance. These factors are appropriate targets of social work preventive and interventive actions.

There is increasing evidence that some conditions cause permanent changes to the brain. Abuse or extreme deprivation in early childhood and trauma at any age may cause permanent alteration in potential or functioning. This may be expressed behaviorally or through chronic physical conditions; for example, some pain syndromes are found more frequently in those with a history of abuse (Drossman, et al., 1995; Curran, et al., 1995). Even relatively mild brain injury (e.g., postconcussion syndrome) may lead to lasting impairment of cognitive function. Social workers have a role in working with victims of these conditions, but an equally important role in prevention of the social factors that place brains and emotions at risk.

Historically, many diseases were attributed to emotions until their precise physiological mechanisms were discovered. As already stated, many people believe that the disease is not "real" until the physical mechanism is found (Morrison, 1997). This history should make us cautions as we consider current debates over whether chronic fatigue syndrome, multiple chemical sensitivities, and Gulf War syndrome are or are not "real." In chronic fatigue, patients experience a debilitating sense of exhaustion frequently associated with decreased cognitive clarity. Chronic fatigue syndrome often follows a viral illness. In multiple chemical sensitivity (environmental hypersensitivity), patients experience debilitating "allergies" to low levels of many common chemicals. There is some overlap between the two syndromes, which may be so severe that patients are disabled (Moutschen, et al., 1994; Sparks, et al., 1994).

Both physical and psychological causes have been suggested for these disorders. Methodological problems are frequent in the research done on these disorders, making it even more difficult to form conclusions. Although psychological features do appear frequently as part of these disorders, it is difficult to know whether they are causal. They could also result from the illness process itself, or the losses that the patients experience due to the illness (Davidoff & Fogarty, 1994).

Social workers who believe in the legitimacy of these entities—whether that legitimacy derives from physiology or psychology—may apply their skills to advocacy, community organization, and empowerment. Public education is also necessary, so that all sufferers in need of care have an opportunity to get their needs met. When treating patients with such disorders, the social worker may find it useful to graph out the psychosomatic continuum already described.

Social workers involved with individuals who have mixed disease states must be aware of the "murky" nature of this field, and must keep their minds open to many possibilities. Respect for the client's experiences and perceptions is vital. This does not mean that the worker must uncritically accept the client's point of view, but that both together should be engaged in a process of inquiry. Again, the psychosomatic continuum can be used to identify situations in which psychological factors may be causing illness or psychological interventions can make the situation better. Particularly when there is no psychiatrist on site, the social worker in a health care setting may function as the front-line mental health professional. Deciding whether a problem is primarily psychological, primarily physical, or a mixture of both requires advanced assessment skills and sometimes a bit of detective work.

Mrs. P, a 78-year-old woman with dementia, entered a nursing home when her family could no longer care for her. Her physician also prescribed a medication designed to decrease her mental confusion. Within a few days she was much more confused, combative, and frightened to eat the food because it might be "poisoned." The social worker was asked to see her. Did this represent a psychological reaction to placement, an attempt to manipulate her family, increased confusion due to a change in environment, or other factors? As part of her assessment process, the social worker checked the description of all Mrs. P's medications in a standard reference book. It showed paranoid psychosis as an uncommon side effect of the new medication. The social worker contacted the physician, who immediately discontinued the medication. She also asked nursing home staff to be especially attentive and reassuring to Mrs. P. Within a few days, she was much more comfortable in the nursing home.

Factitious Disorder

Sometimes patients present themselves as sick when they are not, cause their own symptoms, or induce their own illness. This behavior is called *Munchausen syndrome* or *factitious disorder* when there does not appear to be any tangible psychosocial gain and the patient seems to get gratification from being sick. *Malingering* is the term used when patients create, exaggerate, or prolong illness to receive tangible gain (e.g., an insurance settlement or disability benefit). Not infrequently, drug addiction is a motivator when patients are seeking specific prescriptions for controlled substances because of "pain." Parents may also feign or create illness in their children; this is known as *Munchausen Syndrome by Proxy* or *Factitious Disorder by Proxy* (Levin & Sheridan, 1995).

A man came to the emergency department complaining of urinary obstruction. He was catheterized and a large amount of urine was drained. He was admitted to the hospital because of other elements in his health history, and a full urinary tract evaluation was begun. All tests proved normal. Later, an emergency room physician who also worked at another hospital recognized the patient. The physician said that this man moved from hospital to hospital, always telling colorful tales about his health and appearing to enjoy the attention to his genitals. The wandering and "tall tales" are typical of factitious disorder, although the sexual element is not.

When deception is possible—which actually means in all situations—social workers should be open to the possibility that things are not as they seem. The social worker's role as patient advocate does not extend to uncritical acceptance of everything that a patient says. A typical presentation by deceptive patients includes: a very convincing story, pieces not fitting together on closer inspection or testing, reliance on the patient for history (records "lost," patient from out of town, etc.) and an often dramatic symptom that cannot be ignored. Deceptive patients present legal and administrative challenges, but ordinarily are not amenable to therapy (though they may pretend to be). Sometimes there is an ingratiating or flattering quality to their story. Managing potential deception includes alertness when situations do not add up, helping to obtain history and old records, and assisting in case management and coordination. Confrontation should be undertaken only with caution, consultation, and a security plan. Staff who have been taken in by deceptive patients often need an opportunity to ventilate or understand more about the dynamics of deception.

Issues in Social Work Treatment of Psychosomatic Disorders

In treating clients with suspected psychosomatic disorders, it is imperative to underline that diagnosis is always dynamic. Organic problems are not always clear-cut, and all clinicians should remain humble and open to new information. Physicians and social workers should develop collegial relationships and work together. Pankratz and Glaudin (1980) observed that, even when negative medical results have been received, mental health clinicians cannot be sure that psychological intervention will be sufficient and that no medical intervention will be necessary.

Whatever the disease entity or work setting, an approach that stresses "here and now" is preferable to one focused on blame. Without excluding medical care, social workers can be pragmatic, focusing on whatever is effective in relieving symptoms.

Social workers most often use individual work with patients who have psychogenic illness. Groups composed of patients and/or families in similar situations can also be useful. Such groups may have educational, therapeutic, or other goals. Social workers also serve as consultants for individual patients or broader issues of patient care.

If social workers are outside health care institutions, effective services to patients with psychogenic symptoms require good relationships with medical consultants. Workers need not be defensive about their lack of medical knowledge, since physicians are often equally ignorant about social work. Mutually respectful communication is the answer.

Of course, social workers never advise beyond their competence and scope of practice about specific medical or surgical treatment, but refer such questions to the patient's physician. It is also unprofessional to undermine patient relationships with their physicians, although at times it is necessary to suggest that patients consider a change. Nor should social workers endorse unproven methods of treatment or attempt treatments that they are not competent to carry out. Finally, while workers may encourage clients to maintain a positive attitude toward their illness, stoicism in the face of undiagnosed or undertreated pain is not appropriate. Painful symptoms always call for medical evaluation and appropriate therapy. Within these broad guidelines, there is great scope for creativity.

The focus of study about psychosomatic illness has shifted from the origins of disease to the psychological elements associated with the course of illness and recovery or adaptation. Wholistic ideas are helping to reunite mind and body. This has led to an expansion of the field of psychosomatic illness to include all illnesses, since all diseases have emotional implications for patients and their families.

Social workers have largely neglected the field of psychophysiological illness. A review of ten years (1988–1997) of *Social Work Abstracts* revealed only a handful of articles on that subject written by social workers or appearing in social work journals. The most pertinent article found was H. L. Kaila's "Psychosomatic Problems and Social Support: Perceptions of Women Whose Husbands Are Abroad on Job" (1996). This study points out an important potential field of research for social workers: the role of social stressors in psychosomatic illness.

Important questions for social work research also relate to the psychological effect of illness on the patient. For instance, to what extent do different illnesses create unique psychological difficulties? How might this change over time? Informally, for example, it appears that many women are not as distressed about mastectomy today as women were 20 or 30 years ago. Is this true? If so, is it the result of more options, the changing role of women in society, or other factors? How could this insight be generalized to other diseases? What influences do cultural and sociological factors have on the presentation of, or the adjustment to, illness? What are the costs of new policies that return patients to their families "sicker and quicker," limit mental health or substance abuse benefits, or build narrow gateways to care? Social workers have both the opportunity and the obligation to help answer these questions.

REFERENCES

Bartol, G. M., & Eakes, G. G. (1995). A study of the meanings assigned to the term psychosomatic among health professionals. *Perspectives in Psychiatric Care, 31,* 1, 25–29.

Biondi, M., & Zannino, L. G. (1997). Psychological stress, neuroimmunomodulation, and susceptibility to infectious diseases in animals and man: a review. *Psychotherapy and Psychosomatics, 66,* 3–26.

Cohen, S., & Herbert, T. B. (1996). Health psychology: Psychological factors and physical disease from the perspective of human psychoneuroimmunology. *Annual Review of Psychology, 47,* 113–142.

Cohen, S., Doyle, W. J., Skoner, D. P., Rabin, B. S., & Gwaltney, J. M. (1997). Social ties and susceptibility to the common cold. *Journal of the American Medical Asociation, 277,* 24, 1940–1944.

Courts N. F., & Bartol, G. M. (1996). Psychosomatic: Connotations for people who are neither nurses nor physicians. *Clinical Nursing Research, 5,* 3, 283–293.

Curran, S. L., Sherman, J. J., Cunningham, L. L., Okeson, J. P., Reid, K. L., & Carlson C. R. (1995). Physical and sexual abuse among orofacial pain patients: Linkages with pain and psychologic distress. *Journal of Orofacial Pain, 9,* 4, 340–346.

Davidoff, A. L., & Fogarty, L. (1994). Psychogenic origins of multiple chemical sensitivities syndrome: A critical review of the research literature. *Archives of Environmental Health, 49,* 5, 316–324.

Drossman, D. A., Talley, N. J., Leserman, J., Olden, K. W., & Barreiro, M. A. (1995). Sexual and physical abuse and gastrointestinal illness. *Annuals of Internal Medicine, 123,* 10, 782–794.

Fukunishi, I., Hosaka, T., & Rahe, R. H. (1996). Are abnormal gastrofiberscopic findings related to hostility with poor social support or to negative responses to stress? *Journal of Psychosomatic Research, 41,* 337–342.

Fukunishi, I., Kaji, N., & Hosaka, T. (1997). Relationship of alexithymia and poor social support to ulcerative changes on gastrofigerscopy. *Psychosomatics, 38,* 20–26.

Hossenlopp, C. M., & Holland, J. (1977). Ambulatory patients with medical and psychiatric illness care in a special medical clinic. *International Journal of Psychiatric Medicine, 8,* 1–11.

Kaila, H. L. (1996). Psychosomatic problems and social support: Perceptions of women whose husbands are abroad on job. *The Indian Journal of Social Work, 57,* 2, 245–258.

Kellner, R. (1992). Diagnosis and treatments of hypochondriacal syndromes. *Psychosomatics, 33,* 3, 278–286.

Koo, J. Y. M. (1995). Psychological factors in skin disorders. *Patient Care, 29,* 77–79, 83–85, 89.

Lask, B. (1996). "Psychosomatic medicine" *not* "psychosomatic disorders." *Journal of Psychosomatic Research, 40,* 457–459.

Lechin, F., van der Dijs, B., & Lechin, M. E. (1996). Plasma neurotransmitters and functional illness. *Psychotherapy and Psychosomatics, 65,* 293–318.

Levenson, J. L., & Bemis, C. (1991). The role of psychological factors in cancer onset and progression. *Psychosomatics, 32,* 2, 124–132.

Levin, A. V., & Sheridan, M. S. (1995). *Munchausen syndrome by proxy: Issues in diagnosis and treatment.* New York: Lexington Books.

Miller, T. Q., Smith, T. W., & Turner, C. W. (1996). A meta-analytic review of research on hostility and physical health. *Psychological Bulletin, 119,* 322–348.

Moran, M. G. (1991). Psychological factors affecting pulmonary and rheumatologic diseases. *Psychosomatics, 32,* 1, 14–21.

Morrison, J. (1997). *When psychological problems mask medical disorders.* New York: The Guilford Press.

Moutschen, M., Triffaux, J. M., Demonty, J., Legros, J. J., & Lefebvre, P. J. (1994). Pathogenic tracks in fatigue syndromes. *Acta Clinica Belgica, 49,* 6, 274–289.

Niaura, R., & Goldstein, M. G. (1992). Psychological factors affecting physical condition. Coronary artery disease and sudden death and hypertension. *Psychosomatics, 33,* 2, 147–153.

Nyklicek, I., Bingerhoets, J. J., & Van Heck, G. L. (1996). Hypertension and objective and self-reported stressor exposure: a review. *Journal of Psychosomatic Research, 40,* 585–601.

Pankrantz, L. D., & Glaudin, V. (1980). Psychosomatic disorders. In R. H. Woody (Ed.), *Encyclopedia of clinical assessment* (pp. 148–168). San Francisco: Jossey-Bass.

Rittenberg, C. N. (1995). Positive thinking: An unfair burden for cancer patients? *Support Care Cancer, 3,* 1, 37–39.

Saarmann, L. (1992). Is it live or is it Memorex? Dealing with patients with somatoform or factitious disorders in the emergency department. *Topics in Emergency Medicine, 14,* 4, 43–45.

Saravay, S. M. (1996). Psychiatric interventions in the medically ill. Outcome and effectiveness research. *Psychiatric Clinics of North America, 19,* 467–480.

Scheier, M. F., & Bridges, M. W. (1995). Person variables and health: Personality predispositions and acute psychological states as shared determinants for disease. *Psychosomatic Medicine, 57,* 255–268.

Sheridan, M., & Kline, K. (1984). Psychogenic and psychophysiologic disorders. In F. Turner (Ed.), *Adult psychopathology* (pp. 466–492). New York: Free Press.

Singer, M. T. (1977). Psychological dimensions in psychosomatic patients. *Psychother Psychosom, 28,* 13–27.

Sparks, P. J., Daniell, W., Black, D. W., Kipen, H. M., Altman, L. C., Simon, G. E., & Terr, A. I. (1994). Multiple chemical sensitivity syndrome: A clinical perspective. *Journal of Occupational Medicine, 36,* 7, 718–730.

Stoudemire, A., & Hale, R. E. (1991). Psychological and behavioral factors affecting medical conditions and *DSM-IV,* an overview. *Psychosomatics, 32,* 1, 5–12.

Surwit, R. S., & Williams, P. G. (1996). Animal models provide insight into psychosomatic factors in diabetes. *Psychosomatic Medicine, 58,* 582–589.

Taylor, S. E., Repetti, R. L., & Seeman, T. (1997). Health psychology: What is an unhealthy environment and how does it get under the skin? *Annual Review of Psychology, 48,* 411–447.

Watzlawick, P., Weakland J., & Fisch, R. (1974). *Principles of formulation and problem resolution.* New York: Norton.

Williams, R. B., & Littman, A. B. (1996). Psychosocial factors: Role in cardiac risk and treatment strategies. *Cardiology Clinics, 14,* 97–103.

11

DEVELOPMENTAL DISABILITIES IN AGING PERSONS

Gary B. Seltzer

To save people from death by measures of public health is
proving relatively easy, but no solution is in sight for the
many problems created by their survival.
—René Dubos, *The Mirage of Health* (1959)

A s an aging society, we struggle with the question of how to translate
longevity into living a better life. Images of physical, mental, and cognitive impairments, the losses so characteristically adumbrated for the final
seasons of one's life, are the feared outcomes that we associate with being
old. Oscar Wilde, in his cynical but insightful manner, observed that "the
tragedy of old age is not that one is old, but that one is young" (Wilde,
1990, p. 162).

How old is old, and what characterizes old age, are questions that,
because of the growing number of centenarians and the heterogenous
developmental pattern of elders, are far too complex to be answered by
simple chronological-age categories.

Many more persons with developmental disabilities are living to an
older age than ever before (Janicki & Dalton, 1993). As a result, social
workers and other service providers, as well as researchers and policy ana-
lysts, have become increasingly interested in how the aging process is manifested in persons with mental retardation/developmental disabilities
(MR/DD) and how their extended life span may affect their families. Social
workers who practice in the community, hospitals, and other settings are
likely to be in contact with this group of individuals (Hanley & Parkinson, 1994) and therefore would benefit from an understanding of their

characteristics, their needs for formal and informal support, and the needs of their families.

In this chapter, the literature about aging in persons with MR/DD is reviewed and issues that are relevant to social work practice are identified. First the definitions of mental retardation and developmental disability are reviewed. Next, the related demographic trends that characterize this group are explored. Third, age-associated changes in functional abilities and cognitive abilities are described. Fourth, the need for formal and informal supports is examined. Last, suggestions for practice, policy development, and research regarding this population are presented. Throughout, special attention is paid to older persons with Down's syndrome (DS) and cerebral palsy (CP) because persons with these disabilities display a different pattern of aging than persons who have no known organic etiology for their developmental disabilities (Burack & Zigler, 1990; Zigman, Seltzer, & Silverman, 1994).

DEFINITIONS AND CLASSIFICATION SYSTEMS

The focus of this chapter on aging in persons with developmental disabilities requires that we begin with definitions of two key terms: *developmental disabilities* and *old age*.

Developmental Disabilities

For better or worse, we diagnose and classify people on the basis of shared, nonarbitrary patterns of behavior and emotions and biological etiologies (Millon, 1991). In different eras, different clinical attributes take precedence, usually because of ideological favor or fiscal motivations. Professionals in the field of MR/DD are remarkable for frequently changing their definition and classification nosology. In the late 1960s the term *developmental disabilities* emerged when new federal legislation was enacted in the United States. The disabilities that were included in the legislation were mental retardation, cerebral palsy, spina bifida, and epilepsy, all of which had to have been manifested before the patient reached age 22. Classifying by the presence or absence of a category of disability is known as the *categorical approach* to classification. Since this categorical approach establishes diagnostic criteria based on an etiological impairment, the categorical approach is typically associated with the medical model.

The medical model works well when there is an acute illness and the signs and symptoms of the illness can be traced back to a pathological process that often has a known etiology, e.g., a bacterial infection that causes pneumonia. For persons with a developmental disability, however, a focus on etiology may have little impact on helping them achieve maximum functioning.

In 1978, the term *developmental disability* was redefined in amended federal legislation. This time, a developmental disability was defined by the severity of impairment rather than by category of disability. With this new emphasis on functional limitations, the definition of a developmental disability corresponded more closely to the constructs used by the aging network.

Specifically, P.L. 83-602 defined a developmental disability as a severe chronic disability of a person, which

A. is attributable to a mental or physical impairment or combination of mental and physical impairments;
B. is manifested before the person attains age 22;
C. is likely to continue indefinitely;
D. results in *substantial functional limitations* in three or more of the following areas of major life activity: (i) self-care, (ii) receptive and expressive language, (iii) learning, (iv) mobility, (v) self-direction, (vi) capacity for independent living, and (vii) economic self-sufficiency;
E. reflects the person's need for a combination and sequence of special, interdisciplinary, or generic care, treatment, or other services, which are of lifelong or extended duration and are individually planned and coordinated.

The largest subgroup of the population with developmental disabilities consists of persons with mental retardation (MR). Most of our available knowledge about older persons with developmental disabilities has been generated from research on older persons with MR. According to the most recent definition of mental retardation (1992), "[M]*ental retardation* refers to substantial limitations in present functioning. It is characterized by significantly subaverage intellectual functioning, existing concurrently with related limitations in two or more of the following applicable adaptive skill areas: communication, self-care, home living, social skills, community use, self-direction, health and safety, functional academics, leisure, and work. Mental retardation manifests before age 18" (Luckasson, et al., 1992, p. 1).

Old Age

The definition of old age in the general population poses conceptual challenges for gerontologists and social workers who work with the elderly.

Interindividual differences, that is, differences in patterns of change across individuals, *increase* as people age. The accumulated interactions among the biological, social, and psychological factors result in greater diversity among people. Thus, the longer people live, the greater the differences among them (Neugarten & Neugarten, 1986).

Defining old age in the population with MR/DD has been even more challenging than defining it in the general population. Definitions based on age alone are problematic because some subgroups of the population with developmental disabilities, notably those with organic etiologies such as Down's syndrome and cerebral palsy, age prematurely (Dalton, et al., 1987).

Clinicians find so much variation in function associated with advancing age that they argue against a single chronological cutoff for old age (Cotten & Spirrison, 1986; Seltzer, G. B., & Luchterhand, 1994). On the other hand, those who engage in developing public policy, plan services, or conduct research need to conform to our society's convention of using chronological age as a marker of old age. Some have argued that age 60 should be used to define old age in the DD population, to be consistent with the Older Americans Act (Rose & Janicki, 1986). Others have used age 55 as the lower age boundary in an attempt to include at least some of those who age prematurely; see M. M. Seltzer & Krauss, 1987, for a review of the literature on this issue.

In the field of MR/DD, *stage of life* is a benchmark for assessing whether an activity or service is appropriate for an individual. Philosophically, the normalization principle has supported the normalization of the environment in which individuals function. By normalizing the environment, persons with mental retardation are given access to social roles opportunities that are *age-appropriate* and normative (M. M. Seltzer, 1998; Wolfensberger, 1985). Service providers who support older persons with MR/DD aim to offer them social, recreational, and vocational opportunities that are socially and developmentally normative.

Retirement is a social role that has become a rite of passage for Americans some time after the age of 60. Recently, retirement has also become an option for older persons with MR/DD, many of whom are employed in sheltered workshops and supported employment. Many of these individuals also live in community residences that are also supported by the formal social service system. The decision to retire, then, usually needs to be coordinated between the residential and work settings. Sutton, Sterns, and Schwartz-Park (1993), after a review of states' MR/DD policies, found that many states have established a policy of subsidized retirement for residents with MR/DD. In spite of the opportunity to retire, some individuals with MR/DD prefer not to, partly because they need their earnings to pay for leisure activities.

Health problems can force someone into "early" retirement. In a study in progress (G. B. Seltzer), some individuals with cerebral palsy in their 40s report experiencing so much fatigue that they are unable to continue working. Thus, old age, and its socially normative roles such as retirement, is defined idiographically by factors such as age, health, and functional ability.

DEMOGRAPHIC TRENDS

Life Expectancy

There has been a marked increase in the life expectancy of persons with MR/DD (Janicki, 1988). This increase is due, in part, to new medical technology and the improved health care provided to this population. For example, fully one-third of all children born with Down's syndrome have congenital heart defects (Pueschel, 1987). In the past, these children generally died at a young age. However, because of improved surgical procedures and changed social attitudes toward medical intervention for persons with disabilities, their length of life has been extended considerably (G. B. Seltzer, & Essex, B.L., 1998).

Little data are available about the current life expectancy of persons with MR/DD as correlated with each of the various organic etiologies for their developmental disabilities. Individuals with an organic basis for their disability and severe to profound retardation have a shorter life expectancy than do persons in the general population, but the differences in life expectancy across the specific disorders (e.g., chromosomal anomalies versus metabolic disorders versus teratogenic effects) have not been adequately described (Eyman, et al., 1990; Granger, et al., 1987). However, those who have no organic basis for their disability and mild or moderate retardation have a life expectancy that is close or equal to that of persons in the general population (Lubin & Kiely, 1985).

Eyman, et al. (1989) described the life expectancy of persons with mental retardation in California. They reported that the death rate in this population is curvilinear, with the highest death rate occurring before age 5 and after age 55. Those with severe or profound retardation have a higher death rate at all ages than do those with mild or moderate retardation.

The Aging of Cohorts

As the elderly population in the United States continues to grow faster and larger than most other segments of society, the subgroup of older persons with MR/DD is expected to grow from an estimated population of 173,000 adults with MR/DD age 60 and older in 1998 to 332,900 by the year 2025 (Rehabilitation Research and Training Center, 1995). This substantial increase in numbers is related not only to increased longevity but also to the large size of the baby-boom generation, who are approaching midlife and who will reach old age during the early part of the 21st century (Baird & Sadovnick, 1985; G. B. Seltzer, 1993a). Since the baby-boom population is substantially larger than the current cohort of older persons and probably has access to better medical care than the present cohort, we can expect the baby-boom's MR/DD cohort to have a different health status and longevity than the current cohort of older people with developmental disabilities.

AGE-RELATED CHANGES

Development across the life span is characterized by both stability and change. This is true for older persons with developmental disabilities as well as for the general population, although the paucity of longitudinal research on this group makes it difficult to characterize their trajectories of stability and change in various behavioral and social domains. The blurring of cohort effects and true age effects have been described for the general population (Schaie, 1993) and for those with developmental disabilities (M. M. Seltzer, 1985; Zigman, et al., 1994). The term *healthy survivor effect* refers to the fact that, as a group, older surviving subjects are healthier than were their peers who died at an earlier age, a fact that would tend to reduce aging effects in cross-sectional studies. This is because the group at greatest risk (i.e., the group who did have the disorder) may not have survived long enough to be included in the study sample. In that healthy survivor and cohort effects have not been disentangled in much of the literature on older persons with developmental disabilities, some descriptions of age-related changes in this population remain confounded by differences within the cohorts.

Functional Abilities

Function is defined most broadly as a person's ability to perform age- and culturally appropriate tasks and to fulfill social roles. Factors that typically contribute to an analysis of function include relevant diagnoses; anatomical, physiological, psychological, and cognitive deficits and strengths; a delineation of available social roles; family and social support systems; and other environmental supports. The functional approach has been influenced by the disability models of Nagi (1975) and Wood (1975), models that have been used by the U.N.'s World Health Organization in its manual *The International Classification of Impairments, Disabilities and Handicaps* and the Institute of Medicine's report, *Disability in America: Toward a National Agenda for Prevention* (Pope & Tarlov, 1991). These models of disability begin with a functional analysis to determine the extent to which a client's impairments are sufficient to explain his or her functional limitations. If they are not, the clinician tries to determine the reasons for the discrepancy—be they personal characteristics, such as motivation, or environmental obstacles, such as demands that exceed the person's capabilities.

Some theorists define *disability* as the gap between a person's capabilities and the environmental demands (Nagi, 1979; Verbrugge, 1990). In this formulation, "disability" is inherently a relational construct, the meaning of which varies according to whether there is a good or bad match between individuals and their environments. For example, when functional limitations are unlikely to be affected by changing personal characteristics, as in the case of Alzheimer's disease, there is a need to provide environmental supports such as assistive devices, environmental modifications, or personal care attendants that meet the client's daily needs (Janicki, et al., 1996). Professionals who use this analytic schema can recognize the potential for some clients to gain skills and maintain social roles while appreciating that for others, an appropriate treatment goal is to support the maintenance or slowing down of deterioration of personal abilities by implementing environmental changes.

Persons with mental retardation continue to develop new functional abilities throughout their adult years, but the acquisition of new skills levels off and begins to decline in older age. In persons with mild and moderate retardation who do not have either Down syndrome or cerebral palsy, declines in activities of daily living are not routinely observed until their mid-70s, but motoric skills tend to begin to decline two decades earlier (Bell & Zubek, 1960; Janicki & Jacobson, 1986). In persons with severe and profound retardation who survive to old age, the declines in functional abilities are not as marked as in those who are less impaired, perhaps because of their more limited initial abilities (Janicki & Jacobson, 1986). Persons with Down's syndrome who manifest the symptoms of Alzheimer's disease begin to decline in their functional abilities in their 40s and 50s (Evenhuis, 1990; Zigman, et al., 1987). At all levels of retardation, regression in self-care skills and mobility is a significant predictor of mortality (Eyman, et al., 1989).

Even though older persons with developmental disabilities manifest a more marked pattern of age-related declines in functional and cognitive abilities than the general population, cross-sectional comparisons of younger and older adults with developmental disabilities reveal unexpected patterns. When Krauss and M. M. Seltzer (1986) compared adults with mental retardation aged 18–54 with those aged 55 and older in both institutional and community-based settings, they found that the younger individuals were significantly more impaired cognitively and functionally than were the older ones. The explanation for these unexpected findings was that the younger and older cohorts were composed of different mixes of persons. These differences were the result of changes in diagnostic practices, placement patterns, and mortality that have occurred during the past century. The members of the younger cohort included a higher proportion of persons with severe and profound retardation, persons who in the past were less likely to survive beyond childhood. The older cohort included a higher proportion of persons having "borderline" mental retardation, who would not be included in the younger cohort as a result of contemporary diagnostic practices. This example illustrates the distinction between true influences of aging versus cohort effects; the latter are particularly marked in the population with developmental disabilities. Furthermore, these findings caution social workers and other service providers to refrain from making service plans solely on the basis of the chronological age of the service recipients.

Cognitive Abilities

Of particular interest to social workers who provide services to older persons with developmental disabilities and their families are age-related changes in cognitive abilities. Studies of cognitive functioning are designed to infer the nature of age-associated changes in the mental processes underlying overt performance and consideration of how aging affects cognitive abilities.

As in the general population, most persons with developmental disabilities maintain their cognitive abilities throughout their adult years and may even show evidence of intellectual development (Eyman & Widaman, 1987; Hewitt, et al., 1986; Janicki & Jacobson, 1986; G. B. Seltzer, 1985), with declines manifested only after age 60 or 70. Persons with Down's syndrome are an exception in that they are at an increased risk for Alzheimer's disease, and, as will be described in the next section, they manifest a pattern of cognitive decline starting in their 40s or 50s. Dalton, et al. (1994) reported, after a review of the research, that persons with Down's syndrome begin to evidence memory loss in their late 40s. However, the variation within this group with respect to memory loss was great, and there are persons with Down syndrome in their 60s who show no evidence of cognitive decline.

Age-Related Changes in Persons with Cerebral Palsy

There are about 500,000 people in the United States with cerebral palsy or CP (Granger, et al., 1987). Cerebral palsy is the third leading cause of the need for assistance with life activities and the fifth leading cause of activity limitation in the United States (NCHS, 1989). Yet, we know almost nothing about how the impairments associated with CP affect the social, psychological, and physical functioning of older adults (G. B. Seltzer, 1993). Cerebral palsy is generally considered to be a nonprogressive disorder. However, the effects of aging on a person's functional abilities may not follow a normative trajectory (Overeynder, Janicki, & Turk, 1994; G. B. Seltzer & Essex, 1998) become progressively worse over time (Pimm, 1992). The research on the effects of CP on developmental progression is almost exclusively focused on infants, school-age children, and adolescents (Janicki, 1989). Almost all of the information we have about adulthood and aging is anecdotal (Overeynder, et al., 1992).

Technical advances, such as antibiotic treatment, survival of very low birth-weight infants, and improvement in the management of respiratory functions has increased the prevalence of CP (Crichton, Mackinnon, & White, 1995). Therefore, larger numbers of people with increasingly severe impairments related to CP are living longer.

The adult generation of persons with CP have begun searching for information about their aging process. They want to know about the relationship between CP and aging. They want to know whether they can prevent or slow down what seems to be a premature aging process in some physical and functional domains. They have begun to appreciate that CP, in contrast to the medical community's definition of it as a *nonprogressive* disorder, is having a progressive effect on how they are aging (Pimm, 1992). Although the pathogenesis of CP may be nonprogressive, an analysis of their functional abilities suggests that patients' age-related changes seem to be related to their CP. Factors such as age-associated physical changes are differentially affected by the presence of lifelong impairments that can speed or alter the expected progression of age-related changes. In turn, these changes can lead to the development of secondary conditions, which also result in additional functional limitations and which can negatively influence quality of life (Pope & Tarlov, 1991).

Age-Related Changes in Persons with Down's Syndrome

As the incidence of Down's syndrome (DS) seems to be declining as a result of improved prenatal diagnosis and the availability of abortion, the prevalence of DS is increasing because of the availability of better health care and generally better living conditions (G. B. Seltzer & Luchterhand, 1994). Antibiotic use, beginning in the late 1940s, and surgical repair of congenital abnormalities in the 1960s, advanced the longevity of persons with DS very significantly. Ironically, though, as these individuals advanced in age into adulthood, they developed health problems such as cataracts, hypothyroidism, sleep apnea, hearing loss, and most remarkably Alzheimer's disease (AD).

Life expectancy for those with DS is approximately 55 years of age. Those with Down's syndrome can be divided into two groups with respect to their life expectancy (Eyman, et al., 1991). Those who have no ambulation or feeding skills have a shorter life expectancy—usually less than 30 years. However, most persons with Down's syndrome are ambulatory and can feed themselves; these individuals have a life expectancy of about 50 to 55 years. A primary reason why the latter group has a shorter life span than does the general population is their increased risk for Alzheimer's disease (Wisniewski & Merz, 1985). Nearly all persons with Down's syndrome who survive to age 35 manifest the neuropathology of Alzheimer's disease, detected upon autopsy (Lott & Lai, 1982), although only about 45% manifest the behavioral symptoms (Thase, 1982). Among middle-aged adults with Down's syndrome, the risk of the behavioral manifestations of Alzheimer's disease appears to increase with advancing age.

FORMAL AND INFORMAL SUPPORTS

For a number of reasons, older persons with developmental disabilities have a greater need for formal and informal supports than the general older population. First, these individuals, by definition, have impairments in their functional abilities and need compensatory supports to manage their daily activities, maintain their health, and enjoy a reasonable quality of life. Second, since most older persons with developmental disabilities do not marry or have children, they lack the basic supports that are provided to most older persons by spouses and adult children. Instead, they must depend on their aging parents or on siblings. Third, their disabilities and advancing age may interfere with their ability to develop or maintain meaningful relationships with friends who could provide support to them (Berkson & Romer, 1980; Krauss, 1989; Landesman-Dwyer, et al., 1980).

For all of these reasons, older persons with developmental disabilities may be especially vulnerable and socially isolated, and therefore have a high need for formal support, as well as for continued informal support from their family of origin and from friends.

Health and Mental Health Service Needs

Health

There appears to be a high incidence of physical health problems among some subgroups of the population with MR/DD. These may also cause or increase functional limitations, especially if not given appropriate medical or therapeutic treatment. It may not be the mental retardation per se that results in the increased probability of morbidity and mortality, but rather the underlying organic etiology or situational complications that predispose the individual to infections and other medical problems (Simila, et al., 1986). For example, individuals with Down's syndrome are prone to cardiac defects, eye and ear infections, obesity, skin and dental problems, and hypothyroidism (Crocker, 1989; Patton, et al., 1990).

Individuals with developmental disabilities present a diverse picture in terms of health care needs. Among those with mental retardation, for example, individuals with mild disabilities have health needs that do not differ from those of their counterparts in the general population (Patton, et al., 1990); however, as the severity of mental retardation increases, there is a greater prevalence of physical impairments and health concerns (Crocker, 1989; Patton, et al., 1990).

A number of studies in the 1980s have documented medical care conditions and needs of individuals with developmental disabilities in institutions and the community (see Hayden & DePaepe, 1991, for a review). In terms of contemporary service delivery, health care for institutional residents has improved in recent years, in response to litigation and increased oversight (Crocker, 1992). Institutionalized individuals represent a small minority of the U.S. population with developmental disabilities (approximately 5%), but their medical care expenses far exceed those of persons who live in the community. Studies that examine the health care needs of persons with developmental disabilities living in state institutions suggest that their costly health care results from the severe level of disabilities found among persons who remain living there (Eyman, Chaney, et al., 1986; Minihan, 1986; Rubin, 1987). Hayden and DePaepe (1991), however, cite a number of studies which report that many of the medical conditions treated in institutions can also successfully be treated in the community. More recently, Strauss and Kastner (1996) using the large longitudinal California database described earlier (see studies conducted by Eyman and his colleagues, e.g., Eyman, et al., 1989), found a greater risk of mortality in the community sample than in the institutional one. This discrepancy in mortality, and the data that describe difference in cost of treatment by type of setting, need further investigation.

Studies that examine the medical status of persons who live in the community use different kinds of samples and different categories of health conditions, a methodological problem that limits inferences across studies (Hayden & DePaepe, 1991). Nevertheless, researchers have begun to document the extent of the unmet health-care needs of this community-dwelling group. For example, the National Consumer Survey of people with developmental disabilities (Jaskulski, et al., 1990) found dental care to be the highest reported unmet service need.

Two projects that studied persons who live in the community provided information on the specific medical needs of their patients. The New Jersey program at Morristown Hospital reported prominent seizures and orthopedic problems (Ziring, 1987; Ziring, et al., 1988). A Pennsylvania project reported the following problems: seizures; ear, nose, and throat problems; cardiac disease; gastrointestinal illnesses; allergies; skin problems; and foot problems (Nowell, et al., 1989).

A survey of community-residing individuals with mental retardation (mainly adults) in Massachusetts found that almost two-thirds had at least one chronic condition requiring medical attention (Minihan & Dean, 1990). The largest percentage (30%) had one condition; 14% had two; 12% three; and 5% four or more conditions. These investigators found that the majority of chronic conditions were being adequately managed by the community health care system. The major service gap was in home-based medical services. Gynecological needs were also a neglected area, with less than 40% of the women in their study known to have received a routine gynecological examination within the past three years.

Mental Health
There is some evidence of a higher prevalence of mental illness among persons with mental retardation than in the general population. However, there is a dearth of knowledge about how older individuals with mental retardation and related developmental disabilities experience psychiatric problems (Zigman, et al., 1994). Knowledge has been limited by difficulties in defining the signs and symptoms of mental illness among persons with mental retardation that are critical to developing a diagnostic nosology of psychiatric disorders in this population (Bruininks, et al., 1988;

Menolascino, 1988). Studies focusing on diagnostic categories (e.g., affective disorders; anxiety disorders) suggest that individuals with mental retardation experience a full range of psychiatric disorders (Nezu, et al., 1992).

While behavior problems have been identified as a significant barrier to community integration (Bruininks, et al., 1988), there has been inadequate attention paid to the mental health needs of people with developmental disabilities. This neglect is related to numerous factors.

Inadequacy of current health insurance mechanisms is also apparent for services related to mental health, which are incompletely covered by both private and public insurance (Crocker, 1992; Rosenberg, 1988). This problem is compounded by the dearth of mental health professionals who are trained to provide mental health services to this population (Szymanski & Crocker, 1985). The result of inadequate health care coverage and a shortage of personnel is that mental health problems tend to go untreated in this population. When treated, treatment is frequently limited to psychopharmacological interventions, the efficacy of which is often dubious. (For a recent edited consensus handbook on the topic, see Reiss & Aman, 1998.)

Informal Supports and Families

It is common for persons with developmental disabilities to live with their families, in many cases for their entire lives (Fujiura, et al., 1989; Lakin, 1985). A great deal of research attention is being paid to aging parents who have provided long-term care to their adult children with developmental disabilities (Heller & Factor, 1988; M. M. Seltzer & Krauss, 1994). This interest is the result of several factors. First, social workers and other human-service professionals are concerned about how these parents cope with the increased longevity of their children with MR/DD. Many parents who have children with MR/DD had expected to outlive their offspring. Consequently, they are now underprepared for the present likelihood that their children will outlive them (G. B. Seltzer, et al., 1993a). The demographic shifts described earlier pose new challenges to family caregivers, the effects of which are not yet well understood.

Second, social workers and gerontologists are increasingly interested in the capacity of older persons to be family resources. In much past research and clinical service practice, elderly persons were viewed as burdens on their families. This perspective is changing (Greenberg & Becker, 1988; Rowe & Kahn, 1987; Rowe & Kahn, 1998; G. B. Seltzer &

Luchterhand, 1994). It is now recognized that intergenerational relationships are often reciprocal, with the older generation providing assistance to, as well as receiving assistance from, the younger generation. For example, a parent with arthritis and functional limitations may rely on her child to perform activities for her that she can no longer manage.

Another unique aspect of the caregiving experiences of aging parents who care for their adult son or daughter with MR/DD is the duration of the caregiving responsibilities. U.S. national data indicate that the period of family caregiving for an elderly relative who is not developmentally disabled averages about five years (Stone, Cafferata, & Sangl, 1987). In contrast, the period of care for an aging son or daughter with MR/DD may span a lifetime: six or seven decades.

In a longitudinal study of 461 aging families who provide care to their sons or daughters with mental retardation, M. M. Seltzer and Krauss (1989) examined a number of the issues just discussed. The overall purpose of the study was to investigate the correlates of well-being in the sample of older caregiving mothers, to identify the predictors of continuing in-home versus out-of-home placement for their adult children with retardation, and to describe the patterns of stability and change in the adults with retardation.

The findings of this study suggest that the older women are coping extremely well with their continuing caregiving responsibilities (M. M. Seltzer, Greenberg, & Krauss, 1995; Kling, et al., 1997). Although it was initially hypothesized that they would be at risk for poor physical and mental health because of their long years of caregiving, it was found that they compared favorably with samples of age peers and samples of other caregivers (Krauss & M. M. Seltzer, 1994). Specifically, the aging mothers in this study were substantially healthier and had better morale than did other samples of caregivers for the elderly. Furthermore, they reported no more burden or stress than did other caregivers. Thus, despite the long duration of their caregiving roles and despite the unique characteristics of their children, many of these mothers appear to be resilient, optimistic, and able to function well in multiple roles.

A second hypothesis of the study pertained to the mothers of sons and daughters with Down's syndrome (37% of the total sample). It was hypothesized that these mothers would have poorer physical and mental health than would the other mothers in the sample because adults with Down's syndrome have a higher rate of chronic health problems and are at risk for premature aging. Contrary to these expectations, the mothers of the adults with Down's syndrome manifested better overall well-being than did those of adult children whose retardation was due to other factors (M. M. Seltzer, Krauss, & Tsunematsu, 1993). Even when between-group differences on socioeconomic and disability factors were controlled, the mothers of the adults with Down's syndrome perceived their families to be more cohesive and less conflicted, were more satisfied with their social supports and with the services provided to their adult children, and were less stressed by their caregiving responsibilities than were the other mothers in the sample.

These differences mirror patterns that have been reported for young families with a child with Down's syndrome compared with other groups with developmental disabilities (Holroyd & McArthur, 1976; Krauss, 1989; Mink, et al., 1983). Although the researchers did not expect that well-being of the mothers of the adults with Down's syndrome would be superior in older age, these differences may be persistent sequelae of the diagnosis. Possible reasons include the greater level of scientific knowledge about Down's syndrome than about other diagnostic groups, the greater prevalence of Down's syndrome than other diagnoses and therefore the possibly greater public familiarity with it, and temperamental differences between children with Down's syndrome and comparison groups of children whose mental retardation is caused by other factors. These "protective factors" may buffer some of the stresses associated with having a child with retardation, which are manifested more negatively by families of children with other diagnoses.

A third hypothesis of the study concerned the involvement of aging siblings with their brother or sister with retardation. It was hypothesized that the involvement of siblings would be positively related to maternal well-being (G. B. Seltzer, A. Begun, et al., 1991). It was found that a mother had significantly better health, was more satisfied with her life, and had less stress and burden associated with caregiving when at least one of her other children provided either affective or instrumental support to her adult child with retardation. Over 80% of the families in which there were siblings reported at least some involvement of siblings, with affective support much more common than instrumental support. About one-fourth of the siblings anticipate that their brother or sister will live with them after both parents die (Krauss, et al., 1996), a prediction borne out in the families in which both parents died during the study period (Gordon, M. M. Seltzer, & Krauss, 1997). Families in which there were no children other than the adult with MR/DD or in which no sibling was involved with the son or daughter with MR/DD appear to be particularly vulnerable and especially in need of assistance from social workers with planning for the future.

Fathers in these families have important caregiving responsibility along with their wives. However, fathers are less effective than their wives in coping with the stresses of caregiving (Essex, et al., 1997), possibly because their primary role for most of their child's life was that of breadwinner rather than caregiver. Nevertheless, the fathers in these families have remarkably favorable well-being, equal to or better than other men their age.

In summary, there is a growing body of knowledge about families of older persons with MR/DD. Data from the study by M. M. Seltzer and Krauss (1997) suggest that resiliency is more characteristic of these families' coping style than vulnerability. Therefore, social workers are challenged to avoid assuming a negative outcome and instead to respond to the range of needs of families at this stage of their clients' lives.

In a survey conducted by McCallion and Tobin (1995), social workers were found to believe that aging parents of adults with disabilities need more services than they currently receive and that their siblings should be encouraged to be involved in family caregiving. Social workers can provide important leadership in working towards these goals, particularly if they use practice skills that maintain the independence of these family systems rather than disarming their strengths with a flood of services over which the families have little control.

CONCLUSIONS: IMPLICATIONS FOR PRACTICE, POLICY, AND RESEARCH

Knowledge about aging in persons with developmental disabilities has begun to accumulate. A great deal is now understood about the characteristics of this population and the extent to which they are similar to and different from the larger population of older Americans. This knowledge has formed the basis of social work practice with older persons with developmental disabilities and their families.

Many clinical, policy, and research issues regarding aging in the population with developmental disabilities warrant additional attention, and social workers can play an important role in resolving them. One particularly important clinical issue pertains to the mental health characteristics and needs of older persons with developmental disabilities. Despite the preliminary understanding of the age-related changes in the cognitive, functional, and health statuses of older persons with developmental disabilities reviewed here, there has been no systematic investigation of the mental health status of this population. Some have hypothesized that there is an increased risk of depression in this group because of their social isolation and advanced age, but this hypothesis has not been tested well, either in research or in clinical practice.

From a policy perspective, it is necessary for older persons with developmental disabilities to gain greater access to services provided by the aging-services network, as well as by the developmental-disabilities service system. Although these clients are at risk of "falling through the cracks," successful case management and advocacy can result in improved coordination of services. Policies that foster interagency collaboration would facilitate this process.

From a research perspective, more descriptive and analytic studies about older persons with developmental disabilities and their families are needed. Both qualitative and quantitative methods are required to enhance our understanding of the course and consequences of the aging process for this group. This research should be multidisciplinary, so that it can address the range of biopsychosocial issues that have emerged in the past decade.

REFERENCES

Baird. P. A., & Sadovnick, A. D. (1985). Mental retardation in over half-a-million consecutive live births: An epidemiological study. *American Journal of Mental Deficiency, 89,* 323–330.

Baird. P. A., & Sadovnick, A. D. (1988). Life expectancy in Down syndrome adults. *Lancet, 2,* 8624, 1354–1356.

Bell, A., & Zubek, J. P. (1960). The effect of age on the intellectual performance of mental defectives. *Journal of Gerontology, 15,* 285–295.

Berkson, G., & Romer. D. (1980). Social ecology of supervised communal facilities for mentally disabled adults: I. Introduction. *American Journal of Mental Deficiency, 85,* 219–228.

Bruininks, R. H., Hill, B. K., & Morreau, L. E. (1988). Prevalence and implications of maladaptive behavior and dual diagnosis in residential and other service programs. In J. A. Stark, F. J. Menolascino, M. H. Abarelli, & V. C. Gray (Eds.), *Mental retardation and mental health: Classification, diagnosis, treatment, service* (pp. 3–30). New York: Springer-Verlag.

Burack, J. A., & Zigler, E. (1990). Intentional and incidental memory in organically mentally retarded, familial retarded, and nonretarded individuals. *American Journal of Mental Retardation, 94,* 5, 540–632.

Carlsen, W. R., Galluzzi, K. E., Forman, L. F., & Cavalieri, T.A. (1994). Comprehensive geriatric assessment: Applications for community-residing elderly people with mental retardations/developmental disabilities. *Mental Retardation, 32,* 334–340.

Cotten, P. D., & Spirrison, C. L. (1986). The elderly mentally retarded developmentally disabled population: A challenge for the service delivery system. In J. S. Brody & C. E. Ruff (Eds.), *Aging and rehabilitation: Advances in the state of the art.* New York: Springer.

Crichton, J. U., Mackinnon, M., & White, C. P. (1995). The life-expectancy of persons with cerebral palsy. *Developmental Medicine and Child Neurology, 37,* 567–576.

Crocker, A. C. (1989). The causes of mental retardation. *Pediatric Annals, 18,* 623–629.

Crocker, A. C. (1992). Expansion of the health-care delivery system. In L. Rowitz (Ed.), *Mental retardation in the year 2000* (pp. 163–183). New York: Springer-Verlag.

Dalton, A. J., Seltzer, G. B., Adlin, M. S., & Wisniewski, H. M. (1994). Association between Alzheimer disease and Down syndrome: Clinical observations. In J. M. Berg, A. J. Holland, & H. Karlinsky (Eds.), *Alzheimer disease and Down syndrome.* Oxford: Oxford University Press.

Dubos, R. (1959). *The mirage of health* (p. 184). New York: Doubleday Anchor.

Essex, E. L., Seltzer, M. M., & Krauss, M. W. (1997). Residential transitions of adults with mental retardation: Predictors of waiting list use and placement. *American Journal of Mental Retardation, 101,* 613–629.

Evenhuis, J. M. (1990). The natural history of dementia in Down syndrome. *Archives of Neurology, 47,* 263–267.

Eyman, R. K., Call, T. L., & White, J. F. (1989). Mortality of elderly mentally retarded persons in California. *Journal of Applied Gerontology, 8,* 203–215.

Eyman. R. K., Call, T., & White, J. F. (1991). Life expectancy of persons with Down syndrome. *American Journal of Mental Retardation, 95,* 603–612.

Eyman, R. K., Grossman, H. J., Chaney, R., & Call, T. L. (1990). The life expectancy of profoundly handicapped people with mental retardation. *New England Journal of Medicine, 323,* 329–336.

Eyman, R. K., & Widaman, K. F. (1987). Life-span development of institutionalized and community-based mentally retarded persons revisited. *American Journal of Mental Deficiency, 91,* 559–569.

Fujiura, G. T., Garza, J., & Braddock, D. (1989). National survey of family support services in developmental disabilities. Unpublished manuscript. University of Illinois at Chicago.

Gordon, R. M., Seltzer, M. M., & Krauss, M. W. (1997). The aftermath of parental death: Changes in the context and quality of life. In R. L. Schalock (Ed.), *Quality of life: Its application to persons with disabilities.* Washington, DC: American Association on Mental Retardation.

Granger, C. V., Seltzer. G. B., & Fishbein, C. (1987). *Primary care of the functionally disabled: Assessment and management.* Philadelphia: J. B. Lippincott.

Greenberg, J., & Becker, N. I. (1988). Aging parents as family resources. *The Gerontologist, 28,* 786–791.

Hanley, B., & Parkinson, C. B. (1994). Position paper on social work values: Practice with individuals who have developmental disabilities. *Mental Retardation, 32,* 6, 426–431.

Hayden, M. F., & DePaepe, P. A. (1991). Medical conditions, level of care needs, and health-related outcomes of persons with mental retardation: A review. *Journal of the Association for Persons with Severe Handicaps, 16,* 188–206.

Heller, T., & Factor, A. (1988). Permanency planning among black and white family caregivers of older adults with mental retardation. *Mental Retardation, 26,* 203–208.

Hewitt, K. E., Fenner, M. E., & Torpy, D. (1986). Cognitive and behavioral profiles of the elderly mentally handicapped. *Journal of Mental Deficiency Research, 30,* 217–225.

Holroyd, J., & McArthur, D. (1976). Mental retardation and stress on the parents: A contrast between Down syndrome and childhood autism. *American Journal of Mental Deficiency, 80,* 431–436.

Janicki, M. P. (1988). Aging and persons with mental handicap and developmental disabilities. *Journal of Practical Approaches to Developmental Handicap, 12,* 9–13.

Janicki, M. P. (1989). Aging, cerebral palsy, and older persons with mental retardation. *Australia and New Zealand Journal of Developmental Disabilities, 15,* 311–320.

Janicki, M. P., & Dalton, A. J. (1993). Aging in mental retardation. *Current Opinion in Psychiatry, 6,* 639–643.

Janicki, M. P., Heller, T., Seltzer, G. B., & Hogg, J. (1996). Practice guidelines for the clinical assessment and care management of Alzheimer's disease and other dementias among adults with intellectual disability. *Journal of Intellectual Disability Research, 40,* 373–382.

Janicki, M. P., & Jacobson, J. W. (1986). Generational trends in sensory, physical, and behavioral abilities among older mentally retarded persons. *American Journal of Mental Deficiency, 90,* 490–500.

Jaskulski, T., Metzler, C., & Zierman, S. A. (1990). *Forging a new era: The 1990 reports on people with developmental disabilities.* Washington, DC: National Association of Developmental Disabilities Councils.

Kling, K. C., Seltzer, M. M., & Ryff, C. D. (1997). Distinctive late life challenges: Implications for coping and well-being. *Psychology and Aging, 12,* 288–295.

Krauss, M. W. (1989). *Parenting a young child with disabilities: Differences between mothers and fathers.* Paper presented at the 22nd Annual Gatlinburg Conference on Research and Theory in Mental Retardation and Developmental Disabilities, Gatlinburg, TN.

Krauss, M. W., & Seltzer, M. M. (1986). Comparison of elderly and adult mentally retarded persons in community and institutional settings. *American Journal of Mental Deficiency, 75,* 354–360.

Krauss, M. W., & Seltzer, M. M. (1994). Taking stock: Expected gains from a lifespan perspective on mental retardation. In M. M. Seltzer, M. W. Krauss, & M. P. Janicki (Eds.), *Life course perspectives on adulthood and aging* (pp. 213–220). Washington, DC: American Association on Mental Retardation.

Krauss, M. W., Seltzer, M. M., Gordon, R., & Friedman, D. H. (1996). Binding ties: The roles of adult siblings of persons with mental retardation. *Mental Retardation, 34,* 83–93.

Lakin, K. C. (1985). Service system and settings for mentally retarded people. In K. C. Lakin, B. Hill, & R. Bruininks (Eds.), *An analysis of Medicaid's ICF-MR program.* Minneapolis: University of Minnesota.

Landesman-Dwyer, S., Sackett, G. P., & Kleinman, J. S. (1980). Relationship of size to resident and staff behavior in small community residences. *American Journal of Mental Deficiency, 85,* 6–17.

Lott, I. T., & Lai, F. (1982). Dementia in Down syndrome: Observations from a neurology clinic. *Applied Research in Mental Retardation, 3,* 233–239.

Lubin, R. A., & Kiely, M. (1985). Epidemiology of aging in developmental disabilities. In M. P. Janicki & H. M. Wisniewski (Eds.), *Aging and developmental disabilities: Issues and approaches* (pp. 95–114). Baltimore, MD: Paul H. Brookes.

Luckasson, R., Coulter, D. L., Polloway, E. A., Reiss, S., Schalock, R. I., Snell, M. E., Spitalnik, D. M., & Stark, J. A. (1992). *Mental retardation: Definition, classification and systems of support.* Washington, DC: American Association on Mental Retardation.

McCallion, P., & Tobin, S. S. (1995). Social workers' perceptions of older parents caring at home for sons and daughters with developmental disabilities. *Mental Retardation, 33,* 153–162.

Menolascino, F. J. (1988). Mental illness in the mentally retarded: Diagnostic and treatment issues. In J. A. Stark, F. J. Menolascino, M. H. Albarelli, & V. C. Gray (Eds.), *Mental retardation and mental health: Classification, diagnosis, treatment, services* (pp. 109–123). New York: Springer-Verlag.

Millon, T. (1991). Classification in psychopathology: Rationale, alternatives, and standards. *Journal of Abnormal Psychology, 100,* 245–61.

Minihan, P. M. (1986). Planning for community physician services prior to deinstitutionalization of mentally retarded persons. *American Journal of Public Health, 76,* 1202–1206.

Minihan, P. M., & Dean, D. H. (1990). Meeting the needs for health services of persons with mental retardation living in the community. *American Journal of Public Health, 80,* 1043–1048.

Mink, I. T., Nihira, K., & Meyers, C. E. (1983). Taxonomy of family life styles: I. Homes with TMR children. *American Journal of Mental Deficiency, 87,* 484–497.

Moos, S., Hogg, J. & Horne, M. (1992). Demographic characteristics of a population of people with moderate, severe, and profound intellectual disability (mental handicap) over 50 years of age: Age structure, IQ, and adaptive skills. *Journal of International Disability Research 96,* 488–501.

Nagi, S. Z. (1975, May). *Disability concepts and prevalence.* Paper presented at the first Mary Switzer Memorial Seminar, Cleveland, OH.

Nagi, S. Z. (1979). The concept and measurement of disability. In E. D. Berkowitz (Ed.), *Disability policies and government programs* (pp. 1–15). New York: Praeger.

National Center for Health Statistics (NCSH). (1989). *Disability statistics report.* Rockville, MD: U.S. Department of Health and Human Services, Public Health Services, Centers for Disease Control.

Neugarten, B. L., & Neugarten, D. A. (1986). Age in the ageing society. *Daedalus, 115,* 31–49.

Nezu, C. M., Nezu, A. M., & Gill-Weiss, M. J. (1992). *Psychopathology in persons with mental retardation: Clinical guidelines for assessment and treatment.* Champaign, IL: Research Press.

Nowell, N., Baker, D., & Conroy, J. (1989). *The provision of community medical care in Philadelphia and northeastern Pennsylvania for people who live in community arrangements and with their families.* Philadelphia: Philadelphia Coordinated Health Care.

Overeynder, J. C., Janicki, M. P., & Turk, M. A. (Eds.). (1994). *Aging and cerebral palsy—Pathways to successful aging: The national action plan.* New York State Developmental Disabilities Planning Council.

Overeynder, J., Turk, M., Dalton, A., & Janicki, M. P. (1992). *"I'm worried about the future . . .": The aging of adults with cerebral palsy.* Albany, NY: New York State Developmental Disabilities Planning Council.

Patton, J. R., Beirne-Smith, M., & Payne, J. S. (1990). *Mental Retardation* (3rd ed.). New York: Merrill.

Pimm, P. (1992). Cerebral palsy: "A non-progressive disorder?" *Educational and Child Psychology, 9,* 27–33.

Pope, A. M., & Tarlov, A. R. (Eds.). (1991). *Disability in America: Toward a national agenda for prevention.* Washington, DC: National Academy Press.

Pueschel, S. M. (1987). Health concerns in persons with Down syndrome. In S. M. Pueschel, C. Tingey, J. E. Rynders, A. C. Crocker, & D. M. Crutcher (Eds.), *New perspectives on Down syndrome* (pp. 113–134). Baltimore, MD: Paul H. Brookes.

Rehabilitation Research and Training Center on Aging with Mental Retardation. (1995). *Older adults with mental retardation/developmental disabilities and their aging family caregivers. Fact sheet and policy recommendations.* Chicago: Author, The University of Illinois at Chicago.

Reiss, S., & Aman, M. G. (1998). *Psychotropic medications and developmental disabilities: The international consensus handbook.* Columbus, OH: Nisonger Center, The Ohio State University.

Rose, T., & Janicki, M. P. (1986). Older mentally retarded adults: A forgotten population. *Aging Network News, 3,* 17–19.

Rosenberg, N. S. (1988). Future litigation strategies. In J. A. Stark, F. J. Menolascino, M. H. Albarelli, & V. C. Gray (Eds.), *Mental retardation and mental health: Classification, diagnosis, treatment, services* (pp. 361–367). New York: Springer-Verlag.

Rowe, J. W., & Kahn, R. L. (1987). Human aging: Usual and successful. *Science, 237,* 143–149.

Rowe, J. W., & Kahn, R. L. (1998). *Successful aging.* New York: Pantheon Books.

Rubin, I. L. (1987). Health care needs of adults with mental retardation. *Mental Retardation, 25,* 201–206.

Schaie, K. W., & Willis, S. L. (1993). Age difference patterns of psychometric intelligence in adulthood: Generalizability within and across ability domains. *Psychology & Aging, 8,* 44–55.

Seltzer, G. B. (1985). Selected psychological processes and aging among older developmentally disabled persons. In M. P. Janicki & H. M. Wisniewski (Eds.), *Aging and developmental disabilities: Issues and approaches* (pp. 211–227). Baltimore, MD: Paul H. Brookes.

Seltzer, G. B. (1993a). Psychological adjustment in midlife: Developmental and quality of life issues for persons with mental retardation. In E. Sutton, T. Heller, A. Factor, B. A. Hawkins, & G. B. Seltzer (Eds.), *Older adults with developmental disabilities: Toward community integration* (pp. 157–184). Baltimore: Paul H. Brookes.

Seltzer, G. B. (1993b). Social and emotional dilemmas faced by older persons with cerebral palsy. *The UCPA Networker, Special Edition on Aging and Cerebral Palsy, 7,* 16–18.

Seltzer, G. B., Begun, A., Seltzer, M. M., & Krauss, M. W. (1991). The impacts of siblings on adults with mental retardation and their aging mothers. *Family Relations, 40,* 310–377.

Seltzer, G. B., & Essex, E. L. (1998). Service needs of mental retardation and other developmental disabilities. In S. Allen & V. Mor (Eds.), *Living in the community with disability: A cross-group perspective* (pp. 197–218). New York: Springer.

Seltzer, G. B., & Luchterhand, C. (1994). Health and well-being of older persons with developmental disabilities: A clinical review. In M. M. Seltzer, M. W. Krauss, & M. P. Janicki (Eds.), *Life course perspective on adulthood and old age* (pp. 109–142). Washington, DC: American Association on Mental Retardation Monograph Series.

Seltzer, M. M. (1985a). Informal supports for aging mentally retarded persons. *American Journal of Mental Deficiency, 90,* 259–265.

Seltzer, M. M. (1985b). Research in social aspects of aging and developmental disabilities. In M. P. Janicki & H. M. Wisniewski (Eds.), *Aging and developmental disabilities: Issues and approaches* (pp. 161–173). Baltimore, MD: Paul H. Brookes.

Seltzer, M. M. (1998). Service utilization patterns and organization of the service delivery system for persons with mental retardation and other developmental disabilities. In S. Allen & V. Mor (Eds.), *Living in the community with disability: A cross-group perspective* (pp. 219–240). New York: Springer.

Seltzer, M. M., Greenberg, J. S., & Krauss, M. W. (1995). A comparison of coping strategies of aging mothers of adults with mental illness or mental retardation. *Psychology and Aging, 10,* 64–75.

Seltzer, M. M., & Krauss, M. W. (1987). *Aging and mental retardation: Extending the continuum.* Washington, DC: American Association on Mental Retardation.

Seltzer, M. M., & Krauss, M. W. (1989). Aging parents with mentally retarded children: Family risk factors and sources of support. *American Journal of Mental Retardation, 94,* 303–312.

Seltzer, M. M., & Krauss, M. W. (1994). Aging parents with co-resident adult children: The impact of lifelong caregiving. In M. M. Seltzer, M. W. Krauss, & M. P. Janicki (Eds.), *Life course perspectives on adulthood and old age* (pp. 3–18). Washington, DC: American Association on Mental Retardation.

Seltzer, M. M., Krauss, M. W., & Tsunematsu, N. (1993). Adults with Down syndrome and their aging mothers: Diagnostic group differences. *American Journal of Mental Retardation, 97,* 464–508.

Simila, S., von Wendt, L., & Rantakallio, P. (1986). Mortality of mentally retarded children to 17 years of age assessed in a prospective one-year birth cohort. *Journal of Mental Deficiency Research, 30*, 401–405.

Stone, R., Cafferata, C. L., & Sangl, J. (1987). Caregivers of the frail elderly: A national profile. *The Gerontologist, 27*, 616–626.

Strauss, D., & Kastner, T. A. (1996). Comparative mortality of people with mental retardation in institutions and the community. *American Journal of Mental Retardation, 101*, 26–40.

Sutton, E., Sterns, H. L., & Schwartz-Park, L. S. (1993). Realities of retirement and preretirement planning. In E. Sutton, T. Heller, A. Factor, B. A. Hawkins, & G. B. Seltzer (Eds.), *Older adults with developmental disabilities: Toward community integration* (pp. 95–106.) Baltimore: Paul H. Brookes.

Szymanski, L. S., & Crocker, A. C. (1985). Mental retardation. In H. I. Kaplan & B. J. Sadock (Eds.), *Comprehensive textbook of psychiatry/IV*. Baltimore: Williams and Wilkins.

Thase, M. E. (1982). Longevity and mortality in Down syndrome. *Journal of Mental Deficiency Research, 26*, 117–192.

Verbrugge, L. M. (1990). The iceberg of disability. In S. M. Stahl (Ed.), *The legacy of longevity: Health and health care in later life* (pp. 55–76). Newbury Park, CA: Sage Publications.

Wilde, O. (1990). *The works of Oscar Wilde*. Leicester, England: Bookmart Limited.

Wisniewski, H. M., & Merz, G. S. (1985). Aging, Alzheimer's disease, and developmental disabilities. In M. P. Janicki & H. M. Wisniewski (Eds.), *Aging and developmental disabilities: Issues and approaches* (pp. 177–184). Baltimore, MD: Paul H. Brookes.

Wolfensberger, W. (1985). An overview of social role valorization and some reflections on elderly mentally retarded persons. In M. P. Janicki & H. M. Wisniewski (Eds.), *Aging and developmental disabilities: Issues and approaches* (pp. 61–76). Baltimore, MD: Paul H. Brookes.

Wood, P. (1975). *Classification of impairments and handicaps*. Geneva: World Health Organization, United Nations.

Zigman, W. B., Schupf, N., Haverman M., & Silverman, W. (1997). The epidemiology of Alzheimer's disease in intellectual disability: Results and recommendations from an international conference. *Journal of Intellectual Disabilities, 41*, 76–80.

Zigman, W. B., Schupf, N., Lubin, R. A., & Silverman. W. P. (1987). Premature regression of adults with Down syndrome. *American Journal of Mental Deficiency, 92*, 161–168.

Zigman, W. B., Seltzer, G. B., & Silverman, W. P. (1994). Behavioral and mental health changes associated with aging in adults with mental retardation. In M. M. Seltzer, M. W. Krauss, & M. P. Janicki (Eds.), *Life course perspective on adulthood and old age* (pp. 67–92). Washington, DC: American Association on Mental Retardation Monograph Series.

Ziring, P. R. (1987). A program that works. *Mental Retardation, 25*, 4, 207–210.

Ziring, P. R., Kastner, T., Friedman, D. L., Pond, W. S., Barnett, M. L., Sonnenberg, E. M., & Strassburger, K. (1988). Provision of health care for persons with developmental disabilities living in the community: The Morristown model. *Journal of the American Medical Association, 260*, 1439–1444.

12

SCHIZOPHRENIC DISORDERS

Joseph Walsh

S chizophrenia is a disorder of the brain characterized by abnormal patterns of thought and perception, as inferred from language and behavior. It is primarily a disorder of *thought,* which distinguishes it from psychotic disorders of *mood,* such as bipolar disorder.

DESCRIPTION

Schizophrenia includes two types of symptoms. *Positive* symptoms represent *exaggerations* of normal behavior. These include hallucinations, delusions, disorganized thought processes, and tendencies toward agitation. The *negative* symptoms represent *diminution* of what would be considered normal behavior. These include flat or blunted affect (the absence of expression), social withdrawal, noncommunication, anhedonia (blandness) or passivity, and ambivalence in decision making. A predominance of positive symptoms is sometimes called *Type 1 schizophrenia,* and a predominance of negative symptoms is sometimes called *Type 2 schizophrenia.* It is not clear whether these are distinct types of the disorder.

Hallucinations are sense perceptions of external objects when those objects are not present. These may be auditory, visual, gustatory (the perception of taste), tactile (feeling an object), somatic (an unreal experience within the body), or olfactory (a false sense of smell). *Delusions* are false beliefs that are maintained even though contradicted by social reality. They include persecutory (people or forces are attempting to harm the patient), erotomanic (another person is in love with the patient), somatic (pertaining to the patient's body functioning), and grandiose (the patient has an exaggerated sense of power, knowledge, or identity) beliefs, thought broadcasting (one's thoughts are overheard by others), thought insertion or withdrawal (others are putting thoughts into, or taking thoughts out of, the patient's head), delusions of being controlled (thoughts, feelings, or actions are being imposed on the patient by an external force), and delusions of reference (neutral events have special significance for the patient).

THE EXPERIENCE OF SCHIZOPHRENIA

The person with schizophrenia experiences pronounced sensory changes (Benioff, 1995). *Visual* changes include heightened sensitivity to light and color, a loss of visual perspective, of illusionary changes in faces and objects, and perceived distortions in size. *Auditory* changes include hallucinations, heightened sensitivity to noise, an inability to screen out background noise, the muting of sounds, and distortions of the sounds of voices. *Physical* changes include heightened sensitivity to touch, an inability to interpret internal sensations, and tactile and olfactory hallucinations. *Cognitive* changes include loose associations, the inability to filter out irrelevant information, distractibility, overstimulation of thoughts (flooding), feelings of enhanced mental efficiency, increased *or* decreased speed of thinking, fragmentation (the inability to create a whole from the parts), delusions, and idiosyncratic explanatory systems.

Persons with schizophrenia function well with a moderate amount of face-to-face interaction with significant others (Leff & Vaughn, 1985). Likewise, they manage moderate amounts of social stimulation well. They respond favorably to attitudes of acceptance, reasonable expectations, the opportunity to develop and practice social and vocational skills, and a relatively small number but broad range of social supports. These include contacts with family members, friends, neighbors, work peers, school peers, informal community relations, and perhaps co-religionists. Fifty percent (50%) of persons with schizophrenia attempt suicide, and 10% eventually succeed.

Effects on the Family

Schizophrenia has profound effects on family functioning (Hatfield & Lefley, 1993). When a person has schizophrenia, a chronic state of emotional burden develops, which is shared by all family members. Common emotional reactions include stress, anxiety, resentment of the impaired relative, grief, and depression. Spouses tend to blame each other for family turmoil, and siblings tend to blame parents. There is little time available for family leisure activities and one adult, usually the mother, becomes the primary caretaker of the impaired relative. Siblings have some reactions other than those of the parents, including emotional constriction in personality development, isolation from peers, and jealousy about the attention given to the impaired relative (National Alliance for the Mentally Ill, 1989). Factors that influence the family's coping well or poorly include the severity of the disorder (greater severity implies better coping), the preservation of time for other activities, the ability to be proactive rather than reactive in seeking assistance, and the availability of outside support.

DIAGNOSIS AND CLASSIFICATION

According to the *Diagnostic and Statistical Manual of Mental Disorders (DSM-IV)* (American Psychiatric Association, 1994), schizophrenia is characterized by at least six months of continuous symptoms. The person must display two or more active or positive symptoms (delusions, hallucinations, disorganized speech, and disorganized or catatonic behavior) for at least one month. The remainder of the six months may feature negative symptoms, and there must also be a decline in social functioning skills. Signs of the disturbance may be limited to negative symptoms during the premorbid (prior to the active phase) or residual (after stabilization from an active phase) periods.

There are five subtypes of schizophrenia, which may represent different disease processes. The *paranoid* type features a preoccupation with delusions or auditory hallucinations and a preservation of cognitive functioning and affect. *Disorganized* schizophrenia is characterized by disorganized speech, behavior, and flat or inappropriate affect. *Catatonic* schizophrenia features psychomotor disturbances of immobility or excessive mobility, mutism, odd gestures, echolalia (repeating the words of others), or echopraxia (repeating the movements of others). The *undifferentiated* type describes persons who do not meet criteria for the first three types. *Residual* schizophrenia describes the person who displays only negative symptoms after an active episode. This may be transient or persist for years. *DSM-IV* also provides six course specifiers for further detailing the client's experience.

The age of onset of schizophrenia is between 15 and 40 years. Men tend to develop the disorder at an earlier age than women (50% of men who develop schizophrenia do so by age 28, while 50% of women do so by age 33). The prevalence of schizophrenia is twice as high in lower than in higher socioeconomic classes. The "downward drift" hypothesis holds that many persons who develop schizophrenia lose occupational and social skills and fall into the lower classes, while others with premorbid personality traits never develop adequate skills to establish themselves in stable social roles. Persons with schizophrenia are more likely to have been born in the winter and early spring than in late spring and summer (Kaplan, Sadock, & Grebb, 1995). The reason for this is unclear, but season-specific risk factors such as dietary changes or a virus may be contributing factors.

There is a 1% worldwide prevalence of schizophrenia. Reliable data are difficult to ascertain across countries because of data collection and diagnostic differences, but still there is consistency among nations of the world. There are some areas where the prevalence is either very low (the southwest Pacific region) or very high (western Ireland and Croatia, in the former Yugoslavia). In 1990 in the United States, 2,009,000 persons, or 1.1% of the population, had schizophrenia or schizophreniform disorder (Bourdon, et al., 1994).

SCREENING INSTRUMENTS

A range of brief scales is available for use by social workers to assess symptoms and symptom changes for persons with schizophrenia. Three are described here. The *Psychiatric Symptom Assessment Scale* (PSAS) includes 23 items, each rated on a seven-point scale, and provides an overall score as well as scores for the domains of anxiety/depression, positive behavior symptoms, positive verbal symptoms, deficit symptoms, and paranoia (Bigelow & Berthot, 1989). The PSAS test can be administered during the course of a 30-minute interview. There is no standardized interview protocol included with the PSAS, but all items, and each point along the rating scale, include assessment and rating guidelines. The *Scale for the Assessment of Negative Symptoms* (SANS) and *Scale for the Assessment of Positive Symptoms* (SAPS) are complimentary instruments (Andreasen, 1982; Andreasen & Olsen, 1982). The SANS includes 25 items rated along a six-point scale with five subscales (affect, poverty of speech, apathy, anhedonia, and impairment of attention). The SAPS includes 35 items, four subscales (hallucinations, delusions, bizarreness, and positive thought disorder), and one global assessment of affect. Both are designed for use in conjunction with client interviews, clinical observations, family member observations, and reports from other professionals.

SCHIZOPHRENIA IN HISTORY

The first written accounts of what is now classified as schizophrenia, by John Haslam in London and Philippe Pinel in France, appeared in 1809

(Gottesman, 1991). During the next 50 years more accounts were documented, and in 1852 Benedict Morel in France introduced the term *démence précoce* to label the disorder. By 1896 the German psychiatrist Emil Kraepelin outlined the symptoms of "dementia praecox," which are largely consistent with those observed today. He specified several subtypes and emphasized its deteriorating course. In 1908, Eugen Bleuler in Switzerland renamed the disorder "schizophrenia" to emphasize the splitting of normally integrated thinking and emotive functions. Bleuler also argued that the disorder was not invariably deteriorating and could include periods of remission.

It is a mystery why schizophrenia apparently did not exist prior to the nineteenth century. Some have speculated that it was caused by the rise of urban societies or the breakdown of traditional family and cultural patterns. Others believe that a schizophrenia virus appeared at that time. Given the age of onset of schizophrenia, it may not have appeared because of shorter life spans prior to 1800 (averaging only 36 years in Massachusetts and New Hampshire). Whatever its origins, schizophrenia has maintained a stable prevalence for the past 100 years.

The classification of schizophrenia and its subtypes has evolved since the *DSM* was introduced in 1952. The term schizophrenic *reaction* indicates the emphasis at that time on psychological and social causes. The disorder became "schizophrenia" in *DSM-II* (1967), but otherwise there was much consistency in subtypes until the current list was introduced in *DSM-III* in 1980. These included *simple* schizophrenia, featuring what are now classified as negative symptoms; *hebephrenic* schizophrenia, featuring disorganized thinking; and *latent* schizophrenia, which highlighted premorbid symptoms and is now classified as *schizotypal personality disorder*. The *schizoaffective* type featured affective symptoms; since 1980 this has been classified as a separate psychotic disorder. The *acute* undifferentiated type (acute schizophrenic episode in *DSM-I*) is now classified as schizophreniform disorder. Two major changes in *DSM-III* included the six-month duration criterion, which limited the diagnosis to more severe cases, and an emphasis on positive symptoms of the disorder. *DSM-IV* focuses greater attention on negative symptoms, and the criterion of deterioration in functioning over the course of the disorder was eliminated.

CAUSAL THEORIES

The causes of schizophrenia are not known. Most research at present is focused in the genetic and biological areas, but psychological factors cannot be ruled out, particularly with regard to the course of the disorder. Biological theories of schizophrenia implicate the brain's limbic system, frontal cortex, and basal ganglia as primary sites of malfunction (Lieberman & Koreen, 1993). Whether symptoms result from abnormal development or deterioration of function is not clear. The dopamine hypothesis, established in the 1960s, asserted that schizophrenia results from an excess of that neurotransmitter in the nervous system. More recently possible causal roles of other neurotransmitters, including serotonin and norepinephrine, have been proposed. Brain imaging techniques have revealed enlarged ventricles in many persons with schizophrenia, which may be contributing causes in the consequent reduction in brain tissue (Lewis & Higgins, 1996). Prenatal viral exposure or brain trauma from birth complications have also been postulated as causal factors.

The genetic transmission of schizophrenia is supported by the higher-than-average risk factors among family members of persons with the disorder (Kendler & Diehl, 1993). A monozygotic (identical) twin of a person with schizophrenia has a 47% chance to develop the disorder; a dyzygotic (nonidentical) twin has only a 12% likelihood, which is the same probability as a child with one schizophrenic parent. A nontwin sibling has an 8% chance of developing the disorder. These statistics, while compelling, suggest that environmental influences also exist.

Various psychological and social factors have been postulated as significant in the development of schizophrenia. Freud (1904/1966) placed neurosis and psychosis on a continuum as resulting from similar psychological mechanisms. He wavered, however, between a defense and a deficit theory of schizophrenia. The defense theory conceptualized the symptoms as a means of adapting to internal conflict. The deficit theory implied a nonspecific organic defect, resulting in one's inability to sustain attachments to others and instead becoming preoccupied with internal experience.

Developmental theorists assert that mental disorders result from the inability to progress successfully through critical life stages. For example, problems with normal separation from the primary caregiver during the first few years of life may result in schizophrenia if developmental arrests result in an inability to distinguish the self from others (Mahler, Pine, & Bergman, 1975). The failure to make the transition from adolescence to young adulthood, with its challenges of forming of peer relationships, patterning sexual behavior, revising personal values, and developing independent living skills, has also been suggested as producing a regression that may result in schizophrenia (Dawson, Blum, & Bartolucci, 1983).

Family theorists have used such terms as "emotional divorce" (Bowen,

1960), "communication deviance" (Singer, et al., 1977), the "double-bind" (Bateson, et al., 1956), and family "schisms" and "skews" (Lidz, 1975) to describe problematic parent–child interactions that cause a child to withdraw into psychosis. These have been discounted as causal influences, although family relationships do have influence on the course of the disorder. Adolf Meyer and Harry Stack Sullivan are examples of early twentieth-century theorists who cited cultural influences as significant in the onset and course of schizophrenia (Faustman, 1995).

In summary, the *stress/diathesis theory* holds that schizophrenia results from a mix of constitutional factors—perhaps 70% due to heritability and biology—and environmental and stress factors—approximately 30% (Gottesman, 1991). Those external factors, however, are not specific to schizophrenia. They may include insults to the brain, threatening physical environments, emotionally intrusive or demanding experiences, emotional deprivation, and disruptions to cognitive processes. Smolar (1984) has summarized research on correlations between social class and schizophrenia, although it is not widely believed that these correlations represent causal relationships.

While the causes of schizophrenia are uncertain, there are clues for differentiating better and worse prognoses (Booth, 1995). Clients with a better prognosis demonstrate sudden onset, perceptual changes that are experienced as strange, and a predominance of positive symptoms. They exhibit normal intellectual functions, good response to medication, adaptability to social situations, and the ability to live independently. Clients with a worse prognosis feature a gradual onset, psychotic activity without subjective distress, and a predominance of negative symptoms. They exhibit intellectual deterioration, a poor response to medications, and poor social and independent-living skills.

CASE EXAMPLES

Rachel (Featuring Positive Symptoms)

Rachel was a 35-year-old single unemployed female, living alone, with a diagnosis of schizophrenia, paranoid type. She was tormented by auditory hallucinations in which persons from her family, as well as strangers, degraded her as worthless. She also heard the voices of angels each night, whispering that she would survive her suffering. Rachel believed that she was the spiritual caretaker for her elderly parents, who lived in another state, and by concentrating on their well-being she maintained a purpose in life.

Rachel had been an energetic, personable child, the second of four children born to a physician and his wife. She was a high academic achiever but was also histrionic, given to temper tantrums and interpersonal conflicts. Rachel had no long-term relationships with boys, and often fought with her girlfriends. During her adolescence she was treated for anorexia for several years. Her symptoms of schizophrenia emerged while she was living away from home, studying for a master's degree in English literature. Rachel was terrified when she began hearing the voices, but told no one about them. They became worse, however, until she could not concentrate on her academic work. Eventually Rachel became so afraid that she begged her friends and family for help. At this point she was hospitalized.

Nate (Negative Symptoms)

Nate was a 25-year-old unemployed male with schizophrenia, undifferentiated type. He lived with his divorced working mother in a suburban neighborhood. Nate was referred to a mental health agency from a psychiatric hospital, where he had been admitted for his first active episode of schizophrenia. After that discharge he intentionally overdosed on his prescription antipsychotic medications. Nate reported afterward that he was upset about experiencing his symptoms and could not bear the idea of having a mental illness.

Nate had been an "odd" child, extremely withdrawn throughout his adolescence and early adulthood, and gradually retreating almost completely from his family and peers. He attended school and managed his basic activities of daily living but otherwise stayed at home in his room. He spent his time reading science fiction novels, playing television video games, and watching movies. He never held a job. In late adolescence he began to experience hallucinations, including two voices (one soothing, the other threatening), and tactile sensations (a sense of being stroked on the leg, and of being suffocated while trying to sleep). Nate became so despondent, and his isolation so pronounced, that he was hospitalized. He retained insight into his "former" self, and knew that he was changing in ways that terrified him.

THE ROLE OF PHARMACOLOGY

Medication is the primary intervention modality for persons with schizophrenia. Such persons have a relatively high concentration of the neurotransmitter dopamine (five subtypes have been identified) in nerve cell pathways extending into the cortex and limbic system. Antipsychotic drugs act primarily by binding to dopamine receptors and blocking its transmission, but the newer drugs affect other neurotransmitters as well (Wilson & Claussen, 1993). The antipsychotic medications differ in their side-effect profiles, in the milligram amounts required in equivalent doses, and in the dopamine subtypes and other neurotransmitters that they target for action. Most of the "first generation" of antipsychotic medications (those introduced from the 1950s through the 1970s) target D2 receptors and are effective at reducing positive, but not negative, symptoms.

The first-generation antipsychotic medications act on all dopamine sites in the brain, but only the sites in the forebrain produce the symptoms of schizophrenia. The other pathways extend from the midbrain to the basal ganglia, which governs motor activity. A reduction in dopamine in these areas causes adverse effects: *akathisia* (restlessness and agitation), *dystonia* (muscle spasms), *parkinsonism* (muscle stiffness and tremor) and *tardive dyskinesia* (involuntary smooth-muscle movements of the face and limbs). *Anticholinergic* medications are often prescribed to combat these effects, even though they have their own adverse effects: blurred vision, dry mouth, and constipation.

Four antipsychotic medications have been introduced in the United States in the past ten years that act differently from those developed earlier. Clozapine (Clozaril), introduced in 1990, is a relatively weak D2 antagonist, but has a high affinity for D4 receptors, as well as interactions with D1, D3, serotonin, and other receptors (Meltzer, 1991). Its sites of action are the limbic forebrain and the frontal cortex; thus it does not carry the risk of side effects for the muscular system. In blocking receptors for serotonin,* it raises the possibility that this neurotransmitter has a role in symptomatology. The U.S. Food and Drug Administration (FDA) mandates that physicians prescribe this drug only if the client does not first respond to more traditional antipsychotic drugs, because of its rare but serious adverse effect of white-blood-cell depletion (agranulocytosis). Risperidone (Risperidol), introduced in 1994, also has fewer adverse effects than the first-generation drugs. It has a high affinity for both D2

---

*For a brief but thorough explanation of brain chemistry, and how psychoactive drugs affect it, see Chapter 4 of this volume.

and serotonin receptors, and supports the hypothesis that the serotonin antagonists diminish many of the adverse effects noted above. Olanzapine (Zyprexa) is an antagonist of all dopamine receptors, some serotonin receptors, and several other receptors. Sertindole (Serlect) is even more specifically targeted, interacting predominantly with D2 receptors, but it does not attach to receptors that produce sedative and anticholinergic effects (Tamminga, 1996). The actions of the newer drugs cast doubt that any single effect is responsible for their clinical activity (Bernstein, 1995). Further, their alleviation of the negative symptoms suggests that serotonin-antagonist activity is significant in this regard.

Despite advances in the pharmacological treatment of schizophrenia, the importance of the psychosocial therapies must not be deemphasized. Recent studies that focus on interactions between medications and individual, group, and family behavioral and educational interventions suggest significantly enhanced outcomes for clients as measured by rates of rehospitalization and symptom relapse (Schooler & Keith, 1993).

Bentley and Walsh (1996) have outlined six roles for social workers with regard to clients using psychotropic medications. In the role of *physician's assistant,* the social worker supports the recommendations of the client's physician regarding medication use. The *consultant/collaborator* performs preliminary screenings to determine clients' possible needs for medication, makes referrals to physicians, and regularly consults with the physician and client. The *advocate* supports the client's expressed wishes regarding medication and presents them to others in the service milieu. The advocate may help clients and family members relate to physicians and others in obtaining services, or to administrative bodies regarding access to medications. The social worker is also a *monitor* of the positive and negative effects of the medication. The *educator* provides clients and significant others with information about issues relevant to medication use, including actions, benefits, and risks. Finally, the *researcher* uses case reports and other research designs to study how medications impact the lives of clients and families and how they interact with other interventions.

SOCIAL WORK INTERVENTION

Clinical Case Management

Case management is a person-in-environment approach to intervention that attempts to ensure that clients with schizophrenia receive the services they need in a timely, appropriate fashion (Rubin, 1992). It includes the

Rachel's Medications

Rachel's psychosis was continuously active. Several first-generation antipsychotic medications were prescribed to control her hallucinations and agitation, but she did not respond well to them. She did not complain of adverse effects so much as experience limited positive benefit. Eventually Rachel was prescribed clozapine (Clozaril), which presented her with a serious physical problem: she experienced a drop in white-blood-cell count and was thus at risk for agranulocytosis. The medication had to be withdrawn, and Rachel was again given a more traditional antipsychotic medication, along with an anticholinergic drug to counter the side effects. The latter medication produced very uncomfortable side effects of dry mouth and constipation. Later Rachel began taking another of the newer antipsychotic medications and experienced greater benefit with fewer side effects. The medication did not, however, eliminate her symptoms.

Nate's Medications

Nate was first prescribed a moderate dose of an antipsychotic medication and experienced pronounced extrapyramidal symptoms. He felt stiff and could not walk comfortably, and complained that he was physically not the same person. Part of the reason Nate became suicidal was his belief that he would have to sacrifice physical well-being to take medications. After the second hospitalization the physician and social worker saw Nate every two weeks to titrate his medications—that is, to test and adjust their strengths. The social worker monitored their positive and adverse effects weekly and reported these to the physician. In the end, all agreed on a type and dosage that seemed to have positive benefits and a minimum of adverse effects. This was in fact a low-dose regimen that controlled, but did not eliminate, his anxiety and hallucinations. They did not alter his symptoms of anhedonia and ambivalence.

functions of client assessment, planning for service acquisition, linkage with appropriate service providers, advocacy on behalf of clients with other providers, monitoring of service quality, and evaluation of the overall process (Intagliata, 1982). Intervention goals tend to focus on empowerment and the development of skills for relationship building, independent living, stress management, and vocational adjustment. Case management, provided independently or by a team, is essential for clients with schizophrenia because the resources and personnel needed for service delivery are spread across agency systems. The range of client needs may include housing, income support, medical care, job training, recreation, and living skills development, as well as counseling and medication. The social worker as case manager may work with physicians, nurses, psychologists, occupational therapists, mental health technicians, and lay resource providers, each of whom has expertise in addressing one or another portion of the client's needs.

Clinical case management emphasizes the role of the social worker as a service provider as well as a broker. Its components include intermittent individual counseling, consultation with caregivers, and crisis intervention activities, plus a commitment to the challenges of long-term intervention (Kanter, 1995). The clinical case manager must be able to develop a longitudinal view of the client's strengths, limitations, and symptoms and know how to facilitate the client's own resourcefulness.

The Clinical Relationship

The person with schizophrenia enters treatment with a pervasive ambivalence. There is an initial mistrust of the social worker because the client has difficulty managing relationships and has learned from experience that others are likely to devalue him or her. The client may feel lonely and detached, but nevertheless so anxious about the stress associated with interpersonal activity that isolation seems preferable. In some instances the client will become dependent, valuing the worker's directives because he or she fears taking initiatives. The worker may be perceived as powerful, but this may lead to disappointment if the worker demonstrates evidence of ineffectiveness. The client's motivation for treatment may include a magical craving for improvement rather than what the worker hopes will be a cooperative striving for change (Lantz, 1987).

The social worker may in turn experience some negative feelings toward the client, which must be acknowledged for the relationship to develop positively. These include reactions to the client's behavior, appearance, passive personality, or dependent traits, all of which are contrary to society's values (Minkoff, 1987). Ambivalence about working with the client and interpersonal distancing are common defenses against frustrations with slow client progress. The social worker may also be uncomfortable with the need to assume a highly active clinical posture. Finally, when this is the client's only significant relationship, the worker may resist intimacy to avoid feeling so responsible for the client's well-being.

Every relationship exists within a symbolic frame of reference, including those shared images and behaviors that make private experiences mutually understandable. With the client having schizophrenia this develops largely through nonverbal behaviors, because the client is ineffective with verbal communication (Arieti, 1974). Some persons with schizophrenia achieve stable mental status and rapidly engage in the treatment process, but it is generally a mistake for the social worker to verbally respond too readily to the client who is too quiet or who communicates psychotic ideas. The worker may be uncomfortable with silence or eager to decode the client's psychotic associations so as to proceed with concrete goal setting. A positive therapeutic climate is promoted most effectively by the worker's nonverbal communication of acceptance. An ambience of warmth will be perceived by the client as affirming and will facilitate the development of a working relationship. Forming such a relationship is not an easy task, as persons with schizophrenia are sensitive to nonverbal behavior and will perceive any negative feelings.

Once a working relationship is established and the social worker understands the client's priorities, supportive interventions are effective in helping the client make positive adjustments. These include education, advice, and suggestion; encouragement and praise; strengthening of adaptive defenses; emphasizing client strengths; and environmental interventions (Farmer, Walsh, & Bentley, 1998). Social-skills training addresses deficits in interpersonal relating through the development of specific skills needed for everyday living. Interventions that employ behavioral assessment, social-learning principles, and skills training improve the course and outcome of schizophrenia as measured by symptom reduction, social functioning, and quality of life (Liberman, et al., 1996). Cognitive-behavioral interventions—based on the premise that a person's affect and behaviors are largely mediated by beliefs—include modifying dysfunctional assumptions, improving coping responses, and relabeling psychotic experiences. These interventions can influence hallucinations and delusions by decreasing their frequency and the distress associated with them, and by increasing the person's belief that the voices are really his or her own thoughts (Kuipers, et al., 1996). All of these interventions emphasize the importance of the social worker's developing a relationship of trust with the client.

Group Interventions

Treatment groups for persons with schizophrenia are effective in achieving goals of improved coping with symptoms and enhanced interpersonal relationships. Interaction-oriented groups are consistently found to be superior to insight-oriented groups in this regard. Kahn and Kahn (1992) categorize groups into four models, including those of convenience (maintenance of current mental status), topic specificity (including specific subject matter, such as medication education), phase-orientation (for clients who face common psychosocial development issues, such as community adjustment following hospital discharge), and eclecticism (integrating broad domains of human behavior in the promotion of coping and growth over a long course). Another typology of groups offered by Bond and DeGraaf-Kaser (1990) differentiates among those that are unstructured (open-ended, with broad subject matter), structured (education and skill development formats), experiential in vivo (self-help and drop-in groups), and structured in vivo groups (such as supported employment).

The most common types of groups for persons with schizophrenia are unstructured and eclectic. These may be open or closed, ongoing or time-limited, and within or outside of residential and hospital settings, but they are characterized by a process of verbal interaction, facilitated by social workers, aimed toward achieving goals related to social adaptation. In these groups, social workers may participate as leaders or facilitators providing support to the client leaders. The range of skills necessary for the social worker leading a treatment group include (Walsh & Hewitt, 1996):

1. maintaining a safe place for clients to reveal difficulties and request help;
2. providing relevant information regarding symptoms, medication, interventions, coping with schizophrenia, and community resources;
3. moving members from the general to the specific regarding the content of their sharing;
4. respecting the reluctance of members to participate at times;
5. affirming positive member contributions;
6. establishing and maintaining clear behavioral limits.

Clients may implement self-help groups, which have the same goals and organization as those noted above. In these groups the social worker may participate in supportive roles, including helping with physical organization (securing a room, resources, supplies, etc.), orienting new members, securing educational materials, monitoring the group process to ensure that all members feel included, and helping to diffuse tensions that arise.

Family Interventions

In recognition of the evidence that family dynamics do not cause schizophrenia but have an impact on its course, most family interventions are now psychoeducational in nature. Goals include educating family members about schizophrenia and its treatment and helping families create a facilitative environment for the client's growth while attending to the needs of all members. Some models incorporate crisis management. Parents, siblings, and adult children of persons with schizophrenia sometimes prefer separate groups. The key elements found in effective family intervention include structure and stability, focusing on the here and now, cognitive restructuring, behavioral approaches, a focus on improving family communication, the social worker's positive attitude, and collaborative working relationships (Lam, 1991).

There is substantial evidence that psychoeducational family interventions reduce the rate of relapse, psychiatric symptomatology, family burden, and financial costs of intervention, and improve both the client member's functioning and the family's well-being (Lefley, 1996; Dixon & Lehman, 1995). Psychoeducation delivered within multiple family groups appears to be more effective with regard to relapse rates than single-family models. (McFarlane, 1994). More research is needed on interventions with specific racial, gender, and ethnic family groups, as well as families that are not in contact with their relative with schizophrenia.

Rachel's Intervention

Rachel's delusions, hallucinations, and anxieties were so intense that she could not sustain ongoing social interaction. She strove to maintain a connection with her family by believing that she was watching over them. Through her delusions she was making efforts to find personal meaning. Some mental health workers categorized her perceptions as merely "symptoms" and discouraged her from talking about them. They felt that only her rational thinking should be reinforced. This was demeaning to Rachel and prevented her from entrusting to others the feelings she experienced with her perceptions.

Rachel and her social worker met every two weeks. She initially tested him by describing her beliefs, to gauge his reactions. When he did not judge her, but expressed interest and asked for more details, she shared her inner world more thoroughly. He focused on the feelings associated with her symptoms. He understood that Rachel would function much better with more accurate perceptions of the external world, but he affirmed the positive intent of her efforts to show caring for others.

For four years he worked to stabilize her thinking and affect through counseling, medication monitoring, and a small number of graduated social activities. This was difficult, as Rachel had a low tolerance for anxiety. For a long while she dismissed his invitations to investigate clubhouse and vocational programs and other social activities. The social worker also maintained regular contact with her parents and siblings so that they could help her achieve purposeful roles within the family. Rachel, who had a graduate degree in English, eventually accepted a volunteer position in a local bookstore, working in the stock room. This was difficult for her, and the social worker consulted routinely with the store manager to support his keeping Rachel on staff when her performance was erratic. The social worker maintained a supportive climate in which Rachel's issues about connection, isolation, and purpose could be discussed.

Nate's Intervention

Nate's negative orientation to relationships was a problem for the social worker. Nate always appeared sullen and withholding. He had a passive-aggressive personality style, being outwardly compliant with directives but then ignoring them. Initially Nate had a few friends, but they all smoked marijuana and drank alcohol, which made his symptoms worse. Still, the social worker maintained regular contact with Nate as his counselor and central point of intervention. In addition to dealing with his schizophrenia, Nate was prone to depression, particularly when his few relationships ended. He met new peers in his rehabilitation programs, but resisted socializing with them. The worker was concerned about Nate's suicide potential, and also wanted, but was not able (because of the reluctance of both) to work with his mother toward repairing the tension in their relationship. However, his mother did attend the agency's family education and support group.

Nate identified three goals: getting a good-paying job, finding his own apartment, and meeting enough "healthy" people so that he could find a few male friends and a girlfriend. These goals were ambitious, but realistic if pursued gradually. The social worker initiated a great deal of referral, linkage, advocacy, and monitoring activities over several years in addressing them. First, as noted earlier, Nate's medications were titrated. Next, his vocational potential was formally assessed. He enrolled in a computer training program, which ended with his referral to a job placement agency. His other activities included a clubhouse program where he addressed his interpersonal goals, a volunteer position where he tested his work readiness, and participation with various material resource providers. There were a half-dozen professionals working with Nate on separate tasks, and while progress was slow, he eventually achieved a level of competence such that he accepted a job.

The issue of timing in the social worker's service linkages was delicate. He needed to carefully assess at what times Nate was ready for another step in the process of rehabilitation, when he needed to be restrained from moving ahead, when he needed to be pushed, and when services should be withheld to encourage Nate to take initiatives. The social worker also routinely assessed the stability of Nate's thought processes to determine when cognitive interventions might be effective in supplementing the behavioral milieu.

Nate worked for three weeks and then began despairing over problems he experienced in managing the stresses of a new job. Success on this job might have led to his acquisition of an apartment and responsibility for his own budget, but Nate feared that he was failing. He made a second suicide attempt, which was fortunately not successful. Following a brief hospital stay Nate returned to the same job with reduced hours. He eventually mastered it with the assistance of a job coach.

CONCLUSION

There is much that remains unknown about the causes, course, and treatment of schizophrenia. While other professions pursue research in the genetic, biological, and pharmaceutical arenas, social workers must focus on developing further knowledge of the psychosocial influences on the disorder. Effective interventions with clients and families have been documented, but more research is needed about the intervention needs of special populations including persons of different races, ethnic groups, age groups, sexual preferences, and socioeconomic status. This will lead to the development of new resources, which enhance the functioning of all clients. The clinical case management modality acknowledges that persons with schizophrenia have multiple psychosocial needs, and thus social workers are in a prime position to further the philosophy of holistic practice through the promotion of these interventions. Above all, social workers need to maintain a commitment to the empowerment of persons with schizophrenia. These clients comprise a group that is devalued by the larger society because of their relative lack of political and economic influence. Few other professions seem as willing as social work to act toward them with the dignity they deserve.

REFERENCES

American Psychiatric Association. (1994). *Diagnostic and statistical manual of mental disorders, fourth edition.* Washington, DC: Author.

Andreasen, N. C. (1982). Negative symptoms of schizophrenia: Definition and reliability. *Archives of General Psychiatry, 39,* 784–788.

Andreasen, N. C., & Olsen, S. (1982). Negative vs. positive schizophrenia: Definition and validation. *Archives of General Psychiatry, 39,* 789–794.

Arieti, S. (1974). *Interpretation of schizophrenia* (2nd Ed.). New York: Basic Books.

Bateson, G., Jackson, D. D., Haley, J., & Weakland, J. H. (1963). A note on the double-bind-1962. *Family Process, 2,* 154–161.

Benioff, L. (1995). What is it like to have schizophrenia? In S. Vinogradov (Ed.), *Treating schizophrenia* (pp. 81–107). San Francisco: Jossey-Bass.

Bentley, K. J., & Walsh, J. (1996). *The social worker and psychotropic medication.* Pacific Grove, CA: Brooks/Cole.

Bernstein, J. G. (1995). *Handbook of drug therapy in psychiatry* (3rd Ed.). St. Louis: C. V. Mosby.

Bigelow, L. B., & Berthot, B. D. (1989). The psychiatric symptom assessment scale (PSAS). *Psychopharmacology Bulletin, 25,* 2, 168–179.

Bond, G. R., & DeGraaf-Kaser, R. (1990). Group approaches for persons with serious mental illness: A typology. *Social Work With Groups, 13,* 1, 21–36.

Booth, G. K. (1995). What is the prognosis in schizophrenia? In S. Vinogradov (Ed.), *Treating schizophrenia* (pp. 125–156). San Francisco: Jossey-Bass.

Bourdon, K. H., Rae, D. S., Narrow, W. E., Manderscheid, R. W., & Regier, D. A. (1994). In R. W. Manderscheid & Sonnenschein, M. A. (Eds.), *Mental health, United States, 1994.* DHHS Publication Number (SMA) 94-3000. Washington, DC: U.S. Government Printing Office.

Bowen, M. (1960). A family concept of schizophrenia. In D. D. Jackson (Ed.), *The etiology of schizophrenia* (pp. 346–372). New York: Basic Books.

Dawson, D. F. L., Blum, H. M., & Bartolucci, G. (1983). *Schizophrenia in focus.* New York: Human Sciences Press.

Dixon, L. B., & Lehman, A. F. (1995). Family interventions for schizophrenia. *Schizophrenia Bulletin, 21,* 4, 631–643.

Farmer, R. L., Walsh, J., & Bentley, K. J. (1998). Schizophrenia. In B. A. Thyer & J. S. Wodarski (Eds.), *Handbook of empirical social work practice. Vol. 1, Mental disorders* (pp. 245–270). New York: John Wiley.

Faustman, W. O. (1995). What causes schizophrenia? In S. Vinogradov (Ed.), *Treating schizophrenia* (pp. 57–80). San Francisco: Jossey-Bass.

Freud, S. (1904/1966). *Introductory lectures on psychoanalysis*. New York: W. W. Norton.

Gottesman, I. I. (1991). *Schizophrenia genesis: The origins of madness*. New York: W. H. Freeman.

Hatfield, A. B., & Lefley, H. P. (1993). *Surviving mental illness: Stress, coping, and adaptation*. New York: Guilford Press.

Intagliata, J. (1982). Improving the quality of community care for the chronically mentally disabled: The role of case management. *Schizophrenia Bulletin, 8, 4, 655–673.*

Kahn, E. M., & Kahn, E. W. (1992). Group treatment assignment for outpatients with schizophrenia: Integrating recent clinical and research findings. *Community Mental Health Journal, 28, 6, 539–549.*

Kanter, J. (1995). Case management with long-term patients: A comprehensive approach. In Soreff, S. (Ed.), *Handbook for the treatment of the seriously mentally ill* (pp. 169–189). Seattle: Hogrefe and Humber.

Kaplan, H. I., Sadock, B. J., & Grebb, J. A. (1994). *Synopsis of psychiatry: Behavioral sciences, clinical psychiatry* (7th Ed.). Baltimore, MD: Williams & Wilkins.

Kendler, K. S., & Diehl, S. R. (1993). The genetics of schizophrenia. *Schizophrenia Bulletin, 19, 2, 261–286.*

Kuipers, E., Garety, P., & Fowler, D. (1996). An outcome study of cognitive-behavioural treatment for psychosis. In G. Haddock & D. Slade (Eds.), *Cognitive-behavioural interventions with psychotic disorders*. London: Routledge.

Lam, D. H. (1991). Psychosocial family intervention in schizophrenia: A review of empirical studies. *Psychological Medicine, 21, 423–441.*

Lantz, J. (1987). Emotional motivations for family treatment. *Social Casework, 68, 284–289.*

Leff, J. P., & Vaughn, C. E. (1985). *Expressed emotion in families*. New York: Guilford.

Lefley, H. P. (1996). *Family caregiving in mental illness*. Thousand Oaks, CA: Sage.

Lewis, S. & Higgins, N. (1996). *Brain imaging in psychiatry*. Cambridge, MA: Blackwell.

Liberman, R. P., Kopelowicz, A., & Young, A. (1996). Biobehavioral treatment and rehabilitation of schizophrenia. *Behavior Therapy, 25, 1, 89–107.*

Lidz, T. (1975). *The origin and treatment of schizophrenic disorders*. London: Hogarth.

Lieberman, J. A., & Koreen, A. R. (1993). Neurochemistry and neuroendocrinology of schizophrenia: A selective review. *Schizophrenia Bulletin, 19, 2, 197–255.*

Mahler, M. S., Pine, F., & Bergman, A. (1975). *The psychological birth of the human infant*. New York: Basic Books.

Meltzer, H. Y. (1991). The mechanism of action of novel antipsychotic drugs. *Schizophrenia Bulletin, 17, 2, 71–95.*

McFarlane, W. R. (1994). Multiple-family groups and psychoeducation in the treatment of schizophrenia. *New Directions in Mental Health Services, 62, 13–22.*

Minkoff, K. (1987). Resistance of mental health professionals to working with the chronically mentally ill. In Myerson, A. (Ed.), *Barriers to treating the chronically mentally ill* (pp. 3–20). New Directions for Mental Health Services, San Francisco: Jossey-Bass.

National Alliance for the Mentally Ill. (1989). *Siblings and adult children's network: Background information and articles booklet*. Arlington, VA: Author.

Rubin, A. (1992). Case management. In S. M. Rose (Ed.), *Case management and social work practice* (pp. 5–24). New York: Longman.

Schooler, N. R., & Keith, S. S. (1993). The clinical research base for the treatment of schizophrenia. *Psychopharmacology Bulletin, 29, 4, 431–436.*

Singer, M. T., Wynne, L. C., & Toohey, M. L. (1978). Communication disorders and the families of schizophrenics. In L. C. Wynne, R. L. Cromwell, & S. Matthysse (Eds.), *The nature of schizophrenia* (pp. 512–516). New York: John Wiley.

Smolar, T. (1984). Schizophrenic disorders. In F. J. Turner (Ed.), *Adult psychopathology: A social work perspective* (pp. 119–147). New York: Free Press.

Tamminga, C. T. (1996). The new generation of antipsychotic drugs. *National Alliance for Research on Schizophrenia and Depression Newsletter*, Winter.

Walsh, J., & Hewitt, H. (1996). Facilitating an effective process in treatment groups with persons having serious mental illness. *Social Work With Groups, 19*, 1, 5–18.

Wilson, W. H., & Claussen, A. M. (1992). New antipsychotic drugs: Hope for the future. *Innovations & Research, 2*, 1, 3–12.

13

AFFECTIVE DISORDERS

Mary Kay O'Neil

Depression is the most common form of adult psychopathology confronting mental health professionals. Since antiquity, depression has been recognized as a painful affective state associated with physical, psychological, and social distress. The extent of the problem is currently reflected in the increasing rate of depression among young adults, the spiraling number of suicide attempts, and the upsurge in suicides and accidental deaths, as well as in the recognition that depression is a potential threat at every age and phase of development. It is estimated that more than 12% of adults will at some point become sufficiently depressed to require treatment and 15–30% will suffer from less severe but nevertheless disabling symptoms; however, only 10–25% of people with depressive symptoms seek professional help for this disorder (Klerman, 1975, 1978). Thus, the majority of clinically depressed individuals, for reasons such as social and/or financial circumstances, psychological resistances, and lack of appropriate treatment resources, fail to receive help. These facts about depression provide a challenge to the social work practitioner.

It is important, therefore, for social workers to be able to recognize depression, especially in its early stages or when the mood disturbance is masked by other symptoms. It is also important, in the light of recent clinical and research developments, for social workers to identify those depressed persons who can be helped by modern drug treatments and who ought to be referred for psychiatric assessment. Social work practitioners will find it easier to recognize depression, make appropriate referrals, and mobilize psychosocial factors in treatment if they are familiar with the epidemiology, etiology, psychopathology, and treatment of depression.

This chapter surveys these topics, paying special attention to advances

I wish to acknowledge with thanks the help of Frederick Lowy, M.D., who provided the author with psychiatric consultation and gave critical review of this chapter.

during the past two decades that have led to changes in the classification, diagnosis, and treatment of depression. These advances, especially in the area of psychosocial factors, have major implications for the social worker confronted with depressed clients.

THE NATURE OF DEPRESSION

Use of the Term "Depression"

"Depression" is a term used in everyday language to connote a well-known dysphoric feeling state. In the medical-psychiatric literature, the word "depression" is used to refer to a mood, a symptom, or a syndrome. A "depressed mood"—the phenomenon of feeling blue, sad, unhappy in response to the difficulties and disappointments of everyday life—is experienced by all people at some point. "Depression as a symptom" is usually more intense, prolonged, varied, or inappropriate to the situation than the common dysphoric mood state. Depressive symptoms can occur in affective disorders, as well as in most other psychiatric and some medical disorders, or even without a concomitant diagnosable disorder. In contrast, a "depressive syndrome" is a cluster of symptoms and behavioral disturbances that meets criteria for a psychiatric diagnosis of one of the subtypes of clinical depression, currently referred to as "affective disorders."

Features of Depression

The signs and symptoms of a depressive syndrome include:

dysphoric mood: feeling sad, unhappy, blue, despondent; unable to enjoy life; sometimes showing irritability, anxiety, intense worry, or fear

cognitive disturbance: low self-esteem; ideas of helplessness, hopelessness, worthlessness, failure, guilt, self-blame, at times to the point of delusional thinking; suicidal ideation, which may lead to suicide attempts (see Chapter 27); desire to be dead or recurrent thoughts about death; indecisiveness and inability to concentrate

behavioral disturbance: psychomotor retardation or agitation

disturbance in social functioning: loss of interest or pleasure in socializing or usual activities; impaired capacity to perform work-related and other tasks

disturbance in physiological functioning: loss of appetite and impaired gastrointestinal function; menstrual disturbance or even amenorrhea; insomnia or hypersomnia; sexual disturbance, possibly including impotence

Table 13–1 DSM-III Classification of Affective Disorders

Major Affective Disorders
  Bipolar disorder
    Manic
    Depressed
    Mixed
  Major depression
    Single episode
    Recurrent
Other Specific Affective Disorders
  Cyclothymic disorder
  Dysthymic disorder (or depressive neurosis)
Atypical Affective Disorders
  Atypical bipolar disorder
  Atypical depression

Source: American Psychiatric Association, *Diagnostic and Statistical Manual of Mental Disorders, Third Edition* (Washington, D.C.: American Psychiatric Association, 1980), pp. 17–18.

Classification of Depression

In recent years, several new diagnostic classifications have been introduced and the area is in a state of flux. *Diagnostic and Statistical Manual of Mental Disorders,* Third Edition (*DSM-III*) (American Psychiatric Association, 1980) classifies depression as shown in Table 13–1. This is likely to be the most frequently used classification for some time, at least in North America. The reason for all the activity in this area and the reason why mental health workers need to pay attention to the subdivisions of depression is that some depressed patients (but not others) have been found consistently to respond favorably to somatic treatment—antidepressant drugs, lithium, and electroconvulsive therapy (ECT).

The symptoms of, and diagnostic criteria for, the various types of affective disorders are reviewed in the standard psychiatric textbooks (e.g., Freedman, et al., 1974) and in *DSM-III.* Essentially the subtypes of depression are distinguished by the specific symptoms of mania and depression, as well as by the number, intensity, and duration of symptoms. For example, the *DSM-III* diagnostic criteria for "major depressive episode" include prominent and persistent dysphoric mood and at least four symptoms of depression that have been present nearly every day for at least two weeks. In contrast, the diagnostic criteria for "dysthymic disorder" require that the person has been bothered most or all of the time for at least a two-year period by symptoms characteristic of the depressive syndrome but not of sufficient severity and duration to meet the criteria for a major depressive episode; there must be relatively persistent manifestations of the depressive syndrome, which may be separated by periods of normal mood lasting a few days to a few weeks, but no more than a few months at a time; finally, the person must exhibit prominent depressed mood during the depressive periods and at least three of the nonpsychotic symptoms of depression.

EPIDEMIOLOGY OF DEPRESSION

Current Rates of Depression

Current epidemiological studies of affective disorders document the extent of the problem of depression. Measurement of these disorders has become more standardized, resulting in more reliable rates for the general population and for subgroups defined by sociodemographic factors such as age, sex, and social class.

The basic epidemiological technical terms are "incidence" (number of new cases per year); "point prevalence" (number of cases measured at one point in time); "period prevalence" (total cases in a specified period of time, e.g., one year—hence "annual prevalence"); and "lifetime expectance," or "morbid risk" (an individual's lifetime risk of having a first episode of illness). A recent review of English-language epidemiological studies of affective disorders summarized the current rates for the general population (Boyd & Weissman, 1981):

1. Point prevalence of depressive symptoms ranges between 9 and 20%
2. Annual incidence of bipolar disorder* is 0.009–.015% for men and 0.007–.03% for women; lifetime risk is less than 1% for both females and males
3. Point prevalence of other nonbipolar depression is 3% for men and 4–9% for women; lifetime risk is 8–12% for men and 20–26% for women*

In the next few years, extensive epidemiological data, based on standardized diagnostic interviews, are expected to be available on depression and other psychiatric disorders from the National Institute of Mental Health (Hirschfeld & Cross, 1982).

Demographic Factors

Correlations between demographic factors and the occurrence of depression are important because they help identify subgroups at risk.

---

*"Bipolar" is the term used to describe the former category of manic-depressive illness, that is, depression followed quickly by a state of excitation or mania.

Sex

The most important demographic finding is the greater prevalence of depressive disorders among women: when all depressive disorders are considered, there is a fairly consistent female-to-male ratio of 2:1 (Weissman & Klerman, 1977b). The preponderance of women among depressed patients seems to be even higher for less severe depression (Klerman, 1978) and is found in all but two age groups: young adult university students (Golin & Hartz, 1979; Hammen & Padesky, 1977; O'Neil, et al., 1982b; Parker, 1979; Radloff, 1980) and older persons (Wasylenki, 1980). It has been suggested that men and women in these two groups are equally likely to be depressed because there is less sex role differentiation among the aged and among students.

Age

The rarer and more serious first manic episode of bipolar disorder usually occurs before age 30; whereas major depression may begin at any age and the age of onset is fairly evenly distributed throughout adult life. Other affective disorders (cyclothymic disorder and dysthymic disorder) usually begin early in adult life. Although there is some controversy as to whether or not young children suffer from diagnosable depression, diagnosable affective disorders have a high prevalence at each stage of the life cycle from adolescence to old age. All age groups are vulnerable to some type of depressive difficulty.

Social Class and Marital Status

Social class, occupation, and education are related to psychiatric illnesses and sometimes determine their treatment. Although there is some tendency for the incidence of affective disorders to be slightly higher in higher social strata, this trend is neither strong nor constant (Klerman, 1978). In fact, depression cuts across all strata of society. The relationship between marital status and the spectrum of depressive illnesses is not clear. There is some disputed evidence that married women tend more toward depression than do single women; single men more than single women; and single men slightly more than married men. The separated, divorced, and widowed have slightly higher rates in both sexes (Radloff, 1980).

Help-seeking and Service Use

Depressed women are twice as likely as men to seek and receive help (Kessler, et al., 1981).

ETIOLOGY OF DEPRESSION

Biological Factors in Depression

Genetic factors in the etiology of depression were suspected for a long time, but the evidence was inconclusive until 10–20 years ago. Greater use of standardized interviewing techniques and operationally defined diagnostic categories has made it clear that in at least two subgroups of depression—bipolar disorder and the major (unipolar) depressions—there is a strong family pattern, along with higher concordance in monozygotic than in dizygotic twins and more depression in the biological than in the adoptive parents of depressed patients who were adopted shortly after birth (Nurnberger & Gershon, 1982). Recently, Weitkamp and associates (1981) reported on a deficit in a specific chromosome in depressed patients with a strong family history of bipolar disease.

Genetic factors likely operate through biochemical pathways, although the biochemical lesion has not yet been identified. A severely depressed patient has many bodily changes, but it is not clear which might play a role in the production of the depression and which are the result of the depression. At present, the evidence suggests abnormalities in the level of biogenic amines, which are a class of neurotransmitters (substances produced at the junction of nerve cells in the central nervous system that permit messages to pass from one nerve cell to another) (see Chapter 4). The principal neurotransmitters whose metabolism may be disturbed in depression are norepinephrine, serotonin, dopamine, and acetylcholine.

There is also evidence that a different biological system, the adrenocortical steroid hormones under the control of the hypothalamus and the pituitary gland in the brain, is disturbed in depression.

Extensive investigation of these and other factors is presently under way, and it seems likely that in the next decade the biological factors that contribute to some types of depression will be identified. Already there are biological tests that promise to distinguish reliably bipolar and major depressions from neurotic characterological depressions.

Social Factors in Depression

In the past decade, there has been a resurgence of interest in the psychosocial factors related to depression. Particular attention has been paid to early loss of a parent or other nurturing person, family history of psychiatric illness (especially the effect of being raised by an emotionally ill parent or with an emotionally disturbed sibling), recent and chronic stressful life events, and presence or absence of social support.

Early Loss of a Significant Other

A relationship between the loss of a nurturing person early in life (childhood through early adolescence) and the subsequent development of depression was first postulated many years ago. This relationship has been supported by a vast clinical literature (for a review see Furman, 1974) and by some population studies. In a recent review, Lloyd (1980a & b) reported that the majority of studies found a higher incidence of early loss among depressed as compared with nondepressed controls. However, Crook and Eliot (1980), in a similar review, came to a different conclusion: "There is no sound base of empirical data to support the theorized relationship between parental death during childhood and adult depression." Most recently, Kennard and Britchnell (1982) concluded that although they had found a link between a poor relationship with the mother and subsequent psychopathology, this link was independent of maternal loss. The research evidence, then, remains controversial.

There is also some evidence linking early loss of a parent by death to severity of depression (Brown & Harris, 1978; Brown, et al., 1977) and to attempted suicide later in life (Adam, et al., 1982). However, other investigators have failed to find an association between loss of a parent in childhood, either by death or by separation, and adult depression (O'Neil-Lowy, 1983; Tennant, et al., 1980). Although these findings are forcing a reassessment of the hypothesized loss–depression relationship, the experience of loss in childhood does, of course, emerge as an important focus in the treatment of some depressed people.

There are several clinically relevant points here. First, it is reassuring to know that early loss does not inevitably lead to depression and that many people (even as children) have a remarkable capacity to handle major loss. In fact, it is well recognized that the circumstances surrounding the loss (quality of the lost parenting, type and handling of the loss, capacity and opportunity to mourn, presence and quality of substitute parenting) are major determinants of later psychological problems, including depression. Second, poor, neglectful parenting may be a greater factor in depression than is actual loss by death or separation, provided that the latter is dealt with sensitively. Third, even if loss does not necessarily predict later depression, the history of loss or recent loss in a particular depressed person may be highly relevant clinically and often constitutes an important focus of treatment.

Family History of Psychiatric Illness

There is much less inconsistency in the evidence for a relationship between family history of psychiatric illness and depression; in fact, the link has been recognized since the nineteenth century. Recent family studies and the identification of some biological indicators make it seem likely that recurrent major depression has a primarily biological basis (Nurnberger & Gershon, 1982).

For the bipolar affective disorders, there is reasonably good evidence of a genetic component. The evidence for the genetic transmission of recurrent major depression is not as strong (Kidd & Weissman, 1976), but some studies have confirmed that a family history of either depression or alcoholism increases the risk for unipolar disorder (Winokur, 1979; Winokur & Morrison, 1973). There is less evidence for a strong genetic component in chronic, or so-called characterological, depression. Rosenthal and colleagues (1981) found that when a group of characterological depressions were compared with primary unipolar controls there was a "significantly lower incidence of familial depressions, but higher frequencies of loss of a parent in childhood, familial alcoholism and parental assortative mating" (p. 183). They commented that "nature and nurture are both implicated in the stormy childhoods and adult lifestyles" of people suffering from characterological depression. Parker and colleagues (1979; Parker & Brown, 1979) also provided evidence that concurs with the findings of Rosenthal and associates.

It is increasingly evident from clinical studies that experiential, as well as genetic, factors contribute to the increased family incidence of psychiatric disorders (e.g., Bowlby, 1978; Winnicott, 1969). Experimental studies relating the psychosocial aspects of family history to depression have lagged behind, but research published in the past decade supports the clinical literature. For example, Rutter (1973) has proposed that vulnerability to psychiatric disorder in children raised by parents (especially mothers) who are emotionally disturbed is increased in several ways. These children are exposed to a distressing and disruptive home life, to the loss of adequate parenting, and to models of depressive and/or otherwise disturbed behavior. This early experience itself and the way in which the family coped with the ill member may well influence how the person deals with an episode of depression in later life.

A family history of psychiatric illness (especially affective disorders) has both diagnostic and treatment implications. In this respect, social workers require an understanding of the genetic and experiential aspects of having had an ill parent or sibling in the family (Jackson, 1965).

Stressful Life Events

A great deal of attention has been paid to the role of stressful life events in the occurrence of depression. A recent review reported that, with few exceptions, the findings support the hypothesis that depressed subjects experience more stressful life events prior to the onset of the disorder than do normal persons (Lloyd, 1980b). Some studies have focused on the presumed causative role of life events in depression. Brown and Harris (1978), for example, placed particular emphasis on understanding the meaning of an event for the individual, given the person's current life circumstances, and pointed out the importance of identifying both chronic and recent life stresses. Other authors are beginning to identify certain life events that are high-risk factors in certain groups. For example, O'Neil-Lowy (1983) found that recent loss of parents and of close relationships, financial problems, and changes in academic or residential situation are specific events that are associated with depression in university students. While there is controversy regarding the relationship between early loss and depression, there is no question that recent loss is a risk factor for all age groups. Even though social workers have always been aware of the contribution of life stresses and strains to problems of functioning—and probably to a greater extent than other mental health professionals—these recent findings are particularly helpful in drawing attention to the effect of certain events in specific depressed populations.

Social Support

Social support has been identified consistently as an important variable in modifying the impact of life events and favorably influencing the risk for depression. For instance, Cobb (1976) reviewed a number of studies supplying evidence that social support is a moderator of life stress. He defined "internal and external social support" as those circumstances that lead the subject to believe that she is cared for and loved, is esteemed and valued, and belongs to a network of communication and mutual obligation. Cobb stated:

> The conclusion that supportive interactions among people are important is hardly new. What is new is the assembling of evidence that adequate social support can protect people in crises from a wide variety of pathological states; from low birth weight to death, from arthritis through tuberculosis to depression, alcoholism and other psychiatric illness. Furthermore, social support can reduce the amount of medication required, accelerate recovery and facilitate compliance with prescribed medical regimes. (p. 310)

Brown and Harris (1978) and O'Neil-Lowy (1983) demonstrated the positive influence of at least one confidant. Other investigators have examined the role of social networks (Meuller, 1980) and of social functioning (Weissman & Paykel, 1974) in the occurrence and course of psychiatric disorders, including depression. Henderson and associates (1981) concluded that it is not the availability but the adequacy of close affectional ties in the presence of distressing experiences that provides a buffer against emotional problems. Aneshensel and Stone (1982) recently provided evidence that "social support instead of merely protecting an individual against stress, may itself be important in ameliorating depressive symptoms" (p. 1392). That is, the absence of social support can directly cause depressive symptoms even in the absence of stressful life events. Social workers have a special contribution to make in the area of understanding and improving social support in a depressed person's life.

Psychodynamic and Personality Factors in Depression

Since the early works of Freud (1896, 1917) and Abraham (1911), psychoanalysts have been interested in the dynamic factors that play a role in episodes of depression. Psychoanalytic views have passed through several distinct phases, reflecting both clinical experience in the analysis and psychotherapy of depressed patients and the evolution of psychoanalytic theory. This development has been well described by Mendelson (1974).

Although there is no unitary psychoanalytic theory of depression, there is consensus among psychoanalysts on some important points:

1. Predisposition to depression is established in infancy and early childhood and results from the interplay between biological vulnerability and disturbances in parent–child interactions. The young child's sense of security—of being loved and wanted—can be threatened by parental rejection (influenced in part by the behavior of the child), leading to early mourning, which may be the prototype of later reactions to loss. The severe childhood depressions that result from separation from love objects are examples of this interrelationship (Bowlby, 1969, 1978, 1980; Spitz, 1946).

2. Although depression can occur in all people, certain personality types seem more prone to serious or recurrent depressions:

a. oral-dependent personalities, who need a constant infusion of "external narcissistic supplies" to retain a sense of well-being (recognition, approval, admiration, demonstrations of love)

b. obsessional, conscience-ridden personalities, who constantly struggle to control bottled-up aggressive impulses, which are readily turned against the self, leading to guilt, self-hate, and self-destructive fantasies

c. cyclothymic personalities, who vacillate between periods of elation and despondence, which states are subclinical episodes of mania and depression.

3. Central to the experience of depression is the psychic pain that results from disturbances in the sense of well-being (Sandler & Joffe, 1965) and self-esteem (Jacobson, 1971). Such disturbances can be provoked, especially in vulnerable people, by a variety of life events, of which losses are the most frequent. When defenses intended to protect against this pain fail, the result includes feelings of helplessness and hopelessness and the wish to give up (Engel, 1962).

4. Anger and aggression play an important part in many, though not all, depressions. Depressed persons torture not only themselves but also the significant others in their lives, whom they blame for having withheld the love, approval, reassurance, and admiration due them. Guilt and self-blame may also be involved here, resulting from the sense of being an unworthy and unlovable person.

5. Psychodynamic factors play an important role in all depressions, especially in determining the mental state that precedes and exists during the depression. However, there is a continuum that ranges from bipolar and psychotic unipolar depressions, in which dynamic factors represent only the psychological dimension of a disorder caused by many factors, to neurotic depression (dysthymic disorder), wherein dynamic factors seem to play the dominant role. Klerman (1978), noting that research evidence supporting the etiological role of psychodynamic factors in depressions is limited, commented that "at the present time, the psychodynamic hypotheses are primarily of great heuristic value, contributing to case formulation, guidance of psychotherapeutic practice, and the design of future research" (p. 272).

DIAGNOSIS OF DEPRESSION

The diagnosis of a full-blown case of depression is not difficult. Most seriously depressed patients have symptoms in the areas of mood, cognition (thinking), and psychomotor and social behavior, as well as certain physiological functions. However, clinical skill is required to recognize depression when it is in an early stage or when it is masked by other symptoms (often called "depressive equivalents") and to diagnose the type of depression. (This is important since, in the light of recent knowledge, the subtypes call for different treatment strategies.)

Recognizing Depression

There is a need to distinguish depression from normal lowerings of mood (e.g., unhappiness, sadness, disappointment, frustration, hopelessness, or helplessness), which task is not always easy because depression is usually an accentuation in intensity or duration of these normal states. Certain symptoms suggest depression: withdrawal from or difficulty performing customary social roles; sleep and appetite disturbance; weight loss; loss of sexual interest; constipation or diarrhea; ideas of self-blame (excessive preoccupation with one's own faults or guilt); suicidal ideas; and, sometimes, disturbance in reality testing, manifested by delusions, hallucinations, or confusion.

Depression can also be associated with some medical disorders or regimens:

> side effects of certain drugs, especially those used to treat high blood pressure
> endocrine disorders (e.g., hypothyroidism, Addison's disease)
> neurological disorders (e.g., brain tumors, Parkinson's disease)
> malignant diseases (e.g., brain tumors, cancer of the pancreas or lung)

If masked depressions are to be recognized, the clinician must investigate the possibility of depression even in clients who do not acknowledge feeling blue or show other clinical symptoms of depression. Masked depression is possible when there is evidence of one or more of the following symptoms (Lesse, 1968):

> uncharacteristic focus on bodily aches and pains, as well as psychosomatic disorders; the patient becomes a hypochondriac and goes from doctor to doctor, not feeling reassured by repeated physical examinations and lab tests
> uncharacteristic accident proneness or risk-taking behavior, as though the patient were looking for trouble
> anorexia nervosa and/or bulimia
> excessive use of alcohol and/or drugs
> anger, rage, and sometimes aggressive behavior
> unexpected states of remission in patients with a long history of suicidal ideation and suicide attempts

Treatment Implications

Social workers need to be able to identify five categories of affective disorder (Lowy, 1980).

Bipolar Affective Disorders

In this category, formerly labeled "manic-depressive disorder," there is a strong likelihood of genetic vulnerability; accordingly, there is typically a family history of depression or mania in first-degree relatives. Such patients respond well to ECT and tricyclic antidepressants while depressed and to lithium when elated. Lithium is also an effective maintenance and prophylactic drug for the majority of these patients. When the drug works, it reduces the frequency not only of frank depressive and maniac attacks but also of subclinical ups and downs of mood. These patients should be referred to a general psychiatrist (not to someone who limits her practice to psychotherapy) for assessment and treatment. Psychotherapy is *not* the treatment of choice and should be offered only if there are specific indications over and above the depression. Support and explanation for the patient and family are useful adjuncts to psychiatric treatment.

Major Depressive Disorder

Patients in this category, which includes unipolar affective disorder and psychotic depression, probably have a genetic vulnerability, but the evidence is not as strong as in the bipolar affective disorders. There is often a history of depression in first-degree relatives but not of mania. There is usually a good response to ECT and tricyclic antidepressants, but lithium is not as effective here in preventing recurrences. These patients should be referred for psychiatric assessment and psychopharmacological treatment, and here psychotherapy when indicated is used in combination with drugs or ECT.

Neurotic Depression

There is no good evidence of genetic vulnerability for this disorder, formerly called "reactive depression" but renamed "dysthymic disorder" in *DSM-III*. There may be psychosocial predisposition as a result of early life experiences, and external precipitants often are clear. The treatment of choice here is psychotherapy; ECT and lithium have no place. The antidepressant drugs can be useful during periods of acute depression. Monoamine oxidase inhibitors are probably better than the tricyclic antidepressants but there is no evidence that long-term drug maintenance is useful.

Characterological Depression

This category, also called "depressive personality disorder" or "chronic dysthymic disorder," includes cyclothymic disorder (see Chapter 16). The evidence for and against genetic vulnerability in this category is inconclusive. These patients may require long-term care. If their personality deficit is not too severe, they will benefit from definitive psychotherapy. If the personality deficit is severe, they likely will not benefit from such an approach. The best strategy is to provide intervention when needed. Long-term, continuous support to patients and family should be offered only if they cannot do without it. Drugs should be used sparingly and only for brief periods in acute phases because of the high addictive potential of many patients in this group.

Depression Secondary to Other Diseases
Depression is often secondary to other major psychiatric disorders such as schizophrenia, acute and chronic brain syndromes, severe obsessive-compulsive disorder, and paranoia. Depression should be distinguished from other affective states, especially anxiety, in such patients (Roth & Mountjoy, 1982). It is not uncommon for depression to be a direct result of certain medical conditions, such as endocrinological or neurological problems, or to represent a drug side effect. There is, as well, a diagnosis known as "postinfluenza depression" (Sinanan & Hillary, 1981). Social workers ought to be alert to the possibility of depression secondary to these psychiatric and medical disorders so that both the primary and the secondary diagnosis can be made and appropriate treatment provided.

Medical and Psychiatric Referrals in the Diagnosis of Depression

In general, when in doubt, obtain a consultation; refer early rather than late; and prepare the patient and the family so as to get the greatest benefit from the consultation. People with the following problems should always be referred for medical or psychiatric assessment:

1. Patients who are very severely depressed, irrespective of diagnosis, but especially if they are psychotic or suicidal
2. Patients who become depressed for the first time after age 40 (brain tumors and other somatic illnesses are more common in this group and need to be ruled out)
3. Patients who request referral for another opinion or for medical assessment
4. Patients with many physical complaints; these need to be evaluated to rule out treatable somatic illnesses (see Chapter 4 and 10). If on investigation the complaints are found not to be due to physical illness, the social worker will be able to concentrate on psychological and social issues without being constantly distracted by concern with the seriousness of the physical complaints. Sometimes it is best for such patients to

see their family physician regularly, concomitant with the social worker's treatment.

5. Patients who are taking medication on an ongoing basis, especially antihypertensive medication or steroids

6. Patients with symptoms suggestive of bipolar affective disorder or major depressive disorder, especially if a strong family history of depression or alcoholism is present

7. Patients with symptoms suggestive of neurotic depression or characterological depression should be considered as potential candidates for intensive psychotherapy or psychoanalysis. However, only the minority of patients within these groups are likely to be suitable candidates. If the worker is not a trained psychotherapist or analyst the patient should be assessed by a mental health worker who is so trained.

SOCIAL WORK TREATMENT OF DEPRESSION

Therapeutic Alliance between Social Worker and Depressed Client

The "therapeutic alliance," or therapist–client working relationship, is the sine qua non of all treatment. Although the nature of the relationship may vary with treatment circumstances (e.g., length, depth, purpose), the helping relationship to be established with depressed individuals has a number of elements and difficulties that apply in all cases. Bear in mind that the feelings of hopelessness, helplessness, pessimism, worthlessness, guilt, self-blame, inadequacy, and failure—the core of the depressed person's inner world and the basis of the need for help—are the very feelings that challenge the establishment of a therapeutic alliance.

All depressed patients need the social worker to convey a sense of hope, support, and qualified reassurance. These can be justifiably supplied since most depressive episodes are time limited and even very severe depressions eventually improve.

Excessive dependence, ambivalent wishes to regress and be cared for, and manipulation represent common therapeutic problems. These can be managed through recognition of the need for respite from daily responsibility, for time to heal, and for understanding, support, and a degree of dependence. At the same time, a measure of structure (regularity and consistency) and encouragement for gradual reinvolvement in activities and social relationships do much to restore independence, as well as feelings of adequacy and self-worth.

Depressed persons' view of themselves as worthless, of the outside world as empty and rejecting, and of the future as bleak and hopeless also present difficulties in treatment. Persistent expression of these dark and hostile sentiments may evoke feelings of anger, frustration, and impotence in the worker. Yet, awareness and containment of such reactions is essential so that the patient gradually perceives the worker as trustworthy, accepting, and helpful instead of rejecting, hostile, and useless.

Suicidal thoughts, self-destructive behavior, and the possibility of successful suicide are ever present features of the treatment of depressed people (see Chapter 27). Their extremely painful expression of hopelessness and worthlessness, of anger and hostility at an uncaring world, always needs to be taken seriously. The worker must deal with these issues in a sensitive and empathic fashion but without allowing the patient to manipulate the worker into feeling guilty and unduly responsible for the patient's life. In particularly difficult cases, involving a psychiatrist or a family physician can be beneficial for both the patient and the therapist.

Social Work Roles with Depressed Patients

The nature of a social worker's involvement with depressed clients varies according to whether the patient is an outpatient or an inpatient and is receiving medication or not. Although the initial goals of treatment—reduction of symptoms; restoration of hope, a sense of adequacy, self-esteem, and social functioning; and exploration of maladaptive patterns of behavior—are the same, the conditions of treatment have important implications for the caseworker's role.

The Hospitalized Depressed Patient

The psychiatrist and ward staff have primary responsibility for the hospitalized patient; the social worker is responsible for the support of the family and the patient–family interaction. Deykin and colleagues (1971) described the differences in the caseworker's role with the hospitalized patient and the outpatient. They noted that the hospitalized person is removed from his/her family, the social structure of everyday life, and familiar roles. The social worker's first responsibility is to pay attention to, and mobilize support from, the patient's social situation. This is done by helping the family understand the illness, adjust to the temporary loss of a member, and maintain contact when the patient is unable to do so, and by facilitating meaningful communication between patient and family. The authors noted that maladaptive communication is often a by-product of the frustration, guilt, and anger evoked by the illness and felt on all sides. By working with the family, the social worker can help alleviate these sentiments, repair relationships, and prepare the family for the patient's reentry into the outside world.

If the hospitalized patient is receiving drug therapy, the caseworker's primary function is to interpret drug therapy to family members, to allay their anxiety when immediate improvement is not evident, to stress the need for continuing medication on home visits, and to educate the family about suicidal drug overdose in patients or dietary restrictions that must be observed with certain drugs.

Two other therapeutic issues arise with the hospitalized patient: the social worker's relationship with the patient's primary therapist (the prescribing physician) and the role of the social worker in the patient's aftercare program. The former is discussed in the following section and the latter is dealt with in the section on social environmental therapy as a treatment modality.

The Depressed Outpatient

The social worker's role with the depressed outpatient depends on who is identified as primary therapist, the quality of the patient–family relationship, and the existence of a drug regimen. The social worker as primary therapist is discussed under treatment modalities. Even though the outpatient remains within the family, the social worker still has tasks to perform with the family: to help the family perceive the patient's symptoms as part of his/her illness, to recognize the extra burden the family bears, and to help family members tolerate their own feelings of guilt, frustration, and fear about having a depressed person in the family and, at times, about having contributed to the patient's breakdown. Gradual resumption of the patient's social roles and duties is facilitated by having the outpatient remain in the family and the social worker encourage improved patient–family interaction.

The social worker's role with the outpatient receiving medication is crucial because medication is not as well controlled at home as in the hospital. To gain the patient's and family's confidence and cooperation with the drug regimen, the social worker should explain the expected course of drug effect, reassure patient and family about delayed effects, and encourage compliance. Equally important is communication with the physician who is prescribing the antidepressant medication. It is essential to inform him or her of unusual or severe side effects and of any indication of increased alcohol intake, impulsiveness, or suicidal ideation.

The professional relationship between social worker and prescribing physician is a critical part of combined drug and casework treatment. In an article on casework and pharmacotherapy in the treatment of depression, Weissman (1972a) noted that

> the problems associated with combining casework with pharmacotherapy arise out of the divergent goals of each treatment. The casework goal is improved social and interpersonal functioning and the goal of drug treatment is symptom reduction. . . . The collaboration of caseworker and psychiatrist will help to decrease misunderstanding and make casework and drug treatment more effective. . . . [This is necessary] because of the inevitable ambiguity as to what treatment is really helping, the patient's loyalties to the two therapists and the patient's variable clinical state. (p. 44)

Content and Level of Therapy in Depression

What do social workers and their depressed patients talk about during their therapeutic contacts? Weissman and Klerman (1973), in a study of psychotherapy with depressed women, identified 10 content themes: physical symptoms, mental symptoms, current treatment, practical problems, family of origin, spouse, sex, children, interpersonal relationships, and early experiences. Weissman and Paykel (1974) also reported that

> discussion of current social adjustment occupied most of the therapy and revolved around practical problems such as work, finance, recreation, as well as relationships with husband, children and close friends. Little time was spent discussing physical symptoms and current treatment. The least time was spent on discussion of early experiences or sexual problems. Therapy discussions were primarily descriptive accounts of daily life and not reflective of insights or childhood developmental material. (p. 192)

Since daily concerns, family issues, and social relationships are strongly associated with depressive illness, it should not be surprising to any therapist, regardless of orientation, that these are the main things a depressed person talks about. In fact, recent research confirming the association between depressive illness and psychosocial factors has helped to heighten awareness of the importance of these factors to the depressed person. The level at which these themes are discussed depends on the patient's primary concerns, needs, and wishes, his orientation to psychological understanding, as well as the modality of treatment. Weissman and Klerman (1973) postulated that therapist and patient may run into difficulty about the content and nature of their discussion

> where the therapist's expectations include preconceptions about what the patient should discuss . . . most writings on psychotherapy stress the value of clarification of problems and their causes. It may be frustrating to the therapist to find that the patient spends most of the time describing everyday problems and not postulations about past experiences. We may underestimate the benefit to the patient derived from being able to share these problems with a nonjudgemental and sympathetic listener. A considerable amount of sharing may be necessary to foster the patient's self-examination. The therapist's listening, rather than the search for clarification, may be the "non-specific" factor in therapy which contributes to psychotherapeutic change. For many patients, particularly from the lower social classes, problems with housing, work and finances can be serious. The therapist should not underestimate their significance and push for what might be considered more important therapeutic topics. (pp. 59–60)

The question arises, then, as to how beneficial it is to attempt understanding of the psychodynamic meaning (conscious and unconscious) of a client's depression. I suggest that the content of the therapy should be determined by the patient and that the level at which the material is discussed (e.g., descriptive, reflective, interpretive) should be determined by the type of therapy that is appropriate and feasible for that patient. Of course, it is valuable for the therapist to gain an understanding of the dynamics of the patient and the social situation, whether or not the therapist decides explicitly to introduce this material during the sessions.

Modalities of Treatment in Depression

The main modalities of treatment available to the social worker as the primary therapist are individual (long- and short-term) psychotherapy or casework, family and marital therapy, group therapy, and social environmental treatment.

Long-term Individual Therapy

Social workers in private practice or associated with a psychotherapy clinic may routinely provide long-term, intensive, psychodynamically oriented psychotherapy. The psychoanalytic literature abounds in information about case selection criteria and techniques and in case examples of process and outcome (Arieti, 1982; Jacobson, 1971; Winnicott, 1969; Zetzel, 1965), but reports are noticeably lacking research.

There is another type of long-term treatment that social workers may be called on to employ. Such treatment is long-term in the sense that the patient is seen for brief periods over many years, often for different bouts of depression or at times of crisis for preventive purposes. Brief psychotherapy, crisis intervention, monitoring of medication, or concrete help may be used at various times during these contacts. The unifying factor here is the reassurance of a long-term relationship, preferably with the same social worker or with someone else at the agency, where the person feels known. When a new social worker must be assigned to the client, familiarity with the patient's history of contacts is important in order to meet the patient's need for a sense of continuity between contacts. Fear of abandonment is often at the psychological core of chronic or recurring depression.

Short-term Individual Therapy

In the past decade, there has been a gradual development of short-term psychological approaches to the treatment of depression. Patient selection criteria, problem assessment, focus, goals, and techniques have been refined for several of these therapies, the main types being behavioral, cognitive, interpersonal, and psychodynamic. Clinical trials and other investigations have provided evidence for the efficacy of these treatments in depressed patients. Theory, research, and clinical applications related to these four approaches were comprehensively dealt with by Rush (1982). Since social workers are frequently employed in settings that use or investigate brief therapies, the reader is referred to Rush for further information about behavioral, cognitive, and psychodynamic brief therapy. Weissman and colleagues (Klerman & Weissman, 1977; Rounsaville, et al., 1979) are at the forefront of the development and investigation of interpersonal psychotherapy, and their work is reviewed here.

Interpersonal psychotherapy (IPT) is based on the premise that depression (regardless of symptomatology, severity, biological vulnerability, or personality) occurs in a psychosocial and interpersonal context and that understanding and renegotiating the interpersonal problems associated with the onset of symptoms is important to the depressed person's recovery and possible to the prevention of further episodes. IPT is a brief (12–16 weeks), weekly psychological treatment of the ambulatory, unipolar, nonpsychotic depressed patient that focuses on improving the quality of the depressed patient's current interpersonal functioning. This approach is suitable for use, following a period of training, by experienced psychiatrists, psychologists, or social workers and it can be applied alone or in conjunction with a pharmacological approach. Two general goals are identified: alleviating depressive symptoms and helping the patient devise more effective strategies for dealing with interpersonal problems. The problem areas focused on are grief, interpersonal disputes, role transition, and interpersonal deficits. Techniques such as reassurance, clarification of emotional states, improvement of interpersonal communication, and reality testing of perceptions and performance are employed. Therapeutic work is aimed at conscious and preconscious levels; unconscious factors are recognized implicitly. Problems are defined in here-and-now terms and childhood experiences are recognized only in relation to presenting problems.

Research has demonstrated the efficacy of maintenance IPT, as compared to low contact, in helping depressive clients improve their social functioning. IPT also has been shown to be more effective than the non-scheduled treatment of acute depressives in achieving symptom reduction and later in enhancing social functioning. (Improvement in social functioning takes at least six to eight months to become apparent.)

The use of IPT and cognitive therapy (Beck, 1976) with primary depressives will be tested in a multicenter, collaborative psychotherapy study sponsored by the National Institute of Mental Health. Clinical trials—IPT alone and in combination with antidepressants compared with cognitive therapy plus antidepressant medication—will be conducted to ascertain whether the treatments are differentially applicable to, and effective with, specific subtypes of depressed patients.

Family and Marital Therapy

Family and marital problems have a cause-and-effect relationship vis-à-vis depressive disorders. The impact of depression is felt between people as well as inside each person, and is often an integral part of the family system. Therefore, family or marital therapy is frequently a treatment of choice for depressed clients. Social workers using this modality should assess and treat the interpersonal context in which the illness is experienced. Byng-Hall and Whiffen (1982) stated that family and marital therapists

> attempt to help families cope with current stress and strengthen the family by facilitating parental (or step-parental) intimacy, improving parent–child relationships, and some also aim to reduce the long-

term effects of post-traumatic experiences, especially losses. Depressive disorder seen from the family or marital perspective is only one element in the web of emotional bonds which have been broken, are breaking or are threatening to break. The techniques for dealing with affective disorder cannot then be isolated from those which are aimed at resolving the conflicts in the regulation of distances between family members. (p. 318)

Lask (1979) and Gurman and Kriskern (1978) reviewed the research in this area. A few well-designed studies have indicated:

1. Marital therapy with drugs in the depressed partner leads to greater improvement in family relationships than do drugs alone (Friedman, 1975)
2. Marital therapy helps improve communication patterns between the depressed and nondepressed spouse (Hinchliffe, et al., 1978)
3. Depressed women with concomitant marital disputes who improve their marriage during the course of treatment also experience an improvement in depressive symptoms, while those whose marriages do not improve experience less improvement or a worsening of symptoms (Rounsaville, et al., 1979)

A number of clinical papers that describe family and marital therapy with depressed clients also could be enlightening to social workers (Feldman, 1976; Hogan & Hogan, 1975).

Group Therapy
Group therapy as a specific treatment for depression has not received much attention in the literature or in research, even though Stein (1982) reported that it is an effective method with certain characterological disorders, unipolar depressive reactions, and bipolar affective disorders. The group provides some important benefits to the depressed patient: through group interaction, the members learn much about their depression and the effect it has on those around them; they give each other some dependence gratification; they provide mutual support, thus minimizing the pain and discomfort that they experience and provoke in others; and, if they are at different stages of managing their depression, they generate hope of improvement in each other. The leader, freed of some of the burden of supporting depressed clients, is able to help group members focus on strengthening individual identity, self-esteem, and coping capacity and on

modifying distorted cognitions and affects, as well as on improving their interpersonal relationships (Stein, 1982).

Levin and Schild (1969) stated that "the group treatment of depressed clients has been found to be therapeutically advantageous. As the group members relate to each other, they tend to be less manipulative of and dependent on the worker." They identified three stages of treatment: mutual mourning, ego reactivation, and mastery. Case examples with the rationale for specific therapeutic interventions are provided. The reader is referred to Stein (1975) and Yalom (1975) for further information about the use of group therapy with depressed people.

Social Environmental Treatment
Treatment of a depressed person by manipulation of the social environment (an old-fashioned social work term) is an approach that should not be forgotten or underestimated by social workers (Bennett, 1982). The capacity of seriously depressed people to cope with the everyday world may be severely, and often chronically, impaired (Bothwell & Weissman, 1977; Weissman & Klerman, 1977). Provision of concrete services may be the treatment of choice for some depressed people, especially those just out of the hospital. Goering (1982), in a study of posthospital outcome in neurotic, mostly depressed women, suggested that legal aid, job counseling, housing services, assertiveness training, budgeting courses, day care, and Parents without Partners are useful, if not essential, adjuncts to traditional psychiatric aftercare. In fact, there is a great need for more aftercare programs (Wasylenki, et al., 1981) and social workers could well be leaders in this important area of care of the depressed person.

Depressed older people are another group for whom environmental manipulation may be a very effective type of therapy. As Wetzel (1980) pointed out: "Social scientists have found institutions to be guilty of accelerating, rather than reducing, the symptoms of helplessness and hopelessness in the elderly" (p. 234). She suggested a number of interventions "for prevention and treatment of depression in aging women and men who are living in institutional settings" (p. 234).

SOCIAL SUPPORT IN DEPRESSION: A SPECIAL SOCIAL WORK CONTRIBUTION

The treatment of depression is a vast and varied field in which social workers can make an important contribution. Developing and using social supports is a particularly appropriate area for social work efforts. Cobb (1976) stated this well:

We should start now to teach all our patients, both well and sick, how to give and receive social support. Only in rare instances of clear psychiatric disability should this instruction require a psychiatrist. It seems to me that this is the real function for which Richard Cabot designed the profession of medical social work. (p. 312)

Problems related to interpersonal relationships are a prime focus of any kind of psychotherapy for depression, but improvement in the patient's supportive, close relationships is frequently a main goal of treatment. Lack of social support is both a cause and a result of depression. Recent loss or lack of warm, dependable people, especially a confidant, increases vulnerability to depression. Moreover, the depressed person may provoke relationship problems; that is, the depressed mood may negatively affect those around her. It is difficult for family and friends to manage the hopeless withdrawal or the demanding, clinging dependence of the depressed person. Providing support for this person is always a burden, but this task is made more difficult when familial or close relationships are chronically disturbed. Fear, rejection, anger, and guilt are not uncommon reactions to another person's depression. At times, these sentiments are difficult for even a confidant to control. In a poor relationship, such reactions may compound the ill person's problems. Social workers can help improve the depressed patient's personal relationships, but different situations call for different strategies.

Supportive Relationships Are Strong and Constructive

In this situation, the social worker provides understanding and interpretation of the illness (its nature, causes and course); helps the close person bear the pain and burden of dealing with a depressed patient, and provides hope for eventual improvement; relieves the pressure upon the close person by sharing the patient's excessive dependence, hopelessness, helplessness, and suicidal ideation, which can be frightening to those around; helps the depressed patient both to moderate expectations and demands and to appreciate the good support that the close person offers; and encourages mutually dependent interaction.

Supportive Relationships Are Weak and/or Destructive

Preexisting problems in the relationship or the depression itself may seriously disturb marriage or family dynamics. In this situation, the social worker has a number of options: determine whether the partner or children themselves need help for individual problems and make appropriate referrals if necessary; relieve the close person of providing support and take responsibility for the treatment of the depression; provide concrete help (e.g., homemaker services); intervene in the destructive interaction by identifying constructive, practical, gradual ways in which at least minimal support can be given to increase the self-esteem and feelings of adequacy on the part of everyone involved; treat the destructive, maladaptive relationship separately from the depression (e.g., through family therapy); or separate the depressed patient from the family or the marriage (e.g., arrange for hospitalization or separate living arrangements).

Supportive Relationships Are No Longer Available

In this situation, the social worker should assess the nature of the recent loss to determine whether it is permanent or temporary and within or outside the patient's control; interpret the effect of the recent loss of social support and explain its association with the current depressive episode; provide transitional support; assess the patient's capacity for relationships and build on this; and, as the depression decreases, encourage reinvolvement in the former support system if possible and/or the establishment of new supports within the patient's capacity for closeness. (This capacity should improve, at least to the pre-illness level, as the depression lifts.)

Supportive Relationships Are Unused

Some depressed patients are characteristically socially withdrawn and when depressed become even more so. This situation is often the most difficult for the social worker to manage because these people are hard to engage. In this case, it is important to assess the patient's capacity for relationships and ability to cope on his own; respect the patient's social isolation, especially if it is evident that ordinarily the independent coping style works for this individual (some people have a well-developed capacity to be alone and prefer this state); and make it clear that the therapeutic relationship is being offered for the purpose of helping with the debilitating depression. (This recognition of the patient's need for distance may decrease the fear of closeness, especially at times when help is needed.)

In all four situations, the social worker's most powerful tool for helping the patient develop or maintain good social support is the helping relationship, which was discussed earlier. This relationship encourages the development of self-esteem, self-sufficiency, and individual identity. The depressed person will have learned something about give-and-take, about realistic needs and expectations, and about ways to meet these through relationships with other human beings.

SEX DIFFERENCES IN DEPRESSION AND HELP-SEEKING

Women are more often the focus of the literature on depression than are men. Although much of what is written about depression in women is applicable to men, in two areas—risk factors and help-seeking behavior or service use—sex differences are evident and have treatment implications.

Roy (1981) identified three vulnerability factors associated with depression in men: parental loss before 17 years of age, poor marriage, and unemployment. Similar factors were also related to depression in women, but parenting factors (the number of children under 14 at home and the woman's not working outside the home) were also significant for women (Brown & Harris, 1978; Roy, 1979; Weissman, 1972b; Weissman, et al., 1973). It seems, then, that sex-specific factors in depression are very much related to sex differences in life situations and role definitions. Close attention should be given to the meaning of sex-related differences in risk factors when assessing depression in men and women.

As I noted earlier, depressed women are more likely to make use of psychiatric services than are depressed men. Kessler and associates (1981) and O'Neil and associates (1982) found that these differences are due neither to sex differences in the occurrence of depression nor to differences in symptom expression but rather to differences in attitudes toward emotional problems and help-seeking and to differential referral patterns by physicians. What all this means is that it is more difficult for men to recognize and acknowledge their depressive symptoms and that physicians tend to be less accurate in assigning psychiatric diagnoses to them. Therefore, proportionately fewer depressed men receive treatment. Social workers involved with male clients for presenting problems other than depression (e.g., marital, family, or unemployment difficulties) are in a prime position not only to detect depression in men but also to help them accept treatment. Frequently, it is difficult to treat a man as the identified patient but much can be done by treating the depressive symptoms indirectly, for example, by therapy aimed at a disturbed family situation.

CONCLUSION

Despite the variety of treatment approaches and techniques available to social workers helping depressed people, it is not yet clear which types of depressed patients do best with which treatment modalities or whether different modalities are equally effective for the various types or subtypes of depression. For example, all four brief psychotherapies have been shown to be effective with unipolar, nonpsychotic affective disorders (Rush, 1982). Are these therapies equally effective? Is it mainly the skilled, sensitive therapist selecting a familiar, well-tested technique and working within a positive therapeutic alliance who determines a good outcome? These questions remain to be answered.

Perhaps social workers can best deal with this somewhat confusing situation by keeping up with developments in the field; by making certain that they are well trained in whatever type(s) of treatment they use; and by doing what social workers have long been known to do best—developing their skills as partners in the therapeutic alliance. Indeed, recent research provided evidence that the therapeutic alliance is one of the main variables predicting positive outcome in psychotherapy (Gomez-Schwartz, 1978; Marziali, 1982). Social workers can further contribute to the understanding and treatment of depression by identifying and researching areas that have always been of prime interest to the profession (e.g., interpersonal relationships and social support). There is much for social workers to write about in this area, especially since a survey of the leading social work journals over the past decade revealed only a handful of articles on the social work treatment of depression.

Winnicott (1969) provided some food for thought for the social work practitioner:

> I suggest that our work becomes intelligible as well as rewarding if we keep in mind the heavy weight of depression which has to resolve itself inside the depressed person, while we try to help with whatever happens to be the immediate problem. There is an economics in our work and we can do what we have to do if we do the right thing at the right moment; but if we attempt the impossible the result is that we become depressed ourselves and the case remains unaltered. (p. 57)

Depression, the most common form of adult psychopathology confronting mental health practitioners, has been discussed here from the perspective of the social worker assessing and treating the depressed patient. It is important, however, not to forget that depressed mood is an inevitable part of the experience of everyday life for both social worker and client. Winnicott (1964) emphasized "the ego strength and personal maturity that is manifested in the 'purity' of the depressed mood" (pp. 56–57). He explained this well:

> Depression belongs to psychopathology. It can be severe and crippling and may last a lifetime and it is commonly a passing mood in relatively healthy individuals. At the normal end, depression which is a common, almost universal, phenomenon relates to mourning, to the capacity to feel guilt and to the maturational process. Always depression implies ego strength and in this way depression tends to lift, and the depressed person tends to recover. (pp. 126–127)

Social workers assist people at each phase of the life cycle and with many depressing situations and experiences. Much can be done to help each client develop the vital capacity to bear the inevitable depressions of life (Craig, 1977; Lebow, 1976; Leonard, 1964; Macon, 1979; Shepherd & Barraclough, 1979; Wallerstein & Kelly, 1980). Zetzel (1965) summed this up beautifully:

> Mature, passive acceptance of the inevitable thus remains a sustained prerequisite to the remobilization of available adaptive resources at all times. While failure in this vital area may be consistent with long periods of successful adaptation, it represents a serious potential vulnerability that becomes increasingly relevant in the later years of life, when experiences of loss, grief, and frustration are not to be avoided. In his conclusion to *Childhood and Society* (1950) Erikson said: "Healthy children will not fear life if their parents have integrity enough not to fear death." I submit that healthy children who do not fear life—in spite of subjective awareness of its limitations—will become adults with integrity enough not to fear death. (p. 273)

REFERENCES

Abraham, K. (1949). Notes on the psychoanalytic investigation and treatment of manic-depressive insanity and allied conditions. In E. Jones (Ed.), *Selected papers on psychoanalysis* (pp. 248–279). London: Hogarth.

Adams, K. S., Bouckoms, A., & Streiner, D. (1982). Parental loss and family stability in attempted suicide. *Archives of General Psychiatry, 39,* 1081–1085.

American Psychiatric Association. (1980). *Diagnostic and statistical manual of mental disorders, third edition.* Washington, DC: Author.

Aneshensel, C. S., & Stone, J. D. (1982). Stress and depression: A test of the buffering model of social support. *Archives of General Psychiatry, 39,* 1392–1396.

Arieti, S. (1982). Individual psychotherapy. In E. S. Paykel (Ed.), *Handbook of affective disorders* (pp. 297–306). New York: Guilford.

Beck, A. T. (1967). *Depression: Clinical, experimental, and theoretical aspects.* New York: Harper & Row.

Beck, A. T. (1976). *Cognitive therapy and the emotional disorders.* New York: International Universities Press.

Bennett, D. (1982). Social and community approaches. In E. S. Paykel (Ed.), *Handbook of affective disorders* (pp. 346–360). New York: Guilford.

Bothwell, S., & Weissman, M. M. (1977). Social impairment four years after an acute depressive episode. *American Journal of Orthopsychiatry, 47,* 231–237.

Bowlby, J. (1969). *Attachment and loss.* Vol. 1: *Attachment.* New York: Basic Books.

Bowlby, J. (1978). *Attachment and loss.* Vol. 2: *Separation.* New York: Basic Books.

Bowlby, J. (1980). *Attachment and loss.* Vol. 3: *Loss.* New York: Basic Books.

Boyd, J. H., & Weissman, M. M. (1981). Epidemiology of affective disorders. *Archives of General Psychiatry, 38,* 1039–1046.

Brown, G. W., Brolchain, M., & Harris, T. (1975). Social class and psychiatric disturbance among women in an urban population. *Sociology, 9,* 225–254.

Brown, G. W., & Harris, T. O. (1978). *Social origins of depression.* New York: Free Press.

Brown, G. W., Harris, T. O., & Copeland, J. R. (1977). Depression and loss. *British Journal of Psychiatry, 130,* 1–18.

Byng-Hall, J. J., & Whiffen, R. (1982). Family and marital therapy. In E. S. Paykel (Ed.), *Handbook of affective disorders* (pp. 318–328). New York: Guilford.

Cobb, S. (1976). Social support as a moderator of life stress. *Psychosomatic Medicine, 38,* 300–314.

Craig, Y. (1977). The bereavement of parents and their search for meaning. *British Journal of Social Work, 7,* 41–54.

Crook, T., & Eliot, J. (1980). Parental death during childhood and adult depression: A critical review of the literature. *Psychological Bulletin, 87,* 252–259.

Deykin, E., Weissman, M. M., & Klerman, G. L. (1971). Treatment of depressed women. *British Journal of Social Work, 1,* 278–291.

Engel, G. (1962). Anxiety and depressive-withdrawal: The primary affects of unpleasure. *International Journal of Psychoanalysis, 43,* 89–97.

Feldman, L. B. (1976). Depression and marital interaction. *Family Process, 15,* 389–395.

Freedman, A. M., Kaplan, H. I., & Sadock, B. J. (Eds.) (1974). *Comprehensive textbook of psychiatry.* (2nd Ed.). Baltimore: Williams & Wilkins.

Freud, S. (1953a). Mourning and melancholia. In *Standard edition* (vol. 14, pp. 243–258). London: Hogarth.

Freud, S. (1953b). Further remarks on neuropsychosis of defense. In *Standard edition* (vol. 3, pp. 167–189). London: Hogarth.

Friedman, A. S. (1975). Interaction of drug therapy with marital therapy in depressive patients. *Archives of General Psychiatry, 32,* 619–637.

Furman, E. (1974). *A child's parent dies.* New Haven: Yale University Press.

Goering, P., et al. (in press). Social support and post hospital outcome for depressed women. *Canadian Journal of Psychiatry.*

Golin, S., & Hartz, M. A. (1979). A factor analysis of the Beck Depression Inventory in a mildly depressive population. *Journal of Clinical Psychology, 35,* 322–325.

Gomez-Schwartz, B. (1978). Effective ingredients in psychotherapy: Prediction of outcome from process variables. *Journal of Consulting and Clinical Psychology, 46,* 1023–1035.

Gurman, A. S., & Kniskern, D. P. (1978). Research of marital and family therapy: Progress, perspective, and prospect. In S. L. Garfield & A. E. Bergin (Eds.), *Handbook of psychotherapy and behavior change: Empirical analyses* (2nd Ed.) (pp. 817–901). New York: John Wiley.

Hammen, C. L., & Padesky, C. A. (1977). Sex differences in the expression of depressive responses on the Beck Depression Inventory. *Journal of Abnormal Psychology, 86,* 609–614.

Henderson, S. (1980). A development in social psychiatry: The systematic study of social bonds. *Journal of Nervous and Mental Disorders, 168,* 63–69.

Henderson, S., Bryne, D. C., & Duncan-Jones, P. (1981). *Neurosis and the social environment.* Sydney & New York: Academic.

Hinchliffe, M. K., Hooper, D., & Roberts, F. J. (1978). *The melancholy marriage: Depression in marriage and psychosocial approaches to therapy.* New York: John Wiley.

Hirschfeld, R. M. A., & Cross, C. K. (1982). Epidemiology of affective disorders: Psychosocial risk factors. *Archives of General Psychiatry, 39,* 35–46.

Hogan, P., & Hogan, B. K. (1975). The family treatment of depression. In F. F. Flach & S. C. Draghi (Eds.), *The nature and treatment of depression* (pp. 197–228). New York: John Wiley.

Jackson, G. (1965). Depression in the family. *British Journal of Psychiatric Social Work, 8,* 32–41.

Jacobson, E. (1971). *Depression.* New York: International Universities Press.

Kennard, J., & Britchnell, J. (1982). The mental health of early mother separated women. *Acta Psychiatrica Scandinavia, 65,* 388–402.

Kessler, R. C., Brown, R. L., & Broman, C. L. (1981). Sex differences in psychiatric help seeking: Evidence from four large-scale surveys. *Journal of Health and Social Behavior, 22,* 49–64.

Kidd, K. K., & Weissman, M. M. (1976). Why we do not understand the genetics of affective disorders. In J. O. Cole, A. E. Schatzberg, & S. H. Frazier (Eds.), *Depression: Biology, psychodynamics, and treatment* (pp. 107–121). New York: Plenum.

Klerman, G. L. (1975). Overview of depression. In A. M. Freedman, H. I. Kaplan, & B. J. Sadock (Eds.), *Comprehensive textbook of psychiatry* (vol. 3). Baltimore: Williams & Wilkins.

Klerman, G. L. (1978). Affective disorder. In A. M. Nicholi (Ed.), *The Harvard guide to modern psychiatry* (pp. 253–282). Cambridge: Belknap.

Klerman, G. L., Rounsaville, B., Chevron, E., et al. (1982). *Short-term psychotherapies for depression.* New York: Guilford.

Lask, B. (1979). Family therapy outcome research, 1972–78. *Journal of Family Therapy, 1,* 87–92.

Lebow, G. H. (1976). Facilitating adaptation in anticipatory mourning. *Social Casework, 57,* 463–465.

Leonard, P. (1964). Depression and family failure. *British Journal of Psychiatric Social Work, 7,* 191–197.

Lesse, S. (1968). The multivariant masks of depression. *American Journal of Psychiatry, 124* (May supplement), 35–48.

Levin, B., & Schild, J. (1969). Group treatment of depression. *Social Casework, 14,* 46–52.

Lloyd, C. (1980a). Life events and depressive disorder reviewed: II. Events as precipitating factors. *Archives of General Psychiatry, 37,* 541–548.

Lloyd, C. (1980b). Life events and depressive disorder reviewed: I. Events as predisposing factors. *Archives of General Psychiatry, 37,* 529–535.

Lowy, F. H. (1980). Use of drugs and other treatments in depression. In F. J. Ayd (Ed.) (pp. 179–186). Baltimore: Ayd Medical Communication.

Macon, L. B. (1979). Help for bereaved parents. *Social Casework, 60,* 558–561.

Marziali, E. (1983, May). Prediction of outcome of brief psychotherapy from therapist's interpretative interventions. Read before the Annual Meeting of the American Psychiatric Association, New York.

Mendelson, M. (1974). *Psychoanalytic concept of depression* (2nd Ed.). New York: Spectrum.

Meuller, D. P. (1980). Social networks: A promising direction for research on the relationship of the social environment to psychiatric disorder. *Social Science and Medicine, 14A,* 147–161.

Nurnberger, J. I., & Gershon, E. S. (1982). Genetics. In E. S. Paykel (Ed.), *Handbook of affective disorders* (pp. 126–145). New York: Guilford.

O'Neil, M. K., Lancee, W. J., & Freeman, S. J. J. (1982, Jan.). Sex differences in depressed university students. Read before the Ontario Psychiatric Association meeting, Toronto.

O'Neil-Lowy, M. K. (1983). Psychosocial factors and depressive symptoms in university students. Doctoral dissertation, University of Toronto.

Paykel, E. S. (Ed.) (1982). *Handbook of affective disorders.* New York: Guilford.

Parker, G. (1979). Parental characteristics in relation to depressive disorders. *British Journal of Psychiatry, 134,* 138–147.

Parker, G., & Brown, L. B. (1979). Repertoires of response to potential precipitants of depression. *Australian and New Zealand Journal of Psychiatry, 13,* 327–333.

Radloff, L. S. (1980). Risk factors for depression: What do we learn from them? In D. Belle & S. Salasin (Eds.), *Mental health of women: Fact and fiction* (pp. 93–109). New York: Academic.

Rosenthal, T. L., Akiskal, H. S., & Scott-Strauss, A. (1981). Familial and developmental factors in characterological depressions. *Journal of Affective Disorders, 3,* 183–192.

Roth, M., & Mountjoy, C. Q. (1982). The distinction between anxiety states and depressive disorders. In E. S. Paykel (Ed.), *Handbook of affective disorders* (pp. 70–92). New York: Guilford.

Rounsaville, B. J., Weissman, M. M., Prusoff, B. A., et al. (1979). Marital disputes and treatment outcome in depressed women. *Comprehensive Psychiatry, 20,* 483–490.

Roy, A. (1979). Vulnerability factors and depression in women. *British Journal of Psychiatry, 133,* 106–110.

Roy, A. (1981). Vulnerability factors and depression in men. *British Journal of Psychiatry, 138,* 75–77.

Rush, J. A. (1982). *Short-term psychotherapies for depression.* New York: Guilford.

Rutter, M. (1973). *Children of sick parents.* London: Oxford University Press.

Sandler, J., & Joffe, W. G. (1965). Notes on childhood depression. *International Journal of Psychoanalysis, 46,* 88–96.

Shepherd, D. M., & Barraclough, B. M. (1979). Help for those bereaved by suicide. *British Journal of Social Work, 9,* 67–74.

Sinanan, K., & Hillary, I. (1981). Post influenza depression. *British Journal of Psychiatry, 138,* 131–133.

Spitz, R. A. (1946). Anaclitic depression. *Psychoanalytic Study of the Child, 2,* 313–314.

Stein, A. (1975). Group psychotherapy in the treatment of depression. In F. F. Flach & S. Draghi (Eds.), *The nature and treatment of depression* (pp. 183–196). New York: John Wiley.

Stein, A. (1982). Group therapy. In E. S. Paykel (Ed.), *Handbook of affective disorders* (pp. 307–317). New York: Guilford.

Stuart, R. B. (1967). Casework treatment of depression viewed as an interpersonal disturbance. *Social Work, 9,* 27–36.

Tennant, C., Smith, A., & Bebbington, P. (1981). Parental loss in childhood: Relationship to adult psychiatric impairment and contact with psychiatric services. *Archives of General Psychiatry, 38,* 309–314.

Wallerstein, J. S., & Kelly, J. B. (1980). *Surviving the breakup: How children and parents cope with divorce.* New York: Basic Books.

Wasylenki, D. (1980). Depression in the elderly. *Canadian Medical Association Journal, 122,* 525–532.

Wasylenki, D., Goering, P., Lancee, W., et al. (1981). Psychiatric aftercare: Identified need versus referral patterns. *American Journal of Psychiatry, 138,* 1228–1231.

Weissman, M. M. (1972a). Casework and pharmacotherapy in treatment of depression. *Social Casework, 53,* 38–44.

Weissman, M. M. (1972b). The depressed woman and her rebellious adolescent. *Social Casework, 53,* 563–570.

Weissman, M. M., & Klerman, G. L. (1973). Psychotherapy with depressed women: An empirical study of content themes and reflection. *British Journal of Psychiatry, 123,* 55–61.

Weissman, M. M., & Klerman, G. L. (1977a). The chronic depressive in the community: Unrecognized and poorly treated. *Comprehensive Psychiatry, 18,* 523–531.

Weissman, M. M., & Klerman, G. L. (1977b). Sex differences and the epidemiology of depression. *Archives of General Psychiatry, 34,* 98–111.

Weissman, M. M., & Paykel, E. S. (1974). *The depressed woman.* Chicago: University of Chicago Press.

Weissman, M. M., Pincus, C., Radding, N., et al. (1973). The educated housewife: Mild depression and the search for work. *American Journal of Orthopsychiatry, 43,* 565–573.

Weitkamp, L. R., Stancer, H. C., Persad, E., et al. (1981). A gene on chromosome 6 influencing behavior. *New England Journal of Medicine, 305,* 1301–1306.

Wetzel, J. W. (1980). Interventions with the depressed elderly in institutions. *Social Casework, 61,* 234–239.

Winnicott, D. W. (1964). The value of depression. *British Journal of Psychiatric Social Work, 7,* 123–127.

Winnicott, D. W. (1969). *The family and individual development.* London: Tavistock.

Winokur, G. (1979). Unipolar depression: Is it divisible into autonomous subtypes? *Archives of General Psychiatry, 36,* 47–52.

Winokur, G., & Morrison, J. (1973). The Iowa 500: Follow-up of 225 depressives. *British Journal of Psychiatry, 123,* 543–548.

Yalom, I. D. (1975). *The theory and practice of group psychotherapy.* New York: Basic Books.

Zetzel, E. (1965). Depression and the incapacity to bear it. In M. Shur (Ed.), *Drives, affects, and behavior* (pp. 243–274). New York: International Universities Press.

ADDENDUM

AFFECTIVE DISORDERS: MOOD DISORDERS

Mary Kay O'Neil

R ereading my 1984 chapter on Affective Disorders in the light of 15 years of intensive research and developments in the understanding, diagnosis and treatment of depression, what comes to mind is the phrase "Plus ça change, plus c'est la même chose."

Depression remains the most common form of adult psychopathology confronting mental health professionals.* The physical, psychological, and social distress inevitably associated with depression remains alarmingly high and, despite recent heightened attention, the majority of clinically depressed individuals fail to receive adequate help. As stated in 1984, these facts about mood disorders provide a challenge to the social work practitioner. Since, over the intervening 15 years, social workers have increasingly become primary care providers, the challenge has only intensified.

The 1984 chapter on affective disorders was written within a biopsychosocial model, in that biological, psychological, and social factors were all considered integral to the etiology and treatment. As the early chapters of this book make abundantly clear, there is no longer the slightest doubt that a biopsychosocial perspective is fundamental to good social work theory and practice. This is especially true for the mood dis-

---

*Of the Affective Disorders (now referred to in *DSM-IV* as Mood Disorders), depressive disorders far outnumber the bipolar disorders. Depression is the most common psychiatric condition encountered in most clinical practices. The focus here is primarily on depression. Manic/bipolar disorders are discussed where relevant.

This Addendum is written as an overview essay on developments in the area of affective disorders since the first edition of this book. Rather than a list limited to specific references, an update reading list useful to social work practitioners is provided. I wish once again to thank Frederick Lowy, M.D., for his assistance in writing this addendum.

orders, where the relative weights of the factors relevant to each case, as well as their interaction, are critical indicators for diagnosis and treatment.

After a brief sampling, within a biopsychosocial framework, of what is new with regard to pertinent facts (e.g., nature, classification, epidemiology, demographics, etiology), and guidelines for diagnosis and treatment, this update will focus on recent developments that are most applicable to social workers' recognition and management of mood disorders. These recent developments will not be discussed in detail or in depth. Nor is an attempt made to be comprehensive in presenting the numerous, complex interdisciplinary advances that have been made in the understanding of mood disorders in the last 15 years. Rather, the purpose here is to suggest a way of thinking about mood disorders that integrates these advances and that might be helpful to social work intervention. The pertinent developments fall into four areas: mood disorders over the life cycle; the relevance of attachment theory to the understanding of depression and the therapeutic relationship; the increased use of psychotropic medication; and social work's contribution to the development of combined treatment methods.

THE NATURE AND CLASSIFICATION OF MOOD DISORDERS

The nature of depression and mania is unchanged since the recognition of these conditions in antiquity. How they are labeled and understood has varied throughout history but the classification of mood disorders has stabilized in the fourth edition of the *Diagnostic and Statistical Manual of Mental Disorders (DSM-IV,* 1994), the standard diagnostic manual utilized in North America. The term *affective disorders* has been replaced by *mood disorders,* which is preferred because it refers to sustained emotional states and not merely to the external (affective) expression of the present emotional state. To review,

> [M]ood disorders encompass a large group of psychiatric disorders in which pathological moods and related vegetative and psychomotor disturbances dominate the clinical picture. They are best considered as syndromes (rather than discrete diseases) that consist of a cluster of signs and symptoms that are sustained over a period of weeks to months, represent a marked departure from a person's habitual functioning, and tend to recur, often in periodic or cyclical fashion. (Akiskal, 1995)

According to *DSM-IV*

> [T]he Mood disorders are divided into the Depressive Disorders (unipolar depression), the Bipolar Disorders, and the two other categories based on etiology—Mood Disorder Due to a General Medical Condition and Substance Abuse Induced Mood Disorder. The Depressive Disorders (i.e., Major Depressive Disorder, Dysthymic Disorder, and Depressive Disorder not otherwise specified) are distinguished from the Bipolar Disorders by the fact that there is no history of a manic, mixed, or hypomanic episode. The Bipolar Disorders (i.e., Bipolar I, or Bipolar II Disorder, Cyclothymic Disorder, and Bipolar Disorder Not Otherwise Specified) involve the presence (or history) of manic episodes, mixed manic and depressive episodes, or hypomanic episodes, usually accompanied by the presence (or history) of Major Depressive Episodes.

More emphasis is placed on the recognition of a major mood episode in making a definitive diagnosis. It is now generally recognized that mood disturbances are frequently concomitant with other diagnostic categories, most especially the Anxiety and Personality Disorders and substance and alcohol abuse so that multiple diagnoses may be applicable. The changes from *DSM-III* to *DSM-IV* diagnostic criteria are subtle. However, it behooves social workers, especially those in the field of mental health, to have a working familiarity with current diagnostic indicators, which have consultation, referral and therapeutic implications. Familiarity with the application of *DSM-IV* and with the chapter on mood disorders in the latest edition of the *Comprehensive Textbook of Psychiatry* (Akiskal, 1995) is useful. As this volume's editor, Francis Turner, noted in the first edition, accurate diagnosis is important to social workers only to the extent that it leads to effective, economical, and nonharmful intervention.

EPIDEMIOLOGY AND DEMOGRAPHICS OF AFFECTIVE DISORDERS

More accurate epidemiological data, based on standardized diagnostic interviews, have become available from National Institute of Mental Health studies and numerous other related studies over the last 15 years. Overall rates vary little from earlier reports. But from these extended studies we now have more detailed information about the relationship of depression and demographic factors (gender, age, social class, culture, marital status) as well as other medical conditions (e.g., AIDS, eating disorders) and psychiatric illnesses (e.g., anxiety and personality disorders). It is not surprising that incidence and prevalence rates, even within subgroups, remain relatively consistent. Much more research is needed to account for the persistently higher rates of depression in women. Both psychosocial and biological factors are thought to contribute to women's greater vulnerability, especially to dysthymic disorders. By contrast, manic and bipolar disorders appear to be more common in men. Despite increased recognition of mood disorders as a public health problem, moderate improvement in persistently low help-seeking rates, and the availability of more efficacious treatment, current data continue to suggest widespread undertreatment of mood disorders.

New data on the correlations between demographics and the occurrence of affective disorders, especially depression, assist in the identification of subgroups at risk. It has been known for some time that mood disorders are on the increase in the younger (18–30) age groups, possibly related to rising rates of alcohol and substance abuse. Children and younger adolescents are now being diagnosed more frequently. Clinical studies suggest higher rates of chronicity, recurrence, and refractoriness than previously documented. Moreover, recent attention has turned to groups whose depression was previously understudied. Within the current psychiatric and social work literatures, there has been a noticeable increase in studies on the complicated relationship between depression and aging. Following the proliferation of studies on women and depression, recent work has begun to cover factors that both contribute to and disguise depression in men.

THE ETIOLOGY OF AFFECTIVE DISORDERS

The 1984 discussion of etiology included biological (genetic and neuropathological), psychosocial (early and current loss of significant others, family history of psychiatric illness, stressful life events, and lack of adequate social support), and psychological (psychodynamic and personality) factors. The discussion in the original chapter about the relative contribution and interaction of these factors provides a basis for the consideration of subsequent findings.

Biological Factors

The results from the extensive investigations of biological factors of the last few decades have relevance for social work practice. Knowledge of brain activity related to mood disorders has been greatly expanded during the past 15 years by neurochemical and pharmacological studies as well as by the use of sophisticated neuroimaging techniques such as Magnetic Resonance Imaging (MRI) and Positron Emission Tomography (PET). The strong genetic contribution to vulnerability to mood disorders has been confirmed by population and twin studies. There is good reason to believe that specific genes associated with these conditions will be identified before long. Then proteins produced by these genes will also be identified and studied—leading to more specific drug treatment.

The important point for social workers to keep in mind is that biological and psychosocial factors converge and interact. Some syndromes (mania and bipolar disorders) likely result from a greater biological contribution; other syndromes (depression disorders, dysthymia, subsyndromal depressive episodes) probably owe more to reactions to psychosocial stresses. Hereditary predisposition, and adverse early-life experiences combine to produce temperamental vulnerability to certain life events, especially losses. Psychodynamic mechanisms are activated which result in the subjective symptoms of depression or mania as well as neurophysiological and neuroendocrine dysfunction manifested in psychomotor, sleep, appetite and other biological symptoms.

Therefore, depending on the type of mood disorder and the particular circumstances of an individual patient, treatment might be predominately biological (drug treatment or electroconvulsive therapy), or psychotherapeutic (cognitive, interpersonal or psychodynamic, group, marital or family) or social (environmental stress reduction, mobilization of social supports) or combined therapies.

Psychosocial Factors

The resurgence of interest in the relationship among the psychosocial factors, the importance of which was already evident decades ago, has resulted in a general acceptance of a multifactorial interactional model that has profound relevance to social work theory and practice. Much of what social workers have known from clinical experience about the contribution of social and environmental factors has now been clarified and supported empirically by sound research.

The link between early loss and depression has been illuminated. The previous inconsistency about the relationship between early loss and depression has been further resolved. For example, many social workers had been puzzled by the discrepancy between their clinical observation that depression is frequently accompanied by a history of early loss and some research findings that early loss does not predict depression. Data are now available which support the notion that early loss does indeed predict depression but only in the face of a current loss (O'Neil, et al., 1987). Studies of resiliency in children and of high achievement as an adaptation to loss and other life stresses have contributed to social work understanding of the effects of early and current loss on adult depression. However, a history of childhood loss can also contribute to the opposite; that is, unresolved mourning and denial of depressive affect can result in hyperactivity in children and hypomania in adults. These loss effects are especially deleterious if the loss represented an ongoing threat to a person's social support system or resulted in an impaired capacity to form relationships.

Attachment theory, which has developed exponentially in the last two decades, adds to the understanding of the effects of loss. A recent study by Hazelton, et al. (1998) on the controversial long-term effects of parental divorce and the role of early attachment is interesting. The study found no direct long-term effect of parental divorce on young adult relationships, supported beneficial effects of reduced exposure to a rejecting father and provided evidence for the salience of the quality of early attachment relationships with parents for the development of self-esteem, resiliency, emotional well-being, and the capacity to establish secure adult relationships. Such studies provide firm support for the long-held social work premise that in many people with depression experiential factors such as inadequate nurturing relationships are equally as important as the precipitating stress or genetic contributions. Attachment theory, which has particular relevance for current social work theories of human growth, development, and psychopathology, is discussed further below.

The genetic and experiential factors of a family history of psychiatric illness are now understood more specifically. Besides a history of major depression and bipolar disorder, a positive family history of affective or schizo-affective disorder carries with it increased risk—especially for depression but also for bipolar disorder. The risk is likely due both to genetic factors and to the effect of growing up in a family that is dysfunctional because of the illness of family members. Thus, a child with inherited vulnerability is further predisposed to future psychiatric illness by a stressful environment in which emotional nurturance and social support are inconsistent and weak. Although social workers do not need an in-depth understanding of the mechanisms of the biological contributors to mood disorders, they must keep in mind the genetic as well as the experiential risk involved in having in the family a parent, grandparent, or sibling with a mood disorder.

Research on the role of stressful life events in precipitating mood disorders has continued, with particular emphasis on the effect of certain events in specific depressed populations. There is emerging evidence that some people (with a family and personal history of mood disorders) are predisposed to react more sensitively to events and have a propensity to attribute negative meaning to life stresses. Further, the nature of their interaction with their environment and within relationships tends to provoke further stress. Studies using cognitive, learned helplessness, and loss of self-esteem models of depression corroborate this view. As social workers well know, loss events of all kinds remain a central theme in clinical depression. The impact of adult losses can be modified (increased or decreased) by such variables as concurrent life events, resultant changes in lifestyle, the meaning of such events, deficient or effective social and coping skills and, most importantly, the presence or absence of social supports. There is less persuasive evidence for a similar link between life stress and the triggering of manic episodes; for the latter hereditary factors are stronger.

Social support remains the single most important factor in the course and reaction to treatment in mood disorders. What was written in 1984 about social support as an etiological factor and therapeutic tool still stands. What is new with regard to social support is even stronger evidence of its centrality in the understanding and therapy of depression. In addition, numerous studies specify the nature and quality of relational supports required to modify mood disturbances at various phases of the life cycle.

Interestingly, psychological theories of depression that have developed over the last few decades (based on object loss, learned helplessness, loss of self-esteem) subsume a relational developmental model in which the variables contributing to a person's predisposition to depression are the quality of early nurturing experiences and the ongoing support system. A number of investigations have also focused on identifying the type of support needed to modify the impact of particularly traumatic life events or medical conditions that precipitate depressive reactions (e.g., posttraumatic stress syndromes, bereavement, AIDS). Such studies have led to age-, phase-, and stress-specific treatment modalities, which the social work profession has frequently developed.

The cognitive model of depression, developed primarily by psychologists, has permeated both psychiatric and social work understanding and treatment of affective illnesses. This model provides a bridge between ego-psychological (including relational) and behavioral models of depression. Cognitive therapy, which in the last two decades has become a prime treatment modality for depression, attempts to alter negative attributional states with the intention of alleviating mood disregulation and eventually protecting against relapses into negative thinking, depression, and despair.

Psychoanalytic theories of depression* have not developed independently but in conjunction with the aforementioned psychological models.

---

*As the first psychological approach to the mental suffering caused by mood disregulation, psychoanalytic theories of depression provided a basis for most contemporary psychological models as outlined in the original version of this chapter.

Currently popular psychoanalytic theories (e.g., self-psychology, intersubjectivity) are extensions of object-relational theories. Psychosocial theories have value for case formulation, guiding interventions, and suggesting areas of future research.

To summarize, research in recent years has provided more support for the multifactorial etiology of mood disorders. Biological (genetic, neurochemical), psychological (reactions to loss, self-directed aggression, negative cognitive style), social (disturbed family interactions, inadequate social supports) and other experiential factors (adverse life events) may all play a part. In a particular person some of these factors will be important and others not. Clinical skill involves the identification of those factors that are relevant to the pathogenesis of mood disorder in a given patient and, more specifically, of those amenable to therapeutic intervention.

DIAGNOSIS OF DEPRESSION

It is not the task of social workers to make definitive psychiatric diagnoses of mood disorders. However, it is essential that they develop the clinical skill to recognize them in their early stages or when moods are masked by other symptoms (i.e., depressive equivalents). Most especially, social workers need to understand the treatment implications of diagnostic classifications. Moreover, they need to know when to make medical and psychiatric referrals. Guidelines for so doing were outlined in the first edition and provide the basis for further discussion below. What can be added rests primarily in the area of the therapeutic use of psychoactive drugs and the other recent developments considered here.

SOCIAL WORK TREATMENT

The basics of social work treatment, the role of the social worker in various settings, modalities of therapy, the content and level of therapy, the therapeutic alliance, and social support as the profession's area of contribution were discussed in the first edition. Recent developments most applicable to the social work treatment of mood disorders fall into four areas, described below.

Mood Disorders Over the Life Cycle

Depression should be considered at every stage of the life cycle. Given that social workers work with adult clients of all ages, they need to be familiar with the particular manifestations and psychosocial complications for each age group. It is now well known that not only are life stresses of etiological significance but, at certain stages, particular stresses make a person more vulnerable.

Depressive affect can cause pain and suffering even when it does not constitute a formal *DSM-IV* disorder. From the life-cycle studies, it is clear that symptoms of depression can accompany the inevitable lowering or heightening of mood often seen during the transitions from one life phase to the next (e.g., leaving home, establishing a couple relationship, the birth of a child, divorce, retirement from work, move to a retirement home, spousal bereavement). That is, "normal" depression can have clinical significance. A person who is helped to name, cope with, and accept the inevitable ups and downs of moods accompanying phase-specific life tasks and stresses will be able to adapt to these and to continue to grow rather than develop more serious symptoms or a full-blown disorder. Suffice it to say that keeping in mind a developmental life-cycle model within an overarching biopsychosocial model is clinically useful.

Attachment Theory and Depression

As Sperling and Berman noted in *Attachment in Adults* (1994), "The study of attachment began as research into the earliest developmental origins of childhood and adult psychopathology, with John Bowlby's (1960) work at the Tavistock [Institute, London] Clinic. This model represented a break from traditional psychoanalytic conceptualizations and investigations, both in its emphasis on prospective study and in its link between parental separation/loss and later emotional disturbances" (p. 3). Attachment theory postulates that some individuals are more at risk for adverse effects of stressful life events while others are resilient. This differential vulnerability is determined by a person's cognitive and affective appraisal of an experience—which, in turn, is dependent upon the nature of early life attachments. According to Bowlby, an internal working model of attachment is constructed which is a set of expectations about how one will be responded to by others and how one will respond in return. These expectations are thought to begin in interactions with primary caregivers and often determine one's relational pattern throughout life. Attachment theory has consistently pointed to a link between insecure attachment patterns and adult affective, cognitive, and relational psychopathology. Further, the experience of an ill parent in the family contributes to the development of an insecure attachment pattern, thereby increasing vulnerability.

Empirical evidence is building to support the notion that the quality (secure or insecure) of these attachment patterns affects the development of self-esteem, resiliency, emotional well-being, and the capacity to establish secure adult relationships. That is, internal working models influence cognitive and relational functioning, and later psychological and social adjustment. Further, an insecure attachment pattern (preoccupied–anxious or avoidant–dismissing) is more salient in determining a person's negative response to life stress than the nature of the life event itself. For example, a person's response to separation and loss can be buffered by a secure relational model or worsened by an insecure internal model. It follows that persons with an insecure internal model will have relational problems, with a concomitant decrease in their social support systems and a reduction of their buffering effect. There is also some evidence that change from an insecure to a secure internal model is possible throughout life, although the factors that bring about this change have yet to be more clearly specified. Presumably successful therapy is one of these. Given social work's traditional developmental and relational model of understanding well-being and emotional illness, attachment theory suggests a model for understanding the interaction of the psychosocial contributors to depression.

What, then, does attachment theory add to a social work perspective on mood disorders? Diagnostically, attachment theory sheds light on specific disorders (e.g., abnormal grief, neurotic depression, agoraphobia) and also has a contribution to make to the understanding of the occurrence and course of other psychopathology. Developmentally, attachment theory underlines the basic social work premise that human beings develop best within a secure relationship and that insecure relationships increase the risk for subsequent emotional illness, especially depression. This premise has obvious therapeutic implications. The type of relationship that a person establishes with the social worker will not only reflect that person's internal working model, providing clues to past and present relational experiences and ensuing problems, but will also provide a guide to the relational needs expressed and to transference issues. These can then be deliberately addressed within the therapeutic relationship. Further, attachment theory identifies features common to therapy generally: individual, group, or family therapy. These include the secure base of a relationship with the social worker within which to explore problems; an explanation or shared narrative that explains the problems; and a method or technique that assists in overcoming the difficulty.

As was stated in this chapter of the 1984 edition, "[T]he social worker's most powerful tool for helping the patient develop or maintain good social support (essential to recovery from depression) is the helping relationship. This relationship encourages the development of self-esteem, self-sufficiency, and individual identity. The depressed person will have learned something about give-and-take, about realistic needs and expectations, and about ways to meet these through relationships with other human beings." Attachment theory provides an empirically supported and rich framework within which social workers can increase their understanding of depressive disorders and continue to develop ever more effective interventions.

Investigations into the etiology of affective disorders have consistently found that relational factors make a greater contribution to certain types of mood disorders, especially dysthymic disorders, and that genetic factors contribute more to other types, especially the manic or bipolar disorders. Recent developments, which better integrate the biological and psychosocial modalities of intervention and treatment, reflect this knowledge.

Psychotropic Medication and Social Work Treatment

The most effective approaches to mood disorders do not limit themselves to separate "mind-"directed (psychotherapy, casework) and "brain-" directed (psychopharmacology) therapy. Both mind and brain must be taken into consideration in diagnosis and treatment planning. More and more, social workers are working with adults and children who are also receiving "brain" therapy in conjunction with the various "mind" therapies offered, as evidence accumulates for the efficacy of combined therapies. Moreover, with greater choice, the refining of which medication is best for each person/illness dyad, and a general increase in the efficacy of treatment with drugs (prescription or nonprescription), social workers require appropriate knowledge to assist clients in effectively utilizing them.

What is the appropriate role for social workers with respect to pharmacotherapy for mood disorders? What should social workers know about the use of drugs, given that most have not received formal training in pharmacology and the use of prescriptions drugs? What about nonprescription over-the-counter drugs and the so-called "alternative" drugs and herbs that are increasingly used by people seeking relief of symptoms instead of, or in addition to, drugs prescribed by professionals?

At present social workers do not have the authority or, for the most part, the knowledge required to prescribe medication (although in the United States there are those who advocate limited prescription privileges for social workers). Yet social workers are helping many outpatients whose ongoing treatment includes maintenance medications, and social workers are integral members of hospital and clinic teams treating patients with acute mood disorders whose therapy is primarily pharmacological. Moreover, many social workers who are psychotherapists in private practice need to be able to assess when medication is needed in conjunction with their "talking" therapy and must make the appropriate referral. They also need to be able to monitor the effect of medication on the therapy, to encourage patients to monitor themselves and to work with the prescribing physician to find the most appropriate drug. In short, the social worker's role is to help patients to take as much responsibility as possible for their own medication.

It is important, therefore, for social workers to be familiar with the basic principles of psychopharmacology and, more specifically, with those medications most frequently used in the treatment of mood disorders. A detailed consideration of these points is beyond the scope of this chapter. Fortunately, while a large number of drugs may be prescribed for some of these patients, especially when they also suffer from concomitant medical and other psychiatric disorders, the majority of patients with mood disorders are treated with drugs that fall into only a few categories. These drugs are described in Chapter 5 of this book; their categories are set forth in tables in Chapter 5.

Psychoactive drugs are those chemicals that achieve a concentration in the brain sufficient to influence the neurotransmitters and the receptors of neurons to which they attach. The neurotransmitters are chemical substances that play a key role in the communication between neurons in the central nervous system. Disturbances in the concentration or interaction among neurotransmitters in specific areas of the brain are associated with the symptoms characteristic of mood disorders. The nature and the function of neurotransmitters are discussed in detail in Chapter 4 of this book.

Ideally, the specific disturbance (excess or insufficiency) would be the target of a highly specific drug that would have no effect on other brain or body functions. Such a drug would achieve the desired result in a known dosage range without producing unintended side effects and would not interact adversely with other drugs or foods that the individual in question is taking. Unfortunately, psychopharmacology has not reached this degree of precision; therefore, prescribing medication is still a matter of clinical judgment as well as pharmacological science. Drugs and dosage levels are selected because most people with symptoms similar to those of the patient respond favorably to them. However, individuals vary greatly. Frequently dosages must be adjusted or medication substituted when the desired antidepressant, antianxiety or antimanic effects do not occur or when unacceptable side effects occur. Although monitoring of blood levels of certain drugs is useful, clinical observation remains the most important way through which a good medication program is initiated and modified. Social workers, who often spend more quality time with patients than other mental health professionals—including the physician who has prescribed the medication—are in a key position to monitor the progress of drug therapy.

Although the safety margin of today's medications is acceptable and, increasingly, psychiatrists and other physicians are more skilled in their prescribing, there are many reasons why drug therapy can be ineffective or dangerous. Some of these have to do with internal processes within the patient (e.g., idiosyncratic absorption, metabolism, or excretion of the drug), which have not been initially identified. Some are due to poor compliance with prescriptions; patients take more or fewer pills, or eat foods they should avoid, or add over-the-counter medications that they believe to be harmless, or visit another physician who prescribes drugs without learning what the patient is already taking.

It is important for social workers, as well as other treating professionals, to be alert to indications that medication is not achieving the desired result. This may call for an increase in the dose of, say, an antidepressant. However, the observed symptoms must be distinguished from those that might be due to adverse drug effects; the latter might call for the opposite strategy, namely, reduction of the dose or discontinuation of the drug.

Because antidepressant drugs are effective in relieving depressive symptoms whatever their cause, because they are the treatment of choice for major depressions, and because antipsychotic medication and lithium are the mainstays of the management of mania, it is important that patients not be denied the benefit of pharmacotherapy. Social workers have an obligation to help reluctant patients accept drug therapy when this is indicated. At the same time, it is important to remember that drug therapy alone is never as effective as combined therapy, in which relevant psychological and social factors are also addressed. Frequently it is the social worker who reminds other members of an interdisciplinary team of the need for psychotherapy and the mobilization of social supports. Sometimes the patients themselves or their families try to rely on drugs alone, using such a focus as a resistance to confronting correctable psychosocial problems. Social workers can play a leadership role in helping such patients and families come to grips with chronic problems that, unattended, could precipitate recurrences of the mood disorder.

A related problem is the increasing use of antidepressants such as fluoxetine (Prozac, etc.) as a "feel-good" drug and a substitute for addressing intrapsychic and interpersonal problems. Here, again, social workers can be of great assistance to patients and their physicians by calling attention to treatable psychosocial pathology that is being covered up.

The drugs used most commonly in the management of acute mania are antipsychotics (e.g., haloperidol/Haldol) and lithium carbonate. Sometimes anticonvulsants (e.g., carbamazepine/Tegretol) are also used. Once the acute hospital phase of treatment is complete manic patients, with both Bipolar I and Bipolar II types, are usually maintained on lithium for indefinite periods. In many cases, especially for Bipolar II patients, an antidepressant is added.

Drug therapy for depressed patients involves the use of one of the drugs from any of three distinct classes of pharmacological products. These are the older tricyclic antidepressants (e.g., amitriptyline [Elavil], imipramine [Tofranil], norpramine); the monoamine oxidase inhibitors or MAOIs (e.g., phenelzine [Nardil], tranylcypromine [Parnate]); or the newer selective serotonin reuptake inhibitors or SSRIs (e.g., Prozac, Paxil, Zoloft, Serzone) that are now most often prescribed because they are efficacious yet have fewer adverse side effects.

Social workers whose patients are taking these drugs should familiarize themselves with the effects and side effects of these products as well as the medications and foods that patients are asked to avoid when taking them. This can be done by discussion with pharmacists or the prescribing physicians, by consulting the *Physician's Desk Reference* (in the United States) or the *Compendium of Pharmaceuticals and Specialties* (CPS) (in Canada), or by reading the relevant chapters in any of the standard textbooks of psychiatry or pharmacology.

Social Work and Combined Treatments

Turner's 1996 edition of *Social Work Treatment* makes it abundantly clear that social work practitioners can no longer follow a single theory or approach but must strive for an eclecticism that is informed, effective, and feasible in their practice with individuals, families, and groups. Through training and experience, skilled clinicians learn to search through this maze of current intervention strategies, without getting bogged down by theoretical arguments about competing approaches, to find a way to most effectively treat their clients with mood disorders. In the 1984 version of this chapter the social work treatment of depression was discussed at length. As stated previously, emphasis was placed on the therapeutic alliance, social work roles, the content and level of the therapy, and the main modalities of treatment. The basic features of social work treatment of depression and bipolar disorders, as outlined then, still stand. Despite the proliferation of new drugs and therapeutic techniques available, and the development and maturation of well tested psychotherapies (e.g., dynamic, interpersonal, and cognitive) much work remains before the question, "Which treatment modalities used by which social workers are most effective for patients with differing types of mood disorders?" can be answered.

It was both reassuring and heartening to discover in the recent literature that social workers are not only becoming more skilled in combining biological and psychosocial modes of therapeutic interventions but some are in the forefront of investigating the integration of discrete psychotherapeutic models. Studies of combining the cognitive and relational techniques of psychotherapy demonstrate the efficacy of this approach. Where indicated, combining drugs and psychotherapy further increases efficacy.

Social workers have also turned their attention to the treatment of mood disorders, which are on the increase and have been undertreated in the populations at certain phases of development, particularly old age. A cursory search of the recent literature reveals that the profession is aware of the needs of various populations identified as being at risk for depression. For example, a number of articles are readily found that focus on interventions for such at-risk groups as AIDS patients, mothers with HIV planning for their children, underserved older people, isolated college students,women in rural areas, men out of work because of plant closings, the homeless, primary-care patients, postpartum women, and the link between maternal depression and child abuse.

Social workers have also contributed to the development of short-term, focal, goal-directed therapy. This modality is particularly relevant, given that social workers are increasingly the primary and often the only caregivers for people suffering from mood disorders. Additionally, increasing restrictions on the amount of psychotherapy allowed under managed care and health insurance plans make the brief therapies a valuable treatment modality. Since mood disorders can occur throughout the life cycle and can be chronic or recurrent, therapeutic techniques that can be used intermittently are needed for effective, efficient service delivery.

Harking back to the centrality of the helping relationship and the relevance of attachment theory, the words of John Bowlby seem an apt way to summarize this update of a social work perspective on mood disorders:

> Whilst some traditional therapists might be described as adopting
> the stance 'I know, I'll tell you', the stance I advocate is one of 'You

know, you tell me' . . . the human psyche, like human bones, is strongly inclined towards self-healing. The psychotherapist's job, like that of the orthopaedic surgeon's, is to provide the conditions in which self-healing can best take place. (quoted in Holmes, 1993, p. 148)

REFERENCES: Addendum

OVERVIEW OF MOOD DISORDERS

Akiskal, H. S. (1995). Mood disorders: Introduction and overview. In Kaplan, H. I., & Sadock, B. J. (Eds.), *Comprehensive textbook of psychiatry* (Chapter 16). Baltimore: Williams & Wilkins.

Bromberger, J. T., & Costello, E. J. (1992). Epidemiology of depression for clinicians. *Social Work, 37,* 120–125.

Edwards, R. L. (Ed.). (1995). *Encyclopaedia of social* work (19th ed.). Washington, DC: NASW Press.

Kaplan, H. I., & Sadock, B. J. (1997). Mood disorders. In *Synopsis of psychiatry (8th ed.).* Baltimore: Williams & Wilkins, 1997.

Paykel, E. S. (Ed.). (1993). *Handbook of affective disorders.* London: Churchill Livingstone.

Shulman, K. I., Tohen, M., & Kutcher, S. P. (1996). *Mood disorders across the life span.* New York: Wiley-Liss.

ATTACHMENT THEORY

Bowlby, J. (1988). *A secure base.* New York: Basic Books.

Holmes, J. (1993). *John Bowlby and attachment theory.* London and New York: Routledge.

Hazelton, R., Lancee, W., & O'Neil, M. K. (1998). The controversial long-term effects of parental divorce: The role of early attachment. *Journal of Divorce & Remarriage, 29,* 1–17.

Goldberg, S., Muir, R., & Kerr, J. (1995). *Attachment theory: Social, developmental and clinical perspectives.* Hillsdale, NJ: Analytic Press.

Karen, R. (1995). *Becoming attached.* New York: Warner Books, 1994.

Parkes, C. M., Stevenson-Hinde, J., & Marris P. (Eds.). (1993). *Attachment across the life cycle.* London and New York: Routledge.

O'Neil, M. K., Lancee, W. J., & Freeman, S. J. (1987). Loss and depression: A controversial link. *Journal of Nervous and Mental Disease, 175,* 354–357.

Sperling, M. B., & Berman, W. H. (Eds.). (1994). *Attachment in adults: Clinical and developmental perspectives.* New York: Guilford Press.

SOCIAL WORK AND PSYCHOPHARMACOLOGY

Austrian, S. G. (1995). *Mental disorders, medications, and clinical social work.* New York: Columbia University Press.

Dziegielewski, S. E. (1998). Psychopharmacology and social work practice: Introduction. *Research on Social Work Practice, 8,* 371–383.

Dziegielewski, S. F., & Leon, A. M. (1998). Psychopharmacological treatment of major depression. *Research on Social Work Practice, 8,* 475–490.

Littrell, J., & Ashford, J. B. (1994). The duty of social workers to refer for medications: A study of field instructors. *Research on Social Work Practice, 30,* 123–128.

Walsh, J. (1998). Psychopharmacological treatment of bipolar disorder. *Research on Social Work Practice, 8,* 406–425.

SOCIAL WORK AND PSYCHOSOCIAL TREATMENT

Coyne, J. C., & Fechner-Bates, S. (1992). Depression, the family, and family therapy. *Australian and New Zealand Journal of Family Therapy, 13,* 203–208.

Jensen, C. (1994). Psychosocial treatment of depression in women: Nine single-subject evaluations. *Research on Social Work Practice, 4,* 267–282.

Littrell, J. (1995). Clinical practice guidelines for depression in primary care: What social workers need to know. *Research on Social Work Practice, 5,* 131–151.

Jensen, C. C. (1993). Treating major depression. *Affilia-Journal of Women and Social Work, 8,* 213–222.

Turner, F. J. (Ed.). (1997). *Social work treatment* (4th Ed.). New York: Free Press.

Wool, M. S. (1990). Understanding depression in medical patients. Part I: Diagnostic considerations. *Social Work in Health Care, 14,* 25–38.

Wool, M. S. (1990). Understanding depression in medical patients. Part II: Clinical interventions. *Social Work in Health Care, 14,* 39–52.

14

ANXIETY DISORDERS

Bert L. Kaplan

Current subject matter in newspapers, magazines, and bookstores reflects a broad-based societal concern about anxiety. Young parents, struggling to balance the conflicting demands of career advancement and "normal" family living, worry that their efforts in either direction interfere with success in the other. Single parents, alternate lifestyles, reconstituted families, sandwich generations, etc., make up such a large part of our population that it is difficult for an individual to find a reference point to evaluate the appropriateness of his or her behavior. Furthermore, rapid technological advances have produced an intensity of knowledge and information transmission to the extent that the experiences of "knowledge explosion" and "information overload" are commonplace, with individuals finding they must deal with a constantly increasing number of choices when making daily decisons.

To complicate matters, the health care industry is forced to struggle with insurance companies and administrators who exert as much influence as medical diagnosis and patient need in determining treatment direction, requiring a focus on "brief" therapies as a condition for payment. Thus, mental health practitioners are influenced to select treatment approaches that focus on symptom relief, unable to study the workings of the client's mind at leisure, with the goal of improving overall functioning.

Discussing anxiety disorders within the context of such societal and professional pressures tempts one to "jump on the bandwagon" of current disposition and concentrate essentially on symptom description, with emphasis placed on treatment approaches aimed at symptom alleviation. While such emphasis can help clients function better, it includes three significant shortcomings. It fails to account for the core of knowledge underlying our understanding of the anxiety experience, within which anxiety is viewed as a normal and potentially helpful feeling state; it fails to promote the client's capacity for anxiety tolerance as a necessary component of everyday living; and it overlooks improving the client's ability to cope by failing to deepen understanding of self within a rapidly changing and over-stimulating social context. In other words, focus on symptom relief can help to diminish anxiety, but does little to enhance the client's appreciation of the need to expand a repertoire of coping skills that enable ongoing adaptive functioning. This chapter, by focusing on anxiety as a subjective phenomenon occurring as part of the client's normal everyday experience, considers anxiety and its disorders within the context of increasing self-understanding and the expansion of coping skills.

Her hands were sweating. She didn't understand what was happening to her, but thoughts were racing through her mind with unbelievable speed. It was as through a locomotive had loosed itself and was running wild in her head. She dimly felt the blood pounding at her temples, surging to break through her skin. Her stomach was knotted, and sweat was pouring down her scalp and face. She gasped for breath. "Oh, God, why isn't he here yet?" She, thought.

Quickly, she reviewed past events in her mind. He had promised to come. He swore nothing would keep him away. In the middle of the night, he had whispered words of love to her. "Why isn't he here?" The words raced through her head. She had visions of him lying in a ditch, body broken, smashed beyond recognition. The next flash saw him being attacked and beaten. She forced herself to stop.

"He said he would come!" she screamed to nobody in particular. She did not realize she had spoken the words aloud until several people around her looked up in astonishment. "Are you all right?" a faceless voice asked. She felt her head nod assent, yet she knew she was not all right. She was getting sick and would not be able to help herself. If only she were home, she would know what to do, but waiting in a strange, new place left her helpless. She felt herself beginning to gag and forced herself to stop. She had to gain control. She could not let all these people see her like this.

Even as she fought for control, she began to feel her eyes cloud over and the room start to spin. Her nausea worsened and the sweating became unbearable. She felt her heart about to burst. "If only I could breathe!" she thought, and her mind raced. "He can't be dead!

He just can't be!" At that moment, the door opened and footsteps approached. Her eyes could not focus but she recognized the walk and the tilt of his head to one side. And the voice had its usual ring. "Sorry I'm late," he said.

PSYCHOLOGICAL ASPECTS OF ANXIETY

The anxiety experience can occur anywhere and at anytime. The young woman in the above vignette was obviously waiting for someone whose arrival was important to her. We can imagine the possible circumstances— a concert, a wedding, a dinner appointment. Her reaction was a subjective experience of stress and apprehension in relation to an event that was about to occur, and her specific mental state was that something terrible was about to happen: in her mind, she would soon find out that her date was dead.

In anticipating disaster, the woman found that her thoughts flowed into one another, her capacity to understand what was going on around her was diminished, and her body seemed to function in atypical and almost uncontrollable ways. Most significantly, she was acutely aware of herself and the way she was feeling. She was so uncomfortable, confused, and out of control that she felt she was floundering and unable to help herself. In short, this woman was experiencing an anxiety attack. While any of us may undergo such an experience on occasion, most of us are not generally subject to such extreme feelings of anxiety and are more used to the kind of apprehension experienced before taking a test, consulting a physician, or waiting for a job interview. We wonder about what could go wrong, anticipate that it might, worry about that to the point of feeling some of the physical reactions described in the vignette—but we basically retain a sense of control about ourselves and are able to attend to the business at hand despite the sense of distress.

PHYSIOLOGICAL ASPECTS OF ANXIETY

As was indicated in the vignette, physiological correlates of the anxiety experience may include any of the following 13 somatic or cognitive experiences:

- palpitations
- sweating
- trembling or shaking

- sensations of shortness of breath or smothering
- feeling of choking
- chest pain or discomfort
- nausea or abdominal distress
- dizziness or light-headedness
- derealization or depersonalization
- fear of losing control or "going crazy"
- fear of dying
- paresthesias
- chills or hot flushes
  (American Psychiatric Association, 1994)

All of these indicators may not be present, but several usually occur in combination. However, some form of motor tension and autonomic hyperactivity is always present, so that the person inevitably experiences a sense of jumpiness, increased heart and breathing rates, and heightened blood pressure.

Of major interest with respect to the physiological correlates of the anxiety experience is that these physical reactions, among others, are not specific to anxiety per se (Krystal, 1997; Lichtenberg, 1991). A person experiencing anger, fear, or a general state of overexcitement (affect storm) may demonstrate similar physical reactions. If one were to monitor physiological responses to anger, fear, anxiety, excitement, or an affect storm of any kind, one would not be able to distinguish among the emotional states without knowledge of the person's mental state. In other words, the physiological correlates of anxiety can be ascribed to anxiety only if they are accompanied by the psychological experience of apprehension with respect to impending doom. Mental ideation and physiological process cannot be conceived of separately; neither by itself defines the anxiety condition.

BASIC CONCEPTS OF ANXIETY

Anxiety is an affect that occurs in all individuals. Like joy, sadness, bemusement, and even grief, anxiety arises and diminishes at various times and under various circumstances. The hallmark of anxiety is a feeling of apprehension, accompanied by the idea that something bad is about to happen.

For Brenner (1974a, 1974b), the distinction between anxiety and depression is that anxiety is an anticipatory feeling of tension, whereas depression is a feeling of tension associated with the idea that something bad has already happened. The essential distinction is that anxiety serves as a warning about whatever doom is supposed to come; depression is felt after disaster has occurred. Within this context anxiety can function as a signal that motivates a person to act, in an attempt to "head off" the unpleasant outcome.

When the experience of anxiety does fulfill its anticipatory and motivating purpose, it can be understood as a way of preparing to deal with other, potentially debilitating aspects of anxiety. And when tolerance for the anxiety experience is available, or psychological defenses are working, anxiety is diminished and the ability to go about normal, daily business remains intact even though some apprehension or worry is felt. When defenses are not working, however, or tolerance is not available, anxiety does not decrease and an anxiety state (panic) occurs, during which it is not possible to continue normal routines. Thus, to fully appreciate the full scope of possible anxiety experiences, it is helpful to view anxiety from two perspectives, as a "signal anxiety" and as a "state." The former is a normal part of daily living, such as occurs during preparation for a job interview or an examination; in this case, anxiety serves as a motivator of activity whose purpose is to diminish apprehension. The latter is more problematic, since constructive functioning is not possible so long as a state of anxiety prevails.

Because correlates (symptoms) of anxiety are observable, it is possible to overemphasize them, designating the experience of anxiety as "a problem," rather than as an experience to be tolerated or as a possible motivating force. Maintaining a focus on the role of anxiety as a motivating force, however, in contradistinction to its experience as a mental or physical problem, permits the inference that an anxiety state occurs when the person is not able to tolerate its intensity (insufficient anxiety tolerance), or protect him/herself from it. In other words, even if the anticipatory function accompanies anxiety (signal anxiety), insufficient tolerance or non-availability of defenses may result in an anxiety attack.

Reviewing the above, then, anxiety can be either tolerated, during which experience the individual, though upset, is able to "go about everyday business" without having to do anything about the emotional distress, or it can be diminished when the person becomes able to invoke defenses for protection against a more intense feeling of anxiety. Most importantly, it is not the presence of the anxiety experience that is to be viewed as problematic; rather, it is the absence of anxiety tolerance or working defenses that results in psychological difficulty.

DISORDERS ASSOCIATED WITH ANXIETY

Fortunately, anxiety is frequently experienced in a relatively mild form in a number of everyday situations, such as when taking a test or visiting a physician. Anxiety in such situations is generally advantageous, requiring a marshalling of our tolerance or protective forces in anticipation of what is to come. However, anxiety often plays a major role in certain defined psychological disorders: *phobic disorders, anxiety states,* and, to some extent, *somatoform disorders.*

Phobic Disorders

Many individuals experience apprehension or even panic when faced with certain objects (see chapters 10, "Psychophysiologic Disorders," and 21, "Phobic Disorders"). Insects, snakes, and mice are three sources of distress that are common enough so that they are rarely the object of phobias. However, *phobia* is defined in *DSM-IV* (American Psychiatric Association, 1994) as a persistent, irrational, excessive fear of a specific object, activity, or situation that results in a compelling desire to avoid it. In this view, even the most common of specific fears constitutes a phobia. However, the diagnosis of a phobic disorder is not considered unless the person's daily routine, occupational functioning, or social life suffers significant interference, or unless the person is markedly distressed about experiencing the phobia. Thus, a phobic condition may be evident but remain undiagnosed unless it causes the person significant distress.

Anxiety is the central affective experience in phobic disorders, and the individual must avoid this anxiety at all costs. By associating the onset of anxiety with a specific object, the person can avoid the experience of anxiety by avoiding the object. Nothing could be more simple, and nothing could be, in some instances, more effective. The etiology, symptoms, and treatment of phobias are discussed at greater length in Chapter 21.

Anxiety States

Panic Disorder

The vignette presented near the beginning of the chapter illustrates a *Panic Attack,* with its constellation of psychological and physiological characteristics. Because panic attacks occur in the context of different anxiety disorders, panic disorder is diagnosed only in the presence of recurrent, unexpected panic attacks followed by at least one month of persistent con-

cern about having another panic attack, worry about the possible implications or consequences of the panic attack, or a significant behavioral
change related to the attacks (American Psychiatric Association, 1994).
Criteria for this diagnosis include the criteria for panic attack (discrete
intense fear or discomfort, in which at least 4 of 13 specified somatic or
cognitive symptoms developed abruptly and reached a peak within ten
minutes).

Certainly, an individual may experience a panic attack on occasion.
Such attacks do not constitute a panic disorder unless they satisfy the
above criteria. The person who reacts with panic at the slightest provocation, perhaps several times daily, is certainly in a very different category.
Thus, it is not the experience of the isolated panic attack that warrants
concern.

Generalized Anxiety Disorder
Excessive anxiety and worry that the person finds difficult to control,
occurring more days than not for at least 6 months, and accompanied by
such phenomena as restlessness, fatigue, difficulty of concentration, irritability, muscle tension, and sleep disturbance (three of which must be present), falls into this category. Once again, this is not an experience
unfamiliar to most people except with respect to duration.

We all can sympathize with the anxious person who is constantly on
guard, for each of us has had periods of ongoing anticipation of a dreaded
outcome. However, for most of us anxiety rarely lasts more than a few
days, easing as the dreaded situation passes or loses its meaning. For the
person experiencing a *generalized anxiety disorder,* however, the dread
does not diminish because new situations of danger are perceived as soon
as the earlier ones ease.

There has been controversy over the concept of generalized anxiety
because some theorists argue that no experience of anxiety ever exists without becoming connected to specified stimuli that are viewed as causing the
anxiety (Beck, 1976). In other words, the person experiencing anxiety is
always able to identify the impending doom that is the (real or perceived)
reason for the anxiety. Such a view is, or course, accurate but overlooks the
reality that some individuals demonstrate ongoing anxiety with changing
stimuli, meaning that there is no consistent cause for the continuing anxiety experience. In such instances, one must look beyond rationality for the
reason why the anxiety persists.

Certainly, ongoing anxiety does not appear without a reason, but the
reason may be related more to the individual's incapacity to maintain a sta-

ble sense of identity and/or being than to a specific, identifiable sense of impending doom. For such individuals, almost anything can signify internal disorganization, with the resulting subjective experience of anxiety. This point will be discussed further in the section dealing with the conditions under which anxiety occurs.

Obsessive Compulsive Disorder

Of the disorders mentioned thus far, the *obsessive-compulsive disorder* is probably the most confusing with respect to anxiety since, if obsessive-compulsive rituals are effective, little anxiety is experienced or observed. Like phobic symptoms, obsessive-compulsive characteristics protect the person from the experience of overwhelming anxiety. Indeed, anxiety remains the central and motivating force in the development of obsessive-compulsive symptoms.

Why some individuals develop phobic mechanisms and others obsessive-compulsive ones in response to similar feelings of distress and ideas of impending doom remains uncertain. The reasons may have to do with both constitutional endowment and environment/experience.

Persons suffering from obsessive-compulsive disorder display *obsessions* (recurrent and persistent thoughts, ideas, images, or impulses), *compulsions* (repetitive behaviors performed in a stereotyped manner), or both. Characteristically, the thoughts and/or behaviors occur involuntarily, and the individual feels them to be uncontrollable. In fact, the person feels helpless. Usually, the thoughts are felt to be intrusive and the individual attempts to overlook or ignore them; however, to succeed in doing so invites intense and persistent distress. The only solution, then, is to follow the dictates of the obsessive or compulsive imperatives.

Very often, the obsessive-compulsive behavioral symptom may not appear unusual to an observer. It can consist of something as simple as locking up the house or apartment in a particular sequence or dressing according to a specific routine. Once done for the day, the ritual may not have to be repeated until the next day. In more severe instances, the sense of intrusion may occur many times daily and may require significant behavioral compliance before a feeling of peace is attained. Classic examples of obsessive thinking involve thoughts of killing someone, becoming infected through handshaking, and continuous doubting. Typical compulsions are hand washing, counting, and touching.

Obsessions and/or compulsions make no sense to the person who feels forced to comply with them, nor do they make particular sense with respect to everyday living activities. Once again, the particular symptom has no a priori meaning and its specific significance can be unearthed only as part of a developing process of increased understanding. Although the generic concept that the disorder serves to allay anxiety is true, as with phobia, the conditions that provoke the obsessive-compulsive experience vary with each individual.

A young woman with serious problems of self-esteem, filled with confusion over her anger toward her husband, and unable to become pregnant, found herself obsessed with the idea that the plants in her house might become infected and die. She found that the only way she could help ease her tension was by examining the plants carefully each morning and evening to be sure none was infected.

When she found possible illness or damage she immediately had to clean and repot the plant. She did not understand her behavior, which she tried to control with little or no success, worrying that it meant she was crazy. She held a responsible job, which she performed well, and was considered a valuable employee. She talked of having several close friends in whom she could confide. In many ways, she appeared to be a sensitive, thoughtful, and considerate person.

Posttraumatic Stress Disorder (Acute and Chronic)

The concept of *trauma*, traditionally part of psychological theory, has undergone some revision in the light of developmental theory focusing on the accumulation of ongoing noxious experiences rather than on single events (Spitz, 1965). Nevertheless, the concept of trauma as a single event has been retained in psychology with the recognition that some people undergo experiences outside the usual that leave them psychologically numb or emotionally anesthetized (Krystal, 1997, 1978). Such people report flashbacks of these experiences, finding themselves hyperalert to their possible recurrence and prone to exaggerated startle responses and/or insomnia.

Experiences associated with *posttraumatic stress disorder* may be primarily psychological or primarily physical (e.g., sensory deprivation, mental torture, rape, military combat, accidents, death camps). While it is clear that the sense of numbness or anesthesia must follow the atypical stressful experience for the diagnosis to be made, what remains unclear is why some individuals react to atypical stress with posttraumatic stress disorder and others do not. Often it is assumed that the person who develops this disorder was predisposed to do so. However, since we are talking about atypical stressors and we must remain aware that each person has a breaking point beyond which normal functioning cannot be maintained, such an assumption is hardly warranted.

The difference between the *acute* and *chronic* forms of this disorder is determined by the duration of symptoms, with the acute form lasting a maximum of three months, after which the diagnosis is changed to chronic. A thorough discussion of posttraumatic stress disorder appears in Chapter 26 of this book.

Acute Stress Disorder

The essential feature of *acute stress disorder* is that it occurs within one month after exposure to the traumatic stressor, demonstrating the characteristic symptoms of posttraumatic stress disorder. In addition, dissociative symptoms must be present. The diagnosis is not made unless the symptoms last for a minimum of two days and a maximum of four weeks. Symptoms lasting longer than four weeks require a diagnosis of posttraumatic stress disorder.

Anxiety Disorder NOS (not otherwise specified)

This is a catchall category used when the symptom of anxiety is a central feature of the person's functioning. However, *anxiety disorder NOS* does not fit the precise diagnostic requirements of those conditions already discussed.

Anxiety Disorder Due to a General Medical Condition

This diagnosis depends on a determination that the experience of anxiety is occurring because of a medical condition already diagnosed; in addition, the anxiety symptoms must be etiologically related to the general medical condition through a physiological mechanism. Because it would be highly likely that any seriously ill person would experience and demonstrate anxiety in some way, this syndrome is difficult to determine.

Substance-Induced Anxiety Disorder

Prominent anxiety symptoms associated with drugs, medications, or exposure to toxins are common. The anxiety symptoms may take the form of any of the diagnostic categories, requiring clarity regarding history and onset of symptomatology for diagnositc accuracy. Because all known mental health approaches have proved futile in the face of substance abuse, clinical wisdom requires the client's voluntary discontinuance of the abuse prior to attempting psychotherapy of any kind.

Somatoform Disorders

It is to be specifically noted that *somatoform disorders* constitute a distinct category of illness in *DSM-IV* (see Chapter 10, "Psychophysiologic Disorders"). However, anxiety is often a part of the somatoform condition (Krystal, 1997) and it can be difficult to determine the significance of this symptom for diagnostic purposes.

Somatoform disorders are closely associated with psychological conditions of stress and are often thought to be the outcome of an inability to otherwise process anxiety-provoking experiences. Whereas the phobic or obsessive-compulsive person has found a means to allay anxiety (albeit not necessarily the most adaptive means), the person demonstrating a somatoform disorder experiences anxiety in its full physical manifestations ("When you're upset, you seem to hurt all over"), expressing this response as physical symptomatology rather than as psychological distress (Schur, 1955). In some instances, the person may be aware that the anxious condition is gradually giving way to physical discomfort (Kaplan, 1988). In other instances, he or she may be aware only of pain. It must be emphasized that the pain is quite real, and prolonged physical stress can lead to permanent and irreversible bodily change (e.g., an ulcer). However, it must be emphasized that the bodily condition can also occur for purely physical reasons; thus, the diagnosis of somatoform disorder is used only when no organic problem can be found.

ANXIETY DISORDERS: THE PROBLEM OF DIFFERENTIAL DIAGNOSIS

From the brief summaries of the diagnostic categories associated with anxiety, it would appear that differential diagnosis would be a relatively simple matter: all one needs to know is the symptomatology in order for the diagnosis to follow. However, real people do not fit categories of disorder. For instance, the young woman in the example of obsessional-compulsive disorder also suffered from severe stomach problems and frequent colitis. Obviously, her obsessive-compulsive manifestations, while they helped her contain some anxiety, did not do so to the extent that somatic problems could be avoided. Clearly, under such circumstances, a choice of diagnosis must be made, a choice that rarely paints a full picture. The same is basically true, for instance, with phobic patients. Few patients present with relatively fixed and specific phobias with little other evidence of complications. Indeed, transient and varied phobic manifestations are common in individuals diagnosed as "borderline" (see Chapter 17 herein; Kernberg, 1975), nor is it unusual for people with chronic and generalized anxiety to evidence a number of phobias. Thus, the experience of anxiety is present in almost all categories of psychological disorder—except when it is notable by its absence, as in some cases of pathological gambling or kleptomania. This being the case, a diagnosis based primarily on symptomatology may overlook the significant role that anxiety is playing. In this situation, behaviors that are needed by the individual for protection against anxiety may become the therapeutic target, although the person needs these behaviors in order to function until anxiety can be otherwise managed.

In other clients, anxiety may appear to be the central and most significant symptom. However, it is still necessary to note other aspects of the person's functioning, since some psychotic conditions are accompanied by significant manifest and pervasive anxiety. Experience usually makes it possible for clinicians to know how to order the information obtained about a client, but it must be emphasized that such ordering should always be subject to ongoing review, particularly with respect to anxiety conditions.

Perhaps the most meaningful errors in diagnosis occur with people who under the stress of intense anxiety lose rationality for a brief period of time. If seen in such circumstances they may be diagnosed psychotic, even though rapid recovery is evidenced. A more accurate assessment would distinguish between people who regress temporarily under significant stress but recover quickly from those who regress and remain regressed for long periods. Unfortunately, such a distinction may be forgotten when a person is seen at the height of the anxiety experience.

In summary, the pitfalls of diagnostic error are many and the likelihood of never making such an error is low, given the current state of knowledge. Nevertheless, clinical judgment can be improved by recognizing that anxiety is present in almost all categories of psychological disorder—and by paying attention to how this affect is experienced and understood by the client.

CHANGING PERSPECTIVES ON ANXIETY CONDITIONS

When Freud first developed his psychodynamic model around the turn of the twentieth century, there was a strong tendency to relate cause and effect in a fairly linear manner. As a result, terms like *energy, impulse, repression, cathexis,* and *discharge,* which reflect force and motion, were used to explain the workings of the mind.

As Freud saw it, there was a biological force, *libido* (sexuality), which required expression and which, for a variety of reasons related to experiential factors, could be subject to *repression* (a term used at that time to refer to all mental operations that relegate impulses to the *unconscious,* where they continue to seek expression). Since Freud's early patients demonstrated anxiety, and since their problems appeared to be related to material of a sexual nature that was unacceptable to them, Freud concluded that their symptomatology was the outcome of the repressed sexuality, which was being expressed in disguised form. For Freud, then, anxiety consisted of *transformed sexuality* caused by repression, which did not permit sexual expression in its original state. Therefore, it was only natural that treatment should focus on fostering expression of the unexpressed, and the idea that repressed energy has to be discharged in order for cure to be achieved became a central theme in treatment. Left unexpressed, or repressed, the accumulated sexual energy would, in this view, eventually find itself a means of disguised expression through either physical symptoms (*conversion hysteria*) or phobias (*anxiety hysteria*).

This formulation, an essential component of Freud's early model of the mind, remained evident in his writings throughout the first two decades of the twentieth century. And while Freud gradually became aware of difficulties with this view, he made no formal changes until 1926, when he wrote *Inhibitions, Symptoms, and Anxiety* (Freud, 1936). By that time, Freud had evolved several more models of the mind, notably the topographic and the structural, and had clarified his meaning of terms like *ego, id,* and *superego,* which had previously been used without much specificity. *Inhibitions, Symptoms, and Anxiety* examined the relationship between anxiety and repression, anxiety's function as a signal, its expression as a state or a condition, and its relationship to defense. Most notably, Freud revised his earlier concept of anxiety as transformed sexuality caused by repression. Instead, he developed the idea that anxiety is an ego function activated whenever the person is faced with a threat that must be managed. Since anxiety can be overwhelming and disintegrating to whatever degree of ego organization available to the individual, repression (defense) is invoked for protection. Thus the ego function of anxiety became the cause of repression (defense) rather than the other way around; a new era of psychodynamic formulation dawned, in which ego functions were emphasized instead of drives. (See Freud, 1936 for further discussion of this issue.)

In summary, Freud (1936) broke new ground by distinguishing between anxiety as a signal (motivating force) and anxiety as a condition. Both responses represent apprehension in the face of anticipated unpleasantness or danger, but the former signifies an adaptive response whereas the latter entails helplessness and psychic collapse.

DEVELOPMENTAL ASPECTS OF ANXIETY

We are prone, for diagnostic purposes, to think of anxiety as a correlate of psychological distress; consequently, we often forget that the anxiety response is evident in the form of the neonatal startle reflex. Since it is impossible to describe the nature of mental activity in newborns, it is more accurate to state that the startle reflex is evidence of the capacity for physical responsiveness without anticipatory ideation, reserving the term *anxiety* for the response that is evident once anticipatory ideation can be reasonably determined to exist. In this context, it is interesting to note that while Freud referred to the birth experience as prototypical of the anxiety response, meaning that physiological reactions may be similar in both situations, he was quite opposed to the idea that birth itself should be considered the initial trauma in life (Freud, 1936).

There is much evidence that anxiety as an anticipatory experience develops during the first months of life and much speculation that the nature of anticipated unpleasantness changes as children grow. Since the newborn is considered to be attuned primarily to internal biologic stimuli, any experience of anxiety that is hypothesized at that stage has to be viewed as a function of physiological stimulation. However, by definition, anxiety requires awareness of anticipated danger. Therefore, the first level of anxiety can be said to occur only after the infant becomes aware that physiological tension can be distressful enough to hurt, and its onset recognizable. If such is the case, and observation indicates that it is, then one can speak of "anxiety with respect to physiological tension" as the most primitive form of this affect. Indeed, there are situations wherein both children and adults have been observed to become terrified over the feeling that they may lose control of themselves and express rage that can only be hurtful. In such instances, anxiety can be quite pronounced.

Moving along the developmental ladder, anxiety can be seen to occur in response to awareness that the caretaking person (object) may become unavailable to the infant. At this point, the infant recognizes that its needs are fulfilled by someone or something "out there," and danger is anticipated when that someone or something is absent. Such anxiety is referred to as *anxiety with respect to loss of the object (person)*. It must be emphasized that the object is not yet specific; thus, the infant will generally accept soothing from any object that fulfills the need at the time.

Subsequently, the infant recognizes that a specific object is the one that provides. The infant begins to value this object and assumes that its needs are met because it is itself a valued object. Thus, concern emerges over loss of value in the eyes of the provider and *anxiety with respect to loss of love of the object (person)* emerges.

The next level of anxiety that has been hypothesized and observed relates to the oedipal phase and was originally termed *castration anxiety.* However, the concept of castration anxiety reflects a perpetuation of Freud's orientation to a male-dominated society, and recent research indicates that children of both sexes become concerned with punishment around the same time that they seem to become more cognizant of themselves as sexual beings. Thus, it is probably more accurate to refer to "anxiety with respect to retribution" than to "castration anxiety" at this stage. Such anxiety is evident when an individual feels that punishment or severe accountability will follow a particular activity, thought, or feeling. "My husband/wife will kill me if he/she finds out" is common enough in this vein.

The highest level of anxiety, which relates to the most complex level of development, occurs after the resolution of the oedipal conflict and is termed *anxiety with respect to the superego.* Most commonly, we refer to this as "conscience."

Thus, a developmental perspective identifies a hierarchy of levels of anxiety corresponding to various developmental stages. More evidence exists for some types of anxiety than for others, but all seem to have clinical utility and are observable in practice. Knowledge of the ideation of the individual evidencing anxiety is necessary in order to identify what kind (level) of anxiety is being experienced; such knowledge serves as a diagnostic clue for treatment direction. In summary, five developmental levels of anxiety have been proposed:

1. Anxiety with respect to physiological tension
2. Anxiety with respect to loss of the object (person)
3. Anxiety with respect to loss of love of the object (person)
4. Anxiety with respect to retribution
5. Anxiety with respect to the superego.

ANXIETY AS A DIAGNOSTIC INDICATOR IN PRACTICE

Many people who fall into a category of psychopathology do not feel upset with themselves. The mental-hospital patient who is so out of touch with reality as to be oblivious to current circumstances demonstrates little personal distress. The character-disordered patient typically experiences little or no distress. And the antisocial personality may be denoted by a lack of concern for the grief his/her behaviors cause others. Indeed the presence or absence of anxiety (i.e., affective distress) as a function of anticipated danger, may or may not serve as a diagnostic indicator.

At the same time, anxiety is not without meaning to the clinician. On the contrary, this response has a great deal of meaning to a clinician who knows how to evaluate it. The first determination to be made relates to whether or not the anxiety represents signal anxiety or a state of anxiety. Signal anxiety, as I have said above, is often adaptive, meaning that defenses are usually working and that functioning is still possible. As a state, anxiety is overwhelming and helpless panic is experienced.

> A client demonstrated intense agitation. He had something to talk about but could not because a taxicab was waiting and he was afraid it would leave without him, leaving him stranded. Of course, he could easily call another cab, but the idea that this taxi might leave terrified him. I asked him whether he felt it would be easier for him to talk if he found out whether or not the taxi would wait. He was afraid the driver would not be honest with him. I then offered to ask the driver myself and wondered whether he could accept the driver's answer to me. He agreed. The driver consented to wait and the client's agitation diminished. We spent the next hour talking.

Anxiety as a state prevents people from testing reality, using their own judgment, or taking steps to correct the conditions causing the anxiety. Signal anxiety manifests itself differently.

> A client called and asked for an appointment because he had beaten his wife on several occasions and was becoming aware that he could not stop himself. He wanted help so that no more incidents of wife abuse occurred.

Were I to ask which client evidenced more intense anxiety, there would be little question that the first client was the more agitated. Were I to ask which demonstrated more severe psychopathology, agreement would not be so readily forthcoming. Thus, the type of anxiety reveals what parts of the mind are working; however, it tells little with respect to the severity of the problem. Likewise, to assign a level of anxiety has limited diagnostic utility. The first client was preoccupied with object loss and abandonment; the second, with the strength of his anger or his inability to control it. The latter developmentally precedes anxiety with respect to object loss, yet the client in the second example seemed better able to prepare himself for the possibility of future danger. Obviously, assessment of anxiety is complex, but whatever determinations are possible can help with treatment direction.

Once it is established that the client's anxiety is functioning as a signal, the next most useful assessment concerns not the level of anxiety but whether the client has any awareness of its reason. In this case, further exploration is readily possible. However, if the client believes the source of anxiety is husband/wife, job, etc., meaning that the problem is located outside the individual, then exploration into the working of the mind must be postponed in favor of developing the capacity for self-observation. For instance, the client who was concerned about the taxicab had to experience conditions of greater ease before he could make use of reason and judgment. Such a detour is a detour only with respect to self-exploration, not with respect to the course of treatment, since a working relationship could not otherwise be established.

One last comment about anxiety and diagnosis: everyday living is filled with anxiety-provoking situations. Hardly a day goes by without some significant experience of internal distress or conflict. In 1939, Heinz Hartmann cautioned that conflict and pathology are not to be equated (Hartmann, 1958). Nor are health and freedom from conflict to be considered synonymous. Usual living includes both conflict and conflict-free experiences. As Hartmann noted, it is useful to consider how conflict experiences and nonconflict experiences are processed in the same person at the same time. In effect, it is not how much conflict exists or how much anxiety is experienced, but how much capacity to cope remains available in spite of the experience of conflict and anxiety.

TREATMENT CONSIDERATION IN ANXIETY

The anxious patient needs to be helped to become less anxious before functioning can be improved. This requires accurate assessment of the subjective experience of anxiety and stress. Consider the client who expressed concern about beating his wife. What information would be helpful? It is already known that he is anxious in anticipation that he might once again lose control. Would it be helpful to know how anxious? Could it be determined whether he felt under control or whether his control was slipping? Certainly, one would want to know all of the above. The clinician might ask, "How are you managing now? Would it be okay if we arranged an appointment next week or do you want to come in right away?" This gives the client an opportunity to consider for himself just how he is coping. If he has not lost control and if his anxiety tolerance is high, he might well decide to wait. However, if physical danger were perceived, it would behoove the clinician to suggest an immediate appointment.

In the example of the abusive husband, issues of anxiety tolerance and internal versus external structure are evident. Usually there is some relationship among these variables such that if anxiety tolerance is high, a reasonable degree of internal structure is probably available to the client and coping can be expected at a reasonably high level. If anxiety tolerance is low, however, internal structure is usually not available and must be brought into the situation from outside. To offer structure to a client who does not need it can be infantilizing and disrespectful of autonomy. Not to offer structure when it is needed can be devastating.

Deciding how to intervene is another exercise in clinical judgment. Does the therapist offer concrete services? Should support be elicited from family and friends? Are they available? To what extent does the therapist become involved with a client to effect immediate change? These questions have less to do with issues of anxiety than with the clinician's overall assessment of which intervention will promote more adaptive functioning in the client, regardless of the presence or absence of anxiety. Which approach will help the client feel and function better? While answers to these questions can be gained during the initial interview, such quick decisions require time and experience, and it is unlikely that a beginner will be able to answer such questions without supervisory help for quite some time.

As I indicated previously, the client's apparent anxiety or lack thereof can be misleading.

A middle-aged client came to the office and requested immediate help in getting some material for his wife. He felt he had to have the material for her that very day, but he was not sure where to get it and had driven himself to distraction trying to find out where it was available. He was rapidly approaching a panic state. I commented on his sense of urgency and wondered how crucial it was to solve the problem immediately. With almost a bewildered look, he replied that there really was no emergency, and was suddenly dumbfounded that he had experienced one. The rest of our session was spent exploring what had happened to him.

Both beginning and experienced workers might find themselves influenced by the client's anxiety in such an instance, unknowingly responding to his feelings with anxiety of their own. For example, such marked client anxiety might cause the worker to offer precipitous help, convince the worker to involve a family member in therapy, or even provoke the worker to dismiss the client. When client anxiety arouses worker anxiety that remains outside the worker's awareness and therefore unmanaged, a cycle is initiated in which the client arouses the worker, who further arouses the client, etc. Obviously, such a cycle is not helpful to either client or worker. However, supervision can bring such problems to the worker's attention, allowing examination of the effect of unconscious processes on performance during the therapeutic session, thereby enabling the worker to shape the intervention in the direction of support of the client's capacity to cope.

THEORETICAL ORIENTATIONS AND TREATMENT APPROACHES TO ANXIETY

One of the most crucial concerns with respect to psychopathology is the recognition that every treatment approach to, or definition of, "pathology" has attached to it a theoretical orientation with regard to causality that supports the particular treatment approach under consideration. This is particularly noteworthy because *DSM-IV* claims to be atheoretical, offering only descriptive statements about various categories of pathology. The rationale for this approach is that no one current theoretical stance can account for the range and complexity of human behavior. Similarly, since different theories of pathology lend themselves to different foci in treatment, some practitioners have fallen into the trap of considering themselves eclectic in that they use all theories and methods of practice in accordance with their perceptions of client need, completely overlooking the problem that constructs inherent in one school of thought may well be antagonistic to constructs in another. Clients have a right to intellectual honesty, which is not met by eclecticism. This trend must be replaced by a commitment to building an adequate theory of behavior.

The Psychodynamic Developmental Model

Presently, there are several major orientations to treatment that need some discussion with respect to problems of anxiety. Clearly, the section on changing perspectives on anxiety disorders above reviewed these orientations from the "psychodynamic developmental model." I selected that model primarily because anxiety is an inner experience, which can therefore be defined and reported only subjectively. In this vein, it must be recognized that the psychodynamic model is the only one that offers an explanatory theory regarding inner experience.*

Thus, the psychodynamic developmental view of anxiety emphasizes the internal workings of the mind and supports a treatment approach that sees pathology with respect to anxiety as a function of mental activity. This view, of course, does not deny that external pressures have significant impact on internal reactions, but the focus of the psychodynamically oriented practitioner would be on furthering understanding and skills within the person, thereby enabling better coping with problematic anxiety. According to this model, anxiety states occur when ego functions are incapacitated. Treatment would be aimed at enabling the client to develop skills to sustain these functions even under stress. Obsessive-compulsive behavior disorders, a particular form of anxiety condition, are seen as symptoms brought into play to prevent the experience of overwhelming anxiety; treatment focus would be on understanding the place of those obsessions and compulsions within the total workings of the mind. Treatment in this model is usually offered in a dyadic or group arrangement; intellectual capacity, as well as the ability to self-reflect, is a necessary client attribute for this treatment model. Obviously, a theory that offers a model of mind and revolves around the way in which the mind works is going to lead to a therapeutic mode that explores these workings.

The Behavioral Model

In contrast to the psychodynamic developmental view, which emphasizes *inner* processes, other orientations see the reason for behavior as primarily a function of occurrences *outside* the individual. The *behavioral model*, resting on learning theory, views behavior as a function of learned responses that have accrued as a result of a combination of rewards and

---

*While the humanistic and existential orientations do take steps in this direction, they do not offer a developmental approach that attempts to explain the purpose of anxiety within the frame of reference of a model of the mind.

punishments. In effect, sequences of behavior that are rewarded remain part of the repertoire of the individual. Inherent in this orientation is the emphasis on external factors as causally related to behavior; thus, little attention is paid to the workings of the mind. Some classical behaviorists completely dismiss concepts like *mind, affect,* and *thought* because they cannot be observed and/or measured. Attention is paid only to those aspects of functioning that can be quantified. Other behaviorists are more moderate and recognize that thoughts and feelings are components of the human condition. Nevertheless, their emphasis is that behaviors and even ways of thinking and feeling are learned and can be unlearned, subject only to the influence of the proper combination of rewards and punishments.

Obviously, such an orientation will develop therapies in which the therapist is in charge, rewarding and punishing, as seems fit, those behaviors that are to be changed (Ulman & Krasner, 1965). Since clients literally place themselves in the hands of the behavior therapist, such an approach can easily lend itself to abuse and, indeed, examples of such abuse are a matter of record (Milgram, 1974). More important for the purposes of this chapter, behaviorists view anxiety as a learned response that can be unlearned. The usual method of treatment, following the principles of behavioral theory, is referred to as *systematic desensitization.* In this approach, the client builds up tolerance to anxiety through a series of graduated exposures to anxiety-provoking stimuli. Once again, no attention is given to client understanding or self-reflection.

The Systems Model

The *systems model* represents a third major orientation to human behavior. It tends to coincide with an "interactional model," wherein, as in the behavioral view, emphasis is placed on factors external to the individual as a way of explaining human behavior. Thus, individual pathology may be viewed as an expression of conflict within the family or even as the entire family's symptom; accordingly, therapy may focus on external influences in order to change existing family interaction patterns. A disorder involving anxiety attacks, phobic symptoms, or obsessive-compulsive behaviors can be interpreted as an interactional problem; for example, a child may protect his mother by evidencing the anxiety the mother disowns. Notably, in this orientation, terms relating to the inner functioning of the mind have no utility since no concept of *mind* is offered. Ironically, many interactional therapists committed to a systems orientation do make use of terms like *ego* and *unconscious* even though they otherwise reject the psychodynamic model from which these terms derive. Of course, an orientation that views pathology as an outcome of interaction patterns will foster an interactional therapy; indeed, the systems model favors marital and family sessions.

The Psychopharmacological Model

The *psychopharmacological model* sees pathology as a function of biological factors, either organic or hormonal; medication is considered necessary to correct the problem. Disorders related to anxiety presently lack a biological explanation; however, therapists who view psychopathology as the result of physiological factors believe that eventually an appropriate biological explanation will be found. They argue that since drugs do alleviate anxiety symptoms, there must be a close relationship between cause and symptom, and view medication as the treatment of choice. The pure physiologist sees no value in any other explanation for psychopathology.

Stress Management

Finally, a new and rapidly growing approach to the problem of anxiety is *stress management*. Biofeedback is a popular form of stress management based on principles of operant conditioning. The client performs a series of exercises designed to foster an ability to enable recognition and attention to various physiologic reactions—reactions which, because they are now subject to recognition, can be subject to conscious control. Such phenomena as heart rate, blood pressure, and muscle tension have proved responsive to this approach. Moreover, clients suffering from anxiety have benefited from training in another form of stress management, *progressive relaxation*, which focuses on enhancing the client's awareness of bodily states.

Admittedly, stress management is primarily educative and symptom oriented. Its sole purpose is to alleviate symptomatology, regardless of origins. With respect to conditions associated with anxiety, stress management seeks to enable clients to control the appearance of anxiety and to keep this response within manageable limits. Stress management techniques make use of the client's cognitive capacity to develop information processing systems that are able to control functions not usually accessible to cognitive control. Interestingly enough, while this approach includes significant input from outside the client and seems to rest on external influence, its thrust is to provide the client with the necessary skills to manage his or her own responses. In this regard, the goals of stress management are not terribly distant from psychotherapeutic goals. At the same time, stress management does not attend to the reasons for the anxiety experience and provides no added understanding of the reasons for the problem behaviors. In this regard, stress management as an approach fails to appreciate the full capacities of the type of client who is capable of and desires such increased awareness and understanding.

INTERDISCIPLINARY COOPERATION IN THE MANAGEMENT OF ANXIETY

Clients experiencing anxiety often present themselves to clinics or family service agencies for treatment. Typically, the treatment process begins with an intake and assessment procedure involving social worker, psychologist, and psychiatrist. All are involved with the client until a treatment plan is worked out, at which time the client may be assigned to one of the three for treatment. It is common practice for the psychiatrist to function primarily as consultant, the psychologist as diagnostician, and the social worker as therapist. The social worker typically functions as a member of a treatment team, regularly reporting to the team on the client's progress. If the social worker knows how to use the other team members as resources, the client will benefit from input from several disciplines.

> Mrs. G came to a family service agency in an extremely agitated state; she was distressed that her son was homosexual, and blamed herself for his "failure." She was almost incoherent as she described how she had failed as a mother and was worthless as a person. Mrs. G entertained thoughts of killing herself. The worker was unsure about Mrs. G's capacity to tolerate the level of anxiety she was experiencing and worried that Mrs. G might commit suicide. Arrangements were made for Mrs. G to see the psychologist for testing to evaluate the intensity of her suicidal ideation. Mrs. G was also seen by the psychiatrist to determine how to alleviate some of her immediate agitation so that she could discuss her concerns more calmly.

In this case, interdisciplinary teamwork proved beneficial to the client, but even when the social worker is not employed by an agency, such cooperation is necessary. For example, social workers cannot hospitalize a client and remain the therapist of record; therefore, cooperation with psychiatrists is mandatory when the worker is involved with a client requiring hospital care. The same is true with respect to the need for medication and/or psychological testing, particularly with clients demonstrating phobias and/or obsessive-compulsive symptoms with accompanying somatic complaints.

TREATMENT OF ANXIETY IN THE ERA OF MANAGED CARE

Although most clinicians are well acquainted with the requirements and constraints imposed by insurance companies, most initially welcomed the financial coverage that enabled a larger pool of clients to partake of the therapeutic endeavor. However, the more recent growth of the managed-care industry has carried participation of third parties to the point of intrusiveness. The once sacred nature of the treatment relationship, upon which the very foundation of treatment process depends, is now influenced strongly by external sources not only with respect to type and length of treatment, but also in regard to lack of confidentiality and limited choice of therapist.

Essentially, for those unfamiliar with the managed-care environment, clients may choose therapists only from among those approved as providers by the managed-care group. A nonapproved provider will not be paid by the insurer. Although this may seem initially harmless, the fact that managed-care plans approve a limited number of providers severely limits the client's choice of therapist. In addition, length of treatment is limited, and only those therapists subscribing to some form of short-term therapy focusing on symptom relief or behavioral change are accepted for approval. Indeed, therapists indicating any sort of allegiance to a psychodynamic approach are frowned upon in favor of those subscribing to behavioral or cognitive-behavioral approaches. Considering that anxiety is intrinsic to the human condition and that its management requires the acquisition of internal processing abilities built over time, the significance of these restrictive circumstances for the treatment of anxiety conditions is profound.

To begin with, there are groups of patients whose ability to cope with anxiety remains dependent on the external support services around them. Whereas those relatively well functioning individuals demonstrating only a simple phobia can benefit from short-term behavioral desensitization programs, the larger group of more severely disturbed patients require repeated therapeutic involvements to restore their coping abilities each time a new perceived threat arises. For these patients, shorter-term engagements do not allow for the building of the necessary ego structures that would more likely enable them to cope with repeated anxiety experiences as they arise.

The same is basically true for all other diagnostic categories related to anxiety. It is important to keep in mind that Axis I diagnoses are made on the basis of the most prevalent symptoms observable. However, a fuller diagnostic picture allows for the recognition that the symptoms consistent with the Axis I diagnosis are being demonstrated by a person with additional psychological characteristics and qualities. In short, the anxiety diagnosis hardly defines the patient's basic psychic structure, and it is that structure which basically determines the ability of the patient to make use of the therapeutic experience.

Four decades ago, Eissler (1953), a noted analyst, arguing for a technique based on a diagnostic assessment of ego organization rather than on symptomatology, stated

> [I]t is not so much the particular combination of symptoms and defenses—that is to say, the structure of the symptoms—which necessitates the specific technique but the ego organization in which the particular symptom is embedded. (p. 177)

Though psychoanalytic constructs have undergone considerable change since that time, the basic tenet that more than symptomatic change is necessary for long-term benefit remains a viable concept (Lazar, 1997). For individuals experiencing an anxiety state who are building a basic foundation of ego strength, anxiety tolerance (Kernberg, 1975) is a major goal of treatment that is not available in a managed-care setting. For the obsessive-compulsive patient, for whom symptomatic behaviors are necessary for anxiety containment, focus can only be on supporting the obsessive-compulsive behaviors. And for the patient suffering from posttraumatic stress disorder, anything more than an immediate sense of relief is not likely.

Challenged by such realities, the therapist role requires persistence in attempting to obtain more time to provide a greater in-depth treatment approach than managed care permits. Consistent with this is the need for therapist clarity about the theoretical underpinnings supporting a longer-term involvement as the treatment of choice. Essentially, the therapist must be prepared to argue substantively—in an articulate, carefully spelled out treatise—for patient need, based on an extensive presentation of the reasons for the patient's current difficulty, and the specific benefits that a more comprehensive therapeutic action can allow. Faced with such a document, administrators may well find difficulty in refusing the request, since refusal in the face of strong professional argument leaves room for their possible legal accountability at a later date. This approach requires the therapist to state with courage and conviction that the longer course of treatment is indeed the most desirable. Though arduous to prepare, a thorough, well-reasoned, theoretically based document seems to be the only current means for challenging the managed-care approach, which is grounded primarily on cost effectiveness. Such advocacy reflects a level of professionalism without which effective therapy for extended change does not occur (Shepard, 1997).

RESEARCH ISSUES FOR SOCIAL WORK

Social work's unique position as both a private-practice and agency-oriented profession offers many opportunities for ongoing research that can contribute to its knowledge base. It would be interesting to consider a study model focusing on structured communication between private and agency practitioners, as well as the impact on worker behavior in shifting from one setting to the other. Aside from other obvious projects such as case studies, which can serve to expand knowledge of theory and practice, social work's emphasis on family orientation, structure, and functioning lends itself naturally to investigating such areas as the impact of client anxiety on other family members, the relationship of phobic behavior to family interaction patterns, the impact of phobic bahavior on child rearing, and the meaning of obsessive-compulsive symptoms to other family members.

The relationships between various case management techniques and the symptoms associated with anxiety should also be considered. For instance, do workers really respond with anxiety to clients in acute states of anxiety? Are more experienced or older workers less affected by client anxiety? Are clients manifesting symptoms of acute anxiety referred for testing and/or medication more frequently than other clients?

Because group theory and organizational processes are part of social work's knowledge base, social workers are in a unique position to develop studies of agency attitudes toward the anxiety-ridden client, the availability of resources for individuals requiring frequent contact, and, of course, the impact of worker anxiety on the client. Although it may appear that agency procedures often increase client distress, we have little empirical evidence to support this contention. Finally, the predominance of social workers on the staffs of most crisis centers should allow them to accumu-

late significant data on how anxiety actually affects all aspects of client, family, and agency functioning.

REFERENCES

Alexander, F., & French, T. (1948). *Studies in psychosomatic medicine.* New York: Ronald.

American Psychiatric Association (1994). *Diagnostic and statistical manual of mental disorders, fourth edition.* Washington, DC: Author.

Beck, A. (1976). *Cognitive therapy and emotional disorders.* New York: International Universities Press.

Brenner, C. (1974a). Depression, anxiety, and affect theory. *International Journal of Psychoanalysis, 55,* 25–36.

Brenner, C. (1974b). On the nature and development of affects: A unified theory. *Psychoanalytic Quarterly, 43,* 532–556.

Compton, A. (1980). Developments in the psychoanalytic theory of anxiety. In L. Kutash & R. Schlesinger (eds.). *Handbook on stress and anxiety* (pp. 81–132). San Francisco: Jossey-Bass.

Eissler, K. R. (1953). The effect of the structure of the ego on psychoanalytic technique. *Journal of the American Psychoanalytic Association, 1,* 104–143.

Freud, A. (1946). *The ego and the mechanisms of defense.* New York: International Universities Press.

Freud, S. (1936). *Inhibitions, symptoms, and anxiety.* London: Hogarth.

Grinker, R. (1973). *Psychosomatic concepts.* New York: Jason Aronson.

Hartmann, H. (1958). *Ego psychology and the problem of adaptation.* New York: International Universities Press.

Kaplan, B. (1988). *The art of intervention in dynamic psychotherapy.* New York: Jason Aronson.

Kernberg, O. (1975). *Borderline conditions and pathological narcissism.* New York: Jason Aronson.

Krystal, H. (1997). Desomatization and the consequences of infantile psychic trauma. *Psychoanalytic Inquiry, 17,* 126–150.

Krystal, H. (1978). Trauma and affect. *Psychoanalytic Study of the Child, 33,* 81–116.

Lazar, S. G. (1997). Prologue—Extended dynamic psychotherapy, making the case in an era of managed care. *Psychoanalytic Inquiry, Supplement:* 1–3.

Lichtenberg, J. (1991). Fear, phobia, and panic. *Psychoanalytic Inquiry, 11,* 395–415.

Milgram, S. (1974). *Obedience to authority.* New York: Harper & Row.

Shepard, B. (1997). The human toll: Managed care's restrictions of access to mental health services. *Psychoanalytic Inquiry, Supplement:* 151–161.

Schur, M. (1955). Comments on the metapsychology of somatization. *Psychoanalytic Study of the Child, 10,* 119–164.

Spitz, R. (1965). *The first year of life.* New York: International Universities Press.

Ulman, L., & Krasner, L. (1965). *Case studies in behavior modification.* New York: Holt, Rinehart and Winston.

15

ADJUSTMENT DISORDERS

Judith Mishne

DEFINITION

The defining feature of an adjustment disorder in adulthood is the development of significant emotional or behavioral symptoms in response to an identifiable psychosocial stressor or stressors. This could include the termination of an important romantic, personal, or professional relationship; marital problems; a business crisis; departure from the parental home; some sort of natural disaster; etc. Stressors obviously can affect a single individual, a family and extended kinship network, or a community. The diagnosis of adjustment disorder implies a lack of biological determinism and a response to environmental or psychosocial factors. The maladaptive reactions to psychosocial stressors, which are identifiable life events, are expected to remit when either the stressful situation ceases or a new level of adaptation and coping is achieved. The symptoms must develop within three months after the onset of the marked distress, and must be in excess of what would be the expected response, given the nature of the stressor. Commonly, impairment is marked by significant alterations or decline in occupational and/or social functioning (American Psychiatric Association, 1994). *DSM-IV* emphasizes that this category is not to be used if the disturbance meets the criteria for another specific Axis I disorder or is an exacerbation of a preexisting Axis I or II disorder. "However, an Adjustment Disorder may be diagnosed in the presence of another Axis I or Axis II disorder if the latter does not account for the pattern of symptoms that have occurred in response to the stressor. . . . By definition, an Adjustment Disorder must resolve within six months of the termination of the stressor (or its consequence)" (p. 623). In some instances the symptoms may persist for a prolonged period (e.g., longer than the above noted six months) if they occur in response to a

chronic stressor like a chronic newly diagnosed disabling general medical condition, or "to a stressor that has enduring consequences, like the financial and emotional difficulties, resulting from a divorce" (ibid.).

> Ms. F, a most intelligent and articulate woman, aged 73, entered psychotherapy to deal with a sense of loneliness since the loss of her husband, dead five years, after a 15-year struggle with cancer. Mr. and Ms. F had been very happily married for 50 years, and had one son, a remarkable and successful performing artist. Ms. F moved into the city to live near her son, daughter-in-law and grandchildren. Given her age, many lifelong friends and relatives were deceased, and Ms. F suffered some age-appropriate social isolation. Ms. F responded well to individual psychotherapy and referral to, and completion of, group therapy in a short-term bereavement group, where she made a number of enduring friendships.
>
> When hit with some health problems, especially a diagnosis of late-onset diabetes, she's suffered adjustment disorder in the first two months after the diagnosis. Her symptoms are persisting longer than the above-noted six-month interval, since this disease has "enduring consequences." She's found it difficult to deal with new dietary programs, to negotiate and deal with her physicians, and to be appropriately assertive with the doctor, especially the new diabetes specialist. She's needed her social worker's atypical active intervention with her physicians as she struggles with new stressors, in taking care of herself, monitoring intake, weight loss, and the like. She can appear excessively exhausted, helpless, and depressed, and thereby disinclined to be active socially, and/or to finalize plans to visit welcoming relatives. Thus she suffers Bereavement V62.82, chronic type (longer than six months duration), and Adjustment Disorder with Mixed Anxiety and Depressed Mood, 309.28.

HISTORY OF THE SYNDROME

The diagnosis of Adjustment Disorder (with Disturbance of Conduct or with Mixed Disturbance of Emotions and Conduct) in childhood and adolescence has been noted since the publication of *DSM-III* in 1980, and is considered appropriate "if clinically significant conduct problems do not meet the criteria for another specific disorder developed in clear association with the onset of a psychosocial stressor" (*DSM-III*, p. 89). *DSM-II*'s comparable label was Transient Situational Disorder, and required that the disturbance be acute, transient, and in response to an overwhelming stress. *DSM-III* and *DSM-IV* recognized acute and chronic stressors, and "mundane," rather than overwhelming stress, all within the range of common experience. Additionally, the disturbances were recognized as not necessarily time limited (Kranzler, 1988).

The age-appropriate vicissitudes of development and growth have resulted in diagnosis of Adjustment Disorder of Childhood and Adjustment Disorder of Adolescence, and more recently Adjustment Disorder has been recognized as occurring at any age. Thus, Adjustment Disorder is apparently common, and "individuals from disadvantaged life circumstances experience a high rate of stressors and may be at increased risk for this disorder" (*DSM-IV*, p. 625).

COMMON CONFUSION OF ADJUSTMENT DISORDER AND POSTTRAUMATIC STRESS DISORDER

Because of the reactive features of Adjustment Disorder, it is important to distinguish it from Posttraumatic Stress Disorder, a syndrome receiving inordinate public attention of late (see Chapter 26). Both syndromes are viewed as outcomes to identifiable stressors, but Posttraumatic Stress Disorder's essential feature is the development of characteristic symptoms following exposure to an *extremely* traumatic stressor, outside the range of usual human experience, involving the direct, immediate, and personal experience of an event that involves actual or threatened death or serious injury, or other threats to one's own physical integrity or to the integrity of another valued person or family member. The person's response to the event must demonstrate intense fear, helplessness, or horror—or, in children, the response must involve disorganized or agitated behavior. "The characteristic symptoms resulting from the exposure to the extreme trauma include persistent re-experiencing of the traumatic event, persistent avoidance of stimuli associated with the trauma and numbing of general responsiveness, and persistent symptoms of increased arousal" (*DSM-IV*, p. 424). The symptom picture must be apparent for longer than a month, and the ensuing problems and distress must seriously impact on the client's social and occupational functioning.

Ms. C consulted a social worker and entered individual psychotherapy in response to mounting rage and distress over her romantic relationship, with an abusive man she'd lived with for seven years, and in regard to her faltering and generally unstable career as an actress. With the general decline of Shakespearean theater, and her age, she was increasingly unemployed. She failed to be successful, as in the past, in mastering auditions and being selected by casting agents for calls in plays she'd hoped to be chosen for.

In the exploration of her relationship with her boyfriend, which she ended abruptly upon her discovery of his unfaithfulness, she had terrifying memories of severe and ongoing sexual abuse, at the hands of a relative, when she was of preschool age. Over time, in individual therapy, and in a brief involvement in a group treating adult survivors of childhood sexual abuse, she repeatedly relived the terror-filled years. There was a persistent reexperiencing of the traumatic experiences. She demonstrates Post-Traumatic Stress Disorder 309.81, with Delayed Onset, and manifested impaired affect modulation, feelings of ineffectiveness, shame, despair; a feeling of being permanently damaged. She can be hostile and sarcastic, socially most withdrawn, and given to feeling threatened by other actors and/or work colleagues at a job. As noted in *DSM-IV* (p. 425), she's at increased risk for any number of disorders, and in fact demonstrates Social Phobia. The original stressor has been re-experienced in various ways, in dreams, and recollections which caused her to wonder about False Memory. Her original trauma far exceeds what are the criteria for precipitating Adjustment Disorder.

DIAGNOSTIC CRITERIA FOR ADJUSTMENT DISORDER

Adjustment Disorders are divided in *DSM-IV* into subtypes that best characterize the predominate symptoms. Overall, an adjustment disorder must follow stress, despite the reality that symptoms do not always appear immediately following the stress, nor do they subside or disappear when the stress ceases. However, the maladaptive reaction must occur within three months from the onset of the stress. All authors observe that the severity of the stress is not always predictive of the extent of the regression and/or the number of remittent symptoms. These variables are in response to group norms, values and cultural expectations, and basic personality organization. Personal ego strengths and deficits always play a major role in response to the struggle and vicissitudes of life. Adjustment Disorder can occur at any age, with a wide spectrum of manifest symptomatology.

"Depression, anxious and mixed features [are] most common in adults. Physical symptoms are most common in children and the elderly, but may occur in any age group" (Kaplan & Sadock, 1981, p. 580). According to *DSM-IV,* the "essential feature of Adjustment Disorder is the development of clinically significant emotional or behavioral symptoms in response to an identifiable psychosocial stressor or stressors" (p. 623). To paraphrase *DSM-IV,* (1) the response must develop within three months after the onset of the stressor (s); (2) the response is in excess of what would be expected, given the nature of the stressor; (3) the client's behavior is marked by substantial impairment in social or occupational functioning; (4) that behavior is not an exacerbation of another more fixed mental disorder; (5) the symptoms are expected to cease or gradually disappear when the stress ceases or a new level of coping is achieved.

SUBTYPES OF ADJUSTMENT DISORDER

DSM-IV codes the subtypes according to the subtype which appears to best characterize the predominant symptoms, which include depression, anxiety, a combination of both, and disturbances of emotions and conduct.

Adjustment Disorder with Depressed Mood (309.0)

This diagnosis indicates that the primary manifestations are depressed mood, hopelessness, and tearfulness. It is essential to distinguish this subtype from similar syndromes, e.g., major depression and uncomplicated bereavement. This classification, Adjustment Disorder with Depressed Mood, replaces the category Neurotic Depression of *DSM-III* (1980). The new category is analogous to situational or reactive depression, because the stressor is perceived as the immediate or contributing cause, and "has temporarily overwhelmed the previously normal individual's capacity to cope and adapt" (Klerman, et al., 1979, p. 58).

Mr. B, aged 23, was referred to a social worker for individual therapy, by the social worker at the Student Mental Health Office, located at the university where he had graduated from college and earned a master's degree in American Studies. He had become depressed, tearful, and overwhelmed when he was rejected from his first-choice university for Ph.D. study. He was suddenly noticeably withdrawn and asocial, avoiding friends, professors, and all social gatherings, and neglecting academic special seminars and colloquiums.

Mr. B appeared markedly indifferent to overtures made towards him, apathetic, even hopeless, convinced as he was that this rejection marked the premature end of his hopes for a career as an academic historian. Gone was his typical enthusiasm and zest for learning, and his final master's thesis was of lesser quality than all of his academic work to date. Mr. B responded very well to treatment; he became more realistic over his very first rejection in academia, and in less than half a year, had gained acceptance to another prestigious Ph.D. program. In the four months that he was depressed he suffered acute type (less than six months duration) Adjustment Disorder with Depressed Mood.

Adjustment Disorder with Anxiety or Anxious Mood (309.24)

This category is used when major symptoms include worry, jitteriness, and nervousness. This subtype is differentiated from "anxiety disorders," which entail panic and generalized anxiety, with symptoms of motor tension, shakiness, jumpiness, tension, inability to relax, hyperactivity, apprehensive expectations, hyperattentiveness, distractibility, insomnia, irritability, and impatience. Despite the similarity of symptoms, the existence of a specific precipitant in Adjustment Disorder is the major variable to distinguish the two.

Ms. J sought therapy at a family service agency in conjunction with the stressors precipitated by a very combative divorce, a divorce she sought and had initiated. She claimed she was shocked by her husband's breaking agreements they had arrived at, specifically, his pursuit of joint custody despite their residing in different states at great distance from one another. A major issue in earlier marital struggles concerned parenting decisions, e.g., her seeking psychotherapy and orthodontia for their children and her husband consistently opposing such measures. Because she did not want to continue their history of strife over the children and things she regarded as necessary for their welfare, she was seeking sole custody and guardianship. In addition to the conflicts over the children, quarrels arose over distribution of family equity and general money matters like child support, funds for future college education for the children, etc. Ongoing conflicts with her separated husband were complicated by her seeming well-founded convictions that she had poor and expensive legal representation.

Consequently Ms. J described and demonstrated panic, insomnia, apprehensive expectations, and problems at her job due to impatience, irritability, and distractibility. She related positively to her social worker and responded well in treatment, which provided her biweekly low-fee psychotherapy and medication; ultimately her symptoms abated. She won her case in court, helped as she was to deal with the ongoing vicissitudes and to take definitive actions, like engaging a new lawyer and therapy for her two children. Her anxious condition over five months was appropriately assessed as acute type Adjustment Disorder with Anxiety or Anxious Mood.

Adjustment Disorder with Mixed Anxiety and Depressed Mood (309.28)

This category is applied when the presenting symptoms involve a combination of anxiety and depression, or other emotions and affects, such as ambivalence, anger, depression, anxiety, and increased dependence.

Ms. F sought individual therapy following her most successful completion of college and graduate school in the Midwest, and her return East to pursue her interest in a journalism career. She had worked successfully on a small, rather obscure weekly, and wanted a better position in print or radio journalism. She was angry and ambivalent as she struggled with the pros and cons of entering a graduate-school journalism program, and cited endless conflicting advice from friends, family, and professional journalists. Though she was admitted to the presumably two best programs in the country, she decided not to attend, given advice from some, her already sizable student loans, and, a disinclination to plunge back into intense academic study. She was extremely depressed and anxious, angry and ambivalent about the long-drawn-out process of job seeking and decision making. Often she experienced insomnia and a sense of panic.

She connected quickly with the therapist, and learned to self-soothe, partialize, and master anxiety and depression over managing the stressors of freelancing, until she found an excellent, prestigious radio job. Quite quickly she rose to the top, and received awards and professional recognition. At times she has short-lived recurrent symptoms like those noted above, which appear in response to particularly tough assignments, where she worries about meeting deadlines, and about maintaining the quality of her work. She aptly has observed her vulnerability as dating back to her mother's death when she was eight years old. She's enjoyed very close and positive ties to her father and longtime stepmother, as well as a circle of good and loyal friends, but nevertheless, when feeling overwhelmed by external stress, responds with Adjustment Disorder with mixed emotional features, chronic type (lasting longer than six months). It is significant to note that her conviction about the source of her vulnerability to recurrent Adjustment Disorder caused her to seek out her social worker by name, whom she had seen cited repeatedly in a popular book on the impact on girls of maternal loss in childhood.

Adjustment Disorder with Disturbance of Conduct (309.3)

This disorder is commonly seen in adolescence and "involves conduct in which the rights of others are violated, or age-appropriate societal norms and rules are disregarded" (Kaplan & Sadock, 1981, p. 580). Behaviors commonly observed are truancy, fighting, vandalism, reckless driving, and/or defaulting on legal responsibilities. The major differential diagnosis is Conduct Disorder and Antisocial Personality Disorder. Personality or Conduct Disorder proper is a personality disorder that is long-standing; it falls into two types: the undersocialized aggressive subtype, and the undersocialized nonaggressive type. The aggressive subtype reflects a failure to establish normal bonds of affection and empathy, with resultant physical assaults on people's property, i.e., a pervasive violation of the basic rights of others. The nonaggressive subtype results from the same failure in bonding, but the repetitive pattern is nonaggressive conduct, like lying, stealing without confrontation with a victim, and sly violation of the rules of school and home. The diagnosis of antisocial personality disorder requires that the individual be at least 18 years old, with a history of three or more years of truancy, school suspension, or expulsion, delinquency, running away, substance abuse, inadequate schoolwork, and severe violation of rules of school and home. Adjustment Disorder with Disturbance of Conduct is shorter lived than either Conduct Disorder or Antisocial Personality Disorder, and is reactive to immediate stressors.

Hal, aged 15, was referred to the worker (who specializes in work with adolescents and their families) for an evaluation, following a sharp decline in his academic work, due, it was stated, to: increased academic demands, recent anti-Semitic slurs and assaults from peers he'd known since first grade, exacerbated familial conflict caused by his parents' recent marital conflict due to financial stressors and the father's unilateral decision to sell their home, to move to a less expensive house, to modify the family's heretofore rather luxurious lifestyle—which, in fact, was beyond their means, due to a combination of father's excessive spending, extravagant presents to family members, and some recent business reverses and losses.

Hal's behavior became increasingly out of control, due to his smoking cigarettes, his use of and dealing in pot, staying out all night, and stealing the family car, which he gave to older friends to use and to chauffeur him, since he was too young to have a driver's license. He began to lie and sneak kids into the house for clandestine all-night pot parties. He avoided any and all homework and school assignments and feigned illness on test days, or manipulated his mother into all but doing his homework and reports for him. Both parents recently were regressed, distracted and overwhelmed; family therapy was recommended, initially, on a crisis basis, until a suitable emergent boarding-school plan could be arranged. Hal is a handsome, articulate, very personable teenager, who easily impressed school admissions officers, due to his skillful manipulation, charm, prior history of good grades, and significant musical talents.

Following his emergent midterm departure to boarding school, out of accurate parental concern that he was suddenly beyond their control, the rest of the family has been seen in family and couples treatment; the father has been referred for medication due to his all-too-frequent volatility, and explosive anger, reactive to his recent financial anxieties. Hal did well away from home and achieved very respectable grades, though when home on vacations he reported in individual therapy sessions that, like his peers, he continued to sneak cigarettes and pot all too frequently. He had no major disciplinary problems at school, but the parents remain concerned that probably the school is both too permissive and overly generous with grade inflation. They've chosen to pursue a more rigorous and traditional boarding school setting for Hal, and he's been accepted at two such places. His parents want him better prepared for college and he's reluctant to enter a more demanding school, after six months of improvement. Since home for recess, he's again actively acting out, seemingly in response to continued family-based problems, which, although somewhat lessened, still are apparent. Hal has resumed violating any and all parental attempts at limit-setting, disregarding their preferences and wishes, and additionally is suspected of stealing sizable sums of money from his parents. He suffers chronic-type Recurrent Adjustment Disorder with Disturbance of Conduct.

Adjustment Disorder with Mixed Disturbance of Emotions and Conduct (309.4)

"This subtype should be used when the predominant manifestations are both emotional symptoms (e.g., depression, anxiety) and a disturbance of conduct" [see above subtype] (*DSM-IV*, 1994, p. 624).

Bill was desperate after the first weeks at college, as he experienced panic, anxiety, and depression, convinced that he could not handle his academic courses. A very bright young man, with a fine academic record, he was suffering the same fears and short-lived poor performance that characterized his entrance into high school, where he had his initial taste of demands for more autonomous functioning.

He received a few low marks on quizzes and tests and threatened to drop out of college. He was drinking excessively, cutting classes, and having explosive exchanges with parents in the increasingly frequent long-distance calls home, and with friends and peers in his college dorm. Bill's parents consulted his therapist of childhood, who referred him on a crisis basis to a social worker in the city in which he was studying.

Bill accepted the referral eagerly, and related warmly. Having an ally at hand brought some immediately relief. Bill punctually attended sessions, demonstrated motivation and a desire to master his situation. He was provided emotional support, and was advised to seek tutoring help and arrange consultative conferences with his professors to stave off any more regressions. He followed all recommendations made by his therapist, save for involving himself in campus Alcoholics Anonymous (AA) meetings.

He compartmentalized his life, studying weekdays, abstaining from drinking, until the weekend, when he binged with peers, in a sort of slavish peer conformity. His slavish peer conformity included his dress, in grunge style, with piercing of ears and nose for earrings, and experimentation with hard drugs. Often he substituted use of alcohol for serious drugs, as on a weekly basis he began to attend "raves" where DJs play special disco music, and drugs like Ecstasy abound. The worker's advice, direction, concern, and interpretations were of no avail in helping Bill curtail his increasingly dangerous drug use, or his dealing drugs to support and finance his own drug use. Bill had considerable insight about his social inhibitions, shyness, and fears of inadequacy, which vanished when he used drugs—whereupon, uninhibited and freed of anxiety and depression, he could transform himself into the life of a party, a champion dancer, a most sought-after, popular "man-on-campus."

Always straight and sober in therapy sessions, Bill remained convinced that he could control and contain his drug usage, and with great pride, rationalized, and pointed to his amazingly excellent academic achievement of an "A-/B+" average. He minimized the significance of his recurrent combative outbursts with peers and parents when substance abusing and his flagrant disregard of college rules, as he substance abused and dealt drugs on campus and in his college dorm. He did as he pleased irrespective of parental expectations, and/or the norms and rules of his university. He hid and housed a runaway teenage girl from his home town in his college dorm, drugged, drank weekends, and continued, despite all, to achieve high academic grades.

Aware of his struggles with separation and individuation, and his continual depression and anxiety, he transferred schools, to complete college in his home town, nearer to his parents—where, nevertheless, he continued his substance abuse. He returned to his therapist of early adolescence, in response to his continued anxiety and depression, and continued to defy any and all similar recommendations made to him that replicated those offered earlier by the social worker he'd seen during his freshman and sophomore years. This treatment was terminated due to Bill's noncompliance. In an interesting follow-up, the original therapist notified the worker of news from Bill's father. Bill had graduated college with honors, and had admitted himself into an inpatient setting, for curtailment, once and for all, of drugs and alcohol. Seemingly, college graduation symbolized to Bill a need to face this developmental milestone and surrender the disorder so frequently seen in adolescence, i.e., Chronic Type Adjustment Disorder, with Mixed Disturbance of Emotions and Conduct.

Adjustment Disorder, Unspecified (309.9)

DSM-IV (p. 624) designates this subtype for maladaptive responses like physical complaints, social withdrawal, or work or academic inhibition, i.e., responses that are not classifiable as one of the specific subtypes of Adjustment Disorder.

Adjustment Disorders with Work Disturbance or Academic Inhibition

This diagnosis is applicable when an individual previously functioned adequately, and is now apparently reacting to a relatively recent set of stressors.

Dr. M, a black successful pediatrician in practice for five years, was married and the father of two small daughters. He indicated great satisfaction, until recently, with his personal and professional life, but in the past three months has been experiencing disturbance in his professional life, conflicts with colleagues and patients' parents, and thus consulted a social worker he knew and often made referrals to. He reported feelings of apathy, disinterest, impatience, and apprehension at his office and/or when making rounds at the hospital. He barked at nurses and interns and residents he was to instruct, and became aware that he was backing away from, skipping, or canceling his obligatory days per week at his affiliated hospital. He also recognized that he was taking more and more time off from his private-practice office.

Treatment revealed the correlation between these behaviors and feelings to the unrecognized despair he was struggling with in response to the news of his father's diagnosis of cancer and his wife's miscarriage of what would have been a long-desired son. He had rationalized that, as a doctor, he "understood/could accept" these medical realities in his family. As he gradually could tolerate the true depth of his emotions, and mourn and grieve, he was able to regain his usual high level of professional and interpersonal functioning.

Adjustment Disorder with Withdrawal

This diagnosis refers to social withdrawal in a previously well-socialized individual who currently is not manifesting significant depression or anxiety.

> Ms. W reported to the intake worker at a mental health clinic that she was seeking an evaluation or consultation at the insistence of her husband. She is Cuban-born, a well-educated, successful dean of students at a small, distinguished girls' college. She has always been gregarious and active socially, and now acknowledges a recent social withdrawal. She described a new disinclination to socialize or participate in routine church and community volunteer activities since her last child departed for college. This event coincided with her mother's recent diagnosis of a small stroke, which required Ms. W to shop for her and frequently visit, although her mother's debilitation was not severe. She described a sense of loss of her mother's companionship; previously they had participated together in community and church activities. Ms. W was seen in ongoing therapy and confronted her reactions to the aging process—her mother's, her son's, and her own. She bemoaned the more idyllic recent past, when she felt youthful and could still mother a child at home, share active companionship with her mother, and lead her own satisfying social life with friends and other couples whom she and her husband enjoyed. Addressing the inevitability of change, with the passage of time, in the context of a warm relationship with the social worker she saw for six months, Ms. W was able to regain her social interests and zest for participation and socialization, at work, in her church and community, and with her husband and their circle of good friends.

DIFFERENTIAL DIAGNOSIS OF ADJUSTMENT DISORDERS

In summary, in Adjustment Disorder proper, the disturbance is not attributable to a preexisting mental disorder. The individual commonly shows reactive symptoms within three months of what is experienced as a stressful event, symptoms that are in excess of normal and expectable reactions. At times it is difficult to distinguish between reactive and long-standing psychopathologic symptomatology, since there are no one-to-one correlations between objective events, on the one hand, and unconscious responses and manifest symptomatology on the other. If a symptom, a sign of mental turmoil taking place, is perceived as purely reactive to stress, a professional might conclude that psychotherapy is not indicated. However, this view neglects the reality that many others, exposed to the same set of stressors, would not develop similar symptoms. A. Freud and her associates (1977) emphasize the misleading quality of manifest symptomatology:

> Symptoms may be no more than the individual's answer to some development stress and as such transitory, or symptoms may represent a permanent counter-cathexis against some threatening drive derivative and as such be crippling to further development. (p. 33)

In summary, manifest symptoms and objective events may appear identical. In reality, however, one set of symptoms can have a wide range of possible latent meaning, and pathological significance; thus different types of intervention will be required. Accordingly, the clinician must make a thorough investigation of the client, studying symptomatology, precipitants, and the symptoms' relevance with "regard to developmental level, structure, dynamic significance, etc. (A. Freud, et al., 1977, p. 35). In distinguishing between patients with (reactive) adjustment disorder and those with a (long-standing) personality disorder, a thorough evaluation is crucial. This in some instances requires a thorough physical exam and appropriate lab tests, to rule out organic causes for the presenting symptoms. Presenting somatic complaints cannot be ascribed to emotional causes without seeking out organic gastrointestinal etiologies such as viral illness, etc. For example, Ms. F's fatigue and weight loss were found to be caused by late-onset diabetes, rather than by any emotional factors.

It must be noted that adjustment disorders are among the most commonly diagnosed disorders in both child and adult outpatient clinics. Kranzler (1988) suggests that the diagnosis is frequently misapplied, and cites Werry, et al. (1983), who found this to be among the most highly unreliable diagnoses, due to overuse because of clinicians' "(1) diagnostic hedging; (2) fear of stigmatizing patients by giving a 'serious diagnosis'; (3) concerns about confidentiality" (quoted in Kranzler, 1988, p. 814). Concern about confidentiality, particularly as applied to third-party reimbursements, suggests the possibility of increased overuse of this safe, nonpejorative label with the spread of managed-care plans. Some clinicians also fear applying a "loaded," more severe label, out of concern that patients will be frightened or misunderstand other labels.

Some researchers, like Andreasen and Hoenk (1982), state that the disorder is not the same in children and adults, and in particular, that the adolescents studied appeared to have a more malignant course than adults. The positive prognosis associated with adjustment disorders did not apply in half of the adolescents in five-year follow-up. "Although 71% of the adults were well, more than half of the adolescents received treatment and other diagnoses from the time of their first contact and the five-year follow-up. Only 44% of adolescents were completely well at follow-up. Presenting symptoms did not accurately prognosticate such syndromes as major depression or the development of an antisocial character disorder. This suggests that although useful for immediate descriptive purposes, the adjustment disorder subtypes do not have clear predictive validity—with the younger client population, especially.

ETIOLOGY

As apparent in the vignettes presented, Adjustment Disorder Proper can and often does appear in competent and well-functioning individuals who are intelligent, well educated, and not victims of chronic psychopathology. Many have solid ego organization and secure familial support systems, and have demonstrated long-standing high achievements educationally, professionally, and interpersonally in terms of long-term positive marriages, superior parenting capacities, and enduring long-term friendships and collegial relationships.

The symptomatology arises in response to environmental, psychosocial, and/or interpersonal stress of different magnitudes. Good genetic and biological endowment is common, and symptoms appear when faced with developmental steps, such as adolescence, separation and individuation, the aging process, etc., when a specific stressor has found a point of vulnerability in a person of otherwise considerable ego strength. Life vicissitudes like illness, economic and employment strain, marital problems, natural disaster, and failure to attain academic or professional goals are common precipitants for the onset of Adjustment Disorder proper, which can occur at any age.

Considerations of causality and precipitants must include the following: personality as an important mediator of reaction to stress, and the duration of the stressor, cognitive factors and the available coping skills (Sommer & Lasry, 1984). Social environmental variables like poverty and public assistance result in higher rates of adjustment disorders in lower-class families, and similar findings are noted in conjunction with the discovery of learning disability in children (Faerstein, 1981).

TREATMENT

A wide range of interventions can be effectively employed in the treatment of adjustment disorders; these would include individual, group and family therapy. Often several interventions can be used simultaneously, as in the case of Ms. F, seen in both individual and group therapy. Medication is appropriate in some instances, as demonstrated in the case of Ms. J. Environmental manipulation or restructuring is also necessary, as when a family milieu cannot successfully provide a safe holding environment for a family member; this is evident in the case of Hal, an adolescent, placed on an emergent basis in a boarding school due to parental incapacity to provide limits, controls, and appropriately modulated responses to his ever-increasing adolescent acting-out behaviors and disturbances of conduct. In the case of Bill, he admitted himself to a rehab center following college graduation when he finally recognized he'd lost control over his experimentation with alcohol and drugs, so much so that he'd become addicted.

One would not suggest alterations of the family milieu or the use of medication until it becomes apparent that other interventions alone cannot stave off regression and/or succeed. Medication may be appropriately used, generally briefly, "provided that a careful assessment is done to avoid masking relevant symptoms, affects, moods or (possible) underlying disturbances" (Mishne, 1984). Individual psychotherapy is the most commonly used intervention, but group therapy for individuals suffering difficulties in common can be useful; examples might include families forced by environmental disasters to relocate, employees recently downsized from the same company, and newly retired individuals.

Behavioral and cognitive treatment approaches have proved successful in some situations. Like individual, family, and group therapy, generally treatment plans begin with a time-limited brief, focused intervention. This is based on the definition of adjustment disorder, i.e., a temporary, reactive condition that does not require long-term intervention. Some authors note that time and events unrelated to therapy, such as changes in the precipitating stressful circumstances, can be crucial factors leading to a client's readjustment. Kranzler (1988) emphasizes these considerations in clinical work with children and adolescents as important to keep in mind before deciding to recommend any therapeutic intervention at all.

There are, however, no clear criteria for determining which cases will be the most responsive to treatment, and therefore a clinical

> determination of the severity of the child's maladaptive response
> should guide the decision whether to treat or to wait. It is likely that
> many cases of adjustment disorders never reach clinical attention
> or improve while on clinic waiting lists. (Kranzler, 1988, p. 825)

Treatment interventions may entail collaboration between two or more
social workers, e.g., one who provides individual and/or family therapy
and another who provides group therapy. Collaboration might also be
interdisciplinary, as between a clinical social worker and a psychiatrist/psy-
chopharmacologist who administers and supervises medications, or
between a social worker and a physician who is supervising the medical
management of a newly diagnosed condition. In work with child or adolescent clients, collaboration might entail collaboration with school personnel and/or learning specialists in cases of newly recognized learning
disability or sudden onset academic decline. The cases previously presented
demonstrate the differential use of treatment modalities, instances of varied collaboration, and the spectrum of strategies used in case management;
this can include referral for other services, such as legal services and/or
mediation services for those undergoing divorces. Child care referrals,
tutoring programs, medical services and the like are also commonly needed
for individuals and/or families suffering environmental or psychosocial
stressors.

Kaplan and Sadock (1981) caution about problems of secondary gain
in adjustment disorder: some highly competent and well-functioning individuals experiencing adjustment disorders may enjoy a bout of incapaci-
tation and relative freedom from responsibility, and therefore resist
interventions. If this resistance is protracted, it undoubtedly indicates an
unrecognized deeper level of disturbance. If the adjustment disorder
includes conduct disturbances, with resultant difficulties with the law,
school, or community authorities, "it is inadvisable for the [therapist] to
attempt to rescue the patient from the consequences of his or her action.
Too often such 'kindness' only reinforces socially unacceptable means of
tension reduction and stands in the way of the acquisition of insight and
subsequent emotional growth" (Kaplan & Sadock, 1981, p. 582). By contrast, many patients often emerge from an adjustment disorder stronger
than they were in the precrisis period. This disorder occurs frequently in
competent and successful individuals, who have sufficient ego strength to
tolerate anxiety and frustration inherent in insight-oriented therapy, which
includes the goals of identifying "the stressor's preconscious and conscious
meanings" (ibid., p. 581).

SOCIAL WORK KNOWLEDGE

Commonly, social workers are well trained in the varied clinical modalities required to treat Adjustment Disorder, and can effectively provide supportive crisis intervention in treating Adjustment Disorder. Social work is the clinical discipline, generally, with the greatest expertise in effectively providing environmental interventions, such as mobilizing and making use of existing support systems in the family and community, and/or creating new support systems. These interventions are often important components in a treatment plan for Adjustment Disorder, as are the needed interactions and collaborations between the therapist and the other important individuals and professionals in the patient's life. Social work training and work experience generally provide and entail experience in collaboration.

RESEARCH CHALLENGES

Despite existent understanding of this syndrome, and skills in traditional interventions, it must be recognized that "research on adjustment disorders, particularly in children, is sparse, and the evidence which guides our clinical interventions is limited" (Kranzler, 1988, p. 326). The reality that this is one of the most commonly utilized diagnostic categories only emphasizes the need for new and additional data about individual vulnerability or resilience in the face of stress, familial patterns, and outcomes. Why members of the same family faced with the same set of stressors respond differently is often only marginally understood.

The research challenges are numerous, and this includes diagnostic and prognostic predictors, and the course and predictive validity of the diagnosis. Kranzler (1988) reminds us that some assumptions associated with the temporary duration of symptoms and good prognosis of treatment of adjustment disorders are not necessarily valid, especially in diagnosis of children. With younger populations, one can often see repeated, even prolonged, bouts of symptoms that are reactively precipitated by recurrent and repeated stressful life events, but that are considered to be of insufficient severity or duration to warrant another diagnosis. The reaction is labeled maladaptive, as defined by an impairment in social, educational, or occupational functioning, or symptoms in excess of what is expected in a normal reaction to the given stress. There is an expectation that the symptoms will abate once the precipitating conditions have improved or when a new level of adaptation has been achieved. Professionals rigidly following the written word on the syndrome may be overly zealous in believing in working through and closure.

Research challenges appear to point out the need for more long-term follow-up studies, to in fact examine what was posited to be a temporary affliction that subsides when growth has occurred and the precipitant events have receded. The extensive research and publications of Judith Wallerstein and Joan Kelly (1980) reveal that young adults reflected the staying power of profound sadness as an aftereffect of parental divorce. The impact of the divorce on their childhood proved to be considerably longer than these researchers had initially suspected for their sample group of healthy, well-functioning youngsters who were advancing normally in their age-appropriate tasks. A. Freud and associates (1977) emphasized the misleading quality of manifest or absent symptomatology. This caution appears appropriate decades later, as we struggle to expand the knowledge base about vulnerability and resilience. Too often clinical work has only focused on psychopathology and symptomatology or their apparent absence, with an incomplete comprehension of the dimensions of genuine recovery. This research focus appears most timely as clinicians struggle with the varied edicts of managed care, which can conceivably cause compliance, with the system and a belief that cure indeed can occur via very brief therapy. Also, frustrations with this new form of third-party reimbursement can blind professionals to the reality that in some situations brief-time ended therapy indeed is sufficient, especially with appropriately diagnosed cases of adjustment disorder. In this time of rationed care we need to undertake research efforts about where and with whom to intervene when a family is stressed by identifiable life events. Is it more effective to see the family together, or the parents alone, or the parents and the children in separate individual therapy?

Future research efforts might also profitably focus on examining similar interventions, across different populations, i.e., of different socioeconomic and ethnic and racial origins, suffering the same environmental stress. These groups might include a range of recent reactions to a natural disaster, newly unemployed downsized individuals, couples suffering marital discord, college freshmen seeking student mental-health services, patients diagnosed with a serious, but non-life-threatening disease, etc. We are in need of more discrete data, beyond resultant symptoms, following specific identifiable stressful life events. Family studies might reveal why one child suffers adjustment disorder with disturbance of conduct while another suffers adjustment disorder with depressed mood, or anxiety, following father's unemployment or the tornado in their home town.

SUMMARY

In sum, we must guard against any uniform treatment prescription, despite the fact that manifest symptoms and external events may appear identical. In reality, external events can have a wide range of possible latent meanings and pathological significance for one person that are not so experienced by another who has endured the same events. Symptoms must be examined to distinguish external, internal, and internalized factors. Only with a careful individualized assessment can a clinician guard against generalizations and uniform prescriptions, to thereby provide appropriate, individualized empathetic interventions.

REFERENCES

American Psychiatric Association. (1994). *Diagnostic and statistical manual of mental disorders, fourth edition.* (pp. 623–627). Washington, DC: Author.

Andreasen, N. C., & Hoenk, P. R. (1982). The predictive value of adjustment disorders: A follow-up study. *American Journal of Psychiatry, 139,* 5, 584–590.

Faerstein, L. M. (1981). Stress and coping in families of learning disabled children: A literature review. *Journal of Learning Disabilities, 14,* 7, 420–423.

Freud, A., Nagera, H., & Freud, W. E. (1977). Metapsychological assessment of the adult personality: The adult profile. In R. Eissler, A. Freud, M. Kris, et al. (Eds.). *The anthology of the psychoanalytic study of the child: Psychoanalytic assessment: The diagnostic profile* (pp. 82–114). New Haven, CT: Yale University Press.

Kaplan, H. I., & Sadock, B. J. (1981). *Modern synopsis of comprehensive textbook of psychiatry,* Vol. 3 (3rd Ed.). Baltimore, MD: Williams & Wilkins.

Klerman, G. L., Endicott, J., Spitzer, R., et al. (1979). Neurotic depressions: A system analysis of multiple criteria and meanings. *American Journal of Psychiatry.* 136.

Kranzler, E. M. (1988). Adjustment disorders. In C. J. Kestenbaum & D. T. Williams, *Handbook of clinical assessment of children and adolescents* (pp. 812–828). New York: New York University Press.

Mishne, J. (1984). Adjustment disorders. In F. J. Turner (Ed.). *Adult psychopathology: A social work perspective* (3rd Ed., pp. 249–259). New York: The Free Press.

Sommer, D., & Lasry, J. C. (1984). Personality and reactions to stressful life events. *Canada's Mental Health,* 19–20.

Wallerstein, J., & Kelly, J. B. (1980). *Surviving the breakup: How parents and children cope with divorce.* New York: Basic Books.

Werry, J. S., et al. (1983). The interrater reliability of DSM-III in children. *Journal of Abnormal Child Psychology, 11,* 3, 341–354.

16

PERSONALITY DISORDERS

Mary E. Woods

The terms *personality disorder* and *character disorder* (sometimes used interchangeably) have been plagued with trouble. Over the years, for clinicians and theoreticians alike, the multifarious personality disorders have created even greater confusion and controversy than many other diagnostic designations. Definitions, classifications, and theories about their etiology and dynamics have been extremely divergent. To add to the problem, in recent times there has been a tendency to equate the personality disorder and the borderline disorder. As this chapter will clarify, the borderline personality is only one of several subcategories of the personality disorders.

Certainly, clinical diagnoses in general have the value of designating a cluster of features—traits, behaviors, thought and feeling patterns—characteristically found together, so that each individual is not viewed as totally different from all others, in spite of his uniqueness. When correctly applied, the diagnosis of a mental disorder conveys certain information about a particular client that may not be immediately apparent. However, such diagnoses are—as we all know—replete with ambiguity and hazard and, at best, are inadequate for understanding the complicated emotional and situational dilemmas to which clients seek solutions (Blanck & Blanck, 1974, 1979; Goldstein, 1990; Millon, 1996; Woods & Hollis, 1990). The assessment of a client cannot be complete without taking into account inner strengths and external resources; a full diagnosis cannot be made without appraising family and social forces, as well as environmental conditions. Fundamental social work values—such as our commitment to understand clients from social systems perspectives and to respect the dignity and individuality of each person—can be affronted by the superficial use of psychiatric classifications.

Moreover, there are three reasons for particular concern about the label *personality disorder*:

1. More than many others, this diagnosis has often been used to describe the *total person* (e.g., "He's an obsessive-compulsive" or "She's a schizoid"). Of course, a person is not a common cold; even if it is serious, a cold is only something a person has or suffers from; the diagnosis tells us precious little about the individual except that he or she is sick and probably will be uncomfortable for several days. Nevertheless, it is not uncommon to hear, "I have a caseload full of personality disorders," implying a homogeneous group of *people* rather than a heterogeneous assortment of *disorders*. Just as one cannot *be* a neurotic conflict, one cannot *be* a personality disorder.

2. A person pegged as having (or being!) a personality disorder is often viewed—either subtly or bluntly—in pejorative terms. It is true that in recent years clients with such disorders are looked upon less disparagingly than they once were, but how often we still hear, "Oh, for the good old days when we saw mostly neurotics!" This attitude stems from a widespread, but as yet empirically unsupported, assumption that patients with personality disorders are peculiarly resistant to change.

3. The clinical diagnosis of a personality disorder—perhaps even more than other diagnoses—focuses on *pathological* traits, behaviors, thoughts, and feelings. In spite of social work's ongoing commitment to a "strengths perspective" (Cowger, 1994; Weick, et al., 1989; Weick & Saleeby, 1995), for the most part diagnostic thinkers have failed to develop a sytematic means for assessing *positive* personality characteristics that bear upon the way individuals handle themselves and approach life's opportunities and challenges. Ego psychology has been most influential in helping us develop some tools to assess particular ego functions (Bellak, et al., 1973; Goldstein, 1995; Woods & Hollis, 1990), but in spite of various efforts, we are not very far advanced toward achieving a common system that describes the essence of the "mature" or "healthy" personality.

In this chapter, I examine personality disorders according to the psychosocial framework, which incorporates several theoretical approaches, including psychoanalytic, ego psychology, object relations, and systems theories, among others. Because this model is an open system of thought, it has been able to incorporate and integrate concepts from many fields, including psychology, sociology, anthropology, and education, among others (for further elaboration see Hollis, 1970; Turner, 1978; Woods & Hollis, 1990; Woods & Robinson, 1996).

PERSONALITY DISORDERS AND DIAGNOSIS

Classifications of Personalities and Disorders

From ancient times to the present, there have been innumerable and diverse attempts to describe and classify personality types, as well as personality disturbances. (The reader is referred to Millon [1996], who has written an outstandingly useful, scholarly, comprehensive volume on disorders of personality, in which he includes a historical review of major personality theories.) Aside from the diagnostic and research value of a taxonomy, it has long been thought important for mental health professionals to have a common language with which to communicate with one another, in order to reduce the risks of ambiguity and misunderstanding.

For the most part, in recent decades psychosocial workers have relied upon two classifications to organize information about personality pathology.

The first classification was developed by psychoanalysts. Surprisingly, perhaps, theories about character or personality were not of major interest to psychoanalytic or psychodynamic thinkers until the 1930s and 1940s. In 1908 however, Sigmund Freud (1953) did develop an idea that connected certain traits—such as orderliness and obstinacy—with an anally oriented instinctual life. In the 1930s, Wilhelm Reich (1949) and others elaborated on Freud's early identification of the anal character, and went on to classify personality disorders according to the level of psychosexual development at which libidinal energy seemed to be fixated. Thus, it was believed, when a child fails to master the tasks of one developmental phase, he is unable to move on easily or completely to the next; energies are still invested in the earlier phase and the child continues to seek satisfactions related to that phase. As the child with the fixation moves into adulthood—still trying to gratify early needs in a repetitive and frustrating manner—dysfunctional traits and patterns develop and produce a personality disorder. Particularly until the 1960s, psychosocial workers tended to use this model for the classification of oral, anal, and the less well defined urethral and phallic disorders. (For further discussion see Fenichel, 1945; Millon, 1996; Stanton, 1978.)

This system addressed etiological and psychodynamic issues but, particularly before the advent of ego psychology, was seriously limited, in that the value of the ego was underemphasized because it was viewed as dependent on the overbearing power of the id—the instinctual (sexual and aggressive) energies. The extent of the ego's capacity to make changes—to creatively adapt to realities, to problem-solve, to resolve conflict—was therefore virtually unrecognized. In large measure, the individual was seen as *passively* shaped by past events, unconscious forces, or environmental assaults. The significance of family and social dynamics was minimized. Ego psychologists (for example, Anna Freud, 1946; Hartmann, 1958; Rapaport, 1958) revised psychoanalytic thinking by viewing the ego as having relative *autonomy* from the id. Thus, reactivity to inner impulses and inner demands could be modified by the ego; through the ego an individual's rational and adaptive capacities could be harnessed to develop self-understanding and creative strategies for coping with life circumstances. Ego psychologists recognized the importance of environmental and interpersonal factors. Psychosocial theory and clinical social work practice were greatly enhanced by the realization that the ego could be worked with directly in treatment and was a powerful resource for change; people no longer were viewed as being at the mercy of the id or unconscious forces. By inference at least, and often in practice, workers could be more optimistic in assisting personality-disordered clients, among others. Erikson's (1950) typology of the eight stages of man was also greeted enthusiastically by many social workers because social and cultural considerations influenced his thinking.

This approach to classifying personality (or character) pathologies, based on *fixation of drives,* which was spearheaded by psychoanalysts, is still considered relevant to some clinicians, but has been overshadowed by another system:

The second classification system separates personality disorders on the basis of *clinical syndromes,* such as schizold, dependent, or obsessive-compulsive. All five editions of the *Diagnostic and Statistical Manual of Mental Disorders* (American Psychiatric Association, 1952, 1968, 1980, 1987, 1994) have followed this approach, although each edition introduced changes in specific syndromes and categories. It is important to point out that, by design, *DSM* takes an *atheoretical* and *descriptive* approach to clinical diagnosis, thereby making the manual useful to researchers and to clinicians across a broad range of theoretical orientations. Theories, considered essential to the psychosocial approach, about etiology of personality disorders—hereditary and biopsychosocial influences of all kinds—are deliberately not addressed in *DSM*. Actually, Millon (1996) has greatly elaborated on the *DSM* descriptive approach. He has expanded the list of personality disorders, discusses subtypes of particular disorders, includes discussions of theoretical antecedents to the specific subcategories, hypothesizes about biogenic factors and experiential histories of those with particular disorders, and gives recognition to family and social dynamics. His book is recommended as a companion to *DSM* for those seeking a rich, informative, detailed study of personality disorders. Nevertheless, in spite of its shortcomings, *DSM-IV* is the most commonly used reference today, and for that reason the discussions that follow will be built upon its outline of subcategories.

Descriptive Definitions of Personality Disorders

Personality disorders have been defined in various ways over the years. Space does not permit discussion of most of the definitions (for more detail see Cameron, 1963; Jackel, 1975; Millon, 1996; Stanton, 1978). Some related terms (such as *neurotic character* and *character neurosis*) were ambiguous and have been discarded. Included here are only those descriptions that serve the purpose of this chapter. These definitions apply to the entire range of specific personality disorders.

Jackel (1975) said that personality disorders are manifested "primarily in the person's characteristic modes of response and behavior." Discussing the history of psychoanalytic thinking on the matter, he wrote: "It became evident that patients could react *unconsciously* with repetitive patterned responses that pushed them into characteristic difficulties. These patterned responses had a marked bearing on choice of career, choice of mate, marital adjustment, and many other aspects of social conduct" (Jackel, 1975, p. 287).

Millon (1996) contrasted the healthy and the unhealthy personality:

> When an individual displays an ability to cope with the environment in a flexible manner, and when his or her typical perceptions and behaviors foster increments in personal satisfaction, then the person is deemed by the larger reference group to possess a normal or healthy personality. Conversely, when average or everyday responsibilities are responded to inflexibly or defectively, or when the individual's perceptions and behavior result in increments in personal discomfort or curtail opportunities to learn and to grow, then we may speak . . . of a pathological or maladaptive pattern. (p. 13)

Millon puts normality and pathology on a continuum, asserting that there is no sharp division between them, but he has identified three behavioral characteristics that distinguish pathological from normal personalities:

1. *Tenuous stability:* the individual with pathological personality patterns is distinguished by fragility and lack of resilience under stress; recurrent failures ultimately lead to less control and a distorted view of reality
2. *Adaptive inflexibility:* the individual with pathological personality patterns has few strategies for adapting to, or coping with, stress, and these are practiced rigidly
3. *Vicious circles:* the maladaptive patterns themselves and the many constraints personality-disordered individuals bring to their social milieu "generate and perpetuate extant dilemmas, provoke new predicaments, and set into motion self-defeating sequences with others, which cause their already established difficulties not only to persist, but to be aggravated further" (p. 15).

An important distinction should be made between *maladaptive personality traits* and *symptoms*. Simply put, maladaptive traits usually have existed over the course of an individual's life and have significantly affected important aspects of functioning. Whether or not the person objects to or complains about a *maladaptive trait*, it is nevertheless seen as an integral part of the personality. A *symptom*, on the other hand, may be episodic or appear abruptly; it often has a beginning and an end, as many physical symptoms do. Without treatment, a symptom may last a long time or recur, but, in contrast to a trait, it is not viewed by the clinician or experienced by the suffering individual as part of the fabric of the personality. According to *DSM-IV*:

> *Personality traits* are enduring patterns of perceiving, relating to, and thinking about the environment and oneself that are exhibited in a wide range of social and personal contexts. Only when personality traits are inflexible and maladaptive and cause significant functional impairment or subjective distress do they constitute Personality Disorders. The essential feature of a Personality Disorder is an enduring pattern of inner experience and behavior that deviates markedly from the expectations of the individual's culture and is manifested in at least two of the following areas: cognition, affectivity, interpersonal functioning, or impulse control . . . . This enduring pattern is inflexible and pervasive across a broad range of personal and social situations and leads to clinically significant dis-

tress or impairment in social, occupational, or other important areas of functioning. The pattern is stable and of long duration, and its onset can be traced back to adolescence or early adulthood . . . and is not better accounted for as a manifestation or consequence of another mental disorder . . . and is not due to the direct physiological effects of a substance . . . or a general medical condition. (p. 630)

Needless to say, a person with maladaptive traits of a personality disorder can simultaneously manifest signs or symptoms associated with other disorders described by *DSM-IV* (Axis 1)—such as some form of depression, anxiety, or phobia, among many others. Depending on the nature or type of the personality disorder, the experience and reactions to these symptoms will differ. For example, posttraumatic stress disorder will undoubtedly be experienced differently by a person with a histrionic disorder than by one with a schizoid disorder. More often than not, people with personality disorders go into therapy for symptom relief rather than for personality change. Some symptoms spring from the fears and frustrations intrinsic to maladaptive patterns; some others derive from specific recent events, such as interpersonal experiences or environmental assaults. In any case, once symptoms are reduced, those who want to may then move on to explore maladaptive patterns.

Subcategories of Personality Disorders: Diagnostic Characteristics

For the reason already explained, the *DSM-IV* subcategories of personality disorders will be employed in this chapter, but the explanations will include matters not addressed in the manual. Because they will be discussed elsewhere in the book, the border line personality (see Chapter 17), the antisocial personality (see Chapter 18), and the paranoid personality (see Chapter 20) will not be covered here as such; from time to time they will be referred to, however, because of frequent overlapping of personality styles and traits. The depressive and passive-aggressive personality disorders are not now part of the *DSM* classification, pending further research; they can be subsumed under the catchall category "personality disorder not otherwise specified," which is not discussed in this chapter.

Social workers familiar with personality disorders and their diagnoses know that in many cases diagnoses do overlap, or criteria of two or more disorders coexist in the assessment of one individual. It is also true that there are vast differences in the quality *and* intensity of maladaptive patterns; thus, two individuals accurately diagnosed as having the same disorder may present themselves very differently. *The concept of a continuum between "normal" and "disordered" personalities should always be kept in mind.* And, as we have said, the full extent of a person's condition cannot be usefully evaluated without taking into account personality strengths—qualities that are outside the realm of the diagnoses, such as values, talents, physical attributes, etc.—as well as external resources and opportunities. Finally, even clinicians who have worked extensively with clients with these disorders and are well versed in *DSM-IV* nosology can have divergent judgments about which label best fits the person in question. Nevertheless, the organization of a single system has been useful; decision making and communication with colleagues are far easier now than when we had to grapple with multiple very diverse classifications that lacked correlation.

An important note of caution: *Personality styles must always be assessed in the context of the individual's cultural background and reference group, including the socioeconomic conditions under which the person has lived.* Behaviors—emotional, cognitive, and adaptive patterns common in one ethnic or geographical community—may appear bizarre or pathological in another.

Schizoid Personality Disorder

The person with this disorder has some of the following characteristics:

- Persistent emotional blandness and aloofness; general coldness and indifference to others and to how they feel toward him; general absence of emotional expression, either tender or hostile; underlying sadness, even when felt, is rarely shown
- Dearth of close relationships; genuine preference to be a loner, unencumbered by relationship demands; mechanical style of interaction with others
- Minimal experiences of pleasure; may think of themselves as "empty" or "without a self" (Clark, 1996; Millon, 1996)
- Absence of severely eccentric modes of behavior or communication (in contrast to the person with a schizotypal personality disorder)

A 60-year-old man lived alone in a rented house on the edge of a small town in a dairy-farming area; he worked as a mechanic at a local creamery. For as long as his neighbors could remember, he had lived this way, having only occasional contacts with others—and these were brief and businesslike. Children called him "the hermit," but his demeanor was not extraordinary; he was neat in dress, well spoken, and conscientious at work. He never would have come to the attention of the community social service agency if his home had not been sold to the state to make way for a turnpike. Once help with relocation was provided, he had no desire for service; he had no complaints in spite of his extreme social isolation.

Beck and Freeman (1990) write that "individuals with schizoid personality disorder consider themselves to to be observers rather than participants in the world around them. They see themselves as self-sufficient loners. Others often view them as dull, uninteresting, and humorless." They add: "Schizoids also have a cognitive style characterized by vagueness and poverty of thoughts" (p. 125).

Schizotypal Personality Disorder

The person with this disorder has some of the following characteristics:

- Persistent eccentricities of thought, speech, perception, and/or behavior, such as magical thinking (e.g., superstitiousness or clairvoyance); ideas of reference; vague, digressive, or circumstantial speech; recurrent illusions; depersonalization; constricted or inappropriate affect; bizarre habits; and hypersensitive reactions
- Some characteristics of the schizoid personality disorder, including social withdrawal and aloofness, but usually accompanied by profound social anxiety and discomfort with others
- Insufficient data for a diagnosis of schizophrenia, although the condition might qualify as "ambulatory schizophrenia" (Zilboorg, 1941), "pseudoneurotic schizophrenia" (Hoch & Polatin, 1949), or "masked schizophrenia" (Strahl, 1980)

A 50-year-old woman receiving public assistance because of her psychiatric disability described herself as the "black sheep" of her upper-middle-class family of origin; she spoke of her relatives with apparent indifference. Her caseworker described her small apartment as "colorful, cluttered, and bizarrely decorated." The client had many statuettes and candles, which she vaguely described as having religious significance. She often gave "readings" to neighbors, saying that she could predict the future. Despite frequent run-ins with the neighbors, she insisted that she did nothing to cause the friction; sometimes she wondered whether her troubles stemmed from some dead relative's spite at work. None of the several jobs she had held over the years lasted long; she had difficulty conforming to employer expectations such as punctuality and appropriate dress. Her religious and mystical thinking were not consonant with the beliefs of any members of her family; she had no coherent social group with which she shared her idiosyncratic beliefs or lifestyle.

Describing individuals with "masked schizophrenia," a condition that parallels the schizotypal disorder, Strahl (1980) writes:

These hypersensitive patients harbor negative feelings and attitudes with regard to self, and invariably interpret the reactions of others in a negative way, self-referentially, or with projection . . . . The self-esteem conflict culminates in massive pan-anxiety, which, of course feeds back to the sources of the withered self-esteem—the faulty integrative capacity. Over the years, the self-esteem falls far below the level which the individual's actual potentials would allow, and this is continually aggravated by the anxiety feedback system. (p. 73)

Histrionic Personality Disorder
The person with this disorder has some of the following characteristics:

- Excessive attention-seeking behaviors; persistent excitability, emotional lability, flair for the dramatic; all emotions may be expressed in extreme terms and may seem distorted or exaggerated; easily influenced by others or by fads; suicidal threats and gestures are not uncommon; a tendency to move from crisis to crisis
- A tendency to be perceived as charming and the life of the party and yet also as shallow, self-centered, insincere, and lacking enduring interest in others; relationships are often stormy and of short duration; opinions may be expressed strongly, but are often guided by feelings, with few facts to support them
- Frequent feelings of helplessness and dependency; craving for reassurance but not satisfied after getting it

- Complaints about health and uncomfortable body feelings; inability to enjoy sexual experiences, even when there is—and there frequently is—promiscuity or seductiveness (Powers, 1972); inclination to sexualize nonsexual relationships (Fenichel, 1945)

A very attractive woman of 48—flamboyantly but meticulously groomed—was taken to the hospital by ambulance after telephoning her daughter that she had "taken some pills." This action followed her discovery that her third husband was having an extramarital affair. As it turned out, she had taken a nonlethal dose of aspirin, but she had "wanted him to know how hurt I am." Her adult daughter, who had many problems of her own, complained that her mother had always been vain, demanding, and unreliable. The woman's husband revealed that his wife was a chronic "tease," playful sexually until he became excited, at which point she "turned cold." The fact that this patient actually had had an extramarital affair before her husband did seem to have no influence on her outrage at her husband's infidelity. Exploratory marital counseling was abandoned because of this woman's volatility and frequent outbursts of temper during sessions and because her husband of less than two years decided to terminate the marriage.

Erich Fromm captured the essence of the person with a "marketing orientation," in many ways analogous to the histrionic personality:

Success depends largely on how well a person sells himself . . . how "nice a package" he is . . . . Since success depends largely on how one sells one's personality, one experiences oneself as a commodity. . . . A person is not concerned with his life and happiness, but with becoming salable . . . his feeling of identity becomes as shaky as his self-esteem; it is constituted by the sum total of roles one can play: "I am as you desire me." . . . The premise of the marketing orientation is emptiness, the lack of any specific quality which could not be subject to change . . . . The marketing personality must be free, free of all individuality." (Fromm, 1947, pp. 69–78)

Narcissistic Personality Disorder
Although the concept of narcissism has long been discussed by psychoanalytic thinkers (Freud, 1953), recent years have witnessed a burst of inter-

est in pathological narcissism (e.g., Chessick, 1985; Cooper & Maxwell, 1995; Kernberg, 1975; Kohut, 1971; Loewenstein, 1977; Masterson, 1981; Palumbo, 1976). There are various viewpoints about the narcissistic personality disorder, but most of the differences relate to etiology and to theories about personality structure, dynamics, and treatment approaches.

The person with this disorder has some of the following characteristics:

- Exaggerated sense of self-importance or uniqueness (e.g., a grandiose view of capabilities or accomplishments); a talent, difficulty, or illness that is seen as "one of a kind"; feelings of superiority; endless striving for perfection; fierce competitiveness
- Preoccupation with fantasies of courageous feats or outstanding achievments; extraordinary need for adulation and attention without which boredom, depression, self-hatred, or rage may surface
- Disturbances in close relationships with others: feelings for others may appear genuine but, in fact, are shallow, nonexistent, or laced with rage, envy, or contempt
- Expectation that needs and feelings of others are the same as one's own; empathy is therefore lacking
- Exploitative, even parasitic, treatment of others, marked by a sense of entitlement to having needs met, regardless of cost to others; deficient social conscience
- Vacillation between extreme idealization and deprecation of others
- In spite of the above qualities: self-esteem is usually very fragile; the person may be successful and charming and not appear disturbed; the desperate, not necessarily conscious, need for attachment is not often apparent to others; underlying shame, frequently hidden from self and others (Morrison, 1989)

A 30-year-old bachelor attorney, who had risen rapidly in a prestigious law firm, began treatment complaining of depression triggered by the death of his widowed mother two months earlier. He was the only surviving child (his older sister had died at age 10). His mother had had "blind" faith that he could do anything; he and she had spoken on the telephone almost every day after he had moved out of her home at age 27.

He was handsome, brilliant, athletically and musically accomplished; he sought and was usually able to get an inordinate amount of admiration. But as talented and successful as he was, the loss of his mother's ever-reliable adulation left him feeling bereft and emotionally adrift. Although his mother had been painfully ill for many months before her death, this client never expressed sympathy for her suffering; instead, he spoke angrily of the unfairness to him that she was gone.

He explained that he had never married because to him commitment was too intense or "sticky"; he "treasured" privacy. He had always made sure, however, to have several women interested in him at one time; he charmed and disarmed them and then did only as much for them as was necessary to keep them "on the hook," available to him for attention and reassurance. His sexual relationships were influenced by the fact that he believed his penis to be smaller than average. (During one anxious meeting with his female social worker, he considered asking whether she would examine his genitals and assure him that they were all right.) His many sexual liaisons were maintained, in part, to convince himself that his unique penis was acceptable.

After three years of intensive treatment, this man was able to commit himself to one woman and to acknowledge his grandiosity and his need to be special. He and his worker agreed that his exaggerated view of himself and self-absorption covered up his fear and his precarious self-esteem, which were abruptly exposed when his mother's consistent adulation was no longer available.

Kernberg (1975) described patients with pathologically narcissistic persdonalities as presenting

an unusual degree of self-reference in their interactions with other people, a great need to be loved and admired by others, and a curious contradiction between a very inflated concept of themselves and an inordinate need for tribute from others. Their emotional life is shallow. They experience little empathy for the feelings of others, they obtain very little enjoyment from life other than from the tributes they receive from others or from their own grandiose fantasies, and they feel restless and bored when external glitter wears off and no new sources feed their self-regard. They envy others, tend to idealize some people from whom they expect narcissistic supplies and to deprecate and treat with contempt those from whom they do not expect anything (often their former idols). In general, their relationships with other people are clearly exploitative and sometimes parasitic. It is as if they feel they have the right to control and possess others and to exploit them without guilt feelings—and, behind a surface which often is charming and engaging, one senses coldness and ruthlessness. Very often such patients are considered to be dependent because they need so much tribute and adoration from others, but on a deeper level they are completely unable really to depend on anybody because of their deep distrust and depreciation of others. (pp. 227–228)

The flavor of the narcissistic condition was captured by Fromm:

Narcissism can . . . be described as a state of experience in which only the person himself, *his* body, *his* needs, *his* thoughts, *his* property, everybody and everything pertaining to *him* are experienced as fully real, while everybody and everything that does not form part of the person or is not an object of his needs is not interesting, is not fully real, is perceived only by intellectual recognition, while affectively without weight or color. A person, to the extent to which he is narcissistic, has a double standard of perception. Only he himself and what pertains to him has significance, while the rest of the world is more or less weightless or colorless, and because of this double standard the narcissistic person shows severe defects in judgment and lacks the capacity for objectivity. (Fromm, 1973, p. 201)

Avoidant Personality Disorder
The person with Avoidant Personality Disorder has some of the following characteristics:

- Extraordinary sensitivity to real or potential criticism or rejection, manifested in extreme feelings of anguish, humiliation, and shame
- Painful shyness; a pervasive pattern of social inhibition; isolation and loneliness are deeply felt; close relationships are avoided unless strong assurance of acceptance is given; mistrust of friendly overtures
- Low self-esteem; extreme self-doubt and self-criticism
- Strong desire for social relationships and affection (in contrast to the person with a schizoid disorder)

A 26-year-old woman, employed as a secretary in a small office and seen by others as very competent, came from an extremely disturbed family situation. Her father and three of her four siblings had been diagnosed as having schizophrenia, and periodically were hospitalized. She chronically devalued herself and her achievements; she was deeply disappointed that she could not make friends or get close to a man. Evenings and weekends were spent painfully alone in her small apartment; relief came when she could return to work on Monday morning.

After a few months of treatment at a mental health clinic, this woman asked to join a therapeutic group led by her worker. She hoped to become more socially comfortable. She was well accepted by other group members, but after two meetings (with one missed in between) she did not return. She explained to her worker that she felt "ashamed" of having talked about herself; she was afraid of being belittled or humiliated. Six months later, she joined the group again, but the pattern repeated itself. Her protective withdrawal from the group paralleled her general life situation: she isolated herself from others because she could not get unconditional guarantees of total acceptance.

Karen Horney (1945) describes what she termed the "detached type," similar to the avoidant personality:

On little or no provocation he feels that others look down on him, do not take him seriously, do not care for his company, and in fact, slight him. His self-contempt adds considerably to the profound uncertainty he has about himself, and hence cannot but make him as profoundly uncertain about the attitudes of others toward him. Being unable to accept himself as he is, he cannot possibly believe that others, knowing him with all his shortcomings, can accept him in a friendly or appreciative spirit.

What he feels in deeper layers is much more drastic, and may amount to an unshakable conviction that others plainly despise him. (p. 134)

Dependent Personality Disorder
The person with Dependent Personality Disorder has some of the following characteristics:

- Perceived need to be taken care of can lead to clinging behavior; passivity; strongly felt need to rely on others for support can result in willingness to permit others to make major decisions affecting his life, submitting even when the decisions are to the person's detriment
- Tendency to adapt behavior to please those on whom the person depends; unwillingness to express her own needs or preferences, particularly if these might conflict with the wishes of others; generally compliant and conciliatory, even to the point of being self-sacrificing or allowing abusive treatment
- Fear of being alone or self-reliant; therefore, attachments may be chosen hastily and indiscriminately in the exaggerated belief that one cannot care for oneself; moral standards may therefore be compromised
- Lack of initiative; perception of self as weak, helpless, and inferior to others; self-esteem rises and falls according to the views of others

Mrs. Jensen, a 52-year-old woman, sought help because she had been in an "absolute panic" since her husband, to whom she had been married for two years, announced that he wanted a divorce. The husband, a minister, had been her confidant and counselor when her first husband was divorcing her, also a time when she had felt extremely frightened. During this period, the minister initiated a sexual relationship with the distraught woman, left his own wife, and persuaded Mrs. Jensen to live with him. When both were divorced, they married one another. Although extremely intelligent, Mrs. Jensen had never worked and did not believe she was capable of becoming self-supporting. For this reason, she said, she had allowed the minister to make decisions for her, even though she knew they were in conflict with her own wishes and values.

"How come I let everyone take advantage of me?" the client repeatedly asked during early months of treatment. Gradually, the question was reframed to help Mrs. Jensen determine what *she* stood for, what decisions *she* wanted to make, what *she* needed to make her life more contented. As she worked with her feelings of helplessness and fears of self-reliance, she slowly became more self-directing. She discovered that she was not incompetent after all and realized that it took less "strength" to be responsible for her own life than to accept the humiliation and pain she had endured through her two marriages, in which she had let others take charge of her.

Writing about the person with the "receptive orientation," akin to the dependent personality, Erich Fromm described the individual who "feels 'the source of all good' to be outside, and he believes that the only way to get what he wants—be it something material, be it affection, love, knowledge, pleasure—is to receive it from an outside source" (Fromm, 1947, p. 67).

Obsessive-Compulsive Personality Disorder

The person with Obsessive-Compulsive Disorder has some of the following characteristics:

- Excessive conscientiousness; drivenness; concern with cleanliness, tidiness, "right and wrong," and "shoulds"; moralistic; pervasive rigidity; perfectionism and concern with detail, often resulting in poor productivity because of fear of making mistakes and inclination to ruminate over all—even inconsequential—decisions; tendency to get lost in minor issues and to lose sight of major ones; concreteness; excessive collecting, refusing to discard even worthless or outdated objects; harsh self-criticism and excessive guilt
- Strong, often stubborn, desire to control or dominate others; impatient with real or perceived shortcomings of others
- Need to control emotions; restrained affect; lack of emotional spontaneity; inability to express warm feelings; emotional and/or material stinginess
- Inability to enjoy free time or to take real pleasure in interpersonal relationships; prone to psychosomatic disorders

A self-employed accountant came to the attention of a mental health clinic because one of his two teenage sons was severely depressed. This man, who worked for himself, had been dismissed from several accounting firms for failing to meet deadlines and for indecisiveness.

In family therapy, his wife and sons complained that he was an "autocrat" whom they could never please. Both boys were excellent students, well liked, and cooperative (to a fault, perhaps), but they could not get the approval from their father that they obviously craved. Generally, he pointed to their imperfections and rarely to their achievements. He complained about his wife's "sloppy" housekeeping and poor budgeting in spite of her apparent adequacy in these areas. Family sessions easily could be dominated by his lectures to his wife and children; he was angry when they disagreed with him or refused to do what he wished. Often, he attempted to engage the worker in a debate on the merits of therapy. Clearly, he was unable to relax and enjoy other family members, who, in fact, were prepared to be caring toward him. After a few meetings, he discontinued family sessions and only reluctantly, when given a grim prognosis about his son by the school psychologist, did he allow the depressed boy, who wanted treatment, to attend the clinic.

ETIOLOGY OF PERSONALITY DISORDERS

A thorough overview of the literature on the etiology of the personality disorders is beyond the limits of this chapter. A comparative analysis is complicated for many reasons. First, there is lack of agreement about personality traits and types; similarly, nomenclature, definitions, and conceptual frameworks differ considerably. Second, some behaviorists and family therapists, among others, have little interest in exploring the relationships between personality or behavior and early childhood influences; they deal only with current etiological influences. Third, the relative roles of hereditary and environmental factors continue to be a subject of disagreement and uncertainty. Fourth, within the same school of thought, a syndrome or disorder may be attributed to various combinations of influences. For example, from the psychosocial view, the suspiciousness associated with the paranoid disorder and the rigid control found in the obsessive-compulsive style may have been influenced most strongly either by family interactions or by pervasive social forces (e.g., deprived or oppressive-conditions such as poverty and lack of opportunity, racism, or repressive climates like that of the McCarthy era of the 1950s). Even among writers with a psychoanalytic/ego psychology/systems approach, there are many major and minor differences. Thus, significant variations in thought can be found regarding the nature of libidinal and aggressive drives, ego organization, and the interrelationships among these. For example, followers of Kernberg (1975) and Kohut (1971) disagree with each other about the developmental issues that contribute to narcissistic conditions. Object-relations theory and ego psychology, on which notions about the origins of personality pathology often rest, also contain differences (see Blanck & Blanck, 1974, 1979; Guntrip, 1961, 1971).

The central interacting influences on the development of all personality disorders, from the psychosocial perspective, will be discussed here first. A review of factors that contribute to specific disorders will follow. Although influences are sometimes discussed as though they were discrete, of course each interacts with the others and either promotes or retards the evolution of the disorder.

Heredity and Personality Disorders

Hereditary factors have been of interest to scientists studying severe psychopathology for years; many have believed that there are genetic predispositions to psychosis (Arieti, 1974; Kallman, 1946; Strahl, 1980). However, when it comes to personality traits and disorders, there is less certainty. According to Millon (1996):

> [M]ost psychopathologists admit that heredity must play a role in personality disorder development, but they insist that genetic dispositions are modified substantially by the operation of environmental factors. This view states that heredity operates not as a fixed constant but as a disposition that takes different forms depending on the circumstances of an individual's upbringing. Hereditary theorists may take a more inflexible position, referring to a body of data that implicate genetic factors in a wide range of psychopathologies. Although they are likely to agree that variations in these disorders may be produced by environmental conditions, they are equally likely to assert that these are merely superficial influences that cannot prevent the individual from succumbing to his or her hereditary inclination.
>
> Despite . . . ambiguities and complications, there can be little question that genetic factors do play some dispositional role in shaping the morphological and biochemical substrate of certain traits. *However, these factors are by no means necessary to the development of personality pathology, nor are they likely to be sufficient in themselves to elicit pathological behaviors.* They may serve, however, as a physiological base that makes the person susceptible to dysfunction under stress or inclined to learn behaviors that prove socially troublesome. (p. 88, italics mine)

Among lay people familiar with newborn babies, there is certainly agreement that enormous differences among them can be perceived immediately. Some newborns are active or fretful whereas others seem passive or contented. Research supports these observations; hundreds of infants studied from birth and followed into adolescence were found to maintain many of their original dispositions over the years (Murphy & Moriarty, 1976; Stern, 1985; Thomas & Chess, 1977).

Of course, as Millon (1996) indicates, inborn factors are influenced by the interactions and systems to which an individual is exposed. For example, if, in fact, there is a genetic predisposition to the dependent personality, this tendency will be either checked or reinforced depending on the style of the caregivers. If they usually satisfy the child's needs before the child has to ask, dependent tendencies will be strengthened; on the other hand, if the child's independent behaviors are encouraged, dependent inclinations are less likely to become disabling. A baby with a happy temperament often provokes cheerful, loving responses; in contrast, the fretful infant tries the parents' patience or undermines their confidence in their caregiving. By the same token temperament, at least to some degree, probably can be reversed; for example, a withdrawn infant may become more active and alert in the context of a supportive, interested family.

Early Developmental Influences and Personality Disorders

In spite of differences among researchers, there is consensus that the child's very early years *crucially* affect subsequent development. Of course, later experiences and environmental conditions can either reinforce or reverse early influences as these interact with the personality.

Spitz (1965) discovered that babies deprived of adequate mothering developed abnormalities of functioning and anaclitic (related to a damaged dependency between mother and child) depression. Bowlby (1969, 1973) stressed the importance of physical closeness and attachment to *one* maternal figure, seeing this as necessary for healthy development. He added: "experiences of separation from attachment figures, whether of short or long duration, and experiences of loss or of being threatened with separation or abandonment—all act, we can now see, to divert development from a pathway that is within optimum limits" (1973, pp. 369–370). Mahler and coworkers (1975) described the child's early developmental phases; many notions about the etiology of ego deficits and pathological personality development have been derived from their work.

Winnicott's (1965) familiar concept of "good enough mothering" covers the theoretical issue of overriding concern to object relations writers. Simply put, it is believed that a satisfactory relationship between the child and his parent or caretaker requires both *consistent* parental availability and support and *age-appropriate* encouragement of the child's independence and self-direction. When dependence needs are not adequately filled by the parent figure or when caretaking is interrupted by separations and losses, psychological damage is expected to ensue. Likewise, when a parent clings to a child or for some other reason discourages autonomous functioning, healthy growth is stunted and deviations occur.

There is sufficient evidence from experimental research and from empirical observation to claim that influences in the child's early years do, indeed, have detrimental effects on personality and adaptive functioning. But it is equally obvious that the personality system is infinitely complex and that we are a long way from being able to predict which children—on the basis of their unique endowments and early experiences—will develop specific personality strengths or disorders. It is possible, for example, that some children with "good enough" or even excellent parenting are unable to get the full benefit of it. "Contributions to the etiology may come from either or both sides of the mother–child equation—from both nature and nurture" (Masterson, 1981, p. 132).

Family Relationships and Personality Disorders

The importance of the family system to personality development has long been recognized by social workers (Richmond, 1917; Towle, 1957). Recent developments in family therapy have added sophistication to our understanding of the complexities of family relationships (Woods & Hollis, 1990). Concepts about family roles and communication have contributed to knowledge about family dynamics. Increasingly, clinical social workers are becoming experts on family, as well as personality, theory, thereby adding understanding to the nature of the reciprocal influences between them.

Just as the early parent-child dyad can affect personality development, so the entire family system can distort or promote a child's healthy growth. Writing about the pathological family triangle, Satir (1983) remarked:

I have been repeatedly struck by how readily the [identified child patient] drops his role as intervener once family therapy is under way. Once he is assured that arguments do not bring destruction and that marital amicability lightens parental demands on him, the [patient] actively helps the therapist help his parents as *mates*, while at the same time he tries to get his parents to recognize him as a separate individual with needs of his own. (p. 71)

Concepts about differentiation have been central to family systems theories and also to ego psychology. Healthy development is presumed to be fostered by the family that helps individuals (children and adults) to see themselves as separate, self-directed people at the same time that they share close or intimate relationships with others. Difficulties arise when one assumes that one must negate one's sense of self in order to avoid abandonment by others or, conversely, when one fears that loss of autonomy stems from intimacy and therefore shies away from close relationships.

Boundaries are the means by which individuals (and family subsystems and generations) protect their separateness and sense of identity (Bowen, 1971; Minuchin, 1974). When boundaries are either too permeable or too rigid, personality problems may develop. For example, if an individual believes that family members will be accepting only if they are allowed to take responsibility for major areas of her life, low self-confidence, passivity, and subservience—traits associated with the dependent personality disorder—may be fostered. By the same token, the individual who attempts to prevent intrusiveness on the part of other family members may develop an aloof or bland style and prefer isolation to companionship—qualities found in the person with the schizoid personality disorder.

When forces in the family shift, individuals usually have to find new ways of functioning and adapting. For example, clinicians frequently see dramatic changes in the behavior or mood (e.g., a depressive reaction) of the spouse of an alcoholic when the latter stops drinking. Similarly, an apparently dependent and weak spouse may become self-reliant and even gain a new lease on life when the domineering, or strong, mate dies.

The Larger Environment and Personality Disorders

The interplay between people and their environments—including those extending beyond the family—has been a major interest of social work theory and practice. It is generally acknowledged that one cannot discuss the etiology of personality disorders without reference to their relationship to community and societal systems (Germain, 1979; Woods & Hollis, 1990; Meyer, 1976). Reiner (1979) noted "that individualism and narcissism are defenses against the latent depression and lack of self-esteem that are fostered by many aspects of society" (p. 3). She added that a sense of personal irrelevance originating in early childhood can be

> recreated or intensified in later life by the struggle to survive emotionally in a society that provides few supports in developmental

crises or times of stress. A sense of personal irrelevance may include having one's needs unrecognized by others, having one's anger considered unjustified or unacceptable, or feeling unloved, isolated or abandoned, insignificant or worthless, and powerless to effect change. (p. 3)

Surely, feelings of loneliness, helplessness, and low self-esteem derived from conditions beyond the individual's control foster rigid traits associated with disorders of personality. People adapt to their environment by conforming to its demands or by attempting to change it to suit their needs and goals. When changes in the larger social system are not possible—as they are not for many people living under deprived, frightening, humiliating, or other severely destructive circumstances—deep personality scars are inevitable.

Generally, the literature attributes personality disorders to influences of nature and nurture in early childhood. Without denying the importance of these factors, it is necessary to emphasize also the roles played by psychologically or physically noxious conditions at *any* stage of life. Whether one is forced to live in a concentration camp, the back ward of a mental institution, a rat-infested or unheated tenement, the street, or a community marked by terrorism, personality damage must ensue. As ego functions of adjusting to reality, mastery, and autonomy are assaulted, maladaptive reactions (which may endure even if the environment improves) are unavoidable.

Etiology and Subcategories of Personality Disorders

It should be emphasized that one of the important factors influencing the perpetuation of any personality disorder is the disorder itself. In other words, *the behavior of the individual with the disorder frequently elicits reactions from others that reinforce maladaptive traits.* The discussion of etiological contributions to specific disorders will elucidate this point.

Schizoid Personality
This disorder is sometimes assumed to derive from meager emotional warmth or body contact in early life (Cameron, 1963; Millon, 1996). Detached and cold parenting, on the one hand, or intrusiveness, on the other, can induce withdrawal and schizoid traits. Inborn temperamental qualities are also thought to contribute to the development of this disorder. Obviously, loners perpetuate their isolation by failing to pursue or attract people with vitality or warmth.

Schizotypal Personality

The eccentricities manifested by the person with this disorder are presumed to have both organic and experiential roots (Millon, 1996; Strahl, 1980); but there is little consensus about the relative weight of these factors. Surely, bizarre communications and ungratifying family relationships of various sorts can create personality traits characteristic of people with this condition. Some of the pioneers of the family therapy movement, such as Jackson, Bateson, and Weakland (Jackson, 1968) stressed the relationship between schizophrenia (on which this disorder is assumed by some to border) and human communication. Frequently, individuals with schizotypal traits are unable to sustain meaningful interpersonal relationships; their isolation serves to exaggerate their peculiarities and a downward spiral is often set in motion, with the end result being hospitalization and/or deterioration of interpersonal skills.

Histrionic Personality

Individuals with Histrionic Personality Disorder are thought to come from a background in which dependency needs were inadequately met; such women, in particular, may have had mothers who had hysterical traits themselves and emotionally distant (either passive or domineering) fathers (Powers, 1972). According to Millon (1996), the person with this disorder "may have had many different caretakers . . . who supplied the child with intense, short-lived stimulus gratifications at irregular or haphazard intervals . . . . The shifting from one source of gratification to another so characteristic of histrionics, their search for new stimulus adventures, their penchant for creating excitement and their inability to tolerate boredom and routine, all may represent the consequences of these unusual early experiences" (p. 383).

In contrast to dependent children, who often had their needs met without exerting effort, it is thought that many children who developed adult histrionic disorders had to actively engage the attention and help of adults—by seductive, dramatic, manipulative, or other means that would be acceptable in their particular families. Thus, for adults with such histories, recognition and approval feel essential and become important interpersonal motivators. The person is often unable to develop solid values or a robust self-definition because of the inconsistency experienced in childhood. The ongoing search for praise and stimulation curtails inner growth, resulting in superficiality; therefore, unless or until significant changes are made, deeply intimate and sustaining relationships are almost impossible to achieve.

Narcissistic Personality

Pathological narcissism traditionally has been viewed by psychoanalysts as a developmental arrest. Simply put, a faulty parent–child connection has two possible outcomes: either, because of a weak bond, the very young child fails to advance from autoeroticism ("primary narcissism") to develop solid attachments to particular objects, or, defending herself against parental coldness or cruelty, the child regresses to an earlier narcissistic phase. Differences about etiology among Kernberg (1975), Kohut (1971), Palumbo (1976), and others are too abstract for this discussion. Millon (1996) quotes Michael Stone:

> Narcissistic traits can develop, curiously, when there are deviations from ideal rearing on either side: pampering or neglecting; expecting too much or too little. Excessive praise of a child can give rise to . . . feelings of superiority, of being destined for greatness . . . . But compensatory feelings of a similar kind can arise where there has been parental indifference and neglect, for in this situation a child may develop an exaggerated desire for "greatness" by shoring up a sense of self-worth in the absence of the ordinary parental praise. Whereas the overly praised child may regard himself as better than he really is, the neglected child may present a dual picture: an outward sense of (compensatory) specialness covering an inward sense of worthlessness. (p. 401)

Millon used social learning theory to explain an important influence on the narcissistic pattern; overvaluation by parents of a child's worth becomes internalized but cannot be sustained or validated in the real world. Horney (1939) said: "Parents who transfer their own ambitions to the child and regard the boy as an embryonic genius or the girl as a princess, thereby develop in the child the feeling that he is loved for imaginary qualities rather than for his true self" (p. 91). Since his self-esteem rests on fantasy, the person is only a breath away from depression and self-hate.

Problems for the person with a narcissistic disorder (as is usually true for those with any disorder) are perpetuated and reinforced. When grandiosity and other illusions cannot be externally validated and when self-centeredness and lack of interest in others leads to isolation, the person may struggle all the harder—often with less and less success—to prove that he is in fact special. Thus disappointments keep building on themselves.

Modern times may play a part in supporting the preoccupation with self. Many have believed that narcissism derives from feelings of alienation, lack of opportunity, cut-throat competitiveness, or the need to retreat from the violence of present life (Lasch, 1978; Reiner, 1979). Some think that self-centeredness in young people is encouraged by current child-rearing practices, such as reluctance to restrain children's behavior, or the need to raise "latchkey" children because parents are working.

Avoidant Personality

As with other disorders, hereditary predispositions may play a part in the development of the avoidant personality, even though the hard evidence is lacking. In large part, the hypersensitive, avoidant pattern is thought to derive from repeated experiences of derogation and humiliation. Whether ridicule came from parents or peers (e.g., when a child is taunted for physical characteristics, for a handicap, or for his racial, class, or ethnic background), the results can be painful sensitivity and self-doubt in social situations. The low self-esteem characteristic of the person with this condition often prevents her from reaching out or even being in close proximity to others; and, or course, the person's withdrawal or frightened demeanor may cause others to retreat or reject, thus reinforcing the pattern.

Dependent Personality

When children are overprotected (for any reason), strivings for competence and individuation may be stunted. An infant with a passive temperament may stimulate excessive caregiving; the most well-meaning, loving parents nurture overdependency. The child's overreliance on one person, rather than on a few—due to family circumstances or childhood illness, for example— may foster a lifelong dependency pattern. On the other hand, confidence can also be undermined when circumstances force children to try to be independent before they are able to be so. In either case, the inclination to lean excessively on others may develop. Since adults with this disorder tend to be overly coooperative and placating, they may find authoritative people to rely on—at least temporarily; the dependent pattern is thereby perpetuated, as is low self-respect and a sense of incompetence. And, of course, when people with this pattern allow others to make detrimental decisions for them, to abuse or exploit them, the vicious cycle of self-deprecation and excessive reliance on others becomes even more extreme.

Obsessive-Compulsive Personality

Controlling—often punitive—parents with high and definite expectations for their children are generally assumed to be influential in the development of the obsessive-compulsive personality. The term *anal character,* closely comparable to this disorder, refers to the fixation at the phase in which bowel training is an issue. Millon (1996) quotes Rado's view of the imact of the anal pattern on obsessive traits:

> If the mother is overambitious, demanding and impatient . . . then the stage is set for the battle of the chamber pot.
>
> Irritated by the mother's interference with his bowel clock, the child responds to her entreaties with enraged defiance, to her punishments and threats of punishment with fearful obedience. The battle is a seesaw, and the mother . . . makes the disobedient child feel guilty, undergo deserved punishment and ask forgiveness . . . . It is characteristic of the child under consideration that his guilty fear is always somewhat stronger; sooner or later, it represses his defiant rage. Henceforth, his relationship to his mother, and soon to the father will be determined by . . . guilty fear over defiant rage or *obedience* versus *defiance.* (p. 509)

Ambivalence, Rado noted, is rooted in the underlying obedience-defiance conflict: the person "ponders unendingly: must he give in, or could he gain the upper hand without giving offense" (p. 509).

If firm and demanding parents, schoolteachers, or others in authority are consistently punitive when children do not meet their expectations, the child's autonomy is undermined; guilt and self-doubt are reinforced, especially when the youngster receives no affirmation—for his accomplishments, or for just being the person he is. Anxiety about performance begets anxiety. Concern with perfection and sticking to the rules—probably based on hopes that parental approval will finally come—promotes the rigidity of the obsessive-compulsive personality. Reluctance to make decisions, to initiate changes, or to take risks can exacerbate the emotional constriction and other qualities associated with this disorder. Because of the tendency to comply (in spite of ambivalence or resentment), the young person may get some praise or acceptance from somewhere; but she often adopts a precocious intellectual style, becomes overly helpful, bossy, or critical, qualities that are rarely endearing. Usually, he does not enjoy warmth and spontaneity in relationships; thus, even after sacrificing so much of his personality to be "good," he may still end up feeling alone. Once the traits are developed, their rigidities—including righteous efforts to control themselves and others—lead people with this disorder to self-perpetuating behaviors and little joy in life.

SUMMARY ON ETIOLOGY

Our knowledge about the etiology of personality disorders is, for the most part, imprecise and impressionistic. However, social work clinicians who have seen large numbers of individuals and families under all kinds of conditions may be particularly well equipped to develop hypotheses about the many forces that interact to create self-defeating personality patterns.

The inflexible, maladaptive life patterns that are the hallmark of personality disorders can be viewed, in one sense or another, as defensive patterns. However dysfunctional the personality style, it seems safe to assume that *at one time* it was a safeguard against intolerable anxiety, self-hate, helplessness, or insecurity, as well as a means for warding off unacceptable impulses. At the time these defensive styles are developed—to protect against inner and outer threats—they may be the *most adaptive alternatives* available to the (usually young) person creating them. While the person with a personality disorder often has forfeited some sense of autonomy or availability for interpersonal relationships, or both, it seems probable that unconsciously the vulnerable child believed the adaptation was necessary to find security in the family or the larger environment.

Defensive life patterns can prevent the development of healthy defense mechanisms (Lidz, 1968). For example, the individual with a dependent disorder may never have developed defenses against separation anxiety, which are necessary for autonomy, individuation, and ability to deal with reality. The therapeutic importance of understanding the function (archaic or ongoing) of defensive and adaptive patterns is discussed in this chapter's section on treatment, which follows.

It is also true that defensive personality patterns may be converted into assets. For example, many clinicians have strong caretaking qualities, which may have been defensive adaptations in early life. Perhaps the future therapist, as a young child, had to defend against feelings of insecurity by becoming protective and looking after dependent, inadequate, or ill adults in the family.

Some features of personality disorders actually may be looked upon as virtues: self-effacement, conformity, and even infantile dependence or masochistic suffering, under some circumstances, are very much admired. In my view, for the adult the issue is whether there is choice in the matter; for example, is excessive modesty or conformity felt as obligatory or is it an expression of preference under particular circumstances? Cameron (1963) discussed the matter further:

To avoid common misunderstandings, it is essential to state here that courage, integrity, dependability, normal self-sacrifice and the ability to accept dependence upon others are not signs of character disorder. It is only when these seeming *qualities* turn out to be demands, upon a human environment which does not want them, and does not gain in warmth or understanding from them, that we call them disorders rather than virtues. (p. 640)

SOCIAL WORK TREATMENT OF PERSONALITY DISORDERS

Treatment and Psychosocial Diagnosis of Personality Disorders

In many instances it can take weeks or even months before the social worker has any degree of certainty about the extent or recalcitrance of a person's difficulties. One may be clear that there is a personality disorder and even know which subcategory or subcategories best describe the person's condition, but information about the complex origins of the problem or about the optimal mode of treatment often comes slowly. Diagnostic tools are not perfect. Complicated interacting and self-perpetuating influences take time to understand. Ego deficits, distortions, and defenses often are not evident right away.

Similarly, while some strengths are immediately apparent, others may be obscured from view and revealed only as treatment progresses. As discussed earlier, less attention has been given to developing tools for the assessment of positive qualities than to the diagnosis of pathological conditions. However, it is often potential strengths that determine the individual's capacity to utilize treatment and improve social functioning. The notion that treatment determines the diagnosis (Blanck & Blanck, 1979; Boyer & Giovacchini, 1967) may be more valid for work with personality disorders than for many other forms of psychosocial treatment.

As treatment progresses, then (in individual, family, or group sessions), it is necessary continually to assess the client and her situation to discover strengths, capacities for change, and limiting influences. The therapist looks for indications of these in the quality of the client–worker relationship and the client's use of the treatment situation; the behavioral, attitudinal, or emotional shifts that occur when there are changes in the family or environmental situation (whether therapeutically induced or not); and the degree to which the environment supports the personality disorder and/or discourages change. Elaboration of these points follows.

The Client–Worker Relationship and the Client's Use of the Treatment Situation

When the worker is attuned to the client's approach to treatment and to the quality of interactions with the worker, over a period of time inferences can be made about personality structure, ego development, capacity for self-observation and self-analysis, capacity to use the therapeutic relationship, honesty, and motivation for change.

On the surface, one client may appear to be more disturbed than another but in the long run prove to be more treatable. The description of the behavior or traits of a particular client may seem to convey a poorly integrated personality structure, but the capacity for a therapeutic alliance and for change may, in fact, be better than for another client who appears to be less disturbed.

A 28-year-old woman, Sally, sought help at a mental health clinic because of extreme anxiety and episodes of disabling panic. A public relations representative for the telephone company (her seventh job in six years), she had begun to feel that the position was too much for her; she often found herself in a rage at customers. A fairly attractive and intelligent woman, she had no close relationships with men but instead was promiscuous in a frantic way; sometimes after drinking too much she could not remember who had come home with her. She "hated" her mother and frequently had furious arguments with her. She had two or three women friends but was feeling "fed up" with them; nevertheless, she was terrified of being alone. Except for the increased feelings of panic, her problems had not changed much over the years. Early in treatment, the caseworker diagnosed Sally as having a borderline personality with histrionic traits.

For the first two months of treatment, Sally made almost daily telephone calls to the worker. Medication prescribed by the clinic psychiatrist did not reduce anxiety. Although not suicidal, she believed she was unable to cope and would die soon. After about four months of twice weekly, primarily supportive treatment, Sally rather dramatically calmed down; now, she added, she wanted to work on "getting my act together." She had grown to trust the worker and relied on her to understand and not judge her. She could then begin to reflect on herself, on her emotional and behavioral patterns, and on her situation. After two more years of therapy, she enjoyed her job, had been promoted, and planned to stay with her company. She joined some organizations, made new friends, and was going out with a man she liked very much; she no longer drank to excess. Her anger at her mother dissipated; mostly, she felt sorry for her now. She said she was handling her life in a way she had never done before.

Phyllis, aged 31, had functioned adequately as a bookkeeper at the same firm for over 10 years. She went to a clinic when her husband left her and their 10-year-old daughter to live with another woman. She was angry and depressed. Phyllis had been in therapy on two previous occasions but had never felt helped. Although she was consciously interested in making changes in her "unhappy and boring" life, very little had changed after a year of treatment. She complained about her situation and other people; she liked her worker but protested that "nothing ever helps." Intellectually, she could see that she was not working very hard to solve her problems, but she believed that she was either unwilling or unable to rally her energies to do so. In spite of the worker's interest, availability, and skilled efforts and Phyllis's general trust in the worker's goodwill, the client never developed a strong therapeutic relationship with her. Treatment terminated after the presenting depression had lifted and an afterschool play group had been located for her daughter.

As these examples illustrate, treatment uncovers prognosis. One cannot be sure how a client will use the treatment relationship and what strengths and capacities will be revealed in the process. To the layman, Phyllis might seem far less disturbed than Sally. One could describe Phyllis as a stable but cranky person leading a humdrum life. Initially, even to a clinician, Sally might seem more troubled because of the instability of her mood and her long-standing pattern of erratic behavior. As it turned out, Sally was able to make a strong connection with the worker, to be come introspective, to gain some sense of mastery over her feelings and behavior, to make changes in her life, and to bolster her self-esteem. Compared to Phyllis, Sally had a greater capacity for trust, more motivation for change, a better ability to understand others and their feelings, a wider emotional range, and a greater ability to enjoy herself. Over the course of treatment, it became evident that Phyllis's defenses were more rigidly set than Sally's.

As treatment proceeds, it often becomes clear that the client who heavily uses defenses such as "splitting" (inability to integrate contradictory feelings or states of mind, in conjunction with a tendency to divide all experiences, perceptions, and affects into extremes of good and bad) and "projective identification" (projection of aggressive, negative feelings about oneself onto others as a means to reduce anxiety) and who rapidly shifts from adoring to blaming the worker may actually be more available for reparative work than the client who never really engages in the treatment relationship. For example, some individuals with schizoid or narcissistic personality styles may be able to see the worker as only a shadowy figure or a pale image. Such clients may function on higher levels in certain areas of life, but they also may be less available for change than those who make strong—even if erratic—connections with others.

First meetings with clients may be misleading in various ways. For example, a client's apparent passivity may reflect initial anxiety, an attempt to conform to the presumed expectations of a person seen to be in authority, or lack of sophistication about social work treatment. Some clients either deliberately or unconsciously present themselves as dependent or deficient in coping ability, perhaps because past or present important people have been threatened by their autonomous functioning. Finally, it may not be evident immediately that a client is consciously dishonest, either to please the worker or to avoid inner anxiety.

Behavioral, Attitudinal, or Emotional Shifts That Accompany Changes in the Family or Larger Environment

The severity of personality disorder may be revealed by the degree to which outer influences affect it. For example, suppose a mildly retarded man is moved from a punitive foster home to a halfway house that promotes self-respect and independence; if long-standing suspiciousness is diminished (at least to some degree), the worker might be more encouraged about the possibility of further change in paranoid traits than if no shift had resulted from the move. Similarly, if, in family therapy, positive changes in one family member are followed by healthy changes in the client assumed to have a personality disorder, greater flexibility may be predicted than if the reaction had been negative or dysfunctional.

Environmental Encouragement of the Personality Disorder

Obviously, if a woman with a dependent disorder is married to a domineering man, personality traits of both may be reinforced by the marital complementarity. Similarly, a paranoid disorder may be aggravated in a client whose relatives or associates behave sadistically or maliciously. By the same token, when the family system discourages differentiation of its members for any reason or requires a scapegoat to keep marital problems concealed, a personality disorder of a family member may be sustained; avoidant or dependent traits may be nurtured. Under these circumstances, an individual attempting to make changes might be discouraged by the family forces militating against them; thus family therapy could become a treatment of choice (Woods & Hollis, 1990).

As already mentioned, social and economic abuses, deprivations, racism, and many other alienating forces nurture many of the traits found in personality disorders. Personality changes are difficult to make (or even to consider) when one lives in any inhumane environment.

Differences in race, age, gender, background, class, or sexual orientation between clinical social workers and their clients can lead some people—even those who know they want assistance—to fear that their needs and circumstances will not be understood. When a client has been the victim of racism, social oppression, or prejudice of any kind, the perception of power differentials between her and the social service system can understandably foster distrust (Pinderhughes, 1989). The responsibility for addressing and resolving clients' perceptions (whether totally realistic or not) must be placed squarely on the shoulders of social and mental health agencies and all clinical social workers who treat individuals and families.

Finally, cultural or family values may discourage help-seeking (e.g., "people should solve their own problems"; "that psychology talk is for crazy people"). Fortunately the past decades have seen positive shifts in attitudes about therapy; some people and groups that shied away from it formerly now view it more favorably. In many instances, men not only are willing to join their wives in therapy but, more frequently than ever before, are initiating contact with agencies, clinics, or social work practitioners. Some estimate that up to 40 million people in the United States are receiving psychotherapy or counseling. This wide use should help remove the stigma that has discouraged some people from seeking help in the past, rendering treatment even more acceptable in years to come.

Special Characteristics of Social Work Treatment of Personality Disorders

Beginning in the 1960s, many of the writings about the diagnosis and treatment of the so-called "less than neurotically structured patient" (e.g., Boyer & Giovacchini, 1967; Giovacchini, 1975; Kernberg, 1975, 1977; Masterson, 1976, 1981) were written by psychoanalytically-trained psychiatrists. At first, there was some concern that psychoanalysts were using methods of treatment for which social workers were not equipped. As it turned out, social workers moved more and more to the forefront of the development of approaches to successful therapy with individuals manifesting severe personality disorders (Blitzer, 1978; Clark, 1996; Freed, 1980; Goldstein, 1990; Palumbo, 1970; among many others). Indeed, these conditions do yield to social work treatment. The case of Mrs. Zimmer demonstrates that psychoanalysis or frequent sessions may not be necessary (or preferable) to provide a therapeutic and reparative experience that results in significant and fulfilling personality changes (Woods & Hollis, 1990). Case examples in this chapter add to the growing body of evidence that personality disorders are amenable to social work intervention. (Furthermore, as time has passed, many psychiatrists have shifted from ongoing treatment to specializations, such as psychopharmacology, consultation, administration, etc.; the fact is that in North America social workers are now delivering most of the direct psychotherapy services to clients, including those with personality disorders.) Successful treatment of personality disorders by social work clinicians may be accounted for in various ways:

First, traditionally, social workers have been attuned to client strengths. In work with personality disorders, it has become apparent that when clients are helped to enlist well-developed ego functions and to bolster or mobilize others, positive personality changes are fostered; clients are thereby better equipped to locate inner and outer resources, to overcome obstacles to adaptive functioning, and to bring direction to their lives. Problem- or deficit-oriented approaches that focus on inadequacies and failures can result in pessimism, feelings of powerlessness, and self-blame—with which many people with disorders are already too heavily burdened.

Second, social workers are often able to engage and treat people whom other professionals do not see. Many non-social-work writers have concentrated almost exclusively on the intrapsychic issues of individuals with personality disorders and on the theoretical and technical aspects of one-to-one treatment. Psychosocial therapy draws on additional knowledge related to social, family, and environmental influences. Outreach, home visits, and the provision of concrete services are all part of the trained social worker's armamentarium. For those clients who would not ordinarily seek psychotherapy but who feel that change is necessary, opportunities for help are made available. Social workers in child welfare, probation, or other services often are able to treat clients or refer them for psychological help; some of these clients might otherwise be too uninformed or too afraid to seek treatment on their own. Even involuntary clients of protective services or prison inmates have been known to engage in treatment once they are presented with social work services and learn that *their* needs and *their* visions and goals will be taken seriously and will be the primary focus of the work; too often, potential clients believe that treatment plans will be imposed upon them.

Family or couple treatment and the provision of other environmental services can be influential in promoting change in individual clients with personality disorders. Rice (1980), a social worker, demonstrated how she used concepts about narcissistic personality disorders in couple therapy; she quoted Nathan Ackerman: "A good marriage is the most effective of all treatment relationships" (p. 271). Social workers have long known the value of working with family members and of improving the climate of family life in order to help a particular client's situation or personality problem. Systems theory now supports social work's years of experience. As Gyarfas (1980) said, in a systems context, it is "possible to examine the psychosocial proposition that there is likely to be an association between an individual's inability to meet his own and other's needs, and severely stressful events in the social systems (primary, secondary, and tertiary) on which he depends" (p. 56).

Third, many social workers have come to recognize that sharp distinctions between the treatment of clients with personality disorders and those with so-called neurotic symptoms may have been overdrawn in the past. It seems safe to say that in spite of variations in emphasis in the approach to people with different clinical diagnoses, psychosocial therapy across all sorts of people has more similarities than dissimilarities (Woods & Hollis, 1990). The Hollis typology of treatment procedures (sustainment; direct influence; exploration-description-ventilation; reflective discussion of the person-situation, and of pattern-dynamic and developmental factors) pertains to every clinical condition. Of course, the actual blend is influenced strongly by the assessment of many factors, only one of which is the clinical diagnosis.

Fourth, social workers, probably more than many other professionals in the mental health field, do not expect every client to want intensive psychotherapy. Even when ego deficits, maladaptive traits, or self-defeating defenses are apparent, the social work clinician does not recklessly seek to engage the client in working on problems which he is not interested in considering. Clients come to agencies—even those equipped to provide intensive treatment—for various reasons: placement of a mentally disabled child, vocational rehabilitation, housing problems, and family life education, to name a few. Meeting these needs is valuable in and of itself. Of course, many such clients with personality disorders eventually do decide that they want to make changes they did not originally envision. But it is contrary to social work principles both to underrate the importance of responding to *specific* client requests, and to urge clinical treatment on clients who clearly do not want it.

Beginning Therapy and Establishing a Relationship with the Personality-Disordered Client

Presenting Problems

Individuals later diagnosed as having personality disorders may come to the clinical social worker's attention for a multitude of reasons. Often, clients seek help in a state of crisis—when they have become excruciatingly anxious, depressed, or phobic. Such symptoms may come on the heels of drastic life changes such as marital separation, death, loss of job, or family illness. In other instances, the distress may be triggered by seemingly minor events. Obviously, the client's approach to recovery will be an important diagnostic clue; the presence of a personality problem may be revealed by the difficulties the client has in regaining equilibrium.

Some people with personality disorders are not accustomed to recognizing (even intellectually) that their difficulties have any connection with their own personality or behavior. Their pain is very real and often extreme, but the cause may be seen as other people, external events, uncontrollable urges, fate, or some combination of these. Many such clients tend to be hopeless about improvement unless the factors that seem to victimize them change. Consequently, some clients with personality disorders may resolutely seek environmental solutions without examining their own part in the difficulty.

As often as not, clients come to facilities in which social workers are employed for services unrelated to psychological treatment. They may come for help with employment problems, day care, the needs of elderly relatives, temporary shelter, traveler's aid, and so on. Often, no further services are needed. In some instances, however, such inquiries rather quickly lead to treatment or referral for problems deriving from a personality disorder.

Jack contacted family court to determine whether he could take "family action" against his father for showing pornographic pictures to Jack's "girlfriend." His presenting request could not be met, but

> Jack's conversation with a sensitive intake supervisor brought to light considerable personal distress. Quite readily, Jack accepted a referral to a clinical social worker in private practice. He wanted help because he felt isolated and afraid of losing his relationship with the woman he loved; he was also aware that his painful sensitivity to criticism gave him problems on the job. As it turned out, he had many traits associated with avoidant and schizotypal disorders.

Jack's case also illustrates that the feelings, behaviors, or defenses of clients with personality disorders are not always as "ego syntonic" as many have thought them to be. Some clients declare right away that they wish to make personality changes. One client in her mid-forties said in a first session that she was "sick and tired" of living "half a life." She believed her "entire personality" needed an "overhaul"; she hated her impulsive rages at her husband and children; she said her perfectionism gave her trouble everywhere; and she put little blame for her problems on others.

Worker Characteristics

Therapist characteristics and attitudes identified by research and clinical observation (e.g., Compton & Galaway, 1994; Woods & Hollis, 1990; Perlman, 1957) as important to successful treatment are essential in work with clients with personality disorders. These include nonpossessive warmth and concern, genuineness, accurate empathy (Truax & Carkhuff, 1967), nonjudgmental acceptance, and optimism that change is possible (Woods & Hollis, 1990). Additional qualities found to take on particular importance when working with clients manifesting personality disorders are reviewed here.

Demonstration of Reliability. Consistency about appointments, punctuality, keeping promises, listening closely, and maintaining the therapeutic attitudes mentioned above are imperative with personality-disordered clients. More often than not, they have had unstable parenting and (as a result of patterns that perpetuate interpersonal problems) erratic adult relationships. Such clients, who usually have not internalized a sense of confidence in others, can find it difficult to believe that the worker can be counted upon to care. People who have not had positive mothering in childhood "often not only lack the internalized 'good mother' but are incapable of feeling reassured that the therapist and/or external environment will provide what is absent" (Paolino, 1981, p. 211). Treatment begins when the reassurance is given by demonstrating reliability; aspects of the diagnosis are revealed by how quickly the client can trust in the continuity of the relationship.

Professional Security and Competence. People with personality problems often have trouble enough trusting without being faced with a worker who feels unsure. Clients who have not had satisfactory people to rely upon will want to know that their worker can understand them before they allow themselves to engage in a dependent therapeutic relationship; often, such clients intuitively perceive a worker's lack of skill or personal vulnerability. With clients with personality disorders, every effort should be made to demonstrate that the worker is not interested in exploiting them (as they often feel others are). This message can be conveyed, for example, in the course of discussing fees and acknowledging realistic needs for fee reduction; in being scrupulous in not attempting to elicit praise or gratitude to serve one's own needs; in being self-revealing *only* when it is in the interests of the client; and in avoiding unclear or evasive communications that could be interpreted by the client as dishonest or manipulative.

Capacity to Reach Out. When a reliable, professionally secure, and competent worker reaches out as a "real" person to another "real" person—by making a call to inquire about a client who has been ill, by paying a home visit, by telephoning if an appointment is missed, by providing concrete services or useful information—the probability that trust will develop (however slowly) and that the client will engage in treatment is greatly enhanced. Furthermore, as Freed (1980) said, the worker who is not passive and who establishes herself as a real person will "reduce fantasies and negative transference" (p. 553).

Capacity to Maintain Respect and Empathy in the Face of Trying Behavior and/or Lack of Progress. The worker who chooses to treat clients with personality disorders may face clinging or distancing and rejecting behaviors, suspiciousness, passive-aggressive attitudes, extreme mood swings, and many other qualities that can test his patience and good humor. Even early on, the client's repetitiveness and the tenacity of rigid defenses and self-defeating behaviors can be frustrating to the worker. The worker can minimize countertherapeutic reactions by remaining aware that the disagreeable qualities are born of fear and despair and usually have little to do with the worker as a person. With very dependent, volatile, or otherwise difficult clients, it is often best to try to help them with short-term goals; if these are achieved, optimism is enhanced and there is less chance that lack of movement will result in angry or disappointed termination. Even when treatment is brief, if it has been successful in achieving its limited purpose, the client is more likely to return if further help is needed later on.

Capacity to Confront One's Own Irrational Reactions and Personal Biases. Although self-awareness is always necessary, for the clinician treating clients with personality disorders it is particularly important. One must be ever on the alert to one's own subjective and possibly countertherapeutic reactions. Displacement of irrational feelings, attitudes, and other unrealistic responses—derived from early or significant experiences—can seriously interfere with the treatment relationship and process. As already indicated, many people who suffer with personality disorders are acutely sensitive, have shaky self-esteem, and will be offended or discouraged by irrelevant worker communications (verbal or nonverbal, overt or covert) that are based on the worker's irrational reactions. By the same token, when working with clients of a different color, background, gender, or sexual orientation, it behooves the social worker to reflect deeply on her own ingrained attitudes and biases derived from family or cultural influences. Self-knowledge about one's own responses to differences can help to resolve or contain them; more accurate empathy for the client necessarily follows when the worker's perceptions are not muddied or skewed by prejudice and distortion (Pinderhughes, 1989).

Family and Group Treatment

Because family interactions can support dysfunctional personality traits or discourage positive changes in the client, either ongoing family therapy or family meetings on behalf of the client seen in individual treatment is an effective approach to facilitating change. Also, since individuals with personality disorders frequently see their problems as functions of the behavior or attitudes of other family members, family treatment may be the preferred method for helping them all to sort out whose thoughts and feelings are whose. This process of differentiation is essential in the treatment of many clients whose self-concepts are not well developed and of those who persistently blame others for their troubles. Sometimes external stresses on families, dysfunctional communication styles, or personal problems of other members are reinforcing feelings of alienation on the part of the client with the personality disorder; these influences are often revealed in the context of family meetings. Accordingly, the worker should have solid grounding in the theory and practice of family therapy. In the initial phase of treatment, decisions about modality are often made. If family therapy is the treatment of choice, it is usually best to begin early on. Otherwise, a client who has been seen over a period of time in individual therapy may feel abandoned by the shift. Family members also may doubt the worker's impartiality if the worker has had a much longer relationship with one member than with the others.

Group therapy has also been found to be very useful in work with clients with personality disorders of various kinds (Freed, 1980; Ormont, 1992; Yalom, 1975). In many instances, such clients are isolated and can get from the group a level of support and mutual understanding that exceeds anything the worker could or should supply. Clients also get an opportunity for feedback and reality testing. Self-centered clients (e.g., many of those with narcissistic or histrionic traits) may begin to enhance their self-esteem when called upon to be more giving and sharing; they may learn more genuine and gratifying ways of relating to others. In my experience, it is often best to wait before suggesting a group experience. Some clients (including many with severe paranoid or avoidant traits) may not be able to tolerate a group until they have been in treatment for a long time, if ever. Some may be too impulsive or abrasive and disrupt the group process or frighten away other members. On the other hand, an occasional client—possibly with a borderline or a schizotypal disorder—is threatened by the face-to-face nature of individual treatment. Some such individuals have benefited from an initial period of group therapy (Strahl, 1980).

In any event, from the first session with a client exhibiting a personality disorder, the possibility of using family or group modalities in conjunction with (or instead of) individual treatment should be considered.

Psychopharmacologic Evaluation and Treatment

For some clients with personality disorders, medication that lifts depression or diminishes anxiety brings relief; the capacity to focus on the work of therapy is often facilitated. On the other hand, many individuals do not benefit at all from drug therapy and even seem to become more symptomatic (e.g., showing increased anxiety or extremely unpleasant side effects). Medication therapy for obessessive-compulsive personality disorders has seen significant advances in recent years. Nevertheless, researchers warn that enthusiasm for the new drugs "must be tempered by the recognition that the relief these medications offer is usually partial at best. Statistically and clinically significant changes in . . . symptomatology rarely reflect full remission" and in a "substantial minority of cases, there is little or no response to these medications" (Klerman, 1994, p. 768). In order to provide the best treatment for people with every type of personality disorder, the social worker needs access to a psychopharmacologist with whom she can work comfortably.

Guidelines

Every person is different. The more quickly a worker finds approaches that suit a particular client, the better the chance of engaging him. For example, many clients with personality disorders (particularly when they are severe) can become very anxious and/or distrustful if the worker is extremely warm, interested, or active or appears to want to get too close to them. On the other hand, the cool, detached, passive stance can arouse feelings of rejection or abandonment. The closeness/distance, active/passive balances most comfortable for the particular client should be determined as quickly as possible.

Often, the risk that negative transference will get out of hand or that the client will sabotage the treatment process can be reduced if attention is paid to these potential problems early. For example, the worker could say, "You may find yourself getting angry or disappointed with me sometimes. It will be very important for our work together if you tell me so. The things that happen right here in the treatment hour between us can be useful in understanding problems that occur for you elsewhere." Resistance and opposition are diminished if the worker enlists the client as an equal in the process of searching for solutions. Clients are helped to take responsibility for any part they may play in interfering with the therapeutic relationship or process.

From the outset, various techniques can be used to establish a therapeutic climate and set the tone for the treatment process. Respect for clients with personality disorders is conveyed not only in traditional ways but also through techniques designed to promote self-awareness, mastery over life and impulses, self-esteem, self-differentiation and self-direction, self-reliance, compassion for oneself, and other ego functions. If interventions suitable to a particular client are discovered early in treatment, progress may be faster and the client's hope for change should be strengthened.

A few sample techniques are illustrated here. They are not all useful in every case, but they do serve to show that, from the start, interventions can bring *focus to the work* and *encourage the participation of the client in the process of change:*

- In the client who assumes that her thoughts or feelings force her to act in particular ways, cognitive functions and the capacity for self-direction and self-control can be promoted by saying, "Perhaps if we both bring our good minds to the job and begin to make sense out of the irrational feelings, you will find that they will not lead you around by the nose as much as they seem to now."
- In the client who has frequent rages, hope for control and respect for the client's distress can be conveyed by saying, "We may find that your anger reflects some kind of fear or sadness about yourself or your life that we can work together to try to understand."
- In the client who feels furious at, or devastated by, the disapproval or insult of another, the sense of autonomy and the development of a more consistent self-concept can be supported by saying, "Do you ever wish you gave more credence to your own view of yourself than to the views of others?" Or, "Do you wish you were less sensitive to other people's opinions?"
- In the client who shows pessimism, distrust, or negativism, or who challenges the worker or the treatment process, the fear of intrusion can be quelled and initiative encouraged by saying, "There is no rush, but when you feel comfortable enough I would like it if you could tell me in what ways you think I can be most helpful to you." Or, "In the long run, you will be the best judge of whether you are getting the help you need here."
- In the client who is harshly self-critical or who whines about never doing things right, the capacity for "self-soothing" (Blanck & Blanck, 1979) can be nurtured by saying, "You sound awfully angry at yourself about something that already hurts so much. How come?"
- In the client who seems ready to begin to shed some maladaptive patterns, this readiness can be fostered by saying, "Do you think it is as important as it used to be for you to feel so diffident (distrustful, afraid of others, hard on yourself, responsible for your adult children's lives, etc.)?"

Ongoing, Intensive Treatment with the Personality-Disordered Client

Setting

For some clients with personality disorders who, for various reasons, cannot or will not engage in long-term treatment, short-term or crisis intervention approaches may be beneficial. These therapies should be valued by the social worker as much as any other type of treatment. However, if clients interested in making basic changes approach an agency that is not equipped to provide intensive, ongoing treatment, appropriate referrals should be sought. Personality shifts take time—often years of treatment. Unfortunately, there may be no family agencies or clinics available to serve such clients; private practitioners may have to make themselves available for clients requiring long-term treatment, even for those who cannot pay full fees. In the face of agency constraints, managed care restrictions, and other impediments to service delivery, it is our professional obligation as social workers to do all we can to advocate for changes that allow us to make treatment decisions based on *need*. Social work's commitment to serve all groups compels workers to press for adequate treatment facilities and to use sliding scales so that first-class treatment is available to all who want it.

Methods and Goals

About 40 years ago, Reiner (a social worker) and Kaufman (a psychiatrist) wrote (Reiner & Kaufman, 1959) about four stages of treatment for clients with personality disorders: establishing a relationship; ego building through identification with the caseworker; self-understanding of behavior and its roots in the past; and separation from the caseworker. Even earlier, Austin (1948) had written about the "corrective" casework relationship and "experiential" treatment. Others have expanded this concept: In short, the client's transference expectations of unsatisfactory "parenting" in the treatment relationship are corrected in the context of the worker's acceptance and ability to understand and empathize; in some cases, reparative experiences such as these can result in significant emotional, internal structural, and enduring changes. Of course, the worker simultaneously makes inquiries and offers explanations and tentative interpretations that help the client reflect on her behaviors, present situation, past life, and future hopes; in a healing relationship, the client is helped to take active charge of her life and situation (Beck & Freeman, 1990; Woods & Hollis, 1990).

Elaborations on the theory of the structure and organization of personality disorders are continually emerging. Yet current viewpoints on treatment of clients with deficits stemming from inadequate early parenting (or caregiver–child incompatibility) have much in common with social work notions of years ago. Writing about the borderline personality, but using concepts that can be applied to treatment of full range of personality disorders, Freed (1980) defined three phases of long-term treatment:

"(1) the testing phase, in which establishment of a working alliance takes place; (2) the working-through phase (by far the longest) which includes especially resolution of the underlying depression; and (3) the separation and establishment of a constructive life direction" (p. 554). Giovacchini (1975) said that the analyst's interpretations demonstrate her ability "to understand and pull together what to the patient was disparate, frightening and unknown. This integrative activity, analogous to the mother's understanding of the child's needs, leads to ego structuralization" (p. 276). Blanck and Blanck (1979) discussed the "reparative emotional experience": "Where the patient lived, as a child, in a 'climate' that failed to encourage ego apparatuses, the therapist provides or helps the patient provide a more favorable or conducive climate. Then the cognitive and emotional capacities combine to make interpretation usable" (p. 118). In her book on borderline disorders, Goldstein (1990) is very clear in her belief that "the revival of stunted needs in transference, which are understood and responded to with empathy, and the repair of whatever disruptions occur, result in transmuting internalizations that give patients a second chance to complete their development and to attain more self-cohesion" (p. 157).

Long-term treatment, then, takes place in the context of a corrective or reparative relationship; trust is nurtured so that healing and growth can proceed. Therapy is an intricate process that varies considerably in accordance with the qualities of both client and therapist. There are no blueprints. Usually no single insight or technique will produce dazzling results or even immediate effects. Rather, the accumulation of therapeutic interactions, along withn the repetitiveness and consistency of the approach, slowly (but often surely) results in progress and even in substantial change. The following methods and goals have been related to the successful long-term treatment of clients with various types of personality disorders.

Emphasis on Collaboration and Mutuality. Active participation by the client in the treatment process is, as psychosocial clinicians see it, not only ethical and respectful, but the most effective way to help clients get relief from initial distress, and to carve out goals and plans for reaching them (Woods & Hollis, 1990). From the beginning, the worker's genuine excitement about the prospect of the joint therapeutic process—devoted to reaching understandings and searching for solutions—can reduce client resistance, build trust, and enhance motivation. Needless to say, even though the worker promotes a climate of equality, this does not mean that he does not bring specialized knowledge to the work. Worker and client are both experts in their own right; they share responsibility for the direction treatment takes. Diagnostic skills help the worker to assess the client's condition; experience and knowledge guide the choice of treatment procedures and approaches. However, it is only the clients who can know how vulnerable or distressed they feel, what their visions are, and what changes in their situations or inner lives they are seeking.

Of course, as Beck and Freeman (1990)—who strongly endorse the concept of collaboration—point out, it is usually the therapist's job to convert and translate the broad or vaguely stated aspirations stated by the client ("I can't go on feeling this way") or patterned assumptions ("if I don't get a perfect test score it will mean I failed") into a realistic approach. (For example, to this client the clinician might ask: "Do you think your need never to err contributes to the way you feel?" And: "Do you wish that you could make a mistake and still feel like a worthwhile person? What are your thoughts about this?") In any event, a collaborative partnership (often better faciliated by questions posed to the client than by interpretations) not only invites participation and promotes motivation, but also usually strengthens ego functions such as thought processes, reality testing, judgment, competence, and autonomy—all of which will be important in helping clients take charge of their lives and maintain an improved quality of life long after treatment ends.

Promotion of Realistic Self-Awareness or Self-Observation. As already indicated, interventions designed to help clients reflect on themselves, their feelings, their patterns of thought and behavior, and their past lives often begin immediately. These same measures are repeated over and over throughout the treatment process. One of the first of many benefits that can come from self-observation early in treatment is the ability to begin to evaluate one's own emotional and behavioral patterns. It then becomes possible for the client to determine which are functional and which interfere with personal and interpersonal satisfaction. The notion that the client is totally at the mercy of outside forces begins to dissolve and motivation to make changes *from within* emerges. *Self-awareness is encouraged by questions*—sympathetically posed and sensitively timed—asked in one form or another over and over again. For example, "Are you hoping to become less frightened when your father get angry?" Or, "Do you think your daughter will feel like confiding in you, as you wish her to, when you call her names?" Gently posed inquiries can have the result that gradually dysfunctional patterns become ego alien and thus are viewed as intrusions.

Encouragement and Reinforcement of Cognitive Capacity. Throughout the treatment experience, generalizations such as "Nobody likes me," "My husband never compliments me," "If I weren't so stupid I would be making more money than I am," "The nicer I am, the more abuse I get," or, "My mother understands me better than I understand myself," are, in one way or another (with an eye to appropriate timing), questioned and examined. For many clients with personality disorders, confidence in being able to think for themselves and to figure out the world around them often needs bolstering. On one level or another, they frequently believe that *other* people are experts on their own experiences. Explanations and interpretations may be offered by the worker to help make sense out of chaotic thoughts and feelings, but every effort is made to encourage clients to begin to challenge and correct their own misconceptions and refine their own thinking.

Fostering the Capacity for Differentiation. As cognitive abilities and the relationship with the worker are strengthened, the issue of differentiation often becomes a major focus of treatment with clients with personality disorders. Frequently, such clients have difficulty *distinguishing between their feelings and their thoughts* or *between feelings and reality.* For example, a client who is rarely late for appointments may rush in five minutes after the hour and say, "I *know* you are angry that I am late," to which the worker may reply, "Are you *afraid* that I am angry or do you *think* that I am angry?" Similarly, a client may say, "If that kid disobeys me one more time, I may break his arm," to which the worker may ask, "Is it that you *feel* that you want to hurt him or that you *think* that you really will? Do you know which it is?" Techniques such as this, repeated over time, help the client learn to differentiate between feelings that are aroused by particular circumstances and what the client knows to be true. Interestingly, once better differentiation is achieved, there is greater integration between thoughts and feelings; unmanageable emotions no longer so readily flood the intellect.

Differentiating among feelings can be perplexing for many clients with personality disorders. Their emotions are often experienced in amorphous, global terms. Rage, emptiness, or general depressive feelings frequently dominate the inner lives of such clients. In conjunction with increased self-esteem and self-understanding that come in other ways, techniques that help clients distinguish one feeling from another become important ego-building measures. For example, "When you say you 'feel terrible,' do you mean you feel sad, scared, guilty, or what?"

Other clients—including many with paranoid disorders—tend to report and manifest predominantly irritable or hostile feelings. In the context of a solid relationship, the worker may gently probe, when indicated, for "softer" feelings: "Do you think you were disappointed when you were turned down for the job?" Or, "Were you afraid to show your wife how touched you were by her concern for you?" On the other hand, clients with avoidant or dependent personality disorders may be filled primarily with feelings of sadness or fear. In these cases, the worker can help the client search for other emotions. With a client who has been crying for hours over a friend's unfounded accusation, the worker might ask, "Do you think you were mad, as well as sad, about what happened?"

Sometimes, through identification with a worker capable of a range of emotional expression, the client begins to internalize this example and differentiate feelings more precisely. Usually, to avoid the possibility of having clients feel misunderstood, the worker recognizes that the predominant feeling states (anger, sadness, fear) are understandable outgrowths of unhappy past experiences (of which most such clients have had more than a fair share); however, clients can also be helped to realize that now more possibilities may be open to them, including the opportunity to enjoy pleasurable feelings—rarely felt by some clients.

In my experience, the encouragement of exhaustive ventilation of anger, sadness, fear, or any other characteristic emotion is usually counterproductive; more often than not, the client ends up feeling worse and becomes more regressed. While *always* acknowledging the validity of the feelings, the worker may be able to help the client use growing self-awareness and reasoning abilities to wonder, for example, why he got angry or sad in response to a loving gesture from another. Even severely impaired clients frequently can link present reactions to past (often childhood) experiences. Other sample interventions might be: "Are those tears of sadness or of pleasure?" "Do you think you have gotten into the habit of showing (feeling) anger because you are afraid you will get hurt if you express warm (or sad, frightened, disappointed, etc.) feelings?" "Do you ever wonder what would make you respond to an insult with a smile?" "Was it anger you were feeling or do you think you were feeling self-conscious about being assertive or expressing a difference of opinion to me (your husband, wife, mother, etc.)?"

Sometimes, efforts to develop a sense of identity can both outwardly and inwardly resemble anger. Just as the infant and the adolescent may seem angry and negative when they are struggling to gain age-appropriate independence, some aggressive feelings in adult clients reflect efforts toward growth, rather than hostility. Interpreting them in this way can be extremely helpful to the client. Family meetings also can help clients learn to differentiate one emotion from another and to develop a broader emotional range.

Distinguishing one person's feelings and thoughts from those of others can be problematic in families in which members are excessively dependent on one another. The boundaries of the individual personalities may be so diffuse that one member may say, "I know Jane's feelings better than she does," or "Joe says he is not angry but I know he is." In family therapy, the worker may suggest that family members ask one another about feelings. By exposing and challenging projections, distortions, and inaccurate assumptions, the worker encourages individuation. In individual treatment also, as illustrated earlier, transference reactions to the worker can be helpful in differentiating the client's feelings from the worker's. When the client was five minutes late and thought the worker was angry, the worker pointed out that these were not necessarily her feelings but perhaps related to the frightened feelings of the client, who expected to be scolded for being late. Similarly, clients often believe that the worker wants either to possess and exploit them or to throw them out in the cold. Obviously, the therapeutic relationship provides the client with a nonthreatening forum in which to learn to identify projections, unrealistic perceptions, and reactions.

Nurturance of Self-Compassion. Clients with personality disorders are sometimes harshly self-critical and unforgiving about their mistakes, real or imagined. They may feel guilty about not living up to unrealistic expectations placed upon them by others; often, assumptions are made about expectations that are not true. Separation and individuation, for most clients with personality disorders, represents a major area of unfinished business. Frequently, therefore, there is a tendency to assume (not always consciously) that others will resent, be hurt by, or ridicule their assertive or independent moves. In the treatment relationship, then, self-criticism or guilt about not living up to the projected expectations of the worker can be exposed and clients often begin to be gentler with themselves. A worker may ask, "Can you think about ways in which you may want to change without being so intolerant of your past or present behavior (feelings, thoughts, etc.)?" Even when interventions are not immediately successful in helping a client become self-comforting, an accumulation of such experiences eventually may be internalized.

Not only is self-compassion in the here and now beneficial, but also it is often helpful to clients who are self-critical about current behavior to begin to cultivate sympathy for themselves regarding past events. For example, "Do you ever feel sad for that little girl who had to spend so much time alone?" Or, "Can you be more understanding of the child who felt confused for so many of those years?" Blanck & Blanck (1979) noted: "Self esteem can probably never be created by means of external confrontation." This is not entirely true in my view. We are in agreement, however, that "when the angry and provocative behavior can be understood and explained in its very formative processes, retrospective self empathy will produce a more positively cathected sense of self" (p. 251).

It should be emphasized that I do *not* recommend encouragement of feelings of helplessness and self-pity. Nor do I suggest that clients be urged to blame their parents; actually, when clients can feel more compassion toward themselves, they can bring more understanding (and sometimes even deeply loving feelings) to their relationships with their parents. The purpose of this approach is to facilitate the development of self-nurturing mechanisms, which can help eliminate the client's negative self-image; as self-esteem increases, heavy reliance on external influences diminishes.

Healing the Split. As discussed earlier, clients with a variety of personality disorders often divide their thoughts and feelings about external events, other people, and themselves into all good and all bad compartments; there are often rapid shifts from one extreme to the other and what was all good can become all bad in a matter of moments. This separation of affects and attitudes requires constant attention in treatment sessions. For example, a man with a histrionic disorder may rant about hating his son and have to be reminded that only the other day (or a few minutes earlier) he spoke very proudly and warmly about the boy. The worker might ask whether it is possible that he is very annoyed by the boy but cares about him at the same time. "Good and bad feelings can coexist" is a reminder that may startle some clients and initially make them very anxious. However, when confronted over and over again with the safety of the merger, they often learn to synthesize extremes.

Clients differ in the tenacity of their denial of the emotional connection between good and bad ego states. For some, the ability to integrate positive and negative feelings and experiences seems to be just below the surface, and tolerance for their coexistence can be achieved relatively quickly. For others, the splitting process is so entrenched that even years of treatment will fail to produce a truly comfortable synthesis.

Two notes of caution might be added here regarding the treatment relationship and the splitting mechanism:

First, for some clients, the worker may be a frequent target of bad feelings. The management of countertransference complications evoked by the client's angry attitudes and projections can become an important aspect of work with clients with personality disorders. Usually, but not always, empathic understanding of the client's defense against anxiety can prevent the worker from feeling like counterattacking or withdrawing concern. When clients are particularly difficult or when the worker for one reason or another feels vulnerable, supervision or consultation with colleagues can help the therapist regain his lost perspective. Even the most skilled and experienced workers can be provoked to react negatively under certain conditions.

Second, it is not unusual for clients with severe personality disorders consistently to idealize or adore the worker even when they manifest extreme fluctuations of feelings in other areas of life. For many months or longer, the all-good feeling for the worker seems to be necessary; this unrealistic but positive attachment may nurture some clients during the early phases of treatment, in some way making up for deficits derived from faulty parent–child connections. Of course, it is always wise to let the client know that there is a possibility that she may feel—possibly suddenly—angered by or disappointed in the worker at some time; these potential reactions should be seen by worker and client alike as providing grist for the mill in treatment. In some instances, however, it may be counterproductive to treatment to press too hard to disabuse the client of idealized feelings for the worker. In due time, as treatment progresses, realistic and balanced reactions will replace the exaggerated attachment.

Support of a Sense of Continuity. Closely connected to the often prolonged process of mending the split is the reinforcement of a sense of continuity in feelings, attitudes, and experiences. In the benign, reliable climate of the therapeutic relationship, the client with impaired object relations may begin to bring into awareness the memory that a caring person is available—even when that person is absent. Clients can be helped to develop the capacity for trust or optimism, even in the face of minor upsets, by being confronted with their overdetermined reactions. For example, "Because your boss was angry with you, you were convinced you were going to be fired even though the day before he praised your work and recommended you for a raise." Or to a man who says he fears that his wife will leave him, "It seems hard for you to get the benefit of the fact that only last week your wife said that the best move she ever made was to marry you. How do you account for such a short emotional memory?"

Encouragement of Individuation. Strong defenses against separation and individuation have been powerful influences in the lives of many people with personality disorders (Masterson, 1976). For example, an adult living with parents or with siblings may function reasonably well until there is some forced disruption. Certain well-structured and secure employment situations can conceal a person's underlying fear of autonomy. Many clients first come into treatment when there has been a shift in the external situation: the parents die or the factory relocates, generating anxiety or depression. By the same token, during the course of treatment, as clients move toward independent goals of their own choosing, separation fears and abandonment depression may emerge. As defenses (e.g., schizoid or compulsive patterns, splitting, denial, projection) weaken and moves are made toward independence and more satisfying (either less clinging or less remote) relationships, some clients may seem to regress. Even after a period of apparent progress, such reversals can occur. (On the other hand, some clients are able to shed maladaptive patterns with few, if any, interim negative consequences.) When depression or anxiety do occur, gentle and consistent understanding and reassurance are required. Explanations about what is happening are essential and can be greatly comforting. For example, to a young woman who recently moved from her parents' home, the worker might say, "It's no wonder that you are feeling scared now. Even though you and your mother fought a lot, you two lived as though you were one. It's probably going to feel frighteningly lonely sometimes for a while until you begin to enjoy your new freedom."

Some clients will react to their moves forward by trying to cling to the worker; frequent telephone calls, requests for additional appointments, and difficulty leaving at the end of a session are familiar clinging behaviors. Patience is necessary, of course, but so is individual assessment of the client's need for additional support; either too much or too little can hamper progress.

Repetitive Positive Reinforcement. When clients develop greater self-understanding, make significant (even if not always immediately successful) efforts toward change, reach important decisions, or provide themselves with new or more constructive life experiences, reinforcement is essential. Statements of general support—"You seem to be feeling better recently," or "You certainly look well," or "You have many fine qualities"—are of limited value, at best, but remarks that are specifically directed to the person and the situation can be extremely bolstering. For example, to a woman who knows she is working below capacity because of fear of greater responsibility and autonomy and yet wants to make changes, the worker might say, "It must have taken a lot of courage to apply for that promotion when it could mean being transferred to a new and unfamiliar department. Good for you!" Or to a woman who was feeling like a prisoner in her own home because her mother insisted on visiting every day and the daughter was too afraid of her mother's anger to set limits, "You must have been feeling more confident about yourself when you told your mother you wouldn't be at home as often this summer." Over and over again, appropriately timed comments such as "You really did a good job on that, didn't you?" or "Are you proud of yourself for working out that problem so well?" contribute to positive self-esteem and encourage clients to begin to reinforce their own choices and changes.

Leaving Room for Disagreement. Explanations, suggestions, or interpretations offered by the worker are often best framed in a way that makes disagreement possible and shows that it is encouraged. As illustrated numerous times in this chapter, it is often best if remarks are put in the form of questions—e.g., "Do you think when your mother died you were so young that you had to put your feelings away in order to find the heart to go on?" "Do you think you still tend to avoid emotions, even though you are now mature and strong enough to handle them?" Or, at the end of a comment or interpretation, one may add: "Does it seem that way to you?" "How do you see it?" This does not mean that the worker negates her own expertise or objectivity about a particular situation. For clients with personality disorders, there must be confidence that the worker knows what he is doing. However, therapeutic goals are supported if the worker offers ideas with a built-in opportunity for the client to refute them. This is so for several interrelated reasons: client autonomy is fostered by the worker's expectation that the client may have a different or better notion; the client is not encouraged to be dependent on the worker for the last word; the client is urged to search for insight and understanding from within; worker–client collaboration is reinforced; the worker may be under a misapprehension that only the client can correct; and the tendency of some clients to get stuck in oppositional resistance is neutralized.

CONCLUSION

This chapter may best be concluded with the reminder that individuals with personality disorders—even those with similar clinical diagnoses—are often very different from one another. Intelligence; motivation and capacity for self-awareness and change; creativity; talents; values; and sense of humor are among the strengths that vary from person to person and that appear in countless combinations. Similarly, maladaptive patterns or defenses vary both in degree and in flexibility.

Broadly speaking, psychosocial treatment is designed to build self-esteem, to repair developmental deficits, to promote self-differentiation, and to help clients learn new ways of mastering their lives. In some cases, the worker may have to be extremely active and reach out; in other instances, clients do a great deal of their own work in the context of a caring relationship. Some make remarkable progress; others—including some who try hard to change—seem tragically stuck and make only modest improvements. Perhaps as our knowledge about the treatment of personality disorders continues to expand, the size of this latter group will shrink.

REFERENCES

American Psychiatric Association. (1952). *Diagnostic and statistical manual of mental disorders.* Washington, DC: Author.

American Psychiatric Association. (1968). *Diagnostic and statistical manual of mental disorders, second edition.* Washington, DC: Author.

American Psychiatric Association. (1980). *Diagnostic and statistical manual of mental disorders, third edition.* Washington, DC: Author.

American Psychiatric Association. (1987). *Diagnostic and statistical manual of mental disorders, third edition—revised.* Washington, DC: Author.

American Psychiatric Association. (1994). *Diagnostic and statistical manual of mental disorders, fourth edition.* Washington, DC: Author.

Arieti, S. (1974). *Interpretation of schizophrenia* (2nd Ed.). New York: Basic Books.

Austin, L. (1948). Trends in differential treatment in social casework. *Journal of Social Casework, 29,* 203–211.

Beck, A. T., & Freeman, A. (1990). *Cognitive therapy of personality disorders.* New York: Guilford Press.

Bellak, L., et al. (1973). *Ego functions in schizophrenics, neurotics, and normals.* New York: Wiley.

Blanck, G., & Blanck, R. (1974). *Ego psychology.* New York: Columbia University Press.

Blanck, G., & Blanck, R. (1979). *Ego psychology II.* New York: Columbia University Press.

Blitzer, J. (1978). Diagnosis and treatment of borderline personality organization. *Clinical Social Work Journal, 6,* 100–107.

Bowen, M. (1977). The use of family therapy in clinical practice. In J. Haley (Ed.). *Changing families: A family therapy reader.* New York: Grune & Stratton.

Bowlby, J. (1969). *Attachment and loss.* Vol. 1. New York: Basic Books.

Bowlby, J. (1973). *Attachment and loss.* Vol. 2. New York: Basic Books.

Boyer, L. B., & Giovacchini, P. L. (1967). *Psychoanalytic treatment of characterological and schizophrenic disorders.* New York: Science House.

Cameron, N. (1963). *Personality development and psychopathology.* Boston: Houghton Mifflin.

Chessick, R. D. (1985). *Psychology of the self and the treatment of narcissism.* New York: Jason Aronson.

Clark, K. R. (1996). The nowhere (wo)man: an example of the defensive use of emptiness in a patient with a schizoid disorder of the self. *Clinical Social Work Journal,* 24, 153–166.

Compton, B. R., & Galaway, R. (Eds). (1994). *Social work processes* (5th Ed.). Pacific Grove, CA: Brooks/Cole.

Cooper, J., & Maxwell, N. (1995). The search for a primary object: making and breaking in the treatment of narcissism. In J. Cooper & N. Maxwell (Eds.). *Narcissistic wounds.* New York: Jason Aronson.

Cowger, C. D. (1994). Assessing client strengths: Clinical assessment for client empowerment. *Social Work, 39,* 262–268.

Fenichel, O. (1945). *The psychoanalytic theory of neurosis.* New York: Norton.

Erikson, E. H. (1950). *Childhood and society.* New York: Norton.

Freed, A. O. (1980). The border line personality. *Journal of Social Casework, 61,* 548–558.

Freud, A. (1946). *The ego and the mechanisms of defense.* New York: International Universities Press.

Freud, S. (1953a). Character and anal eroticism. In J. Strachey (Ed.), *Standard edition of the complete psychological works of Sigmund Freud.* Vol. 9. London, Hogarth.

Freud, S. (1953b). On narcissism: an introduction. In J. Strachey (Ed.), *Standard edition of the complete psychological works of Sigmund Freud.* Vol. 14. London, Hogarth.

Fromm, E. (1947). *Man for himself.* New York: Holt, Rinehart, and Winston.

Fromm, E. (1973). *The anatomy of human destructiveness.* New York: Holt, Rinehart, and Winston.

Germain, C. B. (Ed.). (1979). *Social work practice.* New York: Columbia University Press.

Giovacchini, P. (Ed.). (1975). *Psychoanalysis of character disorders.* New York: Jason Aronson.

Goldstein, E. (1990). *Borderline disorders: Clinical models and techniques.* New York: Guilford Press.

Goldstein, E. (1995). *Ego psychology and social work practice* (2nd Ed.). New York: Free Press.

Guntrip, H. (1961). *Personality structure and human interaction.* New York: International Universities Press.

Guntrip, H. (1971). *Psychoanalytic theory, therapy and the self.* New York: Basic Books.

Gyarfas, M. G. (1980). A systems approach to diagnosis. In J. Mishne (Ed.). *Psychotherapy and training in clinical social work.* New York: Gardner Press.

Hartmann, H. (1958). *Ego psychology and the problem of adaptation.* New York: International Universities Press.

Hoch, P., & Polatin, P. (1949). Pseudoneurotic form of schizophrenia. *Psychiatric Quarterly 23,* 248–276.

Hollis, F. (1970). The psychosocial approach to the practice of casework. In R. Roberts & R. Nee (Eds.). *Theories of social casework* (pp. 33–75). Chicago: University of Chicago Press.

Horney, K. (1939). *New ways in psychoanalysis.* New York: Norton.

Horney, K. (1945). *Our inner conflicts.* New York: Norton.

Jackel, M. M. (1975). Personality disorders. In G. H. Wiedeman (Ed.), *Personality development and deviation.* New York: International Universities Press.

Jackson, D. D. (1968). *Human communication.* 2 vols. Palo Alto, CA: Science and Behavior Books.

Kallman, F. J. (1946). The genetic theory of schizophrenia: An analysis of 691 schizophrenic twin index families. *American Journal of Psychiatry, 98,* 544–550.

Kernberg, O. (1975). *Borderline conditions and pathological narcissism.* New York: Jason Aronson.

Kernberg, O. (1977). Structural change. In P. Hartocollis (Ed.). *Borderline personality disorders*. New York: International Universities Press.

Klerman, G. L., et al. (1994). Medication and psychotherapy. In A. E. Bergin & S. L. Garfield (Eds.). *Handbook of psychotherapy and behavior change*. New York: Wiley.

Kohut, H. (1971). *The analysis of the self*. New York: International Universities Press.

Lasch, C. (1978). *The culture of narcissism*. New York: Norton.

Lidz, T. (1968). *The person: His development throughout the life cycle*. New York: Basic Books.

Loewenstein, S. (1977). An overview of the concept of narcissism. *Social Casework*, *58*, 136–142.

Mahler, M. S. (1975). *The psychological birth of the human*. New York: Basic Books.

Masterson, J. F. (1976). *Psychology of the borderline adult*. New York: Brunner/Mazel.

Masterson, J. F. (1981). *The narcissistic and borderline disorders*. New York: Brunner-Mazel.

Meyer, C. (1976). *Social work practice*. New York: Free Press.

Millon, T. (1996). *Disorders of personality: DSM-IV and beyond*. New York: Wiley.

Minuchin, S. (1974). *Families and family therapy*. Cambridge, MA: Harvard University Press.

Morrison, A. P. (1989). *Shame: The underside of narcissism*. Hillsdale, NJ: Analytic Press.

Murphy, L. B., & Moriarty, A. E. (1976). *Vulnerability, coping, and growth*. New Haven, CT: Yale University Press.

Ormont, L. R. (1992). *The group therapy experience*. New York: St. Martin's.

Palumbo, J. (1976). Theories of narcissism and the practice of clinical social work. *Clinical Social Work Journal, 4*, 147–161.

Paolino, T. J., Jr. (1981). *Psychoanalytic psychotherapy*. New York: Brunner-Mazel.

Perlman, H. H. (1957). *Social casework: A problem-solving process*. Chicago: University of Chicago Press.

Pinderhughes, E. (1989). *Understanding race, ethnicity, and power*. New York: Free Press.

Powers, H. P. (1972). Psychotherapy for hysterical individuals. *Social Casework, 53*, 435–440.

Rapaport, D. (1958). Theory of ego autonomy: A generalization. *Bulletin of the Menninger Clinic, 22*, 13–35.

Reich, W. (1949). *Character analysis* (3rd Ed.). New York: Farrar, Straus & Giroux, 1949.

Reiner, B. S. (1979). A feeling of irrelevance: The effects of a nonsupportive society. *Social Casework, 60*, 3–10.

Reiner, B. S., & Kaufman, I. (1959). *Character disorders in parents of delinquents*. New York: Family Service Association of America.

Rice, C. F. (1980). Marital treatment with narcissistic character disorders. In J. Mishne (Ed.). *Psychotherapy and training in clinical social work*. New York: Gardner Press.

Richmond, M. (1917). *Social Diagnosis*. New York: Russell Sage.

Satir, V. (1983). *Conjoint family therapy* (3rd Ed.). Palo Alto, CA: Science and Behavior Books.

Spitz R. A. (1965). *The first year of life*. New York: International Universities Press.

Stanton, A. H. (1978). Personality disorders. In A. M. Nicholi (Ed.). *The Harvard guide to modern psychiatry*. Cambridge, MA: Belknap Press of Harvard University Press.

Stern, D. (1985). *The interpersonal world of the infant*. New York: Basic Books.

Strahl, M. O. (1980). *Masked schizophrenia*. New York: Springer.

Thomas, A., & Chess, S. (1977). *Temperament and development*. New York: Brunner/Mazel.

Towle, C. (1957). *Common human needs.* New York: National Association of Social Workers.

Truax, C. B., & Carkhuff, R. R. (1967). *Toward effective counseling and psychotherapy: Training and practice.* Chicago: Aldine de Gruyter.

Turner, F. J. (1978). *Psychosocial therapy.* New York: Free Press.

Weick, A., et al. (1989). A strengths perspective for social work practice. *Social Work, 34,* 350–354.

Weick, A., & Saleeby, D. (1995). Supporting family strengths: Orienting policy and practice toward the 21st century. *Families in Society, 76,* 141–149.

Winnicott, D. W. (1965). Clinical study of the failure of an average expectable environment on the child's mental functioning. *International Journal of Psychoanalysis, 46,* 235–236.

Woods, M. E., & Hollis, F. (1990). *Casework: A psychosocial therapy.* New York: McGraw-Hill.

Woods, M., & Robinson, H. (1996). Psychosocial theory and social work treatment. In F. J. Turner (Ed.) *Social work treatment* (4th Ed.). New York: Free Press.

Yalom I. D. (1975). *The theory and practice of group psychotherapy.* New York: Basic Books.

Zilboorg, G. (1941). Ambulatory schizophrenia. *Psychiatry, 4,* 149–155.

17

BORDERLINE PERSONALITY DISORDER

Harriette C. Johnson

People who meet diagnostic criteria for borderline personality disorder (BPD) present for services in almost every type of social work practice setting. Typical presenting problems are suicide attempts and gestures, family violence, substance abuse, eating disorders, reckless spending, and other problems of self-control. Social workers act therapeutically with persons with BPD not only when they are designated "therapist" but also in the roles of case manager or advocate (Goldstein, 1983; Johnson, 1988, 1991; Heller & Northcut, 1996).

Clients with BPD are widely recognized as being difficult and frustrating to work with because of characteristics such as intense hostile-dependent feelings toward the practitioner, overidealization of the social worker alternating with rageful disappointment, suicidal or otherwise violent behaviors, impulsivity and recklessness, and the tendency to terminate treatment abruptly and prematurely when painful issues arise (Stone, 1994; Kaplan & Sadock, 1998).

CHARACTERISTICS

DSM-IV criteria (Table 17–1) have been used throughout the United States, with plans to use the *International Classification of Diseases (ICD-10)* by the year 2000. Moderate support for validity of *DSM-IV* criteria for BPD was found in an evaluation of content validity, related to three domains: affective instability, impulsivity, and interpersonal and identity instability (Blais, et al., 1997). Some writers advocate broader inclusion for people in this diagnostic category (Kernberg, 1984), a dimensional rather than a categorical approach to diagnosis (Tuinier & Verhoeven,

1995; Stone, 1994), or regrouping the nine criteria in Table 17–1 into a different set of characteristics (Linehan, 1993). A dimensional approach identifies all characteristics of an individual's profile, emphasizing specific symptoms or characteristics such as self-mutilation and dissociation, rather than including or excluding people from a diagnosis based on a list of criteria.

Some scholars emphasize certain criteria over others. For example, Cowdry (1997), using research diagnostic criteria, requires the presence of self-injurious behavior for an individual to qualify for the diagnosis, whereas *DSM-IV* requires at least five of nine characteristics which may or may not include self-injurious behavior (Table 17-1).

Table 17–1   Diagnostic Criteria for Borderline Personality Disorder

A pervasive pattern of instability of interpersonal relationships, self-image, and affects, and marked impulsivity by early adulthood and present in a variety of contexts, as indicated by five (or more) of the following:

(1)   frantic efforts to avoid real or imagined abandonment. Note: do not include suicidal or self-mutilating behavior covered in criterion 5.

(2)   a pattern of unstable and intense interpersonal relationships characterized by alternating between extremes of idealization and devaluation

(3)   identity disturbance: markedly and persistently unstable self-image or sense of self

(4)   impulsivity in at least two areas that are potentially self-damaging (e.g., spending, sex, substance abuse, reckless driving, binge eating) Note: do not include suicidal or self-mutilating behavior covered in criterion 5.

(5)   recurrent suicidal behavior, gestures, or threats, or self-mutilating behavior

(6)   affective instability due to a marked reactivity of mood (e.g., intense episodic dysphoria, irritability, or anxiety lasting a few hours and only rarely more than a few days)

(7)   chronic feelings of emptiness

(8)   inappropriate, intense anger or difficulty controlling anger (e.g., frequent displays of temper, constant anger, recurrent physical fights)

(9)   transient, stress-related paranoid ideation or severe dissociative symptoms

Source: Reprinted with permission from the *Diagnostic and Statistical Manual of Mental Disorders, Fourth Edition.* Washington, DC, American Psychiatric Association, 1994.

Linehan (1993) sees psychic dysregulation as the core disorder. She has rearranged *DSM-IV* criteria into five rather than nine characteristics: (1) emotional dysregulation (emotional responses that are highly reactive to stimuli), including episodes of depression, anxiety, irritability, and anger; (2) interpersonal dysregulation, characterized by fear of abandonment and chaotic, intense, difficult relationships; (3) behavioral dysregulation (extreme problematic impulsivity seen in profligate spending, indiscriminate sex, binge eating, self-mutilation, reckless driving, or suicide attempts); (4) cognitive dysregulation (brief nonpsychotic depersonalization, delusion, or dissociation); and (5) dysregulation of the self (feelings of emptiness and problems with self-identity).

Other salient characteristics are intolerance of aloneness (Gunderson, 1996), low levels of emotional awareness, inability to coordinate positive and negative feelings, poor accuracy in recognizing facial expressions of emotion, and intense responses to negative emotions (Levine, et al., 1997).

Almost all observers, no matter what their preferred ideologies, agree that *highly variable mood* (extreme fluctuations in emotion) and *impulsive behavior* (e.g., overdoses, self-injury, other violent acts, and outbursts of rage) are two features that characterize most people with BPD and distinguish them from other, often overlapping, *DSM-IV* personality disorders (Cowdry, 1997). There is agreement that the self-destructive behaviors often engaged in by people with BPD, such as cutting or burning themselves or attempting suicide, are very effective in alleviating psychic pain, especially anxiety and anger (Linehan, 1993). These behaviors also are effective at regulating the environment (for example, by getting others to admit the person with BPD to a hospital or otherwise to express concern and caring).

Because their pain is extreme, people with BPD may engage repeatedly in self-destructive behavior as they learn that it reduces pain. It is not yet known how this mechanism works, but various theories have been proposed to explain it. Studies comparing persons with BPD who experience pain during self-injury with those who do not suggest that analgesia (not feeling physical pain) is related to neurosensory and attitudinal/psychological abnormalities, to cognitive impairment in the ability to distinguish pain, and/or to dissociative mechanisms (Russ, et al., 1996; Kemperman, et al., 1997).

EPIDEMIOLOGY

There are no precise data on the prevalence of BPD, but it is thought to be present in about 1–2% of the population. First-degree relatives of persons with BPD have a higher prevalence than average of major depression and substance use disorders (Kaplan & Sadock, 1998). In contrast with other personality and psychiatric disorders, persons meeting *DSM* criteria for BPD were found in a meta-analysis ($N = 783$) to have significantly higher educational achievement and younger age (Taub, 1996). Differences by race or ethnicity have not been demonstrated, although most recent studies have been based on small samples of subsets of persons meeting criteria for BPD (Grilo, Walker, et al., 1997; Else, et al., 1993; Snyder, et al., 1985).

BPD is estimated to be twice as frequent in females as in males (Kaplan & Sadock, 1998). Cowdry (1997) questions these differences in prevalence by gender, postulating that males with BPD often are in jail and remain undiagnosed, so that the 2:1 ratio overstates prevalence in females as compared to males. Grilo, Becker, et al. (1996) found that among 138 consecutively admitted adolescents, females were significantly more likely to meet criteria for BPD whereas narcissistic personality disorder was diagnosed only in males. Paris (1997b) postulates that a common base of impulsivity in antisocial personality disorder (ASPD) and BPD is expressed behaviorally in different ways due to shaping by gender. Persons with BPD constitute 10 to 25% of all inpatient psychiatric admissions and represent the most common inpatient personality disorder diagnosis (Springer & Silk, 1996).

Long-term prognosis appears to be good for the majority of persons diagnosed with BPD. Four long-term studies following persons with BPD for 15 years showed remarkable concordance of findings (Paris, 1993; Stone, 1987; McGlashan, 1986). BPD is a chronic disorder into middle age, by which time the majority of persons formerly diagnosed with BPD no longer meet criteria. In all four studies, mean Global Assessment Scale scores were in the normal range (mid-60s), and most former patients were working and had a social life. It is unclear whether treatment contributes significantly to outcome or whether the natural course of improvement would occur in any case. To the extent that treatment during crisis periods can deter suicide, however, it would be essential to buy time by "holding" BPD suffers until the risk of suicide has passed.

However, about 10% of persons with BPD have committed suicide by the 15th year of posttreatment follow-up (Paris, 1993). Findings are inconsistent with respect to predictors of suicide and other poor outcomes.

BORDERLINE PERSONALITY DISORDER IS FOUND AT SEVERAL BORDERS

Symptoms of BPD border on several Axis I disorders and also overlap with several Axis II personality disorders (Cowdry, 1997). Axis I disorders commonly co-occur with BPD or are mistaken for it. These include major depressive disorder (MDD) (Links, et al., 1996; Alneas & Torgersen, 1997), the spectrum of bipolar disorders (Akiskal, 1996), substance use disorders (Morgenstern, et al., 1997; Grilo, Walker, et al., 1997; Senol, et al., 1997), dissociative identity disorders (DID) (Sar, et al., 1996; Atlas & Wolfson, 1996), and eating disorders (Verkes, Pijl, et al., 1996; Grilo, Levy, et al., 1996; Davis, et al., 1997; Sansone, et al., 1997).

Affective Disorders

Unstable mood is one of the defining characteristics of BPD. Extensive research supports overlap between BPD and mood disorders. Depression is a major component of many borderline states. A strong positive family history of serious affective disorder is found among persons meeting criteria for BPD. Many have symptoms characteristic of bipolar, cyclothymic, and unipolar affective disorders. Significant improvement on antidepressant medication has been reported for clients whose BPD includes prominent affective components (Kaplan & Sadock, 1998). Phobic-anxious people who meet BPD criteria also respond to antidepressants (Klein, 1977). In Turkey, 45 patients diagnosed with BPD were followed for two to four years after discharge. Prevalence of affective disorder was 76.6%, with substance use disorders the second most common Axis I diagnosis among persons with BPD (Senol, et al., 1997).

Ultrarapid-cycling forms of bipolar disorder, where morose, labile moods with irritable, mixed features constitute the patients' habitual self, are often mistaken for BPD (Akiskal, 1996). De La Fuente and Mendlewicz (1996) found no evidence of an endocrine biological link between BPD and MDD, suggesting that the depressive symptoms in some patients with BPD may have different biological substrates from those found in patients with MDD.

Substance Use Disorders

Substance abuse commonly co-occurs with BPD. For example, high prevalence of BPD was found in a multisite sample of 366 substance abusers in treatment, with BPD and ASPD linked to more severe symptomatology of alcoholism (Morgenstern, et al., 1997).

Dissociative Disorders

Recent studies highlight overlaps between dissociative phenomena and BPD (Atlas & Wolfson, 1996; Paris & Zweig-Frank, 1997; Russ, et al.,

1996; Kemperman, et al., 1997). Dissociation is increasingly being recognized as a characteristic of persons with BPD, and, conversely, among people meeting criteria for dissociative identity disorder (DID), borderline characteristics are very common. In a cross-national study, Sar, et al. (1996) found that among 35 patients diagnosed with DID, an average of 3.8 criteria for BPD were reported, only slightly fewer than the five required to meet *DSM* criteria for BPD. Another study of 26 adolescents with BPD showed both significant depression and dissociation, suggesting the importance of evaluating instability of mood as well as weak continuity in self-experience when identifying and treating BPD (Atlas & Wolfson, 1996). Cowdry (1997) has noted the similarity of dissociative states to complex partial seizures.

Eating Disorders

Persons with eating disorders serious enough to warrant hospitalization often also meet criteria for BPD. Using blood platelet measures of serotonin (5-HT) and monoamine oxidase activity to assess monoamine functions (see Chapter 4), Verkes, Pijl, et al. (1996) found that bulimia could be subdivided into two groups, those with comorbid BPD, who resembled recurrent suicide attempters with BPD in levels of anger, impulsivity, and biochemical characteristics, and those without BPD.

The overlap of BPD with other Axis II personality disorders is widely acknowledged. In fact, Kernberg's *borderline personality organization* (different from the *DSM-IV* BPD criteria) is a large umbrella that comprises all major forms of character pathology and appears to encompass *DSM* categories of borderline, histrionic, narcissistic, and antisocial personality disorders (Kernberg, 1984; American Psychiatric Association, 1994). The wide net cast by Kernberg yields a very high prevalence rate of between 15 and 30% of the population (Gunderson, 1984). To identify overlaps between BPD and other personality disorders, readers can consult tables of diagnostic criteria in the *DSM-IV* (American Psychiatric Association, 1994).

Neurologic Dysfunction

Various investigators have found evidence of neurologic dysfunction in persons meeting criteria for BPD, especially those for whom impulsivity is a salient characteristic (Stein, et al., 1993; Drake, et al., 1992; van Reekum, 1993; Biederman, et al., 1991). It is important to distinguish the terms *neurologic* and *neurobiogical*. All psychic phenomena have neurobiological underpinnings, whereas the term *neurologic* designates specific subtypes of neurobiological dysfunctions that are diagnosed and treated by the subspecialty of neurology rather than psychiatry. These distinctions are becoming increasingly fuzzy as knowledge about the neurobiology of psychiatric disorders advances, but they are rooted medical tradition.

In a study of 91 hospitalized borderline patients, 38% (*n* = 35) had underlying neurologic dysfunction (Andrulonis, et al., 1981), including ADHD (then called minimal brain dysfunction) or learning disability (27%, *n* = 25), and brain trauma, epilepsy, or a history of encephalitis (11%, *n* = 10). Differences by gender were highly significant, with 53% (*n* = 17) of males positive for a history of minimal brain dysfunction or learning disability compared with only 14% (*n* = 8) of females. Females more frequently bordered a major affective disorder.

Residual characteristics of ADHD are also typical of adults with BPD. ADHD often continues into adulthood and may underlie such characteristics as impulsivity, irritability, poor frustration tolerance, aggressive outbursts, temper tantrums, readiness to anger, drug and alcohol abuse, distractibility, mood swings, diminished responsiveness to rewarding events, antisocial behavior, and loneliness. There are as yet no large-scale studies indicating a prevalence of overlap between ADHD and BPD.

NEUROBIOLOGICAL UNDERPINNINGS

The revolution in knowledge about biological bases of psychopathology made possible by the development of scanning and other technologies has contributed to knowledge about borderline phenomena. De La Fuente, et al. (1997) used positron emission tomography (PET scan) to identify characteristics of the physiology (function or process) taking place in borderline states. They found a relative hypometabolism (low level of glucose consumption) in the premotor and frontal cortices, the anterior cingulate cortex, and thalamic, caudate, and lenticular nuclei, indicating significant cerebral metabolic disturbances in BPD. Recent studies have tested relationships between BPD and hormonal responses (Steinberg, et al. (1997); BPD, subthreshold depression, and sleep disorders (Akiskal, et al., 1997); association between platelet monoamine oxidase activity and stable personality traits such as impulsiveness, monotony avoidance, and aggressiveness (Stalenheim, et al., 1997); and a possible neural basis for the phenomenon of splitting so often observed in persons with BPD (Muller, 1992).

Higher levels of platelet serotonin in persons with BPD predict recurrent suicide attempts within a year of follow-up, suggesting an association between suicidality and central serotonergic dysfunction (Verkes, Fekkes, et al., 1997). Platelet 5-HT was higher in patients with BPD than in normal female controls and was positively correlated with experiencing anger.

The current understanding of the biological substrates thought to be present in BPD is reviewed by Figueroa and Silk (1997). In persons with BPD, the type and breadth of the individual's hyperreactivity to the environment, which often manifests itself in hypersensitivity in interpersonal situations, is probably mediated through noradrenergic mechanisms (see Chapter 4). Impulsivity, a major constitutional predisposition to BPD, is mediated through serotonergic mechanisms. The combination of these two mechanisms may lead to a clinical picture, often seen in BPD, where impulsivity and self-destructive behavior are employed to deal with the stress and dysphoria of being hypersensitive to interpersonal and other environmental stimuli.

ETIOLOGY

The preponderance of evidence now supports the view that the borderline personality represents a common or similar picture that is the outcome of a heterogeneous developmental course. Almost all observers agree that interacting biological and environmental factors play a role in the development of borderline personality disorder. In general, the components appear to be biological vulnerability (predisposition for affective instability, impulsivity, or other borderline characteristics) interacting with a childhood history of abuse, loss, lack of validation, or other unidentified environmental inputs (Cowdry, 1997; Linehan, 1993).

The role of childhood trauma as a risk factor for BPD is related to sensitivity to environmental stimuli and is proposed to be acting through noradrenergic mechanisms in the development over time of BPD in individuals with a history of childhood trauma. In multiple regressions of potential predictor variables for the borderline diagnosis, *interpersonal sensitivity* was the only significant predictor of the borderline diagnosis (Figueroa, Silk, et al., 1997). The investigators postulate that at least in some cases, interpersonal sensitivity may be the constitutional/environmental substrate with which traumatic experiences interact to lead to BPD. That is, interpersonal sensitivity makes such individuals specially vulnerable to trauma. Reviewing empirical evidence, Zanarini and Frankenburg (1997) conclude that BPD is an outcome arrived at by interactions between a vulnerable (hyperbolic) temperament, a traumatic childhood (broadly defined), and/or a triggering event or series of events. In any particular situation, any one of these three categories may contribute most strongly.

Neurobiological responses to stress were reviewed by Henry (1997). Delayed responses to severe psychological trauma (posttraumatic stress disorder, or PTSD) present a paradoxical mix of symptoms: continuing elevation in catecholamine response mediating anger and fear, together often with normal levels of hypothalamic-pituitary-adrenal (HPA) axis activity. Reexperiencing the trauma and the arousal may be associated with dysfunction of the locus caeruleus, amygdala, and hippocampal systems. In addition, dissociation of the connections between the right and left hemispheres appears to be responsible for the alexithymia (lack of awareness of one's emotions or moods) and failure of the cortisol response that so often follow severe psychological trauma. In this condition, it appears that the right hemisphere no longer fully contributes to integrated cerebral function. Children with damage to the right hemisphere lose critical social skills. Adults lose a sense of relatedness and familiarity. Henry postulates that these losses of social sensibilities may account for the lack of empathy and difficulties with bonding found in antisocial personality disorder (ASPD) as well as in BPD.

Paris (1997a) critically reviews beliefs pertaining to the relationship between traumatic events in childhood and personality disorders in adulthood. He notes that attributing adult psychopathology primarily to environmental factors is problematic because personality traits are heritable, children are resilient to the long-term effects of trauma, all studies of trauma in personality-disordered persons suffer from retrospective designs, and only a minority of patients with severe personality disorders report severe childhood trauma.

According to Paris, the effects of trauma in the personality disorders can therefore be better understood in the context of gene–environment interactions. Interaction is key because many biologically vulnerable persons do not develop BPD, and many persons with histories of childhood trauma or loss do not develop BPD. In cases of biological vulnerability, it should be theoretically possible to prevent a later onset of BPD by recognizing vulnerabilities early and by supporting parents and educating them about these children's special, idiosyncratic needs. These vulnerable children require parenting efforts *different from* and/or *greater than* the ordinary parenting behaviors that are usually successful with children lacking these vulnerabilities. At present, however, few if any preventive assessments or interventive programs are in place.

Linehan views etiology as the interaction of biological factors (due possibly to genetic factors, intrauterine events, or trauma at an early age, especially head trauma) and environmental factors characterized as "invalidating." Invalidating environments communicate to persons who later develop BPD that their responses to life situations are invalid, inappropriate, or incorrect. In such environments, all problems are viewed as motivational in origin—"If only you were to try harder, the problem would be solved." Typically such environments tell children to "calm down." However, it is very difficult for such children to "calm down." These environments fail to recognize or take seriously the person's (biologically based) emotional vulnerability and overly sensitive responses, seen in children who may be inhibited, irritable, or cry a great deal in infancy, children known as "difficult."

The Role of the Family

For many decades, the parents of persons with BPD were assumed by professionals to have caused their children's disorders. In an early review, Gunderson and Englund (1981) found little evidence to support the literature's messages about parental culpability, and suggested that the tendency of persons with BPD and their therapists to see the mothers as "bad" may be a function of the splitting mechanisms used so frequently by persons with BPD. They might, in fact, be projecting nonexistent negative behaviors or affects onto their mothers in the process of reconstructing their pasts.

Palombo (1983) observed that persons with BPD experience the world as hostile and chaotic and believe that their caretakers have failed to provide a benign environment.

> Regardless of whether or not the parents did fail, [they] were in all likelihood helpless to provide such an environment for the child . . . . [T]he most benign, responsive, caring parents may in that sense be utter failures from the perspective of the child because his needs were not adequately attended to. Conversely, neglectful parents raising a competent, well-endowed child might be experienced as loving and responsible . . . .
>
> [The person with BPD] could, and often does, pin the blame for his suffering on those around him. From his perspective, they are the causes of it. Since [the parents] are perceived as powerful and mighty, they cannot be absolved of the blame for permitting his suffering to occur. Myths are then created about the terrible things that

parents did to the child, even though in reality the parents may have struggled mightily to provide for the child. (Palombo, 1983, pp. 335–336)

In their study, Gunderson and Englund (1981) had expected to find empirical support for the beliefs prevailing in the late 1970s that family psychopathology for persons with BPD was characterized by overinvolved, separation-resistant, dependency-generating mothers. Instead, they found that parental underinvolvement was much more common. Neglectful parenting was also implicated in a recent study (Zanarini, et al., 1997). In comparison with people with other personality disorders, three family environmental factors were significant predictors of a borderline diagnosis: sexual abuse by a male noncaregiver, emotional denial by a male caregiver, and inconsistent treatment by a female caregiver. The results suggested that sexual abuse was neither a necessary nor a sufficient condition for the development of BPD and that other childhood experiences, particularly neglect by caretakers of both genders, represent significant risk factors. Since the majority of children who experience any of these risk factors do not develop BPD, however, other variables clearly must be present as well to account for the later development of BPD.

Gunderson and colleagues (1997) caution against one-sided assessment of BPD.

Much of the preceding literature about the families of borderline patients derived solely from reports provided by the borderline patients and rarely included the families' perspectives. When you consider that borderline patients are by nature often devaluative and that they often find on entering treatment that devaluing past caretakers—past treaters as well as families—is a way to ignite the ambitions and enthusiasm of the new candidates for becoming their caretakers, it is disturbing in retrospect that we have not been more suspicious about their accounts of their families. (Gunderson, et al., 1997, p. 451)

Recently, Gunderson himself offered a *mea culpa* with respect to parents of people with BPD, as had another psychiatrist 14 years earlier with respect to schizophrenia (Gunderson, et al., 1997; Terkelsen, 1983).

I . . . was a contributor to the literature that led to the unfair vilification of the families and the largely unfortunate efforts at either excluding or inappropriately involving them in treatment. So it is with embarrassment that I now find myself presenting a treatment [psychoeducation] that begins with the expectation that the families of borderline individuals are important allies of the treaters. Gunderson, et al., 1997, p. 451)

EFFECTIVENESS OF ALTERNATIVE INTERVENTIONS

By the beginning of the 1990s, only a very limited number of studies of treatment effectiveness had been completed. At that time, interventive options for persons with BPD were limited primarily to inpatient and outpatient psychotherapy (psychodynamic, some early use of cognitive-behavioral strategies), inpatient group therapy, family therapy for members of the person's family, and medication (McGlashan, 1986; Stone, 1987). At that time psychoeducation and cognitive-behavioral interventions were already widely used for persons with schizophrenia and their families, but these approaches were just being introduced for BPD (Schulz, et al., 1988; Linehan, et al., 1989).

Since that time, our repertoire of interventions has expanded. Emphasis is shifting from insight-oriented reflective therapies to skills training targeted on the most common difficulties of persons with BPD, such as intense anger, self-destructive acts, excessive drug use, binge eating and purging, or reckless spending (Springer & Silk, 1996). Treatment components (inpatient or outpatient) may involve some combination of individual and group psychoeducation, behavioral strategies and skills training (such as anger management, relapse prevention, social skills training), medication, peer support groups, family psychoeducation and support, cognitive therapy, individual psychodynamic counseling, environmental changes, and advocacy. In light of the chronicity of BPD, Paris (1997) advocates a wide range of treatment options in a model emphasizing continuous availability and intermittent active intervention.

Advances in neurobiology have amplified and deepened our understanding of major psychiatric disorders, including BPD. Axis I disorders such as major depression and ADHD, now known to be biologically-based brain disorders, often co-occur with BPD and are targeted for treatment (Cowdry, 1997). In addition, specific problem behaviors of persons with BPD arising from mood or impulse control dysfunctions are targets of treatment. Concurrently, psychoeducation and cognitive-behavioral approaches have emerged as first-line interventions (Linehan, 1993; Gunderson, Berkowitz, & Ruiz-Sancho, 1997). Insight-oriented psychodynamic psychotherapy appears to have been effective for a subgroup of persons with BPD who are generally likeable by others, motivated, psychologically minded, focused, free of overwhelming impulsivity and substance craving, and without a history of "grotesquely destructive" early environments (Stone, 1987).

However, impulsivity and/or cravings are among the defining characteristics of BPD, and where present usually appear to require more structured, behaviorally oriented interventions to help persons with BPD control self-destructive or addictive-like impulses that threaten their ability to maintain jobs or intimate relationships. Some persons with BPD may benefit from combining these different approaches (Heller & Northcut, 1996; Patrick, 1993). As yet there are no empirical studies that could measure the relative contributions to outcomes of behavioral versus insight-oriented strategies.

Psychoeducation

Psychoeducation for persons with BPD and their family members is increasingly emphasized, as it has become widely recognized that information is empowering (Gunderson, et al., 1997). The question "Why am I this way?" or "Why is my family member this way?" is a salient preoccupation even if not articulated. Palombo (1983) referred to the person with BPD's "maddening sense of inadequacy at coping with an imperfectly understood environment" (p. 331). The clinician can help the person with BPD understand his or her environment (internal as well as external) by giving information about the role of biological factors in the person's borderline illness and about the ways in which the environment may interact with biological vulnerability to cause symptoms and suffering. For example, when the person with BPD has a history of ADHD, head injury, or other neurological dysfunction, it is helpful to say "You know, your ADHD (head injury, epilepsy) seems to have the effect of making you fly off the handle easily" ("get distracted," "say things you're sorry for," "look for excitement all the time"). When there is a tendency to major affective disorder, the worker can point out that the client seems to have a constitutional proclivity for depression or mania that interacts with stressful life events. It is often useful to suggest reading that can help persons with BPD understand their own vulnerabilities and explain treatment options, including medication. Psychoeducation usually includes specific information about the disorder itself; benefits and risks of medications, side effects, and signs that the medication requires adjustment (larger or smaller doses, or a different medication); alternative treatment options; and information about financial assistance, health benefits, community resources, employment assistance, support groups, and respite care.

Skills Training and Relapse Prevention: Dialectical Behavior Therapy

Dialectical behavior therapy (DBT), now the leading cognitive-behavioral strategy in the treatment of BPD, has shown promise in reducing self-destructive behaviors in people with BPD, reducing hospital admissions, and improving social adjustment (Linehan, et al., 1991). Linehan notes that standard cognitive behavior therapy, like psychodynamic therapy, has a change orientation: it strives to change behavior through learning and experience. Where these therapies fail, according to Linehan, is in the lack of acceptance of clients as they are, a posture that reinforces their own inability to accept themselves. DBT begins with a posture of total acceptance (called *radical acceptance*) borrowed from Eastern religions such as Zen. The word *dialectical* refers to the treatment's philosophical framework, the resolution of polarity and tension between opposites. Persons with BPD must accept themselves as they are and at the same time try to change. That is, the treatment is geared toward a balance involving supportive acceptance combined with change strategies. The treatment is behavioral because it focuses on skills training, collaborative problem solving, contingency clarification and management, and the observable present (Linehan, 1993). It is directive and intervention oriented.

Treatment includes weekly individual visits with a therapist and weekly group sessions. The treatment is manualized to follow several phases. In the *pretreatment phase* (sometimes called the *contracting phase* in other treatments), the therapist focuses on suicidal or other self-harming behaviors. Will the person with BPD agree to stop doing these things? Before other issues can be addressed, he or she must be willing to agree to stop hurting or threatening to hurt herself or himself. Treatment requires collaborative agreement. The worker/therapist emphasizes that there are only two options, to accept one's condition and stay miserable, or to try to change it.

The worker engages with the client in active problem solving, responds with warmth and flexibility, and *validates the patient's emotional and cognitive responses*. For example, the worker recognizes that the client's coping behaviors (such as cutting, burning, or attempting suicide) have been very effective or functional for that person by supplying predictable relief from pain. Treatment focuses on figuring out ways to avoid or escape from pain other than hurting oneself.

The social worker frequently expresses sympathy for the client's intense pain and sense of desperation, creating a validating environment while conveying a matter-of-fact attitude about current and previous self-destructive behaviors (Linehan, 1993). The worker reframes suicidal and other dysfunctional behaviors as part of the client's learned problem-solving repertoire and tries to focus the counseling process on positive problem-solving. In individual and group sessions, workers teach emotional regulation, interpersonal effectiveness, distress tolerance, and self-management skills. They openly reinforce desired behaviors to promote progress, by maintaining contingencies that shape adaptive behaviors and extinguish self-destructive behaviors. They set clear limits to their availability for help. The treatment process emphasizes building and maintaining a positive, interpersonal, collaborative relationship in which the social worker's roles are teacher, consultant, and cheerleader.

Because of frequent crises, following a behavioral treatment plan in the context of individual treatment may be difficult, especially if this plan involves teaching skills that are not obviously related to the current crisis and that do not promise immediate relief. Therefore, behaviorally oriented workers have developed psychoeducational group treatment modules to teach specific behavioral, cognitive, and emotional skills (Linehan, 1993).

Group Therapy

Overall, there are few methodologically sound studies of effectiveness of group therapy for persons with BPD, with one notable exception—Linehan's outpatient dialectical behavior-therapy groups, which are part of an overall multimodal-treatment package (Linehan, Armstrong, et al., 1991). Empirical findings with respect to psychodynamically oriented group therapy for persons with personality disorders have been discouraging (Springer & Silk, 1996). Some researchers have even noted deterioration among patients receiving psychoanalytic group therapy (Beutler, Frank, et al., 1984). However, inpatients with BPD themselves have sometimes evaluated group therapies as the most effective treatment they received (Leszcz, et al., 1985; Hafner & Holme, 1996).

Psychodynamically Oriented Individual Counseling

There has been a long-standing debate about the respective merits of interpretive, insight-oriented individual counseling versus a supportive, structured "holding" environment (Waldinger, 1987). Kernberg (1984) views the origin of borderline pathology in malformed psychic structures, whereas Kohut (1978) viewed it as a deficit in the ability to hold or soothe oneself, arising from early developmental failure. According to the deficit view, the worker must be a "holding self-object" (Kohut, 1978), i.e., he or she must perform the holding and soothing functions that persons with BPD cannot perform for themselves (Waldinger, 1987). Advocates of the holding environment believe that healing occurs not through interpretation, but by being a stable, consistent, caring, nonpunitive person who survives the client's rage and destructive impulses and continues to serve this holding function (Waldinger, 1987, p. 270). According to this view, experiential factors are more important than the content of interpretations. Buie and Adler (1982) advocated implementing the holding function by such supports as hospitalization when needed, extra appointments, phone calls between sessions, provision of vacation addresses, and even postcards sent to the client while on vacation.

Psychiatric Rehabilitation Model

In line with current thinking emphasizing the long-term and chronic nature of BPD, Links (1993) advocates the application of the psychiatric rehabilitation model used for persons with schizophrenia to provide a validating environment, the opportunity to enhance skills, and a mechanism to accept input from families. Specific skills are taught, such as learning to accurately label one's own emotions, general problem-solving skills, and skills to enhance self-esteem and deal with anger, as in Linehan's DBT. Often the person's lack of skills is situationally specific, so the training must be done in relation to a setting in which the deficits lead to dysfunction. Practitioners develop environments and mental health services that validate the person's experience. For example, families can be helped to create more validating environments through psychoeducation about the characteristics of the disorder and the idiosyncratic needs of the person with BPD. Hospitalization in acute psychiatric settings is viewed as not very desirable, as it is may be too emotionally stimulating and not validating. Other settings, such as a community agency or a work environment, must be found that mesh with the patient's characteristics and that can create a sense of validation.

Therapeutic Communities (TCs) versus Day Treatment

A current unanswered question is whether residential and therapeutic communities are still justifiable for BPD, given the success of Linehan's outpatient approach (Hafner & Holme, 1996). The effectiveness of therapeutic programs for BPD appears to be strongly related to the presence of program structures that can meet idiosyncratic needs of persons with BPD (Miller, 1995). What are these structures, and can they be used as effectively in outpatient settings as in residential programs? At this time, the jury is still out on these questions.

Miller (1995) describes four characteristics of successful programming in a day setting for persons with BPD: affect facilitation, holding without overcontaining, ensuring client safety, and providing focused time-limited treatment (three weeks in Miller's program). The first three of these characteristics also typify some therapeutic communities specializing in longer-term treatment of persons with BPD (Schimmel, 1997; Hafner & Holme, 1996).

Yet the high rate of suicide in people with BPD living in the community continues (Paris, 1993; Antikainen, et al., 1995). Can client safety be ensured in outpatient programs? Those who argue that hospitals take away responsibility for individual self care in persons with BPD, by removing "sharps" and other implements of suicide, emphasize the need for service providers to take a strong position that they cannot save clients from themselves; only the individuals can ensure their own safety (Linehan, 1993; Miller, 1995).

Work with Families of Persons with BPD

The emergence of psychoeducation and family support groups as the interventions of choice in work with families of persons with BPD is relatively recent (Gunderson, et al., 1997; Johnson, 1991). Recent research on BPD suggests that average or "good enough" mothering may be insufficient to protect a child with neurobiological vulnerabilities from developing borderline characteristics; conversely, resilient children at high risk due to traumatic environments may grow into well-functioning, successful adults. A borderline outcome may be the cumulative result of interactive biological vulnerabilities and life stresses, with or without parental inadequacies. The blame/shame stigma now beginning to dissipate for other major psychiatric disorders such as schizophrenia and bipolar disorder has been slower to diminish for BPD, in the author's view, because persons with BPD seldom have signs of psychosis and, in addition, frequently exhibit irritating or upsetting behaviors. In the absence of evidence to the contrary, such as widely publicized PET scans shown on all the major networks at the time of the assassination of two security guards at the U.S. Capitol, parents are often *assumed* to be at fault when their children grow up with problematic characteristics. Parents of persons with BPD themselves need to be educated that BPD is a neurobiological disorder, not retribution for toxic parenting; they need the support of others in similar situations to break down their sense of stigma, self-blame, and hopelessness; and they need training in ways to cope with behaviors typical of BPD. As Gunderson has pointed out (Gunderson, et al., 1997), parents should be viewed as collaborators in the treatment process, not objects of therapy.

Medication

Medication may target coexisting Axis I disorders and/or specific symptoms characteristic of people with BPD (Cowdry, 1997; Hirschfeld, 1997). *Major depression* (MD) in people with BPD may be helped with selective serotonin reuptake inhibitors (SSRIs), usually the first-choice antidepressants, newer antidepressants such as venlaxafine (Effexor), monoamine oxidase inhibitors (MAOIs), or tricyclic antidepressants. These agents are also helpful in relieving dysphoria when not all criteria for major depressive disorder are met.

Residual Adult ADHD
In persons with BPD, residual adult ADHD is often responsive to stimulant medications, notably methylphenidate (Ritalin), dexedrine, or pemoline (Cylert). Some symptoms of ADHD—impulsivity, aggressive outbursts, temper tantrums, distractibility, and emotional overreactivity—often can be controlled with stimulant medication such as methylphenidate (Ritalin) in adults whose borderline characteristics arise from ADHD (Cowdry, 1997; Spencer, et al., 1996). Wender, et al. (1981) found that 60% of adults with ADHD responded to methylphenidate with a reduction in impulsivity and hot-temperedness and an increase in concentration, calmness, and energy. Stimulant medication has an alerting effect that may help the individual organize multiple incoming internal and external stimuli that he or she has experienced as chaotic, thus reducing anxiety, increasing confidence, and giving the individual a sense of mastery.

Some persons have ultra-rapid-cycling forms of *Bipolar I*, in which morose labile moods alternate with irritable mixed (manic and depressive) moods. These mood swings constitute the person's habitual self, but are often mistaken for BPD. Such patients with bipolar characteristics may need mood-regulating medications, such as lithium and the anticonvulsants carbamazepine and valproate, which can benefit lifelong temperamental dysregulation combined with depressive episodes (Akiskal, 1996).

Eating Disorders

Several neurotransmitters and neuromodulators (brain chemicals that modify neurotransmission without meeting all criteria to be neurotransmitters) are involved in regulation of eating behavior in animals and have been implicated in symptoms such as depression and anxiety in humans with eating disorders (Mauri, et al., 1996). Antidepressants have been effective in reducing frequency of binge eating, purging, and depressive symptoms in persons with bulimia, even in cases of chronic persistent bulimia in patients who had repeatedly failed courses of alternative therapies, and even in persons with bulimia who do not display concomitant depression (ibid.). Medication for anorexia nervosa has been less successful and few controlled studies have been published (ibid.). Central serotonergic receptor-blocking compounds such as cyproheptadine can cause marked increase in appetite and body weight. For anorexia nervosa, zinc supplementation or cisapride may be helpful in combination with other approaches. Naltrexone, an opiate antagonist sometimes used to treat opiate or alcohol addiction, is also being tried.

SPECIFIC SYMPTOMS OR CHARACTERISTICS OF BPD

Impulsivity and Aggression

Mood stabilizers, venlaxafine (Effexor), MAOIs, and stimulants such as Ritalin have all been found helpful in reducing impulsivity and aggression (Hirschfeld, 1997; Cowdry, 1997).

Depressive Symptoms

The antidepressants as a group, including the selective serotonin reuptake inhibitors (SSRIs), MAOIs, tricyclics, and newer antidepressants like venlaxafine, alleviate depressive symptoms even when the criteria for major depression are not met.

Anxiety

Anxiety is sometimes targeted with anxiolytic (anxiety-reducing) drugs, notably the benzodiazepenes such as alprazolam (Xanax). Results are mixed, with some studies reporting negative effects of anxiolytics, i.e., increased impulsivity and dyscontrol, while others reporting helpfulness (Hirschfeld, 1997; Antikainen, et al., 1995).

Self-Injurious Behavior

Self-injury has been reduced with risperidone (Risperdal, an antipsychotic that blocks certain dopamine as well as serotonin receptors) and naltrexone (an opiate antagonist used to treat addiction to alcohol and opiates) in persons with BPD (Khouzam & Donnelly, 1997; Roth, et al., 1996).

Repetitive self-injurious behavior (SIB) such as wrist-slashing is a dangerous and often treatment-refractory feature of many borderline personality disorders. Khouzam and Donnelly (1997) induced remission of self-mutilation in a patient with BPD by treating with risperidone. Szigethy and Schulz (1997) also found risperidone effective in comorbid BPD and dysthymia. Self-injurious behaviors ceased entirely in six of seven patients receiving naltrexone whose self-injurious behaviors were accompanied by analgesia (feeling no physical pain) and dysphoria reduction (acts of self-injury that temporarily relieve painful feelings of sadness and emptiness) (Roth, et al., 1996). Two of the patients who discontinued naltrexone briefly experienced rapid resumption of SIB, which ceased once again after naltrexone therapy was resumed.

Dissociative States

In persons with BPD, dissociative states suggest underlying neurobiological events, such as complex partial seizures, that may call for treatment with anticonvulsants (Cowdry, 1997). *Schizotypal characteristics* are usually transient and intermittent when they occur in patients with BPD. These clients may improve with low-dose neuroleptic medication (Schulz, Cornelius, et al., 1988).

Cowdry (1997, p. 9) has noted that psychotropic medications in treatment of persons with BPD occasionally result in marked improvement, but more often serve to *modulate affect* enough to make daily experiences somewhat less disruptive and to make psychotherapy more productive. In most cases, medication is only one weapon in an arsenal of individual and group interventions to help persons with BPD develop coping skills. For all persons with BPD, creative combinations of the approaches reviewed above should be individually tailored to the needs of persons with BPD and their families.

IMPLICATIONS FOR SOCIAL WORK

How does this new expanded knowledge fit with our roles as case managers, therapists, family consultants, patient and family advocates, and social and political activists? All the contemporary approaches to work with persons with BPD and their families that were considered above fall within the purview of social work practice. Even with respect to psychotropic medication, social workers perform all critical functions except for writing prescriptions, doing medical evaluations, and interpreting laboratory reports.

Prior to intervening, it is imperative that we familiarize ourselves with current research-based knowledge about characteristics and etiologies of BPD, what interventions are effective for what types of BPD clients, and under what conditions they are effective. Research published during the past few years has given us tools for understanding and treating BPD in ways that were beyond our capability in the past. However, without valid *knowledge* about the diverse forms and different underlying characteristics of BPD, and without *training in specific skills* targeted on troublesome or dangerous characteristics of the disorder, there is no reason to expect that our treatments will be effective.

We should not be discouraged by the fact that we do not know for sure whether our treatments account for the positive outcomes, years later, of many clients who in their teens and twenties were ill with BPD for periods of years. We do know that a significant number of persons with BPD (perhaps 10%) commit suicide outside the hospital, so clearly efforts to prevent suicide are critical. Research suggests that if we can prevent suicide in the crisis phases of the disorder, individuals have a good chance at a satisfying life later. The recovery process is usually very slow and gradual, however. We should have a reasonable expectation that the illness will be chronic for an extended time and that relapses are to be expected. Meanwhile, until the risk of suicide is diminished, intensive therapeutic efforts must be put forth. At the same time, as social workers we can remind ourselves and our clients with BPD that tools of self-destruction are always available in the community, that we cannot save them, and that ultimately only they can choose to stay safe.

The natural course of BPD of gradual diminution of symptoms over a period of years underscores the need for ongoing structure and monitoring in the community and for short-term protected environments (hospitals or some other kind of safe havens) where clients can stay until the immediate threat of suicide has passed. Expansion, rather than the contraction of such services now happening under the aegis of managed care, must be vigorously advocated by social workers in the political sphere as well as on an individual basis. At the time of writing, the American public has begun to voice frustration and anger about the impact of current cost-cutting measures throughout managed-care-dominated health care systems. Some social workers are taking an active role in this effort, but we need to do much more.

Skills necessary to work with persons with BPD and their families are teachable and learnable. However, it appears that training in these skills is not be available in some social work programs, requiring workers to get it elsewhere. In our view, generic social work skills simply are not adequate to address the specific challenges of work related to this painful and often dangerous condition. Given the prevalence of this disorder across social work settings, social-work educators should think of ways to bring these therapeutic skills training modules directly into graduate and undergraduate curricula.

The specific skills that workers may need include

1. how to provide psychoeducation for persons with BPD and their families in group and individual venues, conveying up-to-date information about characteristics and etiology of the disorder, helping clients explore the meaning of this information for their own lives, giving information about treatment options and community resources, and explaining potential benefits and risks associated with these;

2. how to create a validating environment, so as to help the person with BPD accept him- or herself while at the same time working actively to change;

3. how to clearly specify and enforce the conditions under which client and practitioner will work together, especially the boundaries of treatment;

4. cognitive-behavioral skills for teaching impulse control, anger management, relapse prevention, and self-soothing, which can be conveyed well in groups as well as individual sessions;

5. With respect to medication, practitioners must access up-to-date information so they can share this information with clients and their families, so that together with clients and family members they can effectively monitor the client's response to a medication and report to the prescribing physician when necessary. Workers do not need to memorize drug information, as it changes continually, but they should become adept at doing computer searches on Medline to obtain state-of-the-art information about drug effectiveness and side effects. Because these searches can be done on the Internet with only a minimal expenditure of time, technology has made "keeping up" with current knowledge infinitely easier than it was only a few years ago. The easiest method is to get on-line access to Medline at home. Otherwise, Internet access to Medline can be obtained in libraries.

6. Finally, skills in advocacy and political action are required for social workers to join with other activist groups fighting to make services available to thousands of service consumers and their families *when they need them.* At the time of writing, the gap between these goals for service delivery and the reality of their availability is great. All of the above should be available to persons with BPD on an as-needed basis, not only for crisis management but also to provide the continuity of a relationship with a consistent, caring person who can weather the client's outbursts of hostility, self-destructive threats and acts, and can convey hope that a happier future is possible.

REFERENCES

Akiskal, H. S. (1996). The prevalent clinical spectrum of bipolar disorders: Beyond DSM-IV. *Journal of Clinical Psychopharmacology, 16*, 2 Suppl. 1, 4S–14S.

Akiskal, H. S., Judd, L. L., Gillin, J. C., & Lemmi, H. (1997). Subthreshold depressions: Clinical and polysomnographic validation of dysthymic, residual, and masked forms. *Journal of Affective Disorders, 45*, 1–2, 53–63.

Alneas, R., & Torgersen, S. (1997). Personality and personality disorders predict development and relapses of major depression. *Acta Psychiatrica Scandinavica 95*, 4, 336–342.

American Psychiatric Association. (1994). *Diagnostic and statistical manual of mental disorders, fourth edition.* Washington, DC: Author.

Andrulonis, P. A., Glueck, B. C., Stroebel, C. F., Vogel, N. G., Shapiro, A. L., & Aldridge, D. M. (1981). Organic brain dysfunction and the borderline syndrome. *Psychiatric Clinics of North America, 4*, 1, 47–66.

Antikainen, R., Hintikka, J., Lehtonen, J., Koponen, H., & Arstila, A. (1995). A prospective three-year follow-up study of borderline personality disorder inpatients. *Acta Psychiatrica Scandinavica, 92*, 327–335.

Atlas, J. A., & Wolfson, M. A. (1996). Depression and dissociation as features of borderline personality disorder in hospitalized adolescents. *Psychological Report, 78*, 2, 624–626.

Beutler, L. E., Frank, M., Schieber, S. C., Calvert, S., & Gaines, J. (1984). Comparative effects of group psychotherapies in a short-term inpatient setting: An experience with deterioration effects. *Psychiatry, 47* (1), 66–76.

Biederman, J., Newcorn, J., & Sprich, S. (1991). Comorbidity of attention deficit hyperactivity disorder with conduct, depressive, anxiety, and other disorders. *American Journal of Psychiatry, 148*, 5, 564–577.

Blais, M. A., Hilsenroth, M. J., & Castlebury, F. D. (1997). Content validity of the DSM-IV borderline and narcissistic personality disorder criteria sets. *Comprehensive Psychiatry, 38*, 1, 31–37.

Buie, D., & Adler, G. (1982). The definitive treatment of the borderline patient. *International Journal of Psychoanalysis and Psychotherapy, 9*, 51–87.

Cowdry, R. (1997). Borderline personality disorder. *NAMI Advocate*, Jan./Feb., 8–9.

Davis, C., Claridge, G., & Cerullo, D. (1997). Personality factors and weight preoccupation: A continuum approach to the association between eating disorders and personality disorders. *Journal of Psychiatric Research, 31*, 4, 467–480.

De La Fuente, J. M., Goldman, S., Stanus, E., Vizuete, C., Morlan, I., Bobes, J., & Mendlewicz, J. (1997). Brain glucose metabolism in borderline personality disorder. *Journal of Psychiatric Research, 31*, 5, 531–541.

De La Fuente, J. M., & Mendlewicz, J. (1996). TRH stimulation and dexamethasone suppression in borderline personality disorder. *Biological Psychiatry, 40, 5,* 412–418.

Drake, M. E., Jr., Pakalnis, A., & Phillips, B. B. (1992). Neuropsychological and psychiatric correlates of intractable pseudoseizures. *Seizure, 1,* 1, 11–13.

Else, L. T., Wonderlich, S. A., Beatty, W. W., Christie, D. W., & Staton, R. D. (1993). Personality characteristics of men who physically abuse women. *Hospital and Community Psychiatry, 44,* 1, 54–58.

Figueroa, E. F., & Silk, K. R. (1997). Biological implications of childhood sexual abuse in borderline personality disorder. *Journal of Personality Disorders, 11,* 1, 71–92.

Figueroa E. F., Silk, K. R., Huth, A., & Lohr, N. E. (1997). History of childhood sexual abuse and general psychopathology. *Comprehensive Psychiatry, 38,* 1, 23–30.

Goldstein, E. G. (1983). Clinical and ecological approaches to the borderline client. *Social Casework, 64,* 6, 353–362.

Grilo, C. M., Becker, D. F., Fehon, D. C., Edell, W. S., & McGlashan, T. H. (1996). Gender differences in personality disorders in psychiatrically hospitalized adolescents. *American Journal of Psychiatry, 153,* 8, 1089–1091.

Grilo, C. M., Levy, K. M., Becker, D. F., Edell, W. S., & McGlashan, T. H. (1996). Cormorbidity of DSM-III-R and Axis I and II disorders among female inpatients with eating disorders. *Psychiatric Services, 47,* 4, 426–429.

Grilo, C. M., Walker, M. L., Becker, D. F., Edell, W. S., & McGlashan, T. H. (1997). Personality disorders in adolescents with major depression, substance use disorders, and coexisting major depression and substance use disorders. *Journal of Consulting and Clinical Psychology, 65,* 2, 328–332.

Gunderson, J. G. (1984). *Borderline personality disorder.* Washington, DC: American Psychiatric Press.

Gunderson, J. G. (1996). The borderline patient's intolerance of aloneness: Insecure attachments and therapist availability. *American Journal of Psychiatry, 153,* 6, 752–758.

Gunderson, J. G., Berkowitz, C., & Ruiz-Sancho, A. (1997). Families of borderline patients: A psychoeducational approach. *Bulletin of the Menninger Clinic, 61,* 4, 446–457.

Gunderson, J. G., & Englund, D. W. (1981). Characterizing the families of borderlines. *Psychiatric Clinics of North America, 4,* 1, 159–168.

Hafner, R. J., & Holme, G. (1996). The influence of a therapeutic community on psychiatric disorders. *Journal of Clinical Psychology, 52,* 4, 461–468.

Heller, N. R., & Northcut, T. B. (1996). Utilizing cognitive-behavioral techniques in psychodynamic practice with clients diagnosed as borderline. *Clinical Social Work Journal, 24,* 2, 203–215.

Henry, J. P. (1997). Psychological and physiological responses to stress: The right hemisphere and the hypothalamo-pituitary-adrenal axis, an inquiry into problems of human bonding. *Acta Physiologica Scandinavica, Suppl. 640,* 10–25.

Hirschfeld, R. M. (1997). Pharmacotherapy of borderline personality disorder. *Journal of Clinical Psychiatry, 58,* Suppl. 14, 48–53.

Johnson, H. C. (1988). Where is the border? Issues in the diagnosis and treatment of the borderline. *Clinical Social Work Journal, 16,* 3, 243–260.

Johnson, H. C. (1991). Borderline clients: Practice implications of recent research. *Social Work, 36,* 2, 166–173.

Kaplan, H. I., & Sadock, B. J. (1998). *Synopsis of psychiatry* (8th Ed.). Baltimore: Williams and Wilkins.

Kemperman, I., Russ, M. J., Clark, W. C., Kakuma, T., Zanine, E., & Harrison, K. (1997). Pain assessment in self-injurious patients with borderline personality disorder using signal detection theory. *Psychiatry Research, 70,* 3, 175–183.

Kemperman, I., Russ, M. J., & Shearin, E. (1997). Self-injurious behavior and mood regulation in borderline patients. *Journal of Personality Disorders, 11,* 2, 146–157.

Kernberg, O. (1984). *Severe personality disorders.* New Haven: Yale University Press.

Khouzam, H. R., & Donnelly, M. J. (1997). Remission of self-mutilation in a patient with borderline personality during risperidone therapy. *Journal of Nervous and Mental Diseases, 185,* 5, 348–349.

Klein, D. F. (1977). Psychopharmacological treatment and delineation of borderline disorders. In P. Hartocollis (Ed.), *Borderline personality disorders* (pp. 365–383). New York: International Universities Press.

Kohut, H. (1978). *The search for the self.* Vols. I and II. New York: International Universities Press.

Leszcz, M., Yalom, I. D., & Norden, M. (1986). The value of inpatient group psychotherapy: Patients' perceptions. *International Group Psychotherapy, 85,* 411–433.

Levine, D., Marziali, E., & Hood, J. (1997). Emotion processing in borderline personality disorders. *Journal of Nervous and Mental Diseases, 185,* 4, 240–246.

Linehan, M. M. (1993). *Cognitive-behavioral treatment of borderline personality disorder.* New York: Guilford.

Linehan, M. M., Armstrong, H. E., Suarez, A., & Allmon, D. (1989). Comprehensive behavioral treatments for suicidal behaviors and borderline personality disorder. Washington, DC: Association for the Advancement of Behavior Therapy.

Linehan, M. M., Armstrong, H. E., Suarez, A., Allmon, D., & Heard, H. (1991). Cognitive-behavioral treatment of chronically parasuicidal borderline patients. *Archives of General Psychiatry, 48,* 1060–1064.

Links, P. S. (1993). Psychiatric rehabilitation model for borderline personality disorder. *Canadian Journal of Psychiatry, 38,* Feb., Suppl. 1, S35–S38.

Marziali, E., & Munroe-Blum, H. (1995). An interpersonal approach to group psychotherapy with borderline personality disorder. *Journal of Personality Disorders, 9,* 3, 179–189.

Mauri, M. C., Rudelli, R., Somaschini, E., Roncoroni, L., Papa, R., Mantero, M., Longhini, M., & Penati, G. (1996). Neurobiological and psychopharmacological basis in the therapy of bulimia and anorexia. *Progress in Neuropsychopharmacology and Biological Psychiatry, 20,* 2, 207–240.

McGlashan, T. H. (1986). The Chestnut Lodge follow-up study: III. Long-term outcome of borderline personalities. *Archives of General Psychiatry, 43,* 20–30.

Miller, B. C. (1995). Characteristics of effective day treatment programming for persons with borderline personality disorder. *Psychiatric Services, 46,* 6, 605–608.

Morgenstern, J., Langenbucher, J., Labouvie, E., & Miller, K. J. (1997). The comorbidity of alcoholism and personality disorders in a clinical population: prevalence rates and relation to alcohol typology variables. *Journal of Abnormal Psychology, 106,* 1, 74–84.

Muller, R. J. (1992). Is there a neural basis for borderline splitting? *Comprehensive Psychiatry, 33,* 2, 92–104.

Palombo, J. (1983). Borderline conditions: a perspective from self-psychology. *Clinical Social Work Journal, 11,* 4, 323–338.

Paris, J. (1993). The treatment of borderline personality disorder in light of the research on its long term outcomes. *Canadian Journal of Psychiatry, 38,* Feb., Suppl. 1, S28–S34.

Paris, J. (1997a). Childhood trauma as an etiological factor in the personality disorders. *Journal of Personality Disorders, 11,* 1, 34–49.

Paris, J. (1997b). Antisocial and borderline personality disorders: Two separate diagnoses or two aspects of the same psychopathology? *Comprehensive Psychiatry, 38,* 4, 237–242.

Paris, J., & Zweig-Frank, H. (1997). Dissociation in patients with borderline personality disorder. *American Journal of Psychiatry, 154*, 1, 137–138.

Patrick, J. (1993). The integration of self-psychological and cognitive-behavioural models in the treatment of borderline personality disorder. *Canadian Journal of Psychiatry, 38*, Feb., Suppl. 1, S39–S43.

Roth, A. S., Ostroff, R. B., & Hoffman, R. E. (1996). Naltrexone as a treatment for repetitive self-injurious behaviour: An open-label trial. *Journal of Clinical Psychiatry, 57*, 6, 233–237.

Russ, M. I., Clark, W. C., Cross, L. W., Kemperman, I., Kakuma, T., & Harrison, K. (1996). Pain and self-injury in borderline patients: Sensory decision theory, coping strategies, and locus of control. *Psychiatry Research, 63*, 1, 57–65.

Sansone, R. A., Sansone, L. A., & Wiederman, M. W. (1997). The comorbidity, relationship and treatment implications of borderline personality and obesity. *Psychosomatic Research, 43*, 5, 541–543.

Sar, V., Yargic, L. I., & Tutkun, H. (1996). Structured interview data on 35 cases of dissociative identity disorder in Turkey. *American Journal of Psychiatry, 153*, 10, 1329–1333.

Schimmel, P. (1997). Swimming against the tide? A review of the therapeutic community. *Australia and New Zealand Journal of Psychiatry, 31*, 1, 120–127.

Schulz, S. C., Cornelius, J., Schulz, P. M., & Soloff, P. H. (1988). The amphetamine challenge test in patients with borderline disorder. *American Journal of Psychiatry, 145*, 7, 809–814.

Senol, S., Dereboy, C., & Yuksel, N. (1997). Borderline disorder in Turkey: A 2- to 4-year follow-up. *Social Psychiatry and Psychiatric Epidemiology, 32*, 2, 109–112.

Snyder, S., Goodpaster, W. A., Pitts, M. W., Jr., Pokorny, A. D., & Gustin, Q. L. (1985). Demography of psychiatric patients with borderline personality traits. *Psychopathology, 18*, 1, 38–49.

Spencer, T., Biederman, J., Wilens, T., Harding, M., O'Donnell, D., & Griffin, S. (1996). Pharmacotherapy of attention-deficit hyperactivity disorder across the life cycle. *Journal of the American Academy of Child and Adolescent Psychiatry, 35*, 4, 409–432.

Springer, T., & Silk, K. R. (1996). A review of inpatient group therapy for borderline personality disorder. *Harvard Review of Psychiatry, 3*, 5, 268–278.

Stalenheim, E. G., von Knorring, L., & Oreland, L. (1997). Platelet monoamine oxidase activity as a biological marker in a Swedish forensic psychiatric population. *Psychiatry Research, 69*, 2–3, 79–87.

Stein, D. J., Hollander, E., Cohen, L., Frenkel, M., Saoud, J. B., DeCaria, C., Aronowitz, B., Levin, A., Liebowitz, M. R., & Cohen, L. (1993). Neuropsychiatric impairment in impulsive personality disorders. *Psychiatry Research, 48*, 3, 257–266.

Steinberg, B. J., Trestman, R., Mitropoulou, V., Serby, M., Silverman, J., Coccaro, E., Weston, S., de Vegvar, M., & Siever, L. J. (1997). Depressive response to physostigmine challenge in borderline personality disorder patients. *Neuropsychopharmacology, 17*, 4, 264–273.

Stone, M. H. (1987). Psychotherapy of borderline patients in light of long-term follow-up. *Bulletin of the Menninger Clinic, 51*, 3, 231–247.

Stone, M. L. (1994). Characterologic subtypes of the borderline personality. *Psychiatric Clinics of North America, 17*, 4, 773–784.

Szigethy, E. M., & Schulz, S. C. (1997). Risperidone in comorbid borderline personality disorder and dysthymia. *Journal of Clinical Psychopharmacology, 17*, 4, 326–327.

Taub, J. M. (1996). Sociodemography of borderline personality disorder (PD): a comparison with Axis II PDs and psychiatric symptom disorders: Convergent validation. *International Journal of Neuroscience, 88*, 1–2, 27–52.

Terkelsen, K. (1983). Schizophrenia and the family: II. Adverse effects of family therapy. *Family Process, 22,* 191–200.

Tuinier, S., & Verhoeven, W. M. (1995). Dimensional classification and behavioral pharmacology of personality disorders: a review and hypothesis. *European Neuropsychopharmacology, 5,* 2, 135–146.

Van Reekum, R. (1993). Acquired and developmental brain dysfunction in borderline personality disorder. *Canadian Journal of Psychiatry, 38,* Suppl. 1, S4–S10.

Van Reekum, R., Links, P., Mitton, M. J., Federov, C., & Patrick, J. (1996). Impulsivity, defensive functioning, and borderline personality disorder. *Canadian Journal of Psychiatry, 41,* 2, 81–84.

Verkes, R. J., Fekkes, D., Zwinderman, A. H., Hengeveld, M. W., Van der Mast, R. C., Tuyl, J. P., Kerkhof, A. J., & Van Kempen (1997). Platelet serotonin and [3H] paroxetine binding correlate with recurrence of suicidal behavior. *Psychopharmacology Bulletin, 132,* 1, 89–94.

Verkes, R. J., Pijl, H., Meinders, A. E., & Van Kempen, G. M. (1996). Borderline personality, impulsiveness, and platelet monoamine meaasures in bulimia nervosa and recurrent suicidal behavior. *Biological Psychiatry, 40,* 3, 173–180.

Waldinger, R. (1987). Intensive psychodynamic therapy with borderline clients: An overview. *American Journal of Psychiatry, 144,* 3, 267–274.

Wender, P. H., Reimherr, F. W., & Wood, D. R. (1981). Attention deficit disorder ("minimal brain dysfunction") in adults: A replication study of diagnosis and drug treatment. *Archives of General Psychiatry, 38,* 4, 449–456.

Zanarini, M. C., & Frankenburg, F. R. (1997). Pathways to the development of borderline personality disorder. *Journal of Personality Disorders, 11,* 1, 93–104.

Zanarini, M. C., Williams, A. A., Lewis, R. E., Reich, R. B., Vera, S. C., Marino, M. F., Levin, A., Yong, L., & Frankenburg, F. R. (1997). Reported pathological childhood experiences associated with the development of borderline personality disorder. *American Journal of Psychiatry, 154,* 8, 1101–1106.

18

ANTISOCIAL PERSONALITY DISORDERS

Michael Rothery

As with any personality disorder, clients who exhibit patterns of behaving and relating that indicate an Antisocial Personality (*DSM-IV*) are a diverse group. At the same time, certain similarities are evident within their ranks, and the shared tendencies that define the disorder are troubling to other people in their lives: family members, intimate partners, and helping professionals.

Antisocial people trouble us because our normal assumptions about relationships do not apply in our involvements with them; in fact, those assumptions are often disadvantageous. Rather than reciprocating trust and commitment, antisocial people may exploit it. Further, they can be dangerous, to themselves and others, and intimidation may be a preferred strategy for getting others to behave as they wish. Finally, while their capacity for harm is daunting, they are relatively impervious to change; effective interventions to alter antisocial patterns are elusive to say the least.

Estimates of the prevalence of people with antisocial personalities vary somewhat, in part because of differences in definition and approaches to measurement. For the population at large, prevalences of from 1% to 3.7% are reported (Hare, 1996; Paris, 1997). This range encompasses findings for different countries and cultures. The prevalence is lower among women than men (0.8% compared to 4.5%*) though this could be partly a definitional and measurement issue (Forth, et al., 1996).

While this proportion is small, it is not reassuring. First, common social work focuses such as corrections, family violence, addictions, child wel-

---

*Because the disorder seems markedly more common among men, I have felt free to use gender-specific language in this chapter.

457

fare, and mental health are fields of service where the likelihood of encountering antisocial people is elevated. Secondly, if a city of one million people is home to "only" 1% with antisocial personalities, it still has a problem—10,000 citizens—that it should not take lightly. This is because the propensity of antisocial people to be destructive through mistreatment of others and of property means that one such person can do an enormous amount of harm. Professionals whose experience has made them aware of the havoc that one callous and manipulative person can wreak will take small comfort from knowing that such people are a relatively small proportion of the population.

My purpose in this chapter is to explore current understandings of this difficult group: who they are, what we can expect in professional relationships with them, and what can be done to counteract their propensity for harm.

DESCRIPTION, DIAGNOSIS AND TERMINOLOGY

Every country has experience with citizens who act in truly monstrous ways, people who attract public attention due their willingness to inflict suffering without apparent restraint. More than a hundred years after he terrorized London's East End, "Jack the Ripper" remains famous, prominent among many other equally gruesome legends. Novels, movies, and television find, in our disquietude about such people, an inexhaustible market for their stories (Hare, 1993).

There are reasons for our deep interest in extreme expressions of antisocial functioning. Such people frighten us, and one way of dealing with fear is to try to understand. Another reason is our fascination with the exotic. Though they are like us in so many ways, people like John Gacy, Charles Manson, Ted Bundy, Paul Bernardo, and Carla Homulka are also profoundly and disturbingly different—there is a gulf that separates them from ordinary people, and, sensing its importance, we want to explain it.

An infamous extreme example is Clifford Olson, a Canadian serial murderer. In 1997, when he attracted attention through a bid for an early parole, the press covered his hearing with interest:

> A psychiatrist for the crown told the B.C. [British Columbia] Supreme Court hearing that Olson has admitted to more than 100 rapes and sexual assaults of children and adolescents, cataloguing them "not unlike an athlete keeping track of his batting average."

Olson had been convicted of none of the assaults, but he took "considerable pride" in recounting many of them in detail, forensic psychiatrist Dr. Stanley Semrau told a hearing for Olson's early parole eligibility.

Semrau called Olson "completely untreatable" and more dangerous than when he was arrested in 1981 because he enjoys his celebrity as the ultimate serial killer. . . .

. . . Depending on the age of the children, . . . [Olson] used alcohol, tranquilizers, toys and candy to lure or subdue his victims. Yet, he bragged of his abilities as a "sexual athlete" and of his seductive powers. In fact, the doctor said, Olson is currently writing "a manual of seduction techniques."

Olson seemed to have no need to kill his earlier assault victims. That changed as he came to enjoy murder. (Hall & MacQueen, 1997, p. A2)

Thankfully, extreme examples like Clifford Olson are very rare, even within the population of people with antisocial personalities. Such examples are useful, however, because they bring characteristic features of the disorder into stark relief. The *expression* of certain defining characteristics is seldom so cruelly bizarre as in Olson's case: the characteristics themselves, however, are recognizable, in a subtler form, in all antisocial people.

The *DSM-IV* Criteria

The American Psychiatric Association's *Diagnostic and Statistical Manual of Mental Disorders* (1994)—the *DSM-IV*—offers one widely used set of criteria for identifying antisocial personality patterns (see Table 18–1). The checklist is strongly behavioral, which has raised objections from some clinicians and researchers (I will return to this issue shortly).

Clinicians and researchers who object to the *DSM-IV* criteria argue that their behavioral emphasis is misleading, in that they confuse a distinctive patterning of traits (personality) with a history of illegal behavior. Not all criminals, they point out, are antisocial, and not all people with antisocial personalities are criminals. Criminality can occur in response to social and economic circumstances as well as because of predispositions due to personality, and someone with strong antisocial traits may express those in ways that do not provoke the interest of the police (Forth, et al., 1996). "What a man is," says George Bernard Shaw, "depends on his character; but what he does, and what we think of what he does, depends on

Table 18–1

A.   There is a pervasive pattern of disregard for and violation of the
     rights of others occurring since age 15 years, as indicated by three
     (or more) of the following:

   1.   failure to conform to social norms with respect to lawful
        behaviors as indicated by repeatedly performing acts that are
        grounds for arrest
   2.   deceitfulness, as indicated by repeated lying, use of aliases,
        or conning others for personal profit or pleasure
   3.   impulsivity or failure to plan ahead
   4.   irritability and aggressiveness, as indicated by repeated physical
        fights or assaults
   5.   reckless disregard for safety of self or others
   6.   consistent irresponsibility, as indicated by repeated failure
        to sustain consistent work behavior or honor financial
        obligations
   7.   lack of remorse, as indicated by being indifferent to or
        rationalizing having hurt, mistreated, or stolen from another
B.   The individual is at least age 18 years.
C.   There is evidence of Conduct Disorder . . . with onset before age
     15 years.
D.   The occurrence of antisocial behavior is not exclusively during the
     course of Schizophrenia or a Manic Episode.

Source: Reprinted with permission from the *Diagnostic and Statistical Manual of Mental Disorders, Fourth Edition.* Washington, DC; American Psychiatric Association, 1994.

his circumstances." "The faults of the burglar," he continues, "are the qualities of the financier" (Shaw, 1960, pp. 26–27).

It is noteworthy that the *DSM-IV* provides, in addition to the diagnostic checklist, a general description of the antisocial personality. In this, it stipulates that the diagnosis is appropriate only when the behaviors concerned occur within the context of a distinctive pattern of personality traits (*DSM-IV*, p. 649). What is immediately striking about Clifford Olson in the brief portrayal provided earlier is not the specifics of his crimes so much as his apparent total lack of concern for what he has done to other people. The pain inflicted, the lives extinguished casually, and the awful, unnecessary grief of the victims' families mean nothing to him. The *DSM-IV* gives this lack of compassion a central importance: "The essential feature of Antisocial Personality Disorder is a pervasive pattern of disregard for, and violation of, the rights of others

Table 18–2

Personality disorder, usually coming to attention because of a gross disparity between behaviour and the prevailing social norms, and characterized by at least 3 of the following:

(a) callous unconcern for the feelings of others;
(b) gross and persistent attitude of irresponsibility and disregard for social norms, rules and obligations;
(c) incapacity to maintain enduring relationships, though having no difficulty in establishing them;
(d) very low tolerance to frustration and a low threshold for discharge of aggression, including violence;
(e) incapacity to experience guilt and to profit from experience, particularly punishment;
(f) marked proneness to blame others, or to offer plausible rationalizations, for the behaviour that has brought the patient into conflict with society.

Source: Long, 1995–1997a, p. 1.

that begins in childhood or early adolescence and continues into adulthood" (*DSM-IV,* p. 645).

Alternative Diagnostic Criteria

The World Health Organization's *International Classification of Mental and Behavioural Disorders (ICD-10)* describes a "Dissocial (Antisocial) Personality Disorder" as shown in Table 18–2.

Robert Hare has achieved prominence for his research on the Psychopathic Personality, and has developed a widely used checklist for diagnosing this condition. Hare (1996, see also Hare, Hart, & Harpur, 1991) argues that his conceptualization of psychopathy is not synonymous with the *DSM-IV* Antisocial Personality, though the two are clearly strongly related. Hare's main concern, as has already been noted, is that an exclusive reliance on behavioral criteria (i.e., a criminal history) is insufficient for assessing a personality pattern. His Psychopathy Checklist—Revised (PCL) (Hare, 1991) consists of 20 items. Factor analysis of these items suggests that the condition they measure has two dimensions: "Factor 1 measures a selfish, callous and remorseless use of others and contains most of the personality characteristics considered central to the traditional clinical conception of the disorder. Factor 2 measures social deviance, as mani-

Table 18–3   Items in the Revised Psychopathy Checklist

Factor 1
1. Glibness/Superficial charm
2. Grandiose sense of self-worth
4. Pathological lying
5. Conning/Manipulative
6. Lack of remorse or guilt
7. Shallow affect
8. Callous/lack of empathy
16. Failure to accept responsibility for actions

Factor 2
3. Need for stimulation/proneness to boredom
9. Parasitic Lifestyle
10. Poor behavioral controls
12. Early behavior problems
13. Lack of realistic, long-term goals
14. Impulsivity
15. Irresponsibility
18. Juvenile delinquency
19. Revocation of conditional release

Items not included in factor scales
11. Promiscuous sexual behavior
17. Many short-term marital relationships
20. Criminal versatility

Source: Harpur, Hart, & Hare, 1994, p. 152.

fested in a chronically unstable and antisocial lifestyle" (Harpur, Hart & Hare, 1994, p. 152). Table 18–3 lists the PCL items, organized according to the two main factors.

A good deal of research on the diagnosis of antisocial personalities has been and continues to be conducted (Long, 1995–1997b), and eventually there will be clearer agreement on what the most valid and reliable criteria for defining the condition are. At present, both clinical and research wisdom suggest that the Clifford Olsons of the world are extreme examples of a complex set of emotional, cognitive, and behavioral predispositions, expressed in different ways and with varying degrees of severity. Core elements are an emotional shallowness and lack of compassion, manipulativeness and exploitation in relation to others, and a lifestyle marked by impulsivity and a lack of concern for laws or other accepted codes of behavior.

Even when antisocial traits are expressed in relatively prosocial ways, the person may avoid entanglements with the police but is nevertheless likely to do harm. This can be in the form of ruthless treatment of others, exploitation of partners and children, and a reckless disregard for the obligations that come with membership in a human community.

A lack of compassion or empathy is universally acknowledged as a hallmark of antisocial personalities, and this bears elaboration, because the lack of compassion is not always expressed in obvious ways. While a fundamental indifference to the needs and feelings of others is part of the antisocial person's makeup, it is often juxtaposed with an ability to be extremely charming. Such people's skill at manipulation is predicated on an ability to engage easily with victims, to win their trust and friendship.

Victims are often subsequently embarrassed at the ease with which they were taken in by someone who, on reflection, did nothing to deserve trust and may even have provided ample clues suggesting extreme caution. But this painful realization comes after the fact—even, sometimes, to well-educated and experienced professionals who will admit that they should have known better. How is it that a person who lacks a capacity to care about others can be so good at winning their trust and friendship?

Empathy as we commonly understand it consists of responses on two dimensions (Nichols, 1987). When we empathize, we are engaged cognitively, being perceptive of the other person's needs and feelings. Equally importantly, our emotions and values are also engaged, in that the other's needs and feelings matter to us. If the experience to which we are attuned is a painful one, we are ourselves distressed, and are moved to offer support or to facilitate steps that will lead to relief.

The antisocial person may be acutely (sometimes brilliantly) perceptive regarding other people's needs, vulnerabilities, and agendas. Encountering someone who shows a keen understanding of us in this way can be disarming, and we can then easily think that the interest and understanding imply caring. However, the antisocial person is interested in our vulnerabilities only as something to exploit, as leverage to be used in exerting power in the service of his (or her) own egocentrically focused agendas. (See Figure 18–1.)

People who are unfortunate enough to enter into intimate relationships or committed friendships with antisocial people often have difficulty explaining why the attractions such people offer are so strong. Part of the explanation is the antisocial person's capacity for ersatz empathy. Being well attuned to others' needs and vulnerabilities, antisocial people can use that perceptiveness to win trust and commitment. To their social workers

Figure 18–1
Empathy and the Antisocial Personality

Acutely perceptive of others'
needs, vulnerabilities, agendas

Cognitive Dimension:
Perceptiveness of
other's needs

Antisocial
Functioning

Egocentrically indifferent to
experience of others

Responsive to experience of
others: distressed by their pain

Emotional
Dimension:
Compassion

Relatively unaware of others'
needs, vulnerabilities, agendas

they can appear self-reflective and interested in change; to a lover, sensitive and caring; to a parole board, a convert to the values of exemplary citizenship, committed to a new life, attending church and doing volunteer work, steering underprivileged youth away from the delinquent paths on which they themselves strayed.

There is a formulaic quality to this manipulativeness, and it is sometimes easy to detect, since not everyone with these propensities is equally skilled. In an intelligent and well-socialized person, however, the "glib, superficial charm" and verbal fluency of some antisocial people (*DSM-IV*, p. 647) translates into a formidable ability to make others their dupes. It is doubtful that anyone who works with such clients can claim not to have been conned at some point—unless they are new to the business and there has been insufficient time for the inevitable to happen.

With the goal of manipulative behavior being to control others in the service of their own egocentrically focused agendas, antisocial people can change formulas with disconcerting ease when it appears opportune to do so. Charm and the appearance of emotional commitment, since they are not rooted in any real caring or compassion, can be dropped and replaced with other strategies; intimidation, coercion, and bribery are not uncommon. In some abusive intimate relationships, victims report a vacillation between strategies based on seductive charm and coercive strategies based on a willingness to inflict fear and pain (through assaults, threats, and other emotional abuses). From a vantage point outside the relationship, the dishonesty of the false caring is made obvious by the brutality of more direct efforts to intimidate; to the victim, the situation may be profoundly confusing, and outsiders may have difficulty understanding her willingness to remain emotionally tied to her abuser.

CAUSES

There is a good deal of continuing research regarding the causes of anti-social personality traits (*DSM-IV*, p. 648; Gibbs, 1997; Hare, 1993; Long, 1995–1997c; Walter, R., Trainham, A., & LeDoux, L., 1997). Though more (always) remains to be done, current evidence suggests a convergence of multiple influences. Genetic predispositions play a part, as can family history (e.g., partner violence and addictions), personal history (abuse in childhood, for example), and socioeconomic pressures. Neurophysiological abnormalities may explain the characteristic lack of empathy and compassion, and the more general shallowness of affect (Hare, 1995), which is consistent with the observation that biological trauma (causing specific kinds of central nervous system injury) can also cause antisocial traits and behaviors to emerge. Such factors, varying in degree, interact with each other in ways that are not yet fully understood, and with results that remain uncertain. Research is difficult, in part because of definitional and measurement issues alluded to earlier, and the results of any one study need to be considered carefully with respect to those aspects.

INTERVENTION

Studies of the development of antisocial functioning provide evidence that such problems in adults are strongly predicted by similar behavioral and personality problems in childhood and adolescence (Cadoret & Stewart, 1991; Forth, Hart, & Hare, 1990; Hare, 1993; Hare, 1996). Such observations suggest the crucial importance of early intervention, and there is strong accumulating evidence that this can be effective, especially if programs engage parents effectively (Gibbs, 1997; Hare, 1993; Henggeler, et al., 1992; Holland, et al., 1993; Kazdin, et al., 1992; Moretti, et al., 1994; Tremblay, et al., 1991; Walter, et al., 1997). Such programs may prove to be the most effective intervention possible, though there are current impediments to their implementation. Valid and reliable assessment instruments or protocols are essential, for example, since we are rightly reluctant to assign ominous diagnoses to young people whose lives can be adversely affected by labeling. With present imperfect instruments, we face a dilemma, weighing the potential damage done by faulty assessments against the potential benefits that can be accomplished by deflecting a young person from a painful developmental path.

Working with the Antisocial Personality

If Freud's famous dictum is correct, that success in life requires capacities for love and gratifying work, then antisocial people have two serious strikes against them. Many of the traits we have discussed comprise a recipe for failure, over the long term, in both spheres. Impulsivity and a willingness to ignore the rights and expectations of others provide limited short-term rewards, but ultimately often lead to a failure to sustain gratifying relationships and careers (*DSM-IV*, p. 646).

Indeed, it is not uncommon that antisocial people are dissatisfied with their lives, are prone to feelings of boredom, depression, and emptiness, and have problems with substance abuse. However, they will not often ask for help, at least for help that implies personal change. The lack of concern for others that is characteristic of antisocial people means they will not be troubled by their behavior due to its costs to others. Traits typically also include egocentricity, and this often translates into an arrogant assessment of self combined with a devaluing of others. The consequence is a tendency to value one's own behavior despite its costs, and to dismiss efforts to help as interference by inferiors.

Professional contact with antisocial people is nevertheless common for social workers. Legally mandated involvements with workers in justice, corrections, and addictions settings are an obvious basis on which such a client might receive service involuntarily. Problems with employers due to substance abuse or other performance issues may result in involuntary or quasi-voluntary referrals, as can indictments for partner violence or child abuse. Lawyers may commend counseling to clients to create the appearance of good intentions for a court or parole board.

Also, social workers are often involved with clients who have been victimized by an antisocial person. In child abuse and family violence situations, for example, an antisocial perpetrator may be a powerful factor to be contended with, even if he does not see himself as needing (or wanting) to change (Huss, et al., 1997).

What to Expect from the Clinical Relationship

Clinical social workers with strong commitments to establishing helping relationships as they are traditionally understood may not work well with antisocial clients, unless they are willing to reorder their priorities. Though empathic understanding is always important, with an antisocial person this must be combined with an ability to challenge efforts at manipulation and other destructive behaviors, directed at the therapist or at others in the client's life. This places limits on our ability to be supportive which may be more stringent than is normally the case, and may also suggest more care respecting the rules one accepts regarding confidentiality. Maintaining silence when an antisocial client discloses illegal or destructive behavior can easily turn into allowing oneself to be manipulated into colluding with that behavior—and, indeed, this may well be the motive for the disclosure.

Agreeing to provide services to an antisocial client will always entail risks. In the worst case the relationship may involve deceit and efforts at intimidation; more often the risk may be that of incurring considerable costs in terms of time and few benefits in terms of a gratifying outcome. When one's clientele includes antisocial people, there is no avoiding such risks altogether, though they can be minimized if care is taken to establish the client's real purposes in the relationship, to determine if there is the possibility for any common ground respecting objectives, and to work cautiously from those.

When contact is initiated on an involuntary basis or for ulterior purposes, establishing a genuine treatment contract is always difficult. It is doubly so if the client has a propensity for manipulation and denial of personal responsibility. Skill, experience, and good supervision may help the social worker avoid being drawn into a helping relationship where the client's commitment to change is fraudulent, but the risk of deception is always high. Since trust is considered an important element in the helping alliance, and is often misplaced in relations with antisocial people, the dilemma facing the social worker is acute.

Antisocial people do not usually have well-differentiated views of others, including the professional helpers they encounter. Perhaps simplistically, it has been suggested that there are two roles to which such a client will wish to relegate the social worker: the "cop" and the "patsy" (see Wishnie, 1977). We may find ourselves in the first of these roles when we engage in power struggles with the client over behavior that is clearly problematic but that he himself has no desire to change. The second role is ours when we allow ourselves to be deceived and exploited and fail to confront that behavior. In either role, we will be ineffective since we are accommodating to a dysfunctional worldview with someone who has well-developed strategies for resisting authority figures and manipulating people who can be deceived into colluding with him.

It has been noted that the antisocial person's manipulativeness is formulaic. However skilled he or she may be, the strategies relied on become predictable in time, given sufficient observation. Confronted by situations where a formula does not work, the antisocial person may switch to a new strategy from his limited repertoire, and/or escalate his attempts to maintain control. Social workers who succeed in blocking early attempts to manipulate them should anticipate more intense efforts as a response. They should also be alert for the possible emergence of new, more ominous strategies; it is at such points that efforts at coercion through threats and intimidation may be encountered. For example, a social worker who successfully helps a woman extricate herself from a relationship with an abusive antisocial partner will normally spend time helping the woman identify and block manipulative efforts to secure her return. When this is accomplished, the worker will be well advised to anticipate, with the client, ways in which the partner will increase the intensity of his efforts. If they remain successful over time (the time involved varies with the person, and can be quite brief), threats or actual assaults may be attempted in an effort to regain control through intimidation.

As another example, a client in her early 20s decided to put an end to a bad drug habit, and obtained the help of a social worker. As she succeeding in stopping her substance abuse, two men with whom she had frequently used drugs made increasingly intense efforts to undermine her resolve and to draw her back to her earlier lifestyle. When these failed, the men resorted to threats of physical harm, directed at both the client and the social worker. The client needed to relocate in order to maintain her gains in safety. Fortunately, threats against the worker ceased once she did so.

Coercive threats against a social worker by an antisocial client require a careful response. The worker's own safety needs must be taken very seriously, and if agency and community resources are not sufficient in this regard, withdrawal of services may be necessary. We cannot be helpful to someone intent on frightening us, in any event. If efforts to intimidate cannot be confronted and constrained, there is little point in continuing a relationship that will almost certainly be unproductive and that could become increasingly dangerous.

When an antisocial client experiences a situation where his formulas are ineffective, and escalation does not help him regain control, he may decompensate (this may be most common in controlled settings). The form that the decompensation takes varies, but the general possibilities include explosive violence, withdrawal into substance abuse, and severe depression.

Social workers are accustomed to monitoring their own emotional reactions to clients as the helping relationship progresses; this practice is very useful when working with antisocial people. Specifically,

- Feeling fearful may suggest an intuitive perception that one is being threatened.
- Experiencing vicarious gratification from the client's illegal actions or risk-taking may lead the worker to implicitly reinforce antisocial traits and behaviors.
- Vicarious trauma may be experienced by the social worker if an antisocial client has been cruel or violent with others, and this reaction can be incapacitating. Good supervision and access to effective emotional supports are essential to workers engaged with such clients.
- Faced with manipulation, social workers can expect to feel off balance and confused at times. Again, good supervision and other opportunities for reality testing and validating one's perceptions are very important.
- When a client does successfully deceive a social worker, the worker's sense of competence can be undermined. Embarrassment over being taken in is understandable, but should be placed in the context of recognizing that even the most skilled and experienced social worker remains susceptible. The author knows of a situation where a highly antisocial person, released from jail, persuaded a senior social worker with a long career as a probation officer to contribute to his rehabilitation by providing him free room and board. This client was subsequently arrested for passing a series of forged checks in his benefactor's name.
- Hostile feelings in relation to an antisocial client may indicate that an unproductive power struggle has developed. This can be motivated by a desire to prove oneself (a desire to win), by pressures from referring agents, or by a need to forestall the harm that the client threatens to cause and to protect potential victims from his actions.

Realistic Goals

It is argued by some clinicians that antisocial behaviors and traits constitute a defense against an underlying profound depression. For this reason, it is believed, effective work on the presenting impulsivity and manipulativeness leads to the emergence of potentially overwhelming depressive reactions. Dealing with these underlying feelings requires considerable therapeutic attention and skill, and is believed to produce fundamental long-term benefits (Adler, 1979; Kernberg, 1992; Wishnie, 1977).

The issue is clouded somewhat by the fact that clinicians (like researchers) are not always consistent in the diagnostic categories they use and how they apply them. Still, there are case examples in the literature of clients who would almost certainly be considered antisocial being treated according to this psychodynamic model. The strong consensus seems to be, however, that that perspective is not generally applicable: it is likely invalid in many cases (certainly in the clearest and most extreme cases) and may require an unrealistic investment of resources with little reason to expect positive outcomes on a regular basis.

The more conventional wisdom is that when a therapeutic contract is entered into with an antisocial person, it is best if it prescribes modest goals:

> An international panel of experts commissioned by the Canadian government has designed an experimental program for psychopaths and other offenders at high risk for violence. Antisocial and violent acts are conceived as potentially preventable endpoints in a chain of events. The program makes no attempt to train the offenders in empathy, put them in touch with their feelings, or help them develop a conscience. The view that they have gone off track and simply need re-socialization is rejected. The aim is to make them accept responsibility for their behavior and persuade them changing it is in their own long-run interest. The program tries to help them use their abilities to satisfy their needs in socially tolerable ways. (Hare, 1995, p. 2; see also Hare, 1993)

Such goals may be modest, but they are not inconsequential. As Hare goes on to point out, antisocial men become less prone to violence, and their criminality tends to diminish, in midlife. Diverting them from activities that could lead to incarceration in their 20s could "buy time" for them and, thereby, have significant benefits in the long term.

Other Considerations Regarding Intervention

Collaboration
The fields of service in which social workers are likely to encounter antisocial clients include corrections, child welfare, addictions, and family services—especially in family violence situations. Not uncommonly, more than one agency and more than one profession will have had involvements with

the client: a child-welfare worker may share concerns about an abusive parent with an addictions counselor, an employer, and the police, for example.

In work with antisocial clients there will often be a strong need for collaboration among people who do not always have the same priorities. Effective collaboration is often critical in offering protection to victims from further victimization. When rehabilitation of the antisocial person is the goal, arresting his impulsivity and manipulativeness often also requires close collaboration—and vigilance against efforts to play services or professionals off against one another.

Pharmacology

There is no support in the literature for the use of drugs to treat antisocial functioning per se. Medications may be prescribed for related issues, such as depression and irritability (*DSM-IV*, p. 647) but won't change the core behaviors and traits, and since a tendency to abuse substances is often part of the person's difficulties, caution is warranted.

Treatment Modalities

It is likely that the commonest form of treatment that antisocial clients encounter is group counseling, because of conventions prevalent in settings like correctional facilities, addictions agencies, and family violence programs. Appropriate as group services may be for most clients in these settings, they may have little impact on a subgroup of strongly antisocial people—the approximately 15% to 20% who cause the most harm, are least likely to respond to treatment, and are inclined to recidivate quickly after service is ended.

The argument may be made with some validity that a group consisting of other offenders will be best able to detect and confront efforts at manipulation or deceit. This possible benefit is counterbalanced, however, by a concern that a strongly antisocial client's traits may make it difficult for him to benefit from groups not specifically designed to address his agendas and his interpersonal style. Someone who is less inclined to respond to others with respect and compassion than with exploitive manipulativeness represents a risk in group treatments for obvious reasons. Further, if he perceives a benefit to doing so, he may accommodate to the group's program, goals, and expectations in a superficial way, but without committing to lasting change.

In brief, inclusion of someone with strong antisocial traits in groups that greatly benefit other clients—anger management groups, couples' communications groups, parenting skills training, for example—is often contraindicated. One concern is a misallocation of scarce resources. Another is that successful completion of such programs by someone whose goals are manipulative can disarm that person's potential victims and place them at continued risk. The example that comes most easily to mind is a woman who is led to believe her abusive partner is making sincere attempts to change when he is really simply attempting to deceive her into returning to a high-risk relationship.

Similar concerns arise when couples or family therapy is contemplated. As with groups, there is an assumption underlying such work that the clients are (or can be) emotionally committed and responsible toward one another. When that assumption is wrong, inclusion of an antisocial person in the therapy can place other clients at risk: their self-disclosures may be used against them, commitments to change may lead to further betrayals, and challenges to favored interpersonal strategies may lead to escalating coercion or worse.

PRIORITIES FOR FUTURE KNOWLEDGE DEVELOPMENT

Current debates about how our society should respond to citizens who trouble us through their disregard for the rights of others are nothing new. There have always been those who lean toward a punitive or justice response and those who favor treatment or rehabilitation. Whereas many offenders can be helped to change through a combination of such strategies, strongly antisocial people present an unfortunate irony: they are as immune to punishment as they are to the influence of more benign therapeutic efforts. In part, this suggests that continued efforts to design programs be very carefully tailored to the unique challenges they present. One example of such an effort was introduced above. There is unquestionably much more such work to be done, as our understanding of these clients increases and our appreciation grows regarding how they differ from other people we serve—and for whom many of our approaches and techniques were designed.

Present evidence regarding the efficacy of early intervention is encouraging, and suggests ongoing work developing programs and researching their outcomes. As we have noted, such efforts also require continued attention to assessment. Instruments and protocols for detecting young people at genuine risk of consolidating antisocial traits during their preadolescent and adolescent years will make an important contribution, especially if they can be refined enough so that the dangers of mislabeling are minimized.

Social work practitioners, scholars and educators could also profitably devote attention to improved assessment of antisocial functioning in the adult populations they serve. This particular personality disorder is more clearly understood and can be more reliably assessed than any other in the *DSM-IV,* and educating ourselves to detect clients with strong antisocial traits is important for compelling reasons. Programs that effectively serve clients implicated in family violence or other criminal acts may have little impact on the antisocial minority within the larger populations. Careful differential diagnosis therefore allows us to recognize a group for whom special programs must be developed, and to exclude that group from programs to which they are unlikely to respond, and in which they might make it more difficult for other participants to benefit. Finally, protection for potential victims is more effective to the extent that we develop a differentiated understanding of perpetrators, and are quick to identify those who are the greatest ongoing risk to others in their lives.

Services to victims are also an area where much remains to be learned. Extricating oneself from a destructive relationship with an antisocial person and recovering from its effects is a difficult, subtle, and important process—a process we have not analyzed or researched nearly systematically enough. Victims of torture, or sadistic child abuse, or partner violence often claim that the physical pain they endured is easier to recover from than the fact that it was administered with an incomprehensible dispassion, without guilt, with no empathic concern for their suffering. Although social workers involved in helping these clients know their trauma is unique, there is a dearth of research to guide our interventions. But clinical wisdom is accumulating.

REFERENCES

Adler, G. (1979). Psychodynamics of impulsive behavior. In H. Wishnie & J. Nevis-Olesen (Eds.). *Working with the impulsive person* (pp. 3–17). New York: Plenum.

American Psychiatric Association. (1994). *Diagnostic and statistical manual of mental disorders, fourth edition.* (DSM-IV). Washington, DC: Author.

Cadoret, R., & Stewart, M. (1991). An adoption study of attention deficit/hyperactivity/aggression and their relationship to adult antisocial personality. *Comprehensive Psychiatry, 32,* 1, 73–82.

Forth, A., Brown, S., Harpur, S., & Hare, R. (1996). The assessment of psychopathology in male and female noncriminals: Reliability and validity. *Personality and Individual Differences, 20,* 5, 531–543.

Forth, A., Hart, S., & Hare, R. (1990). Assessment of psychopathology in male young offenders. *Psychological Assessment, 2,* 3, 342–344.

Gibbs, W. (1997). Seeking the criminal element. *Scientific American, Mysteries of the Mind, Special Issue, 7,* 1, 102–110.

Hall, N., & MacQueen, K. (1997, August 22). Families relieved Olson ordeal over. *Calgary Herald,* pp. A1, A2.

Hare, R. (1991). *The Hare psychopathology checklist—Revised.* Toronto, ON: Multi-Health Systems.

Hare, R. (1993). *Without conscience: The disturbing world of the psychopaths among us.* New York: Pocket Books.

Hare, R. (1995). *Psychopaths: New trends in research.* [On Line] Available: http://www.mentalhealth.com/mag1/p5h-pe01.html.

Hare, R. (1996). Psychopathy: A clinical construct whose time has come. *Criminal Justice and Behavior 23*, 1, 25–54.

Harpur, T., Hart, S., & Hare, R. (1994). Personality of the psychopath. In P. Costa & T. Widiger (Eds.), *Personality disorders and the five-factor model of personality* (pp. 149–173). Washington, DC: American Psychological Association.

Hare, R., Hart, S., & Harpur, T. (1991). Psychopathy and the DSM-IV criteria for antisocial personality disorder. *Journal of Abnormal Psychology, 100,* 3, 391–398.

Henggeler, S., Melton, G., & Smith, L. (1992). Family preservation using multisystemic therapy: An effective alternative to incarcerating serious juvenile offenders. *Journal of Consulting and Clinical Psychology, 60,* 6, 953–961.

Holland, R., Moretti, M., Verlaan, V., & Peterson, S. (1993). Attachment and conduct disorder: The response program. *Canadian Journal of Psychiatry, 38,* 6, 420–431.

Huss, M., Langhinrichsen-Rohling, J., & Scalora, M. (1997, July). Psychopathology as a useful taxon in the treatment of male batterers. Presented at the 5th International Family Violence Research Conference, Durham, New Hampshire.

Kazdin, A., Siegel, T., & Bass, D. (1992). Cognitive problem-solving skills training and parent management training in the treatment of antisocial behavior in children. *Journal of Consulting and Clinical Psychology, 60,* 5, 733–747.

Kernberg, O. (1992). Psychopathic, paranoid and depressive transferences. *International Journal of Psychoanalysis, 73,* 13–28.

Long, P. (1995–1997a). Antisocial personality disorder: European descriptions. *Internet Mental Health* [On-line]. Available: http://www.mentalhealth.com/icd/p22-pe04.html.

Long, P. (1995–1997b). Antisocial personality disorder: Research re: Diagnosis. *Internet Mental Health* [On-line]. Available: http://www.mentalhealth.com/dis-rsl/p24-pe04.html.

Long, P. (1995–1997c). Antisocial personality disorder: Research re: Cause. *Internet Mental Health* [On-line]. Available: http://www.mentalhealth.com/dis-rs3/p26-pe04.html.

Moretti, M., Holland, R., & Peterson, S. (1994). Long-term outcome of an attachment-based program for conduct disorder. *Canadian Journal of Psychiatry, 39,* 6, 360–370.

Nichols, M. (1987). *The self in the system: Expanding the limits of family therapy.* New York: Brunner/Mazel.

Paris, J. (1997). Antisocial and borderline personality disorders: Two separate diagnoses or two aspects of the same psychopathology? *Comprehensive Psychiatry, 38,* 4, 237–242.

Shaw, G. (1960). *Major barbara.* London: Longmans, Green and Co.

Tremblay, R., McCord, J., Boileau, H., Charlebois, P., Gagnon, C., Le Blanc, M., & Larivee, S. (1991). Can disruptive boys be helped to become competent? *Psychiatry, 54,* 2, 148–161.

Walter, R., Trainham, A., & LeDoux, L. (1997). The relationship of parental battering to violent and other maladaptive behavior among juvenile first offenders. Presented at the 5th International Family Violence Research Conference, Durham, New Hampshire.

Wishnie, H. (1977). *The impulsive personality: Understanding people with impulsive personality disorders.* New York: Plenum

19

DISSOCIATIVE IDENTITY DISORDER

Jim Lantz

Dissociative identity disorder is the term currently used in the *Diagnostic and Statistical Manual of Mental Disorders (DSM-IV)* (American Psychiatric Association, 1994) for what is commonly called multiple personality disorder in the general press and among the general public. Dissociative identity disorder is a chronic human problem that includes dissociative phenomena and is almost always reactive to a traumatic event. Such a traumatic event is frequently a childhood trauma, such as physical, ritual, and/or child sexual abuse (Kaplan, et al., 1994; Ross, 1989). Persons who experience dissociative identity disorder have more than one distinct personality, and each of the two or more personalities determines feelings, thoughts, and behaviors when it takes over the individual and becomes the dominant personality. Popular books and films, such as *The Minds of Billy Milligan* (Keyes, 1981), *The Three Faces of Eve* (Thigpen & Checkley, 1957) and *Sybil* (Schreiber, 1973) have presented the public with an amazingly accurate idea of the personality switching that occurs when a person is suffering with this human problem.

DESCRIPTION OF THE PROBLEM

The current edition of the *Diagnostic and Statistical Manual of Mental Disorders (DSM-IV)* reports that the diagnostic criteria for dissociative identity disorder include: the presence of two or more distinct identities or personality states; at least two of the identities recurrently take control of the person's behavior; the person has an inability to recall important personal information that is too extensive to be explained by ordinary forgetfulness; and the disturbance is not due to the direct physiological effects of substances such as alcohol or drugs. Other indicators for the presence of dissociative identity disorder include: reports of time distortions; hearing reports of behavioral episodes that are not remembered; the client is recognized by people whom the client does not recognize; the client calls himself/herself by a different name or refers to himself/herself in the third person; other personalities can be elicited under hypnosis; the client frequently uses the word "we" during the treatment interview; the client discovers objects among his/her personal belongings that he/she does not recognize; the client has frequent headaches; the client hears voices from within that are not identified as separate or outside the self; and the client has a history of severe emotional and/or physical trauma as a child (Kaplan, et al., 1994). Additional features of dissociative identity disorder may include blank spells, flashbacks, feelings of unreality, emerging from a blank spell in a strange place, and displaying different handwriting styles (Ross, 1989).

HISTORY OF THE PROBLEM

Prior to the 1800s, most people suffering with dissociative identity disorder were understood as being "possessed" and were frequently killed. After 1800, mental health practitioners such as Charcot, Janet, Bleuler, and Freud recognized the dissociative nature of such apparent "possessions" as well as the "trauma connection" and etiology of such symptoms (Bliss, 1986; Caul, 1984; Greaves, 1980; Young, 1988; Herman, 1992). For many years mental health practitioners in North America have debated the reality and/or validity of the diagnosis of multiple personality disorder. In recent years the diagnostic label of *dissociative identity disorder* has gained considerable credence in the mental health professions (including the social work profession); as a result, new understandings, treatment concepts, and treatment approaches are appearing more frequently in the literature.

DEMOGRAPHICS

At the present time, it is generally believed that more women suffer from dissociative identity disorder than men (Greaves, 1988). This may be because women and young girls are more likely to suffer rape and other forms of sexual abuse than men and young boys. It should be noted, however, that men and young boys are probably no less likely to suffer physical assault and other forms of physical abuse than are women and young girls. As a result, we might expect to find a higher incidence of dissociative identity disorder among men in future years (Ross, 1989).

There has been some speculation that there is a greater incidence of dissociative identity disorder in population groups that manifest higher levels of physical violence and child abuse (Ross, 1989). It has been suggested that factors such as long-term unemployment, poverty, alcoholism, and drug abuse may be associated with an increased incidence of violence and dissociative identity disorder (Greaves, 1980; Ross, 1989).

CAUSATION

There is considerable agreement in social work and the other mental health professions that persons suffering with dissociative identity disorder have almost always suffered significant traumatic events during childhood and that these events were often physical abuse, sexual abuse, and/or ritual abuse. Generally, such abuse was not a single, isolated incident but a series of traumatic and overwhelming events experienced over many years (Ross, 1989).

There has been some suggestion that persons who develop dissociative identity disorder are more easily hypnotized than persons who do not develop the disorder; as a result, it has been hypothesized that the disorder may develop reactive to "suggestion" and/or in order to obtain secondary gains (Ross, 1989). This is not the perspective of most social workers who have had experience with the multiple-personality-disorder client, nor that of the author of this chapter! It appears that dissociative identity disorder develops reactive to the experience of severe trauma (usually in childhood) and that the disorder is used by the trauma victim to cope with and overcome the pain, suffering, and terror of the trauma situation.

DIFFERENTIAL DIAGNOSIS

Dissociative identity disorder is frequently misdiagnosed (Greaves, 1980; Greaves, 1988; Ross, 1989). With considerable frequency, dissociative identity disorder has been mislabeled as borderline personality disorder, schizophrenia, bipolar disorder, and schizoaffective disorder. Giving dissociative-identity-disorder clients an incorrect diagnostic label is extremely damaging, as it may lead the treatment process to an overreliance upon medications rather than the treatment relationship and to intervention methods that do not focus upon fusion, co-consciousness and cooperation among the client's different personalities (Greaves, 1980; Kluft, 1984, 1988, 1992). Dissociative-identity-disorder clients are often viewed as exhibiting the characteristics and symptoms of borderline personality disorder (BPD) clients. Although this may be somewhat accurate, treating a dissociative-identity-disorder client as if he or she were "borderline" often decreases focus upon, and empathic understanding of, the experiences of trauma in the client's past, which is an extremely important component of effective treatment (Lantz, 1992; Lantz & Lantz, 1992; Ross, 1989).

INTERDISCIPLINARY ISSUES

The current understanding of dissociative identity disorder and its treatment has truly resulted from interdisciplinary involvement and cooperation. Significant contributions to the understanding and treatment of this illness have come from the professions of social work, psychology, psychiatry, counseling, and nursing, and from pastoral care (Ross, 1989).

The contributions of social work to the understanding and treatment of identity disorders have come primarily from our understandings about the effects of child abuse; the use of the treatment relationship in helping children, adolescents, and young adults to overcome the impacts of trauma and other forms of abuse; and the importance of preventing this disorder by developing preventive programs to decrease the incidence of child abuse, substance abuse, and drug abuse (Lantz, 1978; Lantz & Lantz, 1992).

PHARMACOLOGY

Medications are frequently used in treating dissociative-identity-disorder clients. The amount and type of medications vary greatly depending upon the skill, experience, and treatment philosophy of the psychiatrist prescribing the medication. Medications often used to treat this disorder include antidepressant medications, antipsychotic medications, antianxiety medications, and, on occasion, antimanic medications (Klein & Rowland, 1996). At times medications are extremely difficult to use with dissociative-identity-disorder clients, because the medications may act differently upon each of the client's personalities (Keyes, 1981). A final important issue is that social workers and other mental health providers who are treating dissociative-identity-disorder clients often ask a consulting psychiatrist to medicate the clients—in order to decrease their own "helper's anxiety," which is often extremely high when treating the dissociative-identity-disorder client, rather than for the benefit of the client. In this situation, clinical consultation and supervision for the service provider is often more useful than medication for the client.

THREE TREATMENT ORIENTATIONS

Three basic approaches are frequently described in the social work and mental health literature about the treatment of dissociative-identity-disorder clients. These treatment approaches can be called the reparenting approach, the fusion approach and the internal-cooperation approach (Ross, 1989; Kluft, 1992; Lantz, 1978).

The Reparenting Approach

In the reparenting approach to the treatment of dissociative-identity-disorder clients, it is believed that the client has undergone such a traumatic childhood that empathic reparenting is necessary for the client to overcome the impact of that trauma on his or her life and thus overcome the need for dissociation and multiple personalities to deal with the pain. In the reparenting approach, the central curative factor is considered to be the corrective emotional treatment experience. However, the reparenting approach to the treatment of this disorder has lost considerable favor in recent years among many social workers and mental health professionals (Kluft, 1984, 1988; Lantz, 1978). The approach often results in chaotic treatment, wherein the reparenting mental health helper reacts to the chaos of the client and the client does not experience a stable and consistent treatment relationship and treatment approach (Kluft, 1984, 1988, 1992; Greaves, 1980, 1988).

The Fusion Approach

In the fusion approach to the treatment of the dissociative-identity-disorder client, it is considered to be the task of the mental health worker to help the client overcome dissociation and the process of developing different personalities by helping each of the separate personalities to fuse into one central and complete personality (Kluft, 1992; Greaves, 1988). In this view, it is understood that the client develops different personalities in order to deal with the impact of trauma and that such defenses are both helpful and harmful. In the fusion view, it is believed that insight and awareness can help each personality share with the other personalities knowledge, awareness, memories, skills, information, and capacities, and that eventually such information and skill trading can be done permanently in a way that results in a single personality. In the fusion approach, hypnosis, letters from one personality to another, audiovisual tape recordings of each personality that are shown to the other personalities, and "group" meetings in which all alter personalities are present are utilized to promote fusion among the various personalities (Bliss, 1986; Caul, 1984; Ross, 1989; Wilbur, 1984; Greaves, 1980).

The Internal-Cooperation Approach

In the internal-cooperation approach to the treatment of the dissociative-identity-disorder client, it is believed that: (1) the client develops different personalities and the ability to dissociate reactive to severe and ongoing trauma during childhood; (2) each personality develops one or more "functions" and/or "skills," which the client uses in a crisis or trauma situation; (3) the client switches personalities depending upon the personality skill that is needed; (4) the client's ability to switch personalities to obtain and utilize their skills is both helpful and harmful; (5) the client will not be able to achieve fusion unless he or she first gains a significant level of co-consciousness among personalities about the traumatic events in his or her past; (6) the client also will not be able to obtain fusion until after the different personalities exchange skills with each other and can utilize each other's skills when necessary; and (7) fusion should occur only after the development of co-consciousness and skill trading and after the client decides that fusion ought to occur (Kluft, 1992; Lantz, 1978, 1992; Lantz & Lantz, 1992).

In this view, it is understood that fusion is not the primary treatment goal. In the internal-cooperation approach, co-consciousness and skill training to help the client personalities become a more effective "group" is the primary treatment goal. When this treatment goal has been achieved, fusion is sometimes (not always) the final treatment result (Caul, 1984; Kluft, 1984; Lantz, 1978; Wilbur, 1984). In the internal-cooperation approach to the treatment of the dissociative-identity-disorder client, awareness, insight, and defense analysis treatment strategies, along with hypnosis and internal group therapy sessions, are often used to promote co-consciousness and skill trading (Kluft, 1984; Lantz, 1978).

For many proponents of the internal-cooperation approach, insights and skills from group psychotherapy and family therapy have provided many treatment understandings and treatment benefits for dissociative-identity-disorder clients (Lantz, 1978). The internal-cooperation approach has lost some favor to the fusion approach in recent years (Kluft, 1992). The internal-cooperation approach remains this author's orientation to treatment because the goal of this treatment approach maintains client choice about the goal of fusion as the central bond between client and therapist in the treatment relationship. This central bond and agreement is an extremely important component in this author's existential treatment approach (Harper & Lantz, 1996; Lantz, 1978, 1992; Lantz & Lantz, 1992).

DIFFERENTIAL USE OF THEORIES

There is no clear agreement among social workers and other mental health providers who work with dissociative-identity-disorder clients about which clinical theory works best with this population group (Greaves, 1988). The basic reality is that the important elements of treatment have little to do with the social worker's theoretical orientation but a great deal to do with his/her personal characteristics as a helper and with his/her use of several pragmatic treatment principles—principles discovered and utilized by mental health workers who are experienced and effective in the treatment of the dissociative-identity-disorder client yet who hail from different theoretical orientations. A list of such pragmatic treatment principles has been provided by Kluft (1992) and also by Greaves (1988). The following list of pragmatic treatment principles is adapted from Kluft (1992) but is also indebted to the work of Greaves (1988). The reader should recognize these principles as very compatible with the basic practice methods utilized by many direct-service clinical social workers who come to clinical practice from many different theoretical orientations.

PRAGMATIC PRINCIPLES FOR TREATING DISSOCIATIVE IDENTITY DISORDER

The first basic principle in the treatment of the dissociative-identity-disorder client is to provide the client with *firm boundaries and a consistent treatment structure* (Kluft, 1992). Providing the client with stable and firm boundaries is important, because the client's symptoms and problems are generally reactions to traumas the client has suffered as a result of boundary violations that left the client unable to maintain structure and protection in his or her life. Setting up strong, reliable boundaries in the treatment relationship is necessary to protect the client, to give the client a feeling of safety, and to build mutual trust between client and therapist (Greaves, 1988; Kluft, 1992; Lantz, 1978).

A second basic principle in the treatment of the dissociative-identity-disorder client is to focus upon helping the client to achieve *a sense of mastery and control* over his or her life (Greaves, 1988; Kluft, 1992). Many dissociative-identity-disorder clients experience an external locus of control in their lives; this is a defense reactive to the many unwanted assaults they endured as children (Kluft, 1992). As a result, it is imperative that the therapist work hard to engage the client as an active participant in the treatment process (Harper & Lantz, 1996; Lantz, 1978; Lantz & Lantz, 1992). This can help the client to develop a sense of self and internal control as well as a greater sense of personal empowerment (Lantz, 1978).

A third important principle in the treatment of the dissociative-identity-disorder client is to develop and maintain *a strong treatment alliance between client and therapist* (Greaves, 1988; Kluft, 1992). The client has generally experienced interpersonal relationships with significant others that were unreliable, inconsistent, and filled with danger. As a result, it is extremely important for the therapist to monitor, and help the client to monitor, their working relationship, checking with each other through direct and active discussion whenever the relationship seems to be growing and/or deteriorating (Lantz, 1978).

A fourth important principle in the treatment of the dissociative-identity-disorder client is to help the client *uncover, remember, and deal with buried trauma and trauma affect* (Greaves, 1988; Kluft, 1992; Lantz, 1978; Lantz & Lantz, 1992). Dissociative identity disorder is a condition that is reactive to trauma and the buried trauma experience. The defense of dissociation and the development of different client personalities are best confronted and worked through by uncovering different client trauma experiences and effects and then introducing this information to the different client personalities (Kluft, 1992).

A fifth basic principle when working with the dissociative-identity-disorder client is to work hard to *reduce conflict and separateness among the client's different personalities* (Kluft, 1992; Lantz, 1978). Without cooperation and collaboration, the client's different personalities will not be able to share information, knowledge, skills, and abilities. In this author's opinion (Lantz, 1978), only when the client's different personalities have shared with each other adequate information and skills is there a real chance that personality integration can occur.

A sixth important treatment principle when working with the dissociative-identity-disorder client is to help the client's different personalities to *achieve congruence of perception* (Kluft, 1992). For example, two different personalities may have very different perceptions about the client's father, and these two personalities may have difficulty working together because of their conflicting perceptions. It is the therapist's role to attempt to help the conflicting personalities to gain information, share experiences, and listen carefully to each other so that "together" they can increase the objectivity and accuracy of their perceptions (Kluft, 1992).

A seventh important treatment principle when working with the dissociative-identity-disorder client is to treat *all* of the client's different personalities with consistency and evenhandedness (Kluft, 1992). It is important for the therapist to remember that every client personality was developed to perform a necessary function and that each individual personality is no less important than the others. Therapists with experience in group treatment and family therapy are sometimes better able to be fair with all of the client's different personalities (Lantz, 1978).

An eighth important treatment principle when working with the dissociative-identity-disorder client is to work hard to help the client to *regain some of his or her shattered basic world assumptions* (Kluft, 1992). Dissociative-identity-disorder clients have endured such traumatic and pain-filled experiences that it is important for the therapist to provide realistic hope, restore morale, and help the client to gain a sense of opportunity based upon real experiences with significant persons who will not hurt the client or try to manipulate him or her for their own ends (Kluft, 1992; Lantz, 1978).

A ninth treatment principle to use when working with the dissociative-identity-disorder client is to minimize avoidable overwhelming experiences whenever possible (Kluft, 1992). Dissociative identity disorder is an overwhelming experience in itself, and in many instances the pace of therapy outstrips the client's ability to remember and integrate the many traumatic experiences in his or her past (Greaves, 1980, 1988; Kluft, 1988).

A tenth important concept in the treatment of the dissociative-identity-disorder client is to *reinforce personal responsibility* (Kluft, 1992). As Kluft (1992) has pointed out, dissociative identity disorder results from the irresponsibility of others; as a result, it is extremely important to hold the client to the highest standards of behavior in his or her own life. Since the client has observed a great deal of irresponsibility in his or her life, it is especially important for the therapist to matter-of-factly expect consistent and incorruptible behavior from the client. It is also especially important for the therapist to model ethical behavior so the client may have some examples with which to identify.

An eleventh principle in the treatment of the dissociative-identity-disorder client is to provide the client a *warm, flexible, and active therapeutic atmosphere* (Greaves, 1988; Kluft, 1992). Therapists who are themselves disengaged do not do well in engaging the dissociative-identity-disorder client. As a result, the therapist should generally avoid neutrality whenever possible. To many dissociative-identity-disorder clients, "technical neutrality" will be experienced as rejecting and uncaring behavior and will disrupt the primary healing element of treatment—the therapeutic

Trust is extremely important

relationship itself (Kluft, 1984, 1988, 1992). Although it is important to provide a warm, flexible treatment relationship, under no circumstances should the therapist attempt to "purchase" a client's favor, and the therapist must consistently remain self-aware in order to avoid violating the proper treatment boundaries.

A final principle of treatment with the dissociative-identity-disorder client is to help the client *correct faulty cognitions and/or cognitive errors.* Dissociative identity disorder is a human condition in which the client develops many cognitive errors. As a result, the treatment experience should help the client to correct and overcome such ongoing cognitive problems. Cognitive restructuring activities are especially useful to help the client solve many problems and gain many strengths (Kluft, 1992).

TREATMENT MODALITIES

Most practitioners who work extensively with dissociative-identity-disorder clients recommend individual psychotherapy as the treatment approach of choice (Ross, 1989). Dissociative-identity-disorder clients benefit from a structured yet flexible approach to treatment; thus, the individual-treatment modality is believed most effective when attempting to maximize flexibility and to provide a tailored response to the client's treatment needs while maintaining consistency and treatment rigor. This author does not recommend group treatment for dissociative-identity-disorder clients unless the therapist is extremely skilled and experienced with groups and with this sort of client. This author also does not recommend family treatment for dissociative-identity-disorder clients and their family of origin. Often such clients have experienced physical, sexual, or even ritual abuse at the hands of their family of origin. The mental health worker is advised to be extremely careful when working with the dissociative-identity-disorder client's family of origin.

INNER GROUP THERAPY

An unusual form of group therapy that has had considerable effectiveness with the dissociative-identity-disorder client is the "inner group therapy" experience originated and described by David Caul (1984). Caul's (1984) approach is to get the dissociative-identity-disorder client's alter egos to hold conferences with each other and to talk with each other in a group meeting. The therapist acts as a facilitator and uses the group meeting to help client personalities share information, insight, memories, and skills.

Such an approach can help the client develop co-consciousness, to achieve fusion, and to trade information and skills (Caul, 1984).

HYPNOSIS

Hypnosis is a psychotherapeutic tool that can be utilized effectively in the treatment of the dissociative-identity-disorder client (Ross, 1994; Kluft, 1984; Caul, 1984). It is probably accurate to believe that the dissociative-identity-disorder client most likely spends a considerable amount of his or her life in some form of hypnotic trance, as self-hypnosis and dissociation are the client's major defenses against trauma and trauma pain. As a result, it makes considerable sense for the mental health worker and the client to use hypnotic trance together to help the client remember trauma, process trauma effect, practice coping skills and focus concentration in a healthy direction. Although this author believes that it is not necessary for a social worker to be trained in hypnosis before treating a dissociative-identity-disorder client (one of this author's best friends has treated four dissociative-identity-disorder clients very effectively without knowing hypnosis), he does believe that hypnosis is a useful skills that can be of great benefit to the dissociative-identity-disorder client requesting help. This author does not know how Caul's (1984) "inner group" experience can be utilized without the use of hypnosis.

COMMUNITY MENTAL HEALTH RESOURCES

Starting in the early 1970s, mental health practitioners such as Wilbur (1984), Caul (1984), Greaves (1980), Ross (1989), Kluft (1984), and Lantz (1978) have been somewhat effective in getting practitioners from the community mental health movement to take an interest in the dissociative-identity-disorder client and to begin treating such clients on a regular basis. Often such treatment endeavors have yielded good results (Keyes, 1981; Lantz, 1978; Greaves, 1988). For many years dissociative-identity-disorder clients have been treated successfully in community mental health centers, but this trend has changed in recent years as such centers have suffered massive cutbacks and have begun using case management systems to "contain" service provision and service expansion. The simple fact is that the average competent social work practitioner needs from three to five years, with two appointments per week, to help the average dissociative-identity-disorder client to achieve integration. As the reader can see, managed care and time-limited treatment systems do not work well with the dissociative-identity-disorder client.

Joyce was referred to this author for treatment by her boyfriend, who was concerned with Joyce's depression, her bad dreams, her "spaciness," and her anxiety. Joyce was a junior at a midwestern university and hoped to become a nurse. She had been accepted into nursing school and had also been accepted for numerous student loans. Joyce reported that she did not visit her parents because "they beat me when I was young" and "I am afraid of them."

Over a four-year period of time, Joyce earned excellent grades and graduated from nursing school. During her junior and senior years, she shared with this author 14 distinct personalities that she had developed while growing up in an extremely violent rural family. She revealed that she had been continuously raped, tortured, and abused in other ways by her father, her older brother, and her uncle. Joyce reported that her mother had also been "abused by the men in my family." During treatment Joyce met 13 alter personalities that had helped her to survive over the years. Each personality was a different age and each had a different function and/or job. During treatment all 14 personalities were introduced to each other, gave each other information about each other's experiences, and were able to teach each other skills and how to perform each other's functions. Joyce's personalities fused approximately eight months before Joyce terminated treatment. Joyce was seen in this author's private practice but was also seen in an emergency services unit of a community mental health center on a number of occasions and at an inpatient psychiatric unit for three weeks in the middle of her treatment experience. Joyce has neither requested nor required treatment during the past two years and functions well as a nurse at a local hospital. She is presently considering marriage.

THE FUTURE

It is important to note that the dissociative-identity-disorder client is well understood; that the dynamics of the clinical situation are well understood; that we presently have the knowledge and skill needed to treat such clients with considerable success; and that in spite of our knowledge and skill, we are still not providing such clients with adequate treatment because we have not yet been provided with adequate funding for the treatment they need. The recent focus upon time-limited treatment and the use of time-limited approaches in social service agencies and community mental health centers almost ensures that the dissociative-identity-disorder client will fail to receive the intensive treatment he or she needs and deserves in order to get well. In this author's opinion, this is the central and most important current concern for the dissociative-identity-disorder client in North America today.

REFERENCES

American Psychiatric Association. (1994). *Diagnostic and statistical manual of mental disorders, fourth edition.* Washington, DC: Author.

Bliss, E. (1986). *Multiple personality, allied disorders and hypnosis.* New York: Oxford University Press.

Caul, D. (1984). Group and videotape techniques for multiple personality disorder. *Psychiatric Annals, 14,* 46–50.

Greaves, G. (1980). Multiple personality, 165 years after Mary Reynolds. *Journal of Nervous and Mental Disease, 168,* 577–596.

Greaves, G. (1988). Common errors in the treatment of multiple personality disorder. *Dissociation, 1,* 61–66.

Harper, K., & Lantz, J. (1996). *Cross-cultural practice: Social work with vulnerable populations.* Chicago: Lyceum Books.

Herman, J. (1992). *Trauma and recovery.* New York: Simon & Schuster.

Kaplan, H., Sadock, B., & Grebb, J. (1994). *Synopsis of psychiatry* (7th Ed.). Baltimore: Williams & Wilkins.

Keyes, D. (1981). *The minds of Billy Milligan.* New York: Random House.

Klein, D., & Rowland, L. (1996). *Current psychotherapeutic drugs.* New York: Brunner/Mazel.

Kluft, R. (1984). Treatment of multiple personality disorder. *Psychiatric Clinics of North America, 7,* 9–29.

Kluft, R. (1988). On treating the older patient with multiple personality disorder: Race against time or make haste slowly? *American Journal of Clinical Hypnosis, 30,* 257–266.

Kluft, R. (1992). The perspective of a specialist in the dissociative disorders. *Psychoanalytic Inquiry, 12,* 139–171.

Lantz, J. (1978). *Family and marital therapy.* New York: Appleton-Century-Crofts.

Lantz, J. (1992). Using Frankl's concepts with PTSD clients. *Journal of Traumatic Stress, 5,* 485–490.

Lantz, J., & Lantz, J. (1992). Franklian treatment with adults molested as children. *Journal of Religion and Health, 31,* 297–307.

Ross, C. (1989). *Multiple personality disorder.* New York: Wiley.

Schreiber, F. (1973). *Sybil.* Chicago: Henry Regnery.

Thigpen, C., & Checkley, H. (1957). *The three faces of Eve.* New York: McGraw-Hill.

Wilbur, C. (1984). Multiple personality and child abuse. *Psychiatric Clinics of North America, 7,* 3–7.

Young, W. (1988). Psychodynamics and dissociation: All that switches is not split. *Dissociation, 1,* 33–38.

20

PARANOID DISORDERS

Cheryl Regehr and Graham D. Glancy

In 1997 in a city in Ontario, Canada, an elderly woman stabbed to death the four-year-old son of her neighbors. She believed that the child was creating noise intended to drive her crazy and that the child's parents were persecuting her. The neighbors had attempted unsuccessfully to sell their home prior to the death of their child, as they could no longer tolerate the accusations of the woman. After the child's death, family members of the woman came forward in the press and itemized their fruitless attempts to get her treatment over the past several years.

Paranoia is perhaps the most familiar and most feared of psychiatric illnesses. It is central to the plot of many a suspense film. It is highlighted in the media accounts of many high-profile crimes. It has been considered one of the most difficult disorders to treat due to the inability of sufferers to acknowledge the need for treatment and the intransigence of the disorder. This chapter reviews paranoid disorders, the challenges these disorders present to clinicians, and recent advances in models for treatment.

The term *paranoia* was used by the ancient Greeks over two thousand years ago to describe someone who is beside or beyond the mind (*para* = beyond; *noos* = mind). From this root, it became widely used to describe any form of psychosis. The more modern use of the term derives from the work of Esquirol (1838) who coined the term *monomanie*, referring to a group of disorders characterized by delusions with no associated defects in logical reasoning or general behavior. Kahlbaum in 1863 used the term *paranoia* to describe partial insanity that involved relatively persistent delusions not affecting reasoning or general behavior. Kraepelin (1915) also recognized a condition that he called *paranoid,* defined as a persistent delusional system in the absence of hallucinations and personality deterioration.

In the twentieth century, paranoia can best be understood as a symptom that occurs in a range of disorders. In these disorders beliefs are held in the form of a pervasive distrust and suspiciousness of others. These false beliefs are based on incorrect inferences about external reality that are firmly sustained despite what almost everyone else believes and despite what constitutes incontrovertible and obvious proof or evidence to the contrary. Paranoid beliefs may occur in the setting of a person's enduring pattern of perceiving, relating to, and thinking about the environment and thus may be a reflection of an individual's personality structure. However, paranoid beliefs may slide along a continuum such that they are held with delusional conviction. *DSM-IV* (American Psychiatric Association, 1994) identifies three main forms of paranoid disorders: paranoid personality disorder, delusional disorder, and paranoid schizophrenia.

As with other forms of schizophrenia (see Chapter 12), paranoid schizophrenia is characterized both by "positive symptoms," including delusions and hallucinations, and by "negative" symptoms such as social withdrawal and occupational dysfunction. It is differentiated from other subtypes of schizophrenia primarily by the prominence of the delusions. Paranoid schizophrenia also tends to have a later onset and is considered more amenable to treatment.

Jasmine is a 36-year-old woman who is married, has one six-year-old child, and until recently worked as a legal secretary. Four years ago, she began expressing concerns to family members that co-workers were plotting against her. She believed that due to the malevolent actions of others, her work was being altered during the night and she was being caused to appear inefficient. As time progressed, her performance at work became increasingly chaotic, her appearance deteriorated, and her behavior grew more unusual. She was eventually fired from her job and admitted to a hospital with a psychotic paranoid illness. One year after the symptoms began, she was diagnosed with paranoid schizophrenia. Two years later her twin sister was also similarly diagnosed.

If delusions are not bizarre and persist for at least a month, and an individual does not have any of the other major characteristic symptoms of schizophrenia then a delusional disorder can be diagnosed. *DSM-IV* recognizes subtypes of delusional disorder based on the content material. These types include somatic, erotomanic, jealous, persecutory, and grandiose, mixed, and unspecified. Although delusional disorder may occur at any age, it most commonly presents in individuals in their 40s or in later life. It is hypothesized that many paranoid delusions are formed after a "key experience" in a vulnerable personality (Slater & Roth, 1974). As such, presentation may be after stressful life events particularly ones involving social isolation such as immigration or loss. Considerable debate exists about the course of this disorder and whether delusional disorder (and some cases of paranoid personality disorder) eventually develop into paranoid schizophrenia (Kaplan, et al., 1994; Slater & Roth, 1974).

Isabel is a 45-year-old oversensitive woman who presented with the delusion that she emitted a foul smell. She traced the smell back to an evening with friends, during the course of which somebody stated "There's a funny smell in here." From that moment on, she gradually became more and more preoccupied with the belief that she was emitting a foul smell until, at the time of presentation, the belief was clearly held with delusional conviction. The strength of her belief began to interfere with her ability to work with other people. As an adaptive strategy, she purchased a flower shop due to the belief that her own odor would be undetected in such an aromatic environment.

Paranoid personality disorder occurs in people who display a pervasive distrust and suspiciousness of others such that their motives are interpreted as malevolent. This begins by early adulthood and is present in a variety of contexts. These people tend to suspect that others are exploiting, harming, or deceiving them, perceiving attacks on their character or reputation that are not apparent to others. Remarks of others or events are interpreted as having demeaning or threatening messages. Individuals are preoccupied with doubts about loyalty or trustworthiness and are reluctant to confide in others. This frequently presents as recurrent suspicions (without justification) regarding fidelity of spouse or partner. This diagnosis is differentiated from paranoid schizophrenia and delusional disorder by the absence of psychotic features.

John is a 25-year-old man who has been charged with assault against his employer. He explains that "Those b———s at work are always overlooking me for a promotion. This kind of s—t is always happening to me." He goes on to describe a pattern of interpersonal relationships in which others consistently overlook or undermine his special talents in order to further their own gains.

Paranoid symptoms can also occur as a result of a variety of medical conditions. For instance paranoid ideation is associated with illicit drug use (Singer, et al., 1995; Montoya & Haertzen, 1994) and solvent abuse (Byrne, et al., 1991). Diseases of aging such as Alzheimer's disease may also produce paranoid thinking (Wragg & Jeste, 1989). Evidence also reveals that paranoid symptoms may be related to sensory deprivation caused by such disabilities as deafness or blindness (Slater & Roth, 1974). Finally, several authors have pointed to cultural factors that may produce paranoid thinking, such as immigration status (Newhill, 1990) and threatening social situations that result in experiences of powerlessness (Mirowsky & Ross, 1983; Palmer, 1991). These possibilities should be ruled out before entering into a treatment plan with a person experiencing paranoia.

ETIOLOGY

As noted earlier, paranoid disorders may be thought of as a heterogeneous group of conditions that have in common a pattern of false beliefs. Manschreck (1995) lists a wide variety of psychiatric and medical conditions that should be kept in mind when assessing a patient with delusions. As a result of the diversity of conditions that result in paranoid thinking, the primary cause of paranoid disorders, like many other forms of psychopathology, remains an area of debate. Etiological theories can basically be divided into three categories: biological, sociocultural, and psychodynamic. In general, there is a heavier emphasis on biological models for understanding paranoid schizophrenia, while paranoid personality disorder is more often understood in sociocultural or psychodynamic terms. Theories regarding delusional disorder fall somewhere in the middle of the continuum.

Data from biological-family studies are somewhat inconsistent. Some studies have demonstrated a higher incidence of delusional disorder and paranoid personality disorder in relatives of those with schizophrenia (American Psychiatric Association, 1994) but others have failed to replicate this work (Manschreck, 1995). Further studies suggest that families of people with paranoid disorders demonstrate delusions and paranoid traits (Manschreck, 1995). It appears that genetics do play a role in increasing the vulnerability of a person to delusional disorders although the exact role is unclear. A multiplicity of organic disorders and general medical conditions may lead to paranoia which suggests that in some cases at least, neuropathological disorders may play a role in the genesis of paranoid disorders (Cummings, 1985). This theory may be integrated with theories citing neurotransmitter abnormalities, which postulate that certain brain pathways may be damaged by a variety of causes disrupting the intercellular messages. Thirty years of research on neuropathology, most recently with brain imaging techniques, suggest that the disruption of the normal flow of messages passed from cell to cell by dopamine and possibly other neurotransmitters may make an individual vulnerable to psychotic episodes. In a comprehensive review of this literature, Lawrie and Abukmeil (1997) conclude that there is good evidence that the brain is structurally abnormal in schizophrenia and perhaps in delusional disorder.

Psychodynamic mechanisms dominated the early literature on paranoia initially based on Freud's hypothesis of Judge Schreber's account of his mental disorder (Freud, 1958). He asserted that paranoid delusions involved repression of homosexuality and subsequent projection of emotions. This hypothesis has not been empirically proven and is certainly not universally accepted (Zetner, 1984). Other psychodynamic writers suggest that paranoia is a defense against acknowledging losses and represents a splitting and projection of painful experiences (Carstairs, 1992; Newhill, 1989).

Recent psychological formulations appear to support a more cognitively oriented model, which states that persecutory delusions are a product of attributional processes serving to maintain a positive explicit self-concept. A body of research demonstrates that deluded patients have an implicit negative self-concept that is explicitly denied (Kinderman & Bentall, 1996). This theory has opened up an avenue for cognitive behavioral therapy as an adjunctive treatment for paranoid psychosis (Kuipers, et al., 1997).

Finally, some authors point to the higher incidence rate of paranoid disorders in people of lower socioeconomic status and of some disadvantaged cultural groups and offer a sociocultural explanation for paranoid thinking (Palmer, 1991; Newhill, 1990). From this perspective, social positions characterized by powerlessness and by threat of victimization and exploitation are seen to produce paranoia. That is, powerlessness leads to the belief that important outcomes in one's life are controlled by external forces. This belief in external control interacts with experiences of victimization and exploitation to produce distrust and suspiciousness (Mirowsky & Ross, 1983).

In summary, a number of factors may play a part in the etiology of delusions. Genetic and biological factors when combined with disrupted attachment experiences may make a person more vulnerable to paranoid thinking. When an individual with predisposing vulnerabilities faces socioeconomic deprivation, sensory isolation, or advancing age, paranoid symptoms may emerge. The complex intidigitation of these factors will require elucidation for future research.

PREVALENCE

Precise information about prevalence of paranoid disorders is limited as a result of two main factors. First, many people with paranoid beliefs do not seek treatment and do not admit these disorders on epidemiological surveys. The second problem is that the changing definitions of the disorder makes it difficult to compare demographic evidence over a period of time (Kaplan, et al., 1994). Nevertheless, there is considerable stability in reported estimates of incidence over extended periods of time in this century, leading to the conclusion that they are uncommon but not rare conditions (Manschreck, 1996).

Overall incidence rates for schizophrenia range from .5% to 1% of the population. The percentage of this total that represents paranoid type schizophrenia is approximately 50%. However, paranoid type schizophrenia is more likely to have a later onset (Hafner & an der Heiden, 1997) and have higher rates of premorbid functioning than other types of schizophrenia causing some authors to conclude that it may be more related to an affective disorder (Burack & Zigler, 1989).

Delusional disorder accounts for approximately 1% to 2% of inpatient psychiatric admissions and has an estimated overall prevalence rate of .03%. While the overall incidence is equivalent between men and women, the jealous subtype is more common in males and women have a higher incidence of the other subtypes (*DSM-IV*). These disorders are somewhat more likely to occur in individuals of lower socioeconomic status and/or with lower educational levels than are mood disorders (Manschreck, 1995).

Paranoid personality disorder has an incidence rate of .5% to 2.5% of the population and accounts for 10% to 30% of all inpatient admissions.

Table 20-1 Differentiating Paranoid Disorders

	Paranoid Schizophrenia	Delusional Disorder	Paranoid Personality Disorder
Prevalence			
General population	.25–.5%	.03%	.5–2.5%
Psychiatric admissions	unavailable	1–2%	10–30%
Gender prevalence	approximately equal	overall equal jealous type more males other types more females	primarily male
Onset	mid-late adulthood	mid-late adulthood	early adulthood
Duration required for diagnosis	at least six months	at least one month	all of adult life
Presentation	-preoccupation with delusions -auditory hallucinations -social and occupational dysfunction	-nonbizarre delusions -functioning not markedly impaired -no hallucinations	-pervasive distrust of others view of others as malevolent -no psychotic symptoms

It is more commonly diagnosed in men; although it is usually diagnosed in early adulthood, symptoms may begin in childhood (*DSM-IV*).

ASSESSMENT

Frequently, the person suffering from the delusion does not directly present to mental health workers. Instead, family members or neighbors often contact mental health agencies expressing concerns about the client who is actually suffering from the delusion. This occurred in the case of a 38-year-old man who repeatedly called the police complaining that his neighbor was beaming rays into his house despite the lead shield he had built in the adjoining wall. One of the difficult clinical issues, therefore, is that the person presents with such pervasive distrust that developing a therapeutic alliance and eliciting information about the person's belief system is often an insurmountable problem. Paranoid disorders can thus be difficult to assess and often require corroborative information. For instance, if a person reports that she are being harassed and persecuted at work, this on the face of it may not be delusional. The belief can only be regarded as a delusion when it is so extreme as to defy credibility or the consensus of others. The social worker's strength lies in the approach of seeing a person within the context of their family and wider social environment. Collateral information from friends, family and associates may be vital to the assessment.

All paranoid disorders carry some similar features. The person often presents with self-righteousness, attention to detail and guardedness. This guardedness may be to the point of outright hostility or possibility litigiousness. Individuals may be hypervigilant, carefully scanning the environment for danger continuously. They display little emotion; similarly their thought patterns appear rigid and inflexible. These may be considered associated features of paranoia and can be found in the paranoid personality disorder, paranoid schizophrenia and those suffering from delusional disorders. Other factors, however, differentiate between the paranoid disorders. The following factors are important in the assessment.

Can the beliefs be understood in a cultural context?
As mentioned earlier, individuals from cultures which have experienced systematic discrimination and abuse may legitimately express distrust towards the dominant society and its agents. In addition, beliefs which appear unfounded in the culture of the social worker may have a basis in the culture of the client. One colleague expressed concerns for an elderly Jewish client who was burying cutlery in the backyard. Upon consultation, the

social worker discovered the importance of this ritual for purifying eating utensils in the Kosher tradition. Similarly, a Caribbean client expressed concerns that his mother-in-law was exercising powers to steal his attractiveness. Family members confirmed that the mother-in-law did have such an ability and, due to her feelings towards this man, was likely to be using them.

There is some evidence that paranoid and other psychotic disorders are disproportionately diagnosed in some cultures (Mirowsky & Ross, 1983; Newhill, 1990). Social workers can assist the multidisciplinary team by providing information about the cultural context of the client in order to avoid the pathologizing of culturally specific traits and behaviors and the individualizing of the effects of sociocultural dislocation.

What is the duration of the symptoms?

The next issue to address is whether these beliefs are persistent or transient. A diagnosis of delusional disorder requires a one-month duration of symptoms. Paranoid schizophrenia requires a six-month duration of symptoms, which is often preceded by a five-year prodromal period during which the person experiences a decline in their social functioning (Hafner & an der Heiden, 1997). Paranoid ideation persists throughout adulthood and perhaps has its origins in childhood for paranoid personality disorder.

Are beliefs delusional?

The degree of preoccupation and the resultant changes in behavior and lifestyle help one decide whether the beliefs are held with delusional conviction. How the person responds to the delusion, along with previous responses to stresses and adverse life events, may be important in the assessment of future dangerousness.

Does this person exhibit criterion symptoms for schizophrenia?

In paranoid schizophrenia, the delusion is more likely accompanied by prominent hallucinations and a disorder of the form (as opposed to the content) of the thought as portrayed by disorganized speech. In schizophrenia one might observe disorganized behavior or the so-called negative symptoms of schizophrenia, such as a paucity of expressivity of mood associated with a decline in functioning which would not be attributable to the effects of harboring the delusions.

Is this a mood disorder?

Delusional disorder is differentiated from a mood disorder with psychotic symptoms by the observation that the mood episodes have occurred concurrently with delusions, and their total duration has been brief relative to the duration of delusional periods. Although people with paranoia may be unhappy about their situation and their grievances, they do not display the prolonged, severe mood disorder associated with an affective psychosis. As if the picture were not complicated enough, however, those with paranoid personality disorders *may* develop major depressive disorder—and sometimes the two may co-exist.

Are the delusions caused by drug use?

One of the most important factors to investigate is the use of drugs such as amphetamines, cocaine, or corticosteroids (used in some autoimmune disorders) which can cause delusions. Direct questioning of the client and others, as well as clues of recent drug abuse, may help resolve this issue particularly if the onset of delusions is acute and transient. It is important to note, however, that the delusional state following drug ingestion can appear to last much longer than that would be expected by the direct action of the medication, for example, in amphetamine psychosis (Montoya & Haertzen, 1994). Alcohol abuse is frequently a cause of paranoid beliefs and should be considered in every case, as should any prescribed medications or the use of over-the-counter medications.

Are the delusions related to an underlying medical condition?

Delusions may present in association with dementia or delirium, particularly in older patients. In dementia, the delusions occur in the context of other characteristic symptoms, including memory impairment and disturbances in language, sensory, and executive functions over a period of time. Delirium becomes a possibility if a person displays a disturbance in consciousness such as distractibility, disorientation, or confusion; these often develop acutely and have a fluctuating course. Other possible sources of delusions are head injuries, alcohol and drug withdrawal, infections, epilepsy, and other neurological illnesses. These may have been previously diagnosed or may be prominent in the family history.

ASSESSMENT OF DANGEROUSNESS

Part of the management of a person who suffers from paranoid disorder includes an assessment of dangerousness. This can be the most difficult but nevertheless the most crucial part of the assessment as concerns of harm to a third party, or the therapist, are often raised when working with paranoid clients.

There has been considerable debate about whether people with mental disorders are particularly prone to violence. Comprehensive reviews of the literature by several authors have concluded that, although in general terms persons with serious mental illness are no more or less violent than the average person, psychotic symptoms which induce a feeling of threat are risk factors for violence (Arboleda-Florez, Holley & Crisanti, 1996; Glancy & Regehr, 1992). Individuals with well-developed delusions are more likely to be at risk for inflicting harm on others (DePauw & Szulecka, 1988). Further, morbid jealousy has been demonstrated to lead to physical violence in 50% of cases considered in a comprehensive review article. These assaults tend to be both serious and repetitive, and frequently lead to homicide (Mullen, 1990). Thus, individuals with paranoid delusions represent an obvious threat to third parties and to therapists themselves if they are the target of the delusions.

Bearing this in mind, the social worker is faced with an onerous task. It is necessary to have a framework for the assessment of risk of violence that is routinely included in any assessment of paranoid thinking. Several instruments have been devised to assist with this process and are reviewed in a recent article by Ferris and colleagues (1997). One new instrument, which is not included in the above review, is the HCR-20 (Webster, et al., 1997). This instrument appears fairly user-friendly and may be concise enough to use in clinical practice. Many of the risk factors cited in this and indeed most of the other instruments are those that have been shown to be associated with violence. These factors include previous history of violence and young age for first violence. Psychotic symptoms that override self-control and are threatening to one's safety are powerful predictors, as are other psychotic symptoms such as paranoia, self-aggrandizement, and pathological jealousy. The risk increases proportionately as these are associated with such constructs as psychopathy, impulsivity, and substance abuse. Clinical factors include the presence of active symptoms that are unresponsive to treatment and into which the client lacks insight. Further, if the client lacks personal supports or has few plans for the future, these should also be considered factors that may predict violence. In summary, a number of the significant known risk factors for violent acting out are often found in paranoid clients, such that the issue of dangerousness to a third party or to the therapist is likely to emerge.

Following the assessment of the high risk of violence, the social worker must make a series of decisions about future action, based on his or her professional and legal obligations. Most U.S. jurisdictions have a "duty to warn" legislation requiring a duty to warn third parties. This is based on the well-known *Tarasoff* decision (*Tarasoff v. Regents of the University of California*, 1976). In that case a patient told his treating psychologist that he intended to kill his former girlfriend, Ms. Tarasoff. The therapist, concluding that the patient was dangerous, contacted the campus police but did not warn the intended victim. Ms. Tarasoff was subsequently killed and her family sued the therapist. Despite defense arguments that the duty to warn violated the accepted ethical obligation to maintain confidentiality, the courts ruled in the plaintiff's favor. The court concluded that the confidentiality obligation to a patient ends when public peril begins. This was later codified by amendments to the California Civil Code (California, 1984), which, due to efforts of the California Psychiatric Association, limited the *Tarasoff* liability to a "serious threat" against a "reasonably identified victim."

It was not until some 15 years later that a Canadian precedent-setting case was adjudicated. In *Wenden v. Trikha* (1991) a patient left a psychiatric hospital without the knowledge of hospital staff and drove his car into Ms. Wenden's vehicle, causing her severe injuries such that she was unable to care for her children and lost custody of them. A legal action was subsequently dismissed, as it was determined that there was no prior indication that the patient presented a risk to others and there was no previous relationship between the injured party and the patient. However, the judge suggested that if a clinician becomes aware that a patient presents a serious danger to others, and if that patient has a close relationship, then the clinician owes a duty to protect such a person. Therefore, in most jurisdictions, a duty to warn and protect is now owed to third parties when the threat from the patient is of a serious nature and the diagnosis, history, and opportunity to bring the threat to fruition are such that a reasonable clinician would be concerned. It should be noted that in some jurisdictions breaching confidentiality in this matter could still result in disciplinary action (Carlisle, 1996).

TREATMENT

Traditionally it has been felt that paranoia is notoriously difficult to treat. However, recent research has been much more optimistic. In this section we will review the treatment of paranoid disorders and consider some of the special issues that arise out of the treatment of these disorders. At present, the dominant approaches to dealing with paranoid disorders involve a combination of pharmacology, cognitive therapy with the individual, and psychosocial interventions.

The first stage in the treatment of this disorder, as with all other forms of adult psychopathology, is comprehensive psychosocial assessment. As noted above, careful consideration should be given to the individual's sociocultural context and any other psychiatric or medical condition that may contribute to paranoid thinking. Following this, the treatment plan should address biological, psychological, and social factors (see Chapter 2). Treatment for these disorders may well be best administered by a multidisciplinary team approach. However, good communication within the team is particularly important due to the predominance of distrust and persecutory ideas in the thinking of individuals with paranoid disorders.

One of the inherent difficulties in treating paranoia is building up a therapeutic alliance with someone whose basic pathology dictates that he or she has difficulty trusting others. Sometimes collaboration between therapist and client may take an extended period of time to develop for this reason. An additional problem is that many of these people feel that the problem lies within the outside world or circumstances and therefore they believe that the therapist should apply himself/herself to changing these external factors. Sometimes the therapist may wish to "get a foot in the door" by dealing with the secondary anxiety and depression generated by the paranoia. By using techniques to build up rapport, and at the same time alleviating the client's discomfort, a second stage of treatment may permit work on the paranoid beliefs themselves.

Pharmacotherapy

Medication is widely used in the treatment of paranoia. Indeed, Munro and Mok (1995), in perhaps the most comprehensive outcome study to appear to date, suggest that 80.8% of clients with paranoia will improve simply with medication treatment. A number of options exist for the pharmacological treatment of these disorders. For paranoid schizophrenia and delusional disorder, the mainstay of treatment remains the antipsychotic medications. These medications at the basic level are dopamine antagonists, in other words, they decrease the levels of dopamine in the mesolimbic system, a communication line within the brain (see Chapter 4). It should be noted that antipsychotic medications are powerful and specific. Among the many side effects found in this group of drugs, acute dystonia (painful muscle spasms), pseudoparkinsonian syndrome (paucity of movement and tremor), and the long-term risk of tardive dyskinesia (repetitive movement disorder) may be particularly troublesome. Needless to say, valid informed consent should be obtained before the medication is used.

This informed consent would require a full explanation of any short- and long-term unwanted effects of the medication. It is foolhardy for the clinician to attempt to sidestep the preexisting distrust of the client by omitting information even if one believes that this is in his or her best interest. On the contrary, a prolonged and full dialogue between members of the treatment team and the patient is essential. It is only by being completely truthful with a client can his or her essential trust be earned, thereby ensuring collaboration with members of the treatment team.

Clients with paranoid disorders may have concomitant anxiety or depression. This anxiety and depression may heighten their sensitivity to their paranoia, thereby worsening their situations. These emotional symptoms may therefore be a focus of treatment. Manschreck (1995) recommends use of the serotonin reuptake inhibitors (SSRIs) for delusional disorder. He notes the overlap between obsessive-compulsive disorder, mood disorder, and some of the delusional disorders. This may explain the apparent benefit of these agents in delusional disorders.

In paranoid personality disorder, medications may not be the first line of treatment. However, medication may be used to treat the concomitant anxiety and depression that often accompany this disorder (Reid, et al., 1997). Psychotic decompensation may appear in some cases of paranoid personality disorder; it is not uncommon to treat this with antipsychotic medications.

Although medications may assist in treating some of the intrusive symptoms of paranoid disorders, they are by no means a panacea. There is a significant rate of refusal to take medication in individuals with almost any disorder, but in a long-term disorder, especially one characterized by lack of trust, this problem is exacerbated. Also, approximately 20% of people who have paranoid beliefs do not experience a diminishing of symptoms with medication (Munro & Mok, 1995). Finally, medications do not address the concomitant social problems encountered by individuals with paranoid disorders.

Cognitive Therapy

It is, therefore, gratifying to note that contrary to previous widely held attitudes, new research suggests that various modes of psychotherapy may be helpful in the treatment of paranoia and other psychotic disorders. Hogarty (1997) reports data which suggest that individual therapy combined with medication is beneficial for people with schizophrenia in preventing relapses, increasing compliance with medication, and increasing social adjustment. Of particular interest is cognitive behavioral therapy, which was found in one study to be effective in 50% of medication-resistant psychotic patients (Kuipers, et al., 1997). The authors concluded that cognitive behavioral therapy may well specifically target delusional thinking.

Cognitive therapy is based on the premise that as a result of life experiences, individuals develop self-schemas or a series of complex cognitive structures that affect the processing of information about self and others. These are attempts by the individual to organize and summarize his or her motivations, feelings, and behavior as well as the motivations, feelings, and behavior of others. Schemas govern how interpersonal information is attended to and perceived, which affects are experienced and which memories are evoked (Horowitz, 1991). Self-schemas are also likely to be self-confirming, in that judgments of others affect interpersonal responses. For instance, if an individual believes that others will reject him, he will approach the interaction with anger and hostility, thereby increasing the chance of rejection by others.

In the area of paranoid thinking, recent work by Kinderman and Bentall (1996) suggested that paranoid individuals have discrepancies between their self-perceptions and how they believed their parents perceived them. In their model, which is substantiated by an emerging body of research, Kinderman and Bentall suggest that persecutory beliefs are a product of attributional processes serving to maintain a positive explicit self-concept. For instance, "I am not a failure; other people maliciously stop me from succeeding."

In cognitive therapy, a client is taught to change the attributional processes that lead to emotional upset stemming from their delusions. Chadwick and Trower (1996) suggest a three-stage model of intervention. First the therapist introduces the cognitive model and challenges the negative self-evaluative belief. Following this, the therapist teaches the client to challenge the negative self-evaluation himself. Thirdly, the client is taught to rationally challenge the delusion themselves. In an elegant experimental design, Chadwick and Trower (1996) demonstrate that delusions can be significantly ameliorated by cognitive intervention. Contrary to prevailing theories that the patient's self-esteem would be destroyed by the challenge to the delusions, since the delusion is seen to bolster self-esteem, in actual fact self-esteem and depression scores seemed to improve during the therapy. These authors note that specific delusions require specific treatment and that this model, although illustrative, cannot be used for all types of delusions.

Psychosocial Interventions

Recently there has been a renewed interest in community-based alternatives to traditional hospital-based care for severely mentally ill individuals. One of the most widely studied of these is Assertive Community Treatment. More recently this model has also been used with personality-disordered individuals (Links, 1998). The key elements of this treatment approach include a multidisciplinary team that is on call 24 hours a day, *in vivo* treatment (in the person's own environment), and instruction and assistance with basic living skills (LaFave, et al., 1996). This model then provides flexible, individually tailored treatments, linkages among agencies serving the client and client involvement in service planning (Bachrach, 1993). Outcome studies of individuals with both personality disorders and psychotic illnesses demonstrated reduced rates of hospitalization, increased medication compliance, better quality of life, and decreased legal problems (Links, 1998; LaFave, et al., 1996). In working with paranoid clients, the concept of the multidisciplinary team diffuses transference towards one therapist and shares the responsibility for confronting delusional systems.

A second area of psychosocial treatment is aimed at members of the paranoid individual's social support system. The theoretical basis for this model of intervention was that individuals with families who were critical or anxiously overinvolved tended to higher rates of hospitalization. It was believed that this was because families were managing highly distressing and disruptive behavior in the ill person with little support or training. This approach provides psychoeducational individual and group interventions. These are aimed at educating families about aspects of the illness, teaching family members communication and problem-solving skills for dealing with specific psychotic symptoms, and providing support and individual treatment for family members as required (Neill, 1994). While all these techniques are important for family members dealing with paranoid thinking, an additional issue is raised about the potential for physical risk should the individual become delusional about a family member. Thus, family members must also be taught to identify paranoid delusions, to take delusions seriously, and to develop a safety plan for themselves.

CONCLUSION

While paranoid disorders are relatively rare in the general population, they may constitute a significant proportion of the caseload of any mental health practitioner. The three types of paranoid disorders discussed in this chapter—paranoid schizophrenia, delusional disorder, and paranoid personality disorder—have many similarities but can be differentiated on the basis of duration of symptoms, the conviction with which the paranoid beliefs are held, and the degree to which the individual's social functioning is affected. In the past, this differentiation was viewed as central to the choice of treatment modality. Paranoid schizophrenia was treated almost exclusively with medication, while paranoid personality disorder was addressed specifically with individual psychotherapy. Recent evidence has shown that such a distinction does not exclude treatments other than the conventional ones and that all these disorders are best managed with a combination of pharmocological interventions, individual cognitive therapy, active community-based treatment, and psychoeducational family interventions. Thus, while it was previously held that delusional disorders were notoriously difficult to treat, recent published results on new avenues of treatment have filled this field with therapeutic optimism. Nevertheless, social workers engaging with paranoid clients must face the challenges of developing therapeutic alliances with suspicious individuals, while ensuring that transference issues are cautiously managed and remaining vigilant to the possible risk of harm to anyone who is the subject of a delusional system. These challenges require careful ongoing assessment, clear therapeutic boundaries, and the availability of peer or multidisciplinary consultation.

REFERENCES

American Psychiatric Association (1987). *Diagnostic and statistical manual of mental disorders, third edition—revised.* Washington, DC: Author.

American Psychiatric Association (1994). *Diagnostic and statistical manual of mental disorders, fourth edition.* Washington, DC: Author.

Arboleda-Florez, J., Holley, H. & Crisanti, A. (1996). Mental illness and violence: Proof or stereotype? Ottawa: Health Canada, Health Promotion and Programs Branch.

Bachrach, L. (1993). Continuity of care and approaches to case management for long-term mentally ill patients. *Hospital and Community Psychiatry, 44,* 5, 465–468.

Burack, J. & Zigler, E. (1989). Age at first hospitalization and premorbid social competence in schizophrenia and affective disorder. *American Journal of Orthopsychiatry, 59,* 2, 188–196.

Byrne, A., Kirby, B., Zibin, T., & Ensminger, S. (1991) Psychiatric and neurological effects of chronic solvent abuse. *Canadian Journal of Psychiatry, 36,* 10, 735–738.

California Assembly Bill 1133. (1984). McAllister, Section 43–92.

Carlisle, J. (1996, July/August). Duty to warn: report from council. *Members' Dialogue, Canadian Medical Association.*

Carstairs, K. (1992). Paranoid-schizoid or symbiotic? *International Journal of Psycho-Analysis, 73,* 1, 71–85.

Chadwick, P., & Trower, P. (1996). Cognitive therapy for punishment paranoia: A single case experiment. *Behavioural Research and Therapy, 34,* 4, 351–356.

Cummings, J. (1985). Organic delusions: Phenomenology, anatomical correlations, and review. *British Journal of Psychiatry, 146,* 184–197.

DePauw, K., & Szulecka, T. (1988). Dangerous delusions: Violence and misindentification syndromes. *British Journal of Psychiatry*, 152, 91–96.

Esquirol, J. (1838). *Mental maladies: A treatise on insanity.* Translated by E. K. Hunt. (1845). Philadelphia: Lea & Blanchard.

Ferris, L., Sandercock, J., Hoffman, B., Silverman, M., Barkun, H., Carlisle, J., & Katz, C. (1997). Risk assessment for acute violence to third parties: A review of the literature. *Canadian Journal of Psychiatry*, 42, 12, 1051–1059.

Freud, S. (1958). Psychoanalytic notes on an autobiographical account of a case of paranoia. In J. Strachey, (Ed.). *Standard edition of the complete psychological works of Sigmund Freud.* London: Hogarth.

Glancy, G., & Regehr, C. (1992). The forensic aspects of schizophrenia. *Psychiatric Clinics of North America.* 15, 3, 575–589.

Hafner, H., & an der Heiden, W. (1997). Epidemiology of schizophrenia. *Canadian Journal of Psychiatry*, 42, 3, 139–151.

Hamilton, M. (1978). Paranoid states. *British Journal of Hospital Medicine*, November 1978.

Hamilton, M. (1985). *Fish's clinical psychopathology* (2nd Ed.). Bristol, England: Wright.

Hogarty, G. (1997). Three year trials of personal therapy among schizophrenic patients living independent of family. *American Journal of Psychiatry*, 154, 1504–1513.

Horowitz, M. (1991a). *Person schemas and maladaptive interpersonal problems.* Chicago: University of Chicago Press.

Kahlbaum, K. (1863). *Die Grappierung der Psychischen Krankheiten und die Einteilung der Seelan Storungen.* Danzig.

Kaplan, H., Sadock, B., & Grebb, J. (1994). *Synopsis of psychiatry: Behavioral sciences clinical psychiatry* (7th Ed.). Baltimore: Williams & Wilkins.

Kinderman, P., & Bentall, R. (1996). Self-discrepancies and persecutory delusions: evidence for a model of paranoid ideation. *Journal of Abnormal Psychology*, 105, 1, 106–113.

Kraepelin, E. (1915). *Psychiatrie, Neurologie und Medizinische Psychologie.* Vol. 4., p. 1441.

Kuipers, E., Garety, P., Fowler, D., Dunn, G., Bebbington, P., Freeman, D., & Hadley, C. (1997). London-East Anglia randomized controlled trial of cognitive-behavioural therapy for psychosis. *British Journal of Psychiatry*, 171, 319–327.

LaFave, H., de Sousa, H., & Gerber, G. (1996). Assertive community treatment of severe mental illness: A Canadian experience. *Psychiatric Services*, 47, 7, 757–759.

Lawrie, S., & Abukmeil, S. (1998). Brain abnormality in schizophrenia: A systematic and quantitative review of volumetric magnetic resonance imaging studies. *British Journal of Psychiatry*, 172, 110–120.

Links, P. (1998). Developing effective services for patients with personality disorders. *Canadian Journal of Psychiatry*, 43, 4, 251–259.

Manschreck, T. (1995). Delusional disorder and shared psychotic disorder. In H. Kaplan & J. Sadock (Eds.), *Comprehensive textbook of psychiatry* (6th Ed.). Baltimore: Williams & Wilkins.

Manschreck, T. (1996). Delusional disorder: The recognition and management of paranoia. *Journal of Clinical Psychiatry*, 57, Suppl. 3, 32–38.

Mirowsky, J., & Ross, C. (1983). Paranoia and the structure of powerlessness. *American Sociological Review*, 48, 2, 228–239.

Montoya, I., & Haertzen, C. (1994). Reduction of psychopathology among individuals participating in non-treatment drug abuse residential studies. *Journal of Addictive Disease*, 13, 2, 89–97.

Mullen, P. (1990). Morbid jealousy and the delusion of infidelity. In R. Bluglass & P. Bowden (Eds.), *Principles and practice of forensic psychiatry.* London: Churchill Livingston.

Munro, A., & Mok, H. (1995). An overview of treatment in paranoia/delusional disorder. *Canadian Journal of Psychiatry, 40,* 12, 616–622.

Neill, R. (1994). Social work, helping the family to cope with schizophrenia: Psychoeducational programs in the community. *The Social Worker, 62,* 2, 89–92.

Newhill, C. (1989). Paranoid symptomology in late life. *Clinical Gerontologist, 8,* 4, 13–30.

Newhill, C. (1990). The role of culture in the development of paranoid symptomatology. *American Journal of Orthopsychiatry, 60,* 2, 176–185.

Palmer, H. (1991). Ethnic relations and the paranoid style: Nativism, nationalism and populism in Alberta. *Canadian Ethnic Studies, 23,* 3, 7–31.

Reid, W., Balis, G., & Sutton, B. (1997). *The treatment of psychiatric disorders (3rd Ed. Revised for DSM-IV).* Bristol, PA.: Brunner/Mazel.

Slater, E., & Roth, M. (1974). *Clinical psychiatry* (3rd Ed.). London: Balliere, Tindall & Cassell.

Singer, L., Arendt, R., Minnes, S., Farkas, K., Yamashita, T., & Kliegman, R. (1995). Increased psychological distress in post-partum, cocaine-using mothers. *Journal of Substance Abuse, 7,* 2, 165–174.

Tarasoff v. Regents of the University of California. (1976). 17 Cal.Rptr. 3rd (U.S.).

Webster, C., Douglas, K., Eaves, D., & Hart, S. (1997). *HCR-20, Assessing risk for violence* (Version 2). Vancouver, BC.: Simon Fraser University Press.

Wenden v. Trikha. (1991). 116 A.R. 81 (Altaedez. Q.B.)

Wragg, R. & Jeste, D. (1989). Overview of depression and psychosis in Alzheimer's disease. *American Journal of Psychiatry, 146,* 5, 577–587.

Zetner, M. (1984). Paranoia. In F. Turner (Ed.), *Adult psychopathology: A social work perspective.* New York: Free Press.

21

PHOBIC DISORDERS

Ray J. Thomlison

Many of us have been in a crowded elevator and have found ourselves feeling various degrees of discomfort as a result. Some persons feel that they have to act (escape) in order to reduce their level of discomfort, whereas others may feel uncomfortable with being in a relatively confined space, but do not act on the urge to escape or avoid the confinement to begin with. Depending upon the level of anxiety and the degree to which it impacts a person, both the former and the latter might be identified as having a phobia. In this case, *claustrophobia* or the fear of closed spaces is the appropriate phobia designation.

The word "phobia" has crept into everyday language in recent years. In so doing, it has taken on a very general meaning, and usually tends to refer rather loosely to a person's fears or anxieties about given situations or objects. The increased use of the word in everyday language gives acknowledgment to the fact that we all have certain fears and apprehensions. However, such common usage does misrepresent the severity and intensity of impact on people who suffer with clinically identifiable phobias. Mental-health professionals attest to the extreme measures that some people with phobias must take in order to cope with the high levels of anxiety they experience.

This chapter will provide an overview of the current knowledge and research in the understanding and treatment of phobic disorders. Specifically, this chapter explores the concept of phobia; its historical roots; identifies various types of phobic disorders and their clinical presentations; examines the theoretical and empirical approaches to phobic disorders; and draws specific conclusions regarding the implications of phobic disorders for social work intervention.

The author would like to express appreciation to Cathryn Bradshaw MSW for her valuable research assistance.

The Long History of Phobias

The term *phobia* is not new to the psychopathology literature. According to Marks (1969, p. 7) phobia was first used in a medical context by Celsus, a Roman encyclopedist, in the first century when he coined the term *hydrophobia*. Descriptions of morbid fears and their accompanying behaviors have appeared across the ages in the works of such as Hippocrates, Shakespeare, and Descartes. The word *phobia* derives from the Greek *phobeio* meaning "I fear." It has become one of a large class of suffixes. The practice of coining descriptive labels for every feared object or situation can be carried to extremes; thus, by 1914 Hall had compiled a list of 135 phobias (Levitt, 1967).

Contemporary research into phobic disorders has led to the identification of certain common and unique characteristics of most phobias. These characteristics serve as the basis for classification criteria for differentiating phobias. Although there is some debate regarding the differentiation of the classification criteria (e.g., Salkovskis & Hackmann, 1997), the *Diagnostic and Statistical Manual of Mental Disorders,* Fourth Edition (*DSM-IV*; American Psychiatric Association, 1994), is generally accepted by clinicians as stating the agreed-upon criteria for the assessment and differentiation of the numerous phobias.

Clinical Presentation and Diagnosis

All phobias are characterized by an underlying fear or high level of anxiety that is manifested both physiologically and psychologically. In a general sense, phobias are viewed as irrational and recurrent fears of situations, objects, and/or animals. *DSM-IV* places phobias within the large category of anxiety disorders. Before we can explore diagnostic criteria for phobias, it is important to frame this within a discussion of the distinctions between *anxiety* and *fear* as well as between *fear* and *phobia*. Panic or panic attacks are often associated with responses to phobias, so they will also be discussed in this section.

Anxiety and Fear
Confusion stems from the tendency to use the term *anxiety* in reference to relatively low levels of emotional discomfort and *fear* in reference to high emotional arousal tending toward physical immobilization. Such a distinction would be useful if authors did not also speak about "high levels of anxiety" that inhibit individual performance. For this discussion at least,

these terms are considered synonymous. Anxiety is useful to the individual insofar as it promotes action in response to a challenge or threat. Anxiety mobilizes physiological responses, creating a sharpness of perception that enhances individual performance, and is therefore an adaptive response. In addition, success in meeting the challenge or staving off the threat enhances self-esteem by increasing the individual's sense of competence. All people have an optimal level beyond which the biopsychological responses of anxiety lead to diminished individual performance. In this case, anxiety is dysfunctional and immobilizing for the individual.

Fear and Phobia
Forsyth and Chorpita (1997) suggest a continuum taxonomy of fear responses from adaptive to nonadaptive. They define *fear* as the "adaptive biopsychological response to real threat or danger" and *phobia* as the "biopsychological response in the absence of threat or danger" (p. 298). Using these definitions, the presence or absence of an actual fear-provoking stimulus becomes the feature that distinguishes adaptive fear from maladaptive phobic reactions. This explanation would seem to suggest that the point at which an adaptive fear becomes a phobia is when there is no longer a "real" threat or danger, yet an excessive or unreasonable fear response persists.

Panic
When confronted with a fear-provoking stimulus, both phobic and non-phobic individuals will manifest one or more biopsychological responses: increased heart rate, perspiration, shaking, rapid breathing, desire to urinate, feeling of dizziness or faintness, feeling of suffocation, and sometimes a feeling of dying (perhaps of a heart attack). At an extreme level, some or all of these responses can constitute a *panic attack* (PA). *DSM-IV* defines a panic attack as a rapidly escalating experience of intense discomfort, fear, or terror accompanied by multiple somatic or cognitive symptoms. Panic attacks may result in temporary immobilization and a strong desire to escape the situation in which the attack has occurred. Panic attacks are often obvious to others and represent a loss of self-control to the individual.

Classification of Phobias

DSM-IV lists five categories of phobias under the broader classification of anxiety disorders:

- panic disorder without agoraphobia
- panic disorder with agoraphobia
- agoraphobia without a history of panic disorder
- specific phobia
- social phobia

A detailed account of the specific criteria for each of these classifications of phobias can be found in *DSM-IV* (pp. 393–417). Three symptom classes characterize phobic responses: somatic, affective and/or cognitive, and behavioral (*DSM-IV;* Chapman, 1997; Merckelbach, et al., 1996). All individuals confronted with a fear-provoking stimulus will manifest one or more *somatic responses,* such as increased heart-rate and perspiration or a feeling of suffocation. *Affective and cognitive symptoms* that are associated with phobic reactions include a sense of the surreal or depersonalization, and/or a fear of losing control, of going crazy, even of dying. Phobic individuals are well aware of the unrealistic level of their feeling of fear. The recognition of this deviance further complicates life for the phobic.

Because of the level of the anxiety experienced, the individual's natural inclination will be to escape the situation or object. This *behavioral response* constitutes an attempt to avoid the situation or object in order to minimize the chance of having a phobic response. This avoidance behavior is strengthened by the tendency of phobic individuals to anticipate, think about, and/or rehearse phobic situations. Avoidance of the fear-producing situation may become energy-consuming, as many phobic stimuli are an ever-present element of the individual's world. The consequences of such strong avoidance behavior can be severe, ranging from job loss to curtailment of most social interactions. Phobic anxiety leads to pervasive avoidance or may be endured with marked distress that leads to a significant interference with functioning in the personal, social, and/or occupational realms of life. This functioning impairment is an essential characteristic that separates a fear reaction from a phobic disorder.

Anxiety, fear, physiological, and psychological symptoms and avoidance behaviors are central elements of all phobic disorders. The focus (i.e., object or situation) of the phobia becomes the factor that differs in classifying phobias. The person experiencing a phobic disorder will manifest phobic anxiety in association with specific situations and objects, whether these stimuli are actually encountered or only imagined. It is important to realize that the object of fear may not always be external to the individual but may be experienced as a "fear of fear" (i.e., fear of one's own fear reaction). The major classifications of phobias in the *DSM-IV* are agoraphobia (with or without panic), specific phobias, and social phobias.

Specific Phobias

Specific phobias were formerly known as simple phobias. They are defined in *DSM-IV* by a marked and persistent fear of a specific object or event that elicits a prompt anxiety response. Claustrophobia, as mentioned in the case situation at the beginning of this chapter, is an example of a specific phobia (see Thomlison, 1984, for an extensive list of specific phobias). The major subtypes of specific phobias are animal, natural environment, blood-injection-injury, and situational. *DSM-IV* notes that having one specific phobia is often correlated with having one or more other specific phobias.

Social Phobias

The focus of fear in social phobias is one or more social or performance situations. Fear of speaking in public may be the most common example to which people can easily relate. The "fear of fear" or the fear that the anxiety-response symptoms may embarrass the individual can play a major role in social phobias.

Agoraphobia

The essence of agoraphobic anxiety, as described in *DSM-IV*, is the fear of being embarrassed or unable to escape places or situations. The fear of developing panic-like symptoms in these situations and places can lead to an extreme avoidance. In the general sense, agoraphobic fear is most often referred to as "fear of open spaces" and often leaves individuals with agoraphobia house-bound. Agoraphobia may occur with or without panic attacks.

Panic Disorder

To receive a diagnosis of Panic Disorder (PD), the sufferer must experience recurrent panic attacks (minimum of two) in the absence of specific situational cues. This leads to the anticipation of panic attacks in future situations that are similar. *DSM-IV* lists 13 potential somatic and cognitive symptoms that may occur. A minimum of four of the symptoms listed must be present during panic attacks. Social and specific phobias are usually associated with situational and/or predisposed panic, while agoraphobia may be associated with unexpected panic attacks.

Comorbid Diagnoses

An important issue in the classification of phobias is that of comorbid diagnoses (i.e., associated or tending to occur) with other phobias or mental disorders. As we saw with agoraphobia, it is classified according to its co-occurrence with or without panic attacks. *DSM-IV* (p. 403) notes that over 95% of persons with agoraphobia have a comorbid diagnosis of panic dis-

Table 21–1   Prevalence of Phobias and Panic Disorders

Type of Phobia	Rates	Review Sources
Specific Phobias	0.6% to 12.5%	DSM-IV; Chapman, 1997; Merckelbach et al., 1996
Social Phobias	0.4% to 13.0%	DSM-IV; Chapman, 1997
Agoraphobias	5.6%	Chapman, 1997
Panic Disorders	0.6% to 3.5%	DSM-IV; Acierno, et al., 1993; Chapman, 1997

order in clinical populations. Specific phobias and social phobias often co-occur with various mood disorders, such as clinical depression (DSM-IV; Acierno, et al., 1993; Beck & Zebb, 1994; Turner & Beidel, 1989). Comorbid conditions complicate our understanding of phobias and panic disorders and can lead to under- and misdiagnosis of these disorders.

Prevalence of Phobic Disorders

As reflected in the prevalence rates in Table 21–1, phobia is one of the most common mental disorders defined in DSM-IV. The prevalence ranges represented in Table 21-1 include one-year and lifetime prevalence information. For example, the DSM-IV reported that community-sample studies reviewed indicate that 9% of those sampled met criteria for a specific phobia in the previous year. However, 10% to 11.3% within their lifetime had met criteria for a diagnosis of specific phobia.

The fact that many people hide their phobias prevents accurate estimates of how many people are afflicted. Another factor in the underestimation of phobias is that the levels of anxiety or fear experienced may not reach diagnostic-criteria levels. An example of the difference this may make in prevalence rates can be seen in Acierno and colleagues' (1993) review of the panic disorder literature. They report a 0.6% to 1% prevalence of panic disorders in the studies reviewed, yet 6% to 12% of the general population experienced spontaneous panic attacks. Other factors that influence the prevalence rate reported include how the level of distress is defined and the number of types or subtypes included in the study. These parameters for phobias may vary widely from study to study.

Age, gender, and ethnicity have been suggested as risk factors in the development of phobias and panic disorders (e.g., Chapman, 1997). Children and adolescents have a prevalence rate for anxiety and phobic disorders of 1% to 17% (Silverman, Ginsberg, & Kurtines, 1995). There is a strong female bias for agoraphobia and specific phobias; 55% to 95% of those diagnosed are female. For example, in a review by Bekker (1996), it was reported that 75% to 90% of animal and natural environment types of phobias and 63% to 95% of agoraphobia was diagnosed in women in both clinical and community studies. Explanations for this bias have included increased help-seeking behavior in women; a greater openness to self-report symptoms; and a sociocultural bias towards fear and anxiety responses in females. Bekker also notes that social phobias may vary across cultural and ethnic dimensions, as these often are related to social demands. Chambless and Williams (1995) cite a study that found that agoraphobia was more frequently experienced by Blacks (16.9%) than by Whites (9.1%) or Hispanics (6.2%).

CAUSAL THEORIES OF PHOBIC DISORDERS

There is general agreement that phobic disorders represent a fairly clear and consistent set of behaviors or symptoms that are associated with excessive or unrealistic levels of anxiety. This anxiety is about one or more objects/situations in the person's environment which he or she must in some manner escape or avoid. General agreement exists regarding the clinical descriptions of the different types of phobic disorders. However, questions as to why people develop phobias or how phobias can be explained elicit a wide range of answers. At present, three major theoretical models guide the study and treatment of phobic disorders: cognitive, behavioral-conditioning, and neurobiological.

The psychoanalytic model has contributed much to the understanding of phobic disorders. However, the outcomes of treatment based on this model have been inadequately measured, and this approach has been de-emphasized by clinicians. It is included here because of its historical relevance. For Freud, a phobic reaction occurred when a person displaced a frightening or unacceptable aspect of himself onto some external aspect of his reality. Thus, in the future this situation had to be avoided in order to suppress the unacceptable subjective factor.

In the psychoanalytic model, the phobia is at the same time both the repression of anxiety (or pathological fear) and a defense against the anxiety (Laughlin, 1967b). That is, the anxiety results from an unconscious conflict, usually of a sexual nature. This conflict and the resultant anxiety are automatically repressed, or hidden, from the individual's awareness and unconsciously displaced from the original, internal object of conflict onto an external object or situation—that is, the phobia functions as an escape from the anxiety. To help a phobic client, according to this model, the unconscious conflict must be brought into consciousness so that the real source of anxiety can be discovered and dealt with.

Behavioral-Conditioning Model

Although the behavior literature refers to the cognitive-behavioral model, there is more than one such model. Two behavior frameworks that have been most influential in explaining phobic disorders are the operant and the classical-conditioning models. These models agree that problematic behaviors are learned through interaction between the individual and the environment. Thus, phobic anxiety and phobic avoidance, the major elements of phobic disorder, are considered to be behaviors that have been learned in response to environmental stimuli. Just how this learning is postulated to take place is where the operant and the classical model diverge.

Operant Model

According to the operant theory of learning, behaviors that are freely performed by the person are subject to increases or decreases in frequency of occurrence as a result of the consequences that follow the behaviors. Simply speaking, positive consequences increase the frequency of a behavior, while negative consequences decrease its frequency. Phobic behaviors, according to this paradigm, will increase or decrease in frequency in relation to the consequences that follow. This model emphasizes phobic avoidance. Avoidance behavior is strengthened in at least two ways. First, the sympathetic attention of significant others can be seen as "positive (social) reinforcement" for avoidance behavior. Second, the successful escape from, or avoidance of, the anxiety-provoking object or situation has the same effect as positive reinforcement, although this process is referred to as "negative reinforcement."

Since, according to this model, problematic behavior and desired behavior are both learned in accordance with the same principles, treatment uses the positive reinforcement of approach behavior and/or withdraws positive reinforcement of avoidance behavior. In addition, interventions usually include the development of other social behaviors, e.g., assertiveness training or social skills training, to expand the individual's response repertoire.

Classical Conditioning Model

The classical conditioning paradigm has had a most significant impact on the current understanding and treatment of phobic disorders. In the simplest sense, this model postulates that behavior that is elicited by one stimulus can be brought under the control of another stimulus if both are presented together. Insofar as the learning of phobic anxiety is concerned, this model has strong historical roots in the literature of Freud's famous case of Little Albert (see Thomlison, 1984). Although subsequent studies of this type failed to condition phobias (Emmelkamp, 1979), the stage was set for many years of exploration of phobic anxiety in terms of this early classical conditioning model. Currently, classical conditioning theory is used to explain the physical sensations and anxiety in the absence of the fear-provoking stimulus (Kearney & Silverman, 1992; Merckelbach, et al., 1996). Merckelbach and colleagues (1996) consider this a direct pathway to understanding most specific phobias. In panic attacks, hyperventilation may cause the initial experience of panic symptoms but classical conditioning explains the expression of symptoms in future attacks (Acierno, et al., 1993).

Two-Factor Theory
The contemporary conditioning model emphasizes anxiety but also incorporates the phobic avoidance response, hence its name. First, phobic anxiety is said to be a "conditioned response" (learned). This phobic anxiety response is elicited by the "conditioned stimulus" (phobic object/situation). In other words, the phobic object takes on the power to elicit the anxiety response because this phobic object was present at the same time as some other object that naturally elicited anxiety from the individual.

The greatest impetus to the treatment of phobias, a method known as "systematic desensitization," came from this theoretical model. Although contemporary investigators have been critical of the classical conditioning model, it has served as the framework for a great deal of research into the treatment of phobias.

Cognitive Model

The cognitive model has received a great deal of research attention over the past two decades and has had a significant impact on phobia treatment procedures. Cognitive theory focuses on the beliefs, attitudes, and thoughts that lead to statements individuals make to themselves. In this model, anxiety is assumed to result from statements of a fear-inducing nature that individuals communicate to themselves. For example, when someone, for whom this is anxiety-provoking, goes to a party, he may say to himself, "I'm going to have a miserable time here. I hate these functions. I never know what to talk about and people think I'm dumb." Cognitive theorists argue that such statements become reflected in their behavior.

At a more complex level, the cognitive model posits that persons with a phobia, process a threatening situation and how to escape from it in faulty ways. Some investigators have produced data suggesting that clients with a phobia have an exaggerated misinterpretation of physical cues and anxiety (Acierno, et al., 1993; Arntz, 1997; Beck & Zebb, 1994; Kearney & Silverman, 1992). The fear becomes one of fearing the anxiety symptoms—a "fear of fear" response. The belief is that the autonomic-response symptoms have harmful consequences (e.g., heart palpitations mean impending death). This leads to negative affect, a sense of loss of control, and self-focused attention (Kearney & Silverman, 1992). These cognitions lead to a "anxiety expectancy" that maintains the phobia (Fokias & Tyler, 1995).

Cognitive biases associated with phobias include attentional and judgmental biases (Merckelbach, et al., 1996). For example, clients with social phobia have been found to have fewer positive and more negative cognitions compared to subjects with other phobic conditions, as well as low self-confidence, a critical evaluation of their social performance, and internal attribution of responsibility for social failures (Newman, et al., 1994). Thus, altering clients' cognitions seems essential to the treatment of social phobias.

Neurobiological Models

A unitary neurobiological model for the etiology of phobic disorders does not exist. However, an ever-increasing body of knowledge about psychopharmacological approaches to the treatment of phobias, biological predispositions to fears and phobias, and the development of nonconditioned phobic responses is being assembled.

Psychopharmacology
Research in this area has tended to focus on the cause and control of the anxiety response. Therefore, advances in pharmacological treatment have largely involved the amelioration or management of anxiety and panic responses (see reviews: Hayward & Wardle, 1997; Levin, et al., 1989).

Genetics
The heredity–environment debate, which figures in most discussions of human behavior, also enlivens the discussion of phobic disorders (see review: Bruch, 1989). It seems likely that some biological predisposition does influence the individual's anxiety reactions. Some first-degree relatives

and twin studies suggest a modest though significant genetic association for specific phobias (*DSM-IV*; Merckelbach, et al., 1996), social phobias (*DSM-IV*; Bruch, 1989), and panic disorders (Acierno, et al., 1993; *DSM-IV*; Merckelbach, et al., 1996). However, research in this area tends to have significant methodological and/or conceptual problems.

Evolutionary Model

Also known as the *nonassociative model,* the evolutionary model attempts to explain why some phobias exist in the seeming absence of a direct conditioned event (Forsyth & Chorpita, 1997; Merckelbach & de Jong, 1997). The premise is that we, as a species, have an inborn fear-evoking function that has an adaptive, evolutionary purpose. That is, we are predisposed to having evoked fear responses (i.e., abrupt, autonomic nervous system reactions). The mechanisms by which adaptive fear reactions become maladaptive phobic responses remain unclear.

Neurobiological models will undoubtedly have a considerable impact on our understanding of phobic disorders in the decades to come, particularly in identifying different phobic anxiety processes and in inhibiting or arresting certain aspects of phobic anxiety in order to facilitate psychosocial treatment. As with all theories of etiology, the premise is that as our understanding of how the core problem develops is refined we will be able to then translate this into more successful ways to influence phobias through treatment (Forsyth & Chorpita, 1997).

TREATMENT APPROACHES TO PHOBIC DISORDERS

From a social worker's perspective, two issues arise in discussing the treatment of phobic disorders. First, a review of the major social work practice textbooks and journals reveals a dearth of publications for social workers in this area. Second, models of intervention derived from other disciplines must be evaluated by the social worker for their applicability to social work practice. This section examines two major approaches to the treatment of phobic disorders, each of which has relevance to social work practice: the cognitive-behavioral and the pharmacological. Familiarity with these approaches should help the social worker tailor interventions to the specific needs of phobic clients.

Cognitive-Behavioral Interventions

The application of the cognitive-behavioral approaches to phobic disorders has demonstrated how feedback from controlled clinical studies can improve interventions. Effectiveness of cognitive-behavioral approaches has been established through extensive case-level evaluations, empirical investigations, and well-controlled outcome studies. For example, cognitive-behavioral techniques have been found to be effective with clients with social phobias even when these clients differed in initial symptom presentation (Brown, et al., 1995). There appears to be an indirect cognitive effect even when a "pure" behavioral or exposure intervention is used (Newman, et al., 1994). Cognitive-behavioral treatment usually focuses on the identification and disruption of negative thought patterns as well as exposure to fear provoking situations relevant to the client (fear hierarchy) (Acierno, et al., 1993; Beck & Zebb, 1994; Brown, et al., 1995). Current cognitive-behavioral interventions are characterized by a high success rate, clarity regarding intervention components, self-help manuals to augment treatment, and efficacy when compared to pharmacological treatment approaches (Beck & Zebb, 1994).

Panic management approaches often include breathing retraining for hyperventilation, cognitive restructuring with educational components regarding somatic cues, and *in vivo* or imaginal exposure-based experiences (Acierno, et al., 1993; Dattilio, 1994; Peterson, 1995).

In his review, Heimberg (1989) found that studies suggested that a combination of exposure and cognitive therapies was as effective posttreatment as exposure-based therapy alone. Combined treatment increased clients' repertoire of coping skills, including distraction techniques, relaxation, and rational self-talk. However, at six-month follow-up significant differences were found, with the combined-treatment clients receiving better scores on measures of phobic anxiety and avoidance behaviors, general anxiety, and depression. At one-year follow-up, subjects having the combined treatment had not sought additional help, while 40% of exposure-only clients had. The following sequence for cognitive-behavioral treatment has been suggested (Beck & Zebb, 1994; Dattilio, 1994):

- *Physiological interventions:* Deep relaxation, breathing retraining, and applied relaxation consisting of 'in vivo' practice situations using the person's fear hierarchy.
- *Cognitive interventions:* Education about the disorder; guided imagery; coping strategies; cognitive restructuring; and cognitive therapy interventions.
- *Exposure-based interventions:* Situational exposure; interoceptive exposure (i.e., physical sensations) concurrent with coping skills to manage anxiety.

Butler (1989) concluded that six to twelve weekly sessions of individual or group treatment can produce effective results. It is important to provide guidelines on how to maintain improvement to help clients deal with and prevent relapse. A combination of cognitive and behavioral techniques will help clients to increase their perceived ability to cope as well as decreasing the perceived threat. Homework assignments should be given on a regular basis to reinforce the in-session work.

Cognitive Modification

The cognitive-behavior therapist assumes that the individual's cognitive processes can mediate anxiety reactions. These cognitive processes are thoughts, mental images, beliefs, and expectations—all of which are known to affect behavior in some fashion (Bandura, 1977). Assuming the role of cognition in causally mediating both adaptive and maladaptive behavior, the cognitive approach to treating phobic disorders focuses on altering the faulty cognitions. If the cognitions that are maintaining the phobic anxiety can be altered, anxiety will be reduced and the individual will be able to approach the phobic stimulus.

The cognitive approach requires that client and therapist identify both the negative self-statements that the client makes to himself regarding the phobic stimulus and the way in which these statements maintain the phobic anxiety. The therapist then helps the client reframe the anxiety-producing aspects of the phobic situation in order to discover a "more rational explanation" for the development of the fear response. Finally, the client learns how to use positive self-statements by giving self-encouragement as various goals are achieved. Techniques that can be used include homework assignments, within-session role-plays, social-skills training, activities diary, and thought and mood logs (Butler, 1989).

Reports on the effectiveness of cognitive modification with phobic disorders have been building over the past two decades (see reviews: Wells & Clark, 1997; Steketee & Shapiro, 1995). Recent research has been focused on defining the effectiveness of specific elements of cognitive therapy. For example, Newman and colleagues (1994) indicate that cognitive restructuring can occur with social-phobic clients even when a performance-based exposure intervention is used without a cognitive component. Others have studied the factors that might better predict who could most benefit from which specific cognitive components (see review by Steketee and Shapiro, 1995). Acierno and colleagues (1993) in their review of the literature found that both conditioning-based (exposure and extinction) and cognitively-based interventions reduced anxiety, with a combination of these interventions the most successful intervention.

Exposure-Based Treatment

For a number of years, Wolpe's (1958, 1973) systematic desensitization was the treatment of choice for many professionals working with phobic clients. The approach seemed compatible with social work practice but has received little research attention since the early 1980s (Heimberg, 1989; Thomlison, 1984). However, exposure-based treatment is considered an essential element in the treatment of most phobias (Forsyth & Chorpita, 1997; Heimberg, 1989). Studies indicate that exposure techniques (e.g., systematic desensitization; eye movement desensitization [EMD], image confrontation) have been effective in reducing the levels of anxiety and avoidance behaviors in phobic clients (Forsyth & Chorpita, 1997; Sanderson & Carpenter, 1992). The premise underlying exposure-based treatment is that a phobia is an adaptive response to a perceived threat and that psychophysiological response changes will provide the emotional environment necessary for corrective learning. Exposure protocols include setting appropriate goals, monitoring activities by using behavioral diary, graded *in vivo* exposure during sessions, and graded *in vivo* exposure homework assignments (Taylor, et al., 1997).

Systematic desensitization is based on the hypothesis that phobic anxiety is an autonomic response learned in a situation perceived by the individual to have been anxiety provoking. To alleviate the phobic anxiety, in this view, the individual must learn a new response to the situation that provokes the phobic anxiety. In order to achieve this goal, the person must learn to inhibit her anxiety reaction when she is confronted with the anxiety-provoking stimulus. A logical alternative to an anxiety response is relaxation. Therefore, the procedure of desensitization requires that the individual learn relaxation techniques (e.g., deep muscle relaxation or imagery). During the assessment, the individual's phobic reactions are explored with a view to compiling a list of anxiety-provoking situations—a *fear hierarchy*. The list is divided into categories, and the situations in each category are arranged in a hierarchy so that the least anxiety-provoking stimuli can be presented to the person in graded fashion until the most anxiety-provoking situation is encountered. Using this fear hierarchy, the individual is helped to imagine each situation while she is in a relaxed state. The individual works through each hierarchy systematically, nonverbally signaling to the therapist if any scene arouses anxiety at an uncomfortable level. In this case, the image of the scene is withdrawn and the individual is instructed to return to the state of relaxation. Traditionally, the therapist has assisted the client in the desensitization process but in a review of the treatment literature, Peterson (1995) noted that a number of *in vivo* exposure intervention materials were available: written (self- or therapist-directed), audio- and videotapes as well as computer-generated virtual reality devices. Self-help treatments reinforce therapist-assisted exposure treatment or may be used alone (Beck & Zebb, 1994; Peterson, 1995; Thyer, 1987). Self-directed exposure can be as effective as therapist-directed exposure treatment if the client is able to comply with a self-directed course of treatment (Beck & Zebb, 1994).

The *reinforced practice* approach is based on operant-conditioning theory, using the principle of positive reinforcement for increments of successful behavior. This approach identifies behavioral deficits which, if corrected, will allow the individual to overcome her phobic anxiety. The goal of therapy, then, is not to reduce anxiety but rather to "shape" appropriate approach behavior toward the phobic situation or object. Reinforced practice uses graded exposure to the fear-producing stimulus and performance feedback to the individual, a feature that has proven most helpful in initiating change. It is important for therapists to recognize that behavioral practice can be tedious, time-consuming, and anxiety provoking (Butler, 1989). Increased confidence through reinforced practice can become a building block to further growth.

In the treatment procedure, therapist and client identify the phobic situation or object and each of the steps that the client must move through in confronting this phobic stimulus. From beginning to end, a series of goal lines is identified; these serve as achievement markers for the client. The steps needed to achieve each goal are ordered from the least to the most difficult. Instructions to the client require him actually to move through each step; the accompanying therapist will give praise for client achievement and provide precise feedback on the client's performance. This feedback facilitates the client's self-correction in the actual situation; as the client improves the feedback should demonstrate the degree of improvement session by session.

The Pharmacological Approach

The use of drugs in the treatment of many human problems has become widely accepted; in many cases pharmacotherapy has had most impressive results. An analysis of trends in the phobia literature indicates that by 1988 there was a shift to more published pharmacological research articles. Pharmacological treatment efficacy is widely supported (see reviews: Hayward & Wardle, 1997; Levin, et al., 1989). This suggests a prominent role for the neurochemical system in the maintenance of anxiety. However, a relapse rate of more than 85% suggests that pharmacological interventions relieve symptoms but do not directly affect the underlying mechanisms of phobias and panic disorders (Acierno, et al., 1993).

Certain psychotropic drugs (e.g., benzodiazepines, monoamine oxidase inhibitors, beta blockers) seem to reduce anxiety enough to permit the initiation of structured psychosocial approaches. Many research studies suggest the efficacy of a combined pharmacological and psychosocial treatment approach to phobias, especially cognitive-behavioral interventions.

SOCIAL WORK PRACTICE AND PHOBIAS

The state of contemporary social work knowledge in the area of phobias remains sparse. The social work literature contains few reports on practice with phobic individuals though a recent publication will do much to rectify this situation (Thyer & Wodarski, 1998). This section draws heavily upon the author's own clinical experience, as well as on some published studies.

An Ecological Perspective for Practice With the Phobic Client

The Family
The investigators of phobic disorders tend to overlook the interpersonal functioning of the phobic client. As a social work practitioner, you are well aware of the need to have as clear a picture as possible of the client's relationships with significant others, as well as with the community at large. These subsystems represent both potential causes of phobias and resources to assist the treatment process. In addition, a systems perspective gives the social worker a greater understanding of those in the client's network of relationships who are being negatively affected by their phobic anxiety.

In most cases, the phobic client has a spouse and children. Early research on the marital dyad showed that the spouse is actively involved in the client's phobic disturbance. At one level, this involvement may appear quite innocent; for example, the sympathetic spouse may be attempting to hide some of the role deficits of his partner. However, this helpfulness may be one of the factors maintaining the phobic avoidance. In some cases, the spouse may be content with the dyadic balance and purposefully inhibit or resist the partner's efforts at change (Emmelkamp, 1979). This resistance often comes to the attention of the therapist through client reports about the lack of support the spouse is giving, or about increased ridicule, particularly during at-home practice sessions. On occasion, the therapist may receive a call from the spouse, complaining about changes in the client that "have nothing to do with the phobia." It is most advisable to involve the spouse in some joint sessions at least to help her understand their role. These sessions often evolve into marital therapy, indicating that the phobic anxiety was associated with marital conflict.

The incidence of marital conflict among phobic individuals is difficult to ascertain, but some researchers suggest it is higher than was once thought. Conflict between spouses may be a contributing stressor to panic attacks and anxiety; thus, the need for spousal involvement in the treatment of phobic clients.

The role of children in maintaining or alleviating phobic behavior is almost unknown. However, the family is a social system important to the client and clinical assessment of the children vis-à-vis the phobic parent is necessary. Experience suggests that children take on increased responsibility for family tasks, particularly when it is the mother who has a phobia. Children also have great difficulty explaining the frequent unavailability of their parent at school and community functions and are confused or fearful about what is really wrong with their parent. Therefore, even though the role of children in the onset and maintenance of phobic anxiety is unclear, the family should be seen for assessment, and perhaps periodically during treatment, for the purpose of information sharing.

When marital and/or family conflict is believed not to exist, family members can play an important role by supporting the phobic client during and after the treatment process. The means by which this therapeutic resource can be strengthened needs further investigation. At present, the therapist can best use the family by involving members from the beginning and keeping them abreast of the client's progress and its meaning to them.

The Community
By the time many phobic individuals enter treatment, they have become isolated from their community and their peer group. This is particularly true of the agoraphobic client, for whom visits outside the home are extremely anxiety provoking. For these people the community should be a treatment resource, and reinvolvement of the client in the community should be a therapeutic objective.

Social Work Interventions

Assessment, Monitoring, and Evaluation

Assessment of the phobic client must yield information both on the client's functioning as a member of a larger system and on the phobic disorder itself. In the area of phobias, there has not been a great deal of empirical and practice exchange with a view to facilitating intervention planning, goal setting, monitoring progress, and evaluating outcome of interventions (Beck & Zebb, 1994). What we do know from research and theory is that clients presenting with phobias need to have the cognitive, behavioral, and physiological aspects of their phobic response assessed (Franklin, 1996). A number of assessments methods have been reported in the literature: clinical interviews, observation of behaviors, physiological assessments, self-monitoring, and standardized self-report measures (Beck & Zebb, 1994; Kearney & Silverman, 1992). Beck and Zebb (1994) concluded that structured clinical interviews were most frequently limited to diagnostic settings. They observed that behavioral and physiological assessments are often used during the initial assessment of phobic clients. Although self-monitoring may be initially useful in the treatment process, it is often perceived as an unreliable indicator of progress (i.e., monitoring or outcome evaluation) due to an attentional bias that may lead clients to overestimate the frequency, intensity and/or duration of symptoms.

Because standardized self-report measures are inexpensive and easy to administer, these are of particular interest to social workers in a variety of intervention settings. They can be used in goal setting, monitoring progress, and evaluating intervention outcomes. Presenting these measures in graphic form can provide a visual record that is easily read by the client as well as the practitioner. Standardized instruments—tests—that are frequently used in the assessment of phobias include:

- *State Trait Anxiety Inventory* (STAI; Speilberger, et al., 1970) is a 40-item measure of both state and trait anxiety.
- *Social Avoidance and Distress Scale* (SAD; Watson & Friend, 1969) is a 28-item true-false measure of social avoidance and social distress.
- *Social Phobia and Anxiety Inventory* (SPAI; Turner, et al., 1989) is a measure that assesses somatic, behavioral, and cognitive symptoms. The SPAI also discriminates between social phobia and other anxiety disorders.
- *Fear of Negative Evaluation Scale* (FNE; Watson & Friend, 1969) is a 30-item true/false scale that has been used in many studies to assess negative cognitions.

Besides these symptom dimensions, Arnkoff and Glass (1989) suggest that areas of cognitive functioning may be assessed through examining self-statements, irrational beliefs, attribution style, cognitive schemas and expectations, and self-focused attention. Social-support assessment is often overlooked in the assessment and treatment of phobias, especially agoraphobia. Assessing the types and quality of a wider-than-immediate family social-support network is important (Fokias & Tyler, 1995). Other marital and family factors that may be important to assessment include marital quality, characteristics of partner or parents (for children), and willingness of parent or partner to be involved in the therapeutic process. Acierno and colleagues (1993) indicate that the number and intensity of life stressors are important factors when assessing any anxiety disorder, including phobias and panic disorders.

Treatment Planning

Once the assessment of the phobic anxiety has been completed, the social worker must select the most appropriate means by which to help the client confront these situations. To reach this decision, the worker must determine whether the phobic anxiety should be focused on directly or whether behavioral deficits should be the focus of treatment. Next, a decision must be made as to how much of the exposure to the anxiety-provoking situations will be accomplished through imagery and how much through direct confrontation with the phobic object or situation. Empirically-based criteria for determining the most appropriate approach are only just beginning to appear, and the data are somewhat contradictory. However, the following treatment considerations, based on current research and clinical findings, should inform the social worker's decisions.

- If there is identified marital conflict, marital therapy should be offered concurrently with individual treatment focused on the phobic disorder.
- Although relaxation training is not a requirement for modification of phobic anxiety, many clients report feeling significantly more relaxed after such sessions. Therefore, it is suggested that relaxation training be retained as a technique for clients who are highly anxious and who respond positively to the relaxation instructions.
- Systematic desensitization *in vivo* is useful for certain specific phobias such as fear of flying, fear of animals, and fear of particular objects or situations (e.g., elevators). Although the research has favored some other approaches over desensitization with agorapho-

bics, the results are equivocal, and desensitization remains a viable treatment option for certain agoraphobics even though it may take longer than flooding.

- Flooding *in vivo* appears to be a most effective technique for situational phobics and agoraphobics. Data are lacking, however, as to the relative effectiveness of reinforced practice for phobias. Some social workers find that intense exposure through either imagery or actual contact is an unsatisfactory means to facilitate change.

- There is some evidence that reinforced practice in the natural environment is useful with agoraphobics and social phobics. The stepwise approach to expanding the client's behavioral repertoire should make this technique of reinforced practice particularly attractive for the treatment of those agoraphobics who have been isolated to the point that they have lost many of their interactional skills.

- Cognitive approaches have a particular appeal in that they facilitate reframing of the phobic anxiety. To date, however, the effectiveness of cognitive treatments for phobic clients is unclear. Future research may indicate that the cognitive techniques best serve the individual by restructuring her view of the problem, thereby establishing a base upon which actual exposure to the phobic stimuli may take place.

- There is reason to use family and peer group in the treatment of the phobic client. Both subsystems provide natural support for the phobic client during therapy; continued posttreatment improvement of clients with such support suggests the need for expanded efforts in this area.

It must be underlined that while the social work treatment approach suggested here requires client exposure to the phobic stimulus, this must take place within a positive therapeutic relationship. *In vivo* exposure must be agreed to by the client and carried out sequentially. Finally, the exposure must be accompanied by supportive feedback from the therapist.

CONCLUSIONS

Knowledge about the treatment of phobic disorders has progressed significantly in the past 20 years. Over the past two decades, there has been a multiplicity of scientific investigations into prevalence, theory, and research as well as intervention outcomes (Franklin, 1996). While there is not complete agreement on why phobic disorders arise, the progress in treatment approaches has led to an optimistic conclusion that successful treatment of moderately to severely disabling phobias is attainable.

The professional literature indicates the attention that researchers and practitioners have devoted to attempting to identify and understand the causes and effects of phobias. This understanding has led to more specific criteria and differentiation among various phobias. Treatment approaches have been and continue to be empirically investigated. These studies have begun to lay the foundation for a differential treatment approach to various phobic disorders. Further research is needed on the most appropriate interventions for each phobic type. The prevention of phobic conditions has not yet reached the research agenda. This is a particularly challenging area because it demands a clear understanding of etiology.

Most social workers that have phobic clients are in an excellent position to contribute to research endeavors. This is particularly true in relation to the role of family members, both in terms of their contribution to the maintenance of the phobic and in terms of their supporting the treatment process. One area of much needed research is the function of self-help groups in the treatment of phobias. The social work profession has a long-standing commitment to the use of self-help groups, yet little is known about the role they might play in the treatment of the phobic individual. Perhaps another area of interest to social workers would be client and social worker characteristics that are predictive of better outcomes, such as motivation and readiness to change.

In conclusion, the past two decades of work with phobic disorders have yielded knowledge that, if incorporated into social work practice, will permit the successful and short-term treatment of many people who suffer the debilitating anxiety and limitation of a phobic disorder.

REFERENCES

Acierno, R. E., Hersen, M., & Van Hasslet, V. B. (1993). Interventions for panic disorder: A critical review of the literature. *Clinical Psychology Review, 13, 6,* 561–578.

American Psychiatric Association. (1994). *Diagnostic and statistical manual of mental disorders, fourth edition. (DSM-IV).* Washington, DC: Author.

Arnkoff, D. B., & Glass, C. R. (1989). Cognitive assessment in social anxiety and social phobia. *Clinical Psychology Review, 9, 1,* 61–74.

Arntz, A. (1997). The match–mismatch model of phobia acquisition. In G. C. L. Davey (Ed.), *Phobias: A handbook of theory, research and treatment* (pp. 375–396). New York: Wiley.

Bandura, A. (1977). *Social learning theory.* Englewoods Cliffs, NJ: Prentice-Hall.

Beck, J. G., & Zebb, B. J. (1994). Behavioral assessment and treatment of panic disorder: Current status, future directions. *Behavior Therapy, 25, 4,* 581–611.

Bekker, M. H. J. (1996). Agoraphobia and gender: A review. *Clinical Psychology Review, 16, 2,* 129–146.

Bell-Dolan, D., & Allan, W. D. (1997). Book review: Anxiety and phobic disorders. *Clinical Psychology Review, 17, 4,* 446–448.

Brown, E. J., Heimberg, R. G., & Juster, H. R. (1995). Social phobia subtype and avoidant personality disorder: Effect on severity of social phobia, impairment and outcome of cognitive behavioral treatment. *Behavior Therapy, 26*, 467–486.

Bruch, M. A. (1989). Familial and developmental antecedents of social phobia: Issues and findings. *Clinical Psychology Review, 9*, 1, 37–47.

Butler, G. (1989). Issues in the application of cognitive and behavioral strategies to the treatment of social phobia. *Clinical Psychology Review, 9*, 1, 91–106.

Chambless, D. L., & Williams, K. E. (1995). A preliminary study of African Americans with agoraphobia: Symptom severity and outcome of treatment with in vivo exposure. *Behavior Therapy, 26*, 501–515.

Chapman, T. F. (1997). The epidemiology of fears and phobias. In G. C. L. Davey (Ed.), *Phobias*. New York: Wiley.

Dattilio, F. M. (1994). SAEB: A method of conceptualization in the treatment of panic attacks. *Cognitive and Behavioral Practice, 1*, 1, 179–191.

Emmelkamp, P. (1979). The behavioral study of clinical phobias. *Progress in Behavior Modification, 8*, 55–125.

Fokias, D., & Tyler, P. (1995). Social support and agoraphobia: A review. *Clinical Psychology Review, 15*, 4, 347–366.

Forsyth, J. P., & Chorpita, B. F. (1997). Unearthing the nonassociative origins of fear and phobias: A rejoinder. *Journal of Behavior Therapy and Experimental Psychiatry, 28*, 4, 297–305.

Franklin, M. E. (1996). Book review: Social phobias. *Clinical Psychology Review, 16*, 8, 777–778.

Hayward, P., & Wardle, J. (1997). The use of medication in the treatment of phobias. In G. C. L. Davey (Ed.), *Phobias: A handbook of theory, research and treatment* (pp. 281–300). New York: Wiley.

Heimberg, R. G. (1989). Cognitive and behavioral treatments for social phobia: A critical analysis. *Clinical Psychology Review, 9*, 1, 107–128.

Kearney, C. A., & Silverman, W. K. (1992). Let's not push the "panic" button: A critical analysis of panic and panic disorder in adolescents. *Clinical Psychology Review, 12*, 3, 293–305.

Laughlin, H. (1967a). *The neuroses*. London: Butterworth.

Laughlin, H. (1967b). Unraveling the phobic defense. *American Journal of Psychiatry, 123*, 1081–1086.

Levin, A. P., Schneier, F. R., & Liebowitz, M. R. (1989). Social phobia: Biology and pharmacology. *Clinical Psychology Review, 9*, 1, 129–140.

Levitt, E. (1967). *The psychology of anxiety*. Indianapolis: Bobbs-Merrill.

Lewin, B. (1972). Phobias. *International Encyclopedia of the Social Sciences, 11*, 81–84. New York: Macmillan.

Marks, I. (1969). *Fear and phobias*. New York: Academic Press.

Merckelbach, H., & de Jong, P. J. (1997). Evolutionary models of phobias. In G. C. L. Davey (Ed.), *Phobias: A handbook of theory, research and treatment* (pp. 323–348). New York: Wiley.

Merckelbach, H., de Jong, P. J., Muris, P., & van den Hout, M. A. (1996). The etiology of specific phobias: A review. *Clinical Psychology Review, 16*, 4, 337–361.

Newman, M. G., Hofmann, S. G., Trabert, W., Roth, W. T., & Taylor, C. B. (1994). Does behavioral treatment of social phobia lead to cognitive changes? *Behavior Therapy, 25*, 3, 503–517.

Peterson, L. (1995). Special series: Mechanisms, populations, and treatment innovations in anxiety disorders. *Behavior Therapy, 26*, 3, 451–455.

Salkovskis, P. M., & Hackmann, A. (1997). Agoraphobia. In G. C. L. Davey (Ed.), *Phobias: A handbook of theory, research and treatment* (pp. 27–62). New York: Wiley.

Sanderson, S., & Carpenter, R. (1992). Eye movement desensitization versus image confrontation: A single-session crossover study of 58 phobic subjects. *Journal of Behavior Therapy and Experimental Psychiatry, 23*, 4, 269–275.

Silverman, W. K., Ginsburg, G. S., & Kurtines, W. M. (1995). Clinical issues in treating children with anxiety and phobic disorders. *Cognitive and Behavioral Practice, 2, 1,* 93–117.

Speilberger, C. D., Gorsuch, R. L., & Lushene, R. E. (1970). *State-trait anxiety inventory.* Palo Alto, CA: Consulting Psychologists Press.

Steketee, G., & Shapiro, L. J. (1995). Predicting behavioral treatment outcome for agoraphobia and obsessive compulsive disorder. *Clinical Psychology Review, 15, 4,* 317–346.

Taylor, S., Woody, S., Koch, W. J., McLean, P., Paterson, R. J., & Anderson, K. W. (1997). Cognitive restructuring in the treatment of social phobia: Efficacy and mode of action. *Behavior Modification, 21, 4,* 487–511.

Thomlison, R. J. (1984). Phobic disorders. In F. J. Turner (Ed.), *Adult psychopathology: A social work perspective (1st ed.)* (pp. 280–315). New York: The Free Press.

Thyer, B. A. (1987). Community-based self-help groups for the treatment of agoraphobia. *Journal of Sociology and Social Welfare, 14, 3,* 135–141.

Thyer, B. A., & Wodarski, J. S. (Eds.). (1998). *Handbook of empirical social work practice: Mental disorders* (Vol. I). New York: Wiley.

Turner, S. M., & Beidel, D. C., Dancu, C. V., & Stanley, M. A. (1989). An empirically drived inventory to measure social fears and anxiety: The Social Phobia and Anxiety Inventory. *Journal of Consulting and Clinical Psychology, 1,* 35–40.

Watson, D., & Friend, R. (1969). Measurement of social-evaluative anxiety. *Journal of Consulting and Clinical Psychology, 33,* 448–457.

Wells, A., & Clark, D. M. (1997). Social phobia: A cognitive approach. In G. C. L. Davey (Ed.), *Phobias: A handbook of theory, research and treatment* (pp. 3–26). New York: Wiley.

Wolpe, J. (1958). *Psychotherapy by reciprocal inhibition.* Palo Alto: Stanford University Press.

Wolpe, J. (1973). *The practice of behavior therapy* (2nd ed.). New York: Pergamon.

22

EATING DISORDERS AND SOCIAL WORK

Jan Lackstrom

There have been reports of eating disorders throughout history, but anorexia nervosa and bulimia have captured much attention over the past thirty years because of the growing number of people, mostly women, who have suffered with these illnesses. These are thought to be typically illnesses of adolescence, but it is clear that many young people are entering adulthood still experiencing such problems. Equally clearly, there are a significant number of women who develop anorexia and bulimia in adulthood. Most troubling is the tenacious nature of these disorders; in spite of considerable treatment resources both anorexia and bulimia remain highly resistant to intervention.

The objective of this chapter is to provide the social work practioner with the information necessary to complete an eating disorder assessment and to develop an approach to treatment. The chapter will review the incidence of eating disorders and present the multidetermined model of their causality. The necessity of a multidisciplinary team will be discussed, including some of the team-based impasses that can occur. The chapter will conclude with a discussion of diagnostic criteria, outline in detail the assessment process and content, and conclude with a summary of different approaches and models of treatment.

INCIDENCE AND COST TO SOCIETY

Anorexia nervosa is commonly reported to occur in 0.5% to 1% of women. Bulimia, more common, is reported at rates of 1% to 3% of women. Males appear to comprise anywhere from 5% to 15% of the cases of all eating disorders (Anderson, 1995; Garfinkel, et al., 1995; *DSM-IV*—

see American Psychiatric Association, 1994). Reviewing the research on recovery in anorexia, Steinhausen (1995) reported mean rates of recovery at 43% of patients, with 36% still symptomatic but improved and 20% experiencing chronic anorexia nervosa. A mortality rate of 5% was reported. Hsu (1995) completed a review of outcome associated with bulimia nervosa and reported similar results. It is believed that 50% of individuals with bulimia will recover while 20% experience chronic bulimia and 30% remain symptomatic but improved. Hsu does not report on mortality rates; however, he does predict that they are higher than for the general population.

The starvation and chaotic eating associated with eating disorders affect all aspects of the individuals' lives including their physical health, their academic or work pursuits, and their relationships with family and friends. Because eating disorders typically develop during adolescence and early adulthood the illness disrupts many developmental tasks associated with identity formation and autonomy, which in turn confounds future development. Those individuals whose illness takes a more chronic course become increasingly frail and isolated, and their lives come to revolve around the eating disorder.

The families of eating-disordered females also report being negatively influenced by the illness. As families attempt to help the person with the eating disorder recover from the illness they tend to put other family problems on hold; family members do without attention, family development becomes delayed or abbreviated, and family tensions often increase. Coping with a potentially chronic and life threatening illness seriously challenges individual family members and the family as a whole (Woodside & Shekter-Wolfson, 1990; Woodside, et al., 1993).

Eating disorders also reflect and reinforce society's attribution and beliefs about the value of women. A woman valued for her body alone is dehumanized and objectified. These beliefs perpetuate the disempowerment of women. It is critical for social workers to be aware of the issues of power and gender when working with women with eating disorders. For many a female client this disqualification of the self will have contributed to her predisposition to an eating disorder.

The cost of having women preoccupied with their weight and shape and functioning physically and socially at a less than optimal level is difficult to estimate. In addition to the personal costs and the expense associated with treatment one must also recognize the social costs associated when a sector of the population is unable to participate in citizenship. Perhaps more insidious is the cost associated with women generally being valued primarily for their appearance. Although not as dramatic or life threatening as an eating disorder, the primacy of appearance erodes women's identity and well-being and affects the multiple systems in her life. Social workers must review their own beliefs about weight, shape, and fat prejudice to be able to address this issue in counseling in a meaningful way and to avoid replicating socially condoned oppression by colluding with the drive for thinness.

THE MULTIDETERMINED MODEL OF EATING DISORDERS

First described by Garfinkel and Garner (1982), the multidetermined model of eating disorders is widely accepted. Presented in Table 22–1, the model captures the many factors that appear to predispose the individual to anorexia nervosa and bulimia nervosa, as well as those that precipitate and perpetuate the illness.

The individual, family, and cultural factors that commonly predispose an individual to an eating disorder are outlined in Table 22–1. It is thought that these individual, family, and cultural factors combine in a way that causes the individual to become particularly concerned about and sensitive to issues of weight, shape, and appearance. However, this sensitivity is only acted upon with the addition of some kind of precipitating event. The precipitating event or events may be obvious, for example the death of a family member, moving to a new city or school, a sexual assault, or leaving home for the first time. The precipitating event may, however, be more subtle, such as the advent of menstruation, the expectation to begin dating, and the development of maturity fears. Although the majority of clients will be able to identify precipitating events, some cannot; they often feel an increased sense of shame and confusion because they cannot identify a reason for having an eating disorder. The precipitating events may become clear with improved eating. But it should be noted that most people encounter stressful events in their lives and do not develop eating disorders. The combination of individual, familial, and sociocultural variables occurring at a point of crisis for individuals seems to leave them susceptible to coping by developing an eating disorder (Mackay, 1984; Garfinkel & Garner, 1982). Predisposing and precipitating events are often associated with feelings of being out of control of one's life. This is generally accompanied by a sense of personal ineffectiveness and low self-esteem. It is believed that the client then turns to dieting in an effort to regain some sense of competence, control, and self-esteem. Eating is the one area of the client's life in which no one can successfully interfere. The accompanying weight loss, no

Table 22-1   Common Predisposing Factors for Anorexia and Bulimia Nervosa

Individual
Problems with identity and/or separation
Body image distortion
Weight preoccupation
Chronic medical illness, e.g., diabetes
Perfectionism
Sexual abuse
Stressful life events associated with losses

Family
1. *Biology*
   History of eating disorders, substance abuse, affective disorders
   History of family members being overweight
2. *Magnification of Cultural Factors*
   Appearance, weight, perfection and gender roles
3. *Family Environment*
   Parent–child problems leading to difficulties with identity formation
   and autonomy, e.g., intergenerational boundary violations, poor
   communication, rigid or chaotic family rules, poor conflict resolution

Cultural
Pressure for thinness and appearance
Pressure for performance
Pressure to be superwoman

matter how fleeting or how extreme, is reinforced by the social status attributed to women who appear thin.

Anorexia and bulimia are largely understood to be Western-culture-bound syndromes. Theoretical models that focus on the fear of fatness as the primary motivation for dieting and purging behavior misunderstand the significance of the broader cultural context and the meaning of food refusal in non-Western cultures (Katzman, 1998a). Lee (1998) points out that eating disorders do exist in non-Western societies as more than idiosyncratic cases. Lee proposes that the present-day increase in eating disorders in the non-Western countries is not based on an expansion of Western culture but rather reflects an expansion of modernity. He believes that modernity embodies a growing awareness of appearance, the phenomenon of being empowered and disempowered at the same time, rapid economic growth, political conservativism, and greater homogeneity. Modernization is shaped by the specific location, so is unique to each culture. The specific *DSM* criteria for diagnosis are not always applicable to non-Western cultures. Equally, treatment regimens that are Western bound may not be appropriate either. The social work practioner is well advised to attend to the cultural context if working abroad and when reading the literature.

There has also been a lack of attention given to the issue of diversity in eating disorders within the Western world itself. There is little written about ethnicity, race, sexual identity, or class. Lack of knowledge about these issues and stereotyping on the part of mainstream practioners and researchers has resulted in misdiagnosis or delayed diagnosis (Thompson, 1994; Root, 1990; Silber, 1986). Many explanations of gender socialization, the importance of thinness, and the primacy of sexism over other oppressions may be accurate for middle- and upper-class white Christian women, however it does not apply to women of color, Jewish or Muslim women, those who are poor, and those who are lesbian. For example, complex role expectations are not new for poor women, who have been working and raising their families since long before dual career families became common in the middle and upper classes. Racism and religious persecution are profound experiences for many women and have an impact that cannot be ignored (Thompson, 1994). It is imperative to explore issues of diversity as a source of strength for the client as well.

The development of theory and practice that is well grounded in issues of diversity is in its infancy. Social work practioners are encouraged to ask the question "What is the problem solved?" by the eating disorder when assessing and working with their clients (Katzman, 1998a). In answering this question, with the client, the social worker is in a better position to understand the complex and multifactorial meaning of the eating disorder.

Dieting and attempting to maintain an ideal body image does not improve the client's sense of well-being. Efforts to lose weight become a primary mechanism perpetuating the anorexia or bulimia. The chosen solution to the psychological and interpersonal problems—dieting—becomes an additional problem. Whereas others might examine and critique the solutions they have chosen, eating disordered clients do more of the same, blaming themselves for not dieting well enough. Clients typically lower their ideal weights or diet more rigorously with the belief that if they could only get to that ideal weight their problems would go away. The notion that weight loss and a specific appearance will resolve problems becomes further entrenched in the client's belief systems. With time the effects of starvation and/or chaotic eating also contribute to the individual's sense of ineffectiveness as her educational or vocational pursuits, as well as her health and relationships, become compromised by the effects of the eating disorder.

Biology appears to undermine the client's ability to maintain an ideal weight. There is evidence that the body has a set point (Keys, et al., 1950; Keesey, 1995) which it will return to when given the opportunity. There is a growing body of evidence that indicates that for some individuals dieting may elevate the set point and as a result produce an overall weight gain (Dulloo et al., 1992; Ciliska, 1991). Many are able to maintain the anorexia, but roughly 30% of people with anorexia will develop bulimia in response to the starvation associated with the anorexia (Cooper, 1995; Polivy & Herman, 1985). Once bingeing begins the individual typically takes steps to compensate for the binge, and purging develops. Clients vomit; take laxatives, diuretics, drugs; and exercise in an effort to rid themselves of the calories consumed in the binge. Soon the individuals will find themselves in a binge-purge cycle that they cannot control. This increases their self loathing and sense of being out of control.

When clients present for help they ask for help with the medical, psychological, and interpersonal problems associated with their eating disorder. The social worker using an ecological approach to practice is in a good position to identify an eating disorder. The social worker must be astute when a client presents for help, because many clients will hide their eating disorder because of the shame associated with symptomatic behavior. Clients also fear that they will be told to eat normally, which will result in weight gain. The intense fear of weight gain may be a major obstacle to presenting their problem clearly. Clients do not like the dietary and interpersonal chaos in their lives; they are afraid for their health; they are upset by their family's distress and reaction to their illness. Yet in spite of all of the negative consequences of their eating disorder they will not be willing to give up maintaining a low ideal weight. Any intervention that challenges their ability to reach their target weight will be met with resistance. Because of their ecological approach to practice, social workers are in a good position to identify an eating disorder where other professions may be responding more narrowly to the presenting problem.

THE TREATMENT TEAM AND THERAPEUTIC IMPASSES   *support system*

The treatment of an eating disorder requires a multidisciplinary team. Whether in private practice or hospital based, the social worker will need to collaborate with a number of professionals. Involvement of a family physician is essential. A person who presents with an eating disorder should have a physical examination to rule out any physical causes for the symptomatic behaviors (Mackay, 1984). Clients who are purging need to have their electrolytes and cardiac functioning monitored regularly. Clients who become severely emaciated may have to be admitted to a hospital for weight gain or medical stabilization. The family physician is also responsible for making the final decision about offering medication and monitoring its effectiveness. A psychiatrist who specializes in eating disorders and is familiar with psychiatric medications can play a useful role as consultant to the family physician specifically and the treatment team in general. A family physician can be helpful to the counseling process if the client uses physical concerns to distract from the more dynamic or eating issues. By providing a specific place for physical concerns to be addressed the counseling can remain focused. The social worker will also want to include a registered dietitian as a member of the treatment team. The dietitian will be able to help the client develop a nondieting meal plan and provide education about normalized eating. Depending upon the client's needs and the social worker's skills it would not be unusual to include an occupational therapist, a vocational counselor, family therapist, or group therapist as part of the treatment team.

The team must sort out from the beginning of treatment issues of power, authority, and boundaries. Although time-consuming when working in private practice, it is well worth the investment to deal explicitly with who will be responsible for each component of the treatment and how the team will make decisions together. For those social workers working in hospital settings, where the medical model prevails, these issues must also be worked out. Whereas a private practice team has to deal with problems related to their distance, the hospital-based team must deal with issues related to working so closely together. In either case, unless these issues are clarified problems may ensue that will interfere with treatment.

It is important that the treatment team embrace a similar approach to practice. The team members should bring their different models of practice and unique knowledge to the recovery process. However, they must agree on an approach to three key issues: eating, exercise, and medication. If the treatment team cannot agree on an approach, then a therapeutic impasse can occur (Lackstrom et al., unpublished manuscript). There are many areas for dispute; however, if the team is not together on these three key issues treatment will certainly fail. A nondieting and social exercise philosophy is key with this population and the use of medication can be helpful at times.

Eating

A nondieting approach means no diet products, 30% fat in a meal plan which follows *Canada's Food Guide* (Health and Welfare Canada, 1992). This means things like 2%-fat milk instead of skim, buttered toast rather than dry, a piece of pie for dessert instead of fruit all of the time, regular soda pop instead of diet soda pop, no rice cakes, and no "bad" foods. There is much written in the media about "good" and "bad" foods and low-fat eating. People with eating disorders are eating too little fat and restricting food to the point of compromising themselves nutrionally. Individuals who binge are typically bingeing on the food they restrict. It is better to eat a piece of cake in a controlled way than to eat half a cake in a binge. Clients will need education about the importance of fat for their health and for their sense of feeling satisfied. They will need encouragement to include the forbidden, "bad," and phobic foods in their meal plans. If the entire team does not support this approach the client will not make the attempt to include these challenging foods.

Exercise

Social exercise can only be added when the client has eaten regularly with a wide range of food choices for a minimum of three or four weeks. Because exercise is a purging technique, it should be stopped completely at the beginning of treatment. Many clients will say they are doing exercise for their health; it is true that cardiovascular health and strong bones are of concern, but condoning exercise in the context of the eating disorder is colluding with the illness. Often clients will only acknowledge that they have been purging with exercise when they realize they cannot stop without tremendous distress and effort. Once the individual is eating well she should include social exercise. This would include activities that have a natural ending point, such as tennis or volleyball or activities with friends, such as bike riding or rollerblading. In these activities it is normal to stop partway and have a drink or snack to refresh oneself. Solitary activities such as aerobics or swimming laps only invite overindulgence and can contribute to relapse.

Medication

The team must also support the appropriate use of medication. It is not unusual for a client to resist taking medication. In the end it is the client's decision to take the medication or not. However if she is ambivalent, and a team member supports that ambivalence, the client will likely not take the medication. Although the client should be directed to discuss medication with her physician, all team members can be watching for signs that it is time to consider medication or to review its use. Again, one wants to avoid colluding with the eating disorder.

THE ROLE OF THE SOCIAL WORKER IN CASE MANAGEMENT

Social workers participate in all aspects of the treatment of eating disorders, including individual, group, and family therapy; developing community linkages; teaching; and research (Mackay, 1984). Given that social workers are trained in case management this task typically falls to the social worker. Case management usually entails identifying, with the team, the needs the client has and referring them to the appropriate services. The social worker is a coordinator of service. In most cases the client will pass on accurate information to the team about her treatment and needs. In situations where this does not occur the social worker may be required to facilitate the communication process among team members, including the client. It is important that the client do as much of her own work as possible because she will already feel incompetent. A social worker who does too much for the client will inadvertently reinforce her sense of ineffectiveness and personal inadequacy. Educating a client about how to find an apartment of her own or how to manage the social service bureaucracy will be more time-consuming, but in the long run will help the client develop her self-confidence.

DIAGNOSIS

The diagnostic criteria for anorexia nervosa and bulimia nervosa are outlined in Table 22–2. Although fairly straightforward, they present a number of issues relevant to diagnosis. Because other medical illnesses can mimic anorexia, it is essential that a drive for thinness and a body image disturbance be present before a diagnosis of anorexia nervosa is made. Additionally, the identification of the subtype—restricting or binge-eating/purging—is also necessary. In making a diagnosis of bulimia it is essential to assess the quantity of food being consumed in a binge as well as the quality of the binge episode in an effort to differentiate bingeing from overeating. The client should report eating large quantities of food and feeling out of control just before and while engaging in a binge. Social workers often think of vomiting as the only purging technique. Assessing for other methods of compensation, such as abusing laxatives, exercise, diuretics, and fasting is essential. Again, identifying the subtype of bulimia, purging or nonpurging, is important.

Table 22–2   Diagnostic Criteria for the Eating Disorders

Anorexia Nervosa

1. Refusal to maintain body weight at or above a minimally normal weight for age or height (e.g., weight loss leading to maintenance of body weight less than 85% of that expected; or failure to make expected weight gain during period of growth, leading to body weight less than 85% of that expected.
2. Intense fear of gaining weight or becoming fat, even though underweight
3. Disturbance in the way in which one's body weight or shape is experienced, undue influence of body weight or shape on self-evaluation, or denial of the seriousness of the current low body weight.
4. In postmenarcheal females, amenorrhea i.e., the absence of at least three consecutive menstrual cycles. (A woman is considered to have amenorrhea if her periods occur only following hormone, e.g., estrogen, administration).

Specify Type

Restricting Type: during the current episode of Anorexia Nervosa, the person has not regularly engaged in binge-eating or purging behavior.

Binge-Eating/Purging Type: during the current episode of Anorexia Nervosa, the person has regularly engaged in binge-eating or purging behavior.

Bulimia Nervosa

1. Recurrent episode of binge eating. An episode of binge eating is characterized by both of the following:
   A. Eating, in a discrete period of time an amount of food that is definitely larger than most people would eat during a similar period of time and under similar circumstances.
   B A sense of lack of control over eating during the episode.
2. Recurrent inappropriate compensatory behavior in order to prevent weight gain, such as self-induced vomiting; misuse of laxatives, diuretics, enemas, or other medications; fasting; or excessive exercise.
3. The binge eating and inappropriate compensatory behaviors both occur on an average, at least twice a week for 3 months.
4. Self-evaluation is unduly influenced by body shape and weight.
5. The disturbance does not occur exclusively during episodes of Anorexia Nervosa.

Specify Type

Purging Type: during the current episode of Bulimia Nervosa, the person has regularly engaged in self-induced vomiting or the misuse of laxatives, diuretics, or enemas.

Nonpurging Type: during the current episode of Bulimia Nervosa, the person has used other inappropriate compensatory behaviors, such as fasting or excessive exercise, but has not regularly engaged in self-induced vomiting or the misuse of laxatives, diuretics, or enemas.

Source: Reprinted with permission from the *Diagnostic and Statistical Manual of Mental Disorders, Fourth Edition,* Washington, DC: American Psychiatric Association, 1994.

The diagnosis "Eating Disorder Not Otherwise Specified" may be useful for categorizing someone who does not meet the specific criteria for anorexia nervosa or bulimia nervosa. For example, a woman may not have stopped menstruating yet may meet other criteria for anorexia nervosa, or the frequency of someone's bingeing and purging may not meet criteria for a diagnosis of bulimia nervosa, yet her eating and attitudes may well be creating a great deal of distress for her. This category allows those who are experiencing problematic symptoms to be identified and offered help before reaching full criteria.

A new diagnostic category, "Binge Eating Disorder," is currently being researched. Similar to bulimia nervosa, this category includes those people who binge but do not engage in any compensatory behaviors.

EATING DISORDER ASSESSMENT

An eating disorder assessment must be multidimensional. The social work assessment must be augmented by specific enquiry into eating related topics.

Overview and Initiating Factors
To begin the assessment with a brief discussion of what the client thinks started the eating disorder helps develop the therapeutic alliance and focuses the interview. It will allow the social worker the first opportunity to begin to understand the client's beliefs about causality and provide a base on which to place more objective data. It will also allow the social worker to help the client develop a certain degree of comfort with speaking about behaviors that are often experienced as shameful and embarrassing. By initiating a discussion of vomiting, restricting, shoplifting, diarrhea, constipation, self-loathing, or abuse, for example, the social worker is identifying that difficult subjects are acceptable to speak about. An empathic approach is essential.

Weight History
Taking a weight history is essential. A diagnosis of anorexia cannot be made without knowledge of the client's weight and height. It is wise to weigh the client in your office. This will require using accurate scales. Clients can be weighed in their street clothes with their shoes off. Because clients may find this distressing, taking the weight history and the weight near the beginning of the interview is important as it gives the worker the opportunity to discuss and alleviate the distress associated with weighing.

On *rare* occasions it may be appropriate to delay weighing a client; however, a diagnosis must be made on the basis of an accurate weight and height. If the social worker finds herself not weighing these clients with any frequency, she should review her thoughts about this issue and any dynamics in the counseling that are interfering with the weighing.

It is important to get a sense of the client's premorbid weight, remembering that a premorbid weight dating from adolescence will be limited by the fact that the person would not have reached their adult weight. This is also an opportunity to ask about the client's menstrual functioning and her use of birth-control pills. This is also a time to speak about body image disturbance and ideal versus phobic weights. Exploring the meaning of weight and the fear associated with an increased weight will augment understanding of what issues may underlie the eating disorder.

Daily Intake

The social worker needs to identify a typical day's eating. Some clients will have difficulty discussing this information and will resist. Reviewing in detail what was eaten at each meal, any snacks, and any other eating episodes, is important for diagnosis and provides essential baseline information necessary to track the first step of recovery—normalizing eating. Specific information as to the time of eating and the quantity and quality of food eaten must be taken exactly. For example:

breakfast—0 intake;
lunch—(2 P.M.) cheese sandwich = 1 slice whole wheat bread, 1 slice low fat cheese, no butter, green apple, small glass skim milk;
snack—6 P.M. = diet coke and 1 large low fat muffin;
dinner—8 P.M. = 0 intake;
snack—10 P.M. = turns into a binge begins with 4 crackers and low fat cheese, water

becomes

1 quart vanilla ice cream, 1 row chocolate chip cookies, 3 doughnuts, 2 bowls cereal and skim milk, 6 pieces of bread toasted with low fat cheese slices, 5 chocolate bars, regular size.

Reviewing food avoidances is also important because the restricted food may be eaten in binges later on.

Bingeing

Many clients who are bingeing are acutely ashamed of their behavior. As stated earlier, it is important for the social worker to approach this topic empathically so that it does not remain a taboo subject, possibly leaving the client with the belief that the social worker also thinks this is so disgusting that he or she will not speak of it. Discussing bingeing in a direct fashion normalizes discussion of the issue and begins the process of client self-monitoring. Again, detail is important. When did the bingeing begin? What is the frequency per day? What time of day do binges take place? Where? What initiates an urge to binge? What is eaten in a binge? How does a binge end?

Purging

Purging behavior is another area where clients experience shame. It is important to assess purging because purging tends to cause medical complications. Eliciting details about purging is necessary to get a full picture of what the client must contend with in her efforts to recover. Asking what initiates purging and how often it occurs is necessary. The social worker should review a list of purging techniques with the client rather that waiting for the client to report them. Purging behaviors that lower potassium can be life threatening; these include vomiting, abusing laxatives, and abusing diuretics. In these cases medical monitoring is necessary. When assessing vomiting the social worker should also inquire about the use of ipecac, which is known to contribute to cardiac failure. Detailed information also helps the client begin the process of self-monitoring, which will be necessary once she begins to stop her symptomatic behavior.

Medical and Psychological Complications

Social workers must be prepared to expand their knowledge base to include medical information. The social worker is not responsible for the medical care of the client; nevertheless he or she must be aware of potential medical and psychological complications and their implications for treatment (Kaplan & Garfinkel, 1993). For example, at a certain point of starvation a client will be too cognitively impaired to participate in anything but supportive work and is best served by focusing on normalizing eating and increasing weight. Table 22–3 identifies the primary medical and psychological complications of anorexia and bulimia. Again, it is best for the social worker to ask the client about specific complications, rather than waiting for the client to report them. It is important for the social worker to be able to educate the client in a general way about medical complications that she may not have attributed to the eating disorder, for example feeling light-headed or losing hair. The social worker must also be

Table 22–3   Primary Medical and Psychological Complications of
Anorexia Nervosa and Bulimia Nervosa

Dermatologic
>   Dry skin
>   Thinning hair
>   Lanugo hair—Baby-fine hair covering the body
>   Cyanosis—skin looks bluish because of poor circulation
>   Carotene pigmentation

Cardiovascular
>   Bradycardia—slow heartbeat
>   Hypotension—low blood pressure
>   Peripheral edema—retaining fluid in extremities
>   Arrhythmias—irregular heart beats

Gastrointestinal
>   Delayed gastric emptying—stomach slow to digest food
>   Bloating
>   Early satiety—fills full quickly
>   Constipation

Endocrine
>   Amenorrhea—cessation of menstrual periods
>   Hypothermia—feels cold all the time

Musculoskeletal
>   Weakness
>   Osteoporosis

Cognitive and Behavioral
>   Depression
>   Poor concentration
>   Preoccupied with food
>   Poor sleep
>   Decreased libido

alert for comorbid conditions such as depression, anxiety, or substance abuse. These problems may only reveal themselves once the eating begins to improve or may have been issues the client has dealt with for some time and can be readily identified when taking a medical history. Finally, the social worker needs to recognize a medical emergency and insist that the client go to the emergency room or their family physician for care. For the social worker in private practice this may involve calling an ambulance if the client is in a medical crisis.

Table 22–4   Eating Disorder Components of a Family Assessment

---

1. The family's knowledge of eating disorders in general.
2. The family's knowledge of the specifics of their family member's eating disorder.
3. The family's beliefs about the causes of the eating disorder.
4. The family's efforts to aid in the recovery.
5. The family's eating patterns and exercise habits.
6. The family's attitudes about weight and shape.
7. How the family thinks the eating disorder has affected the individual family members and the family as a whole.

Family History

Family dynamics and family issues are thought to contribute to the development and perpetuation of anorexia and bulimia. The individual should be asked about family functioning and conflicts and how those issues may relate to the eating disorder or not. Family assessments are always valuable because they offer the social worker a view into the family, allowing for a greater understanding of the client's world. Although families and patients report family problems, it is often not clear whether the problems identified predate the eating disorder or are the family's response to the disruptions and fears associated with the illness. Family and marital assessments and therapy are highly recommended for all adolescents and married patients (Woodside, et al., 1993; Woodside & Shekter-Wolfson, 1990; Russell, et al., 1992). Additionally, a family assessment is recommended for clients who are living at home (Shekter-Wolfson & Woodside, 1990). The traditional social work family/marital assessment needs to be augmented by specific questions related to eating and body image. Table 22–4, "Eating Disorder Components of a Family Assessment," provides a summary of additional areas of enquiry that relate specifically to eating related issues. These questions can be asked of the person in individual treatment to gain their perspective on family functioning and can be used as preliminary eating questions in a family assessment. In the process of focusing on the family's behaviors, thoughts and feelings, family process and boundaries are revealed while the family answers the questions.

EATING DISORDER TREATMENT

Recovery from anorexia and bulimia entails a two-track system within a stepped approach to treatment. Track One addresses the eating symptoms and Track Two addresses more dynamic issues in an effort to prevent relapse. Working through the psychological, personal, and interpersonal issues alone will not resolve the symptoms of the eating disorder. The stepped-care approach involves reviewing motivation to change and increasing and decreasing the intensity of treatment as appropriate. It is not uncommon for clients to have many slips in their eating and occasionally to relapse completely, necessitating a return to Track One issues.

(Helping a client understand and increase her motivation to change really begins during the initial assessment and continues through to termination.)Whenever the client is resistant to taking the next step or stumbles on an obstacle to change, reviewing motivation will be necessary. Clients can easily identify wanting to be well and stopping their ego-dystonic symptoms, such as purging. They will need to be well motivated to tolerate the physical discomfort that accompanies normalizing eating and then to tolerate their strong affective reactions to those issues that have been masked by the eating disorder. They can readily identify issues related to physical discomfort and the fear of weight gain. More difficult to identify and work through is the function of the eating disorder, as that entails tolerating affects that to date have been intolerable. Given this dilemma, it is easy to appreciate why slips and relapses are common and predictable as the client returns to old coping mechanisms to provide some relief from her physical and psychological distress.

Track One: Normalizing Eating

The obvious first step in normalizing eating is to seek a consultation with a Registered Dietitian who understands the nondieting approach to recovery. The social worker's task is to help the client begin the process of eating more normally, following her meal plan and stopping purging behaviors.

Psychoeducation

Working from the philosophy of providing the least intrusive treatment and moving to more intensive interventions as necessary, psychoeducation about eating disorders has proven to be an effective step for some clients, especially those with bulimia. Psychoeducation can be provided individually or in a group format. Psychoeducation involves providing the client with accurate information about eating disorders. This includes information about the cause of eating disorders, how one gets a diagnosis, the role of dieting, set point theory, medical complications, defining normal eating, teaching cognitive behavioral strategies for change, and relapse prevention (Olmsted, et al., 1995). Psychoeducation appears to help clients develop a better understanding of what an eating disorder is and what the process of recovery entails. Psychoeducation also allows the individual an opportunity to review her motivation for change; obstacles may become more apparent to the client as she gains more knowledge. Most clients make improvements in some aspect of their eating-disordered symptoms. Research evaluating a six-week once-a-week outpatient psychoeducation group found that 25% of those with bulimia had completely normalized their eating and remained symptom free at six months (Olmsted, et al., 1991).

Cognitive Behavioral Therapy
Cognitive Behavioral Therapy (CBT) appears to be the most effective intervention to help normalize eating. Much studied (Fairburn, Agran, et al., 1992; Fairburn, et al., 1991; Fairburn, et al., 1993), CBT helps clients develop an awareness of their cognitions about eating, food, and body image that affect their eating. A CBT model may use food journals or diaries to help the client initially identify behavioral patterns and link these patterns to disordered eating. The client is encouraged to develop self-monitoring skills in an effort to challenge disordered beliefs and to develop alternative ways of understanding. The client is taught cognitive and behavioral strategies to use to normalize eating. For example clients could be taught to separate thoughts and feelings from behavior and taught new strategies for self soothing to cope with the intensified feelings and racing thoughts that often accompany improved eating. A comparison of CBT, medication, and Interpersonal Therapy (IPT) indicated that CBT and IPT were equally effective in reducing eating disordered symptoms. However the IPT required one full year of treatment compared to 20 weeks for CBT (Fairburn, et al., 1991). CBT can be used in an individual or group format. A symptom strategies group is helpful because clients can both support and challenge each other in a way that the group leader cannot, because of their personal familiarity with the issues. A social worker working with eating-disordered clients would be well advised to develop a thorough knowledge of the CBT model of practice.

Medication
The use of medication in treating anorexia has been disappointing. No medication has been found to be helpful in the restoration of weight or in the reduction of the obsessions associated with the recovery process (Walsh, 1995; Garfinkel, et al., 1997).

The use of antidepressant medication has been helpful in reducing bingeing behaviors in a minority of patients. Patients often relapse when they stop the medication. The pretreatment presence of depression is not necessary to consider the use of antidepressants, as those without depression have done equally well on such medication. Serotonin reuptake inhibitors, at doses higher that those used for depression, for example fluoxetine (Prozac) at 60 mg OD, are preferred because they have fewer side effects that the tricyclic antidepressants or monoamine oxidase inhibitors. Studies comparing the use of antidepressants and CBT found that CBT alone provided greater benefits than medication alone. It is generally understood that the use of therapy which focuses on improving eating and reducing symptoms is the treatment of choice for bulimia. Medication may be added as an adjunct therapy, if the client is having problems controlling her bulimic symptoms (Goldbloom, et al., 1994; Walsh, 1995; Garfinkel & Walsh, 1997). The use of medication to treat truly comorbid conditions such as depression and obsessive-compulsive disorder is recognized.

The use of anxiolytics to help reduce the anxiety associated with eating should be time limited, especially for bulimic clients who have shown a tendency to substance abuse. Prokinetic agents such as domperidone (maleate) are useful in providing some relief for the problems of early satiety and bloating that accompany delayed gastric emptying. Prokinetic agents are thought to aid compliance with eating because they help reduce the physical discomfort that results when eating is normalized. (For a review of psychotropic medications see Garfinkel, et al., 1997; Walsh, 1995.)

Many clients will also experience constipation as they normalize their eating and/or stop taking laxatives. The use of laxatives is obviously contraindicated. A stepped approach, beginning with bulking agents and moving to a stool softener if necessary, is a sound one. If a client does not get relief the use of suppositories will be necessary; in rare situations an enema could be used to prevent a client from becoming impacted.

For clients who are purging it will be necessary for their physician to be monitoring their electrolytes. If the electrolytes are low the client may be asked to take a potassium supplement.

The client who takes a more chronic path will likely experience a number of physical problems. The physician should treat these issues as indicated while also remembering that any improvement in eating will contribute to an improvement in the client's overall health status.

Day Hospital and Inpatient Treatments

Some clients will need more intensive treatment requiring either an outpatient or an inpatient admission. These programs are group treatments.

The type of admission is often dependent on service availability. If both programs are available, an inpatient admission is typically used for those with anorexia nervosa who are at a seriously low weight, are medically compromised, and require an extended time to gain weight. Those with bulimia or anorexia who are not medically compromised are more typically admitted to an outpatient program. They would only be admitted to an inpatient unit if that were all that was available or if they had life-threatening complications associated with purging. Frequent bingeing alone is not sufficient criteria for admission to an inpatient program. Both outpatient and inpatient programs focus primarily on normalizing eating with an intensive group therapy format (Anderson, et al., 1997; Piran & Kaplan, 1990). Patients eat supervised meals in the program with no option to leave food on the plate and bathrooms are locked. A very controlling therapeutic environment creates a safe place where symptomatic behavior is not an option. Group therapies would include meal planning and menu marking, meal outings, symptom strategies, recreation and leisure planning, weighing, body image, and interpersonal psychotherapy groups. The intensive programs appear to be effective for 85% of bulimic clients recovered at discharge; more that 50% remained recovered at two-year follow up (Olmsted, et al., 1994). Anorexic clients do not seem to do as well; however, they do make some improvements (Kaplan, et al., 1995). Both groups of patients may need repeated admissions to recover.

Track Two: Relapse Prevention

Individual Therapy

There are no clear guidelines about the use of individual therapy once a client has normalized her eating. There is no research on specific treatments except for that outlined earlier. What does seem common to the variety of models is the shift of focus to resolving the traumatic or upsetting life events and the personality and developmental issues unique to each client. The client is required to cope with the emotional turmoil associated with the resolution of difficulties without returning to symptomatic behavior, separating feelings from behaviors. The social worker should still be assessing eating, purging, and weight as a way to monitor the client's ability to tolerate the affective work. The individual therapist will find that the focus of sessions will shift from dynamic issues to eating issues and back again, based on how the client is coping with the issues she is dealing with, both in therapy and in her daily life. The client's new coping skills will be tested by the material that has been largely masked by the eating disorder. Slips are not uncommon; they indicate that it is time to slow down the dynamic work and restart some supportive or CBT work to focus on reducing the symptoms. Monitoring symptoms is important in that it allows the social worker to pace the work. When a client does relapse, insight-oriented work should stop and a more supportive approach with the goal of normalizing eating is called for. This might include considering (re)admission to an intensive treatment.

Group Therapy

Some intensive programs have more formalized relapse prevention programs that provide a step down from the intensive ones. At the Toronto Hospital, our program offers a four-days-a-week group program for patients being discharged from the inpatient and outpatient programs. The group members meet for one and a half hours four days a week. They participate in two groups, which support and reinforce the strategies they have learned and implemented in the intensive programs. They also participate in two insight-oriented groups, body image and group's choice, where they choose their own agendas to work on. These groups are more evocative in nature. Following these groups, clients who are completely symptom free are referred to a psychotherapy group, while those who continue to experience symptoms are referred to a contemplation group to explore their obstacles to change.

For clients who do not have the luxury of a formalized relapse prevention program, referral to non-eating-disordered groups—such as an interpersonal psychotherapy group, a body image group, or a sexual abuse group—can complement individual therapy. The social worker and the group therapist should meet to discuss their philosophies of dieting, weight, shape, and exercise in an effort to avoid the client having to deal with conflicting ideas in their therapy.

Family and Marital Therapy

Family functioning and therapy has been widely written about. Unfortunately much of the theoretical literature has not been validated and the empirical research has been dependent on client self report during the illness. Perhaps best known is the work of Minuchin, Rosman, and Baker (1978). The five features of the psychosomatic family—enmeshment, overprotectiveness, rigidity, conflict avoidance, and parental marital distress — have become the hallmarks of the eating disordered family. Additional work by Selvini-Palazzoli (1974) described similar patterns of family functioning and explored the meaning of the anorexic symptom. Work by Root and colleagues (1986) added the importance of considering the social context to the understanding of family functioning while the work of White (1987) added the dimension of multigenerational transmission of issues. Recently, the Maudsley group have developed a new multifactorial model which synthesizes the earlier works and proposes interventions in multiple systems. This group has also undertaken clinical research to evaluate the usefulness of family therapy (Dare & Eisler, 1997).

Evaluation of the psychosomatic model concluded that while the variables Minuchin (1978) identified were present there were other variables as well, indicating that eating-disordered families are a heterogeneous group (Kog & Vandereycken, 1985). In a study evaluating patient and family self-report of family functioning before and after intensive treatment, Woodside and colleagues (1996) found that at pretreatment parents identified their families as only somewhat problematic while patients reported their families as highly dysfunctional. At posttreatment, parental scales were within the normal range and the patients who had normalized their eating reported scores similar to their parents. The family ratings held at two-year follow-up as long as the patient remained symptom free. An earlier study of the same cohort of patients indicated that improvements in family ratings by the patients appeared to be associated with improvement in their mood (Heinmaa, et al., 1992). One set of studies has looked at the usefulness of family therapy in maintaining recovery following intensive treatment. Family therapy was a more effective treatment for those under 18 years who had their illness for less that two years, whereas those who were older and had their illness longer did better with individual treatment (Russell, et al., 1992).

Like individual treatment, it is useful to consider a stepped approach to family and marital therapy beginning with education, moving to a brief-therapy model, and with some clients contracting for longer-term work. All families and couples can use education and most benefit from brief work while a few will need longer-term, more intensive work.

Education can be presented in a group format or done with individual families. Many families seem to make significant changes in their coping strategies after gaining knowledge about set point theory, normalized eating, basic strategies to help, boundaries, medical complications, chronicity, and sociocultural pressures on women.

The brief model of family and marital therapy focuses on how the eating disorder is affecting the family in their day-to-day life and what strategies they can use to help. The goal is to put the person with the eating disorder in control of her recovery, and to negotiate with the family members the kind of support that is helpful. This stage is designed to address issues of over- and underinvolvement at a behavioral level; it reestablishes appropriate boundaries. Most families do well with brief therapy, renegotiating overtly how to manage the symptoms without addressing causality in depth. They appear to develop a new way of functioning that brings satisfaction.

Longer-term family or marital therapy follows the brief therapy, which will have helped the family manage the symptoms but does not result in a general level of improved functioning. The patient and family will recognize that they need to explore the function of the eating disorder within the family context. These families are prepared to explore relationship issues and unfinished business such as parental expectations, intergenerational belief conflicts and relationship patterns, boundary violations, family and personal losses, and expression of affect. These families will have prepared themselves to deal with affectively laden material during the education and brief stages of treatment (Woodside, et al., 1993; Woodside & Shekter-Wolfson, 1990).

CONCLUSION

Social work is well positioned as a profession to work with the adolescents and adults who have anorexia and bulimia. The ecological approach to practice and the social work skill base prepare the social work practitioner to complete assessments; to provide individual, group and family therapy; and to intervene in multiple systems. Equally important is the ability to collaborate in developing and working with a multidisciplinary team. Social work is generally seen as contributing more in the area of family functioning and therapy and in developing community linkages, although today's social workers are conducting individual and group therapy in private practice and in eating disorder treatment programs. It is incumbent on clinicians working in this area to expand their knowledge base about eating disorders as few universities offer more than a brief introduction to the area. There is considerable empirical and theoretical literature which should be read critically. Many treatment facilities that specialize in eating disorders welcome visitors who can observe the program being offered. These facilities often provide consultation to private practitioners and agencies that do not specialize in eating disorders. It is also important that practitioners review their own beliefs about weight prejudice, the importance of appearance, and the meaning of success so as to avoid replicating cultural pressures in the counseling process and to help maintain clear boundaries between possible personal issues and professional practice.

In spite of considerable effort, the treatment of anorexia and bulimia is limited in its success. These disorders remain highly resistant to treatment. Given how tenacious anorexia and bulimia are, more attention needs to be directed to prevention. Prevention needs to be focused at children when they are formulating their beliefs about weight, shape, and control and at adolescents who are acting on those earlier formulated beliefs. Again, social work is well placed to develop these programs. Programs can focus directly on issues seen as contributing to eating disorders or indirectly by working with young women to enhance their sense of identity, self-esteem, and competence.

There is a need to continue development of treatment models and evaluation of practice. Practice-based research should help clarify treatment options and identify which treatments are effective in given circumstances.

Finally, attention needs to be given to those clients who are unable to recover from anorexia and bulimia. Little is known about those who experience these disorders chronically. Quality-of-life issues and potential recovery after many years have not been explored in research.

Working with eating disordered clients can be extraordinarily frustrating, provoking feelings of anger and a sense of impotence. It can also be rewarding and humbling to have the privilege of working with clients as they face a multitude of demons and create a healthy and happy life for themselves.

REFERENCES

American Psychiatric Association. (1994). *Diagnostic and statistical manual of mental disorders, fourth edition.* Washington, DC: Author.

Anderson, A. (1995). Eating disorders in males. In K. Brownell & C. Fairburn (Eds.), *Eating disorders and obesity* (pp. 177–182). New York: Guilford Press.

Anderson, A., Bowers, W., & Evans, K. (1997). Inpatient treatment for anorexia nervosa. In D. Garner & P. Garfinkel (Eds.), *Handbook of treatment for eating disorders* (2nd Ed.) (pp. 327–353). New York: Guilford Press.

Ciliska, D. (1991). *Beyond dieting.* New York: Brunner/Mazel.

Cooper, Z. (1995). The development and maintenance of eating disorders. In K. Brownell & C. Fairburn (Eds.), *Eating disorders and obesity* (pp. 199–208). New York: Guilford Press.

Dare, C., & Eisler, I. (1997). Family therapy for Anorexia nervosa. In D. Garner & P. Garfinkel (Eds.), *Handbook of treatment for eating disorders* (pp. 307–324). New York: Guilford Press.

Dulloo, A., Jacquet, J., & Girandier, L. (1992). Post starvation hyperphagia body fat overshooting in humans: A food for feedback signals from lean and fat tissues. *American Journal of Clinical Nutrition, 65,* 717–723.

Fairburn, C., Agran, W., & Wilson, O. (1992). The research of the treatment of bulimia nervosa: Practical and theoretical implications. In G. Anderson & S. Kennedy (Eds.), *The biology of food and famine: Relevance to eating disorders* (pp. 318–340). Orlando, FL: Academic Press.

Fairburn, C., Jones, R., Peveler R., Carr, S., Solomon, R., O'Conner, M., Burton, J., & Hope, R. (1991). Three psychological treatments for bulimia nervosa: A comparison trial. *Archives of General Psychiatry, 48,* 463–469.

Fairburn, C., Jones, R., Peveler, R., Hope, R., & O'Conner, M. (1993). Psychotherapy and bulimia nervosa: The longer-term effects of interpersonal psychotherapy, behavioural therapy and cognitive behavioral therapy. *Archives of General Psychiatry, 50,* 419–428.

Garfinkel, P., & Garner, D. (1982). *Anorexia nervosa: A multidimensional perspective.* New York: Brunner-Mazel.

Garfinkel, P., Lin, B., Goering, P., Spegg, C., Goldbloom, D., Kennedy, S., Kaplan, A., & Woodside, D. (1995). Bulimia nervosa in a Canadian community sample: Prevalence, co-morbidity, early experiences and psychosocial functioning. *American Journal of Psychiatry, 152,* 1052–1058.

Garfinkel, P., & Walsh, P. (1997). Drug therapies. In D. Garner & P. Garfinkel (Eds.), *Handbook of treatment for eating disorders* (2nd Ed.) (pp. 372–380). New York: Guilford Press.

Garner, D., & Garfinkel, P. (1980). Social cultural factors in the development of anorexia nervosa. *Psychological Medicine, X,* 647–656.

Goldbloom, D., Olmsted, M., Davis, R., & Shaw, B. (1994). *A randomized trial of fluoxitine and individual cognitive behavioral therapy for women with bulimia nervosa: Short-term outcome.* Paper presented at the Sixth International Conference on Eating Disorders. New York.

Health and Welfare Canada. (1992). *Canada's Food Guide to Healthy Living.*

Heinman, M., Davis, R., & Woodside, D. (1992). Depression and the perception of family functioning in the eating disorder. Paper presented at the World Congress of Cognitive Therapy, Toronto.

Hsu, L. (1995). Outcome of bulimia nervosa. In K. Brownell & C. Fairburn (Eds.), *Eating disorders and obesity* (pp. 238–244). New York: Guilford Press.

Kaplan, A., & Garfinkel, P. (1993). *Medical issues and the eating disorders: The interface.* New York: Brunner/Mazel.

Kaplan, A., & Olmsted, M. (1995). Day Hospital treatment of anorexia nervosa. University of Toronto, Department of Psychiatry, Research Day. June 15.

Katzman, M. (1998a). Modern day waif protesters: Self starvation in context. Workshop given in Toronto, March.

Katzman, M. (1998b). Culture, ethnicity and eating disorders. Plenary Session, Eighth New York International Conference on Eating Disorders, April.

Keesey, R. (1995). A set-point model of body weight regulation. In K. Brownell, & C. Fairburn (Eds.), *Eating disorders and obesity* (pp. 46–50). New York: Brunner Mazel.

Keys, A., Brozek, J., Henschel, A., Mickelson, O., & Taylor, H. (1950). *The biology of human starvation.* Minneapolis: University of Minnesota Press.

Kog, E., & Vandereycken, W. (1995). Family characteristics of anorexia nervosa and bulimia: A review of the literature. *Clinical Psychology Review, 5,* 159–180.

Lackstrom, J.; Woodside, D. (1998). Families, therapists and family therapy in eating disorders. In W. Vandereycken, P. J. V. Beumont, & P. J. V. Beumont (Eds.), *Treating eating disorders: Ethical, legal and personal issues.* New York: New York University Press.

Lee, S. (1998). Culture, ethnicity and eating disorders. Plenary session, Eighth New York International Conference on Eating Disorders, April.

Mackay, L. (1984). Eating disorders: Anorexia and obesity. In F. Turner (Ed.), *Adult psychopathology: A social work perspective.* New York: Free Press.

Minuchin, S., Rosman, B., & Baker, L. (1978). *Psychosomatic families: Anorexia nervosa in context.* Cambridge: Harvard University Press.

Olmsted, M., Davis, R., Rockert, W., Eagle, M., & Garner, D. (1991). Efficacy of brief group psychoeducational intervention for bulimia nervosa. *Behavioral Research and Therapy, 29,* 71–83.

Olmsted, M., Kaplan, A., & Rockert, W. (1994). Rate and prediction of relapse in bulimia nervosa. *American Journal of Psychiatry, 151,* 738–743.

Olmsted, M., & Kaplan, A. (1995). Psychoeducation in the treatment of eating disorders. In K. Brownell & C. Fairburn (Eds.), *Eating disorders and obesity* (pp. 299–305). New York: Guilford Press.

Piran, N., & Kaplan, A. (Eds.). (1990). *Day hospital treatment for eating disorders.* New York: Brunner/Mazel.

Polivy, J., & Herman, P. (1985). Dieting and bingeing: A causal analysis. *American Psychologist, 40,* 193–201.

Root, M., Fallon, P., & Fredrick, W. (1986). *Bulimia: A systems approach to treatment.* New York: Norton.

Root, M. (1990). Disordered eating in women of color. *Sex Roles, 22,* 525–536.

Russell, G., Dare, C., Eisler, I., & le Grange, D. (1992). Controlled trials of family treatments in anorexia nervosa. In K. Halmi (Ed.), *Psychobiology and treatment of anorexia nervosa and bulimia nervosa.* Washington, DC: American Psychiatric Press.

Selvini-Palazzoli, M. (1974). *Self starvation: From intrapsychic to the transpersonal approach to anorexia nervosa.* London: Chaucer Publishing.

Shekter-Wolfson, L., & Woodside, D. (1990). Family therapy. In N. Piran & A. Kaplan (Eds.), *A day hospital group treatment for anorexia nervosa and bulimia nervosa* (pp. 76–109). New York: Brunner/Mazel.

Steinhausen, H. (1995). The course and outcome of anorexia nervosa. In K. Brownell & C. Fairburn (Eds.), *Eating disorders and obesity* (pp. 334–337). New York: Guilford Press.

Silber, T. (1986). Anorexia nervosa in Blacks and Hispanics. *International Journal of Eating Disorders. 5,* 121–128.

Thompson. B. (1994). Food, bodies, and growing up female: Childhood lessons about culture, race and class. In P. Fallon, M. Katzman, S. Wooley (Eds.), *Feminist perspectives in eating disorders* (pp. 355–378). New York: Guilford Press.

Walsh, B. (1995). Pharmacotherapy of eating disorders. In K. Brownell & C. Fairburn (Eds.), *Eating disorders and obesity* (pp. 313–317). New York: Guilford Press.

White, M. (1987). Anorexia nervosa: A transgenerational perspective. In J. Harkaway (Vol. Ed.), Vol. 20 of *The Family Therapy Collections* (pp. 117–129). J. Hansen (Series Ed.).

Woodside, D., Lackstrom, J., Shekter-Wolfson, L., & Heinmaa, M. (1996). Long-term follow-up of patient-reported family functioning in eating disorders after intensive day hospital treatment. *Journal of Psychosomatic Research, 41,* 269–277.

Woodside, D., & Shekter-Wolfson, L. (Eds.). (1990). *Family approaches in treatment of eating disorders.* Washington, DC: American Psychiatric Press.

Woodside, D., Shekter-Wolfson, L., Brandes, J., & Lackstrom, J. (1993). *Eating disorders and marriage: The couple in focus.* New York: Brunner/Mazel.

23

PSYCHOSEXUAL DISORDERS

Harvey L. Gochros

An understanding of sexual attitudes, beliefs, and biases is fundamental to the understanding of sexual behaviors variously called adult sexual dysfunctions, sexual disorders, or sexual pathology. This article attempts to explore some of the more significant beliefs that influence the helping professions' understanding of and social work approaches to these conditions.

The word *sexuality* encompasses a wide spectrum of thoughts, feelings, and behaviors—many of which provide joy and fulfillment, but others that can lead to pain and anguish. They subsume such areas and concepts as sensuality, intimacy, reproduction, sexual identity, and sexual preference/orientation.

There are three particular areas of sexual expression, however, that are sometimes confused with each other. Each of these is of especial concern to social workers and will be discussed in this chapter. The first area, sex offenses, includes those sexual behaviors that can *clearly* harm others. This involves sexual activity with children and nonconsenting adults. The second area involves people who engage in sexual behaviors that significant segments of a particular society, at any particular time, deem unacceptable and that thus are labeled sinful, illegal, abnormal, or pathological. The third area involves sexual patterns that individuals experience as subjectively unpleasant or that fail to produce the desired pleasurable effects.

SEX OFFENSES

Diverse behaviors have been subsumed under the category of sexual offenses. Many, it has been argued, are "victimless" offenses ranging from prostitution (both the prostitute and the "john" are viewed as offenders) and adult consensual same-sex contacts to downloading erotic images from the Internet. Such "offenses" are culturally defined and vary along with changing community attitudes toward such activities; as an example, the emergence of sexual harassment as an area of concern for Americans. Sanctions for such victimless behaviors also change over time and from community to community, as do psychotherapeutic approaches to these behaviors (Strean, 1983).

All too often, people engage in sexual contact with unwilling adult partners or with minors, willing or not. These individuals are categorized as sex offenders and are subject to the laws of their communities and states. The usual disposition of such offenses is incarceration with the intent to punish and perhaps rehabilitate. In most correctional facilities, however, relatively little effort is made to rehabilitate this population, and those efforts that are made frequently have little success. Rarely are efforts made to understand and design treatment plans that deal with the motivations for these acts.

Many of these offenders have little or no impulse control, have antisocial personalities, or are substance abusers. Because recidivism for these offenses is high, efforts have been made to identify those offenders who are most likely to repeat their offenses when opportunities arise, and who thus require continued institutionalization, as opposed to those who have a reasonable chance for rehabilitation. A comprehensive review of empirical research efforts that have attempted to identify the factors influencing the risk of sex offenders repeating their offenses has been reported by McGrath (1991).

In recent years, social workers have been active in testing out clinical efforts that seem to be effective in reducing the threat of sex offenders (Salter, 1988; Zastrow, 1995). Among these procedures are encouraging the offenders to be more aware of the harm done by their acts; implementing behaviors that lead to offenders transferring their sexual interest to adult consenting partners; offering anger management—anger is a major factor in rape; cognitive restructuring designed to modify dysfunctional sexual attitudes, values, and rationalizations; sexual counseling to reduce stress regarding sexual dysfunctions in nonoffending sexual acts; and recognizing and avoiding sequential patterns that frequently lead to offenses. Much more effort is needed, however, to understand and treat this population.

Considerable attention has been directed to identifying and treating the victims of sexual offenders, particularly victims of sexual assault and child abuse (Forman, 1980; Koss, 1987). The growing attention to these offenses reflects the rising incidence of these adjudicated offenses—this may be a result of either an actual increase of these offenses, more frequent reporting of these incidents, or a growing public repugnance toward such acts.

Recent trends in the prevention of such offenses and the treatment of their victims includes the following (Byington, 1995):

- Greater public awareness of sexual offenses
- More legal actions against offenders
- Increased focus on "date rapes," particularly on college campuses
- Viewing nonconsensual forced sex in marriage as rape, with consequent prosecution
- Consideration of pornography's possible contribution to sexual offenses
- With the advent of AIDS, mandated testing of assailants
- Awareness of the connection between prior incidents of sexual assault or incest and drug addiction
- Recognition that more males have been molested as children or adults than was previously thought

All the above trends have clear implications for both preventive and therapeutic social work on behalf of the victims of sexual offenses.

SOCIALLY UNACCEPTABLE SEXUAL BEHAVIORS

Many clients of social workers have sex-related problems that do not involve victims, but nevertheless to some degree feel a lack of society's sexual approbation. Attitudes about what are good or bad, healthy or unhealthy, or normal or abnormal sexual behaviors vary over time and across diverse cultures. Economic, political, and religious factors play a large part in the evolution of these attitudes.

To a large extent a reproductive bias has had a major influence in these evaluations. This bias or belief suggests that the only sexual behaviors that are normal, desirable, healthy—and for that matter legal, and free from sin—are those sexual behaviors that approximate what it takes to produce socially approved pregnancies. Thus in the past, at least, appropriate sex was reserved for healthy, young (but not too young) heterosexuals in the context of loving, committed heterosexual marriages. Those who could not approximate these conditions—the old, the too young, the disabled, homosexuals, ambisexuals, and those who would not or could not initiate monogamous sexual relationships—were branded as sinners, criminals, or sick.

Even the specific sexual behaviors that were approved or at least condoned had to meet the demands of this bias. Thus heterosexual intercourse, with the man on top (gravity helps conception) in a monogamous
relationship was permitted, whereas nonreproductive acts such as masturbation and both oral and anal intercourse were condemned.

The reproductive bias is a relic of a time in which the strength of any
family, nation, or religion was measured by the number of well-cared for
children in that family, nation, or religion. It remains as a vestige of an
earlier time—a product of cultural lag. Indeed, the reproductive bias has
diminished in recent years largely because of changing economic and technological factors. Large numbers of children are no longer considered economically desirable in most families (at least in developed countries), and
in most developed nations. As a result, witness the changes in the tabooed
sexual areas referred to previously. Because of culture lag, however, the
reproductive bias still can be detected in many subtle and not so subtle attitudes and behaviors:

- Adult masturbation is still an uncomfortable subject, as is all recreational sex.
- The term *genitals* is used, despite the fact the organs so identified are
  only rarely used for "generating" new life, as distinct from other
  more strictly pleasurable activities.
- Sex education in schools generally begins and often ends with reproduction education.
- Even one of the most feared sexual dysfunctions—premature ejacu-
  lation—has its roots in this bias; the bias insists that there is only one
  right place and one right time for a man to ejaculate—the time and
  place most likely to produce fertilization.

As a result of the reproductive bias many sexual behaviors now
accepted as "normal" have been in varying degrees labeled "pathological" historically by most members of the helping professions. There is still
a segment of the social work community that subscribes to these iatrogenic
sexual beliefs, which are based largely on a medical-disease model that
reflects a reproductive bias (Strean, 1983). Over recent decades, the several
editions of the *Diagnostic and Statistical Manual of Mental Disorders*
(American Psychiatric Association, 1980) has mirrored some of the helping professions' changes in what is perceived as pathological, and how the
reproductive bias has been loosening its hold. The classic example is the
removal of homosexuality as a disease category (unless it is ego dystonic)

by a vote of the American Psychiatric Association in 1973. One only has to look at professional beliefs about masturbation, oral sex, homosexuality, and nonmarital cohabitation to see how beliefs about sexual disorders change over time.

It is clear that as social workers we must constantly view sexual behaviors in their social context. Even the definitions of *pathological sexuality, sexual dysfunctions, deviation, promiscuity,* or *addiction* are reflections of prevailing cultural attitudes. Interventions by helping professionals to curtail those behaviors that do not involve victims must be carefully examined as potentially oppressive vehicles of social control, resulting in large part from a cultural reproductive bias.

Some of the sexual behaviors labeled as pathological—especially those that harm and violate the rights of others, whether the acts are consensual or not—are by definition unacceptable and require professional intervention. Rape, incest, and sexual molestation of children are obvious examples. Other sexual prohibitions, however, reflect society's fluctuating attitudes about what is socially acceptable to the significant power group in that culture. Thus adult masturbation, oral and anal sex, and homosexuality would seem to have received diminished public condemnation and gained greater public and individual acceptance, whereas sexual harassment has gained greater public and professional helper concern, censure, and condemnation.

Two examples of these culturally defined "pathological" behaviors, overt or implicit, are the related reified concepts of promiscuity and sexual addiction, discussed below.

Promiscuity

Promiscuity is a basically sexist and heterosexist label that is widely used to describe socially unacceptable behavior; it is primarily diagnosed in heterosexual women and homosexual men. Although the third edition of the *DSM* (1980) attempted a ludicrous statistical definition of promiscuity— "ten or more sexual partners within a year" (p. 321)—*promiscuity* remains a vague concept. It is generally construed to connote a sexual pattern in which the individual has sexual encounters with too many people, or for the wrong reasons. Despite the fact that the number of sexual partners *alone* does not determine the risk of infection (other variables enter the equation of risk, see Gochros, 1988), an accusation of promiscuity is often coupled with the threat of AIDS.

The condemnation of "promiscuity" is to a large extent a product of a general societal discomfort if not censure of recreational sex—that is, sex involving partners without intense romantic involvement or commitment—and is a product of the reproductive bias. The quality and functionality of sexual activities cannot be measured by frequencies, any more than the form of a sexual relationship determines its outcome for the participants. Monogamy is no more a guarantee of interpersonal satisfaction than is having multiple partners.

Sexual Addiction

One of the most frequently asked questions about sexuality by clients—and their social workers as well—is, "What is normal?" Usually this question seeks a quantifiable answer: how many partners, how frequently; what is too seldom? And what is too often? Recently a label has become popular to identify the disease of too much sex. It is called *sexual addiction* or *compulsive sexuality*. This concept has become a major category in the conceptualizations of sexual pathology.

Sexual addiction implies a pattern of sexual activities that are excessive, preoccupying, and/or hazardous to an individual and those affected by him or her. This label has led to a new area for therapy and 12-step self-help groups along with services for such other recently identified similar pathologies as addictions to relationships, love, and romance (Francoeur, 1996). All such diagnoses lead to the difficult question: where does "good sex" end and addiction begin?

Carnes (1991), a leading proponent of the sexual-addiction diagnosis, suggests that it is not possible to quantify a definition of sexual addiction; rather the clinician should look for a pattern of sexual addictive behaviors. He provides 10 behavioral patterns that identify a sexual addict:

1. A pattern of out-of-control behavior
2. Severe consequences due to sexual behavior
3. Inability to stop despite adverse consequences
4. Persistent pursuit of self-destructive or high-risk behavior
5. Ongoing desire or effort to limit sexual behavior
6. Sexual obsession and fantasy as a primary coping strategy
7. Increasing amounts of sexual experience because the current level of activity is no longer sufficient
8. Severe mood changes around sexual activity
9. Inordinate amounts of time spent in obtaining sex, being sexual, or recovering from sexual experience

10. Neglect of important social, occupational, or recreational activities because of sexual behavior

True, these behavioral patterns can be destructive to the individual displaying them as well as to those affected by the individual. But does it help to label that person and give him/her an illness that only compounds their problems? Our society is increasingly addicted to addiction concepts, and almost everyone now seems "addicted" to something: chocolate, TV, or a certain rock group. It has frequently been pointed out that we are becoming a society of victims; almost everyone supposedly has a psychological "disease" or "addiction" requiring therapy, a support group, or a 12-step program. It is not surprising, given our sexually confused society, that sexuality would fall into our addictive rubric (Henkin, 1991).

The invention and popularization of the label "sexual addict" could well become a vehicle for conservative antisexual protagonists to use to instill sexual guilt, to exercise societal control of sexuality through the helping professions. As social workers, we must continue to support the rights of adults to express and enjoy their sexuality with consenting adults in private, so long as they assume the responsibilities that go along with that right.

SEXUAL DISTRESS

How a person feels about his or her sexual feelings, thoughts, and behaviors is shaped by pervasive cultural expectations and values. Sexual distress occurs when a person's sexual behavior is thought by that person to be inadequate or inappropriate in the context of his or her expectations and/or the standards or those in his or her reference group. Social and emotional factors, therefore, contribute to many of the common subjective sexual concerns—and their resultant physical manifestations—encountered by the clients of social workers.

To a large extent these expectations reflect the influence of the reproductive bias, which dictates that sexual expression should approximate behaviors, and involve people, that could lead to a socially approved pregnancy. This can put a fair degree of pressure on the sexual elite—those young, heterosexual, healthy, attractive, and bonded couples whose sexuality is not only condoned (unlike the widely held negative attitudes expressed about the sexuality of old, homosexually oriented, disabled, nonbonded, or institutionalized populations)—but expected.

In approaching the concerns of both those who don't conform to the reproductive bias and those who do, the social worker must take account of the cultural milieu in which the clients play out their sexual lives. Indeed even the choice of specific sexual activities, and how they are perceived by those engaging in them, is related to relics of the reproductive bias. Thus vaginal penetration by a firm penis and achieving mutual orgasms at the right time and place (for conception to occur) in a bonded relationship are considered necessary or at least desirable, whereas non-reproductive activities with a nonbonded but willing partner are at least suspect.

The term *sexual distress* is used here to label sexual concerns, in deliberate contrast to terms such as *sexual disorder* or *sexual dysfunction,* for several reasons (Gochros, 1995). The terms sexual *dysfunction* and *sexual disorder* have a physical, biological emphasis. They objectify a subjective experience. Different people have different expectations and attitudes toward sexual activities. Such an approach provides a change in emphasis for sex therapy from the problematic objective, physical, and to some degree mechanical manifestations of sex to the subjective experience of each individual associated with sexual behaviors (Woody, 1992).

In the more traditional psychodynamic models of sexual difficulties, sexual problems were often considered to be either "symptoms" of underlying psychological disease in the psychodynamic approach (Strean, 1983) or, more recently, dysfunctional learned behaviors that departed from sexual norms but that could be treated by behavioral retraining (Masters & Johnson, 1970; Kaplan, 1974; LoPiccolo, 1978). Although the pronouncements of both of these approaches have lost some of their authority in recent years, their impact remains in the belief systems of many individuals who suffer from sexual difficulties.

The approach to sexual concerns suggested by the term *sexual distress* moves the emphasis in the assessment, treatment, and prevention of sex-related problems to clients' subjective experiences as they relate to their sexual lives.

ASSESSMENT OF SEXUAL DISTRESS

An assessment of a client experiencing sexual distress includes not only an exploration of those biological-physiological functions that are perceived as not working the way clients or their partners would like but also a search for the source of the discomfort, including clients' self-talk about their experiences and consideration of any unrealistic expectations about their own and their partners' sexuality. This can entail an assessment of the individual client's needs and capacity for intimacy, commitment, and spirituality (Hatfield, 1993).

Fundamental to the assessment of sexual difficulties is a thoughtful exploration of a client's past experiences, current behavior patterns, wishes, desires, fantasies and expectations for themselves and their sexual partners.

In addition, many of the values that underlie clients' as well as professional helpers' beliefs about sexuality have a white middle-class bias—for example, the beliefs that sexual contacts must occur in a romantic context and that they should be extended, exhilarating experiences. Such values must be modified to better understand the sex-related concerns of clients from diverse cultural backgrounds.

Various factors frequently combine to cause sexual distress. The principal ones are discussed below.

Unrealistic and Inappropriate Expectations
These are frequently a product of the media's glamorization of sex and the exaggerated or distorted reports of peers. American media and folklore (especially pornography) tend to exaggerate the potential physical and psychic exhilaration of sexual experiences. Indeed, the helping professions have contributed to this image of sex by deeming disturbed those who are not particularly interested in it. Generally, when a couple presented themselves as sexually incompatible, the partner with the lesser interest in sex was considered the disturbed one and became the focus of the worker's intervention. Many people unrealistically feel that they are missing something if their sex lives are perceived as merely "adequate."

Sexual activity is often used in an attempt to accomplish goals that it generally cannot achieve. It can be used as an attempted "quick fix" for loneliness, feelings of interpersonal inadequacy, powerlessness, boredom, or isolation. People are often disappointed when sex fails to overcome such felt deficiencies.

Adult Consequences of Childhood Sexual Abuse
As they approach adulthood, victims of childhood sexual abuse must develop coping mechanisms to deal with the memories and consequences of their experiences. This is especially true when they feel that they had given implied or explicit consent to their abuse. This can result in adult sexual distress as a result of the confusion, humiliation, and guilt associated with these experiences. Such individuals may grow up not trusting their sexual emotions and judgments and fearing that they are merely sex

objects. They may turn to substance abuse or impetuous sexual contacts in an attempt to cope with their pain (Glover, et al., 1996; Simons & Whitbech, 1991).

To cope with their memories of incest and sexual abuse, people often build a barrier to intimacy and sexual enjoyment. They may also suppress memories of these traumatic experiences. When these memories remain dormant, they can manifest themselves later in the form of sexual distress. Because these memories are so unpleasant, sufferers may avoid situations leading to pleasurable physical contacts—even touch. They may see potential sexual partners as dangerous, think they are only seeking their own gratification, and become unable to form or maintain stable intimate relationships.

Another possible adult consequence of childhood sexual abuse or incest is prostitution. Events occurring in these abusive experiences may lead victims to believe that selling sexual access is morally acceptable. Their childhood experiences provided them with conditioning in the use of "emotional distancing" during sexual activities—a psychological device frequently used by prostitutes while having a sexual encounter with a "trick" (Simons & Whitbeck, 1991).

To the extent that they see themselves as worthless except as sex objects, their low self-esteem will have a deleterious effect on how they allow themselves to be treated by others. Many may not seek treatment because they may see themselves as responsible for their past maltreatment.

Boys as well as girls have abusive childhood sexual experiences but such concerns of male clients may not be brought to the attention of social workers because as adults male clients fear homophobia and the myths they have been exposed to about male sexuality. They encounter, however, many of the same consequences that women abused as girls encounter. Many people, including professional helpers, hold to the myth that "real men" cannot be sexual victims but are—or should be—in control of their sexual availability.

Adult victims of childhood sexual abuse or incest often fail to seek help for their sexual concerns because of guilt, fear, or shame. They may have repressed their memories of their abuse and avoid situations that may threaten their coping mechanisms, however destructive these devices are.

Adult traumatic sexual experiences such as rape or being exposed to an exhibitionist can also haunt one's attempts at sexual fulfillment. Social workers must create an atmosphere in which their clients feel free to divulge events in the past that bear on their current sexual distress.

Fear

Even the thought of sexual expression can provoke fear for many clients, who may avoid opportunities for sexual fulfillment or enter into sexual experiences with hesitation. Among the more common antecedents of fear of sex are distressful childhood experiences and other sexual trauma, fear of revealing perceived sexual inadequacy, pregnancy, and anxiety about intimacy and commitment.

A concern of many people, especially those who engage in male-with-male sex, is the fear of contracting or transmitting HIV (Gochros, 1992). It is important that accurate "safe sex" information be communicated to such clients along with realistic estimates of the relative risk of diverse sexual activities.

Guilt

There is much in middle-American culture, as reflected in its more conservative religious and political viewpoints, that contributes to sex being seen as a guilt-ridden indulgence. Sexual pleasure—especially outside the marriage bed—is often portrayed as sinful and even dangerous. Puritanical elements tend to suggest that "if it feels good, it must be wrong," an approach as dangerous as the 1960s slogan "If it feels good, do it!"

This message often starts with parental prohibitions about self-stimulation and exploratory sexual activities with age mates. Clients may experience dysfunctional guilt over sexual fantasies even when the fantasies are completely separated from actual behavior. Indeed guilt, along with its associated self-talk, is one of the major contributors to sexual distress.

Gender Stereotypes

Cultural attitudes and beliefs about the sexual roles of men and women can provide a fertile ground for sexual distress. Despite the efforts of segments of the feminist movement, women are still often evaluated by many men—and often by each other—largely on the basis of their physical attractiveness and sexual desirability, and men are rated by their sexual prowess, self-confidence, and performance (Barbach, 1975; Zilbergeld, 1992). These social biases are often internalized, and when a client's self-image is lacking in these areas they may manifest themselves as sexual distress.

Lack of Interest

Many professional helpers make the mistake of viewing sexual desire (responsibly exercised) as a sign of health, and lack of interest as pathological. Many people are quite satisfied with little or no sexual activity with or without a partner, despite the media hype of sex. Indeed, the popular media portray sex as an essential ingredient of modern life and at the same time sets standards of sexual ecstasy that are difficult to meet.

Clients may be sexually satiated after many years of more or less satisfying sexual activity or may have a basically low physiological sex drive. Or they simply find sexual activities routine and unstimulating. Or they may or may not continue to enjoy physical touch of some sort, but have little or no interest in orgasm-producing sexual encounters.

They may have been convinced, however, that such sexual apathy is pathological and so may seek professional intervention to kindle or rekindle a sexual flame.

Physical Pain
Gynecological, urological, and other sources of pain in intercourse can obviously interfere with the enjoyment of sexual encounters. Both partners must be sensitive to the physical needs and responses of their partners. Social workers who have clients who experience such pain should consider referring such clients to physicians whom they know to be sensitive, sexually knowledgeable, and nonjudgmental—if no simpler explanation of the problem (such as lack of lubrication) is uncovered.

Homosexually active clients who experience such difficulties may hesitate to approach their social worker or physician about these concerns because of the sometimes realistic fear of encountering a homophobic response.

Effects of Illness and Medications
Many physical illnesses such as diabetes, and/or the medications taken to treat them, may have physiological consequences that can lead to sexual distress. Some medications, such as some taken to treat high blood pressure, can impede sexual responses. Consultations with sexually knowledgeable physicians can help to determine any biological basis for a sexual concern. Often the physician can prescribe an alternative medication with no or less negative sexual side effects.

Aging
The manifestations of aging can impact sexual response in varying degrees and at different times for different people, depending on social, biological, and psychological influences. Although sexual expression can bring pleasure, intimacy, and a celebration of life at any age, adaptations to sex-

ual patterns might be helpful or necessary as people age. For example, some might find that they will approach sexual activities with more vigor if they engage in these activities in the morning, when they are well rested, rather than in the late night hours as they used to do.

Some aging clients may no longer feel a need for genital sex and may be ready to reduce, alter, or terminate their sexual activities. Like many younger clients, they may need help in recognizing that not all erotic contact needs to lead to intercourse and orgasm.

Disability
Some professional helpers working with physically and mentally challenged clients ignore or even attempt to discourage their clients' sexual interests. Disabilities—even serious disabilities—need not signal an end to some forms of sexual enjoyment. Modifications that recognize both the limits and resources of the disabled may be necessary—as well as contacts with family members, who may be uncomfortable about the possible consequences of the client's sexual expression.

Institutionalization
Clients living in virtually any institution, whether a prison, hospital, nursing home, or alcohol or drug rehabilitation facility find that their opportunities for a satisfying sexual life are practically nonexistent. Indeed, residents of such facilities who seek sexual outlets are frequently branded as problematic and are subject to discharge from the facility. A growing number of institutions, however, recognize the sexual needs of their residents and provide responsible structures for them to express their sexuality. Privacy is usually a prerequisite for such sexual opportunities. The development of responsible and satisfying sexual patterns is a need frequently overlooked in the rehabilitation programs offered by such institutions.

Lack of Sexual Skills
Despite the common belief that sexual skills are inborn and natural and that "good sex" should be spontaneous, mutually satisfying sex is usually neither intuitive nor automatic. In both gay and straight relationships, men and women must first learn about their own sexual responses and needs and then their partners' before they can communicate (verbally or nonverbally) in bed about their desires. Such communication does not come easily for many of our clients because of long-standing inhibitions about talking about sex, acknowledging sexual likes and dislikes, and asking for specific sexual behaviors from their partners. These inhibitions may take

years, if ever, to overcome, and may require a professional helper's interventions with the individual or couple to develop mutually enjoyable sexual skills.

Lack of Self-Esteem

Impaired self-esteem may lead some clients to feel that they do not deserve sexual pleasure; therefore they will hesitate to make efforts to satisfy their sexual needs in a sexual relationship. Such clients may defer to their partner's wishes while compromising or ignoring their own. Some homosexually oriented clients with internalized homophobia, for example, may be inhibited from negotiating their sexual activities with their partners, even avoiding the negotiation of safer-sex activities.

Deficiency in Intimacy Skills

Although sexual enjoyment is possible without a coexisting intimate relationship, feelings of closeness and intimacy can enhance sexual experiences. Indeed, for many people sexual experiences outside of intimate ongoing relationships are unacceptable.

Sexual distress is often a result of flaws in clients' overall relationships. It is therefore important to assess an individual's or couple's total relationship—the gestalt in which sexual acts occur. Although good sex can occur in a problematic relationship, and many good relationships exist in which sex is unsatisfactory for one or both partners, the two are usually synergistic.

Many homosexually oriented individuals—especially youth—experience difficulties in initiating, maintaining, and terminating intimate relationships because of the lack of societal sanctions to explore and develop intimate relationships (Loulan, 1987; McWhirter & Mattison, 1984). Individuals of any sexual orientation, however, may be either incapable of or uninterested in long-term intimate relationships. They may enjoy and prefer short-term sexual contacts in which there is a mutual implicit or explicit agreement that no long-term emotional commitment is intended or wanted. Clients with such inclinations should not be confused with those who urgently desire a bonded emotional relationship along with their sexual relationship but lack either the interpersonal skills or the opportunities to develop one.

TREATMENT OF SEXUAL DISTRESS

The treatment of sexual distress can involve many diverse approaches—too numerous and, in some cases too complex to elaborate here. The following list, however, suggests some of approaches to preventing sexual problems, concerns and distress in adults (Gochros, 1995):

- Education at home and in school that goes beyond anatomy, physiology, reproduction, and sexually transmitted diseases, but includes a biopsychosocial focus on sexuality in a sex-positive atmosphere that respects cultural gender and sexual preference diversity
- Cross-gender and same-gender intimacy training in secondary schools
- Enhancement of sexual self-awareness, including an understanding of the effects of past experiences and current beliefs about clients' sexual behavior and concerns
- Support for clients' harmless sexual patterns or desires that may divert from prevailing cultural norms; clients may need their social worker's support in dealing with the consequences of their idiosyncratic interests
- Education about sexual anatomy, physiology, and behavior for clients (and there are many) who lack such knowledge or who have acquired distorted information
- Treatment through intimacy training for clients who have never learned the requisite skills for initiating, maintaining, and enhancing intimate relationships; such training might involve role playing, cognitive restructuring, and assertive and negotiating skills
- Specialized individual and group counseling in related social service agencies regarding the sexual concerns of such diverse sexually oppressed groups as partners of people with Alzheimer's disease, the physically and/or mentally challenged, institutionalized individuals, gays and lesbians (of all ages), and the aged
- Demythologizing sex and overturning agency policies and local, state and national laws that contribute to sex-related distress and supporting efforts to develop and implement reasonable and humane sex-positive policies and legislation

CONCLUSION

Much has changed in how social workers view adult sexual "pathology." Decades ago, sexual problems were seen largely as symptoms of deep-seated psychopathology and labeled as various diseases, with proscriptive approaches to their treatment. Such destructive conceptualizations, which pathologize any sexual behaviors other than bonded couples engaging in mutually orgasmic vaginal/penile intercourse, are still occasionally encountered. (See, for example, Strean, 1983.)

In more recent years, sexual problems have been given a more ecological frame of reference. Especially from the viewpoint of social work, sexual concerns must be seen in the context of individuals' self-talk as well as the interplay of their sexual desires, fears, and behaviors in the context of their relationships and their social environment.

This approach leaves room for considerable diversity in how individuals can overcome unrealistic and unnecessary obstacles to their sexuality and seek a fulfilling sexual life.

REFERENCES

American Psychiatric Association. (1980). *Diagnostic and statistical manual of mental disorders, third edition.* Washington, DC: Author.

Barbach, L. (1975). *For yourself: The fulfillment of female sexuality.* New York: Doubleday.

Byington, D. B. (1995). Sexual assault. *Encyclopedia of social work* (19th Ed.). New York: National Association of Social Workers.

Carnes, P. J. (1990). Sexual addiction: Progress, criticism, challenges. *American Journal of Preventive Psychiatry and Neurology, 2,* 1–8.

Carnes, P. J. (1991). *Don't call it love: Recovery from sexual addiction.* New York: Bantam.

Forman, B. (1980). Psychotherapy with rape victims. *Psychotherapy: Theory, Research and Practice, 17,* 304–311.

Francoeur, R. T. (Ed.). (1996). *Taking sides: Clashing views on controversial issues in human sexuality.* Guilford, CT: Dushkin.

Glover, N. M., Janikowski, T. P., & Benshoff, J. J. (1996). Substance abuse and past incest contact, a national perspective. *Journal of Substance Abuse Treatment, 13,* 3, 185–193.

Gochros, H. (1972). The sexually oppressed. *Social Work, 17,* 16–23.

Gochros, H. L. (1986). Sexuality. *Encyclopedia of Social Work* (18th Ed.). New York: National Association of Social Workers.

Gochros, H. (1988). Risks of abstinence: Sexual decision making in the AIDS era. *Social Work, 33,* 254–256.

Gochros, H. (1992). The sexuality of gay men with HIV infection. *Social Work, 37,* 105–109.

Gochros, H. L. (1995). Sexual distress. *Encyclopedia of Social Work* (19th Ed.). New York: National Association of Social Workers.

Gochros, H. L., Gochros, J. S., & Fischer, J. (1986). *Helping the sexually oppressed.* Englewood Cliffs, NJ: Prentice Hall.

Hatfield, E., & Rapson, R. L. (1993). *Love, sex and intimacy: Their psychology, biology and history.* New York: HarperCollins.

Henkin, W. A. (1991).The myth of sexual addiction. *Journal of Gender Studies,* Spring 1991.

Kaplan, H. S. (1974). *The new sex therapy.* New York: Brunner/Mazel.

Kaplan, H. S. (1979). *Disorders of sexual desire and other new concepts in sex therapy.* New York: Brunner/Mazel.

Koss, M. P., & Harvey, M. R. (1987). *The rape victim: Clinical and community approaches to treatment.* Lexington, MA: Stephan Greene Press.

LoPiccolo, J., & LoPiccolo, L. (1978). *Handbook of sex therapy*. New York: Plenum Press.

Loulan, J. (1987). *Lesbian passion: Loving ourselves and each other*. San Francisco: Spinsters/Aunt Lute.

Masters, W., & Johnson, V. (1970). *Human sexual inadequacy*. Boston: Little, Brown.

McGrath, R. J. (1991). Sex-offender risk assessment and disposition planning: A review of empirical and clinical findings. *International Journal of Offender Therapy and Comparative Criminology, 35,* 4, 329–350.

McWhirter, D., & Mattison, D. (1984). *The male couple: How relationships develop*. Englewood Cliffs, NJ: Prentice Hall.

Simons, R. L., & Whitbeck, L. B. (1991). Sexual abuse as a precursor to prostitution and victimization among adolescent and adult homeless women. *Journal of Family Issues, 12,* 3, 361–379.

Salter, A. C. (1988). *Treating child sex offenders and victims*. Newbury Park, CA: Sage.

Strean, H. S. (1983). *The sexual dimension: A guide for the helping professional*. New York: The Free Press.

Woody, J. (1992). *Treating sexual distress*. Newbury Park, CA: Sage.

Zastrow, C. (1995). *The practice of social work*. Pacific Grove, CA: Brooks-Cole.

Zilbergeld, B. (1992). *The new male sexuality*. New York: Bantam Books.

24

ALCOHOL DEPENDENCE

Donald E. Meeks and Marilyn A. Herie

A lcohol dependence is a multifaceted problem involving many issues, processes, and transactions. These include societal, cultural, and individual attitudes toward alcohol use and abuse; the mechanisms through which alcohol is marketed and made available in a society; and medical, psychological, and social problems associated with alcohol use (Anderson, 1996; National Institute on Alcohol Abuse and Alcoholism [NIAAA], 1997). Massive costs to industry, to law enforcement, and to health and social agencies are also associated with alcohol use; for example, the annual costs of alcohol use in Canada, with a total population of 25,000,000, are estimated at $7.5 billion (Canadian), or 41% of the total costs of controlled-substance use (Single et al., 1996). The various dimensions of these problems require diverse interventions ranging from policies and legislation to individual treatment.

This chapter briefly discusses alcohol's effects, conceptualizations of alcohol dependence, self-help approaches, and research on treatment effectiveness before focusing on clinical applications. Our intention is to provide social work practitioners with an overview of current research and treatment modalities for alcohol-dependent clients, with an emphasis on practical tools and techniques. The following areas are reviewed:

- Alcohol and its effects
- Defining alcohol dependence
- Theories on the causes of alcohol dependence
- Self-help approaches
- Empirical practice guidelines
- Alcohol treatment approaches
- Other treatment considerations:
  - Client-treatment matching

- Women-sensitive treatment
- Working with culturally diverse clients

In the section "Alcohol Treatment Approaches" we provide guidelines and tools for identifying and screening individuals with alcohol problems; accompanied by an overview of four general treatment models: brief, motivational counseling, relapse prevention, cognitive behavioral group treatment, and marital/family therapy. The treatment interventions presented were chosen for their research support and their suitability for use by social workers in nonspecialist settings. Other treatment considerations, such as guidelines for client–treatment matching, women-sensitive treatment, and working with culturally diverse clients are also discussed.

ALCOHOL AND ITS EFFECTS

The active ingredient in beverage alcohol is ethyl alcohol, or ethanol, a depressant drug. Alcohol decreases the activity of parts of the brain and the spinal cord in proportion to the amount of alcohol in the bloodstream. Short-term effects appear rapidly after a single dose and disappear within a few hours or days. Long-term effects appear following repeated use over an extended period. These effects can include metabolic disturbances, impaired responses to infection, impairment of absorption of dietary nutrients, and obstructive sleep apnea; as well as dependence, injury, and diseases of the gastrointestinal, nervous, cardiovascular, and respiratory systems (Rankin & Ashley, 1992).

The long list of the medical problems of heavy drinkers includes acute alcoholic liver disease, peptic ulceration, chronic obstructive lung disease, pneumonia, hypertension, gastritis, epileptiform disorders (seizures), and acute brain syndromes. Adverse pregnancy outcomes and fetal abnormalities caused by alcohol's teratogenic effects, as well as a link between alcohol use and breast cancer, are also concerns (Ashley et al., 1994; Rankin & Ashley, 1992). Psychological and social problems, sometimes severe, are associated with heavy use over time. In many cases there may be confusion and/or loss of memory and blackouts. In extreme cases, the individual may suffer dementia, Wernicke-Korsakoff syndrome, or psychiatric disorders such as alcohol-induced depression (Kahan, 1997). Finally, role performance and interpersonal functioning are impaired as a consequence of problem drinking. Problems may occur in all areas of social functioning. These include family dysfunction and breakdown, stress in other interpersonal spheres, and reduced productivity or difficulty holding employment.

Alcohol consumption can be conceptualized as occurring along a continuum of severity, anchored by no consumption at one end and heavy use at the other (illustrated in Figure 24–1). It is estimated that severely dependent drinkers comprise between 3% and 7% of the adult population (the "thin edge of the wedge" in Figure 24–1), while problem drinkers (defined as individuals with low to moderate dependence without physical dependence) comprise between 15% and 35% (Institute of Medicine, 1990). Although alcohol-related problems range widely in severity, there has been a tendency for both research and treatment resources to be focused on the severely dependent population. However, it is important to consider the health and social consequences of many patterns of alcohol consumption, not just those at the extreme end of the spectrum.

Many of the health, social, and economic problems attributable to alcohol are not caused by persons who could be described as alcoholics. Alcohol problems are distributed throughout the drinking population; and mild to moderate drinkers greatly outnumber heavy drinkers. For this reason, it has been recommended that "[i]f the alcohol problems experienced by the population are to be reduced significantly, the distribution of these problems in the population suggests that a principal focus of intervention should be on persons with mild or moderate alcohol problems" (Institute of Medicine, 1990, p. 215). Treatment interventions should therefore be targeted toward both the smaller numbers of severely dependent individuals *and* the more numerous but less severe population of "problem drinkers."

DEFINING ALCOHOL DEPENDENCE

The World Health Organization has advanced the following definition of dependence:

> A cluster of physiological, behavioral and cognitive phenomena of variable intensity, in which the use of a psychoactive drug (or drugs) takes on a high priority. The necessary descriptive characteristics are preoccupation with a desire to obtain and take the drug and persistent drug seeking behavior. Determinants and the problematic consequences of drug dependence may be *biological, psychological and social and usually interact.* (World Health Organization, 1993, emphasis added)

This definition reflects the importance of multiple factors in the etiology and resolution of alcohol problems. The *Diagnostic and Statistical*

Figure 24–1
Continuum of Severity and Spectrum of Responses to Alcohol Problems

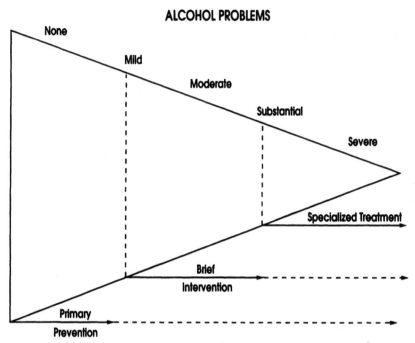

ALCOHOL PROBLEMS

Source: Reprinted with permission from *Broadening the Base of Treatment for Alcohol Problems.* Copyright 1990 by the National Academy of Sciences. Courtesy of the National Academy Press, Washington, DC.

The triangle represents the general population, with the range of problem severity experiences along the upper side. The lower side of the triangle shows the corresponding spectrum of interventive responses. In general, specialized treatment is indicated for individuals with substantial or severe alcohol problems, brief interventions are appropriate for persons with mild to moderate alcohol problems, and prevention efforts should be directed towards the majority of the population who are not experiencing alcohol problems but are at risk of developing them. The dotted lines extending the arrows suggest that brief intervention and prevention efforts may have benefits beyond their target populations. The prevalence of each category of alcohol problem is suggested by the space it occupies on the triangle (e.g., "most people have no alcohol problems, many people have a few alcohol problems, and some people have many alcohol problems").

Manual of Mental Disorders, Fourth Edition (*DSM-IV,* 1994), distinguishes between substance *dependence* and substance *abuse. Dependence* is said to be present if an individual manifests a "maladaptive pattern of substance use, leading to clinically significant impairment or distress," characterized by the presence of three or more of the following seven criteria over a 12-month period:

1. Tolerance
2. Withdrawal distress
3. Drinking in larger amounts or over a longer period than intended
4. Desire or unsuccessful attempts to cut down or control drinking
5. Much time spent in activities related to obtaining alcohol
6. Giving up social, occupational, or recreational activities because of drinking
7. Continuing to drink despite knowledge of an alcohol-related medical problem (*DSM-IV,* p. 181)

Dependence may occur with or without *physiological* dependence (items 1 and 2).

The criteria for substance *abuse* include (a) not meeting the criteria for substance *dependence* (above), and (b) manifesting one or more of the following four characteristics:

1. Drinking that results in the drinker's failure to fulfill major role obligations at work, school, or home
2. Continuing to drink in physically hazardous situations (for example, while driving)
3. Recurrent drinking-related legal problems
4. Continuing to drink in spite of social/interpersonal problems related to alcohol consumption, such as arguments with a spouse or partner about drinking (*DSM-IV,* pp. 182–183)

Although the distinction between substance dependence and substance abuse may be helpful from a diagnostic perspective, treatment should address the client's transactions with people and systems in the environment. Social work intervention is located at the interface between person and environment (De Hoyos, 1989). This dual focus is a unique and critical contribution made by social work to alcohol treatment.

THEORIES ON THE CAUSES OF ALCOHOL DEPENDENCE

There is a good deal of disagreement among scientists and practitioners about the nature and etiology of alcohol problems. Although Hester (1995) identifies no less than 13 conceptual models of alcohol problems, current perspectives can be grouped under *biological, psychological,* and *social/environmental* factors. Biological models emphasize the role of genetic inheritance and neurobiological processes. Studies of twins, family histories, adopted children, and animals provide strong evidence for a genetic component in alcohol dependence; and research on neurotransmitters and enzymes has contributed to our understanding of the biological processes underlying addictive behavior (Ogborne, 1997).

Psychological models assert that dependence is a "mental or behavioural disorder, whose origins are as much environmental as they are physical" (Babor, 1990, p. 28). These formulations stress personality traits, psychodynamic processes, and learned cognitions and behaviors. Sociological definitions emphasize social/environmental factors such as the influence of the dominant culture, family and peer networks, and alcohol availability and cost (Ogborne, 1997). In addition, the sociological perspective takes into account the political dimensions of the term "dependence":

> [A]lcohol and drug use is often considered deviant because it exceeds the established norms of the community. This occurs in part because of inequality in the social structure which, by blocking opportunity and segregating deviants, creates the social conditions for the development and maintenance of dependence. (Babor, 1990, p. 31)

How alcohol dependence is defined shapes prevention and treatment strategies. Biological and psychological perspectives focus on the individual, whereas sociological frameworks point to social-structural variables as foci for interventions.

The *biopsychosocial* model (Donovan & Marlatt, 1988), as its name implies, integrates biological, psychological, and social factors. This approach posits that substance dependence constitutes a "complex, progressive pattern having biological, psychological, sociological and behavioral components" (Donovan & Marlatt, 1988, pp. 5–6). Similarly, Hester (1995) offer a *public health framework* as an integrative solution, with three causal factors taken into account: the *agent* (alcohol), which carries some destructive potential; *host* factors (such as individual differences); and *environmental* factors. Biopsychosocial and public health models reflect the reality that alcohol problems stem from diverse and interacting causes and involve multiple systems.

The above perspectives challenge traditional thinking about alcohol dependence as a moral weakness or a dispositional disease. The moral model ascribes the genesis of alcohol problems to characterological weakness and personal choice, while the disease perspective regards alcoholics as qualitatively different from "normal" drinkers. Orthodox disease concepts tend to focus on the interaction of a person with a drug. Such an emphasis ignores the fact that alcohol problems exist as much in social situations and processes as in people. Environmental factors influence attitudes toward drinking, the availability of alcohol, patterns of consumption, and societal views and self-concepts of alcohol-dependent individuals. Thus, they may reinforce problem drinking behavior.

The disease concept of alcoholism has, nevertheless, been useful to combat moralistic views; many people with alcohol problems would remain untreated if the moral view on alcoholism still held sway. At the same time, a narrow disease concept is limiting: although severely dependent individuals may be regarded as ill, as we have stated, alcohol problems must be viewed from a comprehensive perspective that takes biological, psychological, social, behavioral, and other factors into account. Moralistic views, which are to be discouraged, should be distinguished from the spiritual perspectives that form an important source of strength in the treatment of many individuals.

SELF-HELP APPROACHES

Alcoholics Anonymous (AA) may be the world's leading example of a successful self-help group. Founded in 1935, AA has helped countless alcoholics achieve sobriety. Alcoholics Anonymous is a fellowship of men and women who provide group support within a particular framework of beliefs and philosophies (AA World Services, 1980). Alanon and Alateen are offshoots designed to help families and the teenage children of alcoholics.

AA regards alcoholics as people who have lost control over their drinking. The twelve steps of AA invoke the role of a "higher power," a term not intended to convey a specific concept of God. Its twelve traditions eschew promotion of the organization while affirming the importance of anonymity for its members and the primacy of its helping mission.

AA's contention "once an alcoholic, always an alcoholic" is controversial among many professionals. AA rejects the concept of a recovered alcoholic. The individual's adjustment as a dry alcoholic must always be organized around the label "alcoholic." This posture is interesting in light of AA's major role in destigmatizing alcoholism. A recovering alcoholic, in this view, is a person who cannot handle alcohol and can never drink again. Labeling theory might perceive the permanent assignment of such a label as entrenching the individual in the deviant role.

Women For Sobriety (WFS) is an alternative source of help and support designed specifically for women. Unlike AA, Women For Sobriety asserts that a woman can fully "recover" from alcohol dependence by taking personal control over her problem and putting her past behind her. The thirteen statements of WFS comprise a "New Life Acceptance Program," and emphasize autonomy, empowerment, and competence (Women for Sobriety, 1976).

Two more recent self-help approaches include Rational Recovery (RR) and Moderation Management (MM). Rational Recovery is based on the principles of Havelock Ellis's Rational Emotive Therapy (Ellis & Velten, 1992), and focuses on rational choice (as opposed to spirituality and faith) and the development of self-esteem to maintain abstinence (McCrady & Delaney, 1995). Kishline (1994), a former problem drinker, began Moderation Management as an alternative to abstinence-based self-help programs. MM is not intended for severely dependent chronic drinkers or others for whom alcohol is contraindicated (such as those with health or medical problems); it outlines "nine steps toward moderation and positive lifestyle changes" (Kishline, 1994).

Many professionals find little or no conflict between various self-help approaches and their own. In any case, a focus on ideological differences, where they exist, distorts the issue. Self-help should be considered as an excellent resource for alcohol dependent individuals who find its approach congenial. Nonetheless, it is underutilized by professionals in many locations. Treatment may be further enhanced if self-help involvement is combined with participation in a professional treatment program (McCrady & Delaney, 1995).

EMPIRICAL PRACTICE GUIDELINES

The Importance of Research-Based Treatment

Social work practitioners are increasingly pressed by funders and planners to demonstrate the efficacy of their interventions (Gorey, 1996). Indeed, ethical practice is predicated on the imperative of using the "best available information," which "refers to knowledge that has emerged by means of the scientific process" (Klein & Bloom, 1994, p. 101). In addition to ethical imperatives, there are compelling policy reasons for social workers to demonstrate the efficacy of what they do:

> In an era of political and fiscal conservatism in which cutting social welfare programs heads the agendas of most legislative bodies in

North America, the question of social work's effectiveness is of paramount importance. Integrative empirical evidence is needed . . . especially to cogently refute the colloquial, stereotypical image of social workers as well-meaning but largely ineffective home visitors. (Gorey, 1996, p. 119)

Thus, it is important that social workers offering alcohol treatment select research-based approaches with empirically demonstrated efficacy. It should be noted that any notion of "effectiveness" should take the sociocultural context of the individual into account. This section provides a brief discussion of what is meant by "effective treatment," and summarizes the recent research on "what works" in alcohol treatment.

What Is Effective Treatment?

Effectiveness is typically conceptualized as the extent to which treatment outcome objectives are met. Martin et al. (1990) propose three different levels of treatment goals: (1) recovery, (2) harm reduction, and (3) care. *Recovery* relates to treatment outcome, whereby an individual achieves "a level of improvement which is characterized by prolonged abstinence, or infrequent use of a drug at modest levels of consumption, coupled with the achievement of satisfactory adjustment and functioning in . . . other areas" (Martin, 1990, p. 187). *Harm reduction* refers to the reduction of adverse consequences, either to the individual or to society, as a result of reducing or changing patterns of consumption. The outcome *care* simply means the provision of humane responses to the client's social and health care needs to prevent or slow further deterioration (for example, alcohol detoxification services for chronic users).

Martin (1990) and his colleagues' classification of program effectiveness is a particularly good fit with social work values and ethics. Social workers are well situated to serve marginalized and oppressed groups who do not fit mainstream service systems. Further, the importance of "starting where the client is" may mean accepting the client's goals of harm reduction or care in the short term, while continuing to work towards abstinence-based recovery in the longer term. Furthermore, there is evidence to suggest that for drinkers *at the lower end of the drinking severity continuum* reduced drinking goals are often appropriate (Hester, 1995). However, problem drinkers in this category would not be considered "alcoholic." For individuals with moderate to severe levels of dependence, abstinence goals are most suitable.

What Works in Alcohol Treatment?

Recent comprehensive reviews of the alcohol treatment outcome literature (Finney & Monahan, 1996; Holder, et al., 1991; Miller, et al., 1995) have suggested a number of promising approaches. Both Holder et al. and Miller et al. examined 219 studies selected on the basis of four criteria: (1) specification of a treatment modality being evaluated; (2) the use of control or comparison groups; (3) proper procedures to equate treatment; and (4) the use of a posttreatment, drinking-related outcome measure. Although these three meta-analyses assign somewhat different rankings to the treatment modalities reviewed,* some general practice guidelines can be derived.

Broad-spectrum skill training, particularly social skills training and community reinforcement, were judged to be effective in all of the above meta-analyses. Broad-spectrum approaches focus primarily on the problem areas related to alcohol consumption and relapse, with an emphasis on teaching coping skills (Miller, et al., 1995). Relapse prevention interventions targeting coping skills training and self-efficacy (such as Annis, et al., 1996b; Marlatt & Gordon, 1985) are also well supported (Carroll, 1996); as are brief, motivational interventions (Miller & Rollnick, 1991). In addition, marital/family therapies that focus on communication and positive reinforcement show good empirical support (Finney & Monahan, 1996; Holder, et al., 1991; Miller, et al., 1995).

Finally, pharmacotherapies, particularly antidipsotropic agents, are differentially effective, depending upon client characteristics and whether or not they are offered in conjunction with another treatment (Finney & Monahan, 1996; Miller, et al., 1995). Antidipsotropics are medications that induce aversive symptoms (such as nausea and vomiting) when alcohol is ingested. Popular types are disulfiram (Antabuse), and the less potent and shorter-acting calcium carbimide (Temposil). These drugs are particularly helpful in initiating behavior change and in stabilizing abstinence. The use of other medications such as antidepressants and, more recently, naltrexone hypochloride (ReVia) to decrease cravings in problem drinkers shows some promise (Anton, 1994; Volpicelli, et al., 1994).

ALCOHOL TREATMENT APPROACHES

This section presents a number of practical tools and techniques for social work clinicians in nonspecialist settings: identification and screening tools,

---

*Ranking inconsistencies were primarily due to differences in the classification of treatment interventions.

brief, motivational interventions, relapse prevention strategies, and marital/family therapy.

Brief Screening and Identification of Alcohol-Dependent Clients

Roughly one quarter of the population of North America drinks in a problematic fashion (Institute of Medicine, 1990), and of those, the vast majority never seek specialized addiction treatment (Tucker, et al., 1994). Therefore, chances are good that many of the clients seen in nonspecialist service settings will manifest moderate to severe alcohol-related problems. For this reason, it may be helpful to incorporate the routine use of brief screening/identification procedures. These are generally quick to administer and easy to interpret, and are designed as a preliminary step to a more detailed problem assessment. Our overview of screening techniques and tools is based primarily on the excellent review by Cooney, et al. (1995).

A common screening method involves asking a few questions about the quantity and frequency of an individual's alcohol consumption. It is useful to frame questions in terms of standard drinks: 12 ounces of beer, 5 ounces of wine, and 1.5 ounces of distilled spirits each have equivalent amounts of ethanol. The following are examples of quantity/frequency questions:

- How many days per week did you drink over the last month?
- On a day when you drink alcohol, how many drinks do you have?
- How many times during the last month did you drink more than five drinks (binge drinking)? (Cooney, Zweben, & Fleming, 1995, pp. 47–48)

Individuals' responses are then interpreted based on known levels of risk. "Low-risk" drinking is defined as no more than one or two standard drinks per day, with at least one abstinent day per week. Individuals whose drinking exceeds two drinks on any day are at risk for developing alcohol-related health problems (Addiction Research Foundation [ARF], & Canadian Centre on Substance Abuse [CCSA], 1993). *Any* alcohol use is contraindicated for some individuals:

- People with certain psychological and physical illnesses and conditions
- Those taking certain medications and psychoactive drugs
- People operating vehicles or machinery

- People responsible for public order or safety
- Those who have shown a persistent inability to control their drinking
- Individuals who are legally prohibited from drinking (e.g., under-age persons) (ARF & CCSA, 1993, p. 5)

In discussing alcohol-related health risks with clients, counselors will occasionally be confronted with the assertion that "drinking is good for my heart." Although research has shown that drinking within the limits outlined above can reduce the risk of heart disease for some individuals (NIAAA, 1992), adults who abstain from alcohol do not need to begin drinking for their hearts, since there are other ways to reduce the risk of cardiovascular disease (Ashley, 1996). In addition, research suggests that adverse consequences can occur even at relatively low levels of consumption, and these risks might offset the benefits of moderate drinking (NIAAA, 1992). Potential risks include stroke caused by bleeding in the brain, motor vehicle crashes, interactions with medications, fetal alcohol damage, and possible shifts to heavier drinking. Van Ginnekan (1992) has noted that the notion of a safe drinking limit does not apply to unhealthy people or to high-risk groups. Such individuals should seek alternate ways of reducing their risk of cardiovascular disease—for example, through diet and exercise.

Another popular brief screening tool for alcohol dependence is the CAGE questionnaire, an acronym for four questions about lifetime drinking:

C   Have you ever felt the need to Cut down on your drinking?
A   Have you ever felt Annoyed by someone criticizing your drinking?
G   Have you ever felt bad or Guilty about your drinking?
E   Have you ever had a drink first thing in the morning to steady your nerves and get rid of a hangover (Eye opener)? (Mayfield, et al., 1974)

Reports on the sensitivity of the CAGE range from 40% to 95%, depending upon the definition of dependence used, assessment of lifetime versus current drinking, varying the cut-off from one to four positive responses, and population differences (Cooney, et al., 1995). Because the CAGE does not address current problems, consumption levels, or binge drinking, Cooney, et al. (1995) recommend that it be used in conjunction with quantity/frequency questions.

Later, the TWEAK questionnaire, a modification of the CAGE, was developed by Russell (1994) to screen for alcohol problems in women:

T   How many drinks can you hold? (3 + drinks suggests Tolerance)

W   Have close friends or relatives Worried or complained about your drinking in the past year?

E   Do you sometimes take a drink in the morning when you first get up? (Eye-opener)

A   Has a friend or family member ever told you about things you said or did while you were drinking that you could not remember? (Amnesia or blackouts)

K   Do you sometimes feel the need to K/cut down on your drinking? (Russell, 1994)

The TWEAK is scored by assigning 2 points for a Yes response to the first two questions, and 1 point for a Yes response to each of the last three questions. A score of 2 or greater indicates the likelihood that the respondent has a drinking problem and should be assessed further.

Although various other screening tools have been developed, the quantity/frequency method, the CAGE, and the TWEAK are recommended for their brevity and ease of administration. Because many individuals presenting in nonspecialist service settings may not even be aware of having an alcohol problem, it is imperative that the clinician maintain a nonjudgmental, empathic attitude, provide feedback in a neutral fashion, and avoid labeling (Miller, 1995).

It is important to note that individuals who are identified as having alcohol problems should receive a more detailed assessment. Ideally, this would include a comprehensive psychosocial, legal, and treatment history (ARF, 1997); more precise measures of the amount and frequency of alcohol use (Sobell & Sobell, 1992) and drug use (Wilkinson & LeBreton, 1986) than are provided by simple quantity/frequency questions; and some indicator of the severity of alcohol and drug dependence (Skinner, 1982; Skinner & Horn, 1984).

Brief, Motivational Interventions

In the last decade, there has been an increasing emphasis on the need to "broaden the base" of alcohol treatment approaches (Institute of Medicine, 1990). Instead of focusing on the small minority of individuals clinically diagnosed as alcohol dependent, alcohol consumption can be viewed as occurring along a continuum of severity, as noted above, accompanied by a parallel spectrum of interventive responses. Brief, motivational interventions target the estimated one third of alcohol consumers who could be classified as moderate to heavy drinkers, and who have historically been ignored by traditional alcohol treatment modalities (Skinner, 1990). The ethical considerations of proactive treatment (e.g., not waiting until serious problems develop before treatment is commenced) are especially salient given that socially stable individuals with less severe alcohol-related problems tend to have better prognoses. Perhaps the most compelling justification for the implementation of early identification/brief intervention programs is the growing body of empirical evidence supporting their efficacy (for example, Babor & Grant, 1992; Miller, et al., 1988; Sanchez-Craig, et al., 1989; Wallace, et al., 1988). Although brief interventions may not be suitable for all clients, such as those with chronic, severe dependence and those with concurrent mental disorders, practitioners can adopt strategies to maximize client motivation for change.

"Motivational interviewing" represents a general counseling style developed by Miller (1995), based on the Rogerian principles of therapist empathy, genuineness, and warmth (Rogers, 1959). This perspective suggests that

> [M]otivation should not be thought of as a personality problem, or as a trait that the person carries through the counsellor's doorway. Rather, motivation is a *state* of readiness or eagerness to change, which may fluctuate from one time or situation to another. This state is one that can be influenced. (Miller & Rollnick, 1991, p. 14, emphasis in original)

Whereas traditional perspectives view alcohol dependence as a disease characterized by denial, this alternative approach views motivation as a changeable state over which counselors can exert some influence. From this standpoint, brief interventions work because they can provide a "motivational boost and head start on behaviour change" (Miller, et al., 1988, p. 262).

Miller and Rollnick (1991) outline six "active ingredients" in effective brief counseling, summarized by the acronym FRAMES:

F   FEEDBACK: Providing nonjudgmental feedback about clinical assessment results

R   RESPONSIBILITY: Promoting clients' personal responsibility for change

A   ADVICE: Giving clear advice to the client to change his or her drinking

M   MENU: Offering a menu of behavior change strategies

E   EMPATHY: Maintaining an empathic interpersonal style

S   SELF-EFFICACY: Reinforcing clients' self-efficacy, hope, and optimism (Miller & Rollnick, 1991)

The general counseling style of motivational interviewing is complemented by the transtheoretical model of behavior change developed by Prochaska and DiClemente (1984). Their "stages of change" model outlines six well-defined, predictable experiences through which all individuals pass in resolving a problematic behavior: *precontemplation* (denial/lack of awareness of the problem); *contemplation* (ambivalence toward change, feeling "stuck"); *preparation/determination* (concrete resolution to change, but still somewhat ambivalent); *action* (actually initiating behavior change); *maintenance* (prevention of relapse); and *termination* (complete resolution of the problem) (Prochaska, et al., 1994) or *relapse* (Miller, 1995). Although the model was developed to explain smoking cessation, it has been applied to recovery from a wide range of appetitive disorders, including eating disorders, panic and anxiety disorders, and disorders resulting from brain injury (Prochaska, et al., 1994).

The counselor's therapeutic tasks vary depending upon the client's stage in the change process. These tasks, or motivational strategies, are summarized in Table 24–1. By responding differently to clients at different stages of change, practitioners can tailor their interventions to fit clients' motivational readiness. Attempting to push a client toward change before he or she is ready can engender resistance and hamper motivation (Rollnick, 1985)—for example, encouraging a precontemplator to consider attending a treatment program. Instead, the counselor's goal is to assist clients in moving from one stage to the next: by raising doubt in a precontemplator's mind, the counselor opens the door to contemplating change. By encouraging a contemplator to "tip the balance" in favor of the change, the counselor paves the way to determination, and on to action.

One particularly useful motivational strategy for "contemplators" (clients who are ambivalent about changing their drinking) is the decisional balance (Miller & Rollnick, 1991), where clients are asked to articulate the

Table 24-1 Stages of Change and Therapist Tasks

Client Stage	Therapist's Motivational Tasks
Precontemplation	Raise doubt:- increase the client's perception of risks and problems with current behavior
Contemplation	Tip the balance:- evoke reasons to change, risks of not changing; strengthen the client's self-efficacy for change of current behavior
Determination	Help the client to determine the best course of action to take in seeking change
Action	Help the client to take steps toward change
Maintenance	Help the client to identify and use strategies to prevent relapse
Relapse	Help the client to renew the processes of contemplation, determination, and action, without becoming stuck or demoralized because of relapse

Source: Miller & Rollnick (1991), p. 18. Reprinted by permission.

costs and benefits of their alcohol use. Figure 24–2 presents an example of a decisional balance exercise. This technique is quite different from confrontational approaches, where the counselor focuses attention on the negative aspects of drinking. One major difficulty with confrontation is that

> . . . the natural response of anyone who is challenged about a behavior over which they are ambivalent, is to argue the counter position. In being ambivalent the individual is only too aware of both sides of the argument and if pressed will automatically, and ably, argue the opposite. . . . In motivational interviewing, it is the client's task to convince the therapist that a drug problem exists, and it is not the therapist's role to confront the client into accepting some therapist-determined (usually pre-determined) diagnostic label. (Saunders & Wilkinson, 1990, pp. 136–137)

Instead of encouraging clients to change, confrontation can actually strengthen client resistance. Alternatively, the process by which a client weighs the pros and cons of excessive drinking for him- or herself can present a potent argument in favor of change. Often clients will notice that the benefits of heavy drinking are short-lived, and are accompanied by long-term physical, psychological, social, and occupational costs.

Brief, motivational interventions that include routine screening for alcohol problems, assessment, brief counseling, and supplementary printed

Figure 24–2
Decisional Balance

Decisional Balance:
To Change or Not to Change?

One of the first steps toward successfully changing your drinking is to reach a clear decision that you want to change. In this exercise, you are asked to think about the good and not-so-good things about changing versus not changing your drinking.

Fill in the table below with some of the important advantages and disadvantages of change. What do you have to lose? What do you have to gain? Then "weigh" your reasons for change. Which way does your "decisional balance" tip?

Changing Your Drinking

What's good about it?	What's not so good about it?

Continuing Your Current Drinking

What's good about it?	What's not so good about it?

Source: Adapted from Annis, et al., 1996.

materials (such as self-help manuals) are especially suitable for problem drinkers with mild to moderate levels of severity (Skinner, 1990). In addition to their cost effectiveness, motivational interventions are client-centered, respectful, and empowering. These attributes fit well with social work values and ethics, which emphasize the uniqueness and worth of the individual, and respect for people's value choices (Abramson, 1991).

Relapse Prevention Treatment

Based on social learning theory, particularly on Bandura's theory of self-efficacy, relapse prevention is premised on the notion that effective strategies in *initiating* a change in drinking behavior may not be effective in *maintaining* that change over time (Bandura, 1986). Structured Relapse Prevention (SRP) is a cognitive-behavioral, research-based counseling program that has been developed over the past several years at the Addiction Research Foundation of Ontario (ARF, Annis, 1986; Annis & Davis, 1989a; Annis & Davis, 1989b; Annis, et al., 1996a; Annis, et al., 1996b). Unlike the brief motivational interventions discussed above, SRP is designed for individuals with moderate to severe levels of dependence who are willing to work toward an abstinence goal. SRP treatment is a two-phase intervention, where Phase I introduces clients to powerful techniques designed to initiate and stabilize change, and Phase II focuses on fading their reliance on "initiation" strategies and substituting "maintenance" strategies. SRP is designed as an outpatient intervention consisting of eight to twelve weekly sessions. Research has shown that clients do equally well in both group and individual SRP treatment formats (Graham, et al., 1996).

Pretreatment Considerations
Because not all clients present for treatment in the "determination" stage of change, the motivational interviewing strategies described in the previous section are useful and appropriate precursors to SRP. The counselor's emphasis should be on encouraging clients to "tip the balance" from contemplation to determination to change. Once a client has made a decision to change his or her drinking behavior, the counselor and client collaborate in the design of an individually tailored treatment plan. A client can become an active partner in the treatment planning process by keeping a drinking diary (recording high-risk situations, urges and temptations to drink, and any "slips" or lapses), and by identifying his or her coping strengths and weaknesses.

Coping Skills Training

Because some of the most powerful treatment effects have been noted for interventions that incorporate coping skills training (Finney & Monahan, 1996; Miller, et al., 1995), it is recommended that this element be included in relapse prevention treatment. In SRP, clients are asked to select from a checklist of 16 assignments designed to help expand and enhance their coping repertoire. Many clients identify "Coping with Cravings," "Refusing Alcohol," and "Increasing Social Support" as important during the early weeks of treatment. Later sessions might include "Coping With Unpleasant Feelings and Memories of Trauma," "Anger Management," or "Healthy Relationships." These exercises can be either assigned as homework or used as the basis for discussion during the treatment sessions. Figure 24–3 illustrates one of the SRP coping skills assignments ("Coping With Cravings"). Research has shown that clients with positive treatment outcomes tend to make good use of coping strategies in high-risk situations and have high levels of confidence (self-efficacy) (Moser & Annis, 1996).

Strategies for Initiating Change

Phase I of SRP counseling focuses on powerful strategies useful in initiating change. These include avoiding risky situations (for example, social settings involving drinking), and seeking support from others (such as family, friends, or sponsors). By incorporating the drinking triggers identified in the treatment plan, early sessions help clients to anticipate risky situations for the coming week, and to identify and commit to nondrinking alternatives. A sample of the SRP Weekly Plan for the initiation phase is provided in Figure 24–4. The Weekly Plan is discussed in detail during the treatment session and assigned as homework. The results of coping strategies outlined by the client are then discussed the following week. Clients who experience difficulty stabilizing abstinence in the early weeks of treatment may find an alcohol-sensitizing or anticraving medication (such as Antabuse or naltrexone hypochloride) to be an effective adjunct to treatment (Annis, 1991).

Strategies for Maintaining Change

Clients who have been abstinent from alcohol for several weeks can move on to the second, or "maintenance" phase of SRP counselling. This stage targets strategies suitable for consolidating treatment successes and maintaining long-term gains. Maintenance of change is fostered by: (1) gradual real-life exposure to a hierarchy of frequently encountered high-risk

Figure 24–3
Coping with Cravings Exercise

Name: _____ Substance:_____ Date: _____

Coping with Cravings

Quitting drinking or drug use is likely to generate cravings, especially in high-risk situations. Learning to deal with urges and temptations is a very important part of preventing relapse. We experience urges to use at different levels of intensity, and these can be viewed as being on a continuum.

Mild   Moderate   Severe

<--->

fleeting thoughts   very strong urges

We can decrease cravings for alcohol and other drugs by using specific coping strategies. Remember that cravings do not last forever and will decrease in number and strength over time.

Try some of the following suggestions to help you cope:

Behavior (What I do)	Cognition (What I think)
• Self-monitor - write out your thoughts and feelings • Seek support - Tell someone what you are experiencing. • Distract yourself - do something unrelated to drinking. • Substitute another behavior (e.g., eat something or drink an alternative beverage). • Leave or change the situation • Take deep breaths (in through your nose, out through your mouth) to relax yourself. • Delay the response - put off the decision to drink for 15 minutes.	• Normalize the craving: "I'm experiencing an urge to drink. It's OK to feel like drinking." • Use imagery (e.g., visualize the craving as a wave that rises and falls, and you are riding it out). • Use positive self-statements such as, "I can cope with this. I've been sober for two weeks and I don't want to spoil it now." • Use thought-stopping (e.g., picture a giant STOP sign). • Think of the negative consequences of drinking. • Think of the benefits of not drinking.

continued

Practice Exercise:

Now we would like you to come up with your own plan to deal with urges and temptations. Be specific.

1. Describe a recent high-risk situation that resulted in a craving.

_____

_____

Using your example above, plan ways to deal with urges and temptations to drink.

2. Who are you going to seek support from?

_____

_____

3. What will you do to distract yourself?

_____

_____

4. What messages (positive self-talk) will you give yourself?

_____

_____

5. What else can you do in this situation?

_____

_____

Source: H. Annis, M. Herie, & L. Watkin-Merek, *Structured Relapse Prevention: An Outpatient Counselling Approach*. Toronto: Addiction Research Foundation, 1996.

drinking situations; (2) getting comfortable in each risky situation by experiencing it a few times before moving on to the next one; (3) slowly fading reliance on initiation phase strategies (including reliance on pharmacological agents); and (4) designing homework tasks so that the client takes credit for success. It should be noted that movement from initiation to maintenance does not necessarily occur in a linear fashion: in practice, clients tend to use a combination of both types of strategies. The overall objective is to encourage clients to lessen their reliance on initiation strategies and gain increased confidence in the use of maintenance strategies before treatment ends.

A sample of the maintenance phase Weekly Plan is provided in Figure 24–5. Unlike Phase I assignments (where the focus is on *anticipating* high-risk situations), in Phase II clients are asked to actually *enter* the high-risk situations that they have identified as problematic. For this reason, care should be taken to assist clients in engineering success experiences. In addition, clients should be encouraged to draw upon as wide a variety of coping strengths and resources as possible. As the client's confidence grows, he or she moves up the hierarchy to increasingly more difficult situations. At this later stage, a slip or "lapse" is unlikely to be the major setback it might have been early in treatment, because the client has already begun to experience a snowball effect in the growth of self-efficacy. By the end of treatment, the client should take most of the responsibility for designing his or her own homework assignments (Annis, et al., 1996b).

Cognitive Behavioral Group Treatment

Cognitive behavioral group treatment is an effective means of delivering outpatient, research-based treatment interventions. Research comparing individual with group alcohol treatment modalities suggests that client outcomes do not differ with respect to attendance, completion, and drinking outcome measures (Sobell, et al., 1995; Graham, et al., 1996). This suggests that group clients do not suffer from a lack of individualized counselor attention. Indeed, there are many therapeutic advantages to groups, including behavioral rehearsal and modeling, mutual support, peer acceptance, and a "motivational boost" from other group members (Upper & Flowers, 1994). As Heimberg et al. (1995) point out,

> group members can provide more credible feedback on the quality of an individual's performance than can an individual therapist. During cognitive restructuring, group members often provide evidence to counter a fellow member's distorted thinking. The group may also provide substantial opportunity for vicarious learning and social support. (Heimberg, et al., 1995, p. 297)

In addition, the cost effectiveness of brief (12 sessions or less) group treatment has made it an attractive treatment option within many programs.

Because treatment sessions are limited, realistic goal setting and attention to the task focus are crucial. For example, individuals wishing to explore unconscious motivations and desires, those with lengthy, chronic alcohol abuse histories, and those wishing to gain insight into the childhood precursors of their dependence might benefit from a longer-term, more psychotherapeutically oriented treatment (Dies, 1994). However for

Figure 24-4
Weekly Plan—Initiation Phase

Name: _____ Substance:_____ Date: _____

Structured Relapse Prevention
Initiation Phase – Weekly Plan

The early weeks of changing your alcohol or drug use can be a challenging time. We call this early period of behavior change the "initiation phase," which can last for anywhere from 1 month to much longer. Research has shown that "initiating" a change in your behavior is easier and more effective when you use some of the following powerful strategies.

- Think about what you have to lose if you don't change. What are the factors "pushing" you to change your drinking or drug use at this time?
- Think about situations that could arise that might present a risk for you. Plan ahead of time what you will do so that you aren't caught off guard.
- Avoid risky places and alcohol- or drug-using friends.
- Involve your spouse, another family member, a trusted friend or sponsor.
- During the first couple of weeks of changing your drinking or drug use, living in a supportive environment can be especially helpful.
- If you want to stop drinking, consider discussing the use of alcohol-sensitizing or anticraving medication (such as Antabuse, Temposil, or naltrexone) with your doctor. These drugs can be a big help in getting you over those difficult first few weeks.
- Set a goal for your drinking or drug use—make a commitment to yourself.

Below is some space for you to think about what you would like to accomplish in the coming week and how you will do so.

GOAL:_____ Confidence in achieving this goal: ☐
0% ☐ 20% ☐ 40% ☐ 60% ☐ 80% ☐ 100%

---

many clients, brief, focused group treatment is an appropriate starting point with a number of significant advantages.

A key therapeutic task in time-limited group treatment is maintaining a "here-and-now" focus on helping clients to make changes in their drinking. This means that counselors must look to balancing the activity levels in the group, with attention to both content *and* group process. For exam-

Describe **TWO SUBSTANCE USE TRIGGERS** that are likely to arise over the coming week: **Indicate the following:** Where will you be? What time of day? Who, if anyone, will be present? What will you be doing, thinking, feeling?	Describe **SEVERAL COPING STRATEGIES** for each of the two triggers that you will be prepared to use: **You may want to** use some of the strategies listed above, or plan other ways of coping that will work for you.

Source: H. Annis, M. Herie, & L. Watkin-Merek, *Structured Relapse Prevention: An Outpatient Counselling Approach.* Toronto: Addiction Research Foundation, 1996.

ple, the counselor might manage such content as the exploration of high-risk drinking situations while attending to such process variables as eye contact, effective use of silence, and the facilitation of client-to-client interactions. Counselors can assist the group in maintaining a task-oriented focus by asking questions like the following:

- How does that relate to your drinking?
- Is that something you would like to change about yourself?

Figure 24-5
Weekly Plan—Maintenance Phase

Name: _____ Substance:_____ Date: _____

Structured Relapse Prevention
Maintenance Phase – Weekly Plan

Congratulations! You've successfully made some changes in your drinking or drug use. The next step is to maintain those changes and prevent relapse. Research has shown that two of the most powerful strategies for maintaining behavior change are to:

(1) take stock of all of the high risk situations that you are likely to encounter as a natural part of your lifestyle, and
(2) gradually enter these situations, starting with lower risk and working your way up.

The idea behind planning to enter situations in which you might be tempted to drink or use drugs is that, if these situations are likely to arise at some point, it's better for you to be in control of where and when they do. The following are a few more tips for maintaining behavior change.

- Experience each risk situation a few times before moving on to the next one.
- Make sure that you take the credit for success! For example, in the initiation phase of change, we encouraged you to seek the support of others. Now that you are learning to maintain change, it's important for you to know that you can "do it on your own" if you have to.
- Make sure that the situation you plan to enter is challenging, but not *too* challenging.
- If you find that you are having difficulty with entering high-risk situations, you may be moving too quickly. Take your time! You can always go back to using some of the initiation strategies (like avoiding people, places, and things or relying on the support of others) until you feel more confident.

Setting a goal and planning to enter risk situations are two powerful strategies to help maintain changes in your drinking or drug use. Below is some space for you to plan what you would like to accomplish in the coming week.

GOAL:_____ Confidence in achieving this goal: □
0% □ 20% □ 40% □ 60% □ 80% □ 100%

HOMEWORK ASSIGNMENT Planned Exposure to a Substance Use Trigger	OUTCOME REPORT
Describe triggering situation: _____ _____ _____ Planned Experience: When? _____ Where? _____ Who present? _____ **Coping Plan** (be specific, describe exactly what you will say and do, what you will be thinking, etc.): _____ _____ _____ _____	Did you attempt this assignment? ☐ No ☐ Yes Were you successful? ☐ No ☐ Yes Comment: _____ _____ _____ _____ Did you use? ☐ No ☐ Yes If Yes, how much? _____ What, if anything, might you try doing differently next time?____ _____ _____ _____ _____

continued

- Is what's happening in the group right now helping you make progress on coping with your drinking triggers? (Dies, 1994)

Table 24–2 summarizes feasible client goals for time-limited group treatment, along with procedural and group process guidelines for counselors.

Of the many curative factors in group treatment, the most central include group cohesion, universality (perceived similarity to others), reality testing, mutual aid, vicarious and interpersonal learning, and catharsis (Upper & Flowers, 1994). Of these, building group cohesion is of particular importance in facilitating a well-functioning group. Counselors can increase cohesion among members by identifying similarities among clients, eliciting "I" and "we" statements, reinforcing client-to-client interaction, directing eye contact with clients, and redirecting questions and disclosures to the group (e.g., "How do others feel about . . . ?").

HOMEWORK ASSIGNMENT Planned Exposure to a Substance Use Trigger	OUTCOME REPORT
Describe triggering situation: _____ _____ _____	Did you attempt this assignment? ☐ No ☐ Yes Were you successful? ☐ No ☐ Yes
Planned Experience: When?	Comment: _____ _____ _____
Where? _____	_____
Who present? _____	Did you use? ☐ No ☐ Yes If Yes, how much? _____
Coping Plan (be specific, describe exactly what you will say and do, what you will be thinking, etc.): _____ _____ _____ _____	What, if anything, might you try doing differently next time?____ _____ _____ _____ _____

Figure 24–5 continued

Because the efficacy of unstructured group psychotherapy for treating alcohol problems has not been well supported by research (Finney & Monahan, 1996; Miller, et al., 1995), more structured interventions seem indicated. Integrating structure with group process means guiding members through the stages of group development (preliminary, beginning, middle, and termination phases; see Yalom, 1985), while introducing content that complements these stages. Earlier sessions, which may be characterized by more information sharing and less self-disclosure, should give way to increased client participation and feedback as trust and cohesiveness within the group increase. The effectiveness of cognitive behavioral group treatment lends support to the saying that "it is often easier to act your-

HOMEWORK ASSIGNMENT Planned Exposure to a Substance Use Trigger	OUTCOME REPORT
Describe triggering situation: _____ _____ _____ Planned Experience: When? _____ Where? _____ Who present? _____ **Coping Plan** (be specific, describe exactly what you will say and do, what you will be thinking, etc.): _____ _____ _____ _____	Did you attempt this assignment? ☐ No ☐ Yes Were you successful? ☐ No ☐ Yes Comment: _____ _____ _____ _____ Did you use? ☐ No ☐ Yes If Yes, how much? _____ What, if anything, might you try doing differently next time?____ _____ _____ _____ _____

Source: H. Annis, M. Herie, & L. Watkin-Merek, *Structured Relapse Prevention: An Outpatient Counselling Approach*. Toronto: Addiction Research Foundation, 1996.

self into a new way of thinking than to think yourself into a new way of acting" (Dies, 1994, p. 89).

Marital/Family Therapy

Social supports have consistently been found to be associated with positive treatment outcomes; and families represent one of the most important sources of relational social supports. A number of general approaches to family therapy may be applied to work with families in which one or more members is alcohol dependent. These include structural, strategic, behavioral, solution-focused and multigenerational/Bowenian models (Boudreau, 1997).

Stanton and Todd (1992) have demonstrated the effectiveness of struc-

Table 24–2   Client Goals and Group Guidelines

Client Goals for Treatment	Procedural and Process Guidelines
Symptomatic relief	*Procedural Guidelines*
Development of social skills	Therapist as gatekeeper
Self-concept restructuring	Boundary issues (e.g., lateness,
Learning problem-solving	attendance)
strategies	Member responsibilities
Behavioral skills practice	(e.g., completing homework
(e.g., assertiveness in	assignments)
refusing alcohol)	Confidentiality
Self-reflection	Socializing outside of the group
Experiencing peer acceptance	Nonviolence
Desensitizing interpersonal	No smoking, eating, etc.
anxieties	
Modifying dysfunctional	*Group Process Guidelines*
thoughts	Encourage "I" statements
Emotional catharsis	No "shoulds" or advice-giving
Understanding of others'	Avoid question-and-answer trap
thoughts, feelings, and	Active listening/involvement
actions	Eye contact
Enhancing self-awareness	Openness to risk-taking and
	attempting new behaviors
	Supportiveness
	Sharing feelings about events within
	sessions
	No turn-taking format—
	"think group!"
	Balanced level of member
	participation

Source: Adapted from R. R. Dies (1994), p. 70.

tural approaches in family therapy with substance abusers. Behavioral marital/family therapies with a focus on teaching communication skills and increasing the level of positive reinforcement within relationships also have considerable empirical support (Miller, et al., 1995). While other marital/family approaches with families in which alcohol dependence is an issue are not as well supported, their clinical utility should not be ruled out. More research is needed to determine the relative efficacy of the various approaches.

The analysis of family dynamics in families of alcoholics has moved from a stress theory conception of the alcoholic as villain to a systems perspective that takes into account the contributions of all family members to family strengths and to family dysfunction. Contemporary systems theory views the family of the substance abuser as a small social system in which the substance abuse plays a central role in organizing family interaction. However, the emphasis is shifted from an exclusive focus on the drinker to the changes required to improve the functioning of the system as a whole. Bertalanffy (1956) defined a system as

> ... a complex, hierarchical organization of interacting, interdependent elements characterised by stable, predictable patterns of relating among the elements. Change in one element within a system generates reactions and changes in all components.

Given the complex and reciprocal nature of family interactions, the behaviors of the drinker and other family members cannot be understood by applying simple, linear cause–effect explanations such as stress caused by the drinking. Rather they are understood as the products of *circular causality*. Since the family system is *more than the sum of its parts*, it is perceived, for purposes of analysis, to be an irreducible unit: the problem drinking and other family behaviors cannot be fully understood in isolation from the family system in which they are rooted. It follows from this logic that assessment should uniformly take the important influences of family interaction into account. Nichols and Schwartz (1995) note that where many once believed that alcoholism treatment should be primarily directed toward the individual, most now embrace the view that family counseling should be a central component of the treatment process.

The critical role of family therapy in aftercare is also acknowledged. Having organized its *equilibrium*, or balance of patterned behaviors, around the vicissitudes, unpredictability, resentments, and distrust associated with the drinking, the family might be resistant to change as the now abstinent member seeks reentry into the family circle. Indeed the family's *equilibrium*, once established, may be difficult to change by a family member or by a third party (such as a counselor). A family dynamic that remains unchanged could increase the probability that a newly abstinent family member will experience a relapse. The posttreatment period, far from being a time when family therapy is no longer needed, might be the time when it is most critical.

In family therapy, as in all alcohol treatment, ethnocultural factors play an important role in assessment and in the selection of interventions. Ethnocultural factors influence concepts of family structure, hierarchy, rules, composition, and many other features. The very definition of *family* is a culture-bound concept. In some parts of the world where polygamy is the customary marital form, an entire village might conceive itself to be an extended family. And in some cultures all aunts and uncles are considered parents and all first cousins are brothers or sisters.

Viewed cross-culturally and cross-nationally, family forms might include sibling, grandmother, nuclear, blended, extended, stem, same-sex, single-parent or consensual unions. Acceptance into membership in a family might be by choice as well as by blood or marriage. To deal with these and many other variations, Hartman (1990) offers a "self-determining" definition, where "a family is two or more individuals who define themselves as a family and who over time assume those obligations to one another that generally characterise family life." Ethnocultural influences on family structure and process interact with sociocultural influences on drinking, drinking-related behaviors, and chosen interventions to prevent and treat drinking problems.

OTHER TREATMENT CONSIDERATIONS

Client-Treatment Matching

Clients who require alcohol treatment are a heterogeneous group: there is no single intervention that works for all clients all of the time (Institute of Medicine, 1990). In spite of clients' heterogeneity, however, most treatment effectiveness research does not take individual differences into account: "In evaluating the effectiveness of alcoholism treatment, the tendency has been to look at the *overall outcome* of a particular intervention *averaged* across an *unselected* group of individuals" (Donovan & Mattson, 1994, p. 5, emphasis in original). The only major investigation of matching issues, Project MATCH (*m*atching *a*lcohol *t*reatment to *c*lient *h*eterogeneity, 1997) failed to find strong links between client factors, types of treatment, and client outcome; although the majority of subjects experienced significant and sustained reductions in alcohol use across treatment conditions.

Although definitive research-based guidelines for treatment matching are lacking, six broad principles can guide treatment selection:

1. Alcohol dependent individuals constitute a heterogeneous population, each client presenting with a mix of psychological, social, and perhaps other problems (e.g., medical, economic, legal).

2. Careful assessment will identify the currently most serious problems.
3. No single treatment will be equally effective for all clients with alcohol problems.
4. Treatment settings should provide a menu of treatment options; additional required services can be sought elsewhere through linkages with other agencies in the community.
5. The treatment system should take into account the need to coordinate helping activities, and match clients with needed services.
6. Whatever the treatment and services provided, aftercare is essential.

The choice of treatment methods must take into account, at the least, the client's presenting problems; present alcohol and other drug use patterns; behaviors when abstinent; behaviors when drinking; relationships with family, friends, and associates; education, employment, and financial status; leisure activities; and legal issues (ARF, 1997). In addition, clients may be matched to treatment based on clinical judgment, client preference, type of presenting problem(s), theoretical orientation, empirical evidence, or some combination of the above (Institute of Medicine, 1990).

Women-Sensitive Treatment Considerations

Because women's use of alcohol differs from men's use (Harrison, 1997), it makes sense that attention be given to women's particular treatment needs. A number of guidelines for women-sensitive treatment have been articulated (ARF, 1996). Women-oriented treatment programs should (ideally) offer a broad range of services (including family and children's services), or coordinate these with other programs; take a holistic approach to treatment; ensure that the physical and emotional environment is both comfortable and safe; and encourage empowerment and self-esteem (for example, through job training). Recognizing gender differences in alcohol use and abuse is also important, as is the understanding that women's treatment needs are not homogeneous.

In some cases, women-only treatment groups may be appropriate; for example, women with histories of abuse may feel safer in women-only groups. Programs that employ women in front-line and leadership positions, and that have sexual harassment policies, demonstrate support for women-centered practice at an institutional level. Finally, programs should be sensitive to all women regardless of sexual orientation, culture, age, race, or socioeconomic status (ARF, 1996).

Working with Culturally Diverse Clients

The importance of culture in determining the norms and values surrounding alcohol use cannot be overstated. Heath (1995) notes that viewing alcohol use through the lens of "science" is, itself,

> ... a profound cultural bias. ... How much more does culture influence the ways in which we think about what, where, when, how, and how much to drink; in the company of whom; in what setting; with what utensils; for what purpose; and with what results! (Heath, 1995, pp. 328–329)

It is essential that social work clinicians attempt to suspend mainstream cultural biases when intervening with North America's increasingly diverse client base. Tsang (1997) points out that "diversity" implies not only culture, ethnicity, race, language, and religion, but also people whose *experiences* differ from the mainstream. She argues that, just as culture can determine patterns of alcohol use, it can also shape the type and quality of help people seek (Tsang, 1997). If services are not responsive to culturally diverse clients, such individuals may never cross the treatment threshold.

One way that services can be more responsive is to identify the cultural obstacles to effective treatment. Draguns (1996) suggests that

> Once these barriers are identified, they can be removed and a culturally appropriate solution can be proposed. Cultures may vary in the amount of self-disclosure they may encourage, tolerate, or permit, and they may limit the settings in which such self-disclosure may occur. Admission of negative characteristics may clash with the cultural imperatives of self-presentation. ... The dilemma confronting counsellors is the degree to which they can modify their culturally rooted ideas of effective counseling while retaining the integrity and efficacy of the intended interventions. (Draguns, 1996, p. 7)

The dilemma of how to adapt and tailor research-based interventions has no simple solution. However, counselors can be guided in the process of adaptation by the clients themselves. After all, interventions are only the tools by which practitioner and client bring about change. Flexibility and an openness to alternative approaches are essential in applying structured interventions.

Pedersen and Ivey (1993) have developed a model of culture-centered training that incorporates a three-stage process of *awareness, knowledge,* and *skill. Awareness* refers to the accuracy of people's opinions, attitudes, and assumptions; culturally-defined constraints and opportunities; and individual resources, skills, and limitations. A *knowledge* of the literature necessary to understanding another culture constitutes the second stage. The third stage, *skill,* "provides the ability to do something with the awareness and knowledge people have accumulated" (Pedersen & Ivey, 1993, pp. 20–21). Ridley and Lingle (1996) identify *cultural empathy* as a particularly important skill for clinicians. Cultural empathy is defined as "seeing the world through another's eyes, hearing as they might hear, and feeling and experiencing their internal world" (Ivey, Ivey, & Simek-Morgan cited in in Ridley & Lingle, 1996, p. 27). Even if it is not possible to fully understand another's experience, counselors can and should take steps to ensure that both the treatment services they offer and their counseling style are sensitive to the needs of an increasingly diverse client population.

CONCLUSION

Alcohol problems are multifaceted, involving complex interactions among a person, a drug or drugs, and an environment. The high individual and societal costs of alcohol abuse and dependence require multiple interventions, ranging from prevention to treatment. In addition, research and treatment resources should focus on the health and social consequences of many patterns of consumption, not just on the severely dependent population.

Alcohol dependence can be defined as a cluster of physiological, behavioral, and cognitive phenomena, characterized by a strong desire to drink and continued drinking in the face of adverse consequences. Alcohol dependence has no single cause; it is generally agreed that biological, psychological, and social/environmental factors all play an important role in its etiology.

Alcohol consumption can be conceptualized as occurring along a continuum of severity, accompanied by a parallel spectrum of interventive responses. These range from brief motivational interventions or self-help approaches to longer-term outpatient or residential treatment. It is recommended that practitioners utilize treatment approaches with demonstrated empirical support, given the ethical imperative of using the "best available information," as well as current demands by funders and planners.

Social workers in nonspecialist settings can choose from a variety of effective, simple screening tools to identify clients with alcohol problems.

Screening should be regarded as a preliminary step to a more detailed problem assessment. Consistent with the increasing emphasis on broadening the base of alcohol treatment interventions, treatment approaches focusing on "problem drinkers" have been developed and tested. Brief, motivational interventions provide tools and techniques for motivating ambivalent clients to take action and to make positive changes in their drinking.

Severely dependent clients (those who would traditionally be considered "alcoholics") benefit from more intensive, directive treatment approaches. Relapse prevention helps clients to achieve long-term abstinence by focusing on the factors that initiate and maintain drinking, and by incorporating coping skills training. There are a number of advantages to offering structured interventions in a group format, including behavioral rehearsal and modeling, mutual support, peer acceptance, and a "motivational boost" from other group members. Ideally, counselors will integrate structured content with attention to group process variables. Problem drinking must also be seen in the context of family behaviors and relationships. Accordingly, treatment that includes the family helps to consolidate gains made in individual therapy and to lessen the likelihood of relapse.

Other important treatment considerations include principles of client-treatment matching, offering women-sensitive treatment, and developing awareness, knowledge, and skills in working with culturally diverse clients. Social work's traditional focus on both person and environment provides a unique basis for intervening in the complex of psychological and social problems presented by alcohol-dependent individuals. Because alcohol abuse and dependence play an important role in many other client problems, social workers in nonspecialist settings are well situated to provide alcohol counseling as part of a range of services offered.

REFERENCES

AA World Services. (1980). *Alcoholics anonymous*. New York: Author.

Abramson, M. (1991). Ethics and technological advances: Contributions of social work practice. *Social Work in Health Care, 15*, 2, 5–17.

Addiction Research Foundation. (1997). *Core client interview: Clinical research and treatment institute*. Toronto: Author.

Addiction Research Foundation. (1996). *The hidden majority: A guidebook on alcohol and other drug issues for counsellors who work with women*. Toronto: Author.

Addiction Research Foundation & Canadian Centre on Substance Abuse. (April 30 to May 1, 1993). *Moderate drinking and health. A joint policy statement based on the International Symposium on Moderate Drinking and Health, Toronto, Canada*. Toronto: Author.

American Psychiatric Association. (1994). *Diagnostic and statistical manual of mental disorders, fourth edition*. Washington, DC: Author.

Anderson, P. (1996). WHO Working Group on population levels of alcohol consumption. *Addiction, 91,* 2, 275–283.

Annis, H. M. (1986). A relapse prevention model for treatment of alcoholics. In W. R. Miller & N. Heather (Eds.), *Treating addictive behaviors: Processes of change* (pp. 407–421). New York: Plenum.

Annis, H. M. (1991). A cognitive–social learning approach to relapse: Pharmacotherapy and relapse prevention counselling. *Alcohol and Alcoholism, Suppl. 1,* 527–530.

Annis, H. M., & Davis, C. S. (1989a). Relapse prevention. In T. B. Baker & D. S. Cannon (Eds.), *Handbook of alcoholism treatment approaches* (pp. 170–182). New York: Pergamon.

Annis, H. M., & Davis, C. S. (1989b). Relapse prevention training: A cognitive-behavioral approach based on self-efficacy theory. *Journal of Chemical Dependency Treatment, 2,* 2, 81–103.

Annis, H. M., Herie, M. A., & Watkin-Merek, L. (1996a). *Structured relapse prevention: An outpatient counselling approach.* Toronto: Addiction Research Foundation.

Annis, H. M., Schober, R., & Kelly, E. (1996b). Matching addiction outpatient counselling to client readiness for change: The role of structured relapse prevention counselling. *Experimental and Clinical Psychopharmacology, 4,* 1, 37–45.

Anton, R. (1994). Medications for treating alcoholism. *Alcohol Health & Research World, 18,* 4, 265–271.

Ashley, M. J., & Symposium Participants. (1994). Moderate drinking and health: Report of an international symposium. *Canadian Medical Association Journal, 151,* 6, 809–828.

Ashley, M. J., & Committee. (1996). A Report of the Committee to Recommend Draft Guidelines on Low-Risk Drinking for the Province of Ontario. Low-Risk Drinking Guidelines Project. Phase 1: Review of scientific evidence. Toronto: Addiction Research Foundation.

Babor, T. F. (1990). Social, scientific, and medical issues in the definition of alcohol and drug dependence. In G. Edwards & M. Lader (Eds.), *The nature of drug dependence.* Society for the Study of Addiction Monograph No. 1 (pp. 19–36). Oxford: Oxford University Press.

Babor, T. F., & Grant, M. (Eds.). (1992). *Project on identification and treatment of alcohol-related problems: Report on Phase 2: A randomized clinical trial of brief interventions in primary health care.* Geneva: World Health Organization Division of Mental Health.

Bandura, A. (1986). *Social foundations of thought and action: A social cognitive theory.* Englewood Cliffs, NJ: Prentice-Hall.

Bertalanffy. (1956). General systems theory. *General systems theory yearbook,* Vol. 1.

Boudreau, R. (1997). Addiction and the family. In S. Harrison & V. Carver (Eds.), *Alcohol and drug problems* (2nd Ed.). Toronto: Addiction Research Foundation.

Carroll, K. M. (1996). Relapse prevention as a psychosocial treatment: A review of controlled clinical trials. *Experimental and Clinical Psychopharmacology, 4,* 46–73.

Cooney, N. L., Zweben, A., & Fleming, M. F. (1995). Screening for alcohol problems and at-risk drinking in health-care settings. In R. K. Hester & W. R. Miller (Eds.), *Handbook of alcoholism treatment approaches: Effective alternatives* (2nd Ed., pp. 45–60). Boston: Allyn & Bacon.

DeHoyos, G. (1989). Person-in-environment: A tri-level practice model. *Social Casework,* 131–138.

Dies, R. R. (1994). The therapist's role in group treatment. In H. S. Bernard & K. R. MacKenzie (Eds.), *Basics of group psychotherapy* (pp. 60–99). New York: Guilford Press.

Donovan, D. M., & Marlatt, G. A. (1988). *Assessment of addictive behaviors.* New York: Guilford Press.

Donovan, D. M., & Mattson, M. E. (1994). Alcoholism treatment matching research: Methodological and clinical issues. *Journal of Studies on Alcohol, Suppl. 12,* 5–14.

Draguns, J. (1996). Humanly universal and culturally distinctive: Charting the course of cultural counseling. In P. B. Pedersen, et al. (Eds.), *Counseling across cultures* (4th ed., pp. 1–20). Thousand Oaks, CA: Sage.

Ellis, A., & Velten, E. (1992). *Rational steps to quitting alcohol.* Fort Lee, NJ: Barricade Books.

Finney, J. W., & Monahan, S. C. (1996). The cost-effectiveness of treatment for alcoholism: A second approximation. *Journal of Studies on Alcohol, 57,* 229–243.

Gorey, K. M. (1996). Effectiveness of social work intervention research: Internal versus external evaluations. *Social Work Research, 20,* 2, 119–128.

Graham, K., et al. (1996). A controlled field trial of group versus individual cognitive-behavioral training for relapse prevention. *Addiction, 91,* 8, 1127–1139.

Harrison, S. (1997). Working with women. In S. Harrison & V. Carver (Eds.), *Alcohol & drug problems: A practical guide for counsellors* (2nd Ed., pp. 219–243). Toronto: Addiction Research Foundation.

Hartman, A. (1990). Family ties. *Social Work, 35,* 3, 193–198.

Heath, D. B. (Ed). (1995). *International handbook on alcohol and culture.* Westport, CT: Greenwood Press.

Heimberg, R. G., Juster, H. R., Hope, D. A., & Mattia, M. A. (1995). Cognitive behavioral group treatment for social phobia: Description, case presentation, and empirical support. In M. B. Stein (Ed.), *Social phobia: Clinical and research perspectives.* Washington, DC: American Psychiatric Press.

Hester, R. K. (1995). Behavioral self-control training. In R. K. Hester & W. R. Miller (Eds.), *Handbook of alcoholism treatment approaches: Effective alternatives* (2nd Ed., pp. 148–159). Boston: Allyn & Bacon.

Holder, H., et al. (1991). The cost-effectiveness of treatment for alcoholism: A first approximation. *Journal of Studies on Alcohol, 52,* 517–540.

Institute of Medicine. (1990). *Broadening the base of treatment for alcohol problems.* Washington, DC: National Academy Press.

Ivey, A. E., Ivey, M. B., & Simek-Morgan, L. (1993). *Counseling and psychotherapy* (3rd Ed.). Boston: Allyn & Bacon.

Kahan, M. (1997). Physical effects of alcohol and other drugs. In S. Harrison & V. Carver (Eds.), *Alcohol & drug problems: A practical guide for counsellors* (2nd Ed., pp. 185–201). Toronto: Addiction Research Foundation.

Kishline, A. (1994). *Moderate drinking: The new option for problem drinkers.* Tucson, AZ: See Sharp Press.

Klein, W. C., & Bloom, M. (1994). Is there an ethical responsibility to use practice methods with the best empirical evidence of effectiveness? In W. W. Hudson and P. S. Nurius (Eds.), *Controversial issues in social work research.* Boston: Allyn & Bacon.

Marlatt, G. A., & Gordon, J. R. (1985). *Relapse prevention: Maintenance strategies in the treatment of addictive behaviors.* New York: Guilford Press.

Martin, G. (Chair). (1990). *Treating alcohol and drug problems in Ontario: A vision for the 90's.* Report of the Advisory Committee on Drug Treatment. Toronto: Minister Responsible for the Provincial Anti-drug Strategy,

Mayfield, D., McLeod, G., & Hall, P. (1974). The CAGE questionnaire: Validation of a new alcoholism screening instrument. *American Journal of Psychiatry, 131,* 10, 1121–1123.

McCrady, B. S., & Delaney, S. I. (1995). Self-help groups. In R. K. Hester & W. R. Miller (Eds.), *Handbook of alcoholism treatment approaches: Effective alternatives* (2nd Ed., pp. 160–175). Boston: Allyn & Bacon.

Miller, W. R. (1995). Increasing motivation for change. In R. K. Hester & W. R. Miller (Eds.), *Handbook of alcoholism treatment approaches: Effective alternatives* (2nd Ed., pp. 89–104). Boston: Allyn & Bacon.

Miller, W. R., et al. (1995). What works? A methodological analysis of the alcohol treatment outcome literature. In R. K. Hester & W. R. Miller (Eds.), *Handbook of alcoholism treatment approaches* (pp. 12–40). Toronto: Allyn & Bacon.

Miller, W. R., & Rollnick, S. (1991). *Motivational interviewing*. New York: Guilford Press.

Miller, W. R., Sovereign, R. G., & Krege, B. (1988). Motivational interviewing with problem drinkers: II. The drinker's check-up as a preventive intervention. *Behavioural Psychotherapy, 16,* 251–268.

Moser, A. E., & Annis., H. M. (1996). The role of coping in relapse crisis outcome: A prospective study of treated alcoholics. *Addiction, 91,* 8, 1101–1113.

National Institute on Alcohol Abuse and Alcoholism. (1997). *Ninth special report to the U.S. Congress on alcohol and health.* Rockville, MD: Author.

Nichols, M. P., & Schwartz, R. C. (1995). *Family therapy: Concepts and methods.* Boston: Allyn & Bacon.

Ogborne, A. C. (1997). Theories of "addiction" and implications for counselling. In S. Harrison and V. Carver (Eds.), *Alcohol & drug problems: A practical guide for counsellors* (2nd Ed., pp. 3–18). Toronto: Addiction Research Foundation.

Pedersen, P., & Ivey, A. E. (1993). *Culture-centered counseling and interviewing skills: A practical guide.* Westport, CT: Praeger.

Prochaska, J. O., & DiClemente, C. C. (1984). *The transtheoretical approach: Crossing traditional boundaries of therapy.* Homewood, IL: Dow Jones/Irwin.

Prochaska, J. O., Norcross, J. C., & DiClemente, C. C. (1994). *Changing for good.* New York: William Morrow.

Rankin, J. G., & Ashley, M. J. (1992). Alcohol-related health problems. In J. M. Last & R. B. Wallace (Eds.), *Public health and preventive medicine* (pp. 741–767). Norwalk, CT: Appleton & Lange.

Ridley, C. R., & Lingle, D. W. (1996). Cultural empathy in multicultural counseling. In P. B. Pedersen, et al. (Eds.), *Counseling across cultures* (4th Ed., pp. 21–46). Thousand Oaks, CA: Sage.

Rogers, C. R. (1959). A theory of therapy, personality, and interpersonal relationships as developed in the client-centered framework. In S. Koch (Ed.), *Formulations of the person and the social context.* Vol. 3 of *Psychology: The study of a science* (pp. 184–256). New York: McGraw-Hill.

Rollnick, S. (1985). The value of a cognitive-behavioral approach in the treatment of problem drinkers. In N. Heather, I. Robertson, & P. Davies (Eds.), *The misuse of alcohol: Crucial issues in dependence treatment and prevention* (pp. 135–157). New York: New York University Press.

Russell, M. (1994). New assessment tools for drinking in pregnancy: T-ACE, TWEAK, and others. *Alcohol Health & Research World,* 55–61.

Sanchez-Craig, M., et al. (1989). Superior outcome of females over males after brief treatment for the reduction of heavy drinking. *British Journal of Addiction, 84,* 395–404.

Saunders, B., & Wilkinson, C. (1990). Motivation and addiction behaviour: A psychological perspective. *Drug and Alcohol Review, 9,* 133–142.

Single, E., et al. (1996). *The costs of substance abuse in Canada.* Ottawa: Canadian Centre on Substance Abuse.

Skinner, H. (1990). Spectrum of drinkers and intervention opportunities. *Canadian Medical Association Journal, 143,* 10, 1054–1059.

Skinner, H. A. (1982). *Drug abuse screening test.* Toronto: Addiction Research Foundation.

Skinner, H. A., & Horn, J. L. (1984). *Alcohol dependence scale: User's guide.* Toronto: Addiction Research Foundation.

Sobell, L. C., & Sobell, M. B. (1992). Timeline followback: A technique for assessing self-reported ethanol consumption. In J. Allen & R. Z. Litten (Eds.), *Measuring alco-*

hol consumption: Psychosocial and biological methods (pp. 41–72). Totowa, NJ: Humana Press.

Sobell, L. C., et al. (1995, November). A randomized trial comparing group versus individual guided self-change treatment for alcohol and drug abusers. Paper presented at the Annual Meeting for the Association for the Advancement of Behavior Therapy, Washington, DC.

Stanton, M. D., & Todd, T. C. (1992). Structural-strategic family therapy with drug addicts. In E. Kaufman & P. Kaufman (Eds.), Family therapy of drug and alcohol abuse (2nd Ed., pp. 46–62). Toronto: Allyn & Bacon.

Tsang, B. (1997). Counselling culturally diverse clients. In S. Harrison & V. Carver (Eds.), Alcohol and drug problems: A practical guide for counsellors (2nd Ed., pp. 359–397). Toronto: Addiction Research Foundation.

Tucker, J. A., Vuchinich, R. E., & Gladsjo, J. A. (1994). Environmental events surrounding natural recovery from alcohol-related problems. Journal of Studies on Alcohol, 55, 401–411.

Upper, D., & Flowers, J. V. (1994). Behavioral group therapy in rehabilitation settings. In J. R. Bedell (Ed.), Psychological assessment and treatment of persons with severe mental disorders (pp. 191–214). Washington, DC: Taylor & Francis.

van Ginnekan, S. (1992). Arguments against a safe drinking limit. Paper presented at the 36th International Congress on Alcohol and Drug Dependence, Glasgow, Scotland. Rijswijk, The Netherlands: Ministry of Welfare. Alcohol, Drugs and Tobacco Policy Division.

Volpicelli, J. R., et al. (1994). Naltrexone and the treatment of alcohol dependence. Alcohol Health & Research World, 18, 272–278.

Wallace, P., Cutler, S., & Haines, A. (1988). Randomized controlled trial of general practitioner intervention in patients with excessive alcohol consumption. British Medical Journal, 297, 663–668.

Wilkinson, D. A., & LeBreton, S. (1986). Early indicators of treatment outcome in multiple drug users. In W. R. Miller & N. Heather (Eds.), Treating addictive behaviors: Processes of change (pp. 239–261). New York: Plenum.

Women for Sobriety. (1976). AA and WFS. Quakertown, PA: Author.

World Health Organization. (1993). Technical report series. Geneva: Author.

Yalom, I. D. (1985). The theory and practice of group psychotherapy (3rd Ed.). New York: Basic Books.

25

DRUG ADDICTION: A BPSI MODEL

M. Dennis Kimberley and Peter Bohm

Canst thou minister to a mind diseased;
pluck from the memory a rooted sorrow;
raze out the written troubles of the brain;
and with some sweet oblivious antidote
cleanse the stuff'd bosom of that perilous stuff
which weighs upon the heart?

—Shakespeare, *Macbeth*

The perspective used in this chapter represents a biopsychosocial-interactional model (hereafter abbreviated as BPSI). It describes the interaction of intrapsychic dynamics with interpersonal relationship patterns, within the context of other social-environment transactions associated with the use and abuse of drugs. All converge to inform an integrated perspective on psychopathology that transcends more unitary visions, such as a personality-disorder model. In the *Diagnostic and Statistical Manual of Mental Disorders, Fourth Edition* (DSM-IV, American Psychiatric Association, 1994), a psychopathology paradigm, is acknowledged; however, the emphasis here is on further developing a BPSI conceptualization of social work practice. *Vignettes are based on real cases, with material disguised to protect confidentiality; there is no intention to stereotype or further marginalize any social group.*

SOCIOPOLITICAL HISTORICAL CONTEXT

Most societies and communities control or influence the use and abuse of drugs that impact biological functioning, mood, behavior, cognitive functioning, interpersonal relationships, or social functioning. In some cultures there were once legal sanctions associated with the use of low-risk caffeine (McKim, 1996). Confirmed risks, such as drug-induced psychoses, or perceived risks, such as cannabis use as a "gateway" to more risky substance use, have been sufficient to justify normative and legal proscriptions (restrictions) to control the production, distribution, and use of such drugs (Szasz, 1974). Juxtaposed are norms that legalize and prescribe the use of acceptable drugs for managing medical or mental health problems, managing addictions or drug withdrawal, supporting religious practices, or sanctioning limited personal or interpersonal recreational use (Malcolm, 1971; Rublowsky, 1974).

The public perception, both reality based and socially constructed, has been that the use and abuse of drugs "cause" risks and harm. Units of risk assessment include individuals, families, organizations, and society. In taking social responsibility for policies to control the manufacture, the distribution, and the use or abuse of controlled substances, communities must balance concern for personal, social, and economic costs with individual rights, as well as with the social and economic costs of law enforcement (Doweiko, 1996, pp. 399–414; Chein, 1964).

Within this sociopolitical context, as well as that of social humanism (Crawford, et al., 1989), early feminism (Sandmaier, 1992), structuralism (Leukefeld & Battjes, 1992; Barber, 1994) and ecosystems theory (Wallace, 1989), social workers have became actively involved in social action (e.g., in the temperance movement), promotion of legislation and formulation of policy (e.g., control of drugs), prevention (e.g., early intervention with "crack cocaine babies"), crisis intervention (e.g., detoxification services that go beyond alcohol withdrawal), assessment, treatment, and follow-up (continuing care). In the first quarter of the twentieth century, social workers expressed concern regarding the personal, marital, familial and social risks or harm associated with the use of psychoactive substances (Addams, 1912, pp. 29–31, pp. 120–145, 204; Abbott, 1927, pp. 229–234). It was not uncommon for "harm" to be framed within a concern for social problems, such as marginalization and street gangs; child abuse; social deviance such as prostitution or property crime; and community mental health problems, including parental social functioning, associated with child protection concerns (Addams, 1912; Freeman, 1992).

The concerns expressed by the clinical helping professions converged in the 1960s to guide management of what was perceived to be a "youth drug culture" crisis (Whitaker, 1969). After the 1960s, social workers were also more involved in addressing the use and abuse of mood-altering prescription drugs (MacLennan, 1976). In the absence of significant pre-existing research and practice standards, social workers were active in developing practice wisdom by immersing themselves in the problem at the street level.

DEMOGRAPHICS

The demographic characteristics of use, abuse, harm, risk, and success in treatment vary in time and place. In one era cocaine might be the preferred drug of affluent professionals; in another era crack cocaine could be observed as being the choice of the unskilled poor and highly marginalized people (White, 1991, pp. 164–205). Cannabis derivatives may be used by particular subcultures in one period (Whitaker, 1969). Today the use of cannabis in Western society appears to be more widespread.

Males dominate what is referred to as "heavy drug" abuse activities and they are more likely than females to die of overdose or other complications (Lester, 1992). The onset and path that women drug users present may be different from those of men. Females enter treatment through mental health services and are overrepresented among users of prescription drugs (Doweiko, 1996, pp. 259–267). Whereas females are more likely to attempt suicide using chemicals, males are more likely to be successful in their suicide attempt (Lester, 1992). In caseloads, beyond addiction treatment programs, suicide prevention programs, and mental health centers, males are likely to be charged in property crime and assault cases; females are likely to be charged in prostitution and child protection cases.

In North America, patterns of drug use in African-American and Hispanic communities appear to have varied from one period to another. African-Americans and Hispanics may be overrepresented in their use of illicit drugs, especially heroin and cocaine. What is equally significant is the overrepresentation of African-Americans and Hispanics in the marginalized and criminalized subgroups. In their communities access to prevention, assessment, and treatment programs, cultural sensitivity of such programs, and openness to treatment may vary from middle-class and "white community" norms. For in-depth analysis of these issues the reader is referred to John, et al. (1997), Ruiz and Langrod (1997), and Westermeyer (1997).

TERMS, DIAGNOSIS, CLASSIFICATION, AND ASSESSMENT

Problems of Use

There is no universally supported classification for drugs or for BPSI problems associated with use and abuse of drugs, drug dependence, or drug addiction. Beyond the issue of legal prohibition, both use and abuse may be associated with risk and harm. The risk and harm may be in relation to significant others in the person's social life and also to other members of the community. For example, if a treated sex offender uses a drug that, at low concentrations, is associated with disinhibition, impaired judgment, or sensate stimulation, then his risk of reoffense may increase significantly. Furthermore, social work assessment of risk, harm, need, and strengths must be individualized and contextual.

Constructively confronting *problems of use* is sensitive in that the client's right to self-determination may conflict with the social worker's concerns about risks to self and others. Risks and observable harmful effects associated with use, even if concrete and persistent, are easy for the "user" to deny or minimize. A worker's decision not to intervene because the risks do not involve directly harming others must be considered in context. For example, how well can a parent whose judgment is impaired by low concentrations of cannabis or normal concentrations of diazepam (Valium) supervise a preschool child consistently, safely, and effectively? Such clinical decisions are important and complex.

There is no single system of diagnosis, assessment, or classification that constitutes a universal standard of practice for social workers. However, useful *perspectives for classification and assessment* for social work practice include

- behavioral pharmacology classification (McKim, 1996; Doweiko, 1996)
- mental disorder diagnosis (*DSM-IV*)
- BPSI Functioning Assessment (Kimberley, et al., 1996; Clarke & Kimberley, 1997)

Behavioral Psychopharmacology Classification

A *drug* may be conceptualized as a chemical substance that, when ingested, acknowledging individual differences and interactive effects, results in a relatively predictable range of biochemical, neurological, affective, cognitive and/or behavioral responses (Doweiko, 1996; McKim, 1996; White, 1991).

When the drug is absorbed into the body, the user experiences those responses, some of which are more available to consciousness than others (e.g., agitation versus numbing anesthetization). Treatment must be sensitive to dose-response patterns, as users typically choose drugs to achieve specific effects on BPSI functioning. The more direct effects are often mediated by a set of expectations regarding interpersonal "effects" of the drug as well.

Blood concentrations of the psychoactive components of the drug are associated with variables such as harm or risk associated with use, and patterns of use to which one may apply the term *abuse*. This term is often associated with excessive intake (based on social, medical, or psychosocial functioning norms) or excessive dose responses: response speed, intensity, lag time, duration and dissipation of effects associated with the dose and form of the drug. Clinical judgments take into account medical use as prescribed, biomedical harm or risk, psychosocial functioning, harm or risk; or social functioning problems and associated social risks (White, 1991, pp. 6–8; Doweiko, 1996; McKim, 1996).

The application of the term *abuse,* from a clinical perspective, is also related to *modes of ingestion* and the harm or risks related to the avenue chosen to get the drug into the body. For example, the sharing of needles with others is more clearly risky to self and others for HIV transmission than is eating a "hash brownie." Modes of use that increase rate and intensity of impact are often likely to be defined as being more risky or more harmful. For example, "snorting" cocaine increases the speed and intensity of the user's subjective euphoria but it injures the membranes of the nose.

The class of drug that is used (assuming relatively low doses and low concentrations) is associated with complex judgments regarding potential harm and risk, including the risk of "addiction"—tolerance, physical dependence, chronicity, compulsivity, and withdrawal effects. Each of these phenomena is associated with variations in relatively direct impacts of drugs on affect, cognitive functioning, perception, behavior and social functioning, let alone biomedical risks.

The following *classification system* is close to that suggested by McKim (1996). The following notes on the use and short-term effects of the major classes of psychoactive drugs are paraphrases that summarize the work of several authors (McKim, 1996; Doweiko, 1996; and White, 1991):

- *Alcohol* reduces inhibitions, induces euphoria, and impairs cognitive functioning.
- *Benzodiazepines,* such as diazepam (Valium), reduce anxiety, induce relaxation, and promote sleep.

- *Barbiturates,* such as phenobarbital, impair consciousness and induce sleep.
- *Tobacco* promotes a subjective sense of relaxation.
- *Caffeine and the methylxanthines,* found in tea, coffee, and chocolate, stimulate and maintain cognitive arousal.
- *Psychomotor stimulants,* such as methamphetamine and cocaine, improve mood, induce "high spirits" or euphoria, and promote alertness, attention, or extended sexual performance.
- *Opiates,* such as morphine, heroin, and synthetic opiates like (Demerol), create a "sleepy sensation," promote intense pleasure resembling orgasm, promote vivid daydreams, and inhibit the subjective sensation of pain. This inhibition is often referred to as "numbing."
- *Antipsychotics,* also referred to as neoroleptics, or major tranquilizers such as phenothiazines, are rarely abused in a dependent pattern but may be used to induce dissociative responses and sedating effects.
- *Antidepressants and antimanics,* such as Prozac and lithium carbonate (Lithium) respectively, are used to create a sense of elation, generalized improved mood and/or a sense of normalcy.
- *Cannabis* induces "placid dreaminess" and feelings of euphoria, as well as the subjective effect of increased sensory sensitivity (McKim, 1996, pp. 293–299).
- *Hallucinogens,* such as LSD and mescaline, alter perceptions of "reality," including visual, auditory, and tactile perceptions.
- *Solvents and gases,* such as gasoline or glue, are used to induce euphoric effects and/or a subjective sense of numbing.

Drugs are used to alter normal-range affect, cognitive functioning, perception, and behavior. There may be an interactive effect with conscious expectations, social function, or unconscious desires (e.g., the wish to abdicate adult responsibility). Some levels of use may be defined as abusive or problematic; BPSI functioning, including reality testing, is impacted negatively, and risks, including medical risks (or harm), may be increased for the user. The social worker must not only help assess dose response issues, risks, and level of abuse but must also determine whether the client's *drug of choice* is significant for psychodynamic reasons (e.g., reinforcing dissociative responses or defensive routines) or psychosocial reasons (e.g., inhalant abuse associated with the social support of marginal group membership). Multiple drug use and cross-tolerances among chemicals may render differential assessment and risk management more complex and less reliable.

Problem use of drugs is usually associated with excessive use in terms of frequency and dose, as well as with the intensity and duration of response at affective, cognitive, behavioral, relational, and social functioning levels. Chronicity and medical complications add to confidence in the application of the term *problem*. In addition, contextual variables may expand the boundary of problem definition; for example, a person who engages in prostitution to support a "habit," or who puts others at risk in the workplace, would likely have his or her use defined by professionals as *abuse* or *problematic*. Uncertainties of differential assessment in the convergence of use, abuse, and problem patterns is complex—and is compounded by uncertain rules of clinical observation and judgment. Although there is a constructionist process in definition, there is also empirical validation of the application of the above classifications in that drug use/abuse is associated with verifiable harm and risks, such as: sleep disorders (benzodiazepines); seizures (e.g., opiates); organ failure (e.g., cocaine abuse); coma (e.g., barbiturates), death (e.g., accidental "suicide" with barbiturates), anxiety disorder (caffeine, amphetamines); depression or suicidal feelings (psychomotor stimulants); tardive dyskinesia (antipsychotics); sexual and reproductive dysfunction (antidepressants and antimanics, respectively); short-term memory problems, dissociation, and attention deficits (cannabis); psychosis (e.g., hallucinogens); central nervous system and kidney damage (solvent-inhalants). For more detail the reader is referred to McKim (1996) and Doweiko (1996).

The concepts of *addiction, withdrawal, tolerance,* and *physical dependence* are associated (Doweiko, 1996). At a subjective level, users describe their "psychopathology" or "illness" in terms of "urges," "habits," "compulsions," and "lost control." The vagueness of the terms is useful in supporting part of the addict's defensive routine—which includes denial, minimization, and externalization.

Repeated use of many drugs is associated with the development of some pattern of *tolerance*. One indicator of heavy and repeated use of a mood-altering chemical is that more of the drug is required to ensure a response or to maintain related effects (pharmacodynamic tolerance). Other drugs within a pharmacological class may exhibit cross-tolerance effects, which have a compond effect on the development of tolerance. Development of tolerance is also associated with the "withdrawal syndrome."

[T]he withdrawal syndrome is caused by the absence of the chemical the central nervous system had previously adapted to. When the
drug is discontinued, the central nervous system goes through a
period of readaptation as it learns to function normally again.
(Doweiko, 1996, p. 4)

The dynamic interplay of tolerance and withdrawal is partially responsible for the user's subjective feeling of being physically dependent. Biochemical adaption may be framed as being the objective experience of
dependence. The dependence observed when tolerance and withdrawal
dynamics are not operating, or are weak, is usefully framed as *psychological dependence*. Below, the authors address an integrative notion, consistent with the person-in-environment theories of social work—a model of
BPSI dependence.

In ending this section, it is important that we reflect on the issue of
psychopharmacological determinism and the attribution of personal and
social responsibility. A person may consciously choose to ingest a drug,
often aware of at least some of its expected effects. On the other hand,
both objectively and subjectively, most drugs impact affect (e.g., disinhibition or irritability) and cognitive function (e.g., impaired judgment or
perception, blackouts, or increased arousal). To assess that the client's BPSI
function is fully under conscious self-control would be a disservice to the
client. There are limits to self-determination for many clients until they
achieve sufficient sobriety that they are able to resume more self-control
over the expression of their affect, cognitive functioning and behavior.
Notwithstanding interaction with expectation effects, the social worker
may be called upon to offer a clinical judgment regarding the responsibility, culpability, and self-control of a client who acted while under the influence of drugs. In the extreme, detoxification and residential or institutional
treatment may be recommended until the client feels less "out of control"
and more self-efficacious, within the context of self-control and active self-
determination.

Mental Disorder Diagnosis (DSM-IV)

The *Diagnostic and Statistical Manual of Mental Disorders* (DSM-IV,
American Psychiatric Association, 1994) conceptualizes *substance-related
disorders* in part using drug classifications as described above (pp.
176–181). Within the context of each drug class, emphasis is on differential diagnosis based on notions of *physical dependence* similar to those

addressed in the discussion of psychopharmacology. In addition, *DSM-IV* criteria for substance dependence deal with the *importance of intentionality.* Ingesting larger amounts of a substance than intended, failure to control use when "there is a persistent desire to do so" (p. 181), much energy spent in obtaining the drug, displacing normal activities, and the decision to continue to use a chemical in the face of harm or risk are all viewed as maladaptive indicators of physical or psychological dependence.

The diagnostic system of "disorders" in *DSM-IV* is clear that substance abuse should be assessed even in the absence of indicators of physical dependence. Recurrent drug use associated with risk and harm, criminal-justice problems, interpersonal problems, social problems, or failures in social functioning are all considered to be indicators of abuse. These considerations acknowledge the interaction of biological factors, psychological characteristics, and the social variables.

It is clear that differential diagnosis of indicators of intoxication juxtaposed to indicators of withdrawal is at times difficult. Notwithstanding the difficulty, the *DSM-IV* model encourages observations and judgments of "complications" associated with dependence, abuse, intoxication, withdrawal, and related paths, courses or patterns that may be expected. Using "opioid-induced disorders" as the exemplar (*DSM-IV*, p. 248), differential diagnoses suggested include:

- Opioid intoxication
- Opioid withdrawal
- Opioid intoxication delirium
- Opioid-induced psychotic disorder, with hallucinations
- Opioid-induced mood disorder
- Opioid-induced sexual dysfunction
- Opioid-induced sleep disorder

DSM-IV's mental-disorder paradigm and medical-model bias, even with the concept "disorder" displacing the "disease" metaphor, limit assessment and treatment. This psychopathology model minimizes the importance of social variables and interactional dynamics. From a BPSI functioning perspective, for example, one may consider the positive functions of use and abuse, even under conditions where the "disease-oriented" clinician might be tempted to label use or abuse as "dysfunctional."

BPSI Functioning Assessment

Beyond Disease and Psychopathology
Most often the presenting problems, or presentation of "self" of the client system, are related to personal and social functioning problems that are interactive with use of drugs. Assessment and intervention, to begin where the client is, must consider biopsychosocial interaction. Assessment must get beyond psychopharmacological "drug logs" (focusing on the drugs and effects); treatment must get beyond abstinence and behavior control; prevention must get beyond the delivery of information regarding harm and positive alternatives.

Achievement of abstinence with more control or containment of harm is a beginning that sets the stage for more substantive treatment effects. Programmatic cognitive-behavioral approaches, such as relapse prevention, may prevent relapse, but may not help the client in equally significant ways. Notions of intrapsychic disorder, mental disease, or psychopathology are not sufficient to guide all assessment or intervention. One problem level (e.g., biomedical) need not be defined as primary or causal and another (e.g., social distress) as secondary. By transcending notions of pathology, normal, noncompulsive and nonchronic use of substances may be assessed as problematic in terms of BPSI functioning. The BPSI model embraces the notion that treatment does not stop with sobriety (Cork, 1969, pp. 53–55; Clemmens, 1997).

The Biological Dimension
Assessment of the biological dimension of both problem and intervention must consider the *direct psychopharmacological effects* of a drug, such as altering visual perception, as well as biophysical effects that may "cause" medical complications. Of serious concern, for example, are effects on fetuses and on newborns of maternal drug use and drug interactions. At issue is, who constitutes the primary client? There is a competing objective of preventive measures for the unborn, as well as for those infants and young children who suffer the effects of maternal drug use (Finnegan & Kandall, 1997). Additionally, parents who continue to become less psychologically and socially functional may be confronted by a social worker providing testimony regarding harm or risks associated with parental drug use. But clients' denial, with respect to drug addiction or dependence, is often further confounded by a high degree of minimization regarding risks and impact on children. In the extreme, there are cases where children have been sexually exploited or sold to support parental drug habits.

The Psychological Dimension

The social worker must consider the interaction of three dimensions with drug use and abuse: affect, cognition, and actions. As drugs are used to modify emotions, sensations, and perceptions; consideration of interaction between affect and cognition is necessary to give direction to effective assessment and treatment.

Each drug grouping may be associated with the *creation and maintenance of a particular range of feelings and related sensations.* When the governing function of the "ego" is impaired, many clients learn to use drugs on a self-medication schedule to avoid experiencing even normal ranges of affect (Malcolm, 1971). On the other hand, even though the drugs themselves are associated with promoting and maintaining feelings such as relaxation, carelessness, numbing, or euphoria, many clients report becoming dependent on drugs to address difficult emotional states or strong emotional states that are defined by them as being "overwhelming" (Daley, 1989, pp. 8–10).

In addition there is a form of conditioning associated with "feeling good" or "feeling bad" that is partly psychosocial and interpersonal. Positive affect—"feeling good"—may be associated with social relationships and transactions related to obtaining drugs. Negative feelings of self-worth—"feeling bad"—may contribute to dependence on a chemical in order to "feel like myself." Within a marginalized community positive self-messages (dependent on an ability to buy and share drugs) reinforce a deviant identity and normalize deviance. The "successful" client may not only be giving up drugs and a lifestyle, but may also suffer from the anxiety and pain associated with loss of identity, status, and (deviant) social support.

Interacting with affect are *cognitive functioning* and *cognitive content* The clinician must attend to realities associated with disinhibition, arousal, impairment, distorted perception, and some types of cognitive degeneration. It is important to qualify that cognitive degeneration is often associated with lifestyle and nutrition as well as with chronic or heavy use of dangerous drugs such as heroin, crack cocaine, or solvents.

Of equal importance is attention to the client's beliefs, attitudes, values, motivational statements, and other "cognitive scripts" that may promote, maintain, support denial of, or encourage his minimization of the impacts of drug use. Ability for reality testing is impaired, psychodynamically (e.g., unconscious processes), psychosocially (e.g., *folie à deux*) and psychopharmacologically. The client may act out a set of drug "procuring" and "using" behaviors for which there are mutually reinforcing sets of cognitive scripts, including cognitive distortions.

Denial and minimization are to be expected and are functional in defending the stability and integration of the client's self. Unconscious processes to control anxiety are a major function of such defensive routines. In contrast, some behavioral theories do not acknowledge the significance of unconscious determinants of affect and behavior; workers may interpret clients' defensive routines as conscious and purposeful cognitive distortions. Treating defenses as if they are either maladaptive or fully available to consciousness may have serious implications for both the therapeutic relationship and for fragile egos, which may require these routines to maintain an integrated and stable self as "drug user" or an identity as a person "in control and not addicted."

A major contribution from cognitive behavioral theory is the concept of "expectation effect" (Daley, 1989; Chiauzzi, 1991, pp. 38–39). The theory is that the effect of mood- and perception-modifying chemicals, in part, is related to beliefs associated with needing, obtaining, and using the drug, as well as expectations regarding immediate effects and consequences of the drug use. The feelings, cognitive functioning, and cognitive scripts converge in mutual interaction with drug-related behavior, drug effects, and concomitant action sets.

It is important to differentiate between actions or experiences that may be

1. directly related to drug effects (e.g., agitation with stimulants);
2. related to withdrawal or chronic effects (e.g., depression with withdrawal from cocaine);
3. related to precipitating use or abuse (e.g., peer group membership);
4. associated with obtaining the drug and maintaining supply (e.g., theft or prostitution);
5. activities while disinhibited, aroused, impaired, or in an altered state of consciousness (e.g., breaching safe sex rule);
6. activities associated with attempting to control drug use or to become abstinent.

For the clinician, it is also useful to consider the onset, progression, and path of use and abuse from a behavioral perspective, even though there are obvious convergences with affect, cognition, and life situations. Contextual questions—regarding how and when use and/or abuse began and under what conditions—are significant considerations. Once the use or abuse began, what was the pattern of activity associated with obtaining drugs, maintaining the desired effect, and participating in a marginal or deviant subculture? It is important to understand parallel activities that are reflective of other, seemingly reinforcing, aspects of self-identity (e.g., being a student). Such functional analysis of relationships among onset, progression, path, context, and consequences of the development of use and abuse patterns and lifestyle are significant to both assessment and treatment (expansion of McCready, 1992). Consider the convergences and some interactions in the following case.

Carly presented as a well-groomed and exceptionally intelligent professional woman of 24 years. Presenting problems included multiple drug use and sexual activity with multiple partners. Patterns of dissociation were reinforced by the effects of alcohol and tranquilizers. High eroticization, associated developmentally with multiple experiences of sex abuse and early eroticization, was reinforced by the disinhibiting effect of alcohol and the arousing effect of cocaine. Interacting with the above was disinhibition, impairment, and the desire for euphoria and escape, as well as the expectation that she would attract and reject multiple partners. Drugs were also used to control panic and terror associated with severe sleep disturbances—revivification of trauma.

Interpersonal Relationships

Interacting with the biological, affective, cognitive, and behavioral dimensions are a number of social dimensions, the most important of which is interpersonal relationships. The interactive BPSI concept enables the observation of a mutual, though not necessarily equal, impact of each dimension on interpersonal dynamics, as well as the impact of interpersonal dynamics on every other dimension. Applying interactional theory, these dynamics and mutual impacts must be appreciated to ensure comprehensive understanding of treatment goals, targets for change, and intervention strategies (Shulman, 1992).

Psychodynamic and psychopathological orientations would suggest exploration of BPSI history and development of interpersonal relationships, the most significant often being in the formative years, with parents, siblings, and extended family. Clients might also benefit from exploration (through oral responses, interpretations of nonverbal behavior, and transference patterns) of developmental experiences that may help in understanding the progression and maintenance of drug use. Insight into developmental dynamics may also help to understand successes and failures in clients' attempts to control drug use and its consequences. Three aspects of interpersonal relationships are dominant in the development and maintenance of many drug problems: (1) anxiety and insecurity in interpersonal relationships, (2) interpersonal conflict, and (3) trauma inflicted by others.

Anxiety and *insecurity* may set the stage for the use of drugs to control feelings, create modified feelings, and manage interpersonal relationships. As in the case of Carly, children whose parents have used drugs are more likely to use and abuse drugs themselves, partly due to possible genetic determinants and partly due to modeling. She was physically and sexually abused by both parents, as well as exploited. She was "parentified" to the extent that by the age of eight she was responsible for caring for a mother who, due to multiple drug use and depression, was largely incapacitated, a father who was impaired on most days, and a dependent six-year-old brother. Interpersonal relationships were a source of insecurity, anxiety, and distrust. By the age of 13 Carly handled such feelings by using alcohol and street drugs. Her current relationships are characterized by distrust, superficiality, apprehension, and insecurity. Her drug use actually reinforces her insecurity (e.g., "Will I be found out and lose my [professional] license?"). The interaction between drug use and biophysical response confounds her sense of anxiety as she both desires sexual contact and fears the consequences of both intimacy and multiple sexual relationships.

Many who use drugs claim that either the onset and/or the maintenance of use and abuse coincides with *interpersonal conflict,* which is ameliorated through drug effects (Chiauzzi, 1991, pp. 65–68). Clients do not deny intrapsychic conflict but emphasize that it is often aggravated by interpersonal conflict. Peer pressure is often part of such conflict dynamics. Avoidance and management of interpersonal conflict is often significant to efficacious treatment. To treat a drug problem as if it were predominantly intrapsychic would not be in the best interest of the client.

Persons who have experienced significant physical, emotional, or sexual trauma are overrepresented among those with chronic, compulsive, highly risky and harmful drug use patterns (Saladin, et al., 1995). Trauma effects are largely determined by BPSI and must be addressed parallel with drug use activities. For example, one of the defensive routines associated with trauma is dissociation; this in turn may be reinforced by the use of various drug types such as alcohol, barbiturates, or heroin. In short, posttrauma effects and drug use may be interactive and mutually reinforcing.

Not only are attachment and bonding issues evident, but the link between expressed intimacy/sexual expression and drugs is one that has permeated the literature since the early 1900s (Addams, 1912). On the one hand drug use is observed to be highly correlated with the disinhibition, arousal, and impairment that give the client "permission" to experiment. Some may become more vulnerable to the influence of others when impaired, aroused, or disinhibited. Once sexual behavior is associated at a cognitive, affective, and behavioral level with drug effects, the two can be mutually reinforcing (Winick, 1992).

As well, some drugs are subjectively felt to create sensations that are erotic, sensual, orgiastic, or otherwise sexual in nature, independent of any actual activity that would be defined as primarily sexual. Among these drugs are heroin, cocaine, marijuana, and methamphetamine. On the other hand, some drugs impair sexual functioning, either as one of their properties (e.g., antipsychotics) or as the result of heavy dosage and chronic use (e.g., heroin and cocaine). Sexual dysfunction is associated with heavy and chronic drug use in both males and females. In extreme cases the therapist must address some clients' reality that intimacy and sexual expression without drug effects is anxiety provoking because it presents a novel experience and situation—not to mention other dynamics such as the recall of childhood trauma during sexual intercourse, which may not be moderated by drug effects (Winick, 1992).

As with alcohol, marriages and families whose problems are interactive with parental and/or adolescent drug use are more subject to risks associated with abandonment, marital dissolution, domestic violence, child abuse and neglect, poverty, and the redirection of family resources into drug use (Stanton & Heath, 1997). Neglect and conflict are dominant complaints by both adult partners and children. These patterns are often related to intergenerational repetition of drug use, abuse, and toxic relationship patterns as well as intrapsychic conflicts. For the social worker, the client may often be a child in need of protection or a family in need of stabilization.

Social Context and Social Situation
Social contextual variables, social situation, or social structure are often interpreted as determinants or contributing factors that promote or help maintain patterns of drug use and abuse by persons and within social systems. Situational variables are sometimes articulated in terms of social problems and social issues, and as contributing factors to the development of psychopathology and social deviance. Beyond the issue of familial and

peer relationships are a variety of concerns: poverty and lack of economic opportunity; neighborhood and community patterns; shelter and location of housing; problems with the legal and/or justice systems; sexism and homophobia; ageism, racism and ethnocentricism; as well as further disadvantaging the disabled.

It is difficult to assess clear causal dynamics associated with vague notions such as oppression, environmental determination of social behavior, and structural determinism. It has been useful for many clinicians to assume a BPSI interactional perspective where social factors are impacted by individual and familial behavior (e.g., theft to support drug use impacts community self-confidence and security) and where social factors may contribute to the use and abuse of drugs and maintenance of drug problems for the individual and the community (e.g., poverty is associated with prostitution, which is associated with greater perceived need for the mood-modifying effects of drugs). From an assessment perspective it is important to consider determinants of drug abuse outside of the client; from an intervention perspective it is important to also target systems change and the interface between the client and the social environment (Shulman, 1991).

Issues of Identity, Self, and Personality

One of the major developmental tasks, from either ego-functioning or a "self" paradigm, is for the client to develop a relatively stable, integrated and reality-grounded identity, self, or personality. The notion that persons who become problematic users of drugs may be described, and their abuse may be accounted for, by a trait such as *dependent* or *"addictive" personality* has not been supported (Chiauzzi, 1991, pp. 42–43). That is not to say that persons who use drugs may not demonstrate patterns of dependency and interdependency that are interactive with drug use. Dependency patterns may be reinforced by drug use, or may reinforce drug use; therefore, a "dependent personality" cannot alone *account for* drug abuse. Users exhibit a broader range of characteristics than would be accounted for by the concept of a pathological dependent personality.

Of more promise is a self theory that considers the interaction of BPSI factors in a dynamic fashion that helps construct a complex self and a more fluid identity; in turn, each BPSI dimension is impacted by the client's sense of self and identity (expanded from Denzin, 1987; McAdams, 1993). This more dynamic conceptualization of self theory may not be familiar to readers, as it is part of the authors' current research. As a result, more detailed exemplars will be used to demonstrate the convergence in BPSI of dependence and a BPSI concept of identity, self, and development within a drug use context.

Drug users often present a conception of self with a dual and apparently disintegrated identity consisting of both a "me" (self as object) as a drug abuser ("druggie") and a "me" either before acquiring the habit or as an abstainer ("straight"). In clinical practice we have found it useful to reframe the client's identity in terms of a more integrated self that acknowledges multiple sides or expressions (similar to Polster, 1995). Paradoxically both the "straight" self and the "druggie" self may have positive characteristics (functional, effective, well, and healthy) and negative characteristics (risky, harmful, hurtful, disordered, "dysfunctional," or otherwise described through pathological labels).

The complexity and fluidity involved in applying such a paradigm is further confounded if the assessment includes a dual diagnosis or multiple concomitant problems (Asaad, 1995). For example, a client might be suffering from a clinical depression for which she/he self-medicates by using cocaine, thereby giving a false impression of having a bipolar affect problem. Possible confounding problems may be social rejection as well as legal difficulties. At times the client's subjective sense of a stable and "integrated" self (paradoxically) may be dominated by an identity associated with negative labels such as "loser," "disintegrated," and "unstable," even in the face of being relatively successful. Applying the BPSI paradigm, it may be useful to the client and the clinician to begin considering self and identity issues by evaluating the relationship between drug use and the sense of self that comes with ingestion activities and drug responses.

Clients define how their social context or social situation contribute to them "having had to use drugs" or "having to continue to use drugs." Context does stimulate cue reactivity, a drug "high," or withdrawal sensations without the user having used drugs over a significant period (Chiauzzi, 1991, pp. 36–37, 55–57). Some accounts of social experiences from a clinical perspective are valid contributing factors for adaptation by using drugs. For example Carly experienced some vaginismus related to having been raped; she accounted for some of her drug use by declaring that it enabled her to relate sexually by making her more relaxed. On the other hand, superficial insight into her wish to avoid intimacy led her to apply labels to herself like "slut" because she "did it with so many guys." In addition, Carly had lived in poverty for part of her life and saw herself as "poor white trash" even though she now had a professional education, a professional career, and a professional income. The convergence of identity issues with social interactional factors is obvious.

Part of the integration of the self may be expressed pathologically in the form of narcissism, where the defensive routines impede or preclude genuine empathy for others. The patterns of narcissistic expression are often associated with maintaining status in the marginal subculture. These patterns are often associated with ensuring access to drugs "at all costs," including social relationship costs. Within such contexts, the expression of genuine empathy becomes a social cost; the expression of strategic empathy is more of a benefit.

At another level, both under conditions of use and abuse and under conditions of recovery, part of the integrated sense of self is constructed around issues of *spirituality* or *existence* (Doweiko, 1996, pp. 233–244). In treatment it is important to explore the meaning of life and existential issues. On the one hand they may act as barriers to recovery if not addressed; on the other hand they may support recovery solutions to the extent that expressions of spirituality may help the client to feel more efficacious and hopeful. In the clients' terms this may be regarded as more "faith and hope in myself," or "faith, hope and strength, because I have put my destiny in the hands of a power higher than me."

The BPSI model not only acknowledges that a client's apparently maladaptive expressions may be functional, it also emphasizes the importance of recognizing resilience and building on strengths (Bohm, 1976). A positive focus on solutions, without denying "pathology" or the negatives, enables the social worker to promote change and well-being

MULTIDISCIPLINARY TREATMENT AND CASE MANAGEMENT

Primary Prevention

A strategy utilized by social workers in the interest of primary prevention has been a psychosocial educational approach (Bloom, 1996). Whether the preventive strategy is with an individual, family, group, organization, or community, the social work emphasis is to get beyond information about drugs and their effects to gain knowledge regarding the interaction of biological, psychological, and social realities in either promoting or maintaining drug use and abuse. In psychosocial education, the emphasis transcends prescriptive-informational messages to enable the client system to change attitude, motivation, cognitive scripts, affect, interpersonal relationships, and sense of self and identity, as well as to address social-context variables that increase risk. The emphasis in such preventive work also includes a focus on concomitant variables (e.g., unemployment) that put the client at risk and that increase drug use risks. Effective prevention engages potential users or abusers at a BPSI level to mediate personal choice and to utilize natural support systems (Kail, 1992; Bloom, 1991). The targets may be groups of individuals with similar problems or broader populations at risk.

Early Detection and Case Finding

Secondary prevention is often operationalized through early detection, early case finding, and early brief intervention. The basic belief supporting this strategy is that if the client is engaged at the early stages of hazardous use or risky abuse, at a point where personal strengths and social supports may be optimized, then chronicity and compulsivity may be avoided. Early detection and case finding may reduce problems and risks by using a combination of psychosocial education and informed directive counseling. The basic goal is to prevent problems from escalating to the point that the client's intrapsychic and social functioning are severely compromised through dependence on drugs (Sisson & Azrin, 1993).

Brief Intervention

Early brief therapy takes many forms: psychodynamic, solution focused, interactional approaches, cognitive behavioral strategies, crisis intervention, and task-oriented social work. The goal is early intervention and short-term intervention to promote secondary prevention. The former often emphasizes informational-educational sessions and directive (goal oriented) counseling with individuals, families or groups; the latter involves more counseling and therapy, but of short duration, to prevent problems or risks from becoming worse, and may have an objective of ameliorating or controlling harm (Berg, 1994).

Crisis Intervention

One form of brief intervention, which might be applied either early or at a later stage, is *crisis intervention*. It is not uncommon for a client system to appear for help at a point where there is a biological crisis (e.g., withdrawal effects), a psychological crisis (e.g., uncontrollable and terrorizing hallucinations or flashbacks), a social crisis (e.g., the risk of being beaten or killed), or a complexly interactive crisis (e.g., spousal violence under conditions of impairment and threat of incarceration). The individual, family, group, organization, or community may be in a state of crisis cognitively, affectively, and at times biomedically; overwhelmed by problems, risks, threats, and harm associated with excessive drug use and concomitant problems. The goal of crisis intervention is to control harm and risk, in the interests of stabilizing the client system at a BPSI level, as well as increasing the self-efficacy of the client system (Parad & Parad, 1992; Cocores & Gold, 1990).

Psychopharmacological Maintenance

In a program of psychopharmacological maintenance, "addicts" with a range of problems of use and abuse may be offered psychopharmacological treatments (e.g., legalized heroin or methadone to manage opiate abuse) that enable withdrawal and/or maintain some type of psychoactive drug effect. The goal is to reduce criminalization and to maintain social support, as well as to promote strength and effective personal and social functioning (Doweiko, 1996, pp. 376–386).

Case Management

Social workers who work with "addicted" persons often have a primary responsibility that goes beyond assessment, prevention, or therapy. Both case management and therapy must enable the client to manage problems of everyday life (e.g., finding shelter for the homeless; enabling a prostitute to disengage). Additionally, most social workers have responsibilities to secondary client systems (e.g., parents dealing with the shock of a drug overdose by their teenager; a community that requires critical-incident debriefing after a group of teen males strategically used potent substances to enable coerced sex with an unsuspecting, drug-incapacitated female). Advanced case management issues, then, transcend responsibilities for psychosocial education, coordination, counseling and therapy (Rothman, 1992; Scheffler, 1993).

Community-Based Outpatient Counseling and Therapy

Early in the evolution of the provision of counseling, therapy, medical management, and rehabilitation for drug abusers many believed that inpatient and institutional care were required. This was to ensure emotional stabilization; to achieve control and amelioration of biomedical symptoms and effects; and to ensure for the recovering patient a return to basic psychological and social functioning. Drug intervention knowledge has improved to the point that today most substance-using or -abusing clients may be assessed and treated on an outpatient basis. As well, dual diagnoses may be addressed as parallel and interactive problems (e.g., mania and cocaine use). Outpatient counseling that acknowledges client strengths may enhance treatment effect (Bohm, 1976; Tatarsky and Washton, 1992).

Family and Couple Therapy

Often, the partner or other family members have been significant in promoting a problem, or in maintaining the problem at a significant risk level. On the other hand, treatment effect in the primary client (the drug abuser) may be maintained and reinforced if the partner and/or other family members are engaged in supporting the therapeutic enterprise. As well, even if primary relationship dynamics have not been a contributing factor in promoting or maintaining substance abuse, the active involvement of significant others in the helping process may help ensure and maintain treatment effect. Both initial and progress assessment may be enhanced, in terms of validity and reliability, by the active involvement of a partner and/or other family members (McIntyre, 1993; Zweben and Barrett, 1993; Zelvin, 1993).

Group Therapy

Effective treatment appears to be based on balancing constructive confrontation, support, motivation, the utilization of client's strengths, and the reduction or control of problems associated with intrapsychic and psychosocial functioning. The literature suggests that group therapy has the potential for being very effective with a range of drug abusers, especially in reinforcing reality testing, constructive confrontation, reducing denial and minimization, increasing social support, and improving the client's ability to participate in effective interpersonal relationships that promote psychosocial well-being. The process enables the client to learn what it means to be an effective member of a social group, and to both give and receive support (Flores, 1996; Khantzian, et al., 1990).

Residential Treatment and Milieu Therapy

For clients who have severe problems with chronicity and compulsivity but who do not require intense medical management, residential treatment may provide a stable and supportive venue to enable more complete assessment in vivo, as well as a reduction in those stimuli and stressors that reinforce a cycle of drug abuse. Residential programs may be useful if a client is living in a highly conflictual, unstable, relatively unsupportive, or otherwise transitory social environment. Residential programs offer individual, group, and self-help approaches, often supported by creating therapeutic routines out of the activities of daily living (referred to as *milieu therapy* or *the therapeutic community*). To enhance treatment effect, active participation of a postdischarge social network is essential (Weidman, 1992).

Institutional Care

Depending on the severity of their condition, a minority of drug abusers may require institutional care to address a crisis (e.g., detoxification from heroin or hallucinogenic flashbacks), a chronic problem of compulsivity (e.g., multiple failures of outpatient relapse prevention) or confounding concomitant problems such as dual diagnoses. Institutional care may vary from many hours of monitoring with psychoeducation, treatment, and progress assessment to a full range of multidisciplinary services, such as medical detox with nursing supervision; psychosocial education by a social worker; counseling or therapy by a social worker, psychologist, pastoral counselor or psychiatric nurse; physiotherapy to reverse muscular atrophy; preparation to return to occupational activity under the guidance of an occupational therapist; and concomitant social or mental disorder problem management with a psychiatrist, psychiatric social worker, or clinical psychologist.

ISSUES, CHALLENGES, AND OPPORTUNITIES

The field of drug abuse and drug dependence has been faced with an internal policy–program conflict associated with the use of drugs (especially psychoactive drugs), in the treatment of compulsive and chronic use, as well as withdrawal effects. It is not uncommon for social workers in the field to be faced with the conflict between a demand by the client for medications and an agency policy of rehabilitation without further "dependence on yet another mood-modifying substance."

The homosexual community, especially male homosexuals, appears to be overrepresented with respect to recreational drug use and abuse. On face value, the homosexual client requires the same range of services as those provided for heterosexuals. Even under conditions of sex-orientation-sensitive assessment, treatment, or self-help service heterosexual members of those client communities may express homophobic beliefs, attitudes, and values that are not only hurtful but may be countertherapeutic for the homosexual client, who must focus additional energy on more complex recovery dynamics associated with oppression.

Another contentious issue in the addictions field is the use of recovered or recovering counselors in assessment, counseling, therapy, and case management roles. Some recovered persons who provide service have little or no training in assessment or counseling, let alone therapy. Although they might be helpful in engaging the client and in promoting abstinence and self control, few have the training or skills necessary to effectively help the client with more complex, concomitant, and interactive problems.

One of the main issues for social workers within the context of clinical and helping relationships in the addictions field is balancing support with constructive confrontation. Some drug rehabilitation programs promote a level of confrontation that could be considered unethical within the context of a helping profession. The skill needed is to utilize strategies to overcome denial and minimization and to increase motivation–*but* without alienating the client or increasing resistance.

If a social worker is to undertake a comprehensive assessment, then each BPSI dimension of the client's life and development must be considered in terms of being a contributing factor in the promotion, maintenance, and potential recovery from the problems, risks, and harm associated with use and abuse of psychoactive or controlled substances. Within this context the dynamics of denial and minimization must be understood in a functional rather than a moralistic sense. The social worker must recognize that the label "unmotivated client" is a superficial and moralistic judgment, and that clinical assessment must determine the range of the client's motivation. Motivational conditions, and strategies to enhance motivation, in the best interests of abstinence and control as well as to improve personal and social functioning, must be identified (Miller & Rollnick, 1991).

The addictions field is dominated by the psychopathological diagnostic and treatment models. However, although intrapsychic disorder is important to consider, social conflict, interpersonal relationships, and systemic factors must not be discounted. Assessment of client strengths, abilities, and effective solution patterns must be integrated into a comprehensive social ecological understanding of the problems, needs, harm, risks, opportunities, and solutions (Bohm, 1976). *DSM-IV* classifications may be integrated when they are in the best interest of the client and increase his or her opportunity for recovery. The use of functional analysis may also be helpful.

Clients who suffer from problems associated with use and abuse of drugs present with complex problems, needs, developmental dynamics, and current risks and difficulties. The challenge for social work is to promote respect for a more integrated assessment and treatment model that meets a wide variety of the client's needs in a more holistic fashion; the position of the authors is that a BPSI model provides a basis for integration and for more comprehensive assessment and treatment. Such a move implies integrating those aspects of the medical model that are of benefit to the client and displacing its limited thinking with a broader BPSI and integrated-intervention approach.

Social workers have an opportunity to offer more direction to the field as well as to learn more advanced approaches to practice such as hypnosis, neurolinguistic programming, paradoxical therapy, and strategic therapy. Part of the challenge for the next millennium is to redefine social work's comprehensive contribution in a field where we have demonstrated much leadership since the early 1900s.

REFERENCES

Abbott, E. (1927). The civil war crime wave of 1865–1870. *Social Service Review, 1, 2,* 212–234.

Addams, J. (1912). *New conscience and an ancient evil.* New York: Macmillan.

American Psychiatric Association (1994). *Diagnostic and statistical manual of mental disorders, fourth edition. (DSM-IV).* Washington, DC: Author.

Asaad, G. (1995). *Understanding mental disorders due to medical conditions or substance abuse.* New York: Brunner/Mazel.

Barber, J. G. (1994). *Social work with addictions.* New York: New York University Press.

Berg, I. K. (1994). *Family-based services: A solution-focused approach.* New York: Norton.

Bloom, M. (1991). *Primary prevention: The possible science.* Englewood Cliffs, NJ: Prentice Hall.

Bloom, M. (1996). *Primary prevention practices.* Thousand Oaks, CA: Sage.

Bohm, P. (1976). Accounting for the positive: Strength oriented treatment. *Addictions, 23,* 22–29.

Carter, I. (1977). Social work in industry: A history and viewpoint. *Social Thought, 3, 1,* 7–11.

Chein, I. (1964). *The road to H: Narcotics, delinquency and social policy.* New York: Basic Books.

Chiauzzi, E. J. (1991). *Preventing relapse in the addictions: A biopsychosocial approach.* New York: Pergamon.

Clarke, B., & Kimberley, D. (1997). *Biopsychosocial assessment in addictions: Course manual.* St. John's, Newfoundland: Memorial University of Newfoundland, School of Continuing Education.

Clemmens, M. C. (1997). *Getting beyond sobriety: Clinical approaches to long-term recovery.* San Fransico: Jossey-Bass.

Cocores, J. A., & Gold, M. S. (1990). Recognition and crisis intervention treatment with cocaine abusers: The Fair Oaks Hospital model. In A. R. Roberts (Ed.), *Crisis intervention handbook: Assessment, treatment and research* (pp. 177–195). Belmont, CA: Wadsworth.

Cork, R. M. (1969). *The forgotten children.* Toronto: Addiction Research Foundation and PaperJacks.

Crawford, J. R., Thompson, N. A., Guillionn, F. E., & Garthwaite, P. (1989). Does endorsement of the disease concept of alcoholism predict humanitarian attitudes to alcoholics? *International Journal of the Addictions, 24,* 71–77.

Daley, D. (1989). Five perspectives on relapse in chemical dependency. In D. Daley (Ed.), *Relapse: Conceptual, research and clinical perspective* (pp. 3–26). New York: Haworth.

Denzin, N. K. (1987). *The alcoholic self.* Newbury Park, CA: Sage.

Doweiko, H. E. (1996). *Concepts of chemical dependency* (3rd Ed.). Pacific Grove, CA: Brooks/Cole.

Finnegan, L. P., & Kandall, S. R. (1997). Maternal and neonatal effects of alcohol and drugs. In J. H. Lowinson, P. Ruiz, R. B. Millman, & J. G. Langrod (Eds.), *Substance abuse: A comprehensive textbook* (3rd Ed., pp. 513–533). Baltimore, MD: Williams & Wilkins.

Flores, P. J. (1996). *Group psychotherapy with addicted populations* (2nd Ed.). New York: Haworth.

Freeman, E. M. (1992). "Addicted mothers–Addicted infants and children: Social work strategies for building support networks." In E. M. Freeman (Ed.), *The addiction process: Effective social work approaches* (pp. 108–122). New York: Longman.

John, S., Brown, L. S., & Primm, B. J. (1997). African Americans: Epidemiologic, prevention, and treatment issues. In J. H. Lowinson, P. Ruiz, R. B. Millman, & J. G. Langrod (Eds.), *Substance abuse: A comprehensive textbook* (3rd Ed., pp. 699–704). Baltimore: MD: Williams & Wilkins.

Kail, B. L. (1992). Recreational or casual drug use: Opportunities for primary prevention. In E. M. Freeman (Ed.), *The addiction process: Effective social work approaches* (pp. 96–107). New York: Longman.

Khantzian, E. J., Halliday, K. S., & McAuliffe, W. E. (1990). *Addiction and the vulnerable self: Modified dynamic group therapy for substance abusers.* New York: Guilford Press.

Kimberley, D., Clarke, B., & Cooper, J. (1996). *Social work in addictions: Course Manual* (2nd Ed.). St. John's, Newfoundland: Memorial University of Newfoundland, School of Continuing Education.

Lester, D. (1992). Alcoholism and drug abuse. In R. W. Maris, A. L. Berman, J. T. Maltsberger, & R. I. Yufit (Eds.), *Assessment and prediction of suicide* (pp. 321–336). New York: Guilford Press.

Leukefeld, C. G., & Battjes, R. J. (1992). Intravenous drug use and AIDS: Community approaches to social work revisited. In E. M. Freeman (Ed.), *The addiction process: Effective social work approaches* (pp. 123–135). New York: Longman.

MacLennan, A. (Ed.). (1976). *Women: Their use of alcohol and other legal drugs.* Toronto: Addiction Research Foundation of Ontario.

Malcolm, A. I. (1971). *The pursuit of intoxication.* Toronto: Addiction Research Foundation of Ontario.

McAdams, D. P. (1993). *The stories we live by: Personal myths and the making of the self.* New York: William Morrow.

McCready, B. (1992). Behavioral treatment of the alcoholic marriage. In E. Kaufman and P. Kaufmann (Eds.), *Family therapy of drug and alcohol abuse* (pp. 190–210). Boston: Allyn & Bacon.

McIntyre, J. (1993). Family treatment of substance abuse. In S. L. Ashenberg Straussner (Ed.), *Clinical work with substance-abusing clients* (pp. 171–195). New York: Guilford Press.

McKim, W. A. (1996). *Drugs and behavior: An introduction to behavioral pharmacology* (3rd Ed.). Englewood Cliffs, NJ: Prentice Hall.

Miller, W. R., & Rollnick, S. (1991). *Motivational interviewing: Preparing people to change addictive behavior.* New York: Guilford Press.

Parad, H. J., & Parad, L. G. (Eds.). (1990). *Crisis intervention.* Book 2: *The practitioner's sourcebook for brief therapy* (pp. 3–68). Milwaukee, WI: Family Service America.

Polster, E. (1995). *A population of selves: A therapeutic exploration of personal diversity.* San Francisco: Jossey-Bass.

Prochaska, J. O., & DiClemente, C. C. (1984). *The transtheoretical approach: Crossing the traditional boundaries of therapy.* Homewood, IL: Dow Jones/Irwin.

Rothman, J. (1992). *Guidelines for case management.* Itasca, IL: F. E. Peacock.

Rublowsky, J. (1974). *The stoned age: A history of drugs in America.* New York: G. P. Putnam's Sons.

Ruiz, P., & Langrod, J. G. (1997). Hispanic Americans. In J. H. Lowinson, P. Ruiz, R. B. Millman, & J. G. Langrod (Eds.), *Substance abuse: A comprehensive textbook* (3rd Ed., pp. 705–711). Baltimore, MD: Williams & Wilkins.

Saladin, M. E., Brady, K. T., Dansky, B. S., & Kilpatrick, D. G. (1995). Understanding comorbidity between PTSD and substance use disorders: Two preliminary investigations. *Addictive Behaviors, 20,* 643–655.

Sandmaier, M. (1992). *The invisible alcoholics: Women and alcohol* (2nd Ed.). Blue Ridge Summit, PA: TAB Books.

Scheffler, S. (1993). Substance abuse among the homeless. In S. L. Ashenberg Straussner, (Ed.), *Clinical work with substance-abusing clients* (pp. 291–303). New York: Guilford Press.

Shulman. L. (1991). *Interactional social work practice* (pp. 2–33). Itasca, IL: F. E. Peacock.

Shulman, L. (1992). *The skills of helping individuals, families and groups* (pp. 1–33). Itasca, IL: F. E. Peacock.

Sisson, R. W., & Azrin, N. H. (1993). Community reinforcement training for families: A method to get alcoholics into treatment. In T. J., O'Farrell (Ed.), *Treating alcohol problems: Marital and family interventions* (pp. 34–53). New York: Guilford Press.

Stanton, M. D., & Heath, A. W. (1997). Family and marital therapy. In J. H. Lowinson, P. Ruiz, R. B. Millman, & J. G. Langrod (Eds.), *Substance abuse: A comprehensive textbook* (3rd Ed., pp. 448–454). Baltimore, MD: Williams & Wilkins.

Szasz, T. (1974). *Ceremonial chemistry: The ritual persecution of drugs, addicts and pushers.* Garden City, NY: Doubleday.

Tatarsky, A., & Washton, A. M. (1992). Intensive outpatient treatment: A psychological perspective. In B. C. Wallace (Ed.), *The chemically dependent: Phases of treatment and recovery* (pp. 28–38). New York: Brunner/Mazel.

Wallace, J. (1989). A biopsychosocial model of alcoholism. *Social Casework, 70* 6, 325–332.

Weidman, A. A. (1992). Family therapy and the therapeutic community: The chemically dependent adolescent. In B. C. Wallace (Ed.), *The chemically dependent: Phases of treatment and recovery* (pp. 263–288). New York: Brunner/Mazel.

Westermeyer, J. (1997). Native Americans, Asians, and new immigrants. In J. H. Lowinson, P. Ruiz, R. B. Millman, & J. G. Langrod (Eds.), *Substance abuse: A comprehensive textbook* (3rd Ed., pp. 712–715). Baltimore, MD: Williams & Wilkins.

Whitaker, R. (1969). *Drugs and the law: The Canadian scene.* Toronto: Methuen.

White, J. M. (1991). *Drug dependence.* Englewood Cliffs, NJ: Prentice Hall.

Winick, C. (1992). Substances of use and abuse and sexual behavior. In J. H. Lowinson, P. Ruiz, R. B. Millman, & J. G. Langrod (Eds.), *Substance abuse: A comprehensive textbook* (2nd Ed., pp. 722–733). Baltimore, MD: Williams & Wilkins.

Zelvin, E. (1993). Treating the partners of substance abusers. In S. L. Ashenberg Straussner (Ed.), *Clinical work with substance-abusing clients* (pp. 197–213). New York: Guilford Press.

Zweben, A., & Barrett, D. (1993). Brief couples treatment for alcohol problems. In T. J. O'Farrell (Ed.), *Treating alcohol problems: Marital and family interventions* (pp. 353–380). New York: Guilford Press.

26

POSTTRAUMATIC STRESS DISORDER CONCEPTUALIZED AS A PROBLEM IN THE PERSON–ENVIRONMENT SYSTEM

Cathryn Bradshaw and Barbara Thomlison

There is a growing body of empirical evidence that describes posttraumatic stress reactions in a significant percentage of adults who have experienced a traumatic event. Depression, anxiety, dissociation, somatic complaints, and global psychological distress are common symptoms. Traumatized individuals reexperience the stressor event through ongoing intrusive thoughts; marked avoidance of feelings and activities; and everpresent arousal and anxiety. The severity of symptoms, as well as the nature and perception of the traumatic experience itself, may vary, but the meaning the victim attaches to the experience is important and is associated with long-term sequelae and psychopathology (Briere, 1996; Bryant & Harvey, 1997). This chapter reviews the diagnostic criteria of posttraumatic stress disorder (PTSD) and highlights the theoretical basis for assessment and treatment services to promote positive recovery.

The essential feature of posttraumatic stress disorder (PTSD) is the development of disabling psychological symptoms following a severe traumatic event. Symptoms in each of the following categories must be present: intrusive thoughts, reexperiencing the trauma (flashbacks), persistent avoidance of stimuli associated with the trauma, and persistent increased anxiety. PTSD appears in the *Diagnostic and Statistical Manual of Mental Disorders, Fourth Edition* (*DSM-IV*; American Psychiatric Association, 1994) as a differential Anxiety Disorder diagnosis.

PREVALENCE

Wylie (1996) estimates that 50% to 75% of Americans have been exposed to a traumatic event of the magnitude described in the *DSM-IV* under Posttraumatic Stress Disorder (PTSD). Studies of urban American youth indicate that nearly 40% of youth surveyed have been involved in some form of personal violence or severe victimization (Breslau, et al., 1991). However, research has also shown that not all persons exposed to severe trauma have long-lasting adverse outcomes. Epidemiological studies using large community samples indicate that approximately 1.3% to 2.6% of the general population report symptoms consistent with PTSD at some point in their lifetime. When studies are conducted on definable trauma populations who have been exposed to severe violence, the prevalence rates for PTSD increase; but they vary greatly among the selected studies. Prevalence rates vary from 3.6% of those present at a natural disaster (Shore, et al., 1986) to 59% in a sample of Cambodian-Americans who survived massive war-related trauma as children (Hubbard, et al., 1995).

Trauma populations are as diverse as those who witnessed or experienced "ethnic cleansing" in the former Yugoslavia (Weine, et al., 1995), Australian firefighters (McFarlane, 1989), women seeking refuge from domestic violence (Tutty & Rothery, 1997) and children who have been abused or neglected (Kiser, et al., 1991). Mental health professionals note that the disorder may be especially severe or have especially long-lasting negative effects when the stressor or trauma is personal, as in torture, sexual assault, abuse, rape, or other forms of one-on-one violence.

DEFINITION OF A STRESSOR

Posttraumatic stress reactions can appear in anyone in the aftermath of a severe trauma outside the "normal range" of human experience. Traumatic events that are experienced directly include, but are not limited to, violent personal assault (sexual assault, rape, physical attack, robbery, torture), suicide, kidnapping, incarceration as a prisoner of war, terrorism, exposure to mass murder, hostage captivity, or severe automobile accidents—as well as military (battlefield) action, industrial catastrophes, natural disasters, or being diagnosed with a life-threatening illness. These are traumas that produce intense fear, terror, and feelings of helplessness in anyone. Accordingly, *DSM-IV* indicates that the definition of *stressor* should involve both objective and subjective dimensions. Responses of individuals are associated with both objectively severe stressors and subjective perceptions of threats or stressors (Bryant & Harvey, 1997).

Trauma can cause postincident symptoms in anyone. Changes in behavior and feelings due to trauma are most often temporary, and can be upsetting to the person and to those close to him or her. Intense feelings of anxiety, fear, and losing control are normal reactions to overwhelming threats or danger. Trauma-related fears and anxiety may be expressed in a variety of ways depending upon environmental and personal factors. Symptoms affecting emotional and behavioral functioning fall along a continuum according to the severity and duration of the stressor or trauma and the victim's perception of the stressor. The continuum ranges from effects that include slight, short-term anxiety to the polar extreme of acute stress disorder,* to chronic or delayed onset of posttraumatic stress disorder (PTSD). Individuals of all ages can have PTSD.

A diagnosis of PTSD requires that the individual satisfy criteria including reexperiencing, avoidance, and arousal symptoms. PTSD is not thought to be an inordinate response to a normal event but rather an *ordinary* response to an *extraordinary* trauma or stressor. There are many examples of PTSD symptoms occurring following less severe trauma, but it is the perceived threat that is important in predicting posttraumatic stress disorder (Briere, 1992; Briggs & Joyce, 1997; Browne & Finkelhor, 1986; Deblinger, et al., 1996). Consequently, traumatic stress responses are associated with both severe stressors and perceived threats, accounting for why it is that some trauma survivors experience symptoms years or even decades postincident (Bryant & Harvey, 1997; Rowan & Foy, 1992; Sutker, et al., 1995; Tutty & Rothery, 1997).

HISTORICAL OVERVIEW OF TRAUMA

Herman (1997) identified three forms of psychic trauma described in the nineteenth and twentieth centuries. *Hysterical neurosis* was the first psychic trauma response to be examined in a consistent way. Based on the cases of several women suffering from hysteria, Freud hypothesized that hysteria was the result of incest, which explained the psychological response. Then

---

*Acute stress disorder (ASD) is a recently developed diagnosis which describes posttraumatic stress reactions that occur in the first month following a trauma, but distinguished from PTSD by its emphasis on a minimum of three dissociative symptoms: numbing, reduced awareness, depersonalization, derealization, or amnesia.

shell shock or *combat neurosis* emerged in individuals as part of the after-math of two World Wars. Later, research with American Vietnam veterans sought both to understand their ongoing difficulties and to validate the existence of trauma such as theirs. The third wave of interest in psychic trauma came in the late 1960s with the feminist movements of Western Europe and North America. *Sexual and domestic violence* of adults and children produced feelings of detachment, withdrawal, helplessness, depression, emotional numbness, and fear; these were perceived as producing effects similar to that of shell shock. Comparisons between these experiences still prevail (e.g., Cameron, 1994; McNew & Abell, 1995).

In 1980, the American Psychiatric Association recognized PTSD in its *Diagnostic and Statistical Manual of Mental Disorders, Third Edition* (*DSM-III*, American Psychiatric Association, 1980). Through research efforts and clinical observation in case studies, a common understanding arose across the experiences of hysteria, shell shock and sexual or domestic violence, namely that such symptoms are trauma driven, that is, they are essentially defensive adaptations to the traumatic experience (van der Kolk, 1989). Though psychic trauma is traditionally associated with the experience of war and rape, other severe trauma situations are now recognized as being associated with posttraumatic stress; a posttraumatic stress diagnosis applies particularly to the survivors of child maltreatment trauma. PTSD is indicated when predictable patterns of psychological symptoms develop subsequent to the experience of extraordinary or life-threatening trauma.

THE SYMPTOMS OF POSTTRAUMATIC STRESS

Trauma is a broad descriptor of physical injury or shock but also of painful emotional experience, which can often produce a lasting psychic effect. Posttraumatic symptoms that involve ways of thinking, feeling, and coping serve to perpetuate anxiety, fear and helplessness (Briere, 1992; Singer, et al., 1995). Anxiety or fear is the primary symptom and serves as one of the maintaining causes of posttraumatic stress. For a diagnosis of PTSD, *DSM-IV* outlines three clusters of symptoms that must develop following an identifiable severe traumatic event: (1) reexperiencing (flashbacks), (2) avoidance and/or numbing, and (3) autonomic hyperarousal.

Reexperiencing Symptoms in PTSD

Reexperiencing intrusive thoughts is considered a key symptom in the diagnosis of PTSD. The *DSM-IV* diagnosis of PTSD requires that the trauma be reexperienced in ways such as flashbacks or recurrent recollections, images, thoughts, dreams, nightmares, a sense of reliving the experience, or distress on exposure to reminders of the traumatic event. These symptoms are often referred to as intrusive. The role of reexperiencing symptoms is to facilitate the modification of the trauma event; such flashbacks conceptually function as an adaptive process to the trauma. Bryant and Harvey (1997) indicate that "available evidence suggests that the distressing and intrusive nature of reexperiencing symptoms may be associated with more severe posttraumatic symptomatology" (p. 764). They also suggest that the extent of initial intrusive thoughts may be related to the presence of avoidance activities in the acute trauma phase.

Avoidance Symptoms in PTSD

Avoidance behaviors arise in order to escape reminders—people, places, activities and emotions—associated with the trauma. Avoidance is conceptualized as the primary response to intrusive thoughts, because it can provide temporary relief or respite from the memories. Persistent avoidance is associated with chronic PTSD because it impairs resolution of the trauma and maintains the ongoing disturbance (Bryant & Harvey, 1997). Among the variety of symptoms that can occur, at least three specified avoidance symptoms must be present. The following are particularly common symptoms: attempts to avoid thoughts or feelings associated with the trauma; attempts to avoid activities associated with the trauma; emotional numbness or being disconnected from one's feelings; losing interest in activities that used to provide pleasure. These behaviors and symptoms can lead to depression, dissociation, restricted emotions, detachment, and suppression of memories.

Arousal Symptoms in PTSD

Sensitivity to distress upon exposure to actual or symbolic reminders of the traumatic event is associated with a number of somatic complaints: sleep disturbances, concentration deficits, elevated startle response, increased anxiety, hypervigilance, and other autonomic hyperarousal symptoms. These factors may lead to associated or secondary features such as despair and hopelessness, depression, risk-taking behaviors, and a sense of powerlessness and self-blame for the traumatic event or the consequences of the event.

Differential Diagnosis

Duration of Symptoms
Duration of the symptoms suggests a differential diagnosis. If the disturbing symptoms cause clinically distressing symptoms, or impair social or occupational functioning, the following criteria apply:

- *Acute onset*—if the duration of symptoms is less than three months;
- *Chronic*—if the duration of symptoms is three months or more;
- *With delayed onset*—if the duration of the symptoms is at least six months after the stressor.

PTSD is diagnosed only after symptoms have persisted for six months. A diagnosis of *acute stress disorder* (ASD) is given if symptoms emerges within six months following trauma exposure, namely a minimum of three of these dissociative symptoms: numbing, reduced awareness, depersonalization, or amnesia. An individual may display acute symptoms initially after a traumatic event, process the traumatic memories in an adaptive manner in the next days, and may or may not experience responses predictive of long-term symptomatology. However, diagnosed acute stress disorder (ASD) is regarded as a predictor of longer-term posttraumatic psychopathology (Bryant & Harvey, 1997). Table 26–1 summarizes the diagnostic criteria for posttraumatic stress disorder.

Symptomatology Issues
Three issues continue to be debated in the literature: (1) distinct categories of PTSD according to trauma population; (2) presence of dissociative responses within the symptom repertoire; and (3) PTSD categories based on the duration of trauma. These issues share the common focus of attempting to account for variations in symptom presentation. Some researchers hypothesize that response differences may be related to distinct trauma populations and that generalizing from findings of one trauma population to others may be unjustified (e.g., Bryant & Harvey, 1997). As an illustration, some researchers have attempted to develop a classification of posttraumatic stress that more clearly represents the symptom profile of maltreated children and of adults who were severely maltreated as children. *Postabuse trauma syndrome* or *child abuse accommodation syndrome* has been suggested as a subcategory of PTSD. However, research into which abuse experiences are associated with PTSD symptomatology has been limited. Some clinicians suggest that symptoms of PTSD are universal in adult survivors of child sexual abuse (Herman, 1997), whereas

Table 26–1   Diagnostic Criteria for Posttraumatic Stress Disorder (Summary)

Criteria	Symptom
Stressor (both required)	Threatening event experienced or witnessed Intense fear, helplessness, or horror
Reexperiencing (minimum of one required)	Recurrent images/thoughts/distress Intrusive thoughts, distressing recollections Flashbacks, hallucinations, or illusions Physiological reactions: rapid heartbeat, high blood pressure
Avoidance (minimum of three required)	Avoid thoughts/conversations Avoid people/places Amnesia or lack of recall of the event Diminished interest or participation Estrangement from others or detachment Restricted affect Sense of shortened future
Arousal (minimum of two required)	Insomnia Concentration deficits Hypervigilance Elevated startle response, angry outbursts
Dissociation	Not applicable
Duration	Persistence for at least 6 months post trauma

These symptoms cause clinically important distress or impair work, social, or personal functioning.

Source: Adapted from the *Diagnostic and Statistical Manual of Mental Disorders,* Fourth Edition (*DSM-IV*), Washington, DC: American Psychiatric Association, 1994.

others conclude that only the most severely traumatized individuals exhibit PTSD symptoms (Briggs & Joyce, 1997).

Herman (1997) and van der Kolk (1989) found evidence that dissociative responses are more frequently observed in prolonged and severe trauma. Bryant and Harvey (1997) argue for further revisions of acute stress disorder criteria, based on evidence of the role of dissociative symptoms in acutely traumatized individuals. The question of the fundamental role of dissociative responses in PTSD, or some category of PTSD, has yet to be resolved.

Subtypes of PTSD have been suggested by Terr (1991) and Herman (1997) based upon the differential impacts of short- and long-term exposure to a traumatic situation. Terr (1991) distinguishes between Type I trauma—defined by a single event involving a sudden shock (e.g., rape)—and Type II trauma—created by repeated or prolonged exposure to an overwhelming traumatic situation, as in many cases of incest or domestic violence. Herman (1997) suggests that the single designation of PTSD is insufficient and recommends the establishment of a spectrum of post-trauma-related diagnoses. For example, she suggests a category of *complex posttraumatic stress disorder* for persons who have experienced the prolonged and often repeated traumas referred to under Terr's Type II designation. Additional research in this direction may greatly increase our understanding of the specific contribution of various trauma exposure characteristics and the various PTSD symptoms that can follow trauma.

THEORETICAL PERSPECTIVE OF PTSD

Posttraumatic stress is best conceptualized as a problem in the person-environment system. To understand PTSD and its impact on individuals, we must analyze the ways in which individuals respond to the environments they interact with after the traumatic stressor. As well, interest in understanding the distinction between normal and pathological responses to traumatic, life-threatening, and otherwise stressful events is valuable. The model of causality used to explain how trauma increases vulnerability to posttraumatic stress is derived primarily from social learning and cognitive-behavioral theories in psychology.

Cognitive-Behavioral Models

Research indicates that the cognitive schemas of survivors of trauma constitute an important component of their adaptation to extremely threatening and traumatic events (Foa, et al., 1989; Spaccarelli, 1995; Spaccarelli & Kim, 1995; van der Kolk, 1989). Common trauma-related cognitive changes include negative self-evaluation and guilt as well as perceived helplessness and hopelessness. Learning theory provides the conceptual basis of the fear responses experienced by trauma victims and the emergence of avoidance strategies to deal with these responses. Cognitive-behavioral theory, in the form of cognitive appraisals of the patient's trauma-related beliefs and schemas, information processing, and stress and coping, helps to explain many of the symptoms typical of PTSD as well as the patient's choice of certain adaptation strategies.

Learning Theory
Social learning theory considers PTSD symptoms in terms of classical and operant conditioning. The traumatic event serves as an aversive unconditioned stimulus, leading to extreme tension. These then become conditioned stimuli that provoke anxiety reactions and a heightened state of alertness. This leads to the avoidance of these conditioned stimuli (Emmelkamp, 1994). This accounts for the emergence of fear and anxiety symptoms. Avoidance strategies may be employed by the individual in order to minimize exposure to cues that evoke a conditioned fear response (McCann & Pearlman, 1990; Peterson, et al., 1991; Shapiro & Dominiak, 1992). While this avoidance may temporarily reduce the fear and anxiety, it also negatively reinforces the avoidance response (Berliner & Saunders, 1996). This conditioned response may become generalized to include an aversion to many more people, places, emotions, situations and activities as these become associated with trauma stimuli. However, the use of avoidance strategies does nothing to alter the very nature of the conditioned stimuli.

Cognitive Appraisals
An important aspect of cognitive coping is appraisal—the process of evaluating salient dimensions of the stressful event. Appraisal includes such dimensions as assessing the traumatic event's potential threat, meaningfulness, predictability, and controllability. Foa and colleagues (1989) suggest that perceived controllability is a critical cognitive factor in attempts to cope with extreme trauma. Trauma victims may come to view the world as hostile and unpredictable. The process of appraising may extend beyond the trauma situation to include the breakdown or accommodation of their assumptions about self, others, and the world.

Individuals perceive and make sense of their experience through cognitive structures or schema. These schemas determine the focus of attention as well as how experience is perceived, organized, stored, and retrieved (McCann & Pearlman, 1990). If the trauma occurs to a child when his or her cognitive schema is being formed initially, the child's trauma-impacted assumptions may be especially intransigent. Appraisals resulting from the trauma may lead to the development of cognitive schemas that include a "victim" identity; feeling personally and interpersonally vulnerable; and a random, unpredictable, uncontrollable, and unjust worldview (Foa, et al., 1989; McCann & Pearlman, 1990; Peterson et al., 1991). The resulting trauma-modified schemas may explain symptoms of fear and anxiety.

Information Processing. Reexperiencing and avoidance symptoms are considered from an information-processing perspective. From this perspective, severe trauma may lead to information overload or incomplete information processing. Repression of the trauma material may occur in the first instance and reexperiencing phenomena in the latter. Unprocessed material is thought to remain in an active though unconscious mode, but may be manifested through flashbacks, nightmares, anxiety, and depression (McCann & Pearlman, 1990; Peterson, et al., 1991). Powerlessness may result from the cycling reexperiencing and avoidance phenomena. A learned helplessness construct explains posttrauma symptoms such as chronic depression, passivity, and a sense of futility.

Stress and Coping. Cognitive appraisals of the trauma and trauma-related events influence the choice of coping or adaptation strategies. Resilience has been associated with fewer negative appraisals of the trauma event and the inclination to engage in purposeful coping activities, such as problem solving and support seeking (Spaccarelli & Kim, 1995). PTSD symptoms have been found to be associated with avoidance coping strategies (Sutker, et al., 1995). There seems to be a relationship between having uncontrollable traumatic memories, wishful thinking, and self-blame and the use of self-isolation as coping strategies.

Cognitive appraisals of self in relation to others that promote an expectancy of uncontrollable outcomes in the future result in learned helplessness. Competence, power, and self-esteem have been linked to clients' perception of being able to influence their social and physical environments. Self-esteem, attributional style, and problem-solving coping strategies have been related to locus of control and self-efficacy. Perceived helplessness tends to become an internal, stable, and global attributional style. This style tends to facilitate guilt, self-blame, depression, and a hopelessness feedback loop.

MECHANISMS OF IMPACT

It is recognized that the precise nature of the trauma is insufficient to explain its impact on some people. A framework for understanding why some persons seem to manage, adapt, and even grow in response to traumatic life events whereas others seem to disintegrate, is needed. This leads to the consideration of an encompassing, multidimensional model of stress and coping in order to account for the variability seen in responses to trauma across individuals. PTSD is the one *DSM* diagnosis that clearly regards the interaction of the person with his or her environment as essential in its etiology. By definition, PTSD is caused by environmental events that overwhelm the person's abilities to cope effectively. The effects of any trauma event must be understood within the interactions of (1) risk factors in the environment, including the traumatic event, (2) personal factors and developmental triggers, and (3) protective or compensatory factors (e.g., Mrazek & Haggerty, 1994; Wachtel, 1988). From this perspective, intervention is directed towards reducing risk factors, while increasing protective factors so as to promote healthy coping.

RISK AND PROTECTIVE FACTORS

Posttraumatic stress is a disorder with a unique set of risk and protective factors for the development of psychopathology (Mrazek & Haggerty, 1994). Although they are not fully understood, risk and protective factors for mental disorders appear to act antagonistically or synergistically to produce a variety of effects on diverse individuals (Coie, et al., 1993). *Risk factor* is a process concept which refers to those factors that "increase the probability of onset, digression to a more serious state, or maintenance of a problem condition" (Kirby & Fraser, 1997, p. 10). Risk factors influence the likelihood of an outcome rather than determining the outcome. Protective factors need not be desirable or pleasant qualities, and environmental circumstances do not necessarily have to be positive or beneficial to act protectively. Each life setting exposes individuals to risk and protective factors as they interact with various events, processes, and relationships at differing times and intensities throughout childhood and beyond. A risk-factor approach examines these systematic sources of influence and their combination. Interventions focus on alteration of the risk factor so as to have a broad impact on the outcome (Thomlison, 1997). /

Life stressors and other traumatic events, both perceived and actual, are seen as the precipitating factors that may impair a vulnerable individual and lead to PTSD. The number and interaction of risk and protective factors determines whether PTSD will develop. Resilience appears to be affected by both environmental and biological conditions; but resilience is dynamic: it changes under differing conditions and over time. A risk-resilience ecological model makes several predictions. First, PTSD symptoms are more likely to emerge in cases where the total amount of risk is greater than the protective influences. Second, this cumulative risk influences the likelihood that maladaptive coping strategies will be employed.

For children, the experience of traumatic events, such as witnessing violence or undergoing sexual abuse, can suppress the developmental processes that affect the child's ability to understand the world (Garbarino, et al., 1992). Finally, negative perceptions of the trauma will impact self-image, sense of security, and trust in others (Briere, 1996; Spaccarelli & Kim, 1995).

The risk and protective model of trauma impact suggests that the number of the risk factors directly influences the strength that the traumatic event will exert (Kirby & Fraser, 1997). Research tends to support this cumulative effect. For example, Garbarino and colleagues (1992) and Nicholson (1997) found that individuals who experienced the largest number of traumatic events had the most severe levels of PTSD symptoms. Briggs and Joyce (1997) report that women who experienced multiple abusive episodes involving sexual intercourse had increased symptoms of PTSD. Also, PTSD symptoms seemed more sensitive to the number of cumulative trauma events than did symptoms of anxiety or depression. The findings of Deblinger and colleagues (1996) emphasize the value, in treating posttraumatic stress symptomatology, of parental participation in the direct therapeutic intervention with their children. Parental support systems serve as a protective factor.

Developing Resilience

Resilience is envisioned as a capacity that can develop over a lifetime in the context of person–environment transactions (Egeland, et al., 1993). The term *protective factors* refers to those internal and external influences that assist individuals in restoring or maintaining effective coping in the face of the negative effects of risks (Egeland, et al., 1993; Kirby & Fraser, 1997). Effective coping includes managing thoughts, emotions, and behavior. Identifying the protective factors in the development of resilience has received sparse attention in the trauma-related literature; risk factors have been more prominent.

Environmental Factors

Environmental variables that have occupied the interest of researchers include pretrauma conditions such as family background and social support, characteristics of the traumatic event, and posttrauma resources. However, the dominant avenue of research exploration has been to assess the impact of specific trauma event characteristics on the emergence of symptoms. Mental health disorders are seen to share some risks with other problems as well as having a problem-specific risk structure (Mrazek & Haggerty, 1994).

Traumatic Events. Characteristics of the trauma experience that have received research attention and that may have impact on the person's adaptation to the trauma include the presence or perceived presence of life threat, duration, intensity, and whether the trauma is of natural or man-made origin (e.g., Goenjian, et al., 1995; Hartman & Burgess, 1986; Hubbard, et al., 1995; Kiser, et al., 1991; Singer, et al., 1995; Tutty & Rothery, 1997). For example, in a sample of 3,735 adolescents exposed to violence, researchers found a significant and consistent association between exposure to violence and trauma symptoms (Singer, et al., 1995). This study described symptoms of depression, anxiety, posttraumatic stress, and dissociation, and found that the greater the violence exposure, the higher the scores for total trauma. The strongest association between symptoms and violence was for those who had witnessed or experienced the violence at home, who had been beaten or mugged in the past, or who had been a victim of sexual abuse/assault. It is important to remember that the level or type of trauma exposure does not stand alone in predicting a PTSD outcome. For example, Garrison and colleagues (1995) suggest that common stressful events occurring after the trauma may be more strongly associated with PTSD than the intensity of the trauma event itself.

Recovery-Environment Factors
Environmental and background factors that have been explored as contributing to recovery from PTSD symptoms include early life history, other experiences of trauma, family functioning, social supports, societal attitudes re trauma events, and additional stressors. Parental warmth and support were found to act as resilience factors in mediating the effects of sexual abuse on girls (Spaccarelli & Kim, 1995). Other environmental resources, such as social support networks, are thought to moderate the impacts of trauma (Coie, et al., 1993). In a study of risk and resilience, social support influenced children's emotional and behavioral functioning following exposure to family violence (Kolbo, 1996). In a longitudinal study of high-risk children and their families, Egeland and colleagues (1993) found that emotionally responsive caregiving mediated the negative effects of high-risk environments (i.e., poverty, family stress, and maltreatment). Adverse family and cultural factors have been associated with generic risk for mental health status. Baldwin and colleagues (1993) explored the relationship between parenting behaviors, other family factors, social class and minority status, and mental health.

They found that each of these factors contributed to risk and resiliency in adolescents for the development of psychopathology.

Personal Factors

Variables that protect against mental disorders which have been explored in trauma research include genetic markers and gender (Cameron, 1994; Garrison, et al., 1995; Goenjian, et al., 1995; Singer, et al., 1995); comorbid mental and medical health issues (Hubbard, et al., 1995; Nicholson, 1997); developmental triggers (Wachtel, 1988); informational processing of the event; and personality variables such as locus of control, self-esteem, intelligence, and value placed on success or failure (Baldwin, et al., 1993). Wachtel (1988) suggests that developmental tasks may act as risk factors for the onset or maintenance of PTSD. For example, puberty, marriage, or the birth of a child may trigger PTSD symptoms in someone who was sexually abused as a child when the person needs to rework the trauma situation in the light of his emerging developmental tasks. In a conceptual exploration, Mrazek and Mrazek (1987) hypothesized that the ability to recognize and adapt to the situation in order to avoid harm or punishment, a precocious maturity that increases a sense of self-esteem and self-efficacy, dissociation of affect as a coping strategy to handle overwhelming feelings, and holding on to the conviction that one is loved are among the factors that should be considered to promote resilience.

Biological Factors

Gender has been linked with increased vulnerability to PTSD following exposure to natural disasters (Garrison, et al., 1995; Goenjian, et al., 1995) and various forms of "man-made" violence (Berton & Stabb, 1996; Hubbard, et al., 1995; Singer, et al., 1995). Berton and Stabb (1996) observed that female adolescents showed the highest PTSD scores; this may signal that females respond to violence with more PTSD symptoms then do males. Singer and others (1995) concluded that gender was the only significant and powerful contributor to the higher scores of adolescent females following exposure to violence.

The question of genetic markers (fixed markers) that predispose individuals to a PTSD reaction has been explored by a number of researchers. Sack and colleagues (1995) noted a trend to transgenerational occurrence of PTSD in two generations of Cambodian refugees, which increased when both parents had a diagnosis of PTSD; a study of identical twins found that PTSD was the result of exposure to severe trauma rather than a genetic susceptibility (Goldberg, et al., 1990).

A diagnosis of PTSD has been linked to a comorbid diagnosis of depressive disorders (Briere, 1992; Goenjian, et al., 1995; Hubbard, et al., 1995). For example, 59% of young adults who survived massive war-related trauma as children with a diagnosis of PTSD also had one or more additional diagnosed disorders. Major depression and generalized anxiety diagnoses were the most common disorders comorbid to PTSD. Perceived comorbid medical conditions on health assessment have also been associated with higher symptom levels of PTSD (Nicholson, 1997).

In cases where trauma was unacknowledged, characteristics often noted as persisting for years include nervousness, tensions, feelings of terror and apprehension, somatic manifestations associated with anxiety, and hyperarousal of fear response (van der Kolk & Kadish, 1989). Van der Kolk (1989) suggests that these responses may be the result of physiological changes to the autonomic nervous system (ANS) following prolonged uncontrollable trauma. These physiological changes may lead to the tendency to act with motor discharge (angry outburst or startle response) or with emotional and social withdrawal.

Biology of Fear. Lasting changes in brain chemistry may be associated with the cycle of reexperiencing and avoidance. Butler (1996) reviewed research into the biology of fear and reported that PTSD includes the expression of persistent deregulation of body and brain chemistry. She highlighted three recent types of developments in the biological arena: the deregulation of the flight-or-fight response, changes in memory, and damage to brain structure. Research suggests that when stress becomes overwhelming, there is an increase in the levels of epinephrine and norepinephrine. These neurochemicals tend to induce confusion as well as impair memory and learning. When this sequence is repeated, as with prolonged trauma, the brain becomes increasing sensitive; floods of these brain chemicals are released at lower-than-normal thresholds and may continue to do so for years after the trauma. Hippocampus changes have been documented in traumatized persons, such as veterans and severe childhood abuse survivors (see review in Butler, 1996). The hippocampus is involved with the sorting and storing of short-term memory. Researchers found that scans of brain function during flashbacks revealed that sensory memory was very active while brain areas governing verbal behavior remained quiet. Van der Kolk suggests that survivors of trauma recall the trauma event in a state of *speechless terror* (see review in Butler, 1996). Taken together, these biological mechanisms may help to account for the diverse array of PTSD symptoms.

Contributions of the Risk Factor Approach

Based on the interplay of biological and physiological influences, personal characteristics, and forces in the social environment, the ecological perspective highlights human behavior as the result of transactions between individuals and their environments. The risk-resilience ecological model predicts that symptoms of PTSD and behavioral problems are more likely in cases where the total amount of stressful life events is higher. Higher stress is assumed to have an indirect effect on symptoms by increasing the likelihood that victims will employ maladaptive coping strategies and will perceive abuse events in ways that erode their positive self-image, sense of security, and trust in others. Sorting out the relative influences of biological factors, learned patterns, social interactions, and various contextual conditions, it may never be possible to fully identify causes and their effects (Fraser, 1997). Assessing potential risk and protective factors is important for the development of effective interventions.

RECOVERY: AN INTEGRATED APPROACH

The social ecology of person–environment practice in social work organizes the myriad of facts, forms a basis for understanding, draws inferences, and makes clinical judgments concerning interventions for posttraumatic stress recovery. There are many and varied maintaining causes of PTSD. Such factors operate at the level of the body (muscle tension, shallow breathing), emotions (withheld feelings), behavior (avoidance), mind (self-talk and mistaken beliefs), and whole self (low self-esteem). Thus, the most effective approach for treating PTSD is one that addresses the full range of factors contributing to the condition.

Assessment of PTSD

A multisystemic assessment framework for initial and ongoing clinical assessment addresses the risk and protective factors that must be employed for recovery. That means that the individual, family, and community system levels must be considered. Interventions addressing two primary levels—environmental factors and personal factors—are essential. The assessment content should focus both on environmental strengths and obstacles and on personal strengths and obstacles. Cowger (1997) suggests that the following exemplars of strengths be considered: cognition, emotion, motivation, coping, and interpersonal as well as physiological strengths. This assessment will facilitate the design of interventions that target the reduction of key risks and the enhancement of protective mechanisms.

Focus on Strengths

The aim of a social work assessment of strengths is to identify what is needed for confidence building in the individual. Assessment through unstructured clinical interviews must first determine whether or not a clinical diagnosis of PTSD is likely. The use of self-report inventories is also helpful. Assessment at this stage is fact finding; techniques involve gathering information to determine whether an individual is unsafe and/or in need of medical attention, and identifying strengths, supports, and resources for the mobilization of competencies for building self-confidence.

Activities of the social worker include

- Interviewing and employing measures to determine both environmental strengths and obstacles and personal strengths and obstacles
- Assessing stress in the interactions of the person and his environments and their current contribution to posttraumatic stress reactions, including life cycle transitions, cultural issues, and adequacy of resources
- Evaluating the type and quality of support available from family, relatives, friends, and neighbors in the immediate environment
- Making decisions about ongoing services

Cognitive-behavioral approaches with the individual are viewed as the most effective modality in treatment (Bourne, 1990; Friedrich, 1996). The process should also include any family members who can contribute to assessing strengths, resources, and supports within the context of various life settings. To capture the breadth and depth of strengths, the assessments involve the use of multiple sources of information and multiple methods of data collection. The use of clinical measures can assist in treatment assessment and monitoring.

Clinical Measures of PTSD

Development of measures for many aspects of trauma responses is still relatively limited. Taken together, all the current measures that index PTSD do not encompass the full range of symptoms. Each of the measures indexes aspects of the traumatic response, and different trauma populations may report differences in trauma severity. For a complete list of measures the reader is referred to Carlson (1997). Some common examples include

- *Clinician Administered PTSD Scale* (CAPS) (Blake, et al., 1956) is highly rated for psychometric properties and is recommended for use in clinical or research settings to measure PTSD and ASD symptoms related to up to three identified traumatic events. The CAPS can also be used to make *DSM-IV* PTSD and ASD diagnoses. This is a structured interview, but it can be administered by paraprofessionals. The CAPS allows for assessment of impact of symptoms on social and occupational functioning. Very easy to use.
- The *Impact of Events Scale* (Horowitz, et al., 1979) has been employed to index intrusive and avoidance symptoms in the acute posttraumatic phase.
- The *Dissociative Experiences Scale* (Branscombe, 1991; Carlson & Putnam, 1993) measures dissociation and indexes identity, perceptual, and memory disturbances. It does not index intrusive, avoidance, or arousal symptoms.
- The *Trauma Symptom Checklist* (TSC) (Briere & Runtz, 1989) was developed to assess the impact of trauma in adults, particularly the long-term effects of childhood sexual and physical abuse.
- The *PTSD Symptom Scale* (Foa, et al., 1993) has been employed to index intrusive, avoidance, and arousal symptoms.

Although knowledge about recovery is limited, it is essential to deliver service in a timely manner and to readminister measures later in the treatment process to monitor for change.

Successful Coping with Trauma

Recovery from trauma is painful and difficult and can potentially be a lengthy experience. It is complicated by the fact that individuals may appear to be asymptomatic until much later, and this has implications for service. Referral for treatment is often made only when serious social, cognitive, or other developmental problems emerge. Assessment of the client's readiness to do the trauma-related work must be determined at many points throughout the recovery process (Briere, 1996; Carlson, 1997). Briere (1992, 1996), Carlson (1997), and Falsetti (1997) provide valuable treatment planning reviews for PTSD. Recovery planning should include many of the following goals and strategies:

Goal 1: Increase Self-Capacities
- Address identity and boundary issues before entering on trauma-specific treatment.
- Mobilize supportive networks and assist in development of a more assertive interpersonal and conflict resolution repertoire.
- Promote positive self-talk and self-trance, including ego-supportive suggestions and affirmations.
- Increase instrumental coping skills through assertiveness, social skills, and problem-solving training.

Goal 2: Normalize the PTSD Reactions
- Educate about the numbing and intrusive cycles of symptoms and maladaptive coping strategies, as well as the classical conditioning and generalization of fear responses. The client's understanding can increase a sense of control by normalizing these as predictable, given the patient's trauma experience.
- Use dissociative experiences as a skill base upon which to advance conscious trance-induction.

Goal 3: Alter Cognitive Appraisals
- Develop alternative meanings that increase self-efficacy through reframing and reinterpretation of trauma memories and symptoms.
- Use cognitive restructuring exercises to reevaluate underlying beliefs and promote a more realistic perspective.
- Teach thought stopping and guided self-dialogue techniques to reduce anxiety.

Goal 4: Increase Affect Regulation
- Create a climate of safety for trauma-work through developing a trusting relationship between the client and the social worker. For some clients, pharmacological interventions may be necessary to deal with their anxiety and depression before being able to effectively access traumatic materials.
- Utilize relaxation and breathing techniques to assist in controlling intrusive thoughts and behaviors as well as expand their repertoire of conscious distraction techniques.
- Use systematic desensitization and flooding techniques to facilitate safe exposure to traumatic memories. Reviewing their experience

and telling their story should be done within this therapeutic framework.

- Use behavioral rehearsal to practice adaptive coping skills, such as problem-solving, assertiveness, social skills, and anger management.
- Identify and express feelings verbally and in writing. The use of journaling to focus on reflecting and exploring feelings can be used as a basis for change.
- Identify traumatic memory triggers and situations where the client feels "out of control" as well as necessary safety conditions.

Individual and/or group treatment modalities may be used in the recovery process. Group experiences may be especially helpful in presenting the educational, normalizing, and interpersonal components of intervention.

Social workers must be sensitive to ethnocultural aspects of PTSD symptom presentation and recovery. An excellent resource for these issues is identified in Carlson (1997, p. 187). Numerous potential issues related to the social worker–client relationship and treatment process include issues of trust, intimacy, interpersonal safety, and countertransference. Useful readings that focus on the relationship in trauma and treatment are Briere (1996), Carlson (1997), and Turner (1996).

CONCLUSIONS AND FUTURE DIRECTIONS

The underlying theory of PTSD is that posttraumatic stress is a coping mechanism for managing traumatic experiences. Individuals minimize the adverse emotional consequences of trauma by restricting their awareness of the experience. Denial becomes a primary coping strategy. Fear structures evolve that contain mental representations of the traumatic event, such as intrusive memories, hypervigilance, and avoidance. Recovery from the trauma depends on activating the fear structure so that the cognitions are modified. With the introduction of new information, the fear structures are challenged and modified.

Future Directions

Research and clinical observations have indicated that a predictable pattern of psychological symptoms, labeled posttraumatic stress disorder or PTSD, may develop subsequent to the experience of serious or life-threatening trauma, yet empirical research continues to search for evidence to support this trauma condition. As well, there are a number of shortcomings in the current description and theoretical basis of the impact of traumatic stress and effective interventions. Given the prevalence of exposure to violence in our society, for young and old alike, social workers need to be aware of and trained to screen for posttraumatic stress-related symptoms. Social workers are ideally situated to screen and treat adults with posttraumatic stress reactions. Treatment does require the skills of a clinical MSW social worker, and BSW professionals need to be able to refer clients to services designed to address violence-related trauma symptoms. A person–environment framework provides a way to examine survivors' experiences; and it directs interventions to aspects of the trauma experience that might otherwise be overlooked. Further research is needed to explore both pre- and posttrauma factors that may influence the severity and pattern of PTSD symptoms. Such studies would further refine our understanding of the biopsychosocial risk and of any resilience influences that may impact assessment and treatment.

Although PTSD has been established as an appropriate diagnosis for a number of trauma survivors, many questions of under- and overdiagnosing PTSD remain. In clinical settings, PTSD is slowly being recognized for its utility in conceptualizing and diagnosing reactions to trauma. Clinical denial may remain the most serious obstacle to accurate diagnosis and intervention. Many professional social workers would like to cling to the rare and extraordinary nature of serious trauma or fail to make connections between events that may have occurred years ago with present symptoms. Overdiagnosing may be the particular bias of abuse- and trauma-focused social workers. Given the prevalence of abuse and violence, social workers should routinely screen for such trauma as a potential underlying root of current problems. Secondary trauma exposure is a reaction that may be manifested in social workers who work intensively with many survivors of severe trauma. Social workers can guard against this potential by maintaining clear boundaries. This reaction relates to relationship boundary issues and can be prevented by ensuring that quality clinical supervision is available. Along with monitoring the outcomes of clients treated, social workers need to stay alert to ongoing treatment and research developments to improve their practice.

REFERENCES

American Psychiatric Association. (1994). *Diagnostic and statistical manual of mental disorders, fourth edition. (DSM-IV)*. Washington, DC: Author.
American Psychiatric Association. (1980) *Diagnostic and statistical manual of mental disorders, third edition. (DSM-III)*. Washington, DC: Author.

Baldwin, A. L., Baldwin, C. P., Kasser, T., Zax, M., Sameroff, A., & Seifer, R. (1993). Contextual risk and resiliency during late adolescence. *Development and Psychopathology, 5,* 741–761.

Berliner, L., & Saunders, B. E. (1996). Treating fear and anxiety in sexually abused children: Results of a controlled 2-year follow-up study. *Child Maltreatment, 1,* 4, 294–309.

Berton, M. W., & Stabb, S. D. (1996). Exposure to violence and post-traumatic stress disorder in urban adolescents. *Adolescence, 31,* 489–498.

Blake, D., Weathers, F., Nagy, L., Kaloupek, D., Charner, D., & Keane, T. (1995). The development of a clinician-administered PTSD scale. *Journal of Traumatic Stress, 8,* 75–90.

Bourne, E. J. (1990). *The anxiety and phobia workbook.* Oakland, CA: New Harbinger Publications.

Branscombe, L. (1991). Dissociation in combat-related post-traumatic stress disorder. *Dissociation, 4,* 1, 13–20.

Breslau, N., Davis, G. C., Andreski, P., & Peterson, E. (1991). Traumatic events and posttraumatic stress disorder in an urban population of young adults. *Archives of General Psychiatry, 48,* 216–222.

Briere, J. (1992). *Child abuse trauma: Theory and treatment of lasting effects.* Newbury Park, CA: Sage.

Briere, J. (1996). A self-trauma model for treating adult survivors of severe child abuse. In J. Briere, L. Berliner, J. A. Bulkley, C. Jenny, & T. Reid (Eds.), *The APSAC handbook on child maltreatment* (pp. 140–157). London: Sage.

Briere, J., & Runtz, M. (1989). The trauma symptom checklist (TSC-33): Early data on a new scale. *Journal of Interpersonal Violence, 4,* 2, 151–163.

Briggs, L., & Joyce, P. R. (1997). What determines post-traumatic stress disorder symptomatology for survivors of childhood sexual abuse? *Child Abuse & Neglect, 21,* 6, 575–582.

Browne, A., & Finkelhor, D. (1986). Impact of child sexual abuse: A review of the research. *Psychological Bulletin, 99,* 66–77.

Bryant, R., & Harvey, A. (1997). Acute stress disorder: A critical review of diagnostic issues. *Clinical Psychology Review, 17,* 7, 757–773.

Butler, K. (1996). The biology of fear. *The Family Therapy Networker, July/August,* 39–45.

Cameron, C. (1994). Veterans of a secret war: Survivors of childhood sexual trauma compared to Vietnam war veterans with PTSD. *Journal of Interpersonal Violence, 9,* 1, 117–132.

Carlson, E. (1997). *Trauma assessments. A clinician's guide.* New York: Guilford Press.

Carlson, E., & Putnam, F. (1993). An update on the Dissociative Experiences Scale. *Dissociation, 6,* 16–27.

Coie, J., Watt, N., West, S., Hawkins, J. D., Asarnow, J., Markman, H., Ramey, S., Shure, M., & Long, B. (1993). The science of prevention: A conceptual framework and some directions for a national research program. *American Psychologist, 48,* 1013–1022.

Cowger, C. (1997). Assessing client strengths: Assessment for client empowerment. In D. Saleebey (Ed.), *The strengths perspective in social work practice* (2nd Ed., pp. 59–77). White Plains, NY: Longman.

Deblinger, E., Lippman, J., & Steer, R. (1996). Sexually abused children suffering posttraumatic stress symptoms: Initial treatment outcome findings. *Child Maltreatment, 1,* 4, 310–321.

Egeland, B., Carlson, E., & Sroufe, L. A. (1993). Resilience as process. *Development and Psychopathology, 5,* 517–528.

Emmelkamp, P. (1994). Behavior therapy with adults. In A. E. Bergin & S. L. Garfield (Eds.), *Handbook of psychotherapy and behavior change* (4th Ed., pp. 428–466). New York: Wiley.

Falsetti, S. A. (1997). The decision-making process of choosing a treatment for patients with civilian trauma-related PTSD. *Cognitive and Behavioral Practice, 4,* 1, 99–121.

Foa, E., Riggs, D.,Dancu, C., & Rothbaum, B. (1993). Reliability and validity of a brief instrument for assessing post-traumatic stress disorder. *Journal of Traumatic Stress, 6,* 459–473.

Foa, E., Steketee, G., & Rothbaum, B. (1989). Behavioral/cognitive conceptualizations of post-traumatic stress disorder. *Behavior Therapy, 20,* 155–176.

Fraser, M. W. (1997). The ecology of childhood: A multisystems perspective. In M. W. Fraser (Ed.), *Risk and resilience in childhood: An ecological perspective* (pp. 1–9). Washington, DC: National Association of Social Workers.

Friedrich, W. N. (1996). Clinical considerations of empirical treatment studies of abused children. *Child Maltreatment, 1,* 4, 343–347.

Garbarino, J., Dubrow, N., Kostelny, K., & Pardo, C. (1992). *Children in danger: Coping with the consequences of community violence.* San Francisco, CA: Jossey-Bass.

Garrison, C. Z., Bryant, E. S., Addy, C. L, Spurrier, P. G., Freedy, J. R., & Kilpatrick, D. G. (1995). Posttraumatic stress disorder in adolescents after Hurricane Andrew. *Journal of the American Academy of Child and Adolescent Psychiatry, 34,* 9, 1193–1201.

Goenjian, A. K., Pynoos, R. S., Steinberg, A. M., Najarian, L. M., Asarnow, J. R., Karayan, I., Ghurabi, M., & Fairbanks, L. A. (1995). Psychiatric comorbidity in children after the 1988 earthquake in Armenia. *Journal of the American Academy of Child and Adolescent Psychiatry, 34,* 9, 1174–1184.

Goldberg, J., True, W. R., Eisen, S. A., & Henderson, W. G. (1990). A twin study of the effects of the Vietnam war on post-traumatic stress disorder. *Journal of the American Medical Association, 263,* 1227–1232.

Hartman, C. R., & Burgess, A. W. (1986). Child sexual abuse: Generic roots of the victim experience. *Journal of Psychotherapy and the Family, 2,* 2, 83–92.

Herman, J. (1997). *Trauma and recovery.* New York: Basic Books.

Horowitz, M., Wilner, N., & Alvarez, W. (1979). The Impact of Event Scale: A measure of subjective stress. *Psychosomatic Medicine, 41,* 209–218.

Hubbard, J., Realmuto, G. M., Northwood, A. K., & Masten, A. S. (1995). Comorbidity of psychiatric diagnoses with posttraumatic stress disorder in survivors of childhood trauma. *Journal of the American Academy of Child and Adolescent Psychiatry, 34,* 9, 1167–1173.

Kirby, L. D., & Fraser, M. W. (1997). Risk and resilience in childhood. In M. W. Fraser (Ed.), *Risk and resilience in childhood: An ecological perspective* (pp. 10–33). Washington, DC: National Association of Social Workers.

Kiser, L. J., Heston, J., Millsap, P. A., & Pruitt, D. B. (1991). Physical and sexual abuse in childhood: Relationship with post-traumatic stress disorder. *Journal of the Academy of Child and Adolescent Psychiatry, 30,* 5, 776–783.

Kolbo, J. R. (1996). Risk and resilience among children exposed to family violence. *Violence and Victims, 11,* 2, 113–128.

McCann, L., & Pearlman, L. (1990). *Psychological trauma and the adult survivor: Theory, therapy, and transformation.* San Francisco, CA: Jossey-Bass.

McFarlane, A. C. (1989). The aetiology of posttraumatic morbidity: Predisposing, precipitating and perpetuating factors. *British Journal of Psychiatry, 154,* 221–228.

McNew, J. A., & Abell, N. (1995). Posttraumatic stress symptomatology: Similarities and differences between Vietnam veterans and adult survivors of childhood sexual abuse. *Social Work, 40,* 1, 115–126.

Mrazek, P. J., & Haggerty, R. J. (Eds.). (1994). *Reducing risks for mental disorders: Frontiers for preventive intervention research.* Washington, DC: National Academy Press.

Mrazek, P. J., & Mrazek, D. A. (1987). Resilience in child maltreatment victims: A conceptual exploration. *Child Abuse & Neglect, 11,* 357–366.

Nicholson, B. L. (1997). The influence of pre-emigration and post-emigration stressors on mental health: A study of Southeast Asian refugees. *Social Work Research, 21,* 1, 19–31.

Peterson, K., Prout, M., & Schwarz, R. (1991). *Post-traumatic Stress Disorder: A clinician's guide.* New York: Plenum.

Rowan, A., & Foy, D. (1992). Post-traumatic stress disorder in child sexual abuse survivors: A literature review. *Journal of Traumatic Stress, 6,* 3–20.

Sack, W. H., Clarke, G. N., & Seeley, J. (1995). Posttraumatic stress disorder across two generations of Cambodian refugees. *Journal of the American Academy of Child and Adolescent Psychiatry, 34,* 9, 1160–1166.

Shapiro, S., & Dominiak, G. (1992). *Sexual trauma and psychopathology: Clinical intervention with adult survivors.* New York: Lexington Books.

Shore, J. H., Tatum, H., & Vollmer, W. M. (1986). Psychiatric reactions to disaster: The St. Helen's experience. *American Journal of Psychiatry, 143,* 590–595.

Singer, M. I., Anglin, T. M., Song, L. Y., & Lunghofer, L. (1995). Adolescents' exposure to violence and associated symptoms of psychological trauma. *Journal of the American Medical Association, 273,* 6, 477–482.

Spaccarrelli, S. (1995). Measuring abuse stress and negative cognitive appraisals in child sexual abuse: Validity data on two new scales. *Journal of Abnormal Child Psychology, 23,* 6, 703–727.

Spaccarrelli, S., & Kim, S. (1995). Resilience criteria and factors associated with resilience in sexually abused girls. *Child Abuse & Neglect, 19,* 9, 1171–1182.

Sutker, P. B., Davis, J. M., Uddo, M., & Ditta, S. R. (1995). War zone stress, personal resources, and PTSD in Persian Gulf War returnees. *Journal of Abnormal Psychology, 104,* 3, 444–452.

Terr, L. C. (1991). Childhood traumas: An outline and overview. *American Journal of Psychiatry, 148,* 1, 10–20.

Thomlison, B. (1997). Risk and protective factors in child maltreatment. In M. W. Fraser (Ed.), *Risk and resilience in childhood: An ecological perspective* (pp. 50–72). Washington, DC: National Association of Social Workers.

Turner, F. J. (1996). *Social work treatment: Interlocking theoretical approaches* (4th Ed.). New York: The Free Press.

Tutty, L. M., & Rothery, M. A. (1997). Women who seek shelter from wife assault: Risk assessment and service needs. Paper presented at the Fifth International Family Violence Research Conference, Durham, NH, June 29–July 2.

van der Kolk, B. (1989). The compulsion to repeat the trauma. *Psychiatric Clinics of North America, 12,* 389–411.

van der Kolk, B. A., & Kadish, W. (1987). Amnesia, dissociation, and the return of the repressed. In B. A. van der Kolk (Ed.), *Psychological trauma.* Washington, DC: American Psychiatric Press.

Wachtel, A. (1988). *The impact of child sexual abuse in developmental perspective: A model and literature review.* Ottawa: National Clearinghouse on Family Violence.

Weine, S., Becker, D. F., McGlashan, T. H., Vojvoda, D., Hartman, S., & Robbins, J. P. (1995). Adolescent survivors of "ethnic cleansing": Observations on the first year in America. *Journal of the American Academy of Child and Adolescent Psychiatry, 34,* 9, 1153–1159.

Wylie, M. S. (1996). Going for the cure. *The Family Therapy Networker, July/August,* 21–37.

27

SUICIDE

Howard M. Turney

Insomnia, erratic blood pressure, blinding headaches, and severe depression were the genetic heritage of Ernest Hemingway, his sisters and brother. They carried it as a legacy from both sides of the family. Eventually three of the Hemingway children took their own lives: Ernest in 1961; Ursula in 1966; Leicester in 1982. Though Marcelline's death in 1963 was reported to be from natural causes, Leicester suspected suicide. When Ernest Hemingway put the muzzle of his double-barreled shotgun to his forehead that morning in late July, he suffered from all his father's ills: erratic high blood pressure, insomnia, hypertension, mild diabetes, paranoia, and severe depression. Under stress, real or imagined, the idea of suicide recurred insidiously.

—Michael S. Reynolds, *Hemingway's Home* (1985)

Suicidal behavior is one of the most complex and perplexing forms of human behavior social workers face. These critical situations are highly complicated, and providing appropriate intervention at these crucial times is imperative in order to accurately assess the manner in which clients present themselves. Approximately 75% of those who successfully commit suicide provide an advance communication of their intentions (Litman, 1996). For those who consider ending their lives, suicide is seen as a solution for problems they are experiencing.

Clients' suicidal thoughts and attempts are presented to social workers in a variety of settings. Work with children reveals that a family history of suicide increases the risk of that family's children attempting suicide (Gutierrez, et al., 1996). Adolescent exposure to another adolescent's suicidal behavior is a relevant factor. Most of those who attempted suicide were aware of someone known to them who had attempted suicide. Similarly for the elder population, suicide in older adults has increased significantly over the past 15 years (Adameck & Kaplan, 1996). Interestingly, the largest number of the suicides committed by older women have been committed with firearms. This fact contradicts popular assumptions that women use less violent methods of suicide (Adameck & Kaplan, 1996). The prevalence rate for suicide among older people is, at a minimum, four times higher than for other adult populations (Schatzberg & Nemeroff, 1995).

Throughout the life span suicide is evident in all but the youngest age group (ages one through four) at a rate of 11.8 per 100,000 population (Rosenberg, Ventura, et al., 1996). Suicide is the eighth leading cause of death in the United States (Ivanoff & Riedel, 1995). Unfortunately, it is not known why human beings commit suicide. Theorists have speculated historically about the factors most commonly associated with suicide and suicidal behavior. However, suicide remains a riddle and a problem continuously posed to social work practitioners.

ETIOLOGY

The etiology of suicide has been discussed for centuries. However, research on the explanation of suicide began in the latter part of the nineteenth century with Emile Durkheim, the French social philosopher. Durkheim suggested that suicide occurred because of the "fit" an individual experiences with society (Stillion & McDowell, 1996). He proposed three classifications that explain his sociological perspective on suicide (Maris, 1975).

- *Egoism*—a lack of social interaction; individuals who are socially isolated; results from excessive individualism; too few ties to community
- *Anomie*—lost integration through trauma; when the traditional relationship between an individual and her/his society is disrupted precipitously
- *Altruistic*—the result of excessive integration, e.g., *hara-kiri*; a high degree of social integration; suicide that is required by society

Durkheim's influence on research of suicide has been profound. Most later sociologists studying suicide attempt to develop or alter some portion of Durkheim's theory.

Intrapsychic processes have been suggested as the etiological factor associated with the act of suicide. For Freud, suicide occurred primarily within the mind (Shneidman, 1985). This psychodynamic theory describes suicide as an intrapsychic process, based on unconscious intentions. Karl Menninger (1938) described the hostility directed toward oneself as the wish to kill, the wish to be killed, and the wish to die. Further analysis of Freud's ideas on suicide shows that rage, guilt, anxiety, dependency are additional psychodynamic factors related to suicide (Shneidman, 1985).

A psychological approach to understanding suicide is described as a set of certain circumstances that must be present for a person to take her or his own life. These features include the following:

1. An increased state of upset
2. Increased self-deprecation (self-hate, self-blame) seen in behavior that is obviously counter to the person's own best interest
3. The inability to see viable options that are normally available
4. The notion that it is possible to end suffering by ending the flow of consciousness (Shneidman, 1985)

From this theoretical perspective, suicide is seen as an escape from unbearable emotion.

Cognitive theorists suggest that suicide is an effort to express or to solve problems. The salient feature of this theory is hopelessness. With no alternatives to problems, death provides the solution (Ivanoff & Riedel, 1995). Dichotomous thinking has been noted by Beck (1979) to be characteristic of severely depressed people. This either/or type of thinking has been noted as characteristic of the thinking patterns of persons who are suicidal.

Both serotonin levels and genetic factors have been linked to a biological basis for suicidal behavior. Deficiencies in serotonin levels have been noted in persons who have committed suicide. And persons with family members who have exhibited suicidal behavior have a higher than usual suicidal incidence of suicidal behavior (Stillion & McDowell, 1996). Although these biological factors are not conclusive, they suggest a link between these two factors and suicidal behavior. Interestingly, bipolar disorder, schizophrenia, and alcoholism represent the psychiatric disorders most often identified with suicide (Kaplan & Sadock, 1991).

Although much has been written in efforts to build a comprehensive theory that explains suicidal behavior, it is not known why humans commit this act of self-destruction (Leenaars, 1996). To date, neither sociology, psychology, psychodynamic theory, cognitive theory, nor biology has developed a thorough explanation of this human phenomenon.

PREVALENCE

In 1994, 32,410 people committed suicide in the United States (Centers for Disease Control). The age groups showing the greatest growth in suicide are adolescents and people over 65 years of age. In any typical day, 84 people die of suicide and on any typical day 1,900 adults attempt suicide. During 1992, white males accounted for 73% of all suicides. Coupled with white females, white people account for 91% of all suicides. Almost 60% of all suicides are committed with a firearm, with 74% of men using this method and 31% of women (Centers for Disease Control). For the elderly, suicide rates are highest for those widowed and divorced.

Eighteen older Americans take their lives each day. This accumulates to a total of 6,300 elderly annually (McIntosh, 1993). Because older males have lower involvement with family, friends, and community and are the most socially isolated group in our society, they are at greatest risk for suicide (Mercer, 1992). Older people as a group face social isolation and loneliness. Other factors include loss, chronic pain, and change in economic status, employment, or independence.

Rates of suicide for African-Americans are the lowest for any minority group in this country (Mercer, 1992). Native Americans have the highest suicide rate of any racial/ethnic group in the United States for all age groups (Ivanoff & Riedel, 1995). It is unfortunate that aggregate data on other minority populations are difficult to analyze because they have been neglected in the literature on suicide.

Clearly, suicide is a prevalent occurrence in our society that systemically affects thousands of people. Evidently young people born in the 1950s and before were less susceptible to suicide than those born more recently (Stillion & McDowell, 1996). Over the past four decades young people have in increasingly significant numbers engaged in self-destructive behavior.

ASSESSMENT OF SUICIDAL CLIENTS

Social work practitioners rely on observation of clients to assess the lethality of a situation. Observing a client's behavior and language, the clinician should carefully assess the potential for self-harm in any thorough assessment. Often suicidal clients will use specific language that provides pathways into understanding a client's potential for self-harm. Naturally, most people have, at least once, considered what life would be like if they did not exist. However, social workers must first develop an awareness of the signs and symptoms of a potentially suicidal client.

It is essential that the practitioner be willing to broach the issue of suicide with clients. Failure to do so is a flagrant omission by the social worker. Bringing up the idea does not in any way suggest to the client that the practitioner is promoting such an idea. On the contrary, bringing the issue to the forefront provides an abundance of information in assessing the client's mental status. At the same time, an honest discussion of possible self-destructive behavior helps both clients and practitioners to distinguish fantasy from reality.

In assessing potentially suicidal clients, the social worker must listen intently, noting the use of language. Comments from clients take a variety of forms that provide indications of how the client views his or her future. Comments such as "I can't go on," "There is no use," or "I have no other options," represent language that conveys a sense of hopelessness and helplessness. Further, they convey a sense of finality, which must be explored.

To assess such clients, the social worker must gather historical data regarding the client's past concerning suicidal ideation and attempts. Interviewing clients factually about past thoughts and/or attempts provides the social worker with a sense of the client's ego strengths, use of impulsivity, and relationship to reality. For clients who have successfully constrained past suicidal thoughts, building on this strength can provide a foundation for coping with the current situation. The ability to control impulses to inflict self-harm historically provides important information about the client's decision-making style. Clarifying the client's relationship to reality is imperative to determine the presence of psychotic processes or processes related to personality disorders. By understanding the function of the past suicidal gestures, the clinician is in a better position to assess the client's current suicidal ideation and to contrast past gestures with current functioning. Asking "What is different now that would lead you to take your own life?" provides a stark contrast to past functioning and establishes a context for the client–worker relationship.

Thinking systemically about the client's interpersonal relationships is an essential part of a complete assessment. Understanding the client's interpersonal relationships and the role these relationships play in the client's current level of functioning provides a framework for assessment. Pinpointing the people who provide support for the client and understanding the way that this support is manifested can serve as an indicator of the level of isolation or integration the client is experiencing. Clients may cry out for help to significant others while giving few clues to the social worker. Comprehending the depth of the client's interpersonal relationships and the meaning attached to these relationships gives the worker a broader understanding of potential attempts at self-harm. Similarly, the social worker, who is in an interpersonal relationship with the client, must carefully examine his/her own feelings about suicide and the impact of those feelings on the client. The clinician's professional experience, life experiences, and family history are all factors that contribute to his/her frame of reference about suicide. By incorporating a systemic perspective into the assessment, social workers are better prepared to recognize the lethality of a client's situation.

Making an accurate assessment of a suicidal client can be difficult. Given that suicide is a relatively rare occurrence, predicting who will or will not successfully destroy himself is difficult. It is also difficult to apply general factors to highly idiosyncratic circumstances and events of an individual's life (Fremouw, de Perczel, & Ellis, 1990). Assessment should err on the side of caution to avoid unnecessary risk to clients.

RISK FACTORS

Undoubtedly, psychiatric and addictive disorders play a prominent role in the lives of persons who attempt and commit suicide. Not surprisingly, as many as 80% of those who commit suicide have shown evidence of having suffered from depression (Fremouw, de Perczel, & Ellis, 1990). Mortality rates are high within the population of those suffering from affective disorders. Less clear evidence exists linking physical illness to suicide, and the incidence of suicide may vary across populations and illnesses (Fremouw, de Perczel, & Ellis, 1990). It is unfortunate that at the time of the event the precise mental status of the person committing suicide is not known, since many of those who do commit suicide have never sought psychiatric treatment (Lester, 1989).

Previous suicide attempts are strong indicators for completed suicide (Moscicki, 1995). Interestingly, the rate of successful completion of suicide is higher for children and adolescents than among older persons. Substance abuse is characteristic of suicide for both attempted and completed acts. Of concern are research findings which indicate that increased substance abuse in the past quarter century has been a major factor contributing to the increased suicide rate among youth (Hepworth, et al., 1995).

For adolescents, factors most often associated with suicide include the loss of a relationship, loss of membership in a peer group, lack of acceptance by others, or having lost friends to death. Clearly, there are predisposing factors that, in effect, account for suicide in adolescents. Traumatic losses and child abuse would no doubt influence an adolescent's decision to take his or her own life. A general lack of warmth and security within the family may predispose adolescents to suicide (Hepworth, et al., 1995).

Adult suicide has been associated with dramatic changes in lifestyle including divorce, the death of a loved one, unexpected legal involvement, and financial loss. Nevertheless, in a number of suicidal events there is no evidence of a precipitating stress (Klugman, et al., 1997). Suicide may occur on a continuum from those who act impulsively to those who have contemplated it for years (Kaplan, et al., 1994). These complex and unpredictable factors further challenge the clinician to examine carefully the nature of human existence and to understand how suicide may manifest itself in a presenting problem.

Factors associated with suicide by older persons include the death of a loved one, physical illness, intolerable pain, fear of the implications of dying after a lengthy and costly illness, loneliness and isolation, and role change (McIntosh, 1993). Successful suicides are most common in older people and are attributable to restricted choices and limited alternatives (Kaplan, et al., 1994). Mercer (1992) suggests that suicides in nursing homes are lower than for older persons living in other settings. This could be attributed to the closer observation that occurs in nursing homes or to the possibility of inaccurate reporting by nursing homes.

INTERVENTION

Social workers should be alert to the lethality of any given clinical situation. Whether working with clients by telephone or face to face, clinicians should be prepared to intervene appropriately. Appropriate responses to clients include the duty to protect clients from self-harm (National Association of Social Workers, 1996). In instances where clients have threatened self-harm, interventions should promote the safety of those clients. Approximately 95% of people who commit suicide or attempt to commit suicide have a diagnosable mental disorder (Kaplan, et al., 1994). This, combined with the fact that 80% of that group are people diagnosed with some type of depressive disorder, gives the clinician important insight into the ways that risk factors support interventions. The first step in intervention would be for the clinician to successfully recognize and differentially understand the diagnostic criteria for mental disorders. Accurate diagnosis forms the basis for the application of any meaningful intervention. Be aware that a psychiatric illness does not have to be present for suicide to occur (Slaby, 1994).

A number of factors need to be assessed immediately when dealing with the potentially suicidal client. Information to be obtained early in the intervention include: gender of the client, family system constellation, availability of support systems, any history of recent losses, the client's coping patterns, and the client's age-related developmental level (Stillion & McDowell, 1996). These factors provide the basis for questioning and intervening with the client in a meaningful way. When the threat of suicide is present, the social worker should take a directive and active stance. Such a stance includes not only the deescalation of the current crisis, but preparation for increased availability to that client. Encouragement to live is provided to clients when they receive needed support during periods of instability.

Intervening with a potentially suicidal client may require medical backup. Medical backup could include medication management and/or hospitalization (Klugman, et al., 1995). The worker must determine the following: suicidal ideation is present, and if it is, on what level: with thought, with intent, or with a plan. Carefully exploring this continuum initiates a process to assist the clinician in determining the potential for lethality. Any verbal cue by the client of intent to harm himself should be taken seriously. The clinician must discover how the client's suicidal thoughts, intentions, and plans fit into the contextual framework of the client's life.

John was a 35-year-old, married, male, with a history of depression, anger, rage. The client was accompanied by his spouse who revealed serious concern for the welfare of her husband. Judy reported that John had recently become focused on feelings of worthlessness; increasingly his self-esteem had eroded, and his hope for the future was dim in his eyes. He had been terminated by his employer for reasons he did not understand. John reported having worked in an environment where he was constantly ridiculed by his coworkers. Due to limited resources, he faced financial ruin. Having an infant son, John feared for the future of his family. The only option he saw was to kill himself. He appeared dejected and defeated. This man had begun to abuse alcohol, and during those times he was at greater risk as he verbally expressed wishes to end his life. No words could convince John to view his current circumstances differently. Although his plan was vague, he described vividly how well off his family would be without him.

This brief example provides a window to clues that assist the social worker in determining the course of action that protects the suicidal client from him/herself. Depression, anger, and rage are not prerequisites to suicidal behavior, but certainly provide valuable evidence to be explored with clients to ensure the client's safety. In this case, a strength was that his wife was closely involved and keenly aware of the risks presented by this situation. Her description of the events associated with the current episode were salient facts that supported the clinician's need to fully understand the dangerous nature of the current situation. Hopelessness is a concept often associated with clients who lack the capacity to see any vision for the future. Clients give many clues to clinicians about their view of the future. Paying special attention to the language used by this client and understanding the intentional nature of his communications was essential in understanding how this client intended to respond to his own emotional pain. Clearly this man had developed a belief system that corresponded directly to the implications of being ridiculed at work. For John, his self-worth was closely tied to his ability to provide for his family. Facing financial ruin led the client into a downward spiral that was further exacerbated by alcohol abuse.

This is but one example of the manner in which suicidal states present to social workers. These states must be managed in a manner that protects the life of the client. A direct referral from the social worker's office to an inpatient psychiatric treatment facility was indicated. With the assistance of the client's spouse and the use of crisis intervention, hospitalization was facilitated.

PHYSICIAN-ASSISTED SUICIDE

One of the most challenging issues to face social workers in the future will be physician-assisted suicide. Historically, physician-assisted suicide has been hotly debated both from a legal and from a moral point of view. Challenged in the courts and voted on in some states, this phenomenon presents an ethical issue that challenges the basic values that undergird social work practice—the right to self determination and social justice. Professional social workers in hospitals, home health agencies, rehabilitation centers, treatment facilities, and long-term care facilities will all eventually be faced with the dilemma presented by physician-assisted suicide.

Because people can be kept alive long after their age of productivity and comfort, the question of rational suicide is opened. The "right to die" has become the issue that provides the pathway to an understanding of the client's right to self-determination (Stillion & McDowell, 1996). Complicated by living wills and advanced directives to medical caregivers, requests to withhold life-sustaining treatment sets the stage for end-of-life decisions. Both *palliative care* and *comfort care* are terms used to describe conditions in which no additional life-sustaining efforts will be made. Because the debate over the right to die is an emotional one, social workers should be prepared to deal with both clients and their family members in a manner that enables the worker to differentially understand the systemic effects of such decisions. Whether active or passive, the end-of-life decisions challenge both clients and clinicians to examine traditional beliefs regarding death.

Suicide, the deliberate act of taking one's own life, is a different phenomenon from assisted suicide and euthanasia. *Assisted suicide* is knowingly providing the information and means to another person to commit the act of suicide. *Euthanasia* is causing death to persons suffering incurable conditions for the purpose of preventing uncontrollable suffering. In cases of euthanasia, clients may actively consent to such or may be incapable of giving consent (Report of the Committee on Physician-Assisted Suicide, 1996).

Social and cultural factors, along with depression, play an important role in understanding end-of-life decisions. The economically disadvantaged often live in a world of depression, discouragement, and despair. For many of the poor, adequate health care is unavailable. For some, the request for physician-assisted suicide is based on a need to avoid financially burdening the family in order to preserve family resources.

The role of depression in a client's request may be a motivating factor in the client's determination to die. If, in fact, symptoms of a depressive disorder are present, the clinician must recognize and treat that cluster of symptoms before any consideration can be given to assisted suicide. The wish to die may indeed be a symptom of a depressive disorder. Unfortunately, very little is known about the prevalence of the wish to die among the terminally ill. In extreme forms of depression, one's ability to think rationally may be impaired.

The potential criteria (Quill, 1993) to be assessed for physician-assisted suicide to be a viable alternative include the need for the request to die to be made at the client's own initiative, repeatedly, with the primary mission to end suffering. Assessment should always ensure that the judgment of the client is in no way impaired. This would prevent persons diagnosed with depression from implementing assisted suicide. Any decision to implement assisted suicide should examine the level of palliative care and ensure that the request is not the result of inadequate care. Consultation with other professionals, especially social workers, who are professionally prepared to evaluate the mental status of individuals is essential in making these decisions. Documentation that supports the decision-making process should be clear and should detail how the professionals and the client came to such a decision.

> William was a 34-year-old male who was diagnosed with HIV six years ago. His disease process progressed to the active stage of AIDS two years ago. Most recently William lived with his partner and was cared for in their home. A home health care worker monitored William's condition. For the last three months of his life William required extensive medical attention. William requested that his physician provide him with a lethal dose of medication in order to end his life. His partner was supportive of this decision, having watched William suffer for the past few months. However, the physician refused to participate in any assisted-suicide procedure, citing legal issues. In order to hasten death, William refused to take any further antiviral medication. The decision was, in effect, a passive suicide. Within weeks of ceasing the medication, William died.

This case provides an example of the complex nature of assisted suicide. William was keenly aware that his wish to die would not be honored by his physician. This request to die had been made at William's own initiative. He had discussed the desire to end his life with both his social worker and his partner at length. His sole rationale for wanting to die was to end his suffering. Interviews with the client did not reveal the presence of a depressive disorder or any other mental illness. Although the physician would not participate in assisting the client, William was able to take matter into his own hands and fulfill his wishes, ending his life with dignity. The role of the social worker in such cases is yet to be clearly delineated; however, in this case example, the social worker was directly involved in the end-of-life decisions. At this time (1999) it is not clear what legal liability social workers may have in such cases.

Both overtly and covertly, social workers participate in the end-of-life process. Given the large number of social work professionals who deal directly with clients who have a limited time to live, the role of social workers is evident. Laws governing assisted suicide have been proposed in several states. In Oregon in 1994 death-with-dignity legislation narrowly passed by popular vote. That legislation was challenged in the Supreme Court, which referred the legislation back to Oregon, where voters have recently reaffirmed physician-assisted suicide as an option for end-of-life decisions. Many of the arguments for and against assisted suicide fall under the purview of spiritual debates and often become highly controversial. Questions of rights emerge in these debates, as does the right to self-determination. The breadth of the concept of self-determination will be challenged repeatedly as the right-to-die controversy continues.

CONCLUSION

Social work practitioners are in the forefront delivering services in a variety of settings facing clients who wish to die. A working knowledge of the *Diagnostic and Statistical Manual of Mental Disorders, Fourth Edition (DSM-IV)* (1994) is imperative. Understanding how a psychiatric diagnosis relates to observable behavior aids the clinician in understanding the contextual framework from which the client is operating. In instances where suicidal ideation is present, it is incumbent on practitioners to protect clients from themselves. Competency in the use of interviewing skills prepares the worker to listen attentively to evidence of suicidal ideation.

With the powerful influence of managed care, a philosophy of "least restrictive environment" has prevailed. The least-restrictive-environment approach has been used to minimize the high cost of hospitalization. This philosophy dramatically increases the liability of practitioners who deal with suicidal clients. Never before have the skills of advocacy played a more important role in the delivery of quality mental health care. Protecting clients from self harm requires social workers to articulate conditions accurately and in a manner that is consistent with diagnostic criteria. The ability to meaningfully convince both providers and clients of the appropriateness of hospitalization is essential in an age of diminished services. Our knowledge of resources and our ability to activate those resources in times of crisis support the well-being of clients. Social workers should remain keenly aware of the signs and symptoms associated with suicide. Ignoring them can lead to irreversible errors in judgment.

REFERENCES

Adameck M. E., & Kaplan, M. S. (1996). The growing use of firearms by suicidal older women, 1979–1992: A research note. *Suicide & Life-Threatening Behavior, 26,* 1, 71–77.

American Psychiatric Association. (1994). *Diagnostic and statistical manual of mental disorders, fourth edition.* Washington, DC: Author.

Centers for Disease Control (CDC). National Center for Injury Prevention and Control. (1992). Suicide in the United States. *SA/VE CDC Statistics Page.* Author.

Fremouw, W. J., de Perczel, M., & Ellis, T. E. (1990). *Suicide risk: Assessment and response guidelines.* Needham Heights, MA: Allyn & Bacon.

Gutierrez, P., King, C. A., & Ghaziuddin, N. (1996). Adolescent attitudes about death in relation to suicidality. *Suicide & Life-Threatening Behavior, 26,* 1, 8–17.

Hepworth, D. H., Farley, O. W., & Griffiths, K. J. (1995). Clinical work with suicidal adolescents and their families. In Francis J. Turner (Ed.), *Differential diagnosis and treatment in social work* (4th Ed., pp. 684–695). New York: Free Press.

Ivanoff, A., & Riedel, M. (1995). Suicide. In Richard L. Edwards (Ed.), *Encyclopedia of social work* (19th Ed., Vol. 3, pp. 2358–2372). Washington, DC: National Association of Social Workers.

Kaplan, H. I., & Sadock, B. J. (1991). *Synopsis of psychiatry* (6th Ed.). Baltimore: Williams & Wilkins.

Kaplan, H. I., Sadock, B. J., & Grebb, J. A. (1994). *Synopsis of psychiatry* (7th Ed.). Baltimore: Williams & Wilkins.

Klugman, D. J., Litman, R. E., & Wold, C. I. (1995). Answering the cry for help. In Francis J. Turner (Ed.), *Differential diagnosis and treatment in social work* (4th Ed., pp. 674–683). New York: Free Press.

Leenaars, A. A. (1996). Suicide: A multidimential malaise. *Suicide & Life-Threatening Behavior, 26,* 3, 221–235.

Lester, D. (1989). *Questions and answers about suicide.* Philadelphia: The Charles Press.

Litman, R. E. (1996). Suicidology: A look backward and ahead. *Suicide and Life-Threatening Behavior, 26,* 1, 1.

Maier, T. (1997). Election 97/Death by choice/Oregon voters back MD-aided suicide. *Newsday,* November 6, p. A5.

Maris, R. (1994). Sociology. In Seymour Perlin (Ed.), *A handbook for the study of suicide* (pp. 93–109). Northvale, NJ: Jason Aronson.

McIntosh, John L. (1995). Suicide prevention in the elderly (age 65–99). *Suicide & Life-Threatening Behavior, 25,* 1, 180–190.

Menninger, K. A. (1938). *Man against himself.* New York: Harcourt, Brace.

Mercer, S. O. (1992). Elder suicide. In Francis J. Turner (Ed.), *Mental health and the elderly* (pp. 425–453). New York: Free Press.

Moscicki, E. K. (1995). Epidemiology of suicidal behavior. *Suicide & Life-Threatening Behavior, 25,* 1, 22–31.

National Association of Social Workers (NASW). (1996). *Code of Ethics.* Washington, DC: Author.

Quill, T. E. (1993). *Death and dignity: Making choices and taking charge.* New York: Norton.

Report of the Committee on Physician-Assisted Suicide and Euthanasia. (1996). Suicide and euthanasia. *Suicide & Life-Threatening Behavior, 26,* Supp., 2–17.

Reynolds, M. S. (1985). Hemingway's home: Depression and suicide. *American Literature, 57,* 4, 600–610.

Rosenberg, H. M., Ventura, S. J., et al. (1996). Births and Deaths: United States, 1995. *Monthly Vital Statistics Report, 45,* 3, Supp. 2, 31. Hyattsville, MD: National Center for Health Statistics.

Schatzberg, A. F., & Nemeroff, C. B. (1995). *Textbook of pharmacology.* Washington, DC: American Psychiatric Press.

Shneidman, E. (1985). *Definition of suicide.* New York: Wiley.

Slaby, A. E. (1994). Psychopharmacotherapy of suicide. In A. A. Leenaars, J. T. Maltsberger, & R. A. Neimeyer (Eds.), *Treatment of suicidal people* (pp. 141–149). Washington, DC: Taylor & Francis.

Stillion, J. M., & McDowell, E. E. (1996). *Suicide across the life span* (2nd Ed.). Washington, DC: Taylor & Francis.

Yeager, M. Court leaves right to die up to states. (1997). *Amarillo Globe-News,* June 27.

INDEX

I thank Ann-Marie Turner Dacyshyn and Dr. Sarah E. Turner for their help in preparing this index.

CPSIA information can be obtained at www.ICGtesting.com
Printed in the USA
LVOW06s1234180714

394828LV00001B/46/P